E D I T I O N  *4*

Interpersonal Communication and Human Relationships

Mark L. Knapp
University of Texas at Austin

Anita L. Vangelisti
University of Texas at Austin

Allyn and Bacon
Boston • London • Toronto • Sydney • Tokyo • Singapore

Senior Editor: Karon Bowers
Vice President: Paul A. Smith
Editorial Assistant: Jennifer Becker
Marketing Manager: Jackie Aaron
Editorial Production Service: Chestnut Hill Enterprises, Inc.
Manufacturing Buyer: Megan Cochran
Cover Administrator: Jennifer Hart

Internet: www.abacon.com

Between the time web site information is gathered and then published, some sites may have closed. Also, the transcription of URLs can result in typographical errors. The publisher would appreciate notification where these occur so that they may be corrected in subsequent editions.

Library of Congress Cataloging-in-Publication Data

Knapp, Mark L.
    Interpersonal communication and human relationships / Mark L.
Knapp, Anita L. Vangelisti.—4th ed.
        p.   cm.
    Includes bibliographical references and indexes.
    ISBN 0-205-29573-8
    1. Interpersonal relations.   2. Interpersonal communication.
I. Vangelisti, Anita L.   II. Title.
HM1111.K59   1999
302—dc21   99-41211
                                                            CIP

Credits: p. 109 © 1973 Screen Genis-EMI Music Inc. and Summerhill Songs, Inc. All rights controlled and administered by Summerhill Songs, Inc. All rights reserved. International copyright secured. Used by permission. p. 231 *Time Magazine*, December 8, 1998, p. 244. Author: Roger Rosenblatt; p. 258, reproduced by special permission of *Playboy Magazine*, copyright © 1968 by *Playboy*, p. 268 *New York Times Magazine*, June 9, 1991, pp. 15–18. Author: Paul Thaler

Printed in the United States of America

10 9 8 7 6 5 4 3 2 1   04 03 02 01 00 99

Once a human being has arrived on this earth, *communication is the largest single factor determining what kinds of relationships she or he makes with others and what happens to each in the world.* How we manage survival, how we develop intimacy, how productive we are, how we make sense, how we connect with our own divinity—all depend largely on our communication skills.

Virginia Satir
The New Peoplemaking

Contents

Part VI Toward More Effective Communication in Relationships   397

Preface

This is a book about the way people communicate in developing and deteriorating relationships. We chose to discuss the processes and principles of interpersonal communication in the context of developing relationships for two reasons: (1) There seems to be a widespread concern in this country and abroad for understanding the forces that bring people together and keep them together, and those that divide and separate them; and (2) students of human communication find concepts and principles easier to learn when they can analyze and test them in the context of common experiences. Whether it is with our roommates, our lovers, or our parents, we are constantly experiencing how communication behavior affects our relationships. It is within the context of our relationships with others that abstract concepts like feedback, perception, and conflict resolution become increasingly relevant and important for students of communication.

The book is divided into six parts. The first part has two objectives: (1) to identify several important patterns of communication and (2) to show how these patterns of communication manifest themselves at different stages of a relationship. Part II shows how the characteristics of each individual (e.g., gender, age, needs) and the characteristics of the environment where the relationship develops can affect the way we communicate. The three chapters constituting Part III discuss various communication patterns in the context of relationships that are moving toward increased intimacy or closeness. Part IV examines a number of communication patterns that partners perceive as crucial to the adequate maintenance of relationships.

And Part V takes a look at communication patterns in the context of relationships that are moving toward less intimacy. Although the concept of effective communication behavior is implicit in the preceding chapters, the last part of the book explicitly examines the subject. We believe that any discussion of how to be an effective communicator makes more sense if preceded by chapters detailing the variety of communicative goals and activities that characterize our relationships.

The chapter order was designed to emphasize the developmental theme of the book rather than to suggest a rigid chronology to our communication behavior in relationship development. Greeting behavior, as Chapter 6 points out, takes place between friends *and* enemies even though the discussion of greeting behavior is placed in the section labeled "coming together." Similarly, lying is not a type of behavior found only in the maintenance of relationships even though it is discussed in that section of the book. Further, it should be noted that the terms *growth* and *decay* are meant to be descriptive rather than evaluative. In other words, relationship "growth" is not inherently "good" and relationship "decay" inherently "bad." Positive and negative consequences can accrue from either process.

The concepts presented in this book were not originally designed for generalization beyond our contemporary United States culture, but future explorations may uncover some extensions to other cultural contexts. It is clear that each culture imposes slightly different rules on the development and deterioration of relationships—parental selection of potential marriage partners, prohibiting intimate same-sex relationships, severely sanctioning the termination of marriages, and so on. It is equally clear that specific behaviors utilized to accomplish interpersonal goals may differ greatly from culture to culture. Compare these greeting rituals with your own:

> An Ainu, meeting his sister, grasped her hands in his for a few seconds, suddenly released his hold, grasped her by both ears and gave the peculiar Ainu greeting cry; then they stroked one another down the face and shoulders. . . . Adamanese greet one another by one sitting down in the lap of the other, arms around each other's necks and weeping for a while. . . . At Matavai a full dress greeting after long absence requires scratching the head and temples with a shark's tooth, violently and with much bleeding.[1]

Or consider these friendship rituals:

> To celebrate friendship in other parts of western Africa, men throw excrement at each other and comment loudly on the genitals of their respective parents when they meet; this behavior, perhaps unnatural and obscene to us, is a proof

[1]W. LaBarre, "Paralinguistics, Kinesics and Cultural Anthropology." In T. A. Sebeok. A. S. Hayes, and M. C. Bateson, Eds., *Approaches to Semiotics* (p. 199). (The Hague: Mouton, 1964).

of love to friends. In Tanzania, if a man meets a woman who is his special friend, he has the right to insult her and playfully pummel her like a punching bag. These rowdy displays express an element of strain and fragility often found in friendships, and betray a latent sentiment of aggression that is not always absent from loving relationships.[2]

Thus, although the behaviors used to achieve the goal of initiating contact or showing friendship with others may differ dramatically, the functions served by these behaviors and the ends sought may have some cultural overlap.

This book contains a preponderance of examples from male-female relationships and relationships where people "voluntarily" seek contact with, or disengagement from, one another. While such examples came to us easier and seemed most understandable for readers, the interaction stages outlined in the book are not limited to these applications. Lovers and tennis buddies have gone through the same stages; lovers have simply gone further. Business partners and sorority sisters find different topics, but both engage in a lot of small talk. All people drawn into, or pulled out of, relationships by forces outside their control will like that occurrence or not like it and communicate accordingly. For instance, a child's relationship with his or her parent may, at some point, be very close and loving (Integrating Stage) and at another time be cold and distant (Stagnating Stage).

The "Dear Dr. Knapp" and "Dear Dr. Vangelisti" letters that precede each chapter are from actual letters written by students. The problems posed in these letters have been analyzed and discussed in a university class without the writer's identity being revealed. In this book the letters are used to forecast some of the issues treated in each chapter. The boxed inserts scattered through the text are designed to provide amusing and/or thought-provoking asides associated with the adjacent material. The Instructor's Manual for this edition is based on extensive classroom experience with this text. The behavioral objectives, participative exercises, and test questions should be most helpful in tailoring this text to classroom learning experiences.

This edition, like the last, was written with several expectations: (1) We hope that some readers will reflect on the ideas presented and compare them against what they have experienced and seen in others, but certainly not blindly accept everything. (2) We hope that some readers will not only reflect on the ideas in this book, but will find them challenging enough to actively initiate a lifelong process of analysis and reanalysis of their everyday communicative behavior and that of others. (3) We hope that still other readers will be stimulated to formulate testable hypotheses and submit some of the speculation and undocumented thoughts presented here to the rigors of social science research. The references at the end of each

[2]R. Brain, "Somebody Else Should Be Your Own Best Friend," *Psychology Today* 11 (1977, October): 83–84, 120, 123.

chapter will provide an appropriate initial step in determining what others have found.

In the final paragraph of the Preface, authors normally thank those people "without whom this book would never have been completed." Then authors often go on to thank people who didn't actually work on the book. In this case, it is undeniably clear that the first author would indeed never have brought this edition to print were it not for the exhaustive efforts of Anita Vangelisti. The first author is deeply thankful for the expertise, insight, efficiency, good humor, and plain hard work she brought to this collaboration. In this case, two heads were better than one. Since this book is about relationships, the first author's new and ongoing relationships also need to be thanked for their part in the development of the book. In a book like this, the first place an author looks for examples of concepts is in his or her own relationships. Therefore, I'd like to formally acknowledge a few key people who constitute the treasury of my examples: to my longest and strongest relationship, Mom and Dad; to the miracle baby, Avery—my newest and most energizing relationship; to my brother, Herb, and my sister, Maralee, who for as long as I can remember have kept alive in me the feeling that they are prepared to drop everything if I ever need them; to my daughter, Hilary, and my son, Eric—for the wonderful richness of our relationship and for ever-expanding my understanding of love; and to Lillian, that one-of-a-kind ideal spouse who nobody really believes exists (especially after twenty years), but I know different.

The second author would like to begin her list of "thank yous" with Mark Knapp—for his wisdom, understanding, intuition, and honesty about personal relationships. Few people are given the opportunity to talk, think, or write with their professional "heroes." Working on this book has allowed me to do all three. Thank you. I am also indebted to several relationships (and the people in them) for some important lessons. Thank you to my mother and father, for teaching me how to stick together through thick and thin; to Claire and Serena, for showing me that being best friends is as important as being best sisters; to Carlos, Charlie, John, Laurie, and Marcia (my "first" class)—though you've gone your separate ways, your unfailing support for each other still brings me hope and laughter; and to John, Johnny, and Erin, for making my life more full (especially to John for carrying extra luggage, stopping for cappuccino, and bringing us a little closer each day). And, thank you to Mark and Lillian, for showing the rest of us that it can work.

We appreciate the thoughts and suggestions provided by the following reviewers: Mary Banski, University of Houston; Melanie Booth-Butterfield, West Virginia University; and Karen Roloff, DePaul University. Finally, we would both like to especially thank our editor, Karon Bowers, for making the development of this edition so sane, efficient, and conflict-free—a rare and beautiful talent.

Mark L. Knapp
Anita L. Vangelisti

Human Communication in Developing Relationships

Communication: The Lifeblood of Relationships

Dear Dr. Knapp,

Why is it so difficult for people to express their true feelings to other people they are close to? My boyfriend drives me nuts sometimes because he can't seem to figure out how he feels about things. He'll say, "No, I don't think you're being too sensitive . . ." and think that he really believes what he's saying. But if I keep talking to him, I find that he's feeling something very different . . . which is what I thought in the first place! Even though he usually admits I was right not to believe what he says at first, I find this confusing and irritating. Why doesn't he know how he really feels about things? Why does he spout off and say things that aren't true? Is he afraid to express himself to me?

Bewildered and Bothered

Sometimes our communication with others is bewildering. It is the purpose of this chapter to explore some of the subtle and sometimes indirect, along with the more direct, ways we use to discuss the nature of our relationships with others. In general, then, this chapter is designed to provide the reader with some realistic expectations for the many ways we communicate with our relationship partners and how these patterns change when the relationship changes.

> *The study of everyday life quickly focuses on interpersonal communication—the sequencing of messages in conversations and the sequencing of conversations into relationships—as the primary activity in human sociation and has demonstrated that apparently simple acts of conversation are in fact incredibly complex feats which even social scientists can perform better than they can explain.*
>
> —*W. Barnett Pearce*

People meet and separate. But funny things happen in between. It's almost as if mysterious forces are pushing and pulling us—sometimes muddling our minds, sometimes captivating our souls. Abstract? Definitely. Poetry? Perhaps. The introduction to a scholarly textbook bent on demystifying human communication in developing relationships? Unlikely.

Fortunately, however, the foregoing introduction serves one rather important function. The abstract references to "things" and "mysterious forces" serve to remind all of us how frequently we avoid concrete and detailed descriptions of our own interpersonal relationships. For example, lovers may say, "What we have is so beautiful—to try to explain it, is to ruin it"; a divorcee might reflect: "I can't pinpoint anything specific . . . the relationship just wasn't making it for me anymore"; friends, too, may balk at detailed examination of their relationships: "I don't know. I just like him. Isn't that enough?"[1]

For those who study human communication, it is not enough. Such statements only raise questions: (1) Are there regular and systematic patterns of communication that suggest stages on the road to an intimate relationship? Are there similar patterns and stages that characterize the deterioration of relationships? (2) Can we identify communication strategies that attract and repel us at various stages in a relationship? Specifically, how do people talk to each other when they are building, maintaining, or tearing down a relationship? (3) What are these mysterious forces that propel us in and out of relationships? And what determines how fast or slow a relationship progresses or dissolves? It is the purpose of this book to seek answers to these questions.

One important issue that seems logically to precede tackling any of the aforementioned questions, is the rationale for carefully scrutinizing the communication-relationship interface in the first place. Why devote an entire book to the communication behavior manifested at various stages of a relationship? Is it simply because this is a popular topic which reflects the climate of the times—surfacing in such diverse sources as the songs of Whitney Houston, the pages of *True Romance,* or the *Journal of Personality and Social Psychology*? If mere popularity were the sole justification for our concern, the idea would soon be stripped of any relevance to our daily lives. Instead, we are grappling with a phenomenon that has been, and always will be, with us; one that is inherent in everything we say and do and one that reflects the very nature of human communication itself.

Relationship Messages

It is difficult, if not impossible, to think of any message sent by one person to another that does not, in some way, also carry a commentary on the relationship between the two parties. In a sense, then, each message carries information at two levels. Watzlawick, Beavin, and Jackson call these the *content level* and the *relationship level*.[2] To illustrate this concept, consider the following example. When I say, "Come in. Have a seat," the content indicates some rather specific behaviors to follow. However, there may also be a *relationship message* (combination of vocal, verbal, and nonverbal cues), which says: "I don't know you very well; you probably want a lot from me, but won't give much in return; let's keep this brief and formal; state your business and get out; I am in control of this situation and this is just the first of several directives I'll be issuing in the next few minutes; because of my position, I expect you to follow my orders." In short, the relationship message tells us how to interpret the content. It should also be noted that message content may carry some important relationship information. In the phrase, "Get me a cup of coffee," the content itself involves one person doing something for the other and the form is a direct injunction. This may be taken by the recipient as a message indicative of a superior/subordinate relationship.[3] Regardless of their origin, relationship messages provide us with a good deal of information about how we see the other person, how we see ourselves, what kind of relationship the two of us have in this situation, what kind of relationship we have generally, or what kind of relationship is desired in the future.

What we are doing on the relationship level is sending a message about a message—communication about communication—which is called *metacommunication*.[4] Sometimes we receive relationship information through the perception of nonverbal cues enacted during the verbal message—for example, a stern look, a curt voice, a warm handshake, a reduction of physical space separating the communicators. Sometimes messages are verbally altered and adapted to meet the demands of a specific relationship. A student may say, "Ok, uh, Professor Lipid. I can see you have some other students waiting to see you, so I guess I'll leave. Thanks so much for your help. I'll see you tomorrow in class." The same student would no doubt terminate his conversation with a close friend in a much different manner: "Yeah, right. Later." Sometimes we feel the necessity of metacommunicating verbally when we sense our nonverbal cues have not been sufficient. One partner in a dating pair says: "You think I'd go to an x-rated movie with *you*? You must be crazy!" This is followed by a smile, a friendly touch, and a laugh—all of which attempt to communicate: "We have such a warm and understanding relationship I can add a playful dimension and you will understand and accept it." However, if the non-verbal cues did not serve their intended purpose (either through sender or receiver error), it may be necessary for the speaker to metacommunicate by verbally stating his or her intentions were of a "kidding" nature. This example also illustrates the confusion that incongruous verbal and nonverbal cues can cause: "Your words say you love me, but your behavior leaves considerable doubt."

Much of the time we process relationship-level information without much conscious thought—almost automatically. On at least three occasions, though, we are keenly aware of relationship messages. (1) One such occasion is when the message seems to violate drastically our expectations for the relationship in a given situation—being greeted by a stranger with a hello, a hug, and a kiss! (2) A second occasion is when we are involved in relationships characterized by high levels of intensity. The engaged couple, for example, will be particularly sensitive to all communication addressing itself to the nature of their relationship. Likewise, a couple battling the forces pulling their relationship apart will heighten their awareness for any information that impinges on the viability of their two-person community. In these situations we see a fusion of the content and relationship levels—both providing information pertaining to the relationship itself. (3) Finally, a third occasion is when disagreement and conflict arise. During such strife, the combatants may have several reactions: trying to become the sole "winner"; planning strategies to be "one-up" next time and thereby recoup losses incurred from not "winning"; simply enjoying the feeling of being whipped by the other's rhetorical superiority, and so on. The following dialogue, focusing on marital conflict, serves to summarize some of the concepts outlined in the preceding paragraphs:

WIFE: Honey, you really watch too much TV.	*Although the content addresses a specific behavior, the relationship level is saying: I wish you didn't have so many things which take time and attention away from me. TV is only one minor example which happened to strike me at the moment.*
HUSBAND: I do not.	*The relationship message has been ignored completely, and the husband prepares himself for the impending battle over TV watching.*
WIFE: C'mon, honey . . . you do too.	*The wife feels obligated to defend her initial statement. She cannot or will not verbalize the major problem with the relationship but*

tries not to be too argumentative at this point. She is still hoping her husband will respond to her cues that reveal the relationship message—sitting on the arm of his chair with her arm around his shoulders.

HUSBAND: All right, then, I won't watch any TV for a whole week, damn it!

He is still trying to win on the content level. His kick-me-while-I'm-down strategy is clever because if she agrees, she is really a bitch—knowing what a sacrifice it would be. (The "damn it" dramatized the sacrifice.) Besides, if she agrees, he will still "win" because she will feel guilty for having caused him to be one-down—which of course puts him one-up.

WIFE: Oh, just forget it. Do what you want.

The wife sees the trap her husband has prepared on the content level. She gives up on the possibility of positive communication on the relationship level and removes herself from his chair and starts to leave the scene.

HUSBAND: Forget it! How can I forget it? You come in here and make a big deal out of my TV habits. Then, to satisfy you, I agree to cut it out completely and you say, "forget it"! What's wrong with you, anyway?

He realizes he has "won" on the content level and finally tunes in the relationship level—only to find negative cues. As if enjoying a relationship where he dominates, he tries to prolong his "winning" streak by urging continued argument—never realizing he is also prolonging his counterpart's losing streak.

Now the wife assesses her marital relationship. Her husband does not pay enough attention to her; he was insensitive to her metacommunication about their relationship; he enjoys dominating her; and now he has impugned her sanity for wishing to drop an issue she raised in the first place. The forecast for the immediate future is a long, miserable argument about TV watching. The long-range forecast is a frustrated and confused husband who can't understand why his wife is leaving him, especially since the only thing they fought about was so trivial—TV watching. For illustrative clarity, this dialogue focuses our attention on the husband's response to relationship messages. Obviously, this "interaction snapshot" distorts the dynamics of the husband–wife relationship and their mutual contribution to it. We might, for instance, find a link between the husband's desire to watch TV and the wife's previous orientation to *his* relationship messages.

Thus, human communication may be affected by the existing relationship, but it will also structure the nature of any future relationship. You know you must communicate a great deal of affection to your lover because that is the nature of your commitment. In the process of making these messages of affection, however, you may do one of two things, depending on how effective you are at sending or how effective your lover is at receiving: (1) you may affirm the level of your relationship, or (2) you may change the level of your relationship to one of greater or lesser intimacy.

Up to this point, we have focused primarily on relationship messages communicated in the course of everyday conversation. But what about those times when people talk to each other (or third parties) directly and specifically about their relationships? What do they talk about? How do they talk in order to make sense of their relationships? Two studies that gathered information from people in a variety of relationships suggest the following:[5]

- People talk about relationships as *work*—the effort involved, the sacrifices, the energy needed, and so on.
- People talk about the *commitment* associated with relationships. This involves both the commitment necessary to begin a relationship and the commitment needed to sustain it.
- People talk about relationships as *involvement*. Involvement is reflected in such things as the time spent together, the quantity and quality of the talk, and sharing.
- People talk about their relationships as *unique or special*.
- People talk about relationships in terms of *manipulation*. Manipulation is the control of one's partner for one's own gains.
- People talk about relationships in terms of *consideration and respect*.
- People talk about their relationships as a developing *journey of discovery*.
- People talk about their relationships as a *game*.
- People talk about their relationships as *risky and potentially dangerous*.
- People talk about their relationships as *uncontrollable forces*.
- People talk about their relationships as a system of *bargaining and tradeoffs*.

Obviously, different types of relationships will emphasize different themes. And sometimes the interaction will focus on the lack of these factors as well as their presence.

The *involvement* theme noted above seemed to be the overriding issue in a study of fifty-two married couples who were asked to discuss with each other a list of common problems facing married couples.[6] The content of these conversations included *communal themes* (togetherness, interdependence); *individual themes* (emphasizing separate identities and roles); and *impersonal themes* (factors/forces outside the marriage which are believed responsible for shaping it). The couples who manifested more communal themes tended to report a greater satisfaction with their relationships than those who exhibited more individual themes.

In addition to helping us understand the content of couples' talk about their relationships, this study identifies another important feature of interaction—namely, how the two partners combine their efforts as they discuss the content of their relationship. Thus, no matter what content was being discussed, the couples were also communicating a message about their relationship by *how* they interacted. These styles of communication included: (1) *blending* ("mutually confirming and overlapping talk about shared rules, interpretations, activities, backgrounds, and experiences"); (2) *differentiating* ("unintegrated discussion of individual characteristics"); and (3) *balanced* ("discussion of individual characteristics balanced by integrative higher-order themes").

Five Important Misconceptions About Communication in Relationships

Even under the best conditions, communicating effectively in human relationships can be difficult. Even when we try very hard, effective communication may elude us. Sometimes these problems are associated with rigid and inappropriate assumptions about the nature of communication in relationships.

1.   The Assumption of Consistency   ("But that's not what you said yesterday.") Having *others* "be consistent" is highly valued in this society. It should be. It helps us make useful predictions about others so that we can adopt appropriate attitudes and behavior toward them. It is understandable, then, that seeming inconsistencies in others receive far less support than those we perceive in ourselves. On the other hand, we want to be able to change our *own* opinion or behavior; to be both independent and dependent; to be a person who is both stingy and generous; to be fully committed to co-habitation with somebody but also want time alone; to be a "take-charge" person in some things at some times and a willing "follower" on other occasions. And we really like people who understand this. Even though we value consistency in others, we rarely thank someone for pointing out a seeming inconsistency in our own behavior.

One of the reasons we aren't very receptive to another's accusations of inconsistency is that we may not perceive it as an inconsistency. Inconsistency and consistency are in the eye and ear of the beholder. For example, within fifteen minutes a wife makes these statements to her husband: "You spend too much money," and "You don't ever take me out to a nice restaurant anymore." The husband may perceive these as inconsistent—thinking he would have to spend money to take his wife out to dinner. The wife does not see the inconsistency because she is talking about his *personal* spending, not spending for their *mutual* benefit. In addition, to the wife the importance of going out together far supersedes the importance of spending money. Much of what we say omits important personal reservations which listeners would do well to explore before charging the person with inconsistency.

We should expect relationship messages to exhibit both consistency and inconsistency. The so-called "ideal" relationship does not manifest a continual stream of supportive messages. Ideal relationships are those in which the participants understand and appreciate the necessity of both positive and negative messages. Those with less tolerance for seemingly inconsistent behavior may have more trouble maintaining a wide variety of relationships. This intolerance for inconsistency may be especially troublesome in more enduring relationships because we often tend to emphasize our consistency first and reveal contrariety later.

Why do these seeming inconsistencies occur? Because life situations and communication contexts change. You may want to be "wild and crazy" at the party and "quiet and conservative" at home; you may find frequent conversations on the topic of sex rewarding at one point in your life and boring at another. If we assume a person is "always like that" or "always will be like that," we run a high risk of being wrong. We may like somebody more than anyone we know but not want to marry them; we may love somebody more than anyone else but vehemently dislike something about them. While some may wish to view such behavior as "inconsistent," it is more productively viewed as natural—reflecting the continual unfolding and complexity of each human being. When it seems to occur, it may be a valuable opportunity for learning more about the other person and your relationship—rather than a time for trying to straighten out what will never be straight.

*2.   **The Assumption of Simple Meaning***   ("Well, you said it so you must have meant it!"). Most of us are taught to pay attention to what is said—the words. Words do provide us with some information, but meanings are derived from so many other sources that it would hinder our effectiveness as a partner to a relationship to rely too heavily on words alone. Words are used to describe only a small part of the many ideas we associate with any given message. Sometimes we can gain insight into some of those associations if we listen for more than words. We don't always say what we mean or mean what we say. Sometimes our words don't mean anything except "I'm letting off some steam. I don't really want you to pay close attention to what I'm saying. Just pay attention to what I'm feeling." Mostly we mean several things at once.

Doonesbury

A person wanting to purchase a house says to the current owner, "This step has to be fixed before I'll buy." The owner says, "It's been like that for years." Actually, the step hasn't been like that for years, but the unspoken message is: "I don't want to fix it. We put up with it. Why can't you?" The search for a more expansive view of meaning can be developed by examining a message in terms of *who* said it, *when* it occurred, the *related conditions* or situation, and *how* it was said.

The person *who* is making the message influences the meanings associated with it. If a parent says, "I see you're reading *The Joy of Sex*," it may mean "I don't approve of you reading this book. Don't let me see you with it again." But if a friend says the same thing, it may suggest, "I wish I had a copy. Can I have it when you're finished?" When you have several different relationships with a single person (e.g., your teacher is also your friend), it is wise to consider the possibility of different meanings as you move from one type of relationship to another. Males and females may also say the same thing in different ways.[7]

When a message occurs can also reveal associated meaning. Let us assume two couples do exactly the same amount of kissing and arguing. But one couple always kisses after an argument and the other couple always argues after a kiss. The ordering of the behaviors may mean a great deal more than the frequency of the behavior. A friend's unusually docile behavior may only be understood by noting that it was preceded by situations that required an abnormal amount of assertiveness. Some responses may be directly linked to a developing pattern of responses and defy logic. For example, a person who says "No!" to a series of charges like "You're dumb," "You're lazy," and "You're dishonest," may also say "No!" and try to justify his or her response if the next statement is "And you're good looking."

The *related conditions* accompanying any given message are also influential factors in assessing the meaning of messages. For example, the meaning of "you're crazy" may vary greatly depending on whether it is said in the context of a psychiatric evaluation, a marital quarrel, or a playful gesture by a friend. "OK, let's step outside," may mean something very different to two men at a ski lodge wishing to determine the weather conditions or two men in a bar who are arguing intensely. It is also the analysis of the situation that informs us that the statement, "It's cold in here," is not an observation but really a request to close the window.

We would do well to listen for *how* messages are presented. The words, "It sure has been nice to have you over," can be said with emphasis and excitement or ritualistically. The phrase can be said once or repeated several times. And the meanings we associate with the phrase will change accordingly. Sometimes if we say something infrequently it assumes more importance; sometimes the more we say something the less importance it assumes.

The preceding paragraphs illustrate only a few of the factors that affect the meanings we derive from interpersonal communication. In the interests of efficiency we have learned to take a lot for granted as we speak and listen to others.[8] The recognition of this habit should make us especially careful about attributions of meaning when sending and attending to especially important messages in our lives.

3. *The Assumption of Communicator Independence* ("It wasn't my fault."). Many times we talk about our relationships with people as if we had no *relation* or connection to them—as if our behavior had nothing to do with what the other did. In actuality, however, we have a lot more to do with our partner's responses than we may wish to acknowledge. The reason we often fail to acknowledge this interdependence is that it means we have to accept more of the responsibility for our communication problems. It is much easier to describe your partner's behavior as independent of your own—e.g., "He never listens to me"; "She is never serious with me"; "He doesn't tell me the truth." Acknowledging interdependence forces you to ask yourself what you do to elicit such responses and what you can do to get the responses you desire. Communicators who recognize their interdependence also recognize that communication problems are the result of mutual contributions. One person can't be entirely clean and the other entirely dirty. Sometimes it is also hard to admit that our *success* in communicating with our partner may also be related to interdependence. We live in a society that reveres and rewards individual achievement, but whatever excellence in communication we achieve in relationships has to consider the role of our partner. For example, if your partner wasn't such a good audience for your humorous remarks, would you be as funny?

Communicative interdependence of relationship partners can manifest itself in many ways. One of these is called *response matching*. Sometimes response matching is performed almost unconsciously, but at other times it is well thought out. Studies reveal that people tend to match each other's length of utterance; interruptions and silences; the use of certain types of words; the extent to which one reveals information about himself or herself; and certain nonverbal signals like nodding, smiling, posture, and voice loudness. In addition, certain types of responses are often matched. Jokes, showing solidarity, giving opinions, disagreeing and questioning, often lead to more of the same from the other person.[9] Affectionate responses often follow affectionate responses; hostility often follows from hostile responses; distrust commonly leads to distrust. Sometimes one response will bring forth an almost opposite response. Dominance, for instance, often elicits submission, and submissive responses often elicit dominant reactions. To make matters more complex, sometimes we act on what we think a person thinks of us rather than how we see ourselves—e.g., if you think of yourself as a rather conventional person and your friend thinks you are eccentric and expects you to behave that way, you may respond with eccentric behavior when you are with that person.

Matching and other manifestations of interdependent communication do not, of course, always occur. But they happen often enough so we know they play an important role in developing relationship. The longer a relationship endures, the more interdependence plays a role in each partner's behavior. Over time, each partner's behavior becomes so integrally bound up with their partner that questions of what is interdependent and what isn't are no longer useful in analyzing the relationship. The knowledge that each partner's behavior has important effects on the other means we need to consider the important role our own behavior plays in how we feel our relationship partner treats us. As Timothy Leary said:

> What we are saying here to the human being is, You are mainly responsible for your life situation. You have created your own world. Your own interpersonal behavior has, more than any other factor, determined the reception you get from others. Your slowly developing pattern of reflexes has trained others and yourself to accept you as this sort of person—to be treated in this sort of way. You are the manager of your own destiny![10]

4. *The Assumption of Obvious Causation* ("You can't fool me. I know why you said that.") Sometimes people's motives are fairly clear; sometimes the causes of another's behavior don't matter much to the relationship. When it is important to reflect on why people do what they do in order to help us predict future behavior, we should approach our task with considerable tentativeness and humility. Too many of us jump too quickly to conclusions about the causes of another's responses. If these conclusions are the result of assuming such causes are simple and obvious, they may be incorrect and hinder future prediction. But even if you have correctly deduced your partner's motivation for saying or doing something, you may find he or she denies it and gets very defensive if you suggest that the behavior "was *obviously* caused by. . . ."

Motivations and causes are usually complex and sometimes well-hidden. As much as we try to be clear and certain about what we say, ambivalence is a very common experience in today's world. Sometimes we honestly don't know why we say or do things.[11] And if it isn't clear to us, it is difficult to admit that another person might understand—although it is certainly possible. We enact many communication acts and routines at low levels of awareness—making the often-heard charge, "You *knew* what you were saying (doing)," something less of a truism than many people believe.

Your interpretation of your partner's behavior is inevitably filtered through your own needs and expectations. Your partner's perceptions of his or her own behavior are similarly affected, and sometimes the explanation of why something happened only becomes "clear" in retrospect. Each of our responses is overlaid with possible causations stemming from the specific encounter, the demands of the communicator's life stage, the relationship between the communicators, events and people outside the specific encounter, and many other sources. As listeners, we can only approach an understanding of some of these sources—and even then it may take an extended time.

> *Seven-eighths of everything can't be seen.*
> Anonymous

5.   The Assumption of Finality   ("That settles it."). If something is "finished," it no longer requires the same effort, attention, and concern. As a result, we sometimes act *as if* something is finished in order to set other priorities for our available time and energy. This process will be functional until we begin to believe such things are *actually* finished. Then you are in for some surprises.

People can reach a compromise when they disagree, but the issue in some form may arise minutes, months, or years later. A person's trauma over a parent's untimely death may be temporarily concluded with, "I'm over it," but the trauma may recur later. The partner to your relationship may be a person you "know well," but you will never be finished trying to know that person if you want to maintain a high degree of knowledge. The person changes from day to day. If you are mean to a person because you feel that your relationship will soon be "finished" and you'll never see the person again, you may be surprised to find that person in charge of something you want later in life. Divorce should not be expected to finalize your thoughts of the other person. And you should not assume that you have finished learning about certain communication situations just because you've faced them before.

All of these examples point out that both what we communicate about and the messages we make are constantly in process, ever-changing—a reality which prohibits the luxury of dismissing an issue, person, or behavior as forever finished. People who maintain effective relationships do not approach them passively. An understanding of process is just one factor that keeps people from assuming that the satisfying relationship they have today will continue without careful monitoring and adaptation.

Now we can return to one of our initial questions: How do people talk to each other when they are building, maintaining, or tearing down a relationship? A general understanding of this process can be gained by examining some broad dimensions of communication behavior in developing and deteriorating relationships.

How Communication Changes as Our Relationships Develop

In Table 1.1 you will observe eight dimensions along which our communication with other people varies. There may be other important dimensions, but these allow us to discuss important differences in types of relationships and different stages in the development of a single relationship. First, let's define the dimensions.

1. Narrow–Broad   During the process of coming together, we would predict a gradually increasing variety and amount of exchange, or breadth. More topics are covered in more ways. You may choose to talk to another person only about college and sex (Figure 1.1). Within each category many things could be said: facts, ideas, experiences, feelings about yourself or others, opinions, attitudes. These items are represented in Figure 1.1 by the smaller subdivisions within each cate-

TABLE 1.1   Eight Communication Dimensions that Change in Developing and Decaying Relationships[12]

Growth Stages ———————→
←——————— *Decay Stages*

Narrow	___	___	___	___	___ Broad
Public	___	___	___	___	___ Personal
Stylized	___	___	___	___	___ Unique
Difficult	___	___	___	___	___ Efficient
Rigid	___	___	___	___	___ Flexible
Awkward	___	___	___	___	___ Smooth
Hesitant	___	___	___	___	___ Spontaneous
Overt Judgment Suspended	___	___	___	___	___ Overt Judgment Given

Topic Category: Sex

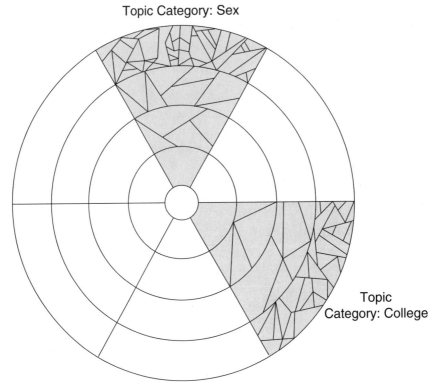

Topic
Category: College

1.1 The Concepts of Communication Breadth and Depth[13]

gory. Thus, for any given situation, the number of categories opened up and the frequency of interaction within each category can be identified. A sampling of possible breadth profiles derived from this concept is:

a. A person who talks about a few topic areas and reveals little within each area. For example, the person who only wants to talk about sports, and within that category only bowling, but won't reveal how he or she got started bowling or what score is usually bowled.

b. A person who talks about a few topic areas and reveals a lot within each area. For example, the person who limits conversation to job and sports categories, but will talk incessantly about both, freely divulging a wide range of nonintimate, superficial information.

c. A person who talks about many topic areas and reveals little within each area. For example, you may discuss sex, family, sports, religion, politics, child rearing, house construction, drugs, and school—all in the space of a short conversation—and come away with the feeling that you really don't know much about that person because as soon as you asked a probing question, the topic was changed.

d. A person who talks about many topic areas and reveals a great deal within each area. This person is probably perceived as a good conversationalist. Interestingly, sometimes this person is also considered a very open person, willing to talk about a wide range of subjects and eager to reveal many items within each category. However, breadth of interaction is only one form of openness and should not be confused with depth or what we are referring to as the Public–Personal dimension.

In the embryonic stages of developing relationships, our communicative options are often limited to a rather restricted range, which is usually determined by culturally accepted modes of exchange. When relationships begin to come apart it is not unusual to note the need to circumscribe the breadth of communication topics and responses—"I just don't want to talk about that." When both parties are bent on destroying the relationship, they do not feel the need to broaden the scope of their interaction. But in attempts to save or rejuvenate a relationship, extending the breadth may be an effort to find other less sensitive areas where nonthreatening interaction can take place and thereby increase the total rewards and offset increasing costs.

2. ***Public–Personal*** This dimension may also be referred to as depth of social penetration. Initially, our public personality is revealed. Should the relationship move forward, we will increasingly uncover more and more of our private or personal selves. This is true for nonverbal as well as verbal communication. In decaying relationships we try to shut off valves that may release personal communication. To require personal communication and accessibility prior to the gradual establishment of a close and trusting relationship will sometimes induce frustration, resistance, rejection, or outright rebellion. Examples where this has occurred are some welfare recipients who are required to hold almost nothing back from state agencies; prisoners who relinquish rights to privacy to their guards and lawyers; and nursing home residents whose dependent status often requires a list of immediate and personal disclosures to their caretakers.

You can visually observe the concept of depth by reexamining Figure 1.1. The concentric circles indicate the possibility of probing the depth of one's personality. The innermost circle represents the core, the most difficult to reach, a place which constitutes a last refuge for our most personal thoughts, feelings, and beliefs. The core and central layers of personality include information about our deepest fears, our most important needs, our basic values, and thoughts about our identity and self-worth. Once revealed, such information may make us very vulnerable. Hence, we often mask, hide, or generally make it difficult for most people to see these central layers. More often than not, the components found in the central layers are not common to many individuals, but have an individual stamp of uniqueness attached to them. When changes occur in the central layers, there will be corresponding changes in the intermediate and outer layers. Once the foundation is changed, the outer structure changes accordingly. This interdependency helps explain some of our communication behavior. For instance, if a person has once penetrated into a central area and is familiar with a basic value held by another person, it is much easier to predict items that may be represented as attitudes in the intermediate area, and as personal history in the outer layer. This also helps explain why a pair, once having achieved penetration to a central layer in a given category, can move easily and swiftly in and out of preceding areas.

As we move outward from the central areas, we come to the intermediate layers. These may contain a wide range of attitudes and opinions on various issues, which decrease in strength as outer layers are approached. The outermost circle represents the most easily accessible parts of an individual's personality and is often largely biographical in nature. The outer layer contains more items than the other layers, but these items will have the least importance or general influence on the total system.

To summarize the concepts of both breadth and depth and to show their usefulness for examining communication at various stages of a relationship, examine Figure 1.2. Here we see the kind of social penetration taking place between a husband, his wife, his friend, and a new acquaintance.

Although the frequency of interaction is not visually illustrated, it is likely that greater breadth and depth will be associated with greater frequency. Several other observations can be made:

a. The wife has the most intimate relationship with her husband, achieving greater breadth and depth. She has penetrated more categories (all but one) and more items within every category. Some categories are special to her relationship and are revealed only to her.

b. The friend has had some breadth and some depth—less than the wife and more than the new acquaintance.

c. The new acquaintance has the most superficial relationship with the husband—little breadth and little depth.

d. The husband has one category that is not open to anyone at any level. He seems to be particularly comfortable with one category, since it has been penetrated by all persons. Should the relationship with the new acquaintance grow in breadth, we might predict the next category to be accessible would be the one already penetrated by the wife and friend.

3. *Stylized–Unique* The process of constructing a more intimate relationship eventually reaches a point where we are interacting with the other person as a

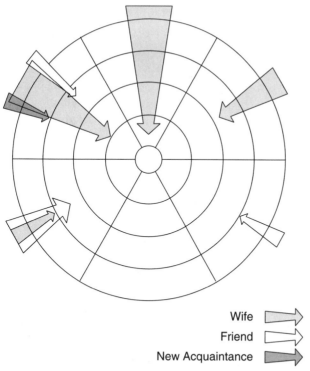

Wife ⇒
Friend ⇒
New Acquaintance ⇒

1.2 Multiple Relationships in the Social Penetration Process

unique individual rather than as a member of a particular society. Uniqueness in communication simply suggests the adoption of a more idiosyncratic communication system adapted to the peculiar nature of the interacting parties. This is not to suggest adaptation is absent in early stages, but that it is adaptation to a more generalized other (an orientation toward another that makes sociological and cultural predictions rather than personal and individual ones) and involves a more stylized behavior acceptable to large groups of people. The handshake is one example of a stylized or conventional behavior which seems to fade away when people label themselves close friends. Actual handshakes or false starts may reappear, however, when close friends have been absent from each other for a long time, if one party is unsure of his or her standing as a close friend, or when the content calls for great formality. In the deterioration process it is not uncommon to see the formalities of stylized communication returning, as if to say: "I am no longer going to acknowledge the peculiar nature of our relationship and will treat you more like I would a large number of people."

4. *Difficult–Efficient*   As a relationship grows and more of the other person is revealed to us, there will be increased accuracy, speed, and efficiency in our communication.[14] Early stages in a relationship hold greater possibilities for less accurate communication and slower progress because we rely so heavily on stereotyped behaviors and fewer channels of communication. There is less reliance on, and ability to interpret nonverbal cues accurately. In short, sensitivity to sending and receiving increases with growing levels of intimacy even though a certain level of inaccuracy may be functional for all types of relationships.[15] Once familiarity with unique styles of communication is obtained, less energy is needed to communicate intended meanings. The decay process is often initiated when *less* energy is assumed to mean *no* energy, which of course precipitates more difficult communication and less efficiency.

5.   *Rigid–Flexible*   Flexibility simply refers to the number of different ways any given idea or feeling can be communicated. The more advanced the stage of growth, the greater the flexibility. For example, anger in long-married couples may take many forms—a frown; a long period of silence; a short, curt "yeah"; a verbal statement; a grunt or growl; a flick of the wrist or arm; the use of the newspaper as a shield; general fidgeting. In the early stages of growth and the later stages of decay there is a greater demand for standardization of communication involving fewer channels.

6.   *Awkward–Smooth*   As knowledge of the other person increases, predictive ability also increases, which leads to greater synchronization of interaction. Each participant is well aware of mutual roles and plays them out in a smooth, complementary fashion. Some have called this phenomenon *meshing*. The comment, "it was all very awkward," is most likely directed at an interaction with a stranger, new acquaintance, or a situation experiencing the strain of decay.

7.   *Hesitant–Spontaneous*   Meeting new people is naturally accompanied by hesitancy. We can make some general predictions about how most people react in this situation, but caution is the byword when little information on a specific person is available. We can also assume that the forces that trigger the deterioration process are, at least in part, related to faulty predictions. When actively engaged in decay processes, we will see an increased hesitancy, whether the participants are trying to save the relationship or whether they both want to terminate it. In close relationships, on the other hand, we find a sort of communicative spontaneity— an informality, an ease of opening up oneself, a comfort in entering areas of the other person, a relationship that flows and changes direction easily. When talking to strangers we seem to reflect caution by using a greater diversity of language choices than we use with friends. With friends we tend to fall back on more habitual verbal behavior.[16] Partners in intimate relationships are expected to grant each other a certain "latitude of understanding" which provides them with a freedom and relaxation that may not exist with newer acquaintances.

8. *Overt Judgment Suspended–Overt Judgment Given*   Although our first impressions of another person probably involve a number of covert judgments, these evaluations are usually unspoken until the relationship reaches a more advanced stage. Large amounts of negative responses between strangers probably mean they have little interest, or opportunity for, developing the relationship further.[17] The closer the relationship, the greater the likelihood of freely giving and receiving positive and negative feedback. Both criticism and praise are much less inhibited in an intimate relationship. Naturally, judgments (usually negative) are an integral part of the initial decay process. Gradually, as the relationship continues to decay, the participants will move toward the suspension of overt evaluation again. "I'd rather just not talk about it."

Now that we have a general understanding of these eight dimensions of communication and how they differ in intimate and nonintimate relationships, let's examine them in greater detail lest we be misled by the seeming simplicity of the process.

Dimensions of Communication: Patterns and Variations

As the arrows in Figure 1.3 suggest, communication behavior typical of any of the eight dimensions moves from left to right (nonintimate to intimate) as people seek closer relationships; communication behavior on any of the dimensions may also move from right to left (intimate to nonintimate) as people become more distant from each other.

Stable and Varied Patterns of Communication

At any given time the communication pattern may reflect deviations on some dimensions that are greater than the expected normal fluctuations. For example, in Figure 1.3, the difficulty and awkwardness of communication are greater than what we would have predicted, given the general similarity of the other dimensions. This configuration may reflect the beginning of communication at a less intimate level, or it may simply reflect the fact that all relationships are composed of coexisting forces which seem in opposition to one another. Intimate relationships have coldness, sadness, and difficulty to accompany the warmth, happiness, and ease. Thus, the behaviors that contribute to relationship decay are normally found in all relationships—but in smaller doses. These "less-pleasant" behaviors may serve a useful function by creating the tension necessary to cause the participants to seek greater intimacy. These temporary fluctuations, however, take place within an overall pattern which reflects the relationship stage (see Chapter 2). Frequent fluctuations over time on many of the dimensions of communication may be the best gauge of instability rather than occasional variations on a few dimensions.

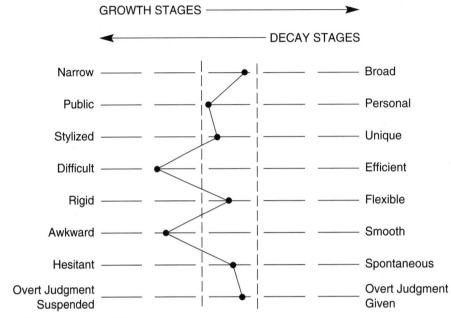

1.3 Plotting Patterns of Communication

It should also be noted that intimate relationships are not likely to sustain communication patterns that represent intimacy extremes. There are limits to which we can communicate uniquely, personally, smoothly, etc. There are also limits or extremes for any type of communication that will vary with the preferences of the couple. One couple's "extreme" of personal communication may be much lower than another's. As relationships become increasingly intimate, some of these extremes may be reached, but they stabilize at lower levels. Figure 1.4 illustrates this idea by showing how the pattern for public/personal communication may develop over time. Other dimensions probably show similar development. As Figure 1.4 shows, we do not continue to reveal more and more of ourselves to another forever. Not only are we limited in what we can and want to reveal, but our desire to know some aspects of our partner may change when we know we can.

Communication Patterns Are Interdependent

The interdependency among the communication dimensions generally means that changes on one dimension will prompt changes on others—e.g., if I am critical about the way you dress (overt judgment given), we may decide to discuss the subject of dress more or avoid it completely (breadth variation); this, in turn, may lead to more or less hesitancy, personal disclosure, etc.

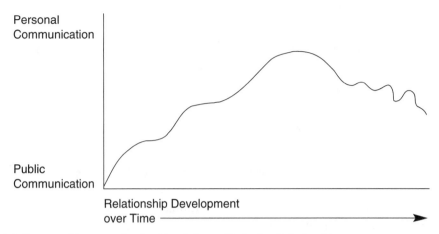

1.4 Pattern of Communication Depth for an Enduring Relationship

Quantity Vs. Quality of Communication

The pattern shown in Figure 1.4 represents the quantity of personal disclosures as well as the quality. When relationships are reaching for more intimacy (during the establishment of a relationship or during periods when efforts are made to rejuvenate a troubled relationship), the quantity or frequency of behaviors is probably the best intimacy indicator.[18] When relationships have stabilized at a particular level of intimacy, the quality of the behavior (perceived sincerity, magnitude of expression, perfect timing, and so on) is more likely to be the best measure of intimacy. For example, many personal disclosures are necessary to establish an intimate relationship; thereafter, occasional disclosures are sufficient to sustain it. A single instance of self-disclosure may be perceived as the equivalent of many earlier disclosures or it may simply serve as a reminder that when important disclosures need to be made, they will be. When intimates wish to recapture a lost level of intimacy, the frequency of personal communications is likely to increase.

Diversity of Communication Characterizes Each Dimension

The fact that there are many ways of communicating at each point on each dimension should be emphasized. You may be operating at the lowest level of intimacy on the public/personal dimension with many people. Even though you communicate many different things in many different ways, the common characteristic is the extremely impersonal or public nature of this communication. The variety of possible communication patterns should increase as intimacy increases. Intimates may use unique and personal patterns, but they may also use patterns from earlier and less intimate stages of development which have less uniqueness and personalness. And, although people who are coming out of an intimate relationship should generally manifest more restricted patterns and patterns of less intimacy, we may occasionally observe a pattern developed during more intimate times.

Accounting for Communication Patterns of Both Relationship Partners

Thus far, we've been describing and plotting communication patterns as if both partners were communicating in the same general way. Partners will not communicate in exactly the same way, but if they are too far apart on these dimensions, they may not perceive the same type of relationship or degree of intimacy. Gross discrepancies will eventually have to be resolved, or the relationship probably has a limited life.

Testing the Model: Perceptions of Communication Behavior

In order to find out if people perceived relationships along the lines of these eight dimensions, we conducted a study.[19] We obtained ratings of communication behavior in various types of relationships (acquaintance, colleague, pal, friend, best friend, and lover) from over a thousand people between the ages of 12 and 90 in eight states of the United States. Their responses revealed three things: (1) As the relationship rated became more intimate, they perceived communication behavior to become increasingly more personalized. *Personalized communication* included: (a) telling another person things we don't tell most people—feelings, secrets, personal things—but not indiscriminately giving opinions of their behavior; (b) relying on a greater variety of channels for sending and receiving messages—including subtle nonverbal channels which may be considered a more specialized or personal domain; and (c) cultivating and using messages that are more personal to the interacting pair only. Personalized communication, then, encompasses some elements of the dimensions of public/personal, stylized/unique, rigid/flexible, and overt judgment suspended/overt judgment given. (2) As the relationship rated became more intimate, these people perceived communication behavior to become increasingly more synchronized. *Synchronized communication* included: conversations that are smooth-flowing, effortless, spontaneous, relaxed, informal, and well coordinated. Synchronized communication, then, included some elements of the dimensions of difficult/efficient, awkward/smooth, and hesitant/spontaneous. (3) The last set of responses these people agreed upon as characterizing communication in relationship development concerned communication difficulty.

Difficulty was not perceived to vary systematically across relationship types from nonintimate to intimate. This is understandable since both intimate and nonintimate relationships alike may have difficulties or "barriers" to effective communication. *Difficult communication,* for these respondents, reflected a general strain, difficulty, and awkwardness of interaction. But this difficulty did not necessarily mean greater inaccuracy in communication. The dimensions of difficult/efficient and awkward/smooth were represented in this factor. Thus, although people organize their perceptions somewhat differently, all but one of the dimensions described earlier are central to judgments of communication in different types of relationships.

Subsequent studies focusing on perceptions of communication behavior at different points in relationship development add support to the communication dimensions we've identified. Baxter's study of relationship deterioration identified the following communication dimensions: *personalized communication; synchronized communication; smoothness of communication; flexibility of communication;* and *uniqueness of communication.*[20] Baxter and Wilmot's factor analysis of the eight dimensions of communication associated with relationship change outlined in this chapter found two central themes: a factor they called effectiveness, which was a combination of *smoothness* and *efficiency,* and *personalness.* Diaries kept by university students indicated that these dimensions were associated with changes in relationship intimacy.[21] Tolhuizen studied eight stages in the evolution of friendships and found communication patterns could be identified along the following dimensions: *breadth of communication; depth of communication; flexibility of communication; ease of communication;* and *evaluation of communication.*[22] In a subsequent study that compared the perceptions of communication between friends to those of acquaintances and those in deteriorating relationships, friends reported significantly more *uniqueness* or other-orientation; more *depth* or personalness; and more ease and comfort (*efficiency* and *smoothness*).[23]

Other studies have focused on particular dimensions of perceived communication behavior—showing how people expect more breadth and depth in developing relationships.[24]

Testing the Model: Actual Communication Behavior

Even though people perceive communication to change along these dimensions at different points in relationship development, the question still remains: Does the *actual* communication behavior vary along the proposed dimensions? Two studies that compared samples of private conversations between acquaintances and between friends say yes.[25]

In one study, friends talked at a faster rate and were able to use "mutual knowledge" in their conversations—suggesting greater *efficiency.* This is not to suggest that mutual knowledge and speed of information exchange won't, on occasion, cause difficulties in communication as well. None of the characteristics of conversations that distinguish different points in a relationship are inevitably associated with a single outcome. The Planalp and Benson study does, however, support the contention that *difficult–efficient* is a useful dimension for examining differences in conversations between acquaintances and friends. This study also supports the use of other dimensions in our model. Intimacy and breadth of self-disclosure, identified more in conversations of friends, fits well with the *public–personal* and *narrow–broad* dimensions. *Overt judgment suspended–overt judgment given* was reflected in several differences: friends offered more opinions and asked for more advice; friends offered more and higher quality feedback; friends expressed more negative judgments and argued more. Friends also seemed to be more *spontaneous*—laughing more and showing more overlaps and interruptions in their interaction. Acquaintances, on the other hand, were tentative. Friends showed *smoothness* in the transitions between topics, and their general style of interaction was judged more relaxed, casual, and friendly. There were few examples of extreme *uniqueness* (e.g., personal idioms) commonly seen in romantic intimates, but friends did use more informal language, jokes, repartee, and slang in contrast to the more *stylized*, polite, and formal communication of acquaintances. Even though the specific types of communication behavior used to characterize the dimensions proposed in this chapter may vary, the dimensions do seem to provide a useful framework for understanding the perceptions of relationship partners and for describing the differences observed in conversations associated with different stages or types of relationships.

In another study of actual conversations, Hornstein compared the structure of talk between friends and acquaintances. Friends showed more *uniqueness* through their implicit ways of opening the conversation; more *breadth* in the form of a greater number of topics introduced; *flexibility* in the greater complexity of conversational closings; and the greater number of questions asked (responsiveness) may have been a good measure of *spontaneity*.

Thus, in studies examining expectations for, perceptions of, and actual communication behavior, the dimensions outlined in this chapter provide useful yardsticks to measure the manner of relating in changing relationships.

SUMMARY

As in most introductory chapters, an effort has been made here to provide a framework for viewing the rest of the book. We started with the premise that most, if not all, messages contain information about the relationship. This, coupled with the fact that all of our communication takes place within the context of some type of relationship, provided the rationale for the focus of this book. Next we explored some common misconceptions about communication in relationships—misconceptions which often impede the understanding, analysis, and effective execution of communication in human relationships. We must be careful not to assume complete consistency in the communication behavior of others (or ourselves); we must be continually watchful for subtle sources of meaning in the messages exchanged; we must be willing to acknowledge our own role in structuring the responses of others to us; we must try to avoid making easy cause-effect attributions before a thorough analysis has been made; and we must learn to deal with people and things that are continually changing—a world in which closure is the exception rather than the rule. The last part of the chapter detailed eight broad dimensions of communication behavior which may help us understand how people communicate in relationships characterized by different levels of intimacy. It was proposed that as relationships reach for more intimacy, this will bring about corresponding communication behavior in the form of more breadth, depth, smoothness, uniqueness, efficiency, flexibility, spontaneity, and more overt judgments. The antonyms of these terms characterize communication in deteriorating relationships. This does not mean that even the most intimate relationships will not also experience difficulty, superficiality, awkwardness, and other patterns more typical of less intimate relationships at times. The model simply argues that such behavior will be less likely to *typify* the partners' communication. The chapter concluded with an examination of several different patterns and configurations possible within the eight dimensions outlined. The title of this chapter says that our communication behavior is the very lifeblood of our relationships. This chapter was designed to illustrate that.

SELECTED READINGS

Interpersonal Communication

Berger, C. R. *Planning Strategic Interaction: Attaining Goals Through Communicative Action.* Mahwah, NJ: Erlbaum, 1997.

Berger, C. R., and Bradac, J. J. *Language and Social Knowledge: Uncertainty in Interpersonal Relations.* London: Edward Arnold, 1982.

Bochner, A. P. "Interpersonal Communication." In E. Barnouw, G. Gerbner, W. Schramm, T. L. Worth, and L. Gross, eds., *International Encyclopedia of Communications*, pp. 336–340. New York: Oxford University Press, 1989.

Burgoon, J. K., Stern, L. A., and Dillman, L. *Interpersonal Adaptation: Dyadic Interaction Patterns.* NY: Cambridge University Press, 1995.

Daly, J. A., and Wiemann, J. M., eds. *Strategic Interpersonal Communication.* Hillsdale, NJ: Erlbaum, 1994.

Fisher, B. A. *Interpersonal Communication: Pragmatics of Human Relationships.* New York: Random House, 1987.

Goffman, E. *Behavior in Public Places.* New York: Free Press, 1963.

———. *Relations in Public.* New York: Basic Books, 1971.

———. *The Presentation of the Self in Everyday Life.* Garden City, NY: Doubleday, 1959.

Grove, T. G. *Dyadic Interaction.* Dubuque, IA: W. C. Brown, 1991.

Knapp, M. L., and Miller, G. R., eds. *Handbook of Interpersonal Communication.* 2nd ed. Thousand Oaks, CA: Sage, 1994.

McLaughlin, M. L., Cody, M. J., and Read, S. J., eds. *Explaining One's Self to Others: Reason-Giving in a Social Context.* Hillsdale, NJ: Erlbaum, 1992.

Montgomery, B., and Duck, S., eds. *Studying Interpersonal Communication.* New York: Guilford, 1991.

Mortensen, C. D. *Problematic Communication.* Westport, CT: Praeger, 1994.

Petronio, S., Alberts, J. K., Hecht, M. L., and Buley, J. *Contemporary Perspectives on Interpersonal Communication.* Dubuque, IA: W. C. Brown, 1993.

Watzlawick, P., Beavin, J., and Jackson, D. D. *Pragmatics of Human Communication.* New York: W. W. Norton, 1967.

Wilmot, W. W. *Dyadic Communication.* 3rd ed. Reading, MA: Addison-Wesley, 1987.

Relationships and Communication

Albrecht, T. L., and Adelman, M. B. and Associates. *Communicating Social Support.* Newbury Park, CA: Sage, 1987.

Altman, I., and Taylor, D. A. *Social Penetration: The Development of Interpersonal Relationships.* New York: Holt, Rinehart & Winston, 1973.

Argyle, M., and Henderson, M. *The Anatomy of Relationships.* London: Heinemann, 1985.

Baxter, L. A. and Montgomery, B. M. *Relating: Dialogues and Dialectics.* New York: Guilford, 1996.

Berscheid, E. and Reis, H. T. "Attraction and Close Relationships." In D. T. Gilbert, S. T. Fiske, and G. Lindzey, eds., *The Handbook of Social Psychology,* vol. 2, pp. 193–281, New York: McGraw-Hill, 1998.

Bochner, A. "Functions of Communication in Interpersonal Bonding." In C. Arnold and J. Bowers, eds., *Handbook of Rhetoric and Communication.* Boston: Allyn & Bacon, 1984.

Buss, D. M. *The Evolution of Desire.* NY: Basic Books, 1994.

Conville, R. L. *Relational Transitions: The Evolution of Personal Relationships.* New York: Praeger, 1991.

Conville, R. L. and Rogers, L. E., eds. *The Meaning of "Relationship" in Interpersonal Communication.* Westport, CT: Praeger, 1998.

Davis, M. S. *Intimate Relations.* New York: Free Press, 1973.

Derlega, V. J., ed. *Communication, Intimacy, and Close Relationships.* New York: Academic Press, 1984.

Duck, S., ed. *Handbook of Personal Relationships: Theory, Research and Interventions.* 2nd. ed. New York: John Wiley & Sons, 1997.

Duck, S., ed. *Individuals in Relationships.* Newbury Park, CA.: Sage, 1993.

———, ed. *Learning About Relationships.* Newbury Park, CA: Sage, 1993.

Duck, S. *Meaningful Relationships.* Thousand Oaks, CA: Sage, 1995.

———, ed. *Social Context and Relationships.* Newbury Park, CA: Sage, 1993.

Duck, S. "Talking Relationships Into Being." *Journal of Social and Personal Relationships* 12 (1995): 535–540.

Duck S., and Gilmour, R., eds. *Personal Relationships. 1: Studying Personal Relationships.* New York: Academic Press, 1981.

———. *Personal Relationships. 2: Developing Personal Relationships.* New York: Academic Press, 1981.

Duck, S. and Wood, J. T., eds. *Confronting Relationship Challenges.* Thousand Oaks, CA: Sage, 1995.

Erber, R., and Gilmour, R., eds. *Theoretical Frameworks for Personal Relationships.* Hillsdale, NJ: Erlbaum, 1994.

Fletcher, G. J. O., and Fincham, F. D. *Cognition in Close Relationships.* Hillsdale, NJ: Erlbaum, 1991.

Fletcher, G. J. O. and Fitness, J., eds. *Knowledge Structures in Close Relationships.* Mahwah, NJ: Erlbaum, 1996.

Fussel, S. R. and Kreuz, R. J., eds. *Social and Cognitive Approaches to Interpersonal Communication.* Mahwah, NJ: Erlbaum, 1998.

Galvin, K. M., and Brommel, B. J. *Family Communication: Cohesion and Change.* Glenview, IL: Scott, Foresman, 1982.

Gilmour, R., and Duck, S., eds. *The Emerging Field of Personal Relationships.* Hillsdale, NJ: Erlbaum, 1986.

Gottman, J. M. *Marital Interaction.* New York: Academic Press, 1979.

Gottman, J. M. *What Predicts Divorce? The Relationship Between Marital Processes and Marital Outcomes.* Hillsdale, NJ: Erlbaum, 1994.

Gottman, J., Notarius, C., Gonso, J., and Markman, H. *A Couple's Guide to Communication.* Champaign, IL: Research Press, 1976.

Gudykunst, W. B., Ting-Toomey, S. and Nishida, T., ed. *Communication in Personal Relationships Across Cultures.* Thousand Oaks, CA: Sage, 1996.

Hendrick, C., ed. *Close Relationships.* Newbury Park, CA: Sage, 1989.

Hinde, R. A. *Relationships: A Dialectical Perspective.* East Sussex, UK: Psychology Press, 1997.

Ickes, W., ed. *Empathic Accuracy.* New York: Guilford, 1997.

Jones, W. H., and Perlman, D., eds. *Advances in Personal Relationships,* Vol. 2. London: Jessica Kingsley, 1991.

Kalbfleisch, P. J., ed. *Interpersonal Communication: Evolving Interpersonal Relationships.* Hillsdale, NJ: Erlbaum, 1993.

Kelly, H. H., Berscheid, E., Christensen, A., Harvey, J. H., Huston, T. L., Levinger, G., McClintock, E., Peplau, L. A., and Peterson, D. R. *Close Relationships.* New York: W. H. Freeman, 1983.

Kowalski, R., ed. *Aversive Interpersonal Behaviors.* New York: Plenum, 1997.

Noam, G. G. and Fischer, K. W., eds. *Development and Vulnerability in Close Relationships.* Mahwah, NJ: Erlbaum, 1996.

Noller, P., and Fitzpatrick, M. A., eds. *Perspectives on Marital Interaction.* Philadelphia: Multilingual Matters Ltd., 1988.

Pearson, J. C. *Lasting Love: What Keeps Couples Together.* Dubuque, IA: W. C. Brown, 1992.

Perlman, D. and Jones, W. H., eds. *Advances in Personal Relationships.* Vol. 4. London: Jessica Kingsley, 1993.

Rawlins, W. K. *Friendship Matters: Communication, Dialectics, and the Life Course.* New York: Aldine, 1992.

Sanders, R. E. "Find Your Partner and Do-Si-Do: The Formation of Personal Relationships Between Social Beings." *Journal of Social and Personal Relationships* 14 (1997): 387–415.

Sarason, B. R., Sarason, I. G., and Pierce, G. R. *Social Support: An Interactional View.* New York: Wiley, 1990.

Spitzberg, B. H. and Cupach, W. R., eds. *The Dark Side of Close Relationships.* Mahwah, NJ: Erlbaum, 1998.

Sternberg, R. J. and Hojjat, M., eds. *Satisfaction in Close Relationships.* New York: Guilford, 1997.

Weber, A. L., and Harvey, J. H., eds. *Perspectives on Close Relationships.* Boston: Allyn & Bacon, 1994.

Yerby, J., Buerkel-Rothfuss, N., and Bochner, A. P. *Understanding Family Communication.* Scottsdale, AZ: Gorsuch, 1990.

NOTES

[1]It isn't hard to see the benefits derived by omitting concrete referents. Lovers may wish to elevate their relationship to cosmic heights lest it become contaminated with the commonplace; the divorcee may derive comfort and protection by avoiding certain unpleasant realities associated with the broken relationship; friends may simply find that specifying what their relationship is, is a difficult and complex process to understand.

[2]P. Watzlawick, J. Beavin, and D. D. Jackson, *Pragmatics of Human Communication* (New York: W. W. Norton, 1967). Other authors have commented on this same phenomenon. Ruesch and Bateson called it *the report and command aspects of messages;* Satir labeled the two levels as *denotative* and *metacommunicative.* See also: J. Ruesch and G. Bateson, *Communication: The Social Matrix of Psychiatry* (New York: W. W. Norton, 1951), and V. Satir, *Conjoint Family Therapy* (Palo Alto, CA: Science & Behavior Books, 1967).

[3]S. W. King and K. K. Sereno, "Conversational Appropriateness as a Conversational Imperative," *Quarterly Journal of Speech* 70 (1984): 264–273.

[4]See C. M. Rossiter, Jr., "Instruction in Metacommunication," *Central States Speech Journal* 25 (1974): 36–42, and G. I. Nierenberg and H. Colero, *Meta-Talk* (New York: Simon & Schuster, 1974).

[5]W. F. Owen, "Interpretive Themes in Relational Communication," *Quarterly Journal of Speech* 70 (1984): 274–287 and L. A. Baxter, "Root Metaphors in Accounts of Developing Relationships," *Journal of Personal and Social Relationships* 9 (1992): 253–275. Another effort to identify the substance of messages that relationship partners

use to define their relationships can be found in J. K. Burgoon and J. L. Hale, "The Fundamental Topoi of Relational Communication," *Communication Monographs* 51 (1984): 193–214. Also see a follow-up study by Burgoon and Hale, "Validation and Measurement of the Fundamental Themes of Relational Communication," *Communication Monographs* 54 (1987): 19–41. The relationship themes identified by Burgoon and Hale are: intimacy, dominance, emotional arousal, composure, similarity, formality, and a task-social orientation.

[6]A. L. Sillars, J. Weisberg, C. S. Burggraf, and E. A. Wilson, "Content Themes in Marital Conversations," *Human Communication Research,* 13 (1987): 495–528; and A. L. Sillars, C. S. Burggraf, S. Yost, and P. H. Zietlow, "Conversational Themes and Marital Relationship Definitions: Quantitative and Qualitative Investigations," *Human Communication Research,* 19 (1992): 124–154.

[7]A. Haas, "Male and Female Spoken Language Differences: Stereotypes and Evidence," *Psychological Bulletin* 86 (1979): 616–626. Also see J. C. Pearson, *Gender and Communication* (Dubuque, IA: W. C. Brown, 1985); R. D. Ashmore and F. K. DelBoca, *The Social Psychology of Female-Male Relations: A Critical Analysis of Central Concepts* (New York: Academic Press, 1986); and D. Tannen, *You Just Don't Understand: Women and Men in Conversation* (New York: William Morrow, 1990).

[8]R. Hopper, "The Taken-for-Granted," *Human Communication Research* 7 (1981): 195–211.

[9]For a summary of these findings, see M. Argyle, *Social Interaction* (New York: Atherton, 1969), 168–179; and J. N. Cappella, "Mutual Influence in Expressive Behavior: Adult-Adult and Infant-Adult Dyadic Interaction," *Psychological Bulletin* 89 (1981): 101–132.

[10]T. Leary, *Interpersonal Diagnosis of Personality* (New York: Ronald Press, 1957), 116–117.

[11]A. Weigert, *Mixed Emotions: Certain Steps Toward Understanding Ambivalence* (Albany, NY: SUNY Press, 1991). C. R. Berger and M. E. Roloff, "Social Cognition, Self-Awareness, and Interpersonal Communication." In B. Dervin and M. J. Voight, eds., *Progress in Communication Sciences,* vol. 2 (Norwood, NJ: Ablex, 1980), 1–49.

[12]Using different terminology, these dimensions are also discussed in I. Altman and D. A. Taylor, *Social Penetration* (NY: Holt, Rinehart & Winston, 1973), pp. 129–135.

[13]Adapted from "Analogue of Personality Structure." In I. Altman and D. A. Taylor, *Social Penetration* NY: Holt, Rinehart & Winston, 1973), 129–135.

[14]J. M. Honeycutt, M. L. Knapp, and W. G. Powers, "On Knowing Others and Predicting What They Say," *Western Journal of Speech Communication* 47 (1983): 157–174. Ickes, W., ed., *Empathic Accuracy* (NY: Guilford, 1997).

[15]A. Sillars and M. D. Scott, "Interpersonal Perception Between Intimates: An Integrative Review," *Human Communication Research* 10 (1983): 153–176. Murray, S. L. and Holmes, J. G. "The Construction of Relationship Realities." In G. J. O. Fletcher and J. Fitness, eds., *Knowledge Structures in Close Relationships* (Hillsdale, NJ: Erlbaum, 1996), 91–120.

[16]W. J. Jordan, R. L. Street, Jr., and W. B. Putman, "The Effects of Relational and Physical Distance on Lexical Diversity," *Southern Speech Communication Journal* 49 (1983): 80–89.

[17]Aune, K. S., Buller, D. B. and Aune, R. K., "Display Rule Development in Romantic Relationships: Emotion Management and Perceived Appropriateness of Emotions Across Relationship Stages," *Human Communication Research* 23 (1996): 115–145.

[18]Perceived frequency of touching seems to follow a similar pattern. See: T. M. Emmers and K. Dindia, "The Effect of Relational Stage and Intimacy on Touch: An Extension of Guerrero and Andersen," *Personal Relationships* 2 (1995): 225–236.

[19]M. L. Knapp, D. G. Ellis, and B. A. Williams, "Perceptions of Communication Behavior Associated with Relationship Terms," *Communication Monographs* 47 (1980): 262–278. A related study compared Japanese and North American perceptions of communication behavior. Both groups perceived relationships in terms of personalized, synchronized, and difficult communication, but cultural orientation played a major role in determining what kind of communication was associated with what kind of relationships. See W. B. Gudykunst and T. Nishida, "The Influence of Cultural Variability on Perceptions of Communication Behavior Associated with Relationship Terms," *Human Communication Research* 13 (1986): 147–166. Additional cross-cultural research on perceptions of relationships can be found in W. B. Gudykunst, S. Ting-Toomey, and T. Nishida, eds., *Communication in Personal Relationships Across Cultures* (Thousand Oaks, CA: Sage, 1996).

[20]L. A. Baxter, "Relationship Disengagement: An Examination of the Reversal Hypothesis," *West-*

ern Journal of Speech Communication 47 (1983): 85–98.

[21]L. Baxter, and W. W. Wilmot, "Communication Characteristics of Relationships with Differential Growth Rates," *Communication Monographs* 50 (1983): 264–272.

[22]J. H. Tolhuizen, "Perceived Communication Indicators of Evolutionary Changes in Friendship," *Southern Speech Communication Journal* 52 (1986): 69–91.

[23]J. H. Tolhuizen, "Affinity-Seeking in Developing Relationships," *Communication Reports* 2 (1989): 83–91.

[24]J. Ayres, "Relationship Stages and Sex as Factors in Topic-Dwell Time," *Western Journal of Speech Communication* 44 (1980): 253–260; and

C. R. Berger, R. R. Gardner, G. W. Clatterbuck, and L. S. Schulman, "Perceptions of Information Sequencing in Relationship Development," *Human Communication Research* 3 (1976): 29–46.

[25]S. Planalp and A. Benson, "Friends' and Acquaintances' Conversations I: Perceived Differences," *Journal of Social and Personal Relationships* 9 (1992): 483–506. S. Planalp, "Friends' and Acquaintances' Conversations II: Coded Differences," *Journal of Social and Personal Relationships* 10 (1993): 339–354. G. A. Hornstein, "Intimacy in Conversational Style as a Function of the Degree of Closeness Between Members of a Dyad," *Journal of Personality and Social Psychology* 49 (1985): 671–681.

2

Stages of Coming Together and Coming Apart

Dear Dr. Vangelisti,

My problem is that I recently broke up with a guy with whom I was previously very close and now he acts like he never even knew me. I've seen this happen with some of my friends too. Why can't people just be friends after they've been closer than that? How can people act so cold to those they've shared so much with? It's really an uncomfortable situation for me and I'd be a lot happier if we could just go back to being friends. Can we?

Not Wanting to Throw It All Away

The author of this letter is seeking an answer to why changing relationships follow the pattern they do. This chapter provides some answers to this question by first describing several possible stages that relationships may follow. When people want to move a relationship from one stage to another, it is probably because they desire to increase certain positive feelings or decrease certain negative feelings. The couple described in the letter above probably perceive differing amounts of positive feelings expected from the friendship; and may have differing expectations for the types of relationships people can have.

> In the development of a human communication system the purpose, function, *or* product *is a* relationship. *The development of a relationship proceeds in rather uniform stages, though the time it takes to pass from the initial stage to a full relationship will vary greatly.*
>
> —*George A. Borden*

We describe our relationships in many ways. Sometimes we rely on conventional intimacy terms like *stranger, acquaintance, buddy, close friend, lover;* sometimes role designations such as *neighbor, boss, hitchhiker, teacher,* or *pickup* are used; sometimes the nature of the relationship is linked to kinship terms such as *mother, sister, cousin,* or *husband.* Inferences about the nature of the relationship may be made from temporal descriptions—e.g., "known him since high school," "going steady," or "just met her once"; or we may assume a reference to ethnicity or personal characteristics will be a sufficient relationship description—e.g., "brothers" or "we think alike." A reference to joint activities or social organizations may provide the initial relationship description—e.g., "we bowl together," "we're in the same sorority," "I work with him," or "I only see her in class."

Types of Relationships

The preceding relationship descriptions do very little to explain a multitude of personal and societal expectations attendant to these relationships. The type of relationship we develop with another person is heavily influenced by mutual and ongoing expectations for the relationship: What is it? What will it become? What should it be now? What should it become? What behavior is expected? What do most people do? Some expectations for relationships are held by many people in this culture—e.g., that family members will most likely have close relationships; that male-female friendships are most likely to be romantic in nature; that same-gender relationships will most likely be limited to friendships (rather than romance); that marriage will most likely be the result of highly intimate feelings between the partners; that participants in various role relationships (teacher–student; doctor–patient) will most likely behave according to those roles. The extent to which such expectations are shared and acted upon helps to explain perceived similarities among relationships described as "friend" or "teacher" or "mother."

Sometimes expectations are not shared—with society or with one's relationship partner. Contrary to the expectations and/or wishes of many people, some family members develop distant relationships; some male–female pairs do not pursue romance; some same-gender pairs seek romantic relationships; some people get married who don't feel intense intimacy; and some people don't fulfill the expectations for their role as doctor, teacher, or mother. When we have difficulty establishing a relationship or in changing an established relationship to one of a different type it is often linked to differing expectations for the relationship held by each party.[1]

Sometimes relationship expectations are confusing because more than one relationship is involved. You may have several relationships with the same person and it is not always clear which relationship is being performed—e.g., a teacher who is also your teammate in tennis. The tennis activity may suggest a new set of expectations for the relationship, but if you make a poor shot, you may hear a comment that sounds more like your teacher than your teammate. Families also present a complex set of relationship expectations. An older parent living in his or her adult child's home may occasionally play parent and occasionally play dependent tenant to the adult son or daughter.

Expectations for relationships change with time and circumstances. The expectations for romantic relationships of today seem to include more physical contact and a greater expression of both positive and negative feelings than people expected fifty years ago.[2] As a child reaches adolescence, he or she expects certain relationship changes with his or her parents. We found that people below age 22 expected more personalized and synchronized communication in all types of relationships than did those people over age 41.[3] A man and a woman may be assigned to work on a task in a corporate environment. The expectations for this relationship are formal, task-oriented, and nonintimate. However, when the task relationship occurs for an extended period, when the pair works together several nights a week, and when they discuss various personal aspects of their life during breaks, the relationship expectations may change.[4] Many of our relationship expectations are rooted in the activities we perform together.[5]

We don't always consciously pursue the relationships we have with others. Sometimes we're "thrown together" with people in certain circumstances. Similarly, we may not actively terminate a relationship, but changes in interests, priorities, or geographical location may contribute to a lack of initiative to keep the relationship going. So it fades away due to mindless inattention rather than planned avoidance.

The variety of relationships we have or could have seems quite diverse. There are, however, some *basic principles that all types of relationships seem to have in common*. These include:

1. Relationship expectations are often altered because of the way people communicate, and the way they communicate often helps to shape the expectations they have for a relationship. This principle establishes the central role of communication behavior in assessing the nature of relationships, but it also recognizes that overt communication behavior may only tell part of the relationship story.

2. Whether our relationships are actively sought or develop out of shared circumstances, each of them reveals fluctuations in closeness or intimacy. Superficial, task-oriented relationships and unfriendly relations can be viewed as less intimate while best friends and lovers are more intimate.

With these foundation concepts in mind, we can return to our initial questions: Are there regular and systematic patterns of communication that suggest stages on the road to a more intimate relationship? Are there similar patterns and stages that characterize the deterioration of relationships?

A Model of Interaction Stages in Relationships

Scientists are forever seeking to bring order to a seemingly chaotic world of overlapping, interdependent, dynamic, and intricate processes. Frequently, the process of systematizing our life and environment is discussed in terms of stages of growth, stages of deterioration, and the forces that shape and act on this movement through stages. For instance, developmental psychologists recount regularized patterns of behavior accompanying stages of infancy, childhood, adolescence, maturity, and old age. Anthropologists and geologists plot the evolutionary stages of human beings and human environments. Biologists note similarities in the life processes of such seemingly diverse organisms as trees and fish. Physical and social scientists talk about affinity and attraction, weak and strong interactions, friction, repulsion, and splitting-up as basic forces acting on matter and people. Rhetorical critics often dissect spoken messages by noting patterns regularly occurring during the introduction, development toward the main points, transitions, and conclusion.

The idea that there are stages in the development of relationships that are characterized by certain patterns of communication is not new.[6] We tried to synthesize as well as expand on this previous work in the development of the model presented in Table 2.1.

Before each stage is described in greater detail, several preliminary remarks about the model are in order. First, we should resist the normal temptation to perceive the stages of coming together as "good" and those of coming apart as "bad." It is not "bad" to terminate relationships nor is it necessarily "good" to become more intimate with someone. The model is descriptive of what seems to happen— not what should happen.

We should also remember that in the interest of clarity the model simplifies a complex process. For instance, the model shows each stage adjacent to the next— as if it was clear when a communicating couple left one stage and entered another. To the contrary. Each stage contains some behavior from other stages. So *stage*

Process	Stage	Representative Dialogue
		TABLE 2.1 A Model of Interaction Stages[7]
	Initiating	"Hi, how ya doin'?"
		"Fine. You?"
	Experimenting	"Oh, so you like to ski . . . so do I."
		"You do?! Great. Where do you go?"
Coming Together	Intensifying	"I . . . I think I love you."
		"I love you too."
	Integrating	"I feel so much a part of you."
		"Yeah, we are like one person. What happens to you happens to me."
	Bonding	"I want to be with you always."
		"Let's get married."
	Differentiating	"I just don't like big social gatherings."
		"Sometimes I don't understand you. This is one area where I'm certainly not like you at all."
	Circumscribing	"Did you have a good time on your trip?"
		"What time will dinner be ready?"
Coming Apart	Stagnating	"What's there to talk about?"
		"Right. I know what you're going to say and you know what I'm going to say."
	Avoiding	"I'm so busy, I just don't know when I'll be able to see you."
		"If I'm not around when you try, you'll understand."
	Terminating	"I'm leaving you . . . and don't bother trying to contact me."
		"Don't worry."

identification becomes a matter of emphasis. Stages are identified by the proportion of one type of communication behavior to another. This proportion may be the frequency with which certain communication acts occur, or proportion may be determined by the relative weight given to certain acts by the participants. For example, a couple at the Intensifying Stage may exhibit behaviors that occur at any of the other stages, but their arrival at the Intensifying Stage is because: (1) the most frequent communication exchanges are typical of the Intensifying Stage and/or (2) the exchanges that are crucial in defining the couple's relationship are statements of an intensifying nature. The act of sexual intercourse is commonly associated with male–female romantic couples at the Intensifying or Integrating Stages, but it may occur as an isolated act for couples at the Experimenting Stage. Or it may occur regularly for a couple at the Experimenting Stage, but remain relatively unimportant for the couple in defining the closeness of their relationship. Thus, interaction stages involve both overt behavior and the perceptions of behavior in the minds of the parties involved. During the formation of a romantic relationship, the couple's overt behavior (to each other and in front of others) may be a good marker of their developmental stage. During periods of attempted rejuvenation of a relationship, we may find that the overt behavior is an effective marker of the stage *desired*. However, in stable or long-established relationships, overt behavior may not be a very accurate indicator of closeness. Instead it is the occasional behavior or memories of past behaviors that are perceived by the couple as crucial in defining their relationship. For example, the married couple of fifteen years may spend much of their interaction time engaging in small talk—a behavior typical of an early developmental stage. And even though the small talk does play an important role in maintaining the relationship, it is the less frequent but more heavily weighted behavior that the couple uses to define their relationship, as at the Integrating Stage. Similarly, close friends may not engage in a lot of talk that outside observers would associate with closeness. In some cases, friends are separated for long periods of time and make very little contact with one another. But through specific occasional acts and the memory of past acts, the intimacy of the friendship is maintained.

The dialogue in the model is heavily oriented toward mixed-gender pairs. This does not mean the model is irrelevant for same-gender pairs. Even at the highest level of commitment, the model may apply to same-gender pairs. The bonding ceremony, for instance, need not be marriage. It could be an act of becoming "blood brothers" by placing open wounds on each other to achieve oneness. Granted, American cultural sanctions against the direct expression of high-level intimacy between same-sexed pairs often serve to inhibit, slow down, or stop the growth of relationships between same-sexed pairs. But when such relationships do develop, similar patterns are reported.[8]

The model (and the remainder of the book) also focuses primarily on relationships where people voluntarily seek contact with, or disengagement from, one another. But the model is not limited to such relationships. All people drawn into, or pulled out of, relationships by forces seemingly outside their control will like or not like such an event and communicate accordingly. For instance, a child's relationship with his or her parent (involuntary) may, at some point, be very close and loving, at another time be cold and distant, and at another time be similar to relationships with other friends.

Our model of relationship development is primarily focused on the interaction patterns of the relationship partners. Nevertheless, we should not forget that these relationships are nested within a network of other social relationships which affect communication patterns manifested by the partners.[9] Friends, co-workers, and/or kin make up the larger social system which influences and is influenced by any single relationship. Sometimes these networks are small, sometimes large; sometimes they are influential on one issue or at one point in time and not so on other issues or at another point in time; sometimes these other relationships tend to serve one relationship partner, and at other times they serve both. What role do social networks play as we develop and maintain a relationship? The people who comprise these networks give us feedback, advice, and support; they act as a sounding board; they help mediate problems; they offer consultation and engage in persuasion. They may, of course, fail to provide these things when they are expected. In short, social networks are comprised of coaches who can dramatically affect our communicative performance as a relationship partner. In addition, they are sources of a social identity which extends beyond the pair bond.

Finally, this model has a close association with the eight dimensions of communication outlined in Chapter 1. Although it is impossible to specify a precise configuration along the eight dimensions (see Fig. 1.1), we would expect the Initiating and Terminating Stages to be characterized by communication that is more narrow, stylized, difficult, rigid, awkward, public, hesitant, and with overt judgments suspended; the stages of Integrating, Bonding, and Differentiating should show more breadth, uniqueness, efficiency, flexibility, smoothness, personalness, spontaneity, and overt judgments given. In short, it is proposed that we communicate within a prescribed range of content, style, and language at different levels of intimacy. Chapters 5 through 11 will further document behavior only briefly noted here.

Interaction Stages

Initiating

This stage incorporates all those processes enacted when we first come together with other people. It may be at a cocktail party or at the beach; it may be with a stranger or with a friend. As we scan the other person we consider our own stereotypes, any prior knowledge of the other's reputation, previous interactions with this person, expectations for this situation, and so on. We are asking ourselves whether this person is "attractive" or "unattractive" and whether we should initiate communication. Next, we try to determine whether the other person is cleared for an encounter—is he or she busy, in a hurry, surrounded by others? Finally, we search for an appropriate opening line to engage the other's attention.

Typically, communicators at this stage are simply trying to display themselves as a person who is pleasant, likable, understanding, and socially adept. In essence, we are saying: "I see you. I am friendly, and I want to open channels for communication to take place." In addition, we are carefully observing the other to reduce any uncertainty we might have—hoping to gain clarification of mood, interest, orientation toward us, and aspects of the other's public personality. Our conscious awareness of these processes is sometimes very low. "Morning, Bob. How ya doin'?" "Morning, Clayton. Go to hell." "Fine, thanks."

Obviously, specific methods and messages used to initiate communication vary with:

1. The kind of relationship and whether the participants have been through this stage before. *Stranger:* "Hello. Nice to meet you." *Friend:* "Hi dude. What's up?"
2. The time allowed for interaction—passing each other on the street versus a formal appointment.
3. The time since last greeting—re-greeting a person you saw just five minutes before versus greeting a relative at the airport who visits once a year.
4. The situational or normative constraints—meeting in the library versus meeting at a rock concert.
5. The special codes of particular groups—fraternity handshake.

In spite of the possibility for considerable variance in initiating behaviors, people generally exercise a good deal of caution and communicate according to conventional formulas.

Experimenting

Once communication has been initiated, we begin the process of experimenting—trying to discover the unknown. Strangers trying to become acquaintances will be primarily interested in name, rank, and serial number—something akin to the sniffing ritual in animals. The exchange of demographic information is frequent and often seems controlled by a norm that says: "If you tell me your hometown, I'll tell you mine." Strangers at this stage are diligently searching for an integrating topic, an area of common interest or experience. Sometimes the strain of this search approaches the absurd: "Oh, you're from Oklahoma. Do you know . . . ?" Obviously, the degree to which a person assists another in finding this integrating topic shows the degree of interest in continuing the interaction and the willingness to pursue a relationship.

Miller and his colleagues have pointed out that we use three bases for predictions in interpersonal encounters.[10] With strangers we may have to rely primarily on *cultural information.* If one's partner is from this culture, they probably share some predictable ways of behaving and thinking. You assume they have knowledge of certain cultural happenings. It is a place to begin, but the potential sources of error are many.

As we gain information about another person, we may begin to use *sociological information* as a basis for conversational strategies and adaptations. This knowledge of a person's reference and membership groups is frequently used in casual social gatherings. When we hear that a person is a feminist, a physician, or a Southern Baptist, we immediately begin scanning associations with these labels that may be useful to us in our conversational pursuits.

The third basis for predictions involves *psychological information*. This information recognizes the individual differences associated with one's conversational partner. It is more likely to occur with conversational partners who are better known to you. These sources of information are important because they will mark differences in the small talk of strangers, people from very different cultures, people who have a close relationship, and people whose relationship is close in name only.

It should be noted that people in established close relationships do spend a lot of time experimenting. It may be an effort to seek greater breadth and understanding of the relationship, to note any changes in current understandings, to pass the time, or to avoid some uncomfortable vibrations obtained at a more intense level of dialogue. Both strangers and friends are searching for possible similarities; both are trying to present a desirable "come-on self" ("If you like the label, you might like what's in the container"); both are concerned about setting up the next encounter where consistency of behavior can be examined.

Small talk is the *sine qua non* of experimenting. It is like exercising; we may hate it, but we may also engage in large quantities of it every day. If we hate it, why do we do it? Probably because we are vaguely aware of several important functions served by small talk:

1. It is a useful process for uncovering integrating topics and openings for more penetrating conversation.
2. It can be an audition for a future friendship or a way of increasing the scope of a current relationship.
3. It provides a safe procedure for indicating who we are and how another can come to know us better (reduction of uncertainty).
4. It allows us to maintain a sense of community with our fellow human beings.

Relationships at this stage are generally pleasant, relaxed, overtly uncritical, and casual. Commitments are limited. And, like it or not, *most of our relationships probably don't progress very far beyond this stage.*

Intensifying

When people achieve a relationship known as "close friends," indicators of the relationships are intensified. Active participation and greater awareness of the process typify this stage when it begins. Initial probes toward intensification of intimacy are often exercised with caution, awaiting confirmation before proceeding. Sitting close, for instance, may precede hugging; holding hands will generally precede holding genitals. Requests for physical or psychological favors are sometimes used to validate the existence of intensity in a relationship. (See pages 53–54 for a discussion of giving and receiving favors.)

The amount of personal disclosure increases at this stage, and we begin to get a glimpse of some previously withheld secrets—that my father was an alcoholic, that I masturbate, that I pretend I'm a rhino when I'm drunk, and other fears, frustrations, failures, imperfections, and prejudices. Disclosures may be related to any topic area, but those dealing most directly with the development of the relationship are crucial. These disclosures make the speaker vulnerable—almost like an animal baring its neck to an attacker.

Verbally, a lot of things may be happening in the intensifying stage:

1. Forms of address become more informal—first name, nickname, or some term of endearment.

2. Use of the first person plural becomes more common—"*We* should do this" or "*Let's* do this." One study of married couples found that the use of "we" was more likely to be associated with a relationship orientation, while the use of "I" was more likely to be associated with a task orientation or the functional requirements and accomplishments of marriage.[11]

3. Private symbols begin to develop, sometimes in the form of a special slang or jargon, sometimes using conventional language forms that have understood, private meanings. Places they've been together, events and times they've shared; and physical objects they've purchased or exchanged; all become important symbols in defining the nature of developing closeness.[12] Such items or memories may be especially devastating and repulsive reminders if the relationship begins to come apart unless the symbols are reinterpreted ("I like this diamond ring because it is beautiful, not because he gave it to me.") or put in a different perspective ("It really was fun when we did _____ , but in so many other ways he was a jerk.").

4. Verbal shortcuts built on a backlog of accumulated and shared assumptions, expectations, interests, knowledge, interactions, and experiences appear more often; one may request a newspaper be passed by simply saying, "paper."

5. More direct expressions of commitment may appear—"We really have a good thing going" or "I don't know who I'd talk to if you weren't around." Sometimes such expressions receive an echo—"I really like you a lot." "I really like you, too, Elmer."

6. Increasingly, one's partner will act as a helper in the daily process of understanding what you're all about—"In other words, you mean you're . . ." or "But yesterday, you said you were. . . ."

Sophistication in nonverbal message transmission also increases. A long verbalization may be replaced by a single touch; postural congruence may be seen;

clothing styles may become more coordinated; possessions and personal space may be more permeable.

As the relationship intensifies, each person is unfolding his or her uniqueness while simultaneously blending his or her personality with the other's.

Integrating

The relationship has now reached a point where the two individual personalities almost seem to fuse or coalesce, certainly more than at any previous stage. Davis discusses this concept, which he calls *coupling*:

> The extent to which each intimate tries to give the other his own self-symbols or to correct the other's self-symbols measures the degree to which he wants to increase their communion.[13]

The experience of former Florida State Senator Bruce Smathers and his fiancée provides one example of movement toward this interpersonal fusion. He switched from Methodist to Presbyterian; she switched from Republican to Democrat. The wire service report indicated this was "a compromise they say will help pave the way for their wedding."

Verbal and nonverbal manifestations of integrating may take many forms:

1. Attitudes, opinions, interests, and tastes that clearly distinguish the pair from others are vigorously cultivated—"We have something special; we are unique."

2. Social circles merge and others begin to treat the two individuals as a common package—one present, one letter, one invitation.

3. Intimacy "trophies" are exchanged so each can "wear" the other's identity—pictures, pins, rings.

4. Similarities in manner, dress, and verbal behavior may also accentuate the oneness.

5. Actual physical penetration of various body parts contributes to the perceived unification.

6. Sometimes common property is designated—"our song," a joint bank account, or a co-authored book.

7. Empathic processes seem to peak so that explanation and prediction of behavior are much easier.[14]

8. Body rhythms and routines achieve heightened synchrony.[15]

9. Sometimes the love of a third person or object will serve as glue for the relationship—"Love me, love my rhinos."

Obviously, integration does not mean complete togetherness or complete loss of individuality. Maintenance of some separate and distinct selves is critical, and possible, due to the strength of the binding elements. One married woman of ten years told us: "I still hold some of myself back from John because it's the only part of me I don't share, and it's important to have something that is uniquely mine."

Thus, we can see that as we participate in the integration process we are intensifying and minimizing various aspects of our total person. Consequently, when we commit ourselves to integrating with another, we also agree to become another individual.

Bonding

Bonding is a public ritual that announces to the world that commitments have been formally contracted. It is the institutionalization of the relationship. There are many kinds of bonding rituals and they characterize several stages of the mixed-sex relationship—going steady, engagement, and ultimately marriage. American society has not widely sanctioned similar rituals for same-sexed romantic pairs, although some exist.

Since bonding is simply the contract for the union of the pair at any given stage of the relationship, one might question why it has been designated as a separate stage. It is because the act of bonding itself may be a powerful force in changing the nature of the relationship "for better or for worse." The institutionalization of the relationship hardens it, makes it more difficult to break out of, and probably changes the rhetoric that takes place without a contract. The contract becomes, either explicitly or implicitly, a frequent topic of conversation. Communication strategies can now be based on interpretation and execution of the commitments contained in the contract. In short, the normal ebb and flow of the informal relationship can be, and often is, viewed differently.

When bonding is an extension of integrating, it is probably seen as a way to help stabilize one's newly formed individuality and integrated selves. It is a commitment to a common future:

> One's future in Western society at least, is one's most prized possession (or particularization). To commit it to another is the most important gift one can give.[16]

Bonding is a way of gaining social or institutional support for the relationship. It enables the couple to rely on law or policy or precedent. Bonding also provides guidance for the relationship through specified rules and regulations.

The way up and the way down are the same.
Heraclitus

Differentiating

Literally, to *differentiate* means to become distinct or different in character. Just as integrating is mainly a process of fusion, differentiating is mainly a process of disengaging or uncoupling. While individual differences are of some concern at any stage in the developing relationship, they are now the major focus and serve as a prelude to increased interpersonal distance. A great deal of time and energy are spent talking and thinking about "how different we really are."

Joint endeavors formerly described by "we" or "our" now assume a more "I" or "my" orientation. Previously designated joint possessions often become more individualized—"my friends," "my daughter," or "my bathroom." Communication is generally characterized by what distinguishes the two persons or how little they have in common. Differences may be related to attitudes, interests, personality, relatives, friends, or to a specific behavior such as sexual needs or picking one's nose. Individuals who persist in interaction at this stage perceive these differences as strongly linked to basic or core values. Hence, we would expect to see less conversation about certain central areas of personality that may reflect these basic values. Persons who move in and out of this stage develop a history of expectations for the manner in which such difficulties will be settled, even if it is simply an agreement to seal off the areas of potential conflict.

When an unusually intense siege of differentiating takes place following bonding, it may be because bonding took place before the relationship achieved sufficient breadth and depth. It may also be due to some unplanned individual or social changes that altered the data upon which the original commitment was made. Advocates of renewable-term marriage argue that couples would be more likely to face, discuss, and work out unexpected changes in their lives if the marriage bond was not a lifelong commitment—if "till death do us part" meant the death of the relationship rather than the death of the participants.

The most visible communication form of differentiating, or affirming individuality, is fighting or conflict, although it is possible to differentiate without conflict. The numerous interpersonal torture tests characteristic of some of this fighting will be more fully discussed in Chapter 11.

Circumscribing

At almost any stage of a relationship we can see some evidence of communication being constricted or circumscribed. In decaying relationships, however, information exchange qualitatively and quantitatively decreases. The main message strategy is to carefully control the areas of discussion, restricting communication to safe areas. Thus, we find less total communication in number of interactions as well as depth of subjects discussed, and communications of shorter duration.

Communication restraint applies to both breadth and depth. As the number of touchy topics increases, almost any topic becomes dangerous because it is not clear whether the new topic may in some way be wired to a previous area of static. When communication does take place, superficiality and public aspects are increasingly the norm. Communications related to one's basic values and hidden secrets may have a history of unpleasantness surrounding them; hence, we see a lot less information exchanged about "who I am and what our relationship is like." A corresponding decrease in expressions of commitment may be seen. When one person ventures such an expression, the echo response may not be so prevalent. "In spite of our differences, I still like you a lot." (Silence)

Familiar phrases typical of this stage include: "Don't ask me about that"; "Let's not talk about that anymore"; "It's none of your business"; "Just stick to the kind of work I'm doing and leave my religion out of it"; "You don't own me and you can't tell me what to think"; or "Can't we just be friends?" The last example is a suggestion that prescribes a whole new set of ground rules for permissible topics in the interaction.

When circumscribing characterizes the relationship, it may also have an impact on public social performances. Sometimes mutual social circles are also circumscribed, sometimes the presence of others is the only time when communication seems to increase—an effort to avoid being seen as not getting along. The following routine is not at all uncommon for some couples at this stage: Driving to a party, the two people exhibit mutual silence, empty gazes, and a general feeling of exhaustion. While playing out their party roles we see smiling, witticisms, and an orientation for being the life of the party. The trip home becomes a replay of the pre-party behavior.

Stagnating

To stagnate is to remain motionless or inactive. Rather than orally communicate, participants often find themselves conducting covert dialogues and concluding that since they "know" how the interaction will go, it is not necessary to say anything. At this stage, many areas are closed off, and efforts to communicate effectively are at a standstill. Even superficial areas have become so infected by previous communicative poison that they are generally left untried. In a sense, the participants are just marking time.

Some of the messages that are sent reflect unpleasant feeling states through the medium of nonverbal behavior. Other messages are very carefully chosen and well thought out. Language choices and message strategies seem to come even closer to those used with strangers, and the subject of the relationship is nearly taboo. In the context related earlier in the discussion of Table 1.1, communication is becoming more stylized, difficult, rigid, hesitant, awkward, and narrow. While there may be many covert judgments made, overt judgments are generally avoided.

Extended stagnating can be seen in many relationships: between alienated parents and children, just prior to divorce, just prior to the termination of a courtship, following unproductive small talk. The main theme characterizing this stage is "There is little sense bringing anything up because I know what will happen, and it won't be particularly pleasant." Experimentation is minimal because the unknown is thought to be known. It is during this time that each partner may engage in "imagined interactions."[17] These imagined dialogues will either take the form of narratives (e.g., "I'll say this and then she'll say this, and then . . .") or perceived actual dialogues (e.g., "I'll do it." "You don't have to." "Ok." "Ok, what?" "Ok, I won't." "Your typical attitude." "And *Your Typical Attitude!*" . . .).

You might legitimately question why people would linger at this stage with so many apparent costs accumulating. Most don't. But when persons continue interacting at this stage they may be getting some rewards outside of the primary relationship, through increased attention to their work or in developing another relationship. They also avoid the pain of terminating the relationship, which they may anticipate will be stronger than the current pain. Others may have hope that they can still revive the relationship. Still others may spend time at this stage because of some perverse pleasures obtained in punishing the other person.

Avoiding

While stagnating, the participants are usually in the same physical environment and avoiding attempts to eliminate that condition. The rhetoric of avoidance is the antithesis of the rhetoric of initiation. Here, communication is specifically designed to avoid the possibility of face-to-face or voice-to-voice interaction. The overriding message seems to be: "I am not interested in seeing you; I am not interested in building a relationship; and I would like to close the communication channels between us." In this sense, then, avoiding suggests a much more permanent state of separation than that communicated by most people in their everyday leave-taking.

When the need to communicate avoidance results from an intimate relationship gone sour, the particular messages may contain overtones of antagonism or unfriendliness. They are more likely to be direct and to the point. "Please don't call me anymore. I just don't want to see or talk to you." This bluntness may naturally evolve from other conditions as well, such as when one person wants to pursue the relationship and ignores the more subtle avoidance cues. These subtle or indirect cues may take the form of being consistently late for appointments or preceding each encounter with, "I can't stay long." Here the avoiding tactics are not motivated so much by dislike of the other as a lack of desire to expend time and energy pursuing a relationship. Sometimes an inordinate number of conflicting engagements can make the point: "I'm so busy I don't know when I'll be able to see you. Friday? I'm going home for the weekend. Monday? I have a sorority meeting. Tuesday? I have to study for a test," etc. etc.

In certain situations physical separation simply cannot be achieved, so a form of avoiding takes place in the presence of the other. It's as if the other person didn't exist. Not surprisingly under such conditions we find the receiver participating less in what interaction is available, not evaluating the other highly, and being less inclined to provide a reward to the other when an opportunity arises. The less obvious result of being ignored is the possibility of a lowered self-concept.[18]

Terminating

Relationships can terminate immediately after a greeting or after twenty years of intimacy. Sometimes they die slowly over a long period of time. The bonds that held the pair together wear thin and finally pull apart. The reasons behind such deterioration may be something obvious like living in parts of the country separated by great distance; or termination may just be the end result of two people growing socially and psychologically at different rates and in different directions. At other times, the threads holding two people together may be abruptly cut. It may be the death of one partner, radically changed circumstances, or an effort by one person to spare both of them the anticipated agony of a prolonged termination period.

Naturally, the nature of the termination dialogue is dependent on many factors: the relative status held or perceived between the two communicators; the kind of relationship already established or desired in the future; the amount of time allowed; whether the dialogue is conducted via the telephone, through a letter, or face to face; and many other individual and environmental factors.

Generally, however, we would predict termination dialogue to be characterized by messages of distance and disassociation. *Distance* refers to an attempt to put psychological and physical barriers between the two communicators. This might take the form of actual physical separation, or it may be imbedded in other nonverbal and verbal messages. *Disassociation* is found in messages that are essentially preparing one or both individuals for their continued life without the other—increasing concern for one's own self-interests, emphasizing differences. Obviously, the amount of distancing and disassociation will vary with the kind of relationship being dissolved, time available, and so on. Chapter 10 details various phases in the process of terminating a relationship which are the result of messages signaling distance and disassociation.

We would also predict that the general dimensions of communicative behavior reviewed earlier in this chapter would polarize more than ever around narrow, stylized, difficult, rigid, awkward, public, hesitant, and suspended judgments.

Finally, we would like to take a finding derived from the study of conversations and apply it to relationships. Thus, we would predict that termination dialogue would regularly manifest: (1) a summary statement; (2) behaviors signaling the impending termination or decreased access; and (3) messages that indicate what the future relationship (if any) will be like.[19] A summary statement reviews the relationship's history and provides the rationale for the imminent termination.

Decreased-access messages clarify what is happening. Addressing the future avoids awkward interactions after parting. Even when dissolving a long-term relationship, the subject of being future friends or enemies must be addressed. "I'll always respect you, but I don't love you anymore," or "I don't ever want to see you again!" Saying good-bye to a long-term relationship may take longer, especially if one party does not want to end it and seeks to delay the final parting. These three functions of conversational leave-taking and their connection to the termination of relationships will be developed more fully in Chapter 10.

Movement: In, Out, and Around Stages

Let us now return to some of our original questions to explain more fully the stages just outlined: What are the forces which help us understand our movement in, out, and around the various stages? What directions for movement are possible at each stage? What is the likely rate of movement through the stages outlined in the model?

The first question focuses on the forces of change. Are relationships always changing? If so, what is a "stable" relationship? When we describe a relationship as stable, we are acknowledging that the changes taking place are occurring at a slower rate or at a low level of intensity. We typically pay less attention to ongoing relationship fluctuations unless they portend a change in stage. These within-stage changes during periods we think of as stable may, however, occur in regular, almost predictable patterns—representing a kind of phase movement within a particular stage. The more dramatic changes which signal movement to a new stage may stem from a buildup of these smaller changes and recurring patterns within a stage, or they may arise without any apparent history.

Two theories provide us with useful perspectives for explaining *movement within and across relationship stages:* (1) dialectical theory and (2) social exchange theories.

Dialectical Theory

From this perspective, change takes place as the result of trying to resolve the inevitable tensions of relationship life. These tensions arise as we try to manage simultaneously two or more desirable, but contradictory, actions. For example, we want to maintain togetherness with our partner, but at any given point we may make autonomy and individual needs a priority. The tension we feel is rooted in the knowledge that we need to have both togetherness and separateness to sustain a relationship, while also recognizing that too much or too little of either (overall or at an inopportune time) can harm the relationship. The way a couple communicatively manages situations like this provides the measure of how and why their relationship changes.

What are the dialectical tensions facing those who are trying to build, maintain, or get out of a relationship? An important source of relevant contradictions is the type of relationship being undertaken.[20] A different set of contradictions, for example, may be at the heart of relationship-change processes for friends, co-workers, and co-workers who are friends. The most likely candidates for contradictions which cut across relationship types are probably similar to those found for other basic human responses to our social environment: involved/uninvolved; dominant/submissive; positive evaluation/negative evaluation (see pp. 74 and footnote 2, Chapter 3). Nevertheless, the most commonly identified dialectical tensions in the research to date are the following:

Integration–Separation.   Relationships require that each partner remain an individual while at the same time merging that self with his or her partner. Obviously, intimate relationships require more integration than those of casual friends, which, in turn, makes this an especially critical dimension for intimates. When there is too much togetherness or too little of it, this will create the tension which will initiate change. Questions about autonomy and connection occur at all relationship stages—whether it involves the decision to become a couple, the rules regarding freedom outside the relationship, or pondering whether staying together is worse than terminating the relationship. Integration–separation tensions also exist for relationship partners and their extended social network as well. They want to blend effectively into the larger social system without losing their unique pair identity.

Expression–Nonexpression.   Even though beginning relationships are often characterized as efforts to seek information from another and provide information about yourself to this other, there is also a counterforce that cautions against revealing too much too soon. This kind of reveal–hide tension continues throughout various relationship stages. We know that on the one hand we need expression and openness to achieve intimacy; we also know that we make ourself and our relationship more vulnerable by doing so. Similarly, there are contradictory demands regarding the expression of relationship information by one or both partners to members of their extended social network. As with the couple itself, the fluctuations associated with sharing relationship information and keeping secrets with members of the extended social network is key to the process of building, maintaining, strengthening, weakening, and terminating the relationships comprising that network.

Stability–Change.   In order to be comfortable with another person, a certain amount of predictability is necessary. Without predictable patterns there is too much uncertainty and ambivalence for a long-term relationship—we need someone we know we can count on in certain predictable ways. But too much predictability (in certain areas or in general) may make the relationship seem stale and prompt a call for something "different." At the same time partners are communicatively wrestling with stable, predictable actions versus changing, novel ones, they are also facing similar tensions as they consider how to relate to larger social systems they are part of. For example, couples may want to be associated with appropriate (and predictable) community relationship norms while simultaneously reaching for a degree of deviance from those norms which identifies *their* relationship as *their* relationship.

Each couple may react to the tensions created on these dimensions in different ways, but it can be a complicated process of negotiation. For example, partner **A** may want a great deal of autonomy and partner **B** may want only a little less. Partner **A** thinks that the survival of the relationship will require even more connectedness than partner **B** wants. But partner **B** thinks if partner **A** emphasized togetherness only a little more, they'd have a fine relationship. Both partner **A** and partner **B** were raised in families which emphasized togetherness as the key to satisfying and close relationships. At this point we are less concerned with how this will be negotiated than we are in pointing out how change or movement in relationships involves: (1) what one person wants for him or herself; (2) what one person wants for the other person; (3) what both parties want for the relationship; and (4) what each party to the relationship wants as a result of past and current experiences with members of their social network. Often, the participants will not be nearly as clear about their wants as the preceding list suggests. In fact, sometimes people don't know what they want until they start talking.

Even though integration–separation, expression–nonexpression, and stability–change are frequently identified tensions associated with relationship change, the discussions that affect these contradictions may be on any topic. For example, suppose two intimates disagree about the need to recycle bottles, cans, and newspapers. They discuss it often and each maintains a disagreeable position to the other. Each realizes that the other's position is not likely to change by continued argument that creates unpleasant feelings for both of them. They develop a tacit agreement not to discuss the issue so often and, when they do, each subscribes to the rule that on this issue they will agree to disagree. The way this couple managed the issue of recycling affected all three tensions discussed earlier—that is, each can be separated on this issue but remain integrated in their relationship; each has agreed to a certain degree of expressiveness when discussing the issue, but each knows it is important to close down the number of times the topic is discussed; and there is a certain stability to their interaction on this issue, but this could change as each feels the need to change the current agreement.

Sometimes the responses of a couple to these tensions will produce dialogue that propels them toward greater intimacy, and sometimes toward less intimacy. It is important to remember that these tensions associated with building and maintaining a relationship are natural—part of what relating is all about. It is equally important to understand that one cannot "solve" relationship problems by seeking greater connectedness or openness or predictability, because the very act of moving toward these goals brings into focus the need for the polar opposite. The more you practice closed behavior, for example, the more salient openness becomes.

Social Exchange Theories

Social exchange theories have been used to explain changes in social behavior for many years.[21] These theories contend: (1) that in social relationships we are constantly exchanging resources (e.g., love, status, information, money, goods, services); (2) that these resources are evaluated by us as rewarding or not; and (3) that people have a tendency to seek those things which will be rewarding to them.

Given these assumptions, what are the rules or principles which govern productive exchange of these resources in developing relationships? One theory believes *equity* is at the heart of effective resource exchange in relationships. This theory predicts relationship partners will be most satisfied with their relationship when the ratio of benefits to contributions is similar for both of them. Inequity occurs when one partner is perceived as underbenefited relative to the other. When this happens, there are several ways equity can be restored by the underbenefited partner: (1) by obtaining increased benefits or rewards within the relationship; (2) by decreasing his or her contributions to the relationship; (3) by psychologically reinterpreting one's position so it no longer seems underbenefited—e.g., "I'm getting a lot more than other people I know" or "Pat deserves more than I do anyway"; (4) by obtaining additional benefits or rewards outside the relationship; or (5) by terminating the relationship. Another theory maintains partners are most satisfied with their relationship when there is an *equality rule* operating—i.e., when each partner is perceived as contributing equally and benefiting equally. A third theoretical perspective argues that the only thing that really matters to people is having the highest *reward level.* This theory is rooted in the belief that the more rewards people get, the happier they are. According to the *need-based rule,* people do not exchange resources because of a desire for equity, equality, or for the most rewards possible. This theory says people exchange resources in response to their perceptions of their partner's needs. The more this is perceived as happening, the more satisfaction is felt for the relationship. All four of these exchange theories have received some support by researchers, but none seems able to account for the entire range of complex responses associated with the exchange of resources in different types of developing and established relationships. On the other hand, it is likely that one of these theories may be very useful in explaining a particular episode or sequence of events in *your* relationship.

Rewards and Costs.   Each of the preceding theories is based on the premise that relationship partners make assessments of what they get and what they give. Has the exchange of resources been a rewarding one or a costly one? In order to better understand this process of evaluating the exchange of resources, let's look more closely at the nature of what we've been calling rewards and costs.

> By rewards, we refer to the pleasures, satisfactions, and gratifications, the person enjoys. The provision of a means whereby a drive is reduced or a need fulfilled constitutes a reward.
>
> By costs, we refer to any factors that operate to inhibit or deter a performance of a sequence of behavior. The greater the deterrents to performing a given act—the greater the inhibition the individual has to overcome—the greater the cost of the act. Thus, cost is high when great physical or mental effort is required, when embarrassment or anxiety accompany the action, or when there are conflicting forces or competing response tendencies of any sort.[22]

Davis proposes an analogous concept when he discusses giving or not giving favors.[23] Favors may be physical or psychological. Although physical favors may certainly have psychological overtones, they include such behaviors as: giving a monetary loan, satisfying sexual desires, having a person to dinner, protecting against physical harm, providing an extra hand when one person is incapacitated or lazy, or offering some expertise the other person lacks. Examples of psychological favors include feeling an integral part of the other's sorrows and joys, giving support for approved behavior, helping to offset or improve unapproved behavior while still communicating support, and helping the other to justify his or her problems (e.g., "You couldn't help it. Everybody goes through the same thing.").

When favors are given, it may be because one participant in the relationship: (1) is dependent on the other; (2) is returning a favor received; (3) wants to obligate the other in the future; or (4) is rewarded by seeing the other person enjoy the favor given.

Withholding favors may occur when one person: (1) doesn't think a similar favor will be needed in return; (2) feels the relationship will suffer by granting the favor; (3) doesn't think the favor can be returned; (4) doesn't have the time or resources to give the favor; or (5) doesn't think the other needs or will benefit from the favor.

It would be a mistake to assume that we are constantly evaluating everything that happens to us as a reward or cost. On the contrary, much of the time we are not consciously processing the substance of our interactions as helping or hurting our relationship. Nevertheless, we are likely to make such evaluations as we try to explain why we *feel* especially good or bad. We also pay particular attention to the reward/cost ratio when we have strong expectations for favorable or unfavorable outcomes. And our conscious awareness of rewards and costs is also likely to be higher with partners we have less experience with—i.e., there is no historical record which assures us rewards and costs will eventually reach an satisfactory state because they always have in the past.

When we do evaluate these rewards (or favors) and costs, we are, of course, relying on our own subjective view of reality. As such, our view of the distribution of rewards and costs may not be shared by our partner. The nature of the interaction between two partners who view the distribution of rewards and costs differently is where important changes occur. Communication about rewards and costs can itself be rewarding or costly. Sometimes the way people talk about rewards and costs in their relationship may be a more powerful reality than any actual exchange of resources. Even though we know the importance of this dialogue, we know very little about how partners to a relationship actually talk about rewards and costs. However, we do know that relationship partners review and weigh one or more of the following and how they affect the relationship as a whole: the current encounter, past encounters, and future encounters.

Analysis of the Current Encounter.

For any given encounter, you might assess the rewards and costs and ask yourself whether the rewards were greater than the costs. Naturally, the greater the ratio of rewards to costs, the more satisfied you are likely to be with the relationship. If your own investment is high, you may have to receive a proportionately high return to evaluate the experience favorably.

Sometimes we seek the highest rewards for ourselves with the least cost, a condition which may also increase the costs for the other person. While frequent application of this strategy sometimes works successfully for transient, short-term, or superficial relationships, it does not seem conducive to achieving greater intimacy because one party in the relationship is always "one down." Of course, you can try to keep the other person from knowing about your increased rewards—keeping the other from knowing that he or she is the "loser"—but daily interaction with intimates makes this chore especially difficult.

When a student tells a professor he or she is one of the best teachers in the school and receives a correspondingly high grade (deserved, of course), the situation could be described as rewarding to the student and the professor while incurring minimal costs for both.

Analysis of Past Encounters.

In any given situation, we may also ask ourselves how this experience compares with all others we have had with this person. You may have an experience in which the costs are very high, but when compared with the multitude of previous rewarding experiences, it does not seem to be a sufficient cause for slowing down the relationship. Sometimes one person has been almost completely dependent on the other for rewards in certain areas. Then when the other person "doesn't come through" or "takes advantage" it may be quite a shock. Conversely, an extremely rewarding experience may not balance an interpersonal economy that has accumulated many costs. It may, however, be an important first step in causing the relationship to grow again. Close friends, lovers, and spouses are less likely to expect a constant balance of rewards and costs because they anticipate that the favors given and received will average out during the course of their relationship. But as these relationships experience problems, the demand for more immediate rewards may increase—particularly in newer relationships, with insecure partners, etc. Sometimes we perceive something as a cost initially (an intense argument), but the long-term effects are rewarding (important issues for the relationship were openly discussed and mutually agreeable decisions were reached).

This analysis of the cumulative rewards and costs obtained in a relationship also provides valuable data for comparison with possible alternatives to the current relationship. For example, poor marriages often continue because the alternatives—divorce proceedings, living alone, division of the children, social criticism—offer potentially greater costs than those currently felt. Thus, not all the rewards and costs that affect the relationship are derived from the partners themselves. Other people in your social network, people you work with, relatives—all provide rewards and costs that may impact on the two-person relationship.

Analysis of Future Encounters.   Finally, we may ask ourselves whether it will be rewarding to interact with this person in the future. What will be the relative rewards and costs derived from interacting at our current stage of the relationship? At a less intimate level? At a more intimate level? Such considerations have a definite impact on the movement through the various stages of growth and deterioration.

One important concept regarding expectations for future encounters concerns the norm of reciprocity.[24] Simply stated, the *norm of reciprocity* tells us that there is a strong tendency on the part of human beings to respond in kind to the behavior they receive. Are you willing to give another certain rewards today in the hope that the norm of reciprocity will be activated and you will be "done unto as you did unto them" sometime in the future?

Reciprocity does not have to be an immediate, unthinking response. It is often one that is conscious and planned. The return volley does not necessarily have to take place immediately following the other's serve–"they had us to dinner last month so we should have them over soon," or "they sent us a Christmas card last year, so maybe we'd better send them one this year." The reciprocated act may not be of exactly equivalent value. **A:** "You're a great person." **B:** "I really admire your artistic talent." The exchange may concern two very different objects—trading access to one's genitals for access to the other's money. Or it may involve almost antithetical behavior—for example, dominance provoking submissiveness and vice versa.

A closely related phenomenon is known as *imitation*. Here, the reciprocated response usually follows soon after the initial response and is generally less conscious. The behavior is similar, but still operates within a basic reward-cost framework.

Have you ever noticed how jokes seem to lead to more jokes; strokes lead to more strokes? **A:** "You really did a good job." **B:** "So did you." Or **A:** "I love you." **B:** "I love you, too." Hostility may evoke hostility. I raise my voice and you counter by raising yours. Nonverbal cues like smiling, nodding, silence, and structural dimensions like interruptions or length of utterance are other examples of imitation that have been documented by research. The phenomenon known as *emotional contagion,* where one person's feeling state is assumed and reflected by others present, would also seem to fall within the realm of imitation.[25]

That a norm of reciprocity exists is evident. The exact manner in which it appears, however, is largely dependent on the nature of the relationship. For instance, some feel there is a reciprocity in disclosing information about oneself. Indeed, during Initiation and Experimentation Stages the obligation for giving tit for tat is high. "I'll tell you my hometown if you'll tell me yours." During Intensifying and Integrating, the parties to the relationship may feel that they can ask and expect greater reciprocity of intimate information. It's almost like saying: "By revealing part of my inner self to you first, I'm showing my trust. This should give you sufficient reward and increase the possibility that you will trust me with an equivalent secret of yours. And if you do, our relationship will grow." Some, however, would argue that during the integrating process the reciprocity norm becomes muddled because it is hard to analyze an exchange of intimate information between two people who see themselves so often as a single entity. It should be obvious that there are many relationships that do not demand reciprocation for a high degree of disclosure—you don't expect your physician, psychiatrist, or priest to exchange intimate information with you.

Rewards and Costs in Enduring Relationships. Several characteristics of more intimate, long-term relationships affect the way these participants deal with rewards and costs.

1. First, the value of both rewards and costs may increase as the relationship becomes more intimate. "I'd sure like to spend an evening just talking to you" may be much more powerful from an intimate than an acquaintance; similarly, "You're so rigid in your beliefs" can be a great cost from an intimate and an unimportant opinion from an acquaintance.

2. Second, intimates exchange a greater variety of resources than casual acquaintances. And seemingly inequitable resources may be equitably exchanged—e.g., a special anniversary dinner is "paid back" by not going to play golf on Sunday. Intimates have had the time to negotiate the relative values of these different resources, but less intimate pairs have not. As a result, exchanges between acquaintances are often of the same type—e.g., you had us over for dinner so we'll have you over for dinner.

3. Third, intimates are more likely to tolerate periods where costs exceed rewards than will acquaintances. Since the relationship is expected to continue, the expectation is that losses can be recouped later. In fact, sometimes people will incur considerable costs during the courtship period in order to win the other's approval for marriage. This may create an imbalance that is difficult to restore immediately and gets the marriage off to a rough start.

4. Fourth, some rewards and costs of intimates may need to be analyzed as a couple rather than two individuals. The wife's career setback or the husband's success in losing weight may more appropriately be considered as costs or rewards for both people rather than the specific individual concerned. If one profits, both are rewarded; if one loses, both are hurt.

5. Fifth, since intimates in long-term relationships have many events over many years to consider in any assessment of overall rewards and costs, it is likely that intimates may find it more difficult to specifically account for an overall feeling of deficit or surplus in rewards and costs. After how much time does one stop expecting "payment" for something? To what extent can the time we spent together when dating be used to balance the time we are apart now?

Observers of people who have maintained a relationship over a long period of time may tend to believe that it is happiness or intimacy that has sustained the relationship over so many years. Some enduring relationships do manifest a high degree of intimacy over the years, but others are far less intimate. A married couple may stay together because the marriage provides needed security or because separation is perceived as more costly than a marriage with little intimacy. Sometimes the mutual commitment to the institution of marriage—rather than the marital partner—will sustain a marital partnership. In short, the rewards necessary to sustain a relationship over a long period of time may be derived from a variety of sources other than feelings of intimacy for one's partner.

An analysis of the rewards and costs in our everyday interpersonal relations can be very useful for understanding why we choose to pursue some relationships, remain at the same level with others, and terminate still others. Most resources we exchange have both a reward and a cost component to them. And some things are only rewarding because they aren't a cost. Some behaviors considered rewarding at one point in a relationship may be perceived as costs at another point. Just because we are rewarded by another person doesn't mean our relationship will continue to increase in intimacy. You may really like to play tennis with someone, but the rewards derived from this activity alone are not sufficient to bring the partners to a more intimate stage. And even if one partner felt the rewards were sufficient to move toward greater intimacy, the other partner may not.

Any analysis of human relationships in terms of an "economic model" of exchange inevitably causes some to feel that the humanness has been taken out of relationships and that the possibility of behavior that is not self-serving has been eliminated. Do people help others without any desire for personal gain? Does altruistic behavior exist? We know that people run into blazing buildings and freezing rivers to save strangers, and we know people donate blood and money to others without any hope of reciprocated gain. Examples like this offer strong testimony to the existence of altruistic behavior. Still, there are questions. Is there something about the act of helping another person which, in itself, is a reward to the helper?

Batson's research shows people experience one of two emotional responses (or some combination of the two) when they confront a distressed person: personal distress or empathic concern.[26] Personal distress involves getting upset, being worried, feeling troubled, and the like. Empathic concern means there is a real feeling of compassion and sympathy for the distressed person. When personal distress predominates, the helper's behavior is grounded in self-interest. When empathic concern predominates, the helper's behavior is designed to reduce the other's distress and qualifies as altruistic behavior. In addition, others have suggested that emotional attachment to another person may trigger altruistic motives even when that person is not suffering distress. Thus, even though we may be motivated by the accumulation of rewards for ourselves, this doesn't necessarily mean we will always act in a selfish manner. Maximizing our own gains may be achieved by maximizing our partner's.

Rewards and costs are determined by many things. We have only touched on a few. Chapters 3 and 4 will explore in more detail some of the situational, psychological, and societal forces that help structure the cost–reward process and, ultimately, our movement through relationships.

Now that we have a general idea of two theories which are useful for understanding why change in relationships occurs, let's examine our model from another perspective—the directions that are available for movement.

Directions Available for Movement Through Interaction Stages

The following propositions about movement possibilities can be derived from the staircase analogy presented in Figure 2.1:

Movement is generally systematic and sequential.

Movement may be forward.

Movement may be backward.

Movement occurs within stages.

Movement is always to a new place.

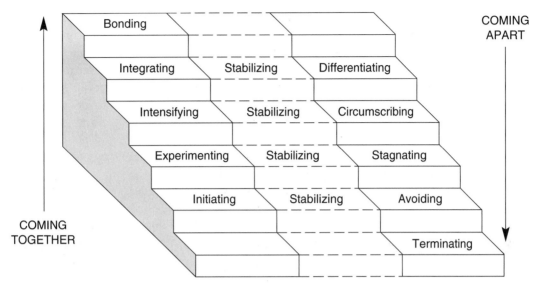

2.1 Staircase Model of Interaction Stages

Movement Is Generally Systematic and Sequential

Typically, when coming together, people follow a process of moving up the left side of the staircase in Figure 2.1; when coming apart, they commonly move down the right side. *This, however, does not suggest that the process is linear or that there is a fixed, unchangeable sequence of movement through stages.* We are dealing with a phenomenon that is never at rest, continually moving and in flux. Of course, the participants may perceive the development of a relationship as chaotic or "out of control"—moved by forces "bigger than either one of us." No doubt some relationships develop in a less orderly fashion than others, but many people experience a general sequencing effect because: (1) each stage contains important presuppositions for the following stage; (2) sequencing makes forecasting adjacent stages easier; and (3) skipping steps is a gamble on the uncertainties presented by the lack of information that could have been learned in the skipped step. Some social norms even help to inhibit skipping steps.

But, of course, sometimes people skip steps during growth processes. Witness the not unfamiliar pickup routine that moves from "Hi, what's your name?" (Initiating) to "Let's get out of this place and get to know each other better at my apartment" (Intensifying). Another familiar skip is for a couple to reach Intensifying and then move to Bonding—only to find out later that their major problem is the lack of integrating in their relationship. Each person "really loves" the other, but one or both are unwilling to move from a primarily "I" orientation to a "we" orientation—risking the merger of self with another.

The termination of relationships may also violate an orderly sequence, achieving sudden death rather than a slow decay. Sudden death is reflected in the situation where a couple is operating at the integration stage, making plans for marriage, and suddenly one party elopes with another person, never to be heard from again. Returning home to a house empty of furniture and finding divorce papers on the last remaining table is another example. As a general rule, movement is to adjacent stages (vertical or horizontal), but any final-state form can be approached from differing initial conditions and through a variety of paths.

Movement May Be Forward

During phases of coming together, one evaluates the various rewards and costs and may decide to advance the relationship to the next logical step upward. The decision might be one of formalizing one's commitments during integration by moving to the Bonding Stage. It is, of course, possible to perform bonding rituals at earlier stages, thus having one foot on Intensifying and one on Bonding. During the phases of coming apart, forward movement means a movement from one of the stairs on the right to one on the left. For instance, a pair may be at the Circumscribing Stage and, after various efforts at rejuvenation, move back to Intensifying, and, in time, perhaps move toward Integrating. Any movement toward greater intimacy is considered *forward*.

Movement May Be Backward

Having once achieved interaction at a level such as Intensifying, the relationship may not be able to stabilize and slips back to a previous step, in this case, Experimenting. The parties may mutually agree that a more superficial relationship is more to their liking. "I like you a lot, Delbert. I still want to go out with you, but I would rather we didn't try to make something out of our relationship which it just isn't right now. Maybe it will develop into something more intimate, but it takes time." Of course, backward movement in the deterioration process is a constant movement down the staircase from Differentiating to Terminating. Backward movement starts laterally, moving from a stair on the left to one on the right. An example is meeting a person at a party and Experimenting, inviting the person over several times until Stagnating sets in, then Avoiding and eventually Terminating the relationship.

Movement Occurs Within Stages

The central staircase represents the possibility of stabilizing relationships at a given level. As with any system, we are constantly fighting the law of nature, which says that all things move toward disorganization and death. We constantly try to arrest possible disintegration by achieving some steady state or equilibrium. This might involve brief forays into communication more characteristic of other stages, while generally maintaining the interaction within a given stage. When lovers quarrel, their disagreement can manifest characteristics more central to the deterioration process. Naturally, to maintain the relationship at the stage more appropriate to lovers, certain forces have to be enacted to counter this disruptive force. In some cases, such disruption may not be as harmful as it first appears. Those who study living systems argue that negative feedback is often needed to keep the system functioning. The absence of negative feedback can cause the steady state to vanish and terminate the system. This is probably why intimates are more apt to provide each other with evaluative judgments.

There will always be a certain degree of instability associated with any stable relationship. Thus, when patterns fluctuate excessively or when they do not fluctuate at all, a condition of instability exists. To complicate things even more, it is likely that there are progressive steps within the stages—a beginning, middle, and end—for each stage.

Movement Is Always to a New Place

Once something has been worked through, it is different. Once communicators have achieved a certain level of interaction, they can never go back to "the way we were." They may, however, work through the same stages or even more intimate ones. Take, for example, a couple who spends considerable time in the experimenting stage. One person wants to move to the Intensifying Stage; the other doesn't. As a result, they gradually move toward Stagnating and, eventually, to Avoiding. Through chance, the couple is later put in adjoining rooms in an experimental coed dorm. Should they choose to renew the relationship and start moving through the Experimenting Stage again, it will be colored by the previous experiences. It may mean some things can be worked through much more quickly but others have to be handled with patience and sensitivity, perhaps due to the pain incurred in the original decay process. The best predictor of who will be friends after an intimate relationship is whether they were friends prior to the romantic involvement. In addition, the extent to which a partner feels "taken advantage of" or manipulated is also an important factor in determining whether romantic partners can be "just friends" after romance.[27]

Now that we have some idea of the directions followed in developing relationships, a few comments about the rate of growth and deterioration are in order.

Rate of Movement Through Interaction Stages

Movement is usually rapid through stages already achieved or exposed. Intimates or close friends can more easily move through or dispense with small talk (characteristic of Experimenting) and move freely into more personal areas.

Movement is usually rapid through areas where positive rewards have been achieved. Those married couples who avoid talking about "why don't you come to church with your family" may be agreeing not to disagree, which may be rewarding in itself. People interested in developing a positive relationship generally avoid conflict (which might elicit high costs or simply provide no reward) until their relationship has a sufficient reward reservoir to manage such conflict.

Movement may be rapid where time is short—for example, summer romances. In a highly mobile and transient society, many efforts are made to short-circuit a lengthy process for getting to know people.

Movement may be facilitated where proximity is high. Seeing someone on a daily basis allows more rapid assimilation of information used in determining whether movement will be forward or backward.

Movement may be facilitated by certain situational features—sensitivity groups, parents-without-partners groups, a newcomer to a block party. In other situations such as attending a church service, movement is inhibited by sanctions regarding what can be talked about.

Movement is generally faster during the early stages. Highly personal information, characteristic of more intimate stages, comes out slowly and acts as a governing agent. In addition, intimates are usually intimates because they have a backlog of rewards. Each reward is tempered by previous rewards, making it harder for dramatic movement to take place as a result of a new reward. "Sure Homer brought me flowers and I appreciate them, but he always does that."

Movement may be slow or rapid depending on individual needs. Two lonely, isolated people with few friends may move quickly; two popular people with a stable of friends may move more slowly.

Movement is bound to be slower if only one party to the relationship desires a change, whether it is to advance or retreat.

Movement during deterioration may be rapid if one person violates a particularly sacred part of their covenant. This is particularly true when (1) the offended person has repeatedly taken a strong stand on the issue and has forecast destruction of the relationship, should violation occur; and (2) if the offended person sees no possibility for offsetting the violation.

Movement from courtship to marriage is accelerated by the time spent together in joint activities and the expression of strong feelings for the other. If the couple feels the reasons for their relationship growth are similar to what is generally expected, this also seems to promote faster movement from courtship to marriage.[28]

Sometimes movement is rapid when both parties agree that they have experienced a relationship "turning point." For example, the mutual expression of serious commitment, the energy each puts into making up after a bad fight, or the way each partner handles an external threat to the relationship, can facilitate movement.[29] If one person thinks it is a turning point and the other does not, it is not as likely to stimulate rapid movement.

These are the major forces that determine how fast or how slow we move in and out of interaction stages and relationships in general. There are many other forces as well.

SUMMARY

This chapter started with the idea that there are many different types of relationships, but all of them seem to have some characteristics in common. For example, relationship expectations change as a result of communication behavior and communication behavior changes as a result of relationship expectations. In addition, each type of relationship appears to fluctuate along a continuum of intimacy or "closeness." With these features in mind, a model of interaction stages covering the growth and decay of relationships was proposed. The model was based on the idea that certain patterns of communication manifest themselves at different points in the life of a relationship. This evolutionary model of message making from greeting to goodbye included the following stages: Initiating, Experimenting, Intensifying, Integrating, Bonding, Differentiating, Circumscribing, Stagnating, Avoiding, and Terminating. An overview of the language, topics, and message strategies relevant to each stage was discussed. The model is closely linked to the eight dimensions of communication discussed in Chapter 1. In the last part of the chapter the concepts of dialectical contradictions and rewards and costs (derived from social exchange theories) were introduced to help explain why, where, and how fast people move through interaction stages. In short, we have taken a quick trip via communication behavior through the birth, adolescence, maturity, sickness, isolation, and death of a relationship.

SELECTED READINGS

Relationship Development

Altman, I., and Taylor, D. A. *Social Penetration: The Development of Interpersonal Relationships.* New York: Holt, Rinehart, and Winston, 1973.

Berger, C. R. "Uncertainty and Information Exchange in Developing Relationships." In S. W. Duck, ed., *Handbook of Personal Relationships,* pp. 239–255. New York: John Wiley & Sons, 1988.

Berger, C. R., and Roloff, M. E. "Thinking About Friends and Lovers: Social Cognition and Relational Trajectories." In M. E. Roloff and C. R. Berger, eds., *Social Cognition and Communication,* pp. 151–192. Beverly Hills, CA: Sage, 1982.

Berscheid, E. and Reis, H. T. "Attraction and Close Relationships." In D. T. Gilbert, S. T. Fiske, and G. Lindzey, eds., *The Handbook of Social Psychology,* Vol. 2, pp. 193–281. New York: McGraw-Hill, 1998.

Blieszner, R. "Close Relationships Over Time." In A. L. Weber and H. H. Harvey, eds., *Perspec-tives on Close Relationships,* pp. 1–17. Boston: Allyn & Bacon, 1994.

Brehm, S. S. *Intimate Relationships.* New York: Random House, 1985.

Brenton, M. *Friendship.* New York: Stein & Day, 1974.

Broderick, C. B. "Predicting Friendship Behavior: A Study of the Determinants of Friendship, Selection and Maintenance in a College Population." Ph.D. dissertation. Cornell University, 1956.

Conville, R. L. *Relational Transitions: The Evolution of Personal Relationships.* New York: Praeger, 1991.

Davis, F. "The Cabdriver and His Fare: Facets of a Fleeting Relationship." *American Journal of Sociology* 65 (1959): 158–165.

Davis, M. S. *Intimate Relations.* New York: Free Press, 1973.

Duck, S. ed. *Handbook of Personal Relationships: Theory, Research, and Interventions.* 2nd ed. New York: John Wiley & Sons, 1997.

Duck, S. *Meaningful Relationships.* Newbury Park, CA: Sage, 1995.

Duck, S., and Gilmour, R., eds. *Personal Relationships. 2: Developing Personal Relationships.* New York: Academic Press, 1981.

Erber, R., and Gilmour, R., eds. *Theoretical Frameworks for Personal Relationships.* Hillsdale, NJ: Erlbaum, 1994.

Fletcher, G. J. O., and Fitness, J. eds. *Knowledge Structures in Close Relationships.* Mahwah, NJ: Erlbaum, 1996.

Galvin, K. M., and Brommel, B. J. *Family Communication: Cohesion and Change.* Glenview, IL: Scott, Foresman, 1982.

Gilmour, R., and Duck, S., eds. *The Emerging Field of Personal Relationships.* Hillsdale, NJ: Erlbaum, 1986.

Gottman, J. M. *What Predicts Divorce? The Relationship Between Marital Processes and Marital Outcomes.* Hillsdale, NJ: Erlbaum, 1994.

Hinde, R. A. *Toward Understanding Relationships.* New York: Academic Press, 1979.

Honeycutt, J. M. "Memory Structures for the Rise and Fall of Personal Relationships." In S. Duck, ed., *Individuals in Relationships,* pp. 60–86. Newbury Park, CA: Sage, 1993.

Honeycutt, J. M., Cantrill, J. G., and Allen, T. "Memory Structures for Relational Decay: A Cognitive Test of Sequencing of De-escalating Actions and Stages." *Human Communication Research* 18 (1992): 528–562.

Ickes, W., ed. *Compatible and Incompatible Relationships.* New York: Springer-Verlag, 1985.

Jones, W. H., and Perlman, D., eds. *Advances in Personal Relationships.* Vol. 2. London: Jessica Kingsley, 1991.

Kellerman, K., and Reynolds, R. "When Ignorance Is Bliss: The Role of Motivation to Reduce Uncertainty in Uncertainty Reduction Theory." *Human Communication Research* 17 (1990): 5–75.

Levinger, G., and Moles, O. C., eds. *Divorce and Separation.* New York: Basic Books, 1979.

Levinger, G., and Rausch, H. L., eds. *Close Relationships: Perspectives on the Meaning of Intimacy.* Amherst, MA: University of Massachusetts Press, 1977.

Lewis, R. A. "A Developmental Framework for the Analysis of Premarital Dyadic Formation." *Family Process* 11 (1972): 17–48.

McCall, G. J., ed. *Social Relationships.* Chicago: Aldine, 1970.

McCall, G. J., and Simmons, J. L. *Identities and Interactions.* New York: Free Press, 1966.

McWhirter, D. P., and Mattison, A. M. *The Male Couple.* Englewood Cliffs, NJ: Prentice-Hall, 1984.

Morton, T. L., and Douglas, M. A. "Growth of Relationships." In S. Duck and R. Gilmour, eds., *Personal Relationships 2: Developing Personal Relationships,* pp. 3–26. New York: Academic Press, 1981.

Newcomb, T. M. *The Acquaintance Process.* New York: Holt, Rinehart, & Winston, 1961.

Noam, G. G. and Fischer, K. W., eds. *Development and Vulnerability in Close Relationships.* Mahwah, NJ: Erlbaum, 1996.

Orbuch, T. L., ed. *Close Relationship Loss: Theoretical Approaches.* New York: Springer-Verlag, 1993.

Perlman, D., and Duck, S., eds. *Intimate Relationships: Development, Dynamics, and Deterioration.* Newbury Park, CA: Sage, 1987.

Perlman, D. and Jones, W. H., eds. *Advances in Personal Relationships.* Vol. 4. London: Jessica Kingsley, 1993.

Planalp, S., Rutherford, D. K., and Honeycutt, J. M. "Events That Increase Uncertainty in Personal Relationships: II. Replication and Extension." *Human Communication Research* 14 (1988): 516–547.

Rands, M., and Levinger, G. "Implicit Theories of Relationship: An Intergenerational Study." *Journal of Personality and Social Psychology* 37 (1979): 645–661.

Rubin, Z. *Liking and Loving.* New York: Holt, Rinehart, & Winston, 1973.

Sanders, R. E. "Find Your Partner and Do-Si-Do: The Formation of Personal Relationships Between Social Beings." *Journal of Social and Personal Relationships* 14 (1997): 387–415.

Simmel, G. *The Sociology of George Simmel.* Translated by K. Wolff. New York: Free Press, 1950.

Weiss, R. "Materials for a Theory of Social Relationships." In W. G. Bennis, D. E. Berlew, E. H. Schein, and F. I. Steele, eds., *Interpersonal Dynamics.* Homewood, IL: Dorsey Press, 1973.

Western Journal of Speech Communication 44 (1980): 86–119. Special Report: Theoretical Explorations of the Processes of Initial Interactions.

Wish, M., Deutsch, M., and Kaplan, S. J. "Perceived Dimensions of Interpersonal Relations." *Journal of Personality and Social Psychology* 33 (1976): 409–421.

Wood, J. T. "Communication and Relational Culture: Bases for the Study of Human Relationships." *Communication Quarterly* 30 (1982): 75–83.

Wright, P. H. "Toward a Theory of Friendship Based on a Conception of Self." *Human Communication Research* 4 (1978): 196–207.

Social Exchange

Adams, J. S. "Inequity in Social Exchange." In L. Berkowitz, ed., *Advances in Experimental Social Psychology,* vol. 2, pp. 267–299. New York: Academic Press, 1965.

Berkowitz, L. "Social Norms, Feelings, and Other Factors Affecting Helping and Altruism." In L. Berkowitz, ed., *Advances in Experimental Social Psychology,* vol. 6, pp. 63–108. New York: Academic Press, 1972.

Blau, P. *Exchange and Power in Social Life.* New York: John Wiley & Sons, 1964.

Burgess, R. L., and Huston, T. L., eds. *Social Exchange in Developing Relationships.* New York: Academic Press, 1979.

Clark, M. S., and Chrisman, K. "Resource Allocation in Intimate Relationships." In A. L. Weber and J. H. Harvey, eds., *Perspectives on Close Relationships,* pp. 176–192. Boston: Allyn & Bacon, 1994.

Crowne, D. P., and Marlowe, D. *The Approval Motive.* New York: John Wiley & Sons, 1964.

Deutsch, M. "Equity, Equality and Need: What Determines Which Value Will Be Used as a Basis of Distributive Justice?" *Journal of Social Issues* 31 (1975): 137–149.

Foa, U. G., and Foa, E. B. "Resource Exchange: Toward a Structural Theory of Interpersonal Communication." In A. W. Siegman and B. Pope, eds., *Studies in Dyadic Communication.* New York: Pergamon Press, 1972.

Gergen, K. J. *The Psychology of Behavior Exchange.* Reading, MA: Addison-Wesley, 1969.

Gergen, K. J., Greenberg, M. S., and Willis, R. H. *Social Exchange: Advances in Theory and Research.* New York: Plenum, 1980.

Gouldner, A. W. "The Norm of Reciprocity: A Preliminary Statement." *American Sociological Review* 25 (1960): 161–178.

Hatfield, E. and Traupmann, J. "Intimate Relationships: A Perspective from Equity Theory." In S. Duck and R. Gilmour, eds., *Personal Relationships. 1: Studying Personal Relationships,* pp. 165–178. New York: Academic Press, 1981.

Hatfield, E., Utne, M. K., and Traupmann, J. "Equity Theory and Intimate Relationships." In R. L. Burgess and T. L. Huston, eds., *Social Exchange in Developing Relationships,* pp. 99–133. New York: Academic Press, 1979.

Holmes, J. G. "The Exchange Process in Close Relationships: Micro-behavior and Macro-motives." In M. J. Lerner and S. C. Lerner, eds., *The Justice Motive in Social Behavior,* pp. 261–284. New York: Plenum, 1981.

Homans, G. C. *Social Behavior: Its Elementary Forms.* New York: Harcourt Brace Jovanovich, 1961.

Huston, T. L., Geis, G., and Wright, R. "The Angry Samaritans." *Psychology Today* 10 (1976): 61–62, 64, 85.

Jones, E. E. *Ingratiation: A Social Psychological Analysis.* New York: Appleton-Century-Crofts, 1964.

Krebs, D. L. "Altruism—An Examination of the Concept and a Review of the Literature." *Psychological Bulletin* 73 (1970): 258–302.

Krebs, D. L. "Empathy and Altruism." *Journal of Personality and Social Psychology* 32 (1975): 1134–1146.

Lerner, M. J. and Mikula, G., eds. *Entitlement and the Affectional Bond: Justice in Close Relationships.* New York: Plenum, 1994.

Macaulay, J., and Berkowitz, L. eds. *Altruism and Helping Behavior.* New York: Academic Press, 1970.

Nye, F. I., ed. *Family Relationships: Rewards and Costs.* Beverly Hills, CA: Sage, 1982.

Reason, P. "Human Interaction as Exchange and Encounter." *Small Group Behavior* 11 (1980): 3–12.

Roloff, M. E. *Interpersonal Communication: The Social Exchange Approach.* Beverly Hills, CA: Sage, 1981.

Sprecher, S. "Social Exchange Perspectives on the Dissolution of Close Relationships." In T. L. Orbuch, ed., *Close Relationship Loss: Theoretical Approach,* pp. 47–66. New York: Springer-Verlag, 1993.

Steil, J. M., and Turetsky, B. A. "Is Equal Better?" In S. Oskamp, ed., *Family Processes and Problems: Social Psychological Aspects,* pp. 73–97. Newbury Park, CA: Sage, 1987.

Thibaut, J. W., and Kelley, H. H. *The Social Psychology of Groups.* New York: John Wiley & Sons, 1959.

Walster, E., Walster, G. W., and Berscheid, E. *Equity: Theory and Research.* Boston: Allyn and Bacon, 1978.

Dialectic Theory

Altman, I., Vincel, A., and Brown, B. "Dialectic Conceptions in Social Psychology." In L. Berkowitz, ed., *Advances in Experimental Social Psychology.* New York: Academic Press, 1981.

Baxter, L. A. "Dialectical Contradictions in Relationship Development." *Journal of Social and Personal Relationships* 7 (1990): 69–88.

Baxter, L. A. and Montgomery, B. M. *Relating: Dialogues and Dialectics.* New York: Guilford, 1996.

Baxter, L. A. and Montgomery, B. M. "Rethinking Communication in Personal Relationships from a Dialectical Perspective." In S. Duck, ed., *Handbook of Personal Relationships.* 2nd ed. New York: John Wiley & Sons, 1997.

Bochner, A. "The Functions of Human Communication in Interpersonal Bonding." In C. Arnold and J. Bowers, eds., *Handbook of Rhetorical and Communication Theory.* Boston: Allyn & Bacon, 1984.

Brown, J. R., and Rogers, L. E. "Openness, Uncertainty, and Intimacy: An Epistemological Reformulation." In N. Coupland, H. Giles, and J. M. Wiemann, eds., *"Miscommunication" and Problematic Talk.* Newbury Park, CA: Sage, 1991.

Cupach, W. R. "Dialectical Processes in the Disengagement of Interpersonal Relationships."

In T. L. Orbuch, ed., *Close Relationship Loss: Theoretical Approaches,* pp. 128–141. New York: Springer-Verlag, 1993.

Masheter, C., and Harris, L. M. "From Divorce to Friendship: A Study of Dialectic Relationship Development." *Journal of Social and Personal Relationships* 3 (1986): 177–189.

Miller, V. D., and Knapp, M. L. "Communication Paradoxes and the Maintenance of Living Relationships with the Dying." *Journal of Family Issues* 7 (1986): 255–275.

Montgomery, B. M. "Relationship Maintenance Versus Relationship Change: A Dialectical Dilemma." *Journal of Social and Personal Relationship* 10 (1993): 205–223.

Rawlins, W. K. *Friendship Matters: Communication, Dialectics, and the Life Course.* New York: Aldine, 1992.

Stamp, G. H. "The Appropriation of the Parental Role Through Communication During the Transition to Parenthood." *Communication Monograph* 61 (1994): 89–112.

Werner, C. M., and Baxter, L. A. "Temporal Qualities of Relationships: Organismic, Transactional, and Dialectical Views." In M. L. Knapp and G. R. Miller, eds., *Handbook of Interpersonal Communication,* pp. 323–379. Thousand Oaks, CA: Sage, 1994.

NOTES

[1]Relationship expectations have been examined from several different perspectives. See R. M. Sabatelli and J. Pearce, "Exploring Marital Expectations," *Journal of Social and Personal Relationships* 3 (1986): 307–321; J. H. Harvey, G. Agostinelli, and A. L. Weber, "Account-making and the Formation of Expectations About Close Relationships." In C. Hendrick, ed., *Close Relationships* (Newbury Park, CA: Sage, 1989). A. L. Vangelisti and J. A. Daly, "Gender Differences in Standards for Romantic Relationships," *Personal Relationships* 4 (1997): 203–219.

[2]M. Rands and G. Levinger, "Implicit Theories of Relationship: An Intergenerational Study," *Journal of Personality and Social Psychology* 37 (1979): 645–661.

[3]M. L. Knapp, D. G. Ellis, and B. A. Williams, "Perceptions of Communication Behavior Associ-

ated with Relationship Terms," *Communication Monographs* 47 (1980): 262–278.

[4]R. E. Quinn, "Coping with Cupid: The Formation, Impact and Management of Romantic Relationships in Organizations," *Administrative Science Quarterly* 22 (1977): 30–45; and J. P. Dillard, "Close Relationships at Work: Perceptions of the Motives and Performance of Relational Participants," *Journal of Social and Personal Relationships* 4 (1987): 179–193. For an analysis of nonromantic friendships between coworkers who differ in status, see T. E. Zorn, "Bosses and Buddies: Constructing and Performing Simultaneously Hierarchical and Close Friendship Relationships." In J. T. Wood and S. Duck, eds., *Under-studied Relationships* (Thousand Oaks, CA: Sage, 1995).

[5]J. G. Delia, "Some Tentative Thoughts Concerning the Study of Interpersonal Relationships

and their Development," *Western Journal of Speech Communication* 44 (1980): 97–103.

[6]Representative works include: F. Lacoursiere, *The Life Cycle of Groups* (New York: Human Sciences Press, 1980); R. Thornton and P. M. Nardi, "The Dynamics of Role Acquisition," *American Journal of Sociology* 80 (1975): 870–885; I. Altman and D. A. Taylor, *Social Penetration: The Development of Interpersonal Relationships* (New York: Holt, Rinehart, & Winston, 1973); B. W. Tuckman, "Developmental Sequence in Small Groups," *Psychological Bulletin* 63 (1965): 384–399; S. W. Duck, *Personal Relationships and Personal Constructs: A Study of Friendship Formation* (New York: John Wiley & Sons, 1973); M. S. Davis, *Intimate Relations* (New York: Free Press, 1973); T. M. Newcomb, *The Acquaintance Process* (New York: Holt, Rinehart, & Winston, 1961); C. B. Broderick, "Predicting Friendship Behavior: A Study of the Determinants of Friendship Selection and Maintenance in a College Population" (Doctoral diss. Cornell University, 1956); G. M. Phillips and N. J. Metzger, *Intimate Communication* (Boston: Allyn & Bacon, 1976), pp. 401–403; C. R. Berger and R. J. Calabrese, "Some Explorations in Initial Interaction and Beyond: Toward a Developmental Theory of Interpersonal Communication," *Human Communication Research* 1 (1975): 99–112; C. R. Rogers, "A Process Conception of Psychotherapy," *American Psychologist* 13 (1958): 142–149; G. Simmel, *The Sociology of George Simmel,* trans. K. Wolff (New York: Free Press, 1950); K. Lewin, "Some Social Psychological Differences Between the United States and Germany," *Character and Personality* 4 (1936): 265–293; J. T. Wood, "Communication and Relational Culture: Bases for the Study of Human Relationships," *Communication Quarterly* 30 (1982): 75–83; D. P. McWhirter, and A. M. Mattison, *The Male Couple* (Englewood Cliffs, NJ: Prentice-Hall, 1984); W. J. Dickens, and D. Perlman, "Friendship over the Life-Cycle." In S. Duck and R. Gilmour, eds., *Personal Relationships: 2. Developing Personal Relationships* (New York: Academic Press, 1981); C. A. VanLear, Jr., and N. Trujillo, "On Becoming Acquainted: A Longitudinal Study of Social Judgment Processes," *Journal of Social and Personal Relationships* 3 (1986): 375–392; J. M. Honeycutt, J. G. Cantrill, and R. W. Greene, "Memory Structures for Relational Escalation: A Cognitive Test of the Sequencing of Relational Actions and Stages," *Human Communication Research* 16 (1989): 62–90; J. M. Honeycutt, J. G. Cantrill, and T. Allen, "Memory Structures for Relational Decay: A Cognitive Test of Sequencing of De-

escalating Actions and Stages," *Human Communication Research* 18 (1992): 528–562; and J. M. Honeycutt, "Memory Structures of the Rise and Fall of Personal Relationships." In S. Duck, ed., *Individuals in Relationships* (Newbury Park, CA: Sage, 1993).

[7]R. B. Rubin and S. A. Welch have begun the process of developing a way to measure people's perceptions of their relationship stage based on this model. Their paper, "Methods of Identifying Relationship Stages: Development of a Coding System and an Index," delivered at the annual convention of the International Communication Association, 1998, detailed their initial effort.

[8]McWhirter and Mattison, *The Male Couple.* S. M. Haas and L. Stafford, "An Initial Examination of Maintenance Behaviors in Gay and Lesbian Relationships," *Journal of Social and Personal Relationships* 15 (1998): 846–855.

[9]T. L. Albrecht, M. B. Adelman, and Associates, *Communicating Social Support* (Newbury Park, CA: Sage, 1987). M. R. Parks and M. B. Adelman, "Communication Networks and the Development of Romantic Relationships: An Expansion of Uncertainty Reduction Theory," *Human Communication Research* 10 (1983): 55–79. R. Klein and R. M. Milardo, "Third-Party Influence on the Management of Personal Relationships." In S. Duck, ed., *Social Context and Relationships* (Newbury Park, CA: Sage, 1993), pp. 55–77. G. Allan, *Friendship: Developing a Sociological Perspective* (Boulder, CO: Westview, 1989). M. R. Parks, "Communication Networks and Relationship Life Cycles." In S. Duck, ed., *Handbook of Personal Relationships.* 2nd ed. (New York: John Wiley & Sons, 1997).

[10]G. R. Miller, and M. Steinberg, *Between People: A New Analysis of Interpersonal Communication.* (Chicago: Science Research Associates, 1975); G. R. Miller, and M. J. Sunnafrank, "All Is for One but One Is Not for All: A Conceptual Perspective of Interpersonal Communication." In F. E. X. Dance, ed., *Human Communication Theory* (New York: Harper & Row, 1982).

[11]H. L. Rausch, K. A. Marshall, and J. M. Featherman, "Relations at Three Early Stages of Marriage as Reflected by the Use of Personal Pronouns," *Family Process* 9 (1970): 69–82.

[12]L. A. Baxter, "Symbols of Relationship Identity in Relationship Cultures," *Journal of Social and Personal Relationships* 4 (1987): 261–280.

[13]M. S. Davis, *Intimate Relations* (New York: The Free Press, 1973), p. 188.

[14]W. Ickes, ed., *Empathic Accuracy* (New York: Guilford, 1997).

[15]H. C. Davis, D. J. Haymaker, D. A. Hermecz, and D. G. Gilbert, "Marital Interaction: Affective Synchrony of Self-Reported Emotional Components," *Journal of Personality Assessment* 52 (1988): 48–57; and K. Grammar, K. B. Kruck, and M. S. Magnusson, "The Courtship Dance: Patterns of Nonverbal Synchronization in Opposite-Sex Encounters," *Journal of Nonverbal Behavior* 22 (1998): 3–29.

[16]Davis, *op. cit.,* p. 195.

[17]Imagined interactions may occur at other points in the relationship as well—and for different purposes. For example, a person may construct an imagined dialogue relative to a date or marriage proposal. See J. M. Honeycutt, K. S. Zagacki, and R. Edwards, "Intrapersonal Communication, Social Cognition, and Imagined Interactions." In C. Roberts and K. Watson, eds., *Readings in Intrapersonal Communication.* Birmingham, AL: Gorsuch Scarisbrick, 1989.

[18]D. M. Geller, L. Goodstein, M. Silver, and W. C. Sternberg, "On Being Ignored: The Effects of the Violation of Implicit Rules of Social Interaction," *Sociometry* 37 (1974): 541–556.

[19]M. L. Knapp, R. P. Hart, G. W. Friedrich, and G. M. Shulman, "The Rhetoric of Goodbye: Verbal and Nonverbal Correlates of Human Leave-Taking," *Speech Monographs* 40 (1973): 182–198.

[20]L. A. Baxter and B. M. Montgomery, *Relating: Dialogues & Dialectics* (NY: Guilford, 1996); L. A. Baxter and B. M. Montgomery, "Rethinking Communication in Personal Relationships from a Dialectical Perspective." In S. Duck, ed., *Handbook of Personal Relationships.* 2nd ed. (New York: John Wiley & Sons, 1997). R. L. Conville, *Relational Transitions: The Evolution of Personal Relationships* (New York: Praeger, 1991). W. R. Cupach, "Dialectical Processes in the Disengagement of Interpersonal Relationships." In T. L. Orbuch, ed., *Close Relationship Loss: Theoretical Approaches* (New York: Springer-Verlag, 1993), pp. 128–141. B. M. Montgomery, "Relationship Maintenance versus Relationship Change: A Dialectical Dilemma," *Journal of Social and Personal Relationships* 10 (1993): 205–223. W. K. Rawlins, *Friendship Matters: Communication, Dialectics, and the Life Course* (New York: Aldine de Gruyter, 1992). G. H. Stamp, "The Appropriation of the Parental Role Through Communication During the Transition to Parenthood," *Communication Monographs* 61 (1994): 89–112. C. M. Werner and L. A. Baxter, "Temporal Qualities of Relationships: Organismic, Transactional, and Dialectical Views." In M. L. Knapp and G. R. Miller, eds., *Handbook of Interpersonal Communication* (Thousand Oaks, CA: Sage, 1994), pp. 323–379.

[21]G. C. Homans, *Social Behavior: Its Elementary Forms* (New York: Harcourt Brace Jovanovich, 1961). M. Deutsch, "Equity, Equality and Need: What Determines Which Value Will Be Used as a Basis of Distributive Justice?" *Journal of Social Issues* 31 (1975): 137–149. E. Walster, G. W. Walster, and E. Berscheid, *Equity: Theory and Research* (Boston: Allyn & Bacon, 1978). J. M. Steil and B. A. Turetsky, "Is Equal Better?" In S. Oskamp, ed., *Family Processes and Problems: Social Psychological Aspects* (Newbury Park, CA: Sage, 1987), pp. 73–97. S. Sprecher, "Social Exchange Perspectives on the Dissolution of Close Relationships." In T. L. Orbuch, ed., *Close Relationship Loss: Theoretical Approaches* (New York: Springer-Verlag, 1993), pp. 47–66. J. G. Holmes, "The Exchange Process in Close Relationships: Micro-behavior and Macromotives." In M. J. Lerner and S. C. Lerner, eds., *The Justice Motive in Social Behavior* (New York: Plenum, 1981), pp. 261–284. M. J. Lerner and G. Mikula, eds., *Entitlement and the Affectional Bond: Justice in Close Relationships* (New York: Plenum, 1994).

[22]J. W. Thibaut and H. H. Kelley, *The Social Psychology of Groups* (New York: John Wiley & Sons, 1959), pp. 12–13.

[23]Davis, *Intimate Relations,* pp. 131–168.

[24]A. W. Gouldner, "The Norm of Reciprocity: A Preliminary Statement," *American Sociological Review* 25 (1960): 161–178. J. K. Burgoon, L. A. Stern, and L. Dillman, *Interpersonal Adaptation: Dyadic Interaction Patterns* (NY: Cambridge University Press, 1995). T. Leary labeled a similar concept the *interpersonal reflex* in *Interpersonal Diagnosis of Personality* (New York: Ronald Press, 1957). W. J. Lederer and D. D. Jackson provide an interesting treatment of the reciprocity phenomenon in marriage in *Mirages of Marriage* (New York: W. W. Norton, 1968), pp. 177–186.

[25]E. Hatfield, J. T. Cacioppo, and R. L. Rapson, *Emotional Contagion* (New York: Cambridge University Press, 1994).

[26]C. D. Batson, *The Altruism Question: Toward a Social-Psychological Answer* (Hillsdale, NJ: Erlbaum, 1991). Also see D. L. Krebs, "Empathy and Altruism," *Journal of Personality and Social Psychology* 32 (1975): 1134–1146.

[27]S. Metts, W. R. Cupach, and R. A. Bejlovec, " 'I Love You Too Much to Ever Start Liking You': Redefining Romantic Relationships," *Journal of Social and Personal Relationships* 6 (1989): 259–274. For an account of male-female nonromantic relationships, see K. Werking, *We're Just Good Friends: Women and Men in Nonromantic Relationships* (New York: Guilford, 1997).

[28]T. L. Huston, C. A. Surra, N. M. Fitzgerald, and R. M. Cate, "From Courtship to Marriage: Mate Selection as an Interpersonal Process." In S. W. Duck and R. Gilmour, eds., *Personal Relationships: 2. Developing Personal Relationships* (New York: Academic Press, 1981). Also see C. A. Surra, "Reasons for Changes in Commitment: Variations by Courtship Type," *Journal of Social and Personal Relationships* 4 (1987): 17–33.

[29]L. A. Baxter and C. Bullis, "Turning Points in Developing Romantic Relationships," *Human Communication Research* 12 (1986): 469–493; and S. A. Lloyd, and R. M. Cate, "Attributions Associated with Significant Turning Points in Premarital Relationship Development and Dissolution," *Journal of Social and Personal Relationships* 2 (1985): 419–436.

Factors Affecting Human Communication Behavior in Relationships

The Nature of the Communicators

Dear Dr. Knapp,

I am currently in a relationship with someone who refuses to take any responsibility for making decisions. She goes along with whatever I want to do, which is fine with me, but I never know what she wants to do or how she feels. I'm the one who is expected to make all of the decisions. The problem is that I sometimes come off sounding like an authoritarian and I don't like that. I've tried being silent, hoping that this would force her into initiating action, but instead we end up doing nothing. Why won't she take charge sometimes? What can I do so I don't have to do everything?

The Man in Charge

One of the factors that affects the way we communicate with our relationship partners involves communicator needs—the need to give and receive control (or dominance), affection, and inclusion. These needs change depending on with whom we are communicating and what other events are occurring in our life. In the case above, the writer may have encountered several people who had strong needs to give control at this time in their life. In addition, the writer may have been a relationship partner whose communication behavior expressed a need to control others. This chapter explores these interpersonal needs as they affect the way we communicate and the development of our relationships.

> *Throughout the life cycle, the developing individual undergoes qualitative change. Both the inner world and the outer world of the individual transform over time. Communication with others is central to the process.*
>
> —Lois M. Tamir

Relationships are created, sustained, moved, and killed by messages. People make and send those messages. But there may be a lot of variance in how individual personalities—each with his or her own special needs, skills, and motivations—choose to make these messages. Individual communicators differ in many ways, but their interpersonal needs are an especially important factor for understanding communication in developing and deteriorating relationships.[1]

The Influence of Interpersonal Needs

A vast body of literature consistently supports the idea that each of us needs: (1) to include others in our activities and to be included in theirs; (2) to exert control over others and have them control us; and (3) to give affection to others and receive it from them.[2] While other needs do exist, most of our *interpersonal* behavior can be directly tied to inclusion, control, and affection.

In many respects, interpersonal needs are like biological needs; they help maintain a satisfactory relationship between ourselves and our environment. Sometimes it is difficult to know exactly how much inclusion, control, or affection we need in order to maintain that satisfactory balance. You can eat or drink too much; similarly, you can give or receive too much inclusion, control, or affection. Too little biological or interpersonal sustenance can cause physical or mental illness. Sometimes, however, we get by without needs being met. For example, we can go without water for a time just as we can adapt to periods when we don't receive all the affection we feel we need.

For most of us, our interpersonal needs do not remain static; their strength or importance varies with the circumstances. For instance, giving and receiving affection may be far more important than inclusion or control needs when a relationship has just reached the integrating stage; inclusion needs may be strongest during early growth stages or during the deterioration process. Our conscious awareness of our own needs and the needs of others also varies with the stage of the relationship, the timing, the context, and so forth. A husband may only become aware of his need for excessive control over others when his wife suggests she can no longer live under such tyranny. With this brief introduction, let's look more carefully at each of these interpersonal needs.

Inclusion

It has been said that abandonment or isolation is the most potent of all interpersonal fears. In order to avoid such situations, we need to construct our lives so that others will include us in their activities. Sometimes we accomplish this goal by asking others to share our social environment, banking on the possibility that they will reciprocate. Frankly, we think it is hard for a person with a satisfying number of contacts to fully understand and empathize with a person who has few or no friends. Most of us try to maintain a balance between being together and being alone—between giving inclusion to others and being included by others.

We tend to associate extroverted behavior with people who have strong inclusion needs. Exhibitionistic tendencies in this frame of reference, then, may be attempts to enhance the possibilities of togetherness and, eventually, acceptance. Verbally, a person may attempt to gain the attention necessary for recognition and inclusion by speaking sooner and more often; discussing a wide variety of topics; engaging in name dropping, startling comments, or exaggerations; and using an abundance of self-references.[3] Extroverts tend to be socially active and have relatively strong social support networks.[4] They usually are seen as cheerful and enthusiastic; they tend to express satisfaction, agree with others, and seek out areas of commonality with their conversational partners.[5] These individuals are fairly confident of their ability to manage interactions.[6] They may use less spatial distance and more eye contact when they converse with others. In the same stereotypical fashion, we tend to associate the opposite pattern of behavior, introversion, with low inclusion needs. People reflecting this pattern are generally seen as reserved and serious[7] and will tend to withdraw from or avoid verbal interaction with others. When in the presence of others, several behaviors may appear: (1) silence; (2) speech errors; (3) rapid and short statements; (4) initiating conversation with "I'm sorry, I can't stay long"; (5) hedging ("Well, I'd sort of like to go"); and (6) presenting an inordinate number of conflicting engagements that prohibit inclusion in the activities of others. In short, there seems to be an inability, unwillingness, or apprehension to communicate with others. Contrarily, in some situations, extroverted behavior may mask a need to be alone and introverted behavior may be exhibited by a person who secretly needs and desires a lot of inclusion. In fact, a number of studies have demonstrated that people who are less expressive tend to be more physiologically reactive to emotional stimuli than those who are highly expressive.[8] It may be that less expressive people sometimes suppress their emotional expression as a way to cope with fairly strong inclusion needs.

Dealing with inclusion needs is not limited to nonintimate relationships. The following situation is not unusual for a married couple where one person leaves the home to work and the other does work around the home. The partner who leaves the home may obtain satisfaction of inclusion needs at work. Hence, when this spouse returns home in the evening, he or she may need some solitude. The other spouse, however, having spent most of the day alone—not being included—wants to socialize and interact.

It should be clear that we are talking about normal patterns of behavior, not pathologies. Each of us moves along a continuum of high and low inclusion needs. Sometimes we manifest a particular pattern long enough so that others label us— "he's a loner," or "she's a social butterfly." Oftentimes the expectations created by these labels make it difficult for the loner to become a joiner and the butterfly to become a caterpillar. Should it reach a point where one's perceived interpersonal needs cannot be satisfied through everyday social interaction, pathologies may develop.

> *Include me out.*
> Sam Goldwyn

At least one physician believes the prolonged absence of inclusion can even be fatal.[9] He documents his contention with statistics that show that single, widowed, and divorced people not only die sooner than married people but have significantly higher death rates for every cause of death. While many people have been involved in marriages (or other relationships) that seem to cause more tension and unhappiness than they alleviate, having a network of social ties often provides us with emotional caring and a sense of personal control over our environment. Studies show that relational support is vital for coping with mental and physical illness, crises, transitions, and various other sorts of life stress.[10]

To some extent, social ties are probably made by those who are already physically and mentally healthy. For example, people who are chronically lonely have been said to close off their own access to social support because they see themselves as relationally incompetent[11] and believe others will see them in similarly negative ways.[12] Not surprisingly, those who interact with or observe lonely people also see them as fairly poor communicators.[13] In such cases, the key to fulfilling inclusion needs may be reciprocity.[14] If we receive a great deal of support from others, but are never able or willing to give support in return, our included needs (and needs for support) may just continue to grow. Likewise, becoming overly involved in giving support to others may prevent us from receiving help when we need it most.[15] In fact, research suggests that people who focus on others to the detriment of themselves tend to experience psychological distress and poor physical health.[16]

Control
Each of us needs the feeling that sometimes we're in charge of a situation; at other times we want others to be in charge and don't mind assuming a more submissive

posture. Most people want to achieve a balance, controlling some situations and topics and being controlled in others.

Sometimes we show an excessive need for dominance or control. The need for dominance may spring from many sources—possibly even a nagging fear or insecurity that we can't control others or that they will take advantage of us if we don't dominate them. Ironically, people who seem to have an extremely high need for control (e.g., spouses in abusive relationships) often see themselves a victims of their partners' verbal aggression.[17] Verbally, dominance might be manifested in such things as interruptions, speaking louder, or holding the floor longer.[18] Mehrabian's research on the nonverbal signals associated with power or status suggests looking for such things as: vast personal territory, arms akimbo, postural relaxation, dress ornamented by status symbols, greater height, and expansive movements.[19] Eye contact may be less since the high-status or powerful person does not feel the need to demonstrate attentiveness and may not be as worried about impression management or feedback. However, when speaking, dominant persons will sometimes use prolonged eye contact as a signal of their strength, trying to create anxiety in the other.[20] Don't be misled by this partial listing of behaviors. Control, once achieved, can be maintained in many subtle ways while giving the illusion of low control and freedom for the other. For example, the statement, "Sure, go ahead and go out with other guys. I don't mind," may actually represent (or be perceived as representing) a form of permission or indulgence from the person in control. Similarly, when individuals "help" others in the right situations, in front of the right people, they have access to a great deal of influence. Researchers note that a pattern of behavior called *overhelping* occurs when individuals explicitly help another person achieve some goal so that observers will attribute the person's success to the help he or she was given.[21] In this way, those who are helping get credit for the success. For instance, some parents give their adult children financial help even though the children are capable of getting along without it. By always being a financial resource, the parents maintain a degree of control over their grown children and may even undermine the children's confidence in their ability to support themselves. Another very subtle way to gain control is what researchers call *sandbagging*.[22] This takes place when people display weakness or low ability so that an opponent will reduce his or her effort. For example, during conflict, one relational partner may act hurt or defeated so that the other will lower his or her guard. Then, when the other is vulnerable, the sandbagger will spring back into action with a hurtful comment or a cutting remark.

Control strategies, in short, come in many different shapes and sizes. Those who wield the most control can appear on the surface to be relatively weak or submissive. Indeed, acting submissive in a relationship may give someone a lot of power if his or her partner comes to depend on that submission as a form of ego gratification.

Occasionally, each of us may gravitate toward a position of oversubmissiveness, helplessness, and avoid almost any form of responsibility and control. We want to be told what to do. At such times, we usually speak less frequently and when verbal messages do occur, their duration will probably be short, accompanied by a lower voice volume. Agreement and acceptance of others' remarks is likely. Nonverbally, the head and eyes are frequently lowered, appeasing smiles increase, and a greater physical distance is maintained.

Affection

To like and be liked by others is important to our interpersonal health. While we may find it momentarily distasteful, the opposite of affection—hostility, coldness, anger—can also be important for us. Experiencing hostility (giving and receiving) provides a useful benchmark for understanding the kind and amount of affection we and others require. Those who have had pleasant experiences with affection will probably be comfortable with both close and distant relationships, recognizing that the absence of affection does not mean they are not lovable people. While the concept of affection is generally associated with intimate behavior, it may incorporate behavior that is known as rewarding, supportive, generous, cooperative, sympathetic, warm, or sensitive. This broadened definition would then encompass such behavior as helping someone with a task, taking an interest in another's problems, or having someone endorse your self-image. The concept of *immediacy*, or the degree of liking between communicators, gives us some further behavioral indicators. Verbally, immediacy is the linkage of the speaker with the content of his or her communication—"we" has more immediacy (or liking) than the separation of the elements into "you and I."[23] Nonverbally, greater liking may be displayed in more touching, increased mutual gazes, decreased distance, a direct body orientation with open arms and body, leaning forward, nodding, and a positive facial expression and vocal tone.

Sometimes we meet someone with an excessive need for affection: "I need a lot of loving." It almost seems as if the person is trying to devour us—to the extent that other friends are resented because they take time away from the relationship. There may be many reasons for such behavior. In one case it may be a fear of rejection; in another, the person may have just terminated a relationship where the satisfaction of affection needs was painful and he or she is trying to recoup past losses.

Low affection may also be triggered by unpleasant experiences (being "burned") with others. Not wanting to get "emotionally involved," feeling that you are "unlovable," or distrusting the affection displays of others may naturally result in distant, superficial relationships. Interestingly, sometimes people who are especially sensitive to rejection will exhibit antagonism or jealousy toward others as a device to avoid getting too personal.[24] This hostility or jealousy then causes others to avoid giving affection, which, in turn, fulfills the person's prophecy that he or she can't trust others to provide for his or her affection needs. Another manifestation of wishing to avoid a high level of affection is found in the person who tries to make friends with everyone so he or she doesn't have to be close to any given individual.

Even in intimate relationships, affection needs are sometimes difficult to satisfy. For example, in marriages where both the husband and wife are pursuing careers outside the home, both partners are trying to satisfy achievement needs at work and affection needs in their relationship. Too much emphasis on the satisfaction of achievement needs is not always compatible with a similar emphasis on affection needs. One partner may desire a great deal of affection after a career setback, but the other person's need for achievement may be soaring and it may be difficult to satisfy the other's affection needs. In other types of relationships, the husband may spend years emphasizing achievement needs while the wife seeks the satisfaction of affection needs; then when the husband wants to spend more time with his family, the wife gets a job that she hopes will fulfill her long-neglected needs for achievement. In some cases, the partners do not agree on what satisfies achievement and affection needs. A husband may say he is showing affection for his wife by working long hours, but the wife may not agree; a wife may think the time spent in raising the children should provide satisfaction for the husband's affection needs, but the husband may not agree.

In summary, interpersonal needs do exist. They do influence and are influenced by communication at various stages of the relationship. While some verbal and nonverbal behaviors which may accompany inclusion, control, and affection have been suggested here, you will find there are many ways to express such needs. Individual differences may only be learned with continued contact over a period of time—"When his moustache twitched, I knew he was mad."

The Role of Interpersonal Needs

For any given situation involving two people, we can plot and analyze the role of interpersonal needs. The example in Figure 3.1 illustrates what one person (A) wants to give and what the other person (B) wants to receive. Similar plots can be developed for self-analysis (what A wants to give and receive) or perception of the other person (what you think B wants to give and receive).

One implication of Figure 3.1 is that interpersonal needs can be used to describe encounters or relationships in terms of compatibility. "Do you have (or want to express) what I don't have (or need)?" Obviously it becomes more complicated (but more accurate) when we add two more lines to the diagram: (1) what A wants to receive and (2) what B wants to give. Schutz's work suggests that a compatibility of inclusion needs is most critical for successful communication where becoming "part of the group" is dependent on mutual agreement—joining a sorority.

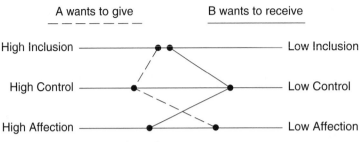

3.1 Plotting Interpersonal Needs

Interacting in close quarters for a short duration calls for compatibility of control needs—a cross-country car trip. Affection compatibility is paramount when there is a close interdependency over a long period of time—roommates. Other researchers have examined these sorts of compatibility issues in terms of loneliness. People who are chronically lonely believe that their interpersonal needs are not being fulfilled—that they lack certain social relationships.[25] They become lonely in part because they perceive that the discrepancy between the social relations they have and the social relations they desire is too large. They may, in reality, have a large number of friends and acquaintances. However, if they believe they have comparatively few relationships (or that they lack a certain type of relationship), they may feel extremely lonely. For some, inclusion may be the problem: they may feel that they aren't really accepted into the social (or task) groups they would like. Others may feel out of control of their interpersonal networks, relegating the cause of their loneliness to external or environmental forces.[26] Yet others may be lacking affection—whether it be from a parent, a friend, or a lover.

Regardless of the type of need, Figure 3.1 illustrates that interpersonal needs occur in the context of a relationship. In some cases, our expectations about what a particular relationship ought to be like may intensify a need (e.g., co-workers should provide inclusion), whereas in others a need may intensify the relationship (e.g., a need for affection may "create" a love relationship). In both instances, however, the compatibility between one person's needs and the other's has substantial effects on the relationship. A number of researchers have discussed this concept in terms of symmetrical and complementary relationships.

Symmetrical Relationships
Symmetrical encounters or relationships are characterized by each participant exchanging the same sort of behavior. Equality is the name of the game. If one person offers to give affection, the other also offers to give affection; if one wants to receive, the other wants to receive; if one has power, the other wants power; if one pleads helplessness, the other counters with an equivalent disability. This type of interpersonal meshing can be and is productive as long as the participants continue

to see each other's individuality and respect each other's rights and needs. It does, however, have competitive overtones which may cause one or both persons to become overly concerned about their own rights and to classify satisfying the other's rights as a duty. Another potential problem concerns the methods used to maintain the "I'm the same as you are" girding necessary for symmetry. Lederer and Jackson outline the problem this way:

> The difficulty is that if A says, "You can't scare me, I've got a gun," and B retorts, "Well, you can't scare me either, I've got two guns," there is danger that this behavior will escalate until the only solution is for A and B to demonstrate their equality by shooting each other.[27]

Complementary Relationships

Complementary encounters or relationships are based on differences. In this case, the partners are exchanging different and complementary sorts of behavior. One person controls, the other submits; one person leads, the other follows; one person gives affection, the other takes it. For example, a mother's need to feed and care for her baby is complemented by the baby's need to be fed and receive affection. Other contexts might include the roles played in doctor–patient or most student–teacher relationships. Since this pattern is completely dependent on the maintenance of the established roles, a potential problem arises when one person no longer wants to exchange behavior consistent with his or her role—there can be no lover without a beloved, no teacher without a student.[28]

Healthy relationships probably have both symmetrical and complementary patterns which vary over time and with topic areas. In situations where one person defines the relationship as symmetrical and the other defines it as complementary, we would expect the probabilities of strife to increase dramatically. For instance, many women are now seeking symmetry in areas where men have traditionally treated the situation as complementary. This same phenomenon can sometimes be seen in the manner parents and children communicate. The smooth-running, complementary pattern between parents and children may take a sharp turn when children reach adolescence. At this time, teenagers increasingly seek symmetrical interactions. Parents who insist on the maintenance of a complementary pattern for all interactions will find the relationship suffering and the communication gap widening.

Analyzing Our Own Needs and Those of Others

One of the obvious implications of our discussion of interpersonal needs is that we must spend time trying to understand our own needs so that we have a better idea of what we need from others and what we can offer them. This doesn't mean we should enter an encounter or relationship with the expectation that we will always be able to satisfy all the needs of the other, or that the other person will always be able to satisfy all our needs. Sometimes only special people at special times can serve these functions. Sometimes we are made aware of our own needs only through the behavior of another person. You may find that you have a need to be very cautious in revealing personal information to others only when you ponder why others never tell you anything very personal. No matter how we obtain such knowledge of our needs, it is safe to say that an understanding of our interpersonal needs will raise the probabilities for successful social interaction.

Telling others to examine and understand their own interpersonal needs is an easy principle to preach, but it is not always easy to do. There are many reasons why it is difficult to analyze our own needs. These difficulties include the following: (1) We are not always aware of our needs, which may be changing from situation to situation, time to time. We are many different selves, *not* a single, *real* self. We can expect different patterns of interpersonal needs as we assess our self in relation to our parents; our self in relation to our lover; our self in relation to our teacher; our self in relation to our employer. Sometimes our lack of awareness of interpersonal needs is due to our inattention to the cycles or rhythms of our life. Although we know virtually nothing about the relationship of a person's biological cycles to his or her social behavior, it seems reasonable to postulate that such effects do occur—e.g., "I don't know why I feel alienated and alone right now. I really have no reason to. People have invited me to parties; I have several really good friends. . . ." (2) For various reasons we may repress certain needs—e.g., not wanting to face the fact that we are often submissive and usually enjoy it. (3) We may distort the strength of a particular need by producing a favorable perception of ourselves to fulfill our need for self-esteem. (4) We may also avoid talking to others about our interpersonal needs which, in turn, provides us with less understanding and awareness of these needs. Sometimes we can only understand these needs by comparing our feelings with those of others. There is, however, a paradox here. For example, our inclusion needs may be best understood by being included in conversations where others discuss such needs. People who are able and willing to discuss their needs with others often understand their needs and are able to garner the social resources necessary to fulfill them.[29] In contrast, those who have difficulty making contact with others are, in all likelihood, the ones who need that contact the most.

Chronically lonely people are a case in point. Whether their needs lie primarily in the area of inclusion, control, or affection, people who are chronically lonely tend to see themselves and others as less competent communicators,[30] less interpersonally attractive, and tend to act less involved in the conversations they have with others.[31] With these sorts of interpersonal difficulties, it is not surprising that lonely people have difficulty communicating with others, understanding their own relational needs, and finding ways of getting their needs met.[32]

> *Trying to define yourself is like trying to bite your own teeth.*
>
> Alan Watts

Closely intertwined with our self-analysis of interpersonal needs is our perception of the needs of the other person, an equally important task if we are to understand what they need and what they have to offer us. The bond between self-analysis and other-analysis is aptly illustrated in Hora's comment:

> To understand himself, man needs to be understood by another. To be understood by another, he needs to understand the other.[33]

Sometimes our own predispositions, needs, and expectations color our perceptions of others. We might engage in selective perception—perceiving what we want to perceive. It is not uncommon, for instance, to see only good in those we like and only bad in those we dislike. Consciously or unconsciously, we sometimes behave in such a way that our perceptions of others must be confirmed. This process, known as a *self-fulfilling prophecy*, might begin with the assumption that another person is hostile. Assuming this is true, we begin to act defensive. Our defensiveness provokes some hostility in the other person, and we take great pride in the confirmation of our original assumption that the person was hostile.

There are many things that may act as barriers to accurate perceptions of others' needs: (1) The other person may wish to conceal his or her needs. (2) The same verbal and nonverbal behavior may be associated with two very different needs—an overbearing person can be reflecting high control and confidence, or deep-seated anxiety and insecurity. (3) The process of selective interaction (interacting only with those like us) may prevent us from experiencing and being able to understand a broad spectrum of needs. (4) We sometimes place undue weight on momentary behavior patterns—we may observe people soon after they have been mistreated, when their self-presentation is focused on making the necessary corrections, and make judgments based on our observations. Despite these and other problems involved in accurate perceptions of others (and ourselves), the value of the process is undeniable, particularly to those who have constantly sought love from one who is incapable of, or unwilling to, return it.

Many communicator characteristics may influence messages exchanged during the course of a relationship. Interpersonal needs form the root system for the more visible manifestations of individual differences, interpersonal skills such as listening, role-taking, role-playing, perceived motivation, and various personality styles.

Interpersonal Needs Across the Lifespan

Throughout life we experience changes and fluctuations in our biological needs. Our interpersonal needs also are affected by the changing demands and experiences associated with different life stages. Thus, we can expect some differences in the communication behavior of people who form relationships at different life stages.

Infancy and Childhood

Interpersonal needs are reflected in our behavior from the day we are born. In fact, some scholars believe our evolutionary heritage provides us with an inborn yearning for contact or inclusion with our world.[34] Infants whose biological needs have been provided for sometimes seem to cry for no reason, but inclusion (holding) and affection (cuddling, soothing sounds) often have a calming effect.

Even before language is understood or spoken, the child is gaining a rudimentary understanding of interpersonal needs. Patterns of being with others and being alone are established.[35] The child soon learns that not all time spent with others is the same. Sometimes good feelings are derived from extended mutual gaze, cuddling, and other displays of affection; sometimes hostile behavior elicits pain; and sometimes there seems to be an absence of affection *or* hostility. In an effort to provide experiences that will ultimately give the child more control over his or her environment, parents shift their children from breast-feeding to solid food, from a baby bed to a "big" bed, from home to school, and so on. For the child, the initial feelings of anxiety and having little control over these new environments are sharply contrasted with the security and control associated with behavioral patterns already mastered. So the infant is scanning his or her world, reacting to the actions of others, and trying to get a grasp on what is expected for getting along.

The developing child also is learning how to signal others that interpersonal needs have not been met. In infancy, these are unfocused expressions (crying, pulling, banging, smiling) of emotional states which may be associated with any number of needs. Gradually, the developing child is able to specify which particular needs are or are not being met. Even infants as young as one year old seem to discriminate among persons with whom they interact—selectively teasing, begging, grabbing, playing, hugging, and aggravating.[36] The ability to *give* inclusion, control, and affection is similarly limited during this time, but develops rapidly as early friendships are formed.

In preschool and early play relationships, the child's repertoire of communication skills associated with interpersonal needs continues to expand.[37] More sophisticated control strategies may characterize the parent–child relationship—e.g., using one parent as leverage on the other; using primitive fear appeals ("I'm not coming home if you don't . . ."). Similarly, the child becomes more sophisticated in giving and withholding affection from his or her parents. Successful strategies are likely to be used again. Sometimes the play behavior of these preschool children reflects interpersonal needs. The actions of the child who continually bosses other children around may be linked to strong parental dominance. Bossing other children may be the only outlet for asserting dominance for that child. In more extreme cases, when a child consistently bullies his or her peers, the child often feels that one or both parents are relatively uninvolved in his or her life.[38] When parents are uninvolved, some children may try to exert control over peers as a way to cope with the fact that their needs for affection and inclusion are not being met by their parents. Childhood is a time for experimenting with various methods of self-presentation. Many of these behaviors stem from basic interpersonal needs—e.g., seeking attention, showing off, requesting things from others, looking for praise, and giving affection.

When the child enters school, he or she will observe a wide variety of social relationships and behaviors. School provides a glimpse at the popular and the unpopular; the liked and the disliked; the in-group and the out-group; and the aggressive and the docile. At about this time first friendships take shape. Up to this point, the child's perspective on friendship has been best described as "the people I'm with." Likes and dislikes are especially important. Often these early friendships are not long-lasting. Rubin gives one explanation:

> Young children, who do not yet understand that one can regard someone both positively and negatively at the same time, are likely to deal with negative feelings by deciding—for the moment—that they aren't friends anymore.[39]

Another reason why some of these early relationships are fleeting concerns the rapidly changing needs of the participants. If a friend is selected because he or she meets your need for inclusion, it may not be long before you desire the company of a less extroverted, outgoing, and intense type of person. One child may like another because he or she is allowed to give as much control as is desired; but the shortcomings of this arrangement may become clear in a short time, and a new friend who is able and willing to give some control in return (but not too much) is favored. Many of these likes and dislikes are based on sharing interests in certain activities rather than sharing values which transcend activities.[40] This is a time of experimenting; a time of finding out about the nature of one's interpersonal needs in the context of a variety of relationships outside the home.

During the period of late childhood several important changes are taking place. First, there seems to be a greater recognition that our own interpersonal needs are closely intertwined with others'. Gradually, we learn that friendship involves the satisfaction of the needs of others as well as our own. Second, our mastery of the language and extensive experience with friendship making and breaking may prompt the gathering of information about the world in other ways. Sometimes we settle on a single "best friend"; sometimes comics, books, magazines, or television take precedence over activities involving other people.

> There seems to be a real need for privacy among many of us during this period, a need to spend more time alone, engaged in solitary activities—reading, sketching, watching television, whatever. This really bothers some parents—mothers in particular—who seem to measure their children's attractiveness and good mental health exclusively by the number of friends they have.[41]

Late childhood is also a time for continued practice in giving inclusion, control, and affection in different ways to different people. We also develop an increased understanding of our own needs and abilities as we face new situations—e.g., being "in charge" of babysitting or mowing the lawn.

Adolescence

Adolescence is a bridge between two very different life stages—childhood and adulthood. Teenagers and young adults often feel conflicts related to the life pattern they are leaving behind and the uncertainty of the one to come. Independence and the commitments and responsibilities that often accompany adolescence provide a major theme during this period. On the one hand, it is gratifying to be treated more like an "adult" and to be breaking away from dependence on parents; on the other hand, it would be nice not to have to contemplate the problems involved in going to college or getting a job or joining the Army or getting married; sometimes we would like our parents to take charge again.

Parent–child relationships during this time are moving from being predominantly complementary to predominantly symmetrical. This relational change, and the conflict sometimes associated with it, often mean that both parents and adolescents express more negativity toward each other than they did in prior years.[42] Yet, even with an increase in expressed negativity, most adolescents feel they have relatively close, positive relationships with their parents.[43] The way adolescents feel about their relationships with their parents depends, in part, on the nature of the relationships they had with their parents when they were children. The growth and the changes that take place during adolescence, in other words, occur as part of an ongoing process that begins long before puberty.

Some researchers have characterized this growth process as one involving a tension between individuality and connectedness. In terms of their verbal behavior, this means that adolescents may alternate between statements of: (1) self-assertion (displaying awareness of one's own point of view and responsibility for communicating it clearly); (2) permeability (expressing responsiveness to the views of others); (3) mutuality (showing sensitivity and respect for others' views); and (4) separateness (expressing distinctiveness of self from others). Once individuation from the parent is achieved, conversations with parents will tend toward a balance among these four types of statements.[44]

Redefining the parent–adolescent relationship as a more symmetrical, individuated relationship often involves difficulties in understanding interpersonal needs. Parental concern on matters of drugs and sex may cause a child to protest that the parent is exercising too much control over his or her life. But parental control in other areas may be more acceptable.[45] Parents may expect a continuation of the affection giving and receiving patterns practiced from early childhood. But the child is establishing other affection and inclusion patterns with peers. Inevitably, these friendships outside the home will alter interpersonal needs in family relationships. It is not unusual for parents to sense this change and criticize the child's new friends. This criticism may only serve to make the new friends seem more desirable and the parents less so. Ironically though, research has shown that friendships formed to compensate for a lack of intimacy at home often fail to fulfill adolescents' interpersonal needs.[46]

It is also interesting to note that the types of communication problems adolescents feel they experience with their parents generally do not determine how satisfied they are with their parental relationship.[47] Both happy and unhappy adolescents report disagreements, misunderstandings, and other communication problems linked to control. The critical factor in distinguishing satisfied from dissatisfied adolescents seems to be the way they interpret these communication problems—e.g., Is my parent to blame? Did my parent have good intentions? Is my parent thinking about my well-being? Struggles between parents and their teenage children are so commonly reported in the popular press, it is understandable that we often ignore the fact that all relationships have periods of turmoil and that most relationships between parents and teenagers are not a constant parade of misunderstandings and fighting.

Friendships play an especially important role in reflecting interpersonal needs during adolescence. This is a time when peer-group comparisons in physical and attitudinal areas are frequent. Do other people my age have the same sexual urges? How many people in my class also hate it when people "assume" something about you without asking first? Social groups are formed and provide a power base and a refuge from unwanted demands from the "outside" world. More than ever before, there is a recognition of the extent to which inclusion in a group can increase your personal leverage and power with other people and institutions. Individual friendships within the group often provide intense pleasure, and sometimes intense pain. Emotional responses are generally less inhibited at this time than they will be later in life. Thus, the emotional highs derived from idealized friends are subject to emotional lows when those friends behave in very normal, but not ideal ways—e.g., lying, not keeping a secret, not accepting you as you are. This may trigger a disillusionment which others may label as "moody" and it may cause the person to go through a period of wanting to be alone. This is only one instance involving changing interpersonal needs relative to adolescent friendships with peers. The interpersonal needs involved in romantic relationships may change need patterns established with friendship groups and individual same-sexed friends. An adolescent's family situation may also affect friendship patterns and needs. An only child may need more friends than one who has several brothers and sisters in his or her own age category. The essence of adolescent friendships seems to be captured by Brenton:

> There is order in the chaos and chaos in the order, of teenage friendships. We want to hang out with the gang, but we want to be close to somebody too. We want to be close to somebody, but we don't want to shut anybody out, either. We want to trust fully, but discover that people let you down—while at the same time we are ready to drop the friendship if our needs aren't being met. We start with shared activities and end up looking at the whole person. We want our friends to help us grow, and find we have to protect ourselves from friends who might put our own vulnerabilities too much to the test.[48]

Despite the inherent complexity and occasional strain in the parent–child relationships and peer friendships which occur during this period, adolescents gradually increase their ability to understand the perspective of the other person and communicate more in terms of their needs.[49]

Adulthood

Just because we are labeled an "adult" does not mean we behave similarly to all others who wear this label. Nor does it mean that all adults follow very different patterns of development. Some regularities in adult life are brought about because many adults in this society face similar decisions about similar tasks at similar times of their life. This research reveals the existence of several distinguishable stages or periods during adulthood.[50] Therefore, let's examine interpersonal needs during early, middle, and late adulthood.

For many adults, early adulthood is a time of adventure, a time to try and "master the world." The feeling of having actually "mastered the world" is not uncommon for young adults who find a compatible partner to live with or who savor the opportunity to live alone; obtain a respectable job and interpret initial successes as the beginning of a brilliant career; or feel they have achieved optimal independence from their parents and other controlling figures of the past. Some couples share the excitement and feeling of accomplishment of having a child during this period. For those who experience this sense of controlling their environment and being firmly in charge of their relationships at home and at work, the desire for control from others will probably be minimal. The one exception may be a mentor at work whose controlling and guiding actions are perceived as having a long-range payoff in promotions and increased responsibilities. In time, however, the partners of these people who want to give a lot of control in their relationships at home and work may want to give more control and receive less. The process of redistributing control needs for a person who feels comfortable and successful giving much and receiving little can be a difficult one. If this issue cannot be satisfactorily resolved, new work environments, new living partners, and even new social groups may be sought. Problems in aligning control needs will surely affect inclusion and affection needs as well. The preceding is only one of the many possible sobering experiences that may arise during this time—e.g., finding out that working hard doesn't always bring success; having to face the fact that people can be treacherous and cruel; confronting the knowledge that life situations are not always "fair"; or being told that "trying" isn't good enough.

Normally, opportunities for giving and receiving inclusion are high during this period of exploring and reaching out. But an occupation that involves moving to a new community may require the effort to establish a new social group. And some people who remain unmarried may desire more inclusion than they are able to achieve. Singles may also desire opportunities to give and receive more affection as well. Cohabiting or married people may experience optimum levels of giving and receiving affection during the early relationship stages, but the introduction of children or increased demands at work may require new efforts to regain satisfactory levels of affection for both partners.[51]

Early adulthood is a time when the analysis of one's own and others' interpersonal needs is probably undertaken in a more superficial way than at other stages in adulthood. It is not uncommon to find a greater emphasis on having one's own needs satisfied than considering how to understand and achieve satisfaction of both partners' needs. It is also a time when the confidence derived from early successes may lead to commitments in the areas of inclusion, affection, and control that are beyond the individual's ability to fulfill.

In contrast, one of the primary themes of middle adulthood is a thorough review and reassessment of established relationships and life goals. What have I done with my life? What can I realistically expect to do? What do I really get and give to my spouse, my children, my friends, my work, my community, and myself? What are my central values and how are they reflected in my life? This is not to say that we don't reflect on such questions at earlier points in our lives. It is likely that the depth of analysis in middle adulthood is much deeper and the answers hold more significance than at earlier times. Answers to these and similar questions provide a basis for putting the past and the future in perspective. People often realize during this stage that decisions concerning possible changes in their life should be made before change becomes too difficult. As a result, some aspects of life are modified; some things are intensified; some are reworked; some are rejected; some new goals may be set; and some new behaviors may be tested. Thus, in some areas the person will be emphasizing his or her strengths from the past—carving out a niche, sinking deeper roots; in other areas, there may be feelings of uncertainty and awkwardness reminiscent of adolescence.

Primary relationships may undergo changes in the composition of interpersonal needs. For example, in traditional husband–wife relationships, the wife may now wish to enter or reenter the world of work outside the home. As a result, she may be able to give and be desirous of giving more control; co-workers may help to satisfy inclusion needs; and affection displays may also change. Communicative exchanges during this time will surely reflect these changing or challenged needs of both husband and wife. People in middle adulthood also are likely to experience interaction changes with their parents and children. Both aging parents and adolescent children are going through life transitions which also involve reevaluation and redirection. Thus, we can expect the parents of the person in middle adulthood to ask for increasing control and certainty not any less inclusion or affection while their teenagers are often looking for less control and inclusion and a different style of affection.

In later adulthood one's aging parents may still be a concern, but children may have left the home. Two themes typically characterize this period: (1) The adult is experiencing clear signals of decreasing strength and other health-related changes, and (2) it is a time when active involvement in civic affairs may be high. While in early adulthood, future-oriented goals encourage people to expand their social network and seek out new relationships with acquaintances, in later adulthood, the situation can be quite different. As individuals age, they begin to see time as more limited and, as a consequence, tend to emphasize goals that are more oriented to the present. These present-oriented goals (e.g., meeting current needs for inclusion or affection) often encourage people to limit more of their social relationships to those that are emotionally satisfying.[52]

Control needs may be low at this time because people may have achieved either the external credentials of power, the sense of internal control of self, or both. Indeed, some research suggests that in many cases, older couples show more personal support and submission than do younger couples in which one partner tries to exert control.[53] In other cases, control may be displayed in a more self-assured manner than it was at earlier life stages. There may be a sense of needing more inclusion in the near future which impels a person during this period to immerse himself or herself more than ever in community activities. The focus has shifted to the satisfaction of the needs of others. The family may be a high priority for giving affection, but if these needs have been neglected for many years, reestablishment may be difficult.

The Older Adult

Interpersonal needs continue to change throughout the period of later life too. Older adults may experience several different need patterns. Certainly the interpersonal needs of a recently retired couple that is active and healthy will differ greatly from those persons who are socially isolated and physically dependent on others.

Generally, the interpersonal needs of these older adults are linked to changes in three areas: (1) health and mobility; (2) social contacts; and (3) financial condition. Naturally, these factors affect interpersonal needs at earlier life stages too, but the impact during this period is often more dramatic. A fourth factor, which often plays a central role in changing needs during the early period of older adulthood, is retirement from work. Established patterns for giving and needing inclusion, affection, and control will be challenged when one or both partners no longer have the satisfactions, irritations, and time spent at work. Although many treat retirement as an opportunity to form new friendships[54] and pursue new interests, it is difficult to ignore the number and variety of social contacts one "leaves behind" in the work environment.[55] This theme of a gradually constricting social life is well known to the older adult.

It is said that we die in this order: socially, psychologically, and biologically. With decreasing health and mobility, older adults are gradually less able to give inclusion to others. Other factors that contribute to the social isolation of the older adult may cause inclusion needs to rise—e.g., the deaths of friends and relatives; leaving friends and acquaintances due to a change of residence or retirement; dropping club memberships due to financial burdens.

Some of the communication behavior associated with the increased inclusion needs of many older adults include the following:

1. To compensate for the decreasing amount of total communication with others, some older adults will "talk your arm off." Those who are bitter about what is happening may communicate very little. Still others, with limited social experiences, may have little to say.

2. When communication does take place, some will be hesitant to discuss controversial topics or to disagree too strongly for fear further alienation and social isolation may occur. Others may express their general resentment with their life situation by being especially disagreeable.

3. With less opportunity for comparing experiences and attitudes with others, some will communicate a lack of trust—fearing others will take advantage of them; others, motivated by the same fear, may communicate in a friendly, docile, and submissive manner.

4. With a constricted social world, it is not unusual for the topics of conversation to focus on oneself—health problems, impact of cold weather, hobbies, etc.

Those who spend much of their time alone may even carry on covert dialogues with themselves. Those who realize that self-oriented communication may grow tiring for listeners will ask questions of the other's life experiences.

5. It is not uncommon for older adults to be more interested in making younger friends than friends their own age. Intergenerational ties between grandparents and grandchildren are sometime very strong. Making new friends in older age categories may have limited rewards. They may have less to give to the friendship, and ill health or death may mean an earlier termination to the relationship than would occur with a younger friend.

6. As the acuity of an older adult's visual and auditory receptors declines, isolation from social processes may occur even in the presence of other people. Many times older adults prefer to talk to only one other person at a time. Memory also plays a part in maintaining a coherent conversation and, when memory fails, the older adult may risk a monologue unrelated to the previous conversation or let others talk until the direction of the conversation is once again pinpointed.

Older adults will also communicate messages that signal decreasing inclusion in the affairs of others. These signals may be similar in nature to those leave-taking cues used to signal the termination of a conversation or a relationship (see Chapter 2, pp. 48–49). Decreasing access may take the form of ordering and dividing up possessions. But indicators may be even more explicit—"Oh, I don't have to worry about that. . . . I won't be around much longer. . . ." The manifestations of supportiveness and salve for the future may be shown in many ways—"You've been a good daughter, Veronica . . . don't fret about me . . . just take care of your family. . . ." There may be additional supportive linkages in one's will, and if there is a desire to express some *non*supportive evaluations of others, a will is the perfect instrument because, unlike everyday leave-taking, there is no possibility of having to face the offended party. The summarizing function of leave-taking may take the form of a life review.[56] Although the life review has been subjected to little systematic study, its occurrence in late life is believed to be a response to a need for reconciling one's past and putting it into an acceptable (to oneself) framework as aligned with earlier goals and values. The extent to which this review manifests itself as dialogue and the depth of that dialogue are unknown. Thus, the processes enacted when one ends a conversation, a relationship, or a life have some distinct parallels. As detailed in an earlier work the communicative processes that characterize the beginning and middle stages of conversations, relationships, and the lifespan may also have remarkable similarities.[57]

Some people respond to their shrinking social world by giving up. Others, however, accept the losses and begin to take steps reminiscent of behavior that characterized earlier growth stages. In an intensive study of male aging Reichard et al. found the following patterns of adjustment to be healthy: (1) mature—constructive rather than defensive or impulsive patterns; (2) rocking chair—taking it easy through dependence on others; and (3) armored—maintaining effective defenses against anxieties. The unhealthy adjustment patterns included: (1) angry—becoming hostile and blaming others for one's life situation; and (2) self-haters—blaming oneself for dissatisfactions with life.[58] Other researchers have found that many elderly people forge new personal ties in the form of dating relationships, friendships, and contacts with people from volunteer organizations.[59] Of course, some older adults live with a spouse or romantic partner. Older people with live-in partners are often less dependent on friends and acquaintances for social support than are those who are formerly married or widowed. For people who live alone, friends, children, and grandchildren play a much more important role in alleviating feelings of loneliness.[60] In fact, research suggests that older adults who participate in community service and social activities tend to be more satisfied with their lives than those who do not.[61] While access to interpersonal relationships may decrease over time, the need for human contact seems to be relatively constant. To illustrate, two sociologists quote a 64-year-old woman as saying:

> I suppose that hope does spring eternal in the human breast as far as love is concerned. People are always looking for the ultimate, perfect relationship. No matter how old they are, they are looking for this thing called love.[62]

Although the focus for most of the preceding discussion of older adults has been on inclusion needs, it should be clear that control and affection needs are also susceptible to the processes of aging. Older adults face gradually less ability to give control and greater needs for control by others. This society has typically invested little interest and credibility in our older population. As a result, control strategies for older adults are sometimes based on making others feel guilty or ashamed. Similarly, the ability to give affection in a variety of ways also decreases, but the need for affection from others may increase greatly.

Interpersonal Needs of Females and Males

As we try to understand our own interpersonal needs and those of others, it may be useful to examine some possible differences between males and females. Some of these differences are related to the way we express the giving and needing of inclusion, affection, and control. Males and females are sometimes taught to express the same feeling or attitude in different ways or to value certain behaviors more than others.

It is not uncommon, for instance, for men and women to communicate affection needs in different ways. Men are sometimes taught to repress emotions, to "stay cool" and express excitement only in certain places—e.g., sports events.

Directly talking about a need for affection from others or admitting the desire to give more affection to others is difficult for men who exhibit these characteristics.[63] Some women, on the other hand, are taught to be more demonstrative about their feelings. These women may feel freer to express emotions—although affection displays must be muted when there is danger of communicating too much intimacy. Men and women may also react differently to the expression of affection in relationships with members of the same sex. Some men fear that any affection displays between men may be associated with homosexuality, thus, male–male friendships among men raised with these values will express affection in very indirect ways.

Men who have stereotypical sex-role characteristics also rely on external signs of control—signs which show everybody "who is in charge." The competition to "get ahead" in sports, school, and work is often measured by one's "accomplishments" for these men. Women who were raised to accept and behave according to the sex-role stereotype for women typically express control indirectly—i.e., willingness to be "in charge" of situations even though it is not obvious to others. For these women, getting ahead and being in control are not so much associated with accomplishments for oneself as with the development of effective interpersonal relationships with others. Figure 3.2 shows one person's view of what men and women who adopt stereotypical sex roles think about.

The traditional male sex role emphasizes inclusion in the activities of others in order to "do things together." Traditional female sex roles emphasize inclusion in the activities of others for sharing emotions and reactions to experiences.[64] As a

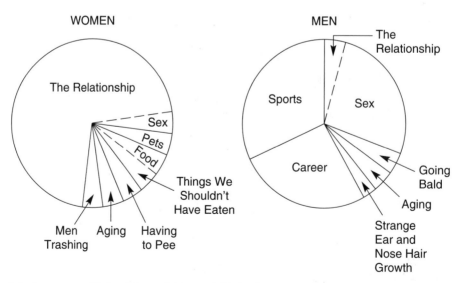

3.2 Stereotype of What Men and Women Think About

result, speed, muscles, coordination, and skills associated with winning various games are important to these men, while looks and communication skills are important for their female counterparts. Men with traditional sex-role orientations typically find it hard to admit they need other people—preferring to express stoically, "I can get along by myself."

A number of scholars describe gender differences in communication by noting that men tend to value instrumental behavior, emphasize individual achievement, and focus on activities, whereas women tend to value affective behavior, emphasize relationships, and focus on communication.[65] Deborah Tannen, a well-known linguist, suggests that women and men define conversation in very different ways. She states that for men, "conversations are negotiations in which people try to achieve and maintain the upper hand if they can, and protect themselves from others' attempts to put them down and push them around." In contrast, for women, "conversations are negotiations for closeness in which people try to seek and give confirmation and support, and to reach consensus. They [women] try to protect themselves from others' attempts to push them away."[66] The complementary nature of these two perspectives allows both women and men to bring important strengths to their cross-gender relationships. However, the differences can also create misunderstandings. Women may wonder why men don't seem to be interested in discussing the details of what happened during the day while they were apart; men may wonder why women want to spend so much time talking about "trivial" issues. Women may feel that intimate talk precedes great sex; men may feel that great sex produces intimacy. Women may ask their male partners why they never say "I love you"; men may respond with frustration because they do a great deal to show their female partners that they care.

In discussing gender differences such as these, it is important to underline two very basic points. First, women and men are more similar to each other than they are different. Men and women both place a great deal of value on interpersonal relationships, both benefit from social support, and both fear isolation and loneliness.[67] The gender differences that have been found between the ways men and women communicate are actually quite small.[68] Of course, small differences can (and do) have important influences in our interpersonal relationships. Second, it is virtually impossible to isolate any behavior that is exclusively performed by males and females. Most of us do not limit ourselves to rigid, unchanging stereotypical behaviors associated with males or females. On the other hand, some patterns of behavior can be linked with the expectations typically associated with male and female performance in this society. When we seek explanations for a person's communication behavior based on interpersonal needs, gender is an important consideration. It is sometimes most inappropriate to judge a member of the opposite sex by your own experiences—i.e., "Well, when I was your age. . . ." Men and women sometimes perform similar tasks with similar needs at different stages in the life cycle. In today's society, many people are trying to break the bonds of stereotypical sex roles. Some men are "taking charge" of household tasks and child care and some women are becoming primary wage-earners.[69] These role changes have changed the way men and women interact. Men are no longer expected to be invulnerable to life's stressors, but instead they are expected to be sensitive to their own and others' emotions. Women are expected to be competent communicators both in the home and in the workplace. While these changes provide people with the opportunity to choose from a variety of behavioral styles, they can be frustrating because the behaviors of females and males are not as predictable as they once were.

Our interpersonal needs, the intensity with which they are felt, and the changes they undergo are heavily grounded in the rewards and costs we associate with our experiences in giving and needing inclusion, control, and affection. When the costs of giving affection to another seem to outweigh the benefits, our need to give affection may decrease and our need to receive affection from that person may increase. The need to give a lot of control may diminish if we feel rewarded by someone when we give little control. Unfortunately, interpersonal needs are not simply determined by our experiences with one other person. A husband's need to give and/or receive control in his relationship with his wife may be a result of his control experiences with friends, relatives, co-workers, and his children. Thus, the rewards and costs accumulated in one relationship for various interpersonal needs may tell only part of the story.

Control, inclusion, and affection can be manifested in a variety of ways. One person's "moderate" need for inclusion may be perceived as "excessive" by another; giving affection in one situation may mean performing the role of a sympathetic listener and giving money in another. Thus, it is important for those who desire to become more effective communicators: (1) to try to observe the various ways we and other people communicate interpersonal needs; and (2) to experiment with various ways of communicating the giving and receiving of inclusion, affection, and control. A person who has not experienced and experimented with giving control in different ways may find it difficult to manage a department of people who desire to be controlled in different ways; a person who limits himself or herself to giving affection in romantic relationships may find it difficult to recognize and give affection in other types of relationships.

SUMMARY

The messages we make and our interpretation of other's messages are affected by many factors. This chapter showed how the nature of interpersonal messages may be affected by the nature of the communicators—particularly the interpersonal needs of those communicators. Each of us wants to give and receive varying amounts and types of affection, control, and inclusion. These interpersonal needs may be expressed in a variety of ways ranging from stereotypical manifestations such as exerting control by ordering people around to highly idiosyncratic messages that may only be shared by the relationship partners, such as putting a hand behind your back to say "I love you."

When both communicators want to give and receive the same sort of behavior, the relationship is labeled a symmetrical one; when one communicator wants to give what the other wants to receive, the relationship is called a complementary one. We noted that one difficulty parents and their teenage children sometimes experience concerns the shifting from a basically complementary relationship to one that is predominantly symmetrical. Many of our relationships have both symmetrical and complementary patterns which vary over time and with topic areas.

The last part of the chapter showed how age and gender affect our interpersonal needs. Throughout our life span we are faced with accomplishing certain tasks and adjusting to certain changes related to finances and health. As we move from infancy through old age, these life conditions will alter our interpersonal needs and our communication behavior among our primary relationships, friendships, acquaintances, and the multitude of store clerks and bureaucrats who pass briefly in and out of our lives. Men and women may show some similarities and some differences in the time and manner in which interpersonal needs are manifested. Those men and women who adhere to conventional sex-role expectations in this society are more likely to reveal the greatest differences in their overt behavior.

Many communicator characteristics can potentially influence the messages we exchange as we move in and out of various relationships. But interpersonal needs form a strong root system for many of the more visible manifestations. The need to understand our own interpersonal needs and those of others is a worthy goal for improving communication in our relationships with others. It is, however, a difficult and never-ending task. Sometimes we aren't aware of our own needs; sometimes we repress or distort them in our messages to others; and sometimes the same style of behavior is associated with very different needs.

SELECTED READINGS

Interpersonal Needs

Alderfer, C. P. "An Empirical Test of a New Theory of Human Needs." *Organizational Behavior and Human Performance* 4 (1969): 142–175.

Frandsen, K. D., and Rosenfeld, L. B. "Fundamental Interpersonal Relations Orientations in Dyads: An Empirical Analysis of Shutz' FIRO-B as an Index of Compatibility." *Speech Monographs* 40 (1973): 113–122.

Horney, K. *Our Inner Conflicts.* New York: W. W. Norton, 1945.

Jacobson, W. D. *Power and Interpersonal Relations.* Belmont, CA: Wadsworth, 1972.

McAdams, D. P. *Intimacy: The Need to Be Close.* New York: Doubleday, 1989.

McAdams, D. P. "Personal Needs and Personal Relationships." In S. W. Duck, S. E. Holofoll,

W. Ickes, and B. M. Montgomery, eds., *Handbook of Personal Relationships: Theory, Research and Interventions*, pp. 7–22. New York: John Wiley & Sons, 1988.

Prager, K. J., and Buhrmester, D. "Intimacy and Need Fulfillment in Couple Relationships." *Journal of Social and Personal Relationships* 15 (1998): 435–469.

Rogers, W. T., and Jones, S. E. "Effects of Dominance Tendencies on Floor-Holding and Interruption Behavior in Dyadic Interaction." *Human Communication Research* 1 (1975): 113–122.

Schutz. W. C. *FIRO: A Three-Dimension Theory of Interpersonal Behavior.* New York: Holt, Rinehart, & Winston, 1958.

Sluzki, C. E., and Beavin, J. "Symmetry and Complementarity: An Operational Definition and Typology of Dyads." In P. Watzlawick and J. H. Weakland, eds., *The Interactional View*, pp. 71–87. New York: W. W. Norton, 1977.

Watzlawick, P., Beavin, J. H., and Jackson, D. D. *Pragmatics of Human Communication.* New York: W. W. Norton, 1967.

Communication Throughout the Life Span

Allen, R. R., and Brown, K. L., eds. *Developing Communication Competence in Children.* Skokie, IL: National Textbook Co., 1976.

Baltes, P. B., and Schate, K. W., eds. *Life-Span Developmental Psychology.* New York: Academic Press, 1973.

Barrett, K. C. "The Self and Relationship Development." In S. Duck, ed., *Handbook of Personal Relationships*, 2nd ed., pp. 81–97. New York: John Wiley & Sons, 1997.

Bigelow, B., Tesson, G., and Lewko, J. *Learning the Rules: The Anatomy of Children's Relationships.* New York: Guilford, 1996.

Birren, J. E. *The Psychology of Aging.* Englewood Cliffs, NJ: Prentice-Hall, 1964.

———., ed. *Handbook of Aging and the Individual.* Chicago: University of Chicago Press, 1959.

Blieszner, R., and Adams, R. G. *Adult Friendship.* Newbury Park, CA: Sage, 1992.

Block, J., and Haan, N. *Lives Through Time.* New York: Bancroft Books, 1971.

Blos, P. *On Adolescence: A Psychoanalytic Interpretation.* New York: Free Press, 1962.

Blurton Jones, N. G. "Non-Verbal Communication in Children." In R. Hinde, ed., *Nonverbal Communication.* Cambridge: Cambridge University Press, 1972.

Brenton, M. *Friendship.* Chapters 5–9. New York: Stein and Day, 1975.

Brim, O. G., Jr. "Adult Socialization." In J. A. Clausen, ed., *Socialization and Society.* Boston: Little, Brown, 1968.

Buhler, C., and Massarik, F., eds. *The Course of Human Life.* New York: Springer, 1968.

Cairns, R. B. *Social Development: The Origins and Plasticity of Interchanges.* San Francisco: W. H. Freeman, 1979.

Cappella, J. N. "The Biological Origins of Automated Patterns of Human Interaction." *Communication Theory* 1 (1991): 4–35.

Chown, S. M. "Friendship in Old Age." In S. Duck and R. Gilmour, eds., *Personal Relationships 2: Developing Personal Relationships*, pp. 231–246. New York: Academic Press, 1981.

Cohen, B., and Klein, J. "Referent Communication in School-Age Children." *Child Development* 39 (1968): 597–609.

Collins, W. A. "Relationships and Development During Adolescence: Interpersonal Adaptation to Individual Change." *Personal Relationships* 4 (1997): 1–14.

Cude, R. L., and Jablin, F. M. "Retiring From Work: The Paradoxical Impact of Organizational Commitment." *Journal of Managerial Issues* 4 (1992): 31–45.

Cumming, E., and Henry, W. E. *Growing Old.* New York: Basic Books, 1961.

Davitz, J., and Davitz, L. *Making It From 40 to 50.* New York: Random House, 1976.

Denham, S. A. *Emotional Development in Young Children.* New York: Guilford, 1998.

Dickens, W. J., and Perlman, D. "Friendship Over the Life-Cycle." In S. Duck and R. Gilmour, eds., *Personal Relationships 2: Developing Personal Relationships*, pp. 91–122. New York: Academic Press, 1981.

Dykstra, P. A. "The Differential Availability of Relationships and the Provision and Effectiveness of Support to Older Adults." *Journal of Social and Personal Relationships* 10 (1993): 355–370.

Elkind, D. *All Grown Up and No Place to Go.* Reading, MA: Addison-Wesley, 1984.

Erikson, E. H. *Identity: Youth and Crisis.* New York: W. W. Norton, 1968.

Fisher, K. W., and Lazerson, A. *Human Development: From Conception Through Adolescence.* New York: W. H. Freeman, 1984.

Frenkel, E. "Studies in Biographical Psychology." *Character and Personality* 5 (1936): 1–34.

Fried, B. *The Middle-Age Crisis.* New York: Harper & Row, 1967.

Glucksberg, S., Krauss, R. M., and Higgins, T. "The Development of Communication Skills in Children." In F. Horowitz, ed., *Review of Child Development Research,* vol. 4. Chicago: University of Chicago Press, 1975.

Gould, R. L. *Transformations: Growth and Change in Adult Life.* New York: Simon & Schuster, 1978.

Grotevant, H. D., and Cooper, C. R. "Individuation in Family Relationships: A Perspective on Individual Differences in the Development of Identity and Role-Taking Skill in Adolescence." *Human Development* 29 (1986): 82–100.

Haslett, B. B., and Samter, W. *Children Communicating: The First Five Years.* Mahwah, NJ: Erlbaum, 1997.

Heckhausen, J., and Dweck, C. S., *Motivational and Self-Regulation Across the Life Span.* New York: Cambridge University Press, 1998.

Hinde, R. A. *Towards Understanding Relationships,* chapters 21 and 22. New York: Academic Press, 1979.

Kimmel, D. C. *Adulthood and Aging.* New York: John Wiley & Sons, 1974.

Kon, I. S. "Adolescent Friendship: Some Unanswered Questions for Future Research." In S. Duck and P. Gilmour, eds., *Personal Relationships 2: Developing Personal Relationships,* pp. 187–204. New York: Academic Press, 1981.

Larson, R., and Richards, M. H. *Divergent Realities: The Emotional Lives of Mothers, Fathers, and Adolescents.* New York: Basic Books, 1994.

Levinson, D. J. *The Seasons of a Man's Life.* New York: Knopf, 1978.

Livesley, W. J., and Bromley, D. B. *Person Perception in Childhood and Adolescence.* New York: John Wiley & Sons, 1973.

Mares, M. L. "The Aging Family." In M. A. Fitzpatrick and A. L. Vangelisti, eds., *Explaining Family Interactions.* Thousand Oaks, CA: Sage, 1995.

Mehler, J., and Dupoux, E. *What Infants Know.* Cambridge: Blackwell, 1994.

Mehrabian, A. *Nonverbal Communication.* Chapter 9, "Child Communication." Chicago: Aldine, 1972.

Montemayor, R. "Family Variation in Parent-Adolescent Storm and Stress." *Journal of Adolescent Research* 1 (1986): 15–31.

Montemayor, R., Adams, G. R., and Gullota, T. P., eds. *Personal Relationships During Adolescence.* Thousand Oaks, CA: Sage, 1994.

Neugarten, B. L., ed. *Middle Age and Aging.* Chicago: University of Chicago Press, 1968.

Neugarten, B. L. and Datan, N. "The Middle Years." In S. Arieti, ed., *American Handbook of Psychiatry,* 2nd ed., pp. 592–608. New York: Basic Books, 1974.

Noller, P., and Callan, V. *The Adolescent in the Family.* New York: Routledge, 1991.

Pawlby, S. J. "Infant-Mother Relationships." In S. Duck and P. Gilmour, eds., *Personal Relationships 2: Developing Personal Relationships,* pp. 123–139. New York: Academic Press, 1981.

Peterson, W. A., and Quadagno, J. *Social Bonds in Later Life: Aging and Interdependence.* Newbury Park, CA: Sage, 1985.

Pinnell, G. S., ed. *Discovering Language with Children.* Urbana, IL: National Council of Teachers of English, 1980.

Reisman, J. M. "Adult Friendships." In S. Duck and P. Gilmour, eds., *Personal Relationships 2: Developing Personal Relationships,* pp. 205–230. New York: Academic Press, 1981.

Roberts, D. F. "Communication and Children: A Developmental Approach." In I. deSola Pool, W. Schramm, F. W. Frey, N. Maccoby, and E. B. Parker, eds., *Handbook of Communication,* Chicago: Rand McNally, 1973.

Rodnick R., and Wood, B. "The Communication Strategies of Children." *Speech Teacher* 22 (1973): 114–124.

Schofield, M. J., and Kafer, N. F. "Children's Understanding of Friendship Issues: Development by Stage or Sequence?" *Journal of Social and Personal Relationships* 2 (1985): 151–165.

Sears, R. S., and S. S. Feldman, eds. *The Seven Ages of Man.* Los Altos, CA: William Kaufmann, 1964.

Sheehy, G. *Passages: Predictable Crises of Adult Life.* New York: E. P. Dutton, 1976.

Shields, M. M. "Parent–Child Relationships in Middle Years of Childhood." In S. Duck and P. Gilmour, eds., *Personal Relationships 2: Developing Personal Relationships,* pp. 141–159. New York: Academic Press, 1981.

Smetana. J. G. "Adolescents' and Parents' Reasoning about Actual Family Conflict." *Child Development* 60 (1989): 1052–1067.

Smith, F., and Miller, G. A., eds. *The Genesis of Language.* Cambridge, MA: MIT Press, 1966.

Valliant, G. E. *Adaptations to Life.* Boston: Little, Brown, 1977.

Vangelisti, A. L. "Older Adolescents' Perceptions of Communication Problems with Their Parents." *Journal of Adolescent Research* 7 (1992): 382–402.

van Tilburg, T. "Support Networks Before and After Retirement." *Journal of Social and Personal Relationships* 9 (1992): 433–445.

White, R. W., ed. *The Study of Lives.* New York: Lieber-Atherton, 1964.

Wood, B. S. *Children and Communication.* Englewood Cliffs, NJ: Prentice-Hall, 1976.

Zietlow, P. H., and VanLear, C. A. Jr. "Marriage Duration and Relational Control: A Study of Developmental Patterns." *Journal of Marriage and the Family* 53 (1991): 773-785.

Male and Female Communication

Aries, E. *Men and Women in Interaction: Reconsidering the Differences.* New York: Oxford University Press, 1996.

Arliss, L. P., and Borisoff, D. J. *Women and Men Communicating: Challenges and Changes.* New York: Harcourt Brace Jovanovich, 1993.

Ashmore, R. D., and Del Boca, F. K. *The Social Psychology of Female-Male Relations: A Critical Analysis of Central Concepts.* New York: Academic Press, 1986.

Broverman, I. K., Vogel, S. R., Broverman, D. M., Clarkson, F. E., and Rosenkrantz, P. S. "Sex-role Stereotypes: A Current Appraisal." *The Journal of Social Issues* 28 (1972): 59–78.

Canary, D. J., and Dindia, K. eds. *Sex Differences and Similarities in Communication.* Mahwah, NJ: Erlbaum, 1998.

Deaux, K. *The Behavior of Women and Men.* Belmont, CA: Wadsworth, 1976.

Eakins, B. W., and Eakins, R. G. *Sex Differences in Human Communication.* Boston: Houghton Mifflin, 1978.

Haas, A. "Male and Female Spoken Language Differences: Stereotypes and Evidence." *Psychological Bulletin* 86 (1979): 616–626.

Henley, N. M. *Body Politics: Power, Sex and Nonverbal Communication.* Englewood Cliffs, NJ: Prentice-Hall, 1977.

Kramarae, C. *Women and Men Speaking.* Rowley, MA: Newbury House, 1981.

Maccoby, E. E., and Jacklin, C. N. *The Psychology of Sex Differences.* Stanford, CA: Stanford University Press, 1974.

Peplau, L. A. "Roles and Gender." In H. H. Kelley, E. Bersheid, A. Christensen, J. H. Harvey, T. L. Huston, G. Levinger, E. McClintock, L. A. Peplau, and D. R. Peterson, eds., *Close Relationships*, pp. 220–264. New York: W. H. Freeman, 1983.

Peplau, L. A., DeBro, S. C., Venigas, R. C., and Taylor, P. L. *Gender, Culture, and Ethnicity: Current Research About Women and Men.* Mountain View, CA: Mayfield, 1999.

Tannen, D. *You Just Don't Understand: Women and Men in Conversation.* New York: William Morrow, 1990.

Thorne, B., and Henley, N., eds. *Language and Sex: Difference and Dominance.* Rowley, MA: Newbury House, 1975.

Wood, J. T. *Gendered Lives: Communication, Gender, and Culture,* 2nd ed. Belmont, CA: Wadsworth, 1997.

NOTES

[1]For example, Prager and Buhrmester found that the fulfillment of certain needs was associated with intimate communication (see K. J. Prager and D. Buhrmester, "Intimacy and Need Fulfillment in Couple Relationships," *Journal of Social and Personal Relationships* 15 (1998): 435–469).

[2]W. C. Schutz, *FIRO: A Three-Dimension Theory of Interpersonal Behavior* (New York: Holt, Rinehart & Winston, 1958). Inclusion, control, and affection not only reflect Schutz's work, but consistently over the last four decades, have appeared in studies of interpersonal relations as major forces that affect human behavior. They seem to be basic responses to our environment and are reflected in the way we assign meaning to both verbal and nonverbal behavior. Osgood labeled the dimensions: *Dynamism, Potency,* and *Evaluation;* Mehrabian called them: *Responsiveness, Power,* and *Immediacy.* Cf. C. E. Osgood, G. J. Suci, and P. H. Tannenbaum, *The Measurement of Meaning* (Ur-

bana: University of Illinois Press, 1957); A. Mehrabian, *Nonverbal Communication* (Chicago: Aldine, 1972).

[3]A. L. Vangelisti, M. L. Knapp, and J. A. Daly, "Conversational Narcissism," *Communication Monographs* 57 (1990): 251–274.

[4]D. D. Von Dras and I. C. Siegler, "Stability in Extraversion and Aspects of Social Support at Midlife," *Journal of Personality and Social Psychology* 72 (1997): 233–241.

[5]A. Thorne, "The Press of Personality: A Study of Conversations Between Introverts and Extroverts," *Journal of Personality and Social Psychology* 53 (1987): 718–726.

[6]L. F. Barrett and P. R. Pietromonaco, "Accuracy of the Five-Factor Model in Predicting Perceptions of Daily Social Interactions," *Personality and Social Psychology Bulletin* 23 (1997): 1173–1187.

[7]Thorne, *op. cit.*

[8]J. J. Gross and R. W. Levenson, "Emotional Suppression: Physiology, Self-Report, and Expressive Behavior," *Journal of Personality and Social Psychology* 64 (1993): 970–986.

[9]J. J. Lynch, *The Broken Heart: The Medical Consequences of Loneliness in America* (New York: Basic Books, 1977).

[10]T. L. Albrecht and M. B. Adelman, *Communicating Social Support* (Newbury Park, CA: Sage, 1987); B. R. Burleson, T, L. Albrecht, and I. G. Sarason, eds., *Communication of Social Support: Messages, Interaction, Relationships, and Community* (Thousand Oaks, CA: Sage, 1994); S. W. Duck, ed., with R. C. Silver, *Personal Relationships and Social Support* (London: Sage, 1991); M. Pilisuk and S. H. Parks, *The Healing Web* (Hanover, NH: University Press of New England, 1986).

[11]B. H. Gottlieb, "Social Support and the Study of Personal Relationships," *Journal of Social and Personal Relationships* 2 (1985): 351–375; H. W. Jones, "The Psychology of Loneliness: Some Personality Issues in the Study of Social Support." In I. G. Sarason and B. P. Sarason, eds., *Social Support Theory, Research and Applications* (The Hague, Holland: Martinus Nijhoff 1985).

[12]P. N. Christensen and D. A. Kashy, "Perceptions of and by Lonely People in Initial Social Interaction," *Personality and Social Psychology Bulletin* 24 (1998): 322–329.

[13]K. J. Rotenberg and J. Kmill, "Perception of Lonely and Non-Lonely Persons as a Function of Individual Differences in Loneliness," *Journal of Social and Personal Relationships* 9 (1992): 325–330;

[14]B. H. Spitzberg and D. J. Cupach, "Loneliness and Relationally Competent Communication," *Journal of Social and Personal Relationships* 2 (1985): 387–402.

[14]B. P. Buunk and K. S. Prins, "Loneliness, Exchange Orientation, and Reciprocity in Friendships," *Personal Relationships* 5 (1998): 1–14.

[15]J. R. Coyne, C. Wortman, and D. Lehman, "The Other Side of Support: Emotional Overinvolvement and Miscarried Helping." In B. H. Gottlieb, ed., *Marshaling Social Support* (Newbury Park, CA: Sage, 1988); J. J. Lynch, *The Language of the Heart* (New York: Basic Books, 1985).

[16]H. L. Fritz and V. S. Helgeson, "Distinctions of Unmitigated Communion from Communion: Self-Neglect and Overinvolvement with Others," *Journal of Personality and Social Psychology* 75 (1998): 121–140.

[17]T. C. Sabourin, D. A. Infante, and J. E. Rudd, "Verbal Aggression in Marriages: A Comparison of Violent, Distressed but Nonviolent, and Nondistressed Couples," *Human Communication Research* 20 (1993): 245–267.

[18]W. T. Rogers and S. E. Jones, "Effects of Dominance Tendencies on Floor Holding and Interruption Behavior in Dyadic Interaction," *Human Communication Research* 1 (1975): 113–122.

[19]A. Mehrabian, *Nonverbal Communication* (Chicago: Aldine, 1972).

20. R. B. Exline, S. L. Ellyson, and B. Long, "Visual Behavior as an Aspect of Power Role Relationships." In P. Pilner, L. Krames, and I. Holloway, eds., *Advances in the Study of Communication and Affect,* vol. 2. (New York: Plenum, 1975), pp. 21–51.

[21]D. T. Gilbert and D. H. Silvera, "Overhelping," *Journal of Personality and Social Psychology* 70 (1996): 678–690.

[22]J. A. Sheppard and R. E. Socherman, "On the Manipulative Behavior of Low Machiavellians: Feigning Incompetence to 'Sandbag' an Opponent," *Journal of Personality and Social Psychology* 72 (1997): 1448–1459.

[23]M. Wiener and A. Mehrabian, *Language Within Language: Immediacy, A Channel in Verbal Communication* (New York: Appelton-Century-Crofts, 1968).

[24]G. Downey and S. I. Feldman, "Implications of Rejection Sensitivity for Intimate Relationships," *Journal of Personality and Social Psychology* 70 (1996): 1327–1343.

[25]L. A. Peplau and D. Perlman, "Perspectives on Loneliness." In L. A. Peplau and D. Perlman, eds.,

Loneliness: A Sourcebook of Current Theory. Research and Therapy (New York: Wiley-Interscience, 1982), pp. 1–20.

[26]J. de Jong-Gierveld, "Personal Relationships, Social Support, and Loneliness," *Journal of Social and Personal Relationships* 6 (1989): 197–221; B. H. Spitzberg and D. J. Cupach, "Loneliness and Relationally Competent Communication," *Journal of Social and Personal Relationships* 2 (1985): 387–402.

[27]W. J. Lederer and D. D. Jackson, *The Mirages of Marriage* (New York: W. W. Norton, 1968), p. 162.

[28]D. C. Dryer and L. M. Horowitz, "When Do Opposites Attract?: Interpersonal Complementarity Versus Similarity," *Journal of Personality and Social Psychology* 72 (1997): 592–603.

[29]M. K. Conn and C. Peterson, "Social Support: Seek and Ye Shall Find," *Journal of Social and Personal Relationships* 6 (1989): 345–358.

[30]Christensen and Kashy, *op. cit.*

[31]R. A. Bell "Conversational Involvement and Loneliness," *Communication Monographs* 52 (1985): 218–235.

[32]R. A. Bell and M. E. Roloff, "Making a Love Connection: Loneliness and Communication Competence in the Dating Marketplace," *Communication Quarterly* 39 (1991): 58–74.

[33]T. Hora, "Tao, Zen, and Existential Psychotherapy," *Psychologia* 2 (1959): 236–242.

[34]I. Eibl-Eibesfeldt, *Love and Hate* (New York: Holt, Rinehart & Winston, 1971).

[35]K. C. Barrett, "The Self and Relationship Development." In S. Duck, ed., *Handbook of Personal Relationships,* 2nd ed. (New York: John Wiley & Sons, 1997), pp. 81–97; J. N. Cappella, "The Biological Origins of automated Patterns of Human Interaction," *Communication Theory* 1 (1991): 4–35.

[36]R. B. Cairns, *Social Development: The Origins and Plasticity of Interchanges* (San Francisco: W. H. Freeman, 1979).

[37]S. A. Denham, *Emotional Development in Young Children* (New York: Guilford, 1998).

[38]L. Bowers, P. K. Smith, and V. Binney, "Perceived Family Relationships of Bullies, Victims and Bully/Victims in Middle Childhood," *Journal of Social and Personal Relationships* 11 (1994): 215–232.

[39]Z. Rubin, *Children's Friendships* (Cambridge, MA: Harvard University Press, 1980), p. 73.

[40]W. K. Rawlins, *Friendship Matters: Communication, Dialectics, and the Life Course* (New York: Aldine de Gruyter, 1992).

[41]M. Brenton, *Friendship* (New York: Stein and Day, 1975), p. 57. Reprinted with permission of Stein and Day Publishers.

[42]D. J. Flannery, R. Montemayor, M. Eberly, and J. Torquati, "Unraveling the Ties That Bind: Affective Expression and Perceived Conflict in Parent-Adolescent Interactions," *Journal of Social and Personal Relationships* 10 (1993): 495–509.

[43]W. A. Collins "Relationships and Development During Adolescence: Interpersonal Adaptation to Individual Change," *Personal Relationships* 4 (1997): 1–14.

[44]H. D. Grotevant and C. R. Cooper, "Individuation in Family Relationships: A Perspective on Individual Differences in the Development of Identity and Role-Taking," *Human Development* 29 (1986): 82–100.

[45]J. G. Smetana, "Adolescents' and Parents' Conceptions of Parental Authority," *Child Development* 59 (1988): 321–335.

[46]M. Gold and D. S. Yanof, "Mothers, Daughters, and Girlfriends," *Journal of Personality and Social Psychology* 49 (1985): 654–659.

[47]A. L. Vangelisti, "Older Adolescents' Perceptions of Communications Problems with Their Parents," *Journal of Adolescent Research* 7 (1992): 382–402.

[48]Brenton, M. (1975), p. 74.

[49]E. M. Ritter, "Social Perspective-Taking Ability, Cognitive Complexity and Listener Adapted Communication in Early and Late Adolescence," *Communication Monographs* 46 (1979): 40–51.

[50]R. L. Gould, *Transformations: Growth and Change in Adult Life* (New York: Simon & Schuster, 1978); D. J. Levinson, *The Seasons of a Man's Life* (New York: Knopf, 1978); R. S. Sears and S. S. Feldman, eds., *The Seven Ages of Man* (Los Altos, CA: William Kaufmann, 1964); G. Sheehy, *Passages: Predictable Crises of Adult Life* (New York: Dutton, 1976); G. E. Valliant, *Adaptation to Life* (Boston: Little, Brown, 1977).

[51]R. C. Barnett and C. Rivers, *She Works/ He Works: How Two-Income Families Are Happier, Healthier, and Better Off* (New York: Harper Collins (1996); R. L. Repetti, "Effects of Daily Workload on Subsequent Behavior During Marital Interaction: The Roles of Social Withdrawal and Spouse Support," *Journal of Personality and Social Psychology* 57 (1989): 651–659; D. N. Ruble, L. S. Hackel, A. S. Fleming, and C. Stangor, "Changes in the Marital Relationship During the Transition to First-Time Motherhood: Effects of Violated Expec-

tations Concerning Division of Household Labor," *Journal of Personality and Social Psychology* 55 (1988): 78–87; P. Schwartz, *Peer Marriage* (New York: The Free Press, 1994).

[52]L. L. Carstensen "A Life-Span Approach to Social Motivation." In J. Heckhausen and C. S. Dweck, eds., *Motivation and Self-Regulation Across the Life Span* (New York: Cambridge University Press, 1998).

[53]P. H. Zietlow and C. A. VanLear, Jr. "Marriage Duration and Relational Control: A Study of Developmental Patterns," *Journal of Marriage and the Family* 53 (1991): 773–785.

[54]T. van Tilburg, "Support Networks Before and After Retirement," *Journal of Social and Personal Relationships* 9 (1992): 433–445.

[55]C. M. Avery and F. M. Jablin, "Retirement Preparation Programs and Organizational Communication," *Communication Education* 37 (1988): 68–80.

[56]J. E. Birren, *The Psychology of Aging* (Englewood Cliffs, NJ: Prentice-Hall, 1964), pp. 273–279.

[57]M. L. Knapp, *Social Intercourse: From Greeting to Goodbye* (Boston: Allyn and Bacon, 1978), Chapter 6.

[58]S. Reichard, F. Livson, and P. G. Petersen, *Aging and Personality* (New York: John Wiley & Sons, 1962).

[59]W. A. Peterson and J. Quadagno, *Social Bonds in Later Life: Aging and Interdependence* (Newbury Park, CA: Sage, 1985).

[60]P. A. Dykstra, "The Differential Availability of Relationships and the Provision and Effectiveness of Support to Older Adults," *Journal of Social and Personal Relationships* 10 (1993): 255–370; T. van Tilburg, J. de Jong Gierveld, L. Lecchini, and D. Marsiglia "Social Integration and Loneliness: A Comparative Study Among Older Adults in the Netherlands and Tuscany," *Journal of Social and Personal Relationships* 15 (1998): 740–754.

[61]R. E. Harlow and N. Cantor "Still Participating After All these Years: A Study of Life Task Participation in Later Life," *Journal of Personality and Social Psychiatry* 71 (1996): 1235–1249.

[62]K. Bulcroft and M. O'Conner-Roden, "Never Too Late," *Psychology Today* 20 (1986): 66–69.

[63]L. A. Peplau, S. C. DeBro, R. C. Venigas, P. L. Taylor, *Gender, Culture, and Ethnicity: Current Research About Women and Men* (Mountain View, CA: Mayfield, 1999); J. T. Wood, *Gendered Lives: Communication, Gender, and Culture,* 2nd ed. (Belmont, CA: Wadsworth, 1997).

[64]R. Martin, " 'Girls Don't Talk About Garages!': Perceptions of Conversation in Same- and Cross-Sex Friendships," *Personal Relationships* 4 (1997): 115–130; W. K. Rawlins, "Communication in Cross-Sex Friendships." In L. P. Arliss and D. J. Borisoff, eds., *Women and Men Communicating: Challenges and Change* (New York: Harcourt Brace Jovanovich, 1993), pp. 51–70; S. M. Rose "Same- and Cross-Sex Friendships and the Psychology of Homosociality," *Sex Roles* 12 (1985): 63–74.

[65]L. K. Acitelli, "Gender Differences in Relationship Awareness and Marital Satisfaction Among Young Married Couples," *Personality and Social Psychology Bulletin* 18 (1992): 102–110; C. Sedikides, M. B. Oliver, and W. K. Campbell, "Perceived Benefits and Costs of Romantic Relationships for Women and Men: Implications for Exchange Theory," *Personal Relationships* 1 (1994): 5–21; S. Sprecher and C. Sedikides, "Gender Differences in Perceptions of Emotionality: The Case of Close Heterosexual Relationships," *Sex Roles* (1993): 511–530; T. A. Wills, R. L. Weiss, and G. R. Patterson, "A Behavior Analysis of the Determinants of Marital Satisfaction," *Journal of Consulting and Clinical Psychology* 42 (1974): 802–811; J. T. Wood and C. C. Inman, "In a Different Mode: Masculine Styles of Communicating Closeness," *Journal of Applied Communication Research* 21 (1993): 279–295.

[66]D. Tannen, *You Just Don't Understand: Women and Men in Conversation* (New York: William Morrow, 1990).

[67]See, for example, A. L. Vangelisti and J. A. Daly, "Gender Differences in Standards for Romantic Relationships," *Personal Relationships* 4 (1997): 203–219.

[68]B. R. Burleson, A. W. Kunkel, W. Samter, and K. J. Werking, "Men's and Women's Evaluations of Communication Skills in Personal Relationships: When Sex Differences Make a Difference—And When They Don't," *Journal of Social and Personal Relationships* 13 (1996): 201–224; D. J. Canary, K. S. Hause, "Is There Any Reason to Research Sex Differences in Communication?" *Communication Quarterly* 41 (1993): 129–144; K. Dindia and M. Allen, "Sex Differences in Self-Disclosure: A Meta-Analysis," *Psychological Bulletin* 122 (1992): 106–124; D. J. Goldsmith and S. A. Dun, "Sex Differences and Similarities in the Communication of Social Support," *Journal of Social and Personal Relationships* 14 (1997): 317–337.

[69]N. Helmich, "Husbands Get Respect for Staying Home," *USA Today* (September 17, 1990), p. D-1; J. H. Pleck, *Working Wives, Working Husbands* (Beverly Hills, CA: Sager, 1985).

4

The Communication Environment: Cultural and Physical

Dear Dr. Vangelisti,

I don't understand why I can't find a guy who is honest with me. It is so easy to say you believe in telling the truth and so hard (for some) to do it. When I grew up, I was encouraged to tell the truth and to treasure that in others. But the last two relationships I've been in have made me wonder if I expect too much. Then I see these politicians who lie to the public and I wonder if honesty is really valued or whether we just say it is.

In Search of Truthfulness

The society or culture within which a relationship develops reflects certain guidelines or "teachings" about how people are expected to behave in various types of relationships. The extent to which individuals are exposed to these guidelines and the extent to which they subscribe to them will affect the type of communication behavior they exhibit with their communication partners. The cultural values and trends associated with honesty may, for some, make this a pivotal issue in the success or failure of a relationship.

Different societies approach relationships and social interaction in different ways.[1] Some societies place more emphasis on the practical aspects of marriage than others;[2] some advocate more indirect communication than others;[3] some see close family ties as more important than others;[4] and some are more tolerant of negative marital communication than others.[5] Most of the time, the assumptions that guide social interaction in various cultural environments are unspoken. As a consequence, people often are unaware of the impact of that their social background has on their interpersonal relationships. This chapter explores several important characteristics of U.S. society that may influence communication. It also examines the possible effects of specific communication environments within the larger U.S. culture and their influence on what people say.

> *The organism, then, is in a sense responsible for its environment. And since organism and environment determine each other and are mutually dependent for their existence, it follows that the life-process, to be adequately understood, must be considered in terms of their interrelations.*
>
> *—George Herbert Mead*

Human communication does not take place in a vacuum. Every time we communicate, we are surrounded and influenced by a set of conditions that help determine why we did or did not interact in a particular way. In Chapter 3 we explored the potential influence of each communicator's interpersonal needs on communication behavior in developing and deteriorating relationships. In this chapter our focus is on the influence emanating from communication environments. These environments range in size from the society at large to a classroom or an elevator. To illustrate, consider a jealous male who confronts a friend he suspects is his competition by saying, "You make me so mad I could *kill* you." Two observers comment on the conditions that prompted such a statement:

Analysis 1. It's just the climate of the times. Today people are generally less patient with others and put less energy into building close relationships. Besides, he probably heard somebody on TV say the same thing in a similar situation.

Analysis 2. I think it was entirely a function of the setting itself—the environment in which the confrontation took place. If his girlfriend and several of his other friends hadn't been around, it would have been different. Because it was a public setting, he felt he had to speak to all the audiences present. In a very real sense he was trying to tell his girlfriend how much he loves her. The fact that the confrontation took place right outside the athletic building may also have contributed to the strength of the statement.

You can probably think of several other explanations—including the possible role of interpersonal needs. But the preceding analyses adequately represent the scope of this chapter. Which analysis is correct? Like most situations involving complex human behavior, there is some truth in each analysis; each contributes a share of the total picture.

The Influence of the Cultural Environment

One of the analyses presented at the beginning of this chapter explained the jealous boyfriend's behavior as a reflection of the climate of the times. What are the current trends in U.S. society that comprise the climate of the times? Trends in many areas go together to make up the climate of the times, but our concern is with four areas: (1) patterns of work; (2) relationship styles; (3) attitudes toward self-fulfillment; and (4) messages from the mass media. How will these societal conditions affect our interpersonal communication directed toward the development of relationships?

Patterns of Work

More than ever before in this nation's history, both husband and wife are employed outside the home. In 1940, less than 28 percent of women worked and only about one-third of those who worked were married. At the time of this writing, almost 60 percent of women work outside the home, and most of those who do work are married. In addition, there are millions of unmarried couples who live together and maintain separate full-time jobs and careers. The monetary gains and increased feelings of self-fulfillment may provide important benefits for a couple's relationship, but this pattern of work may also bring about relationship stress, particularly when two careers are involved.

Work environments can be deceptively alluring. The variety of people and potential relationships may provide a stimulating contrast to a single individual whose habits you know well; the rewards you receive for showing your skill in accomplishing tasks may seem personally more gratifying than the rewards your spouse provides; the topics discussed may somehow seem more "important" than those discussed at home. As a result, the effort expended for maintaining a satisfying relationship may not be enough, and conflict develops. When both parties to a relationship are working, it may take special planning to find the time to talk about and resolve such conflicts. It is not unusual for such couples to have difficulty finding the time necessary to build friendships—although the quantity and variety of people available in the work setting should be high. When friendships with people at work are pursued without the participation of the other spouse, problems may develop. If the friendship is with a member of the opposite sex, jealousy may occur; if it is a friendship with a member of the same sex, a spouse may feel slighted—wondering why that time cannot be spent together. And when dual-career couples decide to have children, many decisions regarding responsibilities and priorities must be agreed upon to head off potential areas of relationship strife.

Many of the problems faced by couples who both work also face couples where only one partner leaves the home to work. However, the intensity of these problems and our general lack of preparation for dealing with these issues forces us to look closely at this trend. Even couples who are able to free themselves of traditional expectations for appropriate marital behavior and who are able to manage their time and support each other's efforts and achievements may face special difficulties in maintaining a rewarding relationship. For example, families and careers develop by stages, and the behavior most advantageous for the family may be counterproductive for enhancing a career or vice versa. To add to the complexity, each spouse may be at a different stage in his or her respective career.

Although the preceding paragraphs seem to emphasize the possible problems in two wage-earner families, many couples are succeeding in such relationships. The senior author and his spouse, Lillian, have for over twenty years now. To succeed, however, couples must adapt their expectations and communication behavior to a set of conditions quite different from the working patterns of our parents. Flexibility and compromise are the by-words for dual-career couples.

Often career advancement is dependent on moving to a new location. This presents dual-career couples with difficult choices. It also has the potential to affect how we view other relationships. During the 1970s and 1980s, this nation experienced a particularly high rate of mobility. As songwriter and singer Carole King so succinctly put it: "Nobody seems to stay in one place anymore." In the late 1980s, to emphasize what one author called our "society of torn roots,"[6] *Chicago Tribune* columnist Blair Kamin noted:

> The average American moves 12 times in a lifetime, according to the U.S. Bureau of the Census. But it is not unheard of for corporate employees to move 10 times in 20 years, or even three times in a single year, according to the transferees themselves.[7]

Although Americans still move more frequently than people in Western Europe or Japan, the trend to relocate has slowed. In the early 1970s, only about 10 percent of the employees who were asked by their corporation to change locations resisted. In recent years, roughly one-third of the employees asked to move resisted—even though they were sometimes promised fatter-than-usual salaries.[8] The U.S. Census Bureau found that movement from one residence to another has decreased from about 20 percent in the mid 1980s, when one in five people moved every year, to slightly over 16 percent.[9]

But while physical mobility has decreased, the rate of change that people encounter in the workplace has not. Today's employee must be prepared to deal with a fast-paced, constantly changing work environment. Phrases like "high-speed management," "reinventing the workplace," and "rapid downsizing" reflect the continual state of flux that characterizes many organizations. Employees in the United

States now are working more hours, earning less, and under more pressure to adapt than they have been in several decades.[10] Job descriptions change quickly to accommodate fluctuations in the marketplace. People constantly have to learn new skills to keep up with advances in technology. For many, job security seems to be a thing of the past. It is not at all uncommon for employees to move from one job to another every three or four years.

How are interpersonal relationships affected by a high degree of change? First, rapid change may affect our expectation for how long relationships will last. Virtually everything we do is based on a culturally taught assumption regarding how long things last. As children, we learn how long Mommy or Daddy spend at the office; how long dinner lasts; how long a vacation is; how long a friend can play at our house. If the pace of life accelerates, we will come to expect things to last for a shorter time. In other words, we can become culturally conditioned toward building and dissolving relationships quickly.

Movement from one relationship to another in rapid succession may also affect the trust, support, and long-term commitment desired in many relationships. If we expect most of our relationships to change, we may feel it necessary to rely less on others and more on ourselves—thus avoiding the very relatedness we seek. The lament of the following song seems to capture the essence of this perspective:

"Songs"

Music by Barry Mann, Words by Cynthia Well

Everyone seems to be movin'
Movin'up and movin'on
Just when you try to touch them
That's when you find they're gone
We pass through each other's lives
And fade into the past
You just don't know who to believe in
No one seems to last. . . . [11]

Another result of frequent change is the possibility of building a wide range of acquaintances and friends. One study, cited by Milgram, asked a number of people from different lifestyles to keep a diary of those with whom they come in contact over a one-hundred-day period. On the average, each person listed some five hundred names. Milgram's own research, based on the idea that "it's a small world," suggested that each American has a pool of five hundred to twenty-five hundred acquaintances.[12] Even more surprising was Milgram's finding that a message given to anyone in the United States, and passed only to people known on a first-name basis, can reach any other person in the United States with an average of about five intermediaries. For example, a wheat farmer in Kansas was trying to get a message to an unknown graduate student in Cambridge, Massachusetts. The farmer gave it to his Episcopal priest who gave it to another priest in Cambridge who happened to know the graduate student. All this seems to suggest that Americans are developing a fantastic repertoire of acquaintances from which to select close friends.

The rapid changes we have seen in technology over the past decade also have affected our relationships by increasing the number of channels we have for communication. While our interactions with others used to be limited to phone calls, letters, or face-to-face conversations, many of us now use cell phones, pagers, fax machines, and e-mail to keep "in touch" with people we care about. Relational partners are able to contact each other more easily—if they can't reach each other on the phone, they can always try leaving a page or a voice-mail message. This increased number of channels not only gives us greater access to those we love, it also gives us access to a larger number of people. For example, we can "meet" and "talk with" individuals from all over the world on the Internet. Cyberspace has created a whole new environment for social interaction. Indeed, research has begun to show that a fairly large proportion of those who use the Internet as a social vehicle form ongoing personal relationships—e.g., friendships or romantic relationships—with some of the people they "meet."[13] Of course, all of these new channels for communication come with risks. The anonymity of the Internet allows individuals to easily conceal their identity and their intentions from each other. Some research suggests that deception is not only common, but is expected among frequent Internet users.[14] Furthermore, the increased access we get to each other with all of these different communication channels may create a need for more privacy. Having a pager go off several times during the course of a romantic evening may spoil the mood of one or both partners. As our privacy needs increase, we will begin to turn off our cell phones, use caller I.D. to screen our calls, and limit the time we devote to answering e-mail messages.

Frequent changes in our social environment also provide an opportunity to "start over" or outlive an undesirable past. In a new social setting, new modes of behavior can be communicated without an audience that is contaminated by, and holding you to, past behavior. You can interact with people anonymously on the Internet without ever revealing anything about your personal history. Similarly, when you move from one city to another or even from one job to another, you can change some of your behaviors without having to explain why. Each of us needs to have some intimate relationships, but we also need to be "the stranger on the train" too—to have situations where commitments are not demanded. In fact, some people are more comfortable if they have only a minimal number of relationships in which strong commitments are necessary. Frequent change serves this need.

In summary, the patterns of work that you and others practice in this society will affect the way your relationships develop. We've only examined two possible forces: employment of both relationship partners and changing work environments. Economists and business forecasters suggest that in the future more couples will be working in their home. The implications of this prolonged proximity to family members will certainly affect the conduct and expectations for these relationships.

Relationship Styles

In today's society we have a greater variety of relationship styles available to us (with social approval) than ever before. It is an Era of Options. Many people still choose to develop and conduct relationships in the manner of previous generations, but the number of people choosing alternative lifestyles is significant. Some are choosing to be married, some aren't; some choose to live alone while others prefer to live with one or more people; some decide to have children, some don't; some live with a partner of the same sex, others choose a partner of the opposite sex; some raise their children with a spouse and some don't; some have a sexual relationship before marriage and some don't. The variety of relationship styles available is quite extensive. To illustrate these trends and to show how dramatic changes have occurred in this society's acceptance of such trends, consider the following findings reported in several national studies:[15]

- In 1990, when asked to define the term *family,* only 22 percent chose the traditional definition: "A group of people related by blood, marriage, or adoption." Almost three-quarters instead felt that a family was "a group of people who love and care for each other."
- Only 3–4 percent of all U.S. households have a breadwinner father and a stay-at-home mother.
- In 1997, 68 percent of children lived with two parents, down from 85 percent in 1970. Nearly 30 percent of children lived with only one parent.
- In 1960, 40 percent of households were made up of four or more persons. By the 1990s, this figure had dropped to 26 percent.
- Fifty-six percent of the adult population in the United States is married, down from 68.4 percent in 1970.
- In 1900, men married at about 26 years of age and women married at about 22. Today, the average groom is 27 years old and the average bride is 25.
- From 1960 to 1990, the number of single-person households in the United States almost doubled.
- Sociologists predict that the number of never-married people will grow from 5 percent to about 10 percent in the years ahead.
- Today, more than 4 million heterosexual couples live together without being married. This number is more than double what it was in the late 1970s.

- In 1970, there were 310,000 marriages in the United States between people of different ethnic origins. By the mid 1990s, this figure was up to 1.3 million.
- Roughly 83 percent of people believe it is acceptable to be married and not have children.
- Seventy-five percent say it is morally acceptable to be single and have children.
- In 1972, 26 percent of people in the United States felt that having sex prior to marriage was "not at all wrong." By the late 1980s, this number had risen to 40 percent.
- Fifty-seven percent reject the idea that a woman should be a virgin when she gets married.
- Less than half of adults report discomfort with having friends who are homosexual.
- Seventy percent of people in the United States rejected the idea that parents should stay together for the children's sake, even if the parents are not getting along with each other.

National pollster Daniel Yankelovich has said that the preeminent question for people entering relationships in today's society is how to preserve warmth and closeness while at the same time holding onto this newfound freedom to choose.[16] Whatever forms of interpersonal communication develop in response to this Era of Options for relationship styles, certain relationship needs will have to be satisfied. And a diversity of relationship types will have to be maintained to meet them. These needs include:

1. Individuals must know people who share their concerns; otherwise they may develop feelings of social isolation or boredom.
2. They must know people they can depend on in a pinch; otherwise they may develop a sense of anxiety and vulnerability.
3. They must have one or more really close friends, with ready access to those friends; otherwise, they may experience emotional isolation or loneliness.
4. They must know people who respect their competence; otherwise, they may manifest a decreased self-esteem.[17]

Attitudes Toward Self-Fulfillment

Up until the late 1950s most Americans adhered to what has been called a "giving/getting" compact with society—that is, you only get out of the system as much as you put in. Self-denial and sacrifice were commonly accepted practices. In the late 1960s and throughout the 1970s, however, a new set of values emerged. Some people called it the "Me Decade"; and others referred to it as cultural narcissism.[18]

People were disenchanted because they felt they weren't getting back as much as they gave; that there was no payoff for self-denial and sacrifice; that individuals had a right to seek self-fulfillment by seeking gratification of whatever needs they felt; that if they didn't satisfy their desires today, tomorrow would be too late. The preoccupation with one's own improvement and satisfaction seemed well on the road to new heights as our society entered the Era of Options. It seemed that everyone would be able to achieve self-fulfillment.

But focusing exclusively on oneself often does not lead to self-fulfillment. As psychologist Marion Solomon notes, "It is assumed that members of both sexes can 'have it all'—a successful career and a happy family life . . . everyone gets what he or she wants. But that is not what most men and women experience."[19] Yankelovich's polls indicate that by the early 1980s, people began to realize that even though they could have many things in life, having "everything" was not necessarily what they wanted. Yet for some, it was not clear what they wanted to have or what they were willing to give up. In Yankelovich's words:

> Among the people I interviewed, many truly committed self-fulfillment seekers focus so sharply on their own needs that instead of achieving the more intimate relationships they desire, they grow farther apart from others. In dwelling on their own needs, they discover that the inner journey brings loneliness and depression. They are caught in a debilitating contradiction: their goal is to expand their lives by reaching beyond self, but the strategy they employ constricts them, drawing them inward toward an ever-narrowing, closed-off "I." People want to enlarge their choices, but seeking to "keep all options open," they diminish them.[20]

Many scholars concur that the me-first, satisfy-all-my-desires attitude often leads to superficial and unsatisfying relationships. Why then, do many of today's young people seek material gain with such great fervor? Some argue that the continued emphasis on materialism is not so much an effort to satisfy desires as it is an effort to find security—security that often eludes people in a world where economic prospects, personal safety, and even interpersonal relationships seem unstable.[21] So, one of the results of a cultural environment that has emphasized social diversity—represented by many alternative (and acceptable) lifestyles—is that the promise of self-fulfillment has been high. But increased social diversity has also meant that some aspects of human contact have been more difficult—for example, we become choosier about social ties, we focus on our own needs to the exclusion of others', we find it harder to identify people with exactly matching interests, values, schedules, and tastes.

The Yankelovich surveys suggest that the 1980s marked the onset of a trend that has developed further during the 1990s and into the twenty-first century—a trend away from self-centeredness and toward a greater commitment to all types of relationships. Today, more than ever, we hear people talking about developing healthy relationships, building bridges between different groups, and strengthening community ties. This is not to say that people will leave self-centeredness completely behind. As Amitai Etzioni, a professor and former white house advisor, notes,

> To suggest that most adults thrive on bonding is not to suggest that their individuality needs to be lost as they become immersed in a relationship. . . . To suggest a higher valuation of the we-ness of being a couple . . . does not entail giving up a personal identity.[22]

Focusing on oneself can play an important role in developing a strong identity and achieving personal ambitions. The current trend suggests not that we subvert ourselves, but rather that we emphasize a commitment to others—that we recognize the centrality of relationships to our lives. This increased focus on relationships may be encouraged by several different factors. For instance, the proliferation of self-help books and magazine articles emphasizing the importance of interpersonal relationships to individuals' health and happiness may encourage people to make a stronger commitment to their associations with others. Also, because many of the relationship types we see today (e.g., cohabitating couples, stepfamilies, gay/lesbian couples) are not supported by our social institutions, it is very possible that the people involved in these relationships will rely on an increased sense of commitment to maintain their ties to each other.[23] Bellah and his colleagues take this claim one step further by arguing that an increased commitment to interpersonal relationships and community is necessary if we are to deal with many of the economic and societal difficulties we face today.[24]

Messages from the Mass Media

Images of what relationships are like and how people should communicate in these relationships are also featured in the daily messages we receive from television, magazines, music, books, and movies.[25] Some of these images reinforce stereotypes while others try to portray preferred or idealized behavior; some capture the reality we live in pretty well while others seem to be mostly fiction; some seem to have a sizable impact on us while others have minimal influence; some we consciously accept, reject, or discuss with friends while others may affect us in more subtle ways. Nevertheless, the images of communication and relationship development in the mass media are based on reciprocal influence: our behavior makes a contribution to what appears in the mass media and the images portrayed in the mass media have an impact on our everyday expectations and behavior.

Popular Literature

All popular magazines in the United States with a circulation over one million were examined by Kidd over a twenty-year period.[26] She was primarily interested in articles that gave advice about interpersonal relations and how they reflected and influenced the climate of the times. She identified what she called *two visions.*

Vision I, prominent from the 1950s to the early 1960s, presented life in this society as relatively unchanging and consistent. If you wanted to be an interpersonal success, all you had to do was learn the ten easy steps and apply them to almost any situation. Articles during this period were often based on the premise that effective interpersonal relations are manifest only when everyone is happy. Therefore, communicators were advised to make every effort to elicit happiness in others. This could be done by giving compliments when you didn't want to; listening attentively and supportively to dull and boring interchanges; and so on. In short, it was argued that one's personal enrichment would be strengthened by trying to make others happy. This, of course, meant constantly thinking of others before yourself and avoiding confrontation, disagreement, and conflict at all costs. People were encouraged to avoid dating those with whom they argued by telling them they were "busy." This strategy was supposed to be in the best interests of both parties because it avoided further immediate conflict arising out of telling the other person you simply didn't want to date them. Wives were advised to pretend to be satisfied during sex with their husband even if they were not. This was described as "the worthiest duplicity on earth" in a 1957 article in *Reader's Digest.* Togetherness was another primary theme. Both men and women were supposed to enjoy their family so much they didn't even want a night out. If you did, there was a problem in your relationship. Thus, Kidd's analysis shows the popular magazines of the 1950s and early 1960s advised American readers on how to create a good impression, put aside genuine personal feelings, and live up to a predetermined standard.

From the early 1960s to the early 1970s a new set of guidelines for interpersonal behavior emerged (Vision II). These guidelines reflected a changing society. The idea of a single ever-effective standard for success was abandoned. Life and relationships were recognized as constantly changing entities. "Not all marriages are alike and cannot be measured by the same standard." Readers were encouraged to forsake the idea of self-sacrifice to make others happy, and to substitute being your real self. Only by being yourself were you ultimately going to be able to make others happy. Again, a corollary prescription followed. Rather than avoid conflict, people were encouraged to feel free to come together in an atmosphere of openness in which *any* feelings, no matter how argumentative, could be aired. The mere act of communication was the elixir for productive human relationships. No matter what our problem is, "we can talk it out."

To investigate whether the guidelines set out by Vision II have changed, a group of researchers conducted another study that followed up on Kidds' findings. Prusank, Duran, and DeLillo examined articles in popular women's magazines published from 1974 to 1990.[27] They found that the vision of interpersonal relationships portrayed during this time period differed from the views portrayed by Vision I and Vision II. Several interesting patterns make up what these researchers called Vision III. First, the content of Vision III articles represented a "softening" of the previous two Visions. For instance, rather than present a strong orientation toward others (Vision I) or toward the self (Vision II), Vision III often took the middle ground, providing readers with relationship-oriented reasons for engaging in self-oriented behaviors (e.g., "it will make your romantic relationship more interesting"). Second, "equality" was an important component of Vision III. Relationship health and stability were obtained when there was a sense of balance between partners. Readers were not necessarily encouraged to distribute tasks equally, but instead to take advantage of their differences by distributing work on the basis of expertise. Third, to have a satisfying relationship with another person, people were told they must first have "knowledge"—both of themselves and of others. Such knowledge was said to provide relational partners with understanding and a realistic view of their own and others' expectations. Fourth, and finally, change in relationships was acknowledged, but it was described as predictable and cyclical (e.g., "all relationships go through difficult times").

Of course, it is important to remember that Vision III, as described here, emerged from popular women's magazines. Magazines typically read by men were not examined. It may be that the orientation toward relationships depicted in Vision III is one that was portrayed only in women's magazines. To examine this possibility, Duran and Prusank conducted another study comparing relational themes in women's and men's popular magazine articles.[28] Although they found that the types of relationships (e.g., romantic, dating) as well as the issues (e.g., sexual relations, understanding the opposite sex) raised in men's and women's magazines were similar, they also found some interesting differences. Articles in women's magazines were more likely to present relationships as complex phenomena and to take a cooperative, accommodating approach to relational issues. By contrast, articles in men's magazines tended to depict relationships as simple and often approached relational issues from a competitive, adversarial stance. The goal of many of women's magazine articles was to help women understand men, whereas the goal of the men's articles often was to offer men a means to protect themselves from women. Findings such as these suggest that while there does appear to be an increased focus on relationships in popular magazines, the way magazines deal with relational issues may depend on their audience.

Another important thing to consider is that none of the three Visions discussed here gave much consideration to issues that talk could not resolve; to individuals who could not conform to disclosure norms; to couples who had difficulty understanding their relational expectations; to situations in which separation would offer satisfactions unattainable by co-presence. Coping with these issues may be the substance of today's society and the content of what historians might call Vision IV.

In another study of romance novels, Hubbard[29] examined the role relationships depicted between men and women across four decades. Not unlike Kidd's study,

Hubbard found that during the 1950s the characters in romance novels played very traditional, complementary roles. Without exception, the hero was portrayed as "masterful, tall, handsome, passionate and powerful, educated, and engaged in a successful career." The heroine, on the other hand, was "young, small, isolated from family and friends, modestly educated, and low in self-esteem." She achieved personal fulfillment through romance, marriage, and family, whereas his needs were met through his own achievements.

In the 1960s and 1970s, these roles began to change. The typical heroine started to recognize the inequality of her relationship with the hero and made tentative efforts to change the situation. She sometimes insulted her partner as "despicable and arrogant," sought a traditionally male-dominated career, or declared that "nature intended her to be more than a docile showpiece." Her efforts, however, were usually destined to failure. In some cases, her own fragility, lack of support systems, or lack of education prevented her from making any independent moves. In others, the hero led her "gradually and forcefully" to see "the error of her ways."

Characters portrayed in the early 1980s were quite different from those of the three previous decades. Both the hero and the heroine became more realistic and lifelike. He was sometimes tall, handsome, and affluent, but was not necessarily so. In many cases he depended on the heroine to "help him reach his full potential." She was sometimes young, other times middleaged; sometimes small, other times nearly six feet tall. She was "most often highly skilled, artistic, or well-educated." The relationship between these two "new" characters also changed. They both became sensitive to interpersonal matters and caring about their relationship. They respected one another's ambitions and treated love, in part, as a pragmatic venture, focusing on "whether a permanent relationship will work, whether the parties are compatible, and whether the needs and desires of both participants can be satisfied."

In short, the characters of the early 1980s portray what two leading trend forecasters identified as the unifying theme of the 1990s: "the triumph of the individual." Individual respect, power, and sexual equality become the basis on which relationships are built. Both men and women "take responsibility for deciding what they want and finding relationships that will meet their needs."[30] While, as Hubbard notes, it may be a number of years before we can accurately assess whether such ideals for romanticism have been accepted by the general public, many trend forecasters and sociologists argue that they have not only been accepted, but that they are thoroughly ingrained in our current understandings of interpersonal relationships.[31]

Television

In the average household the TV set is on about seven hours a day with actual viewing averaging about three hours a day. One of the prominent themes during both day and night programming concerns family and social relationships.

Television today reflects a different set of cultural norms and values than were seen in previous decades. The problems addressed in family situation comedies are less likely to be "Peter breaks Mom's favorite vase" than "Zak's anxiety over upcoming exams renders him temporarily impotent"; the inevitable "happy ending" of the past is often replaced with ambiguous or qualified happiness; the explicit "lesson" ("So always make sure you put a stamp on an important letter.") is often more implicit or hidden among several possible "lessons" to avoid the charge of "preaching." Certainly many of the formal portrayals of days gone by have been replaced with images of a more casual society—(e.g., fathers in family sitcoms of the past usually ate dinner in tie and jacket). Sexual norms have also changed. Analyses of both afternoon (soap operas) and evening programming show that references to or suggestions of sexual intercourse are much more likely when the participants are unmarried than when they are married.[32]

As television programing moves away from happy endings, simple lessons, and conservative sexual norms, the effects of viewing television on our ideas about society and social relationships are also likely to change. Television influences the way we perceive certain social groups and social issues. For instance, one study demonstrated that exposure to different types of media content was associated with different beliefs about minority groups.[33] People who watched more TV entertainment programs felt that African Americans held higher socioeconomic positions, whereas those who watched more TV news believed that the same group held relatively lower socioeconomic positions. Most scholars agree that findings such as these reflect the fact that viewers often accept the portrayals that television presents. TV entertainment programs tend to feature models of financially successful African Americans, while TV news often depicts African Americans in lower socioeconomic contexts.[34] Other studies similarly reveal that viewing certain types of programs can affect people's views about relationships and relational concerns. For example, research shows that people who watch soap operas are more likely than those who do not to overestimate the incidence of divorce, single parenthood, abortions, and sexually transmitted diseases in the real world.[35]

Although findings like these suggest that television strongly influences viewers, researchers are careful to note that people do not automatically accept what they see on television as reality. In some cases, the media influence people's perceptions,[36] in others, they do not.[37] Furthermore, many scholars argue that television is not as much an *influence on* our perceptions as it is a *reflection of* our beliefs and stereotypes. If this is the case, television programming shows us what we expect (or what we want) to see and may reinforce our biases. Whether television is an influence on our perceptions, a reflection of our beliefs, or both, TV programming provides us with interesting information about the way society views interpersonal relationships.

Television programs also can serve as a vehicle for discussions about communication and relationships. The way we respond to what we see on TV can affect those around us. For instance, sometimes children's social skills are influenced by the way parents and children talk about TV characters.[38] Parents can provide guidance concerning characteristics that a child perceives he or she shares with a TV character. A child may identify with the constant victimization that Charlie Brown receives, but parents may point out how Charlie sticks with his relationships and how they all become friends at the end. Children (and adults) may also show identification with characters by imitating them (e.g., Bart Simpson). But again, input from family and friends (positive or negative) may be the critical factor determining the adoption of this behavioral style. Social skills can also be strengthened or weakened by the type of parental participation in a child's reenactment of TV episodes—e.g., the hero saving the heroine or the monster terrorizing the helpless victim. In one study, children who were exposed to television programs portraying families whose members communicated in a concerned and supportive manner were more likely to perceive real-life family communication as similarly affiliative than those who were not exposed to such programs. This was particularly true when the verbal and viewing behavior of their parents endorsed such perceptions.[39]

Finally, it should be noted that TV may also affect our understanding of and participation in various kinds of relationships by what it does *not* show. Studies continue to demonstrate that women, minorities, and nonconventional families are underrepresented characters on television.[40] Interaction patterns common to, for example, blue-collar families or certain ethnic minorities may be so rare (or stereotypical) that the implicit message is that such patterns are "nonstandard" and should gradually be abandoned if the group wants to advance in this society.

Popular Music

What do the words to popular songs tell us about the cultural attitudes toward relationship development? A study of popular music in 1955 was replicated in 1966. By comparing the results of these two studies we can see how courtship patterns were described during two very different periods of our country's history.[41] The lyrics were categorized according to the following stages of a love relationship:

1. **Prologue to Courtship**—in 1955 a number of songs focused on what might be called "wishing and dreaming" about someone to love. In 1966 this stage was virtually absent. No longer were prospective lovers waiting for something to happen. Instead, they took a more active role and began searching for a partner—the primary activity of the next stage.

2. **Courtship**—In 1955 the songs proclaimed that everyone wants love, but there were many obstacles to overcome before finding it. Lyrics expressed a variety of approaches for seeking and establishing love: sentimental appeals, desperation, questions and promises, and impatience. Women were put on a pedestal, and men

were helpless in the face of women who "held the key" to their hearts. The lyrics of 1966 reveal a very different picture. The prerequisites and pre-conditions creating obstacles to love were severely curtailed and people set out directly to satisfy their romantic longings. Women were no longer put on a pedestal, and men took the initiative in starting and terminating most relationships. In short, the 1966 theme was that "we" control our relationship practices; other people and other things do not.

3. The Honeymoon—This is the euphoric or happy stage of courtship. In 1955 the happiness was for a relationship that would last; in 1966 permanence was not expected. In 1955 love was equated with a deep romantic involvement, but by 1966 songs were primarily discussing love in terms of physical attraction and sexual involvement. The 1966 music suggested that you could sleep with someone whether you felt affection for them or not—e.g., "you don't have to say you love me." The theme of freedom for both parties was part of the euphoria of this stage in 1966 which was not operating in 1955.

4. The Downward Course of Love—This stage describes the breakup of the relationship. The primary difference that occurred over the eleven-year period between these two studies was in the speed with which the relationships were expected to terminate. It was no longer, "Are you still mine?" followed by crying and perhaps one more chance; now the attitude was one of, "It's over and there's no use crying" so let's have a quick break and get on with other things. Most of the breakup themes were initiated by the participants in the relationship rather than other people or external events. Dishonesty was a common problem in 1966 contributing to termination.

5. All Alone—This is the isolation following the terminated relationship. In 1955 it was characterized by songs expressing how things will never be right—although some songs did address the possible development of a new relationship. In general, this stage in 1955 songs was a negative experience; in 1966 some pain was expressed, but it was also characterized as a positive first step in exploring various facets of one's real self.

More recent analyses of popular music reveal a number of interesting trends that build upon the findings of the courtship study. For example, Chesebro and his colleagues[42] found that popular songs in the late 1950s were characterized by their innocent view of love and romantic relationships. Romance was a "pure" experience, unsoiled by skepticism or irony. In the 1960s, popular music reflected a more realistic, and perhaps a more ironic view of relationships. Songs such as "We Can Work It Out" also demonstrated a sense of leadership and assertiveness that the songs of the late 1950s lacked. The 1970s represented a period when people were frustrated by both leadership and love. More emphasis was given to lyrics focusing on indifference, loneliness, and broken relationships. The music of the early 1980s, however, provided some practical resolution to these problems. Individual achievement and personal adjustment became paramount, and a renewed interest in romance and in assertiveness was apparent.

Another set of studies examining the most popular country–western songs in recent years shows women as more active participants in seeking the enjoyment of physical love—whether it is within a marriage or outside it. Many of these songs became much more explicit in terms of the language they used to describe physical love, and the sense of guilt associated with extramarital affairs began to fade.[43]

While the use of explicit lyrics—evidenced in part by the banning of some recorded songs from the retail market—represents one trend in popular music, another very different trend has also emerged. Rock stars, in particular, have begun to take a stand on political and environmental issues. One columnist illustrates by noting that "piety—excessive, conspicuous piety—is rock's growth industry.... Pop stars are taking the weight of the world on their own padded shoulders and shooting it from arty angles in their videos.... Rebellion is out; fussy sanctimony is in."[44]

Of course, not all of our exposure to and understanding of the preceding cultural themes is direct. Sometimes friends will interpret these themes for us and, in turn, become a factor influencing our expectations for communication behavior in various kinds of relationships. Or families may act as cultural mediators and establish their own rules and regulations about relationships—e.g., "The only people you can really depend on are members of your own family" or "Marriage is a trap only fools fall for."

These observations about contemporary society only scratch the surface. We have taken a hurried look at how some features of our society may influence what we do and how we influence cultural trends by our behavior. Whether we are acting and reacting within the social movements and media portrayals set forth in this chapter or within some other social configuration, the society will have a profound impact on what we say, how we say it, how often we say it, to whom we say it, when we say it, why we say it, and where we say it. Any examination of messages associated with the development of relationships must contend with the forces exerted by the climate of the times.

The Influence of the Immediate Physical Environment or Setting

Pictured in Figure 4.1 are several settings where people meet and talk. There is also a list of statements. Try to match the statements with the environment you think is most and least likely to stimulate each statement.

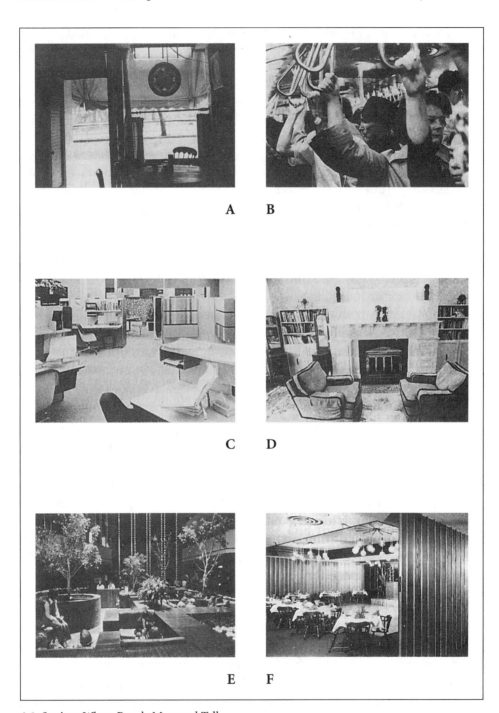

4.1 Settings Where People Meet and Talk

Statement	Most Likely to Appear in Setting:	Least Likely to Appear in Setting:
1. Good morning, Mr. Freedle. How are you today?	_____	_____
2. I just don't want to talk about it here. This just isn't the place to talk about such personal problems.	_____	_____
3. It was indeed a pleasure to make your acquaintance. I hope we meet again sometime.	_____	_____
4. Marge, I just don't know what I'm going to do. I feel so frustrated and confused about my relationship with Willie.	_____	_____
5. Now look, Grover, this is an important job we've been assigned and we have to do it right so let's get to work.	_____	_____
6. Hey, dude . . . what's happenin'?	_____	_____
7. Oh wow! That's really weird!	_____	_____
8. Have you been here before?	_____	_____
9. So you're from Louisville. I remember one time I drove through there. Isn't there a . . . ?	_____	_____
10. I feel so at ease and secure when I'm with you, Tyrone . . . if it isn't love it's so close it doesn't matter.	_____	_____
11. You're not going to believe what I just heard. . . .	_____	_____
12. It really hurts me when you don't listen to me and you continually ask me to do things you know I don't want to do. You make me feel so small and insignificant when you do that.	_____	_____
13. You wanna go someplace this weekend?	_____	_____

You probably found some statements and environments that seemed to go together immediately and others that were more difficult to classify. Some statements may appear to fit several environments and others seem suited to only one.

The ease or difficulty in matching dialogue to setting is closely related to the ease or difficulty you had in answering such questions as: Who is likely to say this? To whom is the statement most likely directed? What environments do these people usually attend? What intimacy level does this statement suggest? What intimacy level does this setting suggest? Like any perceptual task, the job became increasingly difficult as the stimuli became more ambiguous. Environments and verbalizations representing extreme forms of intimacy, formality, etc. were obviously easier to code, but like most situations involving the attribution of meaning, the boundaries were not always so clear.

We do know, however, that each setting contains certain elements that may affect the communication–relationship interface. People's perceptions and past experiences in a particular environment can evoke emotions that influence the way they interact with others.[45] We also know that people enter settings with certain established relationships and communicative intents. The existing relationship (stranger, friend, enemy) and the purpose for communicating (small talk, marriage proposal, counseling) affect one's perception of the environment and may prompt the participants to restructure the environment to more closely approximate their relationship and purpose. Such restructuring can take the form of moving closer or further away; arranging objects to create moods—the last-minute staging of one's home for that special, intimate evening by lighting candles, putting on soft music, preparing drinks, fluffing pillows on the couch, hiding dirty dishes, trash, and other nonintimate material associated with daily living; arranging the objects in the environment to establish or reflect certain role relationships, to demarcate boundaries, or to encourage greater affiliation. The typical "executive suite," for instance, may not be designed to encourage personal counseling, but chairs and other artifacts can be altered and arranged to make it more conducive to a helping relationship rather than a more formal, business relationship. Sometimes communicators will perceive seemingly inappropriate settings as appropriate. This is most often the case when the relationship bond is strong and the urgency to communicate is great. Lovers who will soon be parted sometimes seem oblivious to the rather cold and public features of an airport terminal, as evidenced by their intimate displays of verbal and nonverbal behavior. In short, the environment acts upon us, but we may also act upon the environment.

Any communication setting is comprised of four major components: (1) the natural environment; (2) architectural structure and design features; (3) movable objects; and (4) the presence or absence of other people. Each of these components has the potential for facilitating or inhibiting certain kinds of communication.

To the extent that the natural environment influences our moods, stress-level, and sense of well-being,[46] it may have an effect on how we communicate with others. Most of us have felt unusually depressed on dark, overcast days or felt a surge of good feelings as we experienced the first signs of spring. Similarly, many of us have felt edgy or tense in a crowded urban area or calm and relaxed when on a long drive in the country. Although many factors in the natural environment such as sun spots, moon positions, humidity, and noise may affect our behavior, social scientists have been particularly interested in temperature and barometric pressure. Some believe extremely hot or cold weather will increase irritability and bring on a mild depression; others argue that temperature extremes only affect our irritability when they are prolonged; still others believe that our mood is more negative when barometric pressure drops. In one study, students showed less interpersonal attraction for other students as temperature and humidity increased.[47] Some studies associate aggressive acts with increases in temperature and humidity.[48] But as other researchers point out, there are probably a lot of things that interact with temperature and humidity to bring on aggressive acts—e.g., prior provocation, the presence of aggressive models, perceived ability to leave the environment, and so on.[49]

Extensive research in human ecology affirms the different psychological and social effects of such environmental factors as walls, room size, lighting, materials (wood, metal, tile, cloth), soundproofing, doors, hallways, chairs, desks, tables, fences, and many, many more.[50] The various features that make up our environment can affect our psychological and physiological well-being as well as the way we interact with others.[51] For instance, one investigation demonstrated that children studying in classrooms without windows were more sociable (talkative) in class than were those exposed to some natural light.[52] A potential reason for these findings is that the children in windowless classrooms produced higher levels of a stress hormone (cortisol) than did the other children. Their increased talkativeness may have been a reaction to their comparatively higher levels of cortisol.

In addition to being affected by various aspects of the environment, communication settings may also be affected by the presence or absence of others. When other people are part of the setting, they may be seen as active or passive participants, depending on the degree to which they are perceived as involved (speaking or listening) in the conversation. In most instances, others are perceived as active, if for no other reason than that they are able to overhear what is being said. There are, however, situations when other persons are granted the dubious title of "nonperson" and the main participants behave accordingly. This may occur in high-density situations, but is also common with just one other person. Cab drivers, janitors, and children have been known to achieve nonperson status with some regularity. The presence of nonpersons, of course, allows the free, uninhibited flow of interaction because as far as the active participants are concerned, they themselves are the only human interactants present. Some parents have been known to talk to other people about highly personal aspects of their small children's lives in the children's presence as if they weren't there. Naturally, any perceptible response by the nonperson (verbal or nonverbal) to what is being said automatically reinstates "person" status.

When others are perceived as an active ingredient in the environment, it may facilitate or inhibit certain kinds of communication. The chief difference in communication with active others is that messages must be adapted to multiple audiences rather than to a single listener. Even telephone conversations, where the third party can only hear one of the interactants, are altered to account for the uninvited listener. Sometimes the existence of these additional audiences presents such a strain or threat that one or both communicators leave the scene. On the other hand, the appearance of a third party provides an opportunity to ease out of a conversation with an undesirable other by dumping the focus of interaction on the third party and making a polite exit. The presence of others may increase our motivation to look good in what we say and do—which can be detrimental (distorting information) or beneficial. The benefits of looking good in the presence of others are exemplified in the form of constructive approaches to conflict (see Chapter 8). In numerous cases, the presence of others prohibits overt fighting from arising at all. Certainly such benefits may be temporary in nature—for example, "catching it" later.

Generally, we would expect to find more breadth and depth of communication when the interdependency among those present is high; when interdependency is medium or low, communication will probably be less personal, more ritualistic, and more stereotyped—a form of communication designed for a broader, less specific audience.

Our Perceptions of Communication Environments

Any effort to provide a framework for looking at the interdependency of environmental stimuli and human communication necessitates a consideration of what these environments are. The range of interpersonal settings confronting us is staggering. We communicate in restaurants, public restrooms, classrooms, dormitories, churches, cars, all forms of public transportation, homes, elevators, offices, parks, theaters, bars, hotels, institutions, on street corners. Despite this diversity, each environment has a particular configuration of features which causes us to perceive it in certain ways. These perceptions, in turn, help structure the messages we choose to make. Some perceptions foster communication typical of early stages of development in relationships; some foster communication typical of more intimate stages; some environments generate perceptions that provide an "ideal" setting for communication in deteriorating relationships. The following sections are about different types of perceptions, and include hypotheses about the kind of communication that may flow from these perceptions.[53]

Perceptions of Formality

Sometimes we perceive our environment along a formal-informal continuum. Perceived formality may be based on any number of stimuli within the setting. It may be based on the decor or on the normal functions associated with a particular room—most kitchens offer a more formal setting than do most bedrooms. Perceived formality may derive from the wearing apparel of those present—black tie, come as you are, uniforms. As discussed earlier, the mere presence of others may designate greater formality; it follows that increasing the number of participants many times increases the formality of the setting. Using the dimensions of communication in developing relationships presented in Chapter 1, we would hypothesize that as formality increases, we are more likely to find communication that has less breadth and depth. In addition, we are likely to see communication that is more stylized (the prescribed range of responses is narrower), less relaxed, more hesitant, and generally more difficult.

Perceptions of Warmth

Warmth, as discussed here, is a broader concept than one's physiological reaction to temperature. When environments are perceived as warm, we are more inclined to linger, to feel relaxed and comfortable. Warmth may be associated with plants, woodwork, carpeting, soft chairs, drapes, lack of harsh lighting, or soundproofing. Although most research on human reactions to color has not attempted to alter systematically the color of an entire environment, it does tell us that colors may have a distinct impact on our perceptions of warmth or coldness of a setting. Wexner, for example, found the color blue to be the most frequently associated with the following mood tones: secure, comfortable, tender, soothing, calm, peaceful, and serene.[54] Several experiments have tested the effects of "beautiful" and "ugly" rooms. In many respects, warm and cold settings are analogous to beautiful and ugly ones. The ugly or cold room was described as producing monotony, fatigue, headaches, discontent, irritability, and hostility. Beautiful rooms elicited descriptive words like: pleasure, comfort, enjoyment, importance, and energy. Subjects in the beautiful rooms wanted to continue their activity while those in ugly rooms engaged in a wide range of avoidance or escape tactics. Beautiful rooms also seem to elicit more positive evaluations, better recall, and more effective problem solving.[55] Fast food chains often attempt to design environments that will remain inviting (some warmth) but encourage rapid turnover (some coldness).

The forementioned research does not offer much specific data regarding actual communication behavior. We would, however, predict that the greater the perceived warmth, the more likely we would find personal, spontaneous, and efficient communication patterns.

> *I don't like cold weather, and I found the schools cold, so I selected art. I liked that room because it was so warm. Of course, I loved my teacher too. But it was only years later that I accepted the fact that I generated heat because I was so happy in that room.*
>
> Louise Nevelson

Perceptions of Privacy

Doors and walls (enclosed places) usually connote more private settings. When a person is seen entering an office, and closing a door which is usually left open, curious viewers may ponder the need for privacy and the specific content of the private communication. Privacy may also be perceived in open places—without any doors or walls. The critical determinant is that the setting is not subject to other people freely entering or overhearing the active participants' conversation. However, even enclosed settings, without other people, can sometimes connote a certain publicness—a therapeutic interview in a large lecture hall.

A number of studies have demonstrated that people's ability to manage privacy within their environment is associated with a sense of well-being.[56] Privacy allows individuals the chance to engage in solitary activities (e.g., quiet contemplation), but it also creates an opportunity for intimate communication.[57] Having privacy enables us to share something special with others. For instance, personal objects of one or both communicators in the environment may contribute to perceptions of privacy—family pictures, a toothbrush, trinkets. Accessibility to these objects ("You can use my toothbrush.") will increase as intimacy increases. Giving a loved one access to private objects shows that privacy involves more than just closing ourselves off from the outside world. It also gives us the opportunity to open ourselves up to those we trust.[58] Settings perceived as private usually encourage closer speaking distances, greater depth and breadth of topics discussed, and communication designed to fit the special relationship with the one other person—flexibility and spontaneity.

Perceptions of Familiarity

Unfamiliar environments are much like unfamiliar people—typically calling for more cautious and hesitant communication. The slow, deliberate, and tentative nature of such communication is only compounded when we meet an unfamiliar person in a totally unfamiliar setting. We generally prefer familiar places.[59] Since we are uncertain of the norms or typical responses associated with unfamiliar environments, there is increased pressure to suspend overt judgments of the other person. Hence, initial communication in unfamiliar settings will probably be more awkward and difficult as we try to go slowly until we can associate this environment with one we know. For example, the spontaneity of children is sometimes severely curtailed on that first visit to Grandma's house. We would predict that familiar environments, even though they are also perceived as formal and public, will allow greater flexibility in communicating than unfamiliar environments, even though they are also perceived as informal and private. At least in the familiar environment we know the range of acceptable responses. One explanation given for the stereotyped structures of fast food stops is that they allow a mobile, constantly changing society to readily find a familiar predictable place which will guarantee minimum demands for active contact with strangers. When a relationship is in its early stages of development and the participants are in an unfamiliar setting, we would predict little or no rapid movement toward greater intimacy. This is provided, of course, that the people involved don't perceive a strong outside threat that would throw them together. In fact, in an unfamiliar setting, the most likely topic for small talk will be the environment itself. Even intimates, when confronted with unfamiliar settings, will initially linger longer at the experimenting stage.

Perceptions of Constraint

Part of our total reaction to a setting is based on our perception of whether (and how easily) we can leave it. There can be a definite difference in an individual's perception of confinement or constraint when his or her in-laws are visiting for an evening versus visiting for a month. The intensity with which we perceive an environment as constraining is also closely related to the space available to us and the privacy of that space. Many environments seem to be only temporarily constraining—a long car trip, but there are those which most of us would consider rather extreme cases of environmental constraint—certain institutional settings (prisons, nursing homes), spacecraft, and the settings allowed a sequestered jury during a long trial.

A study by Taylor et al. presents some information about how people communicate in *anticipation* of such conditions. Navy personnel were ostensibly being considered for a stint in an undersea capsule. They were told they would have to live and work with another sailor. Then they were allowed to talk over an intercom for three hours with a person they might be teamed with (actually a confederate). Some subjects were told the confinement would last three weeks; others were told they would live underwater for six months. When the conversations of the subjects were analyzed, there was generally less self-disclosure in the situations where long-term commitment was expected, and especially when the confederate gave negative or unfavorable responses.[60] This study only deals with strangers and the expected environmental constraints, not interaction as it develops within a confined setting. It does suggest the possibility that there will be an initially slow revelation of personal information when physical and/or psychological constraint is perceived as high. In the same manner, we might expect such conditions to extend the duration of other communication behaviors typical of early stages in a relationship.

Perceptions of Distance

Another important environmental perception concerns how close or far away the environment forces us to conduct our communication with another person. Very often there are identifiable facets of the environment that create greater physical distance—tables, chairs, desks, offices on a different floor, houses in different parts of the city. Distance perceptions, however, are based on both physical and psychological proximity, frequently grounded in visibility or eye contact. An individual may be seated close to someone and still not perceive it as a close environment—for example, immovable chairs which are not facing one another. Also, women and men tend to use space in different ways. Women usually interact with each other at closer distances than do men. But when a threat is perceived, women tend to increase their distance from the source of the threat and leave the scene more quickly than do men.[61]

As the intimacy of the relationship increases, there is a gradual shrinking of the distance barrier; in the same manner, shrinking the distance barriers can facilitate more intimate communication. Thus, we can intentionally reduce or extend distances we deem inappropriate. The closest proximity is usually associated with love, comfort, and protection. The corresponding communication behaviors include touching, a softer voice, and so on. When the setting forces us into close distances that are not desired—elevators, eight people in a compact car, crowded buses—we will probably find people making efforts to psychologically increase distance and thereby reflect a less intimate feeling. This may include less eye contact, body tenseness and immobility, cold silence, nervous laughter, joking (often about the intimacy), and other strategies designed to keep the conversation public and directed to all present. If people must talk under such conditions, they usually avoid anything but small talk, trying to offset the unavoidable intimacy messages imposed by the environment.

A few qualifying remarks are in order. The preceding discussions focused on only some of the dimensions along which settings may be perceived. Very little research and a lot of speculation are behind the hypothesis here that intimate communication is more often associated with settings perceived as: informal, warm, private, familiar, unconstrained, and close. The discussion of these perceptions was generally limited to extreme examples—either formal *or* informal, public *or* private. In daily life many of our perceptions are not so polarized and are more accurately represented as points on a continuum. For clarity of discussion, each dimension was discussed separately, but again typically we experience a mixture of these perceptions for any given setting. In an elevator, for instance, you may perceive it as close, familiar, and only temporarily confining, but it may also be public (assuming others are present), formal, and cold. It is this combination of intimate and nonintimate factors that acts on and interacts with the choice of what we ultimately say. In some cases we may perceive one dimension so strongly that it will override other perceptions, provide the critical influence, and possibly even block any awareness that other perceptions were made.

While we know that environments add substance to our perceptions of communication situations, we are unsure exactly how these perceptions relate to the messages we produce. We know that people get used to and adapt to inappropriate settings, but we're not sure how that process works. We also know that careful selection of the environment may make a difference in the outcome of the encounter and the resulting relationship. In fact, sometimes we deliberately select incongruous settings—reprimanding someone in an intimate setting in order to soften the impact or to show personal concern.

SUMMARY

The basic theme of this chapter is a simple one: when we examine the reasons why people communicate the way they do, we must consider the potential influence of the environment within which that communication takes place. Communication and relationships are influenced in different ways by different cultures. This chapter focused on some of the characteristics of U.S. society and how various aspects of the physical environment are used and interpreted in that society. We examined the environment from two perspectives: (1) the cultural environment, represented by behaviors, attitudes, and values shared by enough people to exert an influence on the messages we make; and (2) the physical environment, represented by natural or human constructions which frame our conversations and relationships.

To recapitulate, we discussed four areas within the cultural environment: (1) patterns of work; (2) relationship styles; (3) attitudes toward self-fulfillment; and (4) messages from the mass media. Couples who try to combine a marriage, family, and career may find some personal and financial benefits, but they must also work especially hard to develop the communication skills necessary to offset potential relationship difficulties in such pursuits. Although our society is not as mobile as it was a few years ago, the fast-paced changes that many of us currently encounter in the workplace still affect the way we maintain our relationships and establish new friendships. In today's society, many different relationship styles are acceptable so it should be easier for this generation to satisfy what Weiss believes we all need—relationships with people who share our concerns, people on whom we can depend in a pinch, one or more really close friends who are easily accessible, and those who respect our competence. Some people will no doubt be more confused as the number of relationship options becomes greater, but greater choice is definitely the trend. We also noted that the number of people who are preoccupied with their own self-interests seems to be diminishing. Some trend forecasters even believe we have moved into an era where interpersonal and group commitments will supersede individual commitments—at least to a greater extent than we've experienced in the last twenty-five years in this culture. We concluded our discussion of the culture by reviewing the messages we receive from popular literature, television, and popular music concerning relationship growth and decay. The last part of the chapter discussed the physical environment and its interrelationship with the messages communicators send and receive. Several perceptions were proposed in which are seen the component parts (architecture, objects, people, and the natural environment) of communication settings—formality, warmth, privacy, familiarity, constraint, and distance.

The possible effect of interpersonal needs discussed in the preceding chapter and the possible effect of communication environments in this chapter represent some major forces that influence communication behavior in developing relationships. Obviously, in any given situation or relationship there may be other factors that may have a major modifying influence on message-making—e.g., individual values, roles, expectations, self-images, motivations, past history, reference groups, prescribed or perceived time to communicate, and the repertoire of communication skills available. Thus, like the proverbial blind men examining different parts of an elephant, we may accurately describe some influential factors in a communication situation, but omit others necessary for a full understanding of what happened. It is the nature of human communication to be incomplete; we can't say everything about anything. We can, however, strive to increase the precision, accuracy, and relevance of what we do say. Hopefully, these two chapters have made you aware of the tremendous complexity attending human interaction and the multitude of contingencies attached to each human action. Trying to understand human communication is a humbling experience—with one's certainty of explanation often inversely correlated with one's grasp of the possible influential factors. Each communicator is a party to something different from, yet a part of, both of them—their relationship. A person cannot denounce the insensitivity of a friend or acquaintance without simultaneously denouncing a part of himself or herself. Any individual change in attitudes or behavior is diffused out across every other facet of one's personality which, in turn, affects the partner to the relationship and, eventually, the relationship itself.

SELECTED READINGS

The Sociocultural Environment

Bellah, R. N., Madsen, R., Sullivan, W. M., Swidler, A., and Tipton, S. M. *Habits of the Heart: Individualism and Commitment in American Life.* New York: Harper & Row, 1985.

Bennis, W. G., and Slater, P. E. *The Temporary Society.* New York: Harper & Row, 1968.

Etzioni, A. *The Spirit of Community: Rights, Responsibilities, and Communitarian Agenda.* New York: Crown, 1993.

Howe, N., and Stauss, B. *13th Gen: Abort, Retry, Ignore, Fail?* New York: Vintage Books, 1993.

Lasch, C. *The Culture of Narcissism: American Life in an Age of Diminishing Expectations.* New York: W. W. Norton, 1979.

Naisbitt, J., and Aburdene, P. *Megatrends 2000: Ten New Directions for the 1990s.* New York: William Morrow, 1990.

Packard, V. A. *A Nation of Strangers.* New York: David McKay, 1972.

Reisman, D. *The Lonely Crowd.* New Haven: Yale University Press, 1961.

South, S. J., and Tolnay, S. E., eds. *The Changing American Family: Sociological and Demographic Perspectives.* San Francisco, CA: Westview, 1992.

Toffler, A. *Future Shock.* New York: Bantam Books, 1971.

———. *The Third Wave.* New York: William Morrow, 1980.

Yankelovich, D. *New Rules: Searching for Self-Fulfillment in a World Turned Upside Down.* New York: Random House, 1981.

The Physical Environment

Canter, D. ed. *Environmental Interaction.* London: Surrey University Press, 1975.

Downs, R. M., Liben, L. S., and Palermo, D. S., eds. *Visions of Aesthetics, the Environment* and Development: The Legacy of Joachim F. Wohlwill. Hillsdale, NJ: Erlbaum, 1991.

Evans, G. W. and McCoy, J. M. "When Buildings Don't Work: The Role of Architecture in Human Health." *Journal of Environmental Psychology* 18 (1998): 85–94.

Garling, R., and Golledge, R. G., eds. *Behavioral and Environment: Psychological and Geographical Approaches.* The Netherlands: Elsevier Science Publishers, 1993.

Gudykunst, W. B., S. Ting-Toomey, and Nishida, T., eds. *Communication in Personal Relationships Across Cultures.* Thousand Oaks, CA: Sage, 1996.

Ittehon, W. H., Prohansky, H. M., Rivlin, L. G., and Winkel, G. H. *An Introduction to Environmental Psychology.* New York: Holt, Rinehart & Winston, 1974.

Knapp, M. L. and Hall, J. A. *Nonverbal Communication in Human Interaction.* 3d ed. Fort Worth, TX: Holt, Rinehart & Winston, 1992.

Mehrabian, A. *Public Places and Private Spaces.* New York: Basic Books, 1976.

Pedersen, D. M. "Psychological Functions of Privacy," *Journal of Environmental Psychology* 17 (1997): 147–156.

Prohansky, H. M., Ittehon, W. H., and Rivlin, L. G., eds. *Environmental Psychology: Man and His Physical Setting.* New York: Holt, Rinehart & Winston, 1970.

Sommer, R. *Tight Spaces: Hard Architecture and How to Humanize It.* Englewood Cliffs, NJ: Prentice-Hall, 1974.

Steele, F. I. *Physical Settings and Organization Development.* Reading, MA: Addison-Wesley, 1973.

Stokols, D., Altman, I., eds. *Handbook of Environmental Psychology.* vol. 1. New York: John Wiley & Sons, 1987.

Werner, C. M., Altman, I., and Brown, B. B. "A Transactional Approach to Interpersonal Relations: Physical Environment, Social Context and Temporal Qualities," *Journal of Social and Personal Relationships* 9 (1992): 297–323.

Dual Careers

Aldous, J., ed. "Dual-Earner Families." Special issue of *Journal of Family Issues* 2 (1981).

Barnett, R. C., and Rivers C. *She Works/He Works: How Two-Income Families are Happier, Healthier, and Better Off.* New York: HarperCollins, 1996.

Bell, R. A., Roloff, M. E., Van Camp, K., and Karol, S. H. "Is It Lonely at the Top?: Career Success and Personal Relationships." *Journal of Communication* 40 (1990): 9–23.

Bryson, J. B., and Bryson, R., eds. "Dual-Career Couples." Special issue of *Psychology of Women Quarterly* 3 (1978): 5–120.

Duxbury, L. E., and Higgins, C. A. "Gender Differences in Work-Family Conflict." *Journal of Applied Psychology* 76 (1991): 60–74.

Gerstel, N., and Gross, H. *Commuter Marriage: A Study of Work and Family.* New York: Guilford, 1984.

Gilbert, L. A. *Two Careers/One Family: The Promise of Gender Equality.* Newbury Park, CA: Sage, 1993.

Hall, F. S., and Hall, D. T. *The Two-Career Couple.* Reading, MA: Addison-Wesley, 1979.

Pepitone-Rockwell, F., ed. *Dual Career Couples.* Beverly Hills, CA: Sage, 1980.

Rice, D. G. *Dual-Career Marriage: Conflict and Treatment.* New York: Free Press, 1979.

Schwartz, P. *Peer Marriage.* (New York: The Free Press, 1994).

Silberstein, L. R. *Dual-Career Marriage: A System in Transition.* Hillsdale, NJ: Erlbaum, 1992.

Winfield, F. E. *Commuter Marriage: Living Together, Apart.* New York: Columbia University Press, 1985.

Interpersonal Relations and the Mass Media

Alberts, J. K. "The Role of Couples' Conversations in Relational Development: A Content Analysis of Courtship Talk in Harlequin Romance Novels." *Communication Quarterly* 34 (1986): 127–142.

Bachen, C. M., and Illouz, E. "Imagining Romance: Young People's Cultural Models of Romance and Love." *Critical Studies in Mass Communication* 13 (1996): 279–308.

Chesebro, J. W., Foulger, D. A., Nachman, J. E., and Yannelli, A. "Popular Music as a Mode of Communication, 1955–1982." *Critical Studies in Mass Communication* 2 (1985): 115–135.

Craig, S. *Men, Masculinity, and the Media.* Newbury Park, CA: Sage, 1992.

Douglas, S. J. *Where the Girls Are: Growing Up Female with the Mass Media.* New York: Random House, 1994.

Doyle, M. V. "The Rhetoric of Romance: A Fantasy Theme Analysis of Barbara Cartland Novels." *The Southern Speech Communication Journal* 51 (1985): 24–48.

Duran, R. L., and Prusank, D. T. "Relational Themes in Men's and Women's Popular Nonfiction Magazine Articles." *Journal of Social and Personal Relationships* 14 (1997): 165–189.

Gerbner, G., Gross, L., Morgan, M., and Signorielli, N. "The 'Mainstreaming' of America: Violence Profile No. 11." *Journal of Communication* 30 (1980): 10–29.

Gritzner, C. F. "Country Music: A Reflection of Popular Culture." *Journal of Popular Culture* 11 (1978): 857–864.

Gross, L., and Morgan, M. "Television and Enculturation." In J. R. Dominick and J. Fletcher, eds., *Broadcasting Research Methods: A Reader.* Boston: Allyn & Bacon, 1981.

Hubbard, R. C. "Relationships Styles in Popular Romance Novels." *Communication Quarterly* 33 (1985): 113–125.

Kidd, V. "Happily Ever After and Other Relationship Styles: Advice on Interpersonal Relations in Popular Magazines, 1951–1973." *Quarterly Journal of Speech* 61 (1975): 31–39.

Pichaske, D. *A Generation in Motion: Popular Music and Culture in the Sixties.* New York: Schirmer Books, 1979.

Prusank, D. T., Duran, R. L., and DeLillo, D. A. "Interpersonal Relationships in Women's Magazines: Dating and Relating in the 1970s and 1980s." *Journal of Social and Personal Relationships* 10 (1993): 307–320.

Rogers, J. N. *The Country Music Message: Revisited.* Fayetteville, AR: University of Arkansas Press, 1989.

Silverstone, R. *Television and Everyday Life.* New York: Routledge, 1994.

Zillman, D., Bryant, J., and Huston, A. C., eds. *Media, Children, and the Family.* Hillsdale, NJ: Erlbaum, 1994.

NOTES

1. W. B. Gudykunst, S. Ting-Toomey, and T. Nishida, eds., *Communication in Personal Relationships Across Cultures.* (Thousand Oaks, CA: Sage, 1996); A. L. Sillars, "Communication and Family Culture." In M. A. Fitzpatrick and A. L. Vangelisti, eds., *Explaining Family Interaction* (Thousand Oaks, CA: Sage, 1995), pp. 375-399.

2. R. Goodwin and C. Findlay, " 'We Were Just Fated Together' . . . Chinese Love and the Concept of *yuan* in England and Hong Kong," *Personal Relationships* 4 (1997):85–92.

3. T. Holtgraves, "Styles of Language Use: Individual and Cultural Variability in Conversational Indirectness," *Journal of Personality and Social Psychology* 73 (1997):624–637.

4. S. G. Timmer, J. Veroff, and S. Hatchett, "Family Ties and Marital Happiness: The Different Marital Experiences of Black and White Newlywed Couples," *Journal of Social and Personal Relationships* 13 (1996):335–359.

5. K. W. Halford, K. Hahlweg, and M. Dunne, "The Cross-Cultural Consistency of Marital Communication Associated with Marital Distress," *Journal of Marriage and the Family* 52 (1990): 487–500.

6. V. Packard, *A Nation of Strangers* (New York: David McKay, 1972), pp. 7–8.

7. B. Kamin, "Job Transfer More Than a Moving Experience," *Chicago Tribune* (October 9, 1988), A1, A26–A27.

8. R. C. Barnett and C. Rivers *She Works/He Works: How Two-Income Families are Happier, Healthier, and Better Off.* (New York: Harper-Collins, 1996); A. Toffler, *The Third Wave* (New York: William Morrow, 1980).

9. Associated Press, "Americans Moving Less, Census Bureau Reports," *Austin American Statesman* (December 4, 1997), A28; S. A. Holmes, "People's Roots Sinking Deeper," *Austin American Statesman* (September 12, 1995) A1, 7; R. A. Mosbacher, *Geographic Mobility: March 1986–March 1987,* U.S. Department of Commerce, Bureau of the Census.

10. R. C. Barnett and C. Rivers, *op cit.,* pp. 65–66.

11. © Copyright 1973 by Screen Gems-EMI Music Inc. & Summerhill Songs Inc. All administrative rights for the entire world controlled by Screen Gems-EMI Music Inc. All rights reserved. Used by permission.

12. S. Milgram, "The Small World Problem," *Psychology Today,* 1 (1967): 60–67.

13. M. R. Parks and L. D. Roberts, " 'Making MOOsic': The Development of Personal Relation-

ships On Line and a Comparison to Their Off-Line Counterparts," *Journal of Social and Personal Relationships* 15 (1998): 517–537.

[14]K. M. Wolff, "Impression Management, Anonymity, and Deceptive Communication in Computer Chat." Paper presented at the annual meeting of the Central States Communication Association, Chicago, IL., 1998.

[15]J. Adler, "Tomorrow's Child," *Newsweek* (November 2, 1998), pp. 54–64; Associated Press, "Survey: Married Adults Hang on to Majority," *Austin American Statesman* (January 7, 1999), A7; R. C. Barnett and C. Rivers, *op cit.*, p. 3; N. G. Bennett, D. E. Bloom, and P. Craig, "American Marriage Patterns in Transition." In S. J. South and S. Tolnay, eds., *The Changing American Family: Sociological and Demographic Perspectives* (San Francisco, CA: Westview, 1992), pp. 89–108; R. Farnighetti, ed., *The World Almanac* (Mahwah, NJ: World Almanac Books, 1998); D. A. Gilbert, *Compendium of American Public Opinion* (New York: Facts on File, 1988); R. G. Niemi, J. Mueller, and T. W. Smith, *Trends in Public Opinion: A Compendium of Survey Data* (New York: Greenwood Press, 1989); *Newsweek Special Issue: The 21st Century Family* (Winter/Spring, 1990); D. Popenoe, "American Family Decline, 1960–1990: A Review and Appraisal," *Journal of Marriage and the Family* 55 (1993): 527–542; A. F. Saluter, "Marital Status and Living Arrangements: March, 1994," *Current Population Reports: Population Characteristics* (U.S. Bureau of the Census, February, 1996), p. 484; J. A. Sweet and L. L. Bumpass, "Young Adults' Views of Marriage, Cohabitation, and Family." In S. J. South and S. Tolnay, eds., *The Changing American Family: Sociological and Demographic Perspectives* (San Francisco, CA: Westview, 1992), pp. 143–170; P. Wingert, "I Do, I Do—Maybe," *Newsweek* (November 2, 1998), p. 58; D. Yankelovich, *Searching for Self-Fulfillment in a World Turned Upside Down* (New York: Random House, 1981).

[16]D. Yankelovich, "New Rules in American Life," *Psychology Today* 15 (1981): 40.

[17]R. S. Weiss, "The Fund of Sociability," *Trans-Action* (July–August 1969). Weiss also notes the need for adults to nurture children. In a society with an increasing number of childless couples, we might see this need fulfilled vicariously through social work (the Big Brother program), professional work (nurturing students), the children of other couples, or, we suppose, through pets or plants.

[18]C. Lasch, *The Culture of Narcissism: American Life in an Age of Diminishing Expectations* (New York: Norton, 1979); P. Marin, "The New Narci-

sism," *Harper's* (October, 1975), pp. 45–50. A best-selling book in the late 1970s was: R. J. Ringer, *Looking Out for Number 1* (New York: Fawcett, 1978).

[19]M. F. Solomon, *Narcissism and Intimacy: Love and Marriage in an Age of Confusion.* (New York: W. W. Norton, 1989).

[20]D. Yankelovich, *New Rules,* 1981.

[21]N. Howe and B. Stauss, *13th Gen: Abort, Retry, Ignore, Fail?* (New York: Vintage Books, 1993). See also J. Giles, "Generalizations X," *Newsweek* (June 6, 1994): 62–70; D. M. Gross and S. Scott, "Proceeding with Caution," *Time* (July 16, 1990): 56–62.

[22]A. Etzioni, *The Spirit of Community: Rights, Responsibilities, and Communitarian Agenda* (New York: Crown, 1993).

[23]W. J. Doherty, "Private Lives, Public Values," *Psychology Today* 25 (1992): 35–37.

[24]R. N. Bellah, R. Madsen, W. M. Sullivan, A. Swidler, and S. M. Tipton, *The Good Society* (New York: Knopf, 1991).

[25]C. M. Bachen and E. Illouz, "Imagining Romance: Young People's Cultural Models of Romance and Love," *Critical Studies in Mass Communication* 13 (1996): 279–308.

[26]V. Kidd, "Happily Ever After and Other Relationship Styles: Advice on Interpersonal Relations in Popular Magazines, 1951–1973," *Quarterly Journal of Speech* 61 (1975): 31–39.

[27]D. T. Prusank, R. L. Duran, and D. A. DeLillo, "Interpersonal Relationships in Women's Magazines: Dating and Relating in the 1970s and 1980s," *Journal of Social and Personal Relationships* 10 (1993): 307–320.

[28]R. L. Duran and D. T. Prusank "Relational Themes in Men's and Women's Popular Nonfiction Magazine Articles," *Journal of Social and Personal Relationships* 14 (1997): 165–189.

[29]R. C. Hubbard, "Relationship Styles in Popular Romance Novels, 1950 to 1983," *Communication Quarterly* 33 (1985): 113–125.

[30]J. Naisbitt and P. Aburdene, *Megatrends 2000: Ten New Directions for the 1990s* (New York: William Morrow, 1990).

[31]R. N. Bellah, R. Madsen, W. M. Sullivan, A. Swidler, and S. M. Tipton, *Habits of the Heart: Individualism and Commitment in American Life* (New York: Harper & Row, 1985); P. Schwartz, *Peer Marriage* (New York: The Free Press, 1994).

[32]B. S. Greenberg and R. Busselle, "What's Old, What's New: Sexuality on the Soaps," *Siecus Report* 24 (1996): 14–16; B. S. Greenberg, R. Abelman, and K. A. Neuendorf, "Sex on the Soap Operas:

Afternoon Delight," *Journal of Communication* 31 (1981): 83–89; B. S. Greenberg, D. Graef, C. Fernandez Collado, F. Korzenny, and C. K. Atkin, "Sexual Intimacy on Commercial Television During Prime Time," *Journalism Quarterly* 57 (1980): 30–37.

[33]G. B. Armstrong and K. A. Neuendorf with J. E. Brentar, "TV Entertainment, News, and Racial Perceptions of College Students," *Journal of Communication* 42 (1992): 153–176.

[34]O. H. Gandy and P. W. Matabane, "Television and Social Perceptions Among African-Americans and Hispanics." In M. K. Asante and W. B. Gudykunst, eds., *Handbook of International and Intercultural Communication* (Newbury Park, CA: Sage, 1989).

[35]J. D. Brown and J. R. Steele, "Sexuality and the Mass Media: An Overview," *Siecus Report* 24 (1996): 3–9.

[36]B. J. Wilson, D. Linz, E. Donnerstein, and H. Stipp, "The Impact of Social Issue Television Programming on Attitudes Toward Rape," *Human Communication Research* 19 (1992): 179–208.

[37]W. J. Brown and M. J. Cody, "Effects of a Prosocial Television Soap Opera on Promoting Women's Status," *Human Communication Research* 18 (1991): 114–142.

[38]P. Messaris and C. Sarett, "On the Consequences of Television-Related Parent-Child Interaction," *Human Communication Research* 7 (1981): 226–244. See also D. J. Atkin, B. S. Greenberg, and T. F. Baldwin, "The Home Ecology of Children's Television Viewing: Parental Mediation and the New Video Environment," *Journal of Communication* 41 (1991): 40–52.

[39]N. L. Buerkel-Rothfuss, B. S. Greenberg, C. K. Atkin, and K. A. Neuendorf, "Learning about the Family from Television," *Journal of Communication* 32 (1982): 191–201.

[40]Research conducted by G. Gerbner, reported in "TV Stereotypes Persist, Study Shows," *Austin American Statesman* (June 19, 1993), 3; G. Gerbner, L. Gross, M. Morgan, and N. Signorielli "Living with Television: The Dynamics of the Cultivation Process." In J. Bryant and D. Zillmann, eds., *Perspectives on Media Effects* (Hillsdale, NJ: Erlbaum, 1986), pp. 17–40; A Mulac, J. J. Bradac, and S. K. Mann, "Male/Female Language Differences and Attributional Consequences in Children's Television," *Human Communication Research* 11 (1985): 481–506; R. Riffe, H. Goldson, K. Saxton, and Y. C. Yu, "Females and Minorities in TV Ads in 1987 Saturday Children's Programs," *Journalism Quarterly* 6 (1989): 129–136; T. Skill, J. D. Robinson, and S. P.

Wallace, "Portrayal of Families on Prime-Time TV: Structure, Type and Frequency," *Journalism Quarterly* 64 (1987): 360–398.

[41]D. Horton, "The Dialogue of Courtship in Popular Songs," *American Journal of Sociology* 62 (1957): 569–578; J. T. Carey, "Changing Courtship Patterns in the Popular Song," *American Journal of Sociology* 74 (1969): 720–731.

[42]J. W. Chesebro, D. A. Foulger, J. E. Nachman, and A. Yannelli, "Popular Music as a Mode of Communication, 1955–1982," *Critical Studies in Mass Communication* 2 (1985): 115–135.

[43]J. N. Rogers, *The Country Music Message: Revisited* (Fayetteville, AR: University of Arkansas Press, 1989).

[44]J. Leland, "Johnny B. Goody-Goody," *Newsweek* (February, 1991), pp. 59–60.

[45]D. Amedeo, "Emotions in Person-Environment-Behavior Episodes." In T. Garlin and R. G. Golledge, eds., *Behavior and Environment: Psychological and Geographical Approaches* (The Netherlands: Elsevier Science Publishers, 1993), pp. 83–116; J. A. Russel and J. Snodgrass, "Emotion and the Environment." In D. Stokols and I. Altman, eds., *Handbook of Environmental Psychology* (New York: John Wiley & Sons, 1987), pp. 245–280.

[46]For information on the association between stress and the environment, see G. W. Evans and S. Cohen, "Environmental Stress." In D. Stokols and I. Altman, eds., *Handbook of Environmental Psychology* (New York: John Wiley & Sons, 1987), pp. 571–610; and R. S. Ulrich, R. F. Simons, B. D. Losito, E. Fiorito, M. A. Miles, and M. Zelson, "Stress Recovery During Exposure to Natural and Urban Environments," *Journal of Environmental Psychology* 11 (1991): 201–230.

[47]W. Griffitt, "Environmental Effects of Interpersonal Affective Behavior: Ambient Effective Temperature and Attraction," *Journal of Personality and Social Psychology* 15 (1970): 240–244; W. Griffitt and R. Veitch, "Hot and Crowded: Influence of Population Density and Temperature on Interpersonal Affective Behavior," *Journal of Personality and Social Psychology* (1971): 92–98.

[48]C. A. Anderson and K. B. Anderson, "Violent Crime Rate Studies in Philosophical Context: A Destructive Testing Approach to Heat and Southern Culture of Violence Effects," *Journal of Personality and Social Psychology* 70 (1996): 740–756; C. A. Anderson, B. J. Bushman and R. W. Groom, "Hot Years and Serious and Deadly Assault: Empirical Tests of the Heat Hypothesis," *Journal of Personality and Social Psychology* 73 (1997): 1213–1223; U.S. Government Printing Office, "Report of the

National Advisory Commission on Civil Disorders" (Washington, DC, 1968), p. 71.

⁴⁹R. A. Baron and P. A. Bell, "Aggression and Heat: The Influence of Ambient Temperature, Negative Affect, and a Cooling Drink on Physical Aggression," *Journal of Personality and Social Psychology* 33 (1976): 245–255; R. A. Baron and P. A. Bell, "Aggression and Heat: Mediating Effects of Prior Provocation and Exposure to an Aggressive Model," *Journal of Personality and Social Psychology* 31 (1975): 825–832.

⁵⁰See: R. Sommer, *Tight Spaces* (Englewood Cliffs, NJ: Prentice-Hall, 1974); R. Sommer, *Personal Space* (Englewood Cliffs, NJ: Prentice-Hall, 1969); R. Sommer, *Design Awareness* (San Francisco: Rinehart Press, 1972); O. Newman, *Defensible Space* (New York: Macmillan, 1973); M. L. Knapp, *Nonverbal Communication in Human Interaction* (New York: Holt, Rinehart & Winston, 1978), pp. 94–97; A. Mehrabian, *Public Places and Private Spaces* (New York: Holt, Rinehart & Winston, 1973), pp. 162–165.

⁵¹G. W. Evans and J. M. McCoy, "When Buildings Don't Work: The Role of Architecture in Human Health," *Journal of Environmental Psychology* 18 (1998): 85–94.

⁵²R. Kuller and C. Lindsten, "Health and Behavior of Children in Classrooms With and Without Windows," *Journal of Environmental Psychology* 12 (1992): 305–317.

⁵³A related schema for analyzing *situations* (a broader concept than settings) was advanced by Altman and Taylor. Their framework includes: situational formality, situational confinement, and situational interdependence. Cf. I. Altman and D. A. Taylor, *Social Penetration* (New York: Holt, Rinehart & Winston, 1973), pp. 162–165. Other more recent reviews and conceptualizations of social situations include M. Argyle, A. Furnham, and J. A. Graham, *Social Situations* (Cambridge, MA: Cambridge University Press, 1981); L. C. Miller, M. J. Cody, and M. L. McLaughlin, "The Situations and Goals as Fundamental Constructs in Interpersonal Communication Research." In M. L. Knapp and G. R. Miller, eds., *Handbook of Interpersonal Communication* 2nd ed., (Beverly Hills, CA: Sage, 1994), pp. 162–198.

⁵⁴L. B. Wexner, "The Degree to Which Colors (Hues) Are Associated with Mood-tones," *Journal of Applied Psychology* 38 (1954): 432–435. See also D. C. Murray and H. L. Deabler, "Colors and Mood-Tones," *Journal of Applied Psychology* 41 (1957): 279–283.

⁵⁵A. H. Maslow and N. L. Mintz, "Effects of Esthetic Surroundings: I. Initial Effects of Three Esthetic Conditions upon Perceiving 'Energy' and 'Well-Being' in Faces," *Journal of Psychology* 41 (1956): 247–254. See also N. L. Mintz, "Effects of Esthetic Surroundings: II. Prolonged and Repeated Experiences in a 'Beautiful' and 'Ugly' Room," *Journal of Psychology* 41 (1956): 459–466.

⁵⁶P. B. Harris, B. B. Brown, and C. M. Werner, "Privacy Regulation and Place Attachment: Predicting Attachments to a Student Family Housing Facility," *Journal of Environmental Psychology* 16 (1996): 287–301; C. M. Werner, I. Altman, and B. B. Brown, "A Transactional Approach to Interpersonal Relations: Physical Environment, Social Context and Temporal Qualities," *Journal of Social and Personal Relationships* 9 (1992): 297–323.

⁵⁷D. M. Pedersen, "Psychological Functions of Privacy," *Journal of Environmental Psychology* 17 (1997): 147–156.

⁵⁸I. Altman, *Environment and Social Behavior: Privacy, Personal Space, Territory and Crowding* (New York: Irvington Press, 1975); I. Altman, "A Personal Perspective on the Environment and Behavior Field." In R. M. Downs, L. S. Liben, and D. S. Palermo, eds., *Visions of Aesthetics, the Environment and Development: The Legacy of Joachim F. Wohlwill* (Hillsdale, NJ: Erlbaum, 1991), pp. 113–138; S. Petronio "Communication Boundary Management: A Theoretical Model of Managing Disclosure of Private Information between Marital Couples," *Communication Theory* 1 (1991): 311–335.

⁵⁹U. Ritterfeld and G. C. Cupchik, "Perceptions of Interior Spaces," *Journal of Environmental Psychology* 16 (1996): 349–360.

⁶⁰D. A. Taylor, I. Altman, and R. Sorrentino, "Interpersonal Exchange as a Function of Rewards and Costs and Situational Factors: Expectancy Confirmation-Disconfirmation," *Journal of Experimental Social Psychology* 5 (1969): 324–339.

⁶¹J. R. Aiello, "Human Spatial Behavior." In D. Stokols and I. Altman, eds., *Handbook of Environmental Psychology* (New York: John Wiley & Sons, 1987), pp. 389–504.

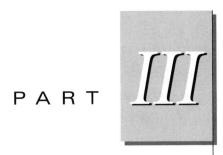

PART **III**

Interaction Patterns for Coming Together

5

The Genesis of Dialogue

Dear Dr. Knapp,

I've been dating this guy and I really enjoy his company. The problem is that we are very different people with very different views on things. For example, he is a "bleeding heart liberal" and I'm a "closed-minded conservative"; he has a Ph.D. in math and I took my one mandatory math class just hoping to get my B.A.; he is militant about cigarette smoking and I don't really care. From big to little issues we seem to be different. At first we ignored the differences, but now that the relationship is getting more intense, we have started to discuss them. Neither of us particularly wants to change or have the other person change. So my question is, what is the chance of us being able to move ahead in our relationship? We're obviously attracted to each other for reasons other than similarities—why do we like each other so much? In the long run, will these differences overrule all the other compatible/good aspects of our relationship?

Wondering if It Will Work

This chapter does not list any human characteristics that will invariably predict relationship success or failure. It does discuss why people get together and how they go about sizing each other up. Perhaps an understanding of these processes may be helpful in setting realistic expectations for how predictable our perceptions of others can be.

> *Getting to know someone, entering that new world is an ultimate, irretrievable leap into the unknown. The prospect is terrifying. The stakes are high. The emotions are overwhelming.*
> —Eldridge Cleaver

To give birth to an encounter is to give life to a relationship. Like the birth of a child, the first moments in the life of a relationship are often critical in determining the length and quality of its life. Psychiatrist Leonard Zunin feels that the first four minutes of interaction with a stranger may well be the most crucial time in determining whether an encounter-relationship will blossom or die. Furthermore, he argues that the quality of a married couple's relationship can generally be predicted by assessing the interaction during the first four minutes after the couple is reunited following a working day.[1] Whether the critical time frame is four seconds, four minutes, or fourteen minutes is not nearly as important as the knowledge that these early moments of coming together may have a significant impact on the communication and relationship that follows.

Like the birth of a baby, some relationships are delivered easily—even routinely; others are wrought with complications. Perhaps it is an understanding of these potential complications and important consequences of initial interaction that often causes us to enter first encounters with feelings of apprehension, uncertainty, and cautious anticipation. Even the first few moments with a friend are charged with some uncertainties: Were there events that may have profoundly affected either of your lives since you were last together and that may alter the original basis for the friendship? What is the friend's present mood? The stress often associated with new encounters causes some people to avoid them like the plague. However, avoidance of encounters with new and unfamiliar people is increasingly difficult in a mobile, high-tech society which requires more and more time to be spent at the early stages of developing relationships. And, as we pointed out in Chapter 2, most relationships do not advance beyond the experimenting stage.

Given the importance and the inescapable frequency of these early phases, we can now address ourselves to the central question for this chapter: What interpersonal processes are enacted when we first come together with other people? The obvious point of departure is to consider the question of why people come together in the first place.

Getting Together

Sometimes people deliberately set out to find a relationship partner, but usually the initial period of relationship development does not involve much prior planning.

Instead, relationships spring to life because people are in proximity to other people. What brings people into contact with other people?

Davis has identified four human *impulses* that seem to push people together: (1) the impulse to receive stimulation; (2) the impulse to express experiences; (3) the impulse to assert oneself; and (4) the impulse to enhance enjoyment of certain activities.[2] While this may not be a comprehensive list, it goes a long way toward answering our question of why people come together.

The Impulse to Receive Stimulation

Many times we seek encounters with others simply to get excitement, variety, or a change of pace from an existence which may be temporarily stale. Such conditions may arise when one has few social contacts—single people, older people—or many social contacts. In the latter case, one may feel conditions are overly familiar or repetitive. "All we seem to do is go to the same places, talk to the same people about the same old things." In the United States, certain time periods seem more apt to trigger this impulse for stimulation—Sundays are a particularly good example. Another is spring, when reruns begin and certain TV addicts seem to socially "come out of the walls."

The Impulse to Express Experiences

A divorced friend of the senior author recently spent the better part of an hour telling him how great it was to be alone and how much he enjoyed the solitude. The author was struck by the fact that possibly a large part of this person's satisfaction with solitude was due to the fact that he had a friend to whom he could relate this experience. Each of us has a reservoir of private experiences that at some point must overflow onto others. Usually we'll try to find specific others who will provide protection, comfort, and security for unpleasant private experiences and who will increase our enjoyment of pleasant experiences. There is a great deal of wisdom in the oft-stated belief that the most intolerable form of punishment is total isolation from human contact. Part of the impulse to express experiences is motivated by a desire to discover how they compare with the experiences of others—the subject of the next section.

The Impulse to Assert Oneself

No matter how we choose to define it, our identity, or our self, is largely the result of testing its potential components against other people.[3] We know ourselves by knowing others, by what they think of us and say to us. Sure, we sometimes talk to ourselves and test out ideas and feelings on our own imagination, but without social comparison we quickly lose our perspective for efficient daily interaction. Each of us has to feel we have some influence or control over our psycho-social environment. Our ability to assert some control and to fulfill our goals affects the way we interpret our social world.[4] Researchers have found that those who do not believe they have such control tend to also feel that they have fewer social relationships than they would like—they are lonely in comparison to other people.[5] The only way for these and other people to develop a sense of control and to measure their social impact is to seek out the actions and ideas of others.

When we find ourselves in a situation where our feelings or environment are confusing, ambiguous, or changeable, the need for social contact and comparison increases dramatically. We are simply trying to reduce the uncertainties surrounding us—trying to make sense out of our world. The anguish felt by one of our students whose father died subsided considerably after she discussed her feelings with other students who had also experienced the death of a parent. It wasn't long before she said to us, "I realize that I'm in much better shape than a lot of people I've talked to, so I've started counseling them." Without knowing it, many of the people this student had talked to provided her with an indirect form of social support. By asserting herself and comparing herself to others, she realized that her situation was not as bad as it could be. Our initial interaction with strangers also reflects how we try to reduce the uncertainty of who they are—"Where are you from?" "What do you do?" "Do you know somebody I know?" It is not as necessary to seek encounters with others when the object of our testing is some physical reality—"Is the sun shining?"—but attitudes, values, and beliefs demand testing in the social arena.

Schachter's classic experiment illustrates how induced anxiety or fear may cause individuals to come together in an attempt to reduce their uncertainties.[6] Some female undergraduates were brought to a laboratory for the alleged purpose of serving as subjects in an experiment dealing with the physiological effects of electric shock. Some subjects were told the shocks would be extremely painful, but "would do no permanent tissue damage." Other subjects were told the shocks would be mild, resembling a tickle or a tingle. While the equipment was supposedly being prepared, the girls were asked to wait in another room. When given the choice of waiting alone or with others, two-thirds of the women in the high-fear treatment group wanted to wait with others; two-thirds of the women in the low-fear group chose to wait alone or said they didn't care what room they waited in. A follow-up study indicated the high-fear subjects did not want to wait with just anybody; they wanted to wait with subjects in their own treatment group. As Schachter observed: "Misery doesn't love just any kind of company, just miserable company." This finding held true even when subjects were not allowed to speak to one another. Just the presence of others and the observation of nonverbal cues seemed to be enough to provide information on how others were reacting, and how it compared with one's own feelings. It should be noted that fear accompanied by the thought that you might be forced to reveal some threatening emotion will likely keep people apart rather than bring them together.

The Impulse to Enhance Enjoyment of Certain Activities

Sometimes the desire to encounter others is associated with an event or an activity that is more fun with others than alone. There may be times when Auto-Bridge or Auto-Monopoly or eating Thanksgiving dinner alone is enjoyable, but usually the participation of others enhances the pleasure. As Davis so aptly stated: "It's hard to be festive alone."

Now that we have some idea of the general impulses that bring people together, we should note that there are certain conditions that facilitate and/or impede the initiation of communication with others. This is not to say that people are typically conscious of these conditions. Most times, we meet and talk with others without thinking about the surrounding circumstances. Our failure to carefully consider these circumstances, however, doesn't prevent them from affecting our relationships. For instance, one of the most important facilitators of social interaction is having something in common. But researchers argue that we often base our selection of romantic partners on infatuation rather than on a careful assessment of the commonalities we have with potential partners.[7] Even though we may not analyze these similarities, they can affect our relationships. The list of things that people may discover in others and consider to be important commonalities is almost endless. A few examples will suffice.

Before you even meet the other person you may find out things about him or her that are also true of you—religion, birthplace, age, sex, group membership (a sociology student), race, attitudinal orientation (liberal), interests (collecting rhinos). These things can be uncovered by a common acquaintance, a newspaper story, a computer web site, a dating service, or a host of other sources. Perhaps you have had previous interaction with this person and found him or her socially attractive. Whether you discover these commonalities beforehand or during the interaction, they will facilitate the initiation or duration of an encounter. Other commonalities may be derived from a common interest in an activity that facilitates the encounter—you both like to play handball. The very fact that you are in the same setting (exposed to the same stimuli) with another person may suggest certain commonalities—a singles bar or the site of a tornado disaster. Or the encounter may be facilitated by a common friend. Sometimes a third person or object provides the catalyst for an encounter—a stalled car or a petition that needs signatures. When this added stimulus has unusual features, it may literally beg for comment. A cast on your arm or leg or some unusual hair style may provide the focus for that often elusive opening line, and walking your pet vulture around the block on a leash would be hard for neighbors to ignore. Obviously, people can also meet by accident—literally. More than one relationship which led to marriage has started when "we just bumped into each other on the street."

Interestingly, the aforementioned facilitators can also impede coming together. There are many instances where this happens. You and another person may both enjoy a common activity, but the activity itself may have certain sanctions against interacting—chess tournaments or attending the symphony. Two very career-oriented individuals may not take the time away from their work to participate in social gatherings. Similarly, two people who are very shy may both avoid social interaction because of the anxiety it causes them. Even if they are not shy, people who are attracted to each other may both decide against "making the first move" because they are both worried about being rejected.[8] At a party, a female may find a great deal in common with an attractive male only to discover later that he is holding hands with another male. Same group membership may also work against coming together; you may not even want to associate with a person in the same group—living in a small university town and desperately wanting to find acquaintances who are not affiliated with the university. Unusual features may also act as barriers to encounters—having some sort of physical handicap, wearing a wedding ring to a singles bar, or reading *Penthouse* in church.[9]

> *At the moment of meeting, parting begins.*
> Patrick Hughes and George Brecht

The process of determining whether a given stimulus is a facilitator or a barrier to an encounter involves establishing your individual criteria for coming together with others. In essence, you are asking yourself whether this person has the characteristics that will make it worthwhile to initiate an encounter. Do the location, the appearance, and behavior of the other and your own mood and purposes suggest an encounter is desirable at this time? Will you have to expend a great deal of energy on this encounter—never to see the person again? Will the other person define the encounter as legitimate under those circumstances? In order to understand more fully some of the things we consider when processing these questions, we need to look at the process of person perception.

Sizing Up the Other Person

The process of perceiving other people is rarely translated (to ourselves or others) into cold, objective terms. "She was 5 feet 8 inches tall, had blonde hair, and wore a plaid skirt." More often, we try to get inside the other person to pinpoint his or her attitudes, emotions, motivations, abilities, ideas, perceptions, and traits. Although research suggests that our methods for assessing others' feelings and behaviors are usually quite imprecise,[10] we sometimes behave as if we can accomplish this difficult maneuver almost instantaneously—perhaps with a two-second glance.[11]

We try to obtain information about others in many ways. Berger suggests several methods for reducing uncertainties about others: unobtrusively watching a person interacting with others, particularly with others who are known to you so you can compare the observed person's behavior with the known others' behavior; observing a person in a situation where social behavior is relatively uninhibited or where a wide variety of behavioral responses are called for; deliberately structuring the physical or social environment so as to observe the person's responses to specific stimuli; asking people who have had or have frequent contact with the person about him or her; and using various strategies in face-to-face interaction to uncover information about another person—questions, self-disclosures, and so on.[12] A study by Miell and Duck demonstrated that of these, the most common strategies people said they used to gather information about one another included asking direct questions, observing each other, and using reciprocal self-disclosure. These respondents also said that they sometimes provoked their conversational partners to discover the partners' true feelings and opinions on a given issue.[13]

Berger and Kellermann note that strategies such as these may be viewed as plans for reaching social goals. When our social goals involve obtaining information about another person, we may also have a number of higher level goals that influence our choice of strategies.[14] For instance, the higher level goal of social appropriateness may prevent us from asking new acquaintances about their age, income, or sexual preferences—even if we would like to obtain that information. Getting to know someone is a never-ending task, largely because people are constantly changing and the methods we use to obtain information are often imprecise. You may have known someone for ten years and still know very little about him or her. If we accept the idea that we won't ever fully know another person, it enables us to deal more easily with those things that get in the way of accurate knowledge such as secrets and deceptions. It will also keep us from being too surprised or shocked by seemingly inconsistent behavior. Ironically, those things that keep us from knowing another person too well (e.g., secrets and deceptions) may be just as important to the development of a satisfying relationship as those things that enable us to obtain accurate knowledge about a person (e.g., disclosures and truthful statements).

Why Perceptions Differ

When several different people look at the same person, it is not unusual for each of them to see different things; when you alone observe one behavior or one person at two different times, you may see different things. The following are but some of the factors that contribute to these varying perceptions:

1. Each person's perceptions of others are structured by his or her own cultural conditioning, education, and personal experiences. Adults teach children what they think are the critical dimensions to look for in other people.[15] In the United States individuals are trained to develop their auditory and visual sensors and to pay less attention to information that could be obtained from touching or smelling. As an individual, a person may have had previous experiences with tall, powerful, red-headed males that cause him or her to recoil in fear. The experiences of another may cause him or her to see the same person as a good lover, a warm and gentle person, a dull person, a dogmatic person, an athlete, etc.

2. Sometimes perceptions differ because of what we choose to observe and how we process what we've observed. It is not necessarily true that person perception is based on observations of a particular person. Your observations may be totally dominated by what others have told you about this person, or you may focus primarily on the situation or role relationships. Most people do not use the same yardstick to measure their parents, their friends, and strangers. It is often difficult to see our own children or spouses as others do. An aggressive child may be perceived very differently at home by his or her parents than by a stranger when the child displays the same behavior. We do not mentally process everything we observe. There are moments when we will look for, see, respond to, and interpret a particular set of cues and other times when the same cues will go unnoticed or will be disregarded. Even when two people attend to the same cluster of cues and receive the same impressions, the language used to express these impressions may be sufficiently different to suspect different perceptions.

3. Sometimes we see only what we want to see or don't see what may be obvious to others because of our own needs, desires, or temporary emotional states. This is a process known as *selective perception*. Selective perception is obviously more difficult when contradictory information is particularly vivid, but it can be done. We can ignore the stimulus—"He's basically a good boy, so what I saw was not shoplifting." We can reduce the importance of the contradictory information— "All kids get into mischief. Taking a comic book from the drugstore isn't such a big deal." We can change the meaning of the contradictory information—"It wasn't shoplifting, because he was going to pay for it later." We can reinterpret previously observed traits to fit the contradictory information—"I can see now how he tried to manipulate and use me. He ran errands for me so I wouldn't report his shoplifting!" Or we can infer new traits—"I still think he's a kind and pleasant kid, but he doesn't seem to be very honest or dependable." In each attempt to deal with seemingly contradictory information, an effort was made to see the boy's behavior as making sense.

When we learn that an old childhood acquaintance has been charged with a mass murder, we may selectively recall a variety of behaviors and incidents that were relatively unimportant to our previous image of this person, but will now help to explain the new image.[16] Factors such as how much time has passed and what our role was in the situation influence the sorts of memories we develop.[17] And there will always be some who, after reconstructing the past, must say: "I always *knew* something like this would happen." Encountering people who are consistently puzzling to us probably leads us to terminate association with them.

In view of these and other factors affecting our perception of others, it is difficult to isolate those characteristics that typify an accurate perceiver or a good judge of other people. While no definitive conclusions from empirical research can be made at this time, the following characteristics have been explored and seem to be possessed by a good judge: breadth of personal experience, ability to process complex stimuli and complex relationships, intelligence, self-insight (seeing and accepting both positive and negative qualities in oneself), and the ability to assume a detached role, like a third-person observer. Certainly it is not a single skill that makes a person a good judge of others. Vernon was probably right when he said that some people are good at knowing themselves; others at understanding their friends; and still others are most accurate in judging strangers.[18] Each procedure seems to involve different perceptual and cognitive operations and few of us are good at all three.

What are these mental gyrations we perform when perceiving others? Several related theories will help us understand how we form impressions of others.

The Processes of Perceiving Others

While it may seem logical that our impressions of others are based on the sum of all we know about them, research and actual experience would suggest that our impressions are often more. In the 1940s Soloman Asch advanced the idea that we organize individual traits to form a whole and this Gestalt impression affects the judgment we make on each individual trait.[19] In short, this theory suggests that if we assess the totality of another person as negative, this will negatively affect our perceptions of individual traits associated with this person.

Kelley's experiment illustrates this concept by showing how the identification of a person as either "warm" or "cold" can affect a wide range of perceptions.[20] Half of Kelley's class received this description of a new instructor who would teach their class:

> Mr. _____ is a graduate student in the Department of Economics and Social Science here at M.I.T. He has had three semesters of teaching experience in psychology at another college. This is his first semester teaching Economics 70. He is 26 years old, a veteran and married. People who know him consider him to be a rather warm person, industrious, critical, practical, and determined.

The other half of the class received the exact same description with the exception of the word *warm,* which was changed to *cold.* A class discussion with the new instructor followed. After the instructor left, the class evaluated him. Those who were told he was warm rated him as significantly more considerate, informal, sociable, popular, good-natured, humorous, and humane than those who were told he was cold. During the actual class discussion only 32 percent of those who felt he was cold participated; 56 percent of those who saw him as warm interacted with him.

As an outgrowth of this work on *central traits,* it was proposed that all human beings operate with an *implicit personality theory.* This simply means that each of us has a mental catalogue of traits in our head. As soon as we obtain information on one trait or a cluster of traits, we seem to assume automatically that other traits will also be characteristic of the person being observed. Given this mental matrix, the knowledge that someone is warm or cold may or may not change our impression of the person, depending on how we weigh and interrelate the characteristics of warmth or cold with other perceived characteristics.[21]

Suppose we told you we were going to fix you up with a blind date who was: very good looking, rich, intelligent, blunt, and independent. How would you assess this person on the following characteristics?

Cautious	_____	or	_____	Rash
Reliable	_____	or	_____	Unreliable
Generous	_____	or	_____	Stingy
Considerate	_____	or	_____	Inconsiderate
Short	_____	or	_____	Tall
Successful	_____	or	_____	Unsuccessful
Conventional	_____	or	_____	Eccentric
Humble	_____	or	_____	Proud
Self-Respecting	_____	or	_____	Servile
Sincere	_____	or	_____	Insincere
Kind	_____	or	_____	Cruel
Quiet	_____	or	_____	Talkative
Romantic	_____	or	_____	Unromantic

How do your answers compare with others'? When regularities are found in person perception, it might be due to an implicit personality theory derived from being a member of this contemporary United States culture. However, there is also evidence to suggest that individuals have rather stable implicit personality theories of their own which may not be grounded in a particular culture. For example, research shows that some people believe personality traits are relatively fixed (unlikely to change), whereas other people see traits as more malleable (likely to change). In at least two different cultures, those who saw personality traits as fixed tended to make stronger predictions about others' behavior (e.g., "She is shy, so she probably won't go to the party") than did those who saw the traits as malleable (e.g., "She is shy, but she still might like to go to the party")[22] People whose implicit theories suggest that personality traits are fixed tend to make more extreme judgments about individuals and groups than do those who believe personality traits are likely to change.[23]

As human beings we each have a need for structuring our world and for finding invariant properties in people so that they can be organized and classified. It would be literally impossible to function socially if we tried to react to each individual stimulus as a separate and unique aspect of our world, in spite of the fact that it probably is. Instead, we choose to say it is often a "difference that doesn't make a difference" and engage in what we know as stereotyping. Stereotyping is a way of simplifying our environment so that we can handle it. Sometimes we *stereotype inductively,* which is inferring personality or group membership on the basis of specific features—height, skin color, vocal resonance, or baldness. Other times we *stereotype deductively:* We start with a more abstract category like group membership or personality and infer specific features—"If he's Jewish, he must have a big nose." Of course, while stereotyping simplifies our social environment and makes our lives more manageable, it can also create more problems. Stereotyping shapes the inferences we make about other people.[24] It affects the type of questions we ask when seeking information about others.[25] Unless we are careful, our stereotypes can prevent us from meeting, interacting, and relating to people we might otherwise care a great deal about.

A slightly different, yet related, approach to identifying how we perceive other people is outlined in the following phases of the inference process.[26] Sarbin, Taft, and Bailey suggest that person perception begins with a system of postulates, or premises, within the perceiver—"Team sports require cooperation; cooperative people tend to have many friends." A syllogistic major premise is then derived from this system of postulates—"People who enjoy team sports tend to be cooperative." Then the perceiver searches for and observes occurrences relevant to the major premise—"Jack plays football." The occurrence must then be converted into a general class—"Football is a team sport." The inferential conclusion, then, is that "Jack is probably cooperative" and the perceiver's prediction is that "Jack probably has many friends."

Sometimes we attribute certain characteristics or qualities to others on the basis of their overt actions. *Attribution theory* is concerned with whether a specific behavior is due to a person's personality (typically recurring patterns of behavior) or whether it is due to the situation or circumstances impinging on the person. Jumping up in the air and giving a "V for victory" sign is certainly appropriate behavior for a cheerleader at a sporting event, but it would seem rather odd as the result of having pointed out a fallacy in your partner's reasoning during cocktail party chatter. Sometimes when we perceive a person's behavior as a deviation from the norms, we consider it as a reflection on his or her personality—he or she did it out of choice rather than in response to constraints of the situation. Sometimes, of course, it is just the opposite; we see more conventional behavior as "typical" of that person while norm violations are seen as "called for by the circumstances." A number of researchers have found that we tend to interpret our own behavior in more positive, generous ways than we do others' behavior. For instance, in performing a task, we sometimes take credit for successful task outcomes, but blame circumstances or other people for failures. This tendency to enhance outcomes associated with our own behavior is called the *self-serving bias*. Although a great deal of research supports the idea that we sometimes engage in the self-serving bias, studies also suggest that we are less likely to do so when it means blaming someone we care about for a failure.[27] Our knowledge of other people and our attitudes toward them affect the judgments we make. Taking those findings a step further, when we are confronted with what seems to be another's undesirable behavior, we probably look for a situational cause. If we can't find a plausible situational cause, then we probably attribute the negative behavior to that individual's personality, and with even more confidence than we would attribute positive behaviors to his or her personality. Studies conducted with individuals who are involved in ongoing relationships reveal another interesting finding. The causal judgments that we make about our partners depend, in part, on how satisfied we are with our relationship. When we are happy with a relationship, we are more likely to attribute our partner's positive behaviors to his or her personality ("She's being polite because she's a wonderful person") and negative behaviors to situational factors ("She's acting irritable because she had a bad day at work"). On the other hand, when we are distressed or unhappy with a relationship, we will use situational factors to explain positive behaviors ("She's only being polite because we have guests over.") and personality variables to explain negative behaviors ("She's acting irritable because she's an inconsiderate person").[28]

As for attributions about our own behavior, we seem to be even more likely to accept situational explanations with the passage of time. With time we also seem to see our own behavior as more similar to others—e.g., "I guess I'm more like my Dad than I ever thought I'd be." Apparently, two things happen as time passes: (1) we tend to consider more of the potentially influential features of a situation on our behavior; and (2) we may have less need to be seen as a person who had control over the situational influences which may have affected our behavior.[29]

Generally, then, we seem more prone to attribute the actions of others to more enduring dispositions and discount situational demands. This tendency to overestimate the influence of dispositional factors and underestimate the role of situational factors in others' behavior is called the *fundamental attribution error*. The reason we often make this error is obvious. If a behavior is part of a person's personality, it is carried from situation to situation and, hence, our predictions about this person are made considerably easier. Although a large amount of research seems to confirm this human predisposition for consistency in judging others, its application to everyday communicative events may be blown out of proportion. For example, some have noted that conversational norms (rather than a tendency to disregard situational cues) contribute to biases in our attributional judgments.[30] Our assumptions about how we are supposed to respond to and interpret questions about others may create biases in our attributional statements.[31] The mood we are in when we interpret others' behavior affects the types of attributions we make.[32] In addition, the artificial conditions and the strong constraints on subjects to be "logical" in most of these experiments may have influenced the findings.[33]

Seeing or Hearing Yourself in Others

We cannot divorce ourselves from the process of person perception. We are at the same time both the observer and the observed, inextricably a part of our own observations. What I think that you think of me reverberates back to what I think of myself. What I think of myself, in turn, affects the way I act toward you. The way I act toward you, in turn, influences how you feel toward yourself and the way you act toward me, etc. Laing, Phillipson, and Lee show how this *spiral of reciprocal perspectives* can operate:

> Jack feels Jill is greedy. Jill feels Jack is mean. That is, Jack feels Jill wants too much from him whereas Jill feels Jack does not give her enough. Moreover, Jack feels that Jill is mean as well as greedy. And Jill feels that Jack is greedy as well as mean. Each feels that the other has and is withholding what he or she needs. Moreover, Jack does not feel he is either greedy or mean himself, nor does Jill. Jack, however, realizes that Jill thinks he is mean, and Jill realizes that Jack thinks she is greedy. In view of the fact that Jack feels he is already overgenerous, he resents being regarded as mean. In view of the fact that Jill feels she puts up with so little, she resents being regarded as greedy. Since Jack feels generous but realizes that Jill thinks he is mean, and since Jill feels deprived and realizes that Jack thinks she is greedy, each resents the other and retaliates. If, after all I've put up with, you feel that I'm greedy, then I'm not going to be so forbearing in the future. If, after all I've given you, you feel I'm mean, then you're not getting anything from me anymore. The circle is whirling and becomes increasingly vicious. Jack becomes increasingly exhausted by Jill's greed and Jill becomes increasingly starved by Jack's meanness. Greed and meanness are now so confused in and between each and both that they appear to take on a life of their own. Like two boxers dominated by the fight that they are themselves fighting, the dyad, the system, the marriage, becomes "the problem" to each of the persons who comprise it, rather than they themselves.[34]

By the nature of human interaction, we are a part of what we are observing. Sometimes, however, we explicitly project our own qualities on others; after all, if the trait is worth being a part of us, it must be true of others—"Everyone is dishonest; it's only human." It is possible, of course, to reverse the process and see characteristics opposite from our own in others—"I may be tough, but most people are spineless." Thus, the needs, values, and desires of the perceiver help to structure and become a part of the perception. Why?

Well, sometimes we are so tuned in to looking for certain aspects of another person, we focus only on those things that will fulfill our current needs. If you see a potential marriage partner only as a "good lay," it may be due to the fact that you are so focused on one dimension, you ignore other potentially important characteristics of the person. In the same manner, we may allow our own needs to magnify or accentuate the characteristics of the other person. We may see available sex partners as somehow sexier than others; fear may cause "people who are out to get me" to appear everywhere.

Perceptual distortion caused by the perceiver's inner drives is particularly evident in the early stages of infatuation. H. L. Mencken called this condition *perceptual anesthesia*. Of course, it doesn't help matters that our partner might try to present only the side that he or she feels we want to see. Bach and Deutsch provide a vivid illustration of this interaction between: (1) seeing what your own needs demand you see, and (2) presenting yourself to others as you would most like to be seen.

The introduction of this couple takes place at a public camera club that also serves as a singles meeting place. He is an old member, and she is new. . . .

They Say	*They Think*
He: Well, you're certainly a welcome addition to our group.	*Can't I ever say something clever?*
She: Thank you. It certainly is friendly and interesting.	*He's cute.*
He: My friends call me Stretch. It's left over from my basketball days. Silly, but I'm used to it.	*It's safer than saying my name is David Stein.*
She: My name is Candy.	*At least my nickname is. He doesn't have to hear Hortense O'Brien.*
Stretch: What kind of camera is that?	*Why couldn't a girl named Candy be Jewish? It's only a nickname, isn't it?*
Candy: Just this old German one of my uncle's. I borrowed it from the office.	*He could be Irish. And that camera looks expensive.*
Stretch: May I? (He takes her camera, brushing her hand and then tingling with the touch.) Fine lens. You work for your uncle?	*Now I've done it. Brought up work.*

They Say	*They Think*
Candy: Ever since college.	*So okay, what if I only went for one year?*
It's more than being just a secretary. I get into sales, too.	*If he asks what I sell, I'll tell him anything except underwear.*
Stretch: Sales? That's funny. I'm in sales, too, but mainly as an executive. I run our department.	*Is there a nice way to say used cars? I'd better change the subject.*
I started using cameras on trips. Last time it was in the Bahamas. I took—	*Great legs! And the way her hips move—*
Candy: Oh! Do you go to the Bahamas, too? I love those islands.	*So I went there just once, and it was for the brassiere manufacturers convention. At least we're off the subject of jobs.*
Stretch:	*She's probably really been around. Well, at least we're off the subject of jobs.*
I did a little underwater work there last summer. Fantastic colors. So rich in life.	*And lonelier than hell.*
Candy:	*Look at that build. He must swim like a fish. I should learn.*
I wish I'd had time when I was there. I love the water.	*Well, I do. At the beach, anyway. There I can wade in and not go too deep.*

In just a few minutes, these two have set a pattern of imaging from which it is going to be hard to retreat. After the meeting, they have a drink and talk until the bar closes, matching, matching, and matching—politics, tastes in clothes, houses, cars, all the impersonal things. Their similarity in height gives them a sense of destined sameness that makes them feel as a unit apart from the world. They forget the world. They go to his apartment, and the sex is so good that they feel very bound to each other.

They spend the weekend together, and by the time it is over they both feel they are in love, and say so. It is the electric magic. It is a fairytale, a dream realized. They are enchanted. They ask few questions of one another, for they do not want to commit themselves to specific answers.

One of the matters they scrupulously avoid is religion. . . .[35]

It was easy to see that "things aren't always what they seem to be" in the get-acquainted dialogue of Candy and Stretch. But it is worth noting that the "things aren't always what they seem to be" phenomenon continues throughout the life of a relationship. The anger in the yelling and screaming apparently directed at you by your partner may be motivated by your partner's anger with himself or herself; your partner may disclose something very personal to you, but the hidden intent may be to see if this information makes you "squirm" rather than because it would be helpful to the relationship; statements apparently designed to support your ego and compliment you may be insincere; feigned weakness may be an attempt to dominate you.

Thus far, we've emphasized how the insertion of oneself into the process of person perception can distort our image of the other person. The disadvantages of such distortions are clear, but on occasion advantages may also accrue. For instance, if you need affection and you underestimate a person's liking for you, you may be extremely happy at the slightest show of interest or acceptance—and, you might not be as disappointed if you are rejected. Similarly, overestimating a person's liking for you may cause you to exert a great deal of energy for that person. That exertion, in turn, may elicit increased liking from your partner.

We can change reality by changing our perceptions; it can work for us or against us. Once again we see the relationship between our initial perceptions, our behavior based on these perceptions, the impact of our behavior on the other person's perceptions and behavior, and our subsequent perceptions based on the responses of the other person. When this cycle, or *chain of reciprocal events,* is structured (usually unconsciously) in such a way that the other person's response possibilities are limited to actions that will only reaffirm initial perceptions, we have a phenomenon Merton called the *self-fulfilling prophecy.*[36] In short, we begin with a false definition of another person, behave toward this person as if our definition were true, and eventually elicit new behavior from the other person which makes the original perception seem true.[37] For instance, I may see you as a very threatening person. Since I cannot trust you and feel that you might cause me harm, I buy a gun to protect myself. You find out that I bought a gun which causes your feelings of insecurity to skyrocket. As a result, you also buy a gun. As soon as I find out you have a gun, it is easy for me to proudly state that my first impression was indeed accurate—you can't be trusted and you pose a definite threat to my welfare. My impression of you has been proven by a self-proving mechanism.

Finally, it should be noted that many of our perceptions of others may have an optimistic bias in them.[38] Apparently many of us are inclined to see the good, the pleasant, and the positive to a far greater extent than we see the less pleasant things. Consider the following findings which Matlin and Stang cite to support the existence of a *Pollyanna Principle.*[39]

- People tend to evaluate other people—students, instructors, strangers—positively.
- Most people describe themselves as optimists, claiming that their present mood is positive, and that their lives are happy at work and at home.

- The average person rates himself or herself as "better than average," even though this is mathematically impossible.

- People judge pleasant events to be more likely to occur than unpleasant events, even when the actual probabilities are equivalent.

- Even when people have seen pleasant and neutral stimuli equally often, they report that the pleasant stimuli were more frequent.

- People remember events as more pleasant with the passage of time.

- People overestimate the importance of pleasant events and underestimate the importance of unpleasant events.

- In a free-association task, people produce a greater number of responses to pleasant stimuli, and they produce them more quickly. Further they recall the responses to pleasant stimuli more accurately.

The reasons why these behaviors occur is not entirely clear, but if we are affected by our observations of others, we may simply be trying to create a positive social environment for ourselves. Looking forward to people and events with the expectation that they will be positive may bring about a self-fulfilling prophecy in some cases where the outcome may have otherwise been less positive. On the other hand, optimism that is grossly unwarranted and unrealistic may cause others to see you as socially inept and out of touch with reality. Although we tend to perceive most of our life events in a positive light, a number of researchers have found that when forming initial impressions of others we tend to weight negative events and characteristics more heavily than positive ones.[40] Initially, many researchers explained this *negativity effect* by noting that negative events and characteristics may be the most informative. Since we believe that most events are positive, negative events are seen as relatively rare. Therefore, when negative events occur, we assume that they will provide us with more information than we usually receive.[41] More recent research on initial interaction, however, has demonstrated that this may not be the case. Negativity alone does not seem to predict how informative an event or characteristic is. Instead, *typicality* (i.e., how unusual an event or characteristic is) seems to be the more important factor. When we observe something that is atypical or unusual in an initial interaction, it stands out in our mind—we tend to remember it and use it in forming our first impressions of others.[42]

First and Last Impressions

Most of us realize how critical first impressions can be. We try to "get off to a good start" when we meet others by presenting ourselves in the best possible light. Unless we have a good supply of friends and really don't care what happens to our relationship with a new person, it is risky business to say: "I don't care what people think of me at first. Let them see my shortcomings right off the bat. Eventually, this strategy will lead to a better relationship." Because first impressions are often so important, this strategy may lead nowhere. Research and everyday observations confirm the fact that first impressions are often lasting ones.

Asch's work shows how important initial information can be in forming an impression of someone.[43] He asked some people to describe a person who was characterized by the following adjectives: intelligent, industrious, impulsive, critical, stubborn, and envious. Other people were asked to describe a person who was: envious, stubborn, critical, impulsive, industrious, and intelligent. The only difference in the two tasks was the order in which the adjectives appeared. Those who received the description beginning with the word *intelligent* described the person in much more positive terms than those who read the adjective list initiated by the word *envious*. The perceivers apparently created an image based on the early adjectives and proceeded to interpret the remaining adjectives so they would fit the first impression.

While first impressions are obviously important, they can be overdone. You can make yourself look so good that unrealistic expectations are set. This may cause problems later in the relationship as witnessed by the following example:

DOUG: I don't understand why you don't want to take the weekend backpack trip with Hal and Gwen. You know, it's been three months since we've been in the woods or the mountains? I really miss it.

HELEN: Well, I was never that much of an outdoor woman, after all. I mean, I love the scenery, but camping out is pretty hard on a woman. It's different for a man.

DOUG: But don't you remember what you said when we met on that Sierra Club Hike?

HELEN: What did I say: That I loved the scenery? That I loved nature: Of course, I do. But carrying a pack is really exhausting for me.

DOUG: But it seems so much like part of us—being alone in the wilderness. Remember how we slipped away, the two of us? Cooked our meals together? Made love in the open?

HELEN: Well, what do you want me to say?

DOUG: I don't know. You seem different now, somehow. It just isn't the same. That's why I want to get into the mountains with you again, bring it back, bring you back. . . .

Plainly, Helen had allowed Doug to believe that she was far more of an outdoor woman than she actually was. Their initiatory experience had been the kind of thing she was not really prepared to sustain. She had been smitten with Doug, but she had not really been too happy with backpacking and trail living. . . .[44]

The issue of first and last impressions is particularly relevant to the early phases of relationship development because we are receiving so much previously unknown information about the person. But people in long-established relationships also grapple with these decisions when hitherto unknown or seemingly contradictory attitudes, behaviors, or habits are revealed. In some cases, people try to ignore or undermine the new information.[45] But even then, the information influences the way they relate to each other. While the topic of Doug and Helen's conversation dealt with perceptions about past behavior, Doug's impression of Helen's interest in camping out will now affect their current relationship.

There are at least two reasons why first impressions can be so dominant: (1) We have a tendency to want to size up another person quickly in order to reduce any uncertainties. (2) We have a tendency to avoid admitting we made a mistake. This is often done by clinging to our first impression rather than revising our opinion according to recent contradictory information.

In spite of the seeming predominance of first impressions, we do judge others by what they did last. Notice how the following dialogue moves rapidly from potatoes to honesty and from today to "ever since we've known each other."

JOHN: These potatoes are kinda bland.

MARY: That's the way I've always fixed them and you've eaten them before and haven't said anything.

JOHN: I've eaten them, but I haven't always liked 'em.

MARY: For God's sake, John, why don't you tell me when you don't like something? You never seem to be honest with me . . . and it's not just the potatoes either . . . it's a lot of things . . . ever since I've known you, you have kept things from me. . . .

Boxer Muhammad Ali was described as "washed up" when he lost a decision to Ken Norton; shortly thereafter Ali was voted Athlete of the Year when he defeated George Foreman. In turn, George Foreman was considered too old and out of shape after more than a decade of boxing inactivity. This changed as soon as he regained the heavyweight championship at age 45. It is not uncommon that last actions are considered most important when they represent a dramatic reversal from a previous impression or there is a compelling reason to believe your first impression was inaccurate.

Obviously, the question of whether we will base our perceptions of another on *primary* (first impressions) or *recency* (last actions) cannot be fully answered unless we know which traits we see as susceptible to change and which traits we see as permanent. It's the difference between "once a cheat, always a cheat" and "sure he cheated in college, but look what he's done lately—he's a U.S. Senator."

The Many Faces of Attraction

While the previous section dealt primarily with the process of perceiving others, it should be clear that one aspect of sizing up another person is deciding whether we are attracted to that person. Judgments concerning another person's attractiveness are made continually throughout each stage of coming together and coming apart. The criteria for such judgments will often change at various stages, but some feelings of attraction or repulsion emerge before (based on reputation) or very early in the encounter or relationship. We make judgments about our attraction to people in both intimate and nonintimate relationships. We even have stable relationships with people we aren't very attracted to. The extent to which you feel attracted to other people will surely affect how you communicate with them and, sometimes, whether you communicate with them.

In everyday conversation, we usually think first of physical attractiveness when someone says they are attracted to a person. While this is perhaps the most obvious referent, interpersonal attraction is a more complex phenomenon. McCroskey and McCain identified three types of attraction: (1) social attraction—"He would fit into my circle of friends"; (2) physical attraction—"I think she's quite pretty"; and (3) task attraction—"My confidence in her ability to get the job done makes me want to work with her."[46]

What factors are the most important in determining our attraction to another individual?

Reward or Punishment?

Some people feel they are attracted to particular others because they obtain personal rewards; they like those who like them, even those who they anticipate will like them. Rewards may also be associated with communication competence[47] or interaction styles—i.e., somebody who listens attentively, who responds directly to your statements and questions. As was noted in earlier chapters, perceived rewards are not always as obvious as simply observing that one person praised or complimented another. The perceiver may feel the flattery is not deserved or phony and question the sincerity of the communicator. Or the perceiver may be so certain that he or she isn't any good at something, that he or she may respond favorably to someone who confirms it. What are rewards for some, then, may be costs for others. Some people may show attraction for others who physically and/or mentally abuse them. Some of these relationships are short-lived; in others there are hidden and offsetting rewards; in still others, the abused person may feel that the relationship isn't particularly good, but it is the "best I can do." Indeed, researchers have found that people with poor self-concepts tend to be more committed to spouses who think poorly of them than they are to spouses who think well of them.[48]

The rewards or costs we perceive to be associated with our attraction for another person do not always emanate from that individual. For instance, one study demonstrated that women who were asked to rate men's physical attractiveness were influenced by ratings made by female peers—particularly when those peer ratings were negative.[49] Other studies have revealed that the quality of both men's and women's dating relationships is affected by family and friends.[50]

Perceptions of relational rewards and costs also sometimes differ for men and women. Some scholars argue that these differences exist because our society teaches females and males to value different aspects of relationships.[51] Others feel that the distinctions are the result of thousands of years of evolutionary forces.[52] Regardless of how they originally developed, it is important to note that these distinctions are often small. By and large, men and women tend to have more relational similarities than differences. For example, when one group of researchers asked people to rate the importance of various relational rewards and costs, they found both women and men felt that some of the most important rewards of romantic relationships were companionship, happiness, and feeling loved or loving another person.[53] The most significant costs reported by both genders were stress and worry about the relationship, sacrifices, and increased dependence on the other. The researchers also noted that although there were far more similarities than differences in men's and women's ratings, several interesting differences did emerge. Women rated intimacy, self-growth, self-understanding, and positive self-esteem more highly than did men, and women saw loss of identity and innocence about relationships as more serious costs. In contrast, men felt sexual gratification was a more important benefit and monetary loss was a more significant cost than did women. While the number of gender differences here may be small, it is easy to imagine how the differences might affect communication between male and female romantic partners.

For many years, conventional courtship wisdom has held that a woman who plays hard to get somehow offers sufficient reward to attract males. Apparently, it is not only a matter of how hard a woman is for a particular male to get, but also how hard she is for other men to get. The greatest attraction, according to Walster and her colleagues, occurs when the woman is easy for the subject to get but hard for others to get. Men seem to ascribe to this woman all the assets of the uniformly hard-to-get woman (selective, popular), all the assets of the uniformly easy-to-get woman (friendly, warm, flexible), and none of the liabilities of either.[54] Other researchers have since qualified these findings, noting that both men and women who are extremely selective (i.e., described as never having "met a guy(girl) she(he) liked enough to go 'steady' with") are less attractive than those who are moderately selective.[55]

Near or Far?

Proximity may also facilitate or curtail attraction. A great deal of research verifies the fact that we are more likely to develop friendships with people we are exposed to more often. ("To know him is to love him.") It may be that you share the same office, attend the same classes, occupy the same dormitory room, or come from the same neighborhood. Conversely, we may try to obtain closer proximity to people we have been attracted to—two students living in two separate dorms who agree to share an apartment. Obviously, increasing exposure by decreasing distance allows us to obtain more information more quickly about another person. And, for this reason, we can think of many examples where we have been in close proximity to someone and have not been attracted to them. This is particularly true when it soon became clear that you differed on some basic and fundamental attitudes or beliefs. ("Familiarity breeds contempt.") However, this fact does not limit the tremendous potential of proximity in fostering and influencing attraction. As one of our colleagues astutely noted, "It's tough to be close when you're far away."

Proximity was found to be a most influential factor in the development and maintenance of romantic relationships in commercial organizations. Sometimes the two people worked in the same area of the building and sometimes they just shared the same elevator every morning and evening; or they were assigned to work on a task together; or the proximity was on an irregular basis—e.g., a receptionist in another office. The proximity of the two participants' work group and supervisor also influenced the course of these relationships. When supervision was not close and when there was little pressure from a work group to terminate the relationship, it was more likely to continue.[56] While these relationships continue, proximity is an advantage; when there is no desire to prolong the relationship, proximity is a problem and efforts will no doubt be made to decrease the possibilities of co-presence.

Similarity or Dissimilarity?

The phrase *birds of a feather flock together* reminds us of another important source of attraction—similarity. Many studies confirm the fact that we often desire and select friends, dates, and spouses who are similar to us—in morals, background (social class, occupation), interests, goals, ways of expressing ideals (language choices, dynamism), attitudes (political leaning, etc.), or appearance (size, features).[57] There are at least three underlying reasons why we seem to gravitate to similar others: (1) We assume similar characteristics will reflect a common view of the world. (2) If we share a lot in common, our interaction will require less hard work. Dissimilar others may ask us to justify our beliefs and force us to keep track of referents for a host of expressions that we can assume with similar others. Similar others also seem to provide a promising information-per-time-unit investment. In a culture where the pressures of getting things done rapidly is high, similarity seems to grease the path. Sometimes we even fake similarities in order to get more information about another. Dissimilarity, it is presumed, bogs you down—trying to straighten out something like that, in the long run, may be a trivial matter. And dissimilar others may have to start learning about each other at more basic levels—e.g., "Now how does that handshake go?"—which inevitably forecasts a long time before the relationship can begin to deal with more personal matters. (3) Similar others also seem to give us a better chance of being liked.

Many of the experiments testifying to the relationship between similarity and attraction have used Byrne's *phantom-other technique.* According to this technique, subjects are asked to inspect a questionnaire supposedly filled out by another person. Actually, the experimenter has filled out the questionnaire, so it will be either similar or dissimilar to the subject's own attitudes and beliefs on a variety of issues. When subjects are asked to indicate how much they like the phantom-other, a greater liking is consistently expressed for those who agree with the subject's opinions.[58] While it is at times true that "opposites attract," the overwhelming evidence seems to point in the other direction; we are drawn to people who are similar to us, and more specifically, to those who agree with us.

Several qualifications regarding this general principle of attitude similarity and attraction are in order.[59] For example, researchers have found that we tend to assume we are more similar to attractive others than we are to less attractive others.[60] If we are very attracted to someone, we may perceive a number of similarities between ourselves and that person that might otherwise go unnoticed. It is also important to remember, however, that perceived similarities do not always lead to attraction. People may be trying to renounce a fate they hope to avoid—the hard of hearing may not want to meet the deaf. In one experiment, people were led to believe that they were very similar in attitudes and beliefs to another person except that the other person had had "a nervous breakdown and was seeing a psychiatrist."[61] In such cases, subjects were more anxious to avoid their partner than if the partner had dissimilar attitudes and beliefs. Here, similarity was threatening. People could not dismiss the idea that "this can happen to me" (because the person is so like me) when they had to face it directly. You may also find that you don't perceive a similarity that others perceive[62] or that you are similar to someone in ways that seem to be of little relevance for a particular kind of relationship (e.g., bowling partners who are both Presbyterian). Attitude similarity may lead to attraction, but other offsetting costs may inhibit relationship development. For example, your similar other may live thousands of miles away; the similar other may express a dislike for you; or the similar other is dissimilar on a single characteristic that overrides any attraction you might feel based on all the similarities.

Other qualifications concerning this general principle of attitude similarity and attraction concern changes in people over time. In the early stages of a relationship similarity may be based on a wide range of background factors and relatively superficial opinions and interests. As the relationship intensifies, certain topics, beliefs, and values may emerge as the most critical areas of similarity—those areas which must be similar if the relationship is to continue. You may find some similarities are initially appealing, but disastrous to a long-term relationship—e.g., similarities on things you don't like about yourself or on the need to dominate. You may initially value your partner's imagination and creativeness but detest it when you find he or she is also a liar. Partners in a relationship do not always grow at the same speed or in the same direction, but changes in the relative importance of external factors, physical attributes, attitude similarity, need similarity, and the like do change with time:

HUSBAND: I don't understand all your proposals for weird and deviant sexual adventures. When we got married we agreed sex was beautiful, not something to be abused.

WIFE: It is beautiful and I'm not proposing we abuse it. All I'm suggesting is some variety—something different from the "same ol' thing."

This dialogue also points up another qualification. Two people may assume similarity on the basis of a general statement (Sex is beautiful), but end up disagreeing about the particular behaviors associated with the general statement (*This* sex is not beautiful). The degree of pleasantness or unpleasantness regarding attitude similarity or dissimilarity obviously depends on how deeply held the attitude in question is. We can like a person generally and still disagree with or dislike certain attitudes or features of them, providing the disliked attributes are not basic, or core, values.

Dissimilarities are not always unattractive. Sometimes exposure to dissimilar attitudes may help to strengthen our own beliefs—shoring up or modifying our position on an issue by examining a contrasting one. At times the dissimilarities are irrelevant for the particular relationship sought. The other person may not rigidly adhere to or argue a dissimilar belief or the dissimilarity may not challenge our most cherished beliefs. Sometimes when dissimilar others say they like us, this positive evaluation may override the perceived differences. And we may be attracted to dissimilar others because they represent something we'd like to be like—an ideal.

Like similarities, dissimilarities can change over time. In one study, the attitude similarity of couples at the time of engagement and after eighteen years of marriage was analyzed.[63] Happily married couples showed more attitude differences at engagement, but became more alike. Unhappily married couples became more unlike each other. Another study demonstrated that female roommates who spent more time talking to each other tended to be more similar than those who did not talk as much.[64] The researchers argued that conversation between friends may be an important way for them to develop and maintain similarity. Of course, conversations also allow people to deal with their differences. Friends and marital partners develop norms to smooth out differences and iron out possible problem areas. In fact, even the act of engaging in the pleasantries of initial interaction with a person known to differ on the subjects of preparedness for war and/or the construction of nuclear power plants seemed to enhance interpersonal attraction. People who didn't have a chance to interact showed significantly less attraction for each other.[65] Some assume these findings are the result of individuals' desire to have a stable, predictable, and controllable communication environment—and that interacting with others helps them to attain this goal.[66] Others feel that similarity on some issues leads to increased interaction and that the interaction then leads to increased similarity.[67] Although it is apparent that quality communication plays an important role in attraction,[68] we clearly have a lot to learn about how interaction affects perceptions of similarity and dissimilarity. After all, it is the way we talk about ourselves—not the comparison of our answers on questionnaires—that causes others to perceive us as similar or dissimilar to them. Some people learn to like each other after a bad start (perceived dissimilarity or negative reactions). Furthermore, we may be more attracted to someone whose reaction toward us has changed from negative to positive than we might be toward someone we liked from the beginning.[69] Similarly, we might be very negative toward someone who originally liked us and then shifted to dislike, even more negative, perhaps, than toward a person we didn't think much of from the beginning.

Another important qualification to the similarity–attraction principle is that there are instances in which we seek out people who are known to be different. Seeking out people with vastly different backgrounds and attitudes is usually an infrequent activity determined by our own free choice as the seeker. We usually engage in this when we don't feel we'll be rejected by the dissimilar other(s), and when we are in need of putting our unique identity in sharp contrast with others—escaping from the another-face-in-the-crowd syndrome. Just as there are times when we wish to emphasize our similarities with others, there are also times when we seek to emphasize our uniqueness.[70]

People can be similar in a variety of ways. Research has tended to emphasize similarities in personal preferences (attitudes, beliefs, values, interests, goals) and personal characteristics (age, race, sex, status, looks, background). But people also perceive similarities and dissimilarities in communication style (ways of expressing ideas, language choices, topic selection); communicative norms (sharing an understanding and acceptance of cultural roles and rituals); personal needs (immediate and long-term individual and interpersonal needs); and situational factors (sharing perceptions of the pros and cons attendant to a particular situation). For example, Burleson and his colleagues found that people with similar communication values were more likely to become friends than were those with dissimilar values[71] and that spouses tended to have relatively similar levels of communication skills.[72] These findings suggest that some degree of similarity with regard to communication issues is important for relationships. But while some of these similarities and dissimilarities may be central to any type of attraction—task, physical, or social— others probably are not. There are likely some similarities that are especially important in one type of attraction and not in others. The factors important for task attraction may take into consideration, for example, the fact that the task may not last long and may demand a type of expertise that a long-term romantic relationship would not profit from.

Beauty or Beast?

We now return to physical attractiveness. It is safe to say that the evidence from contemporary United States culture overwhelmingly supports the notion that *initially* we respond much more favorably to people perceived as physically attractive than to those seen as less attractive. In short, "what is beautiful is good." Summarizing numerous studies in this area, it is not at all unusual to find subjects evaluating physically attractive persons as more likely than unattractive persons to possess a wide range of socially desirable traits—success, personality, popularity, sociability, sexuality, persuasiveness, and often happiness.[73] In other cultures, the positive traits associated with physical attractiveness may differ, but the judgments in favor of "what is beautiful" are fairly consistent.[74] These judgments, linked to a person's attractiveness, begin early in life (preschool, kindergarten) apparently reflecting similar attitudes and evaluations made by teachers and parents. But in addition, it seems that less attractive people will not be discriminated against as long as their performance is impressive: As soon as performance declines, however, the less attractive individual may receive more sanctions than the attractive one. For the less attractive readers of this book, bear with us. The picture is not entirely bleak. For instance, attractive people are not consistently rated more intelligent or more trustworthy. And unattractive couples have been judged by others to be more happily married than physically attractive couples. Handsome men do not seem to score any better on tests measuring happiness, self-esteem, and psychological well-being. And although attractive women seem to score slightly better on such measures than unattractive ones, this doesn't seem to be a lasting result. For example, middle-aged women who had been identified as attractive or unattractive in college were tested later in life. By middle age, the attractive college coeds seemed to be less happy, less satisfied with their lives, and less well adjusted than their plain counterparts.[75]

In management positions, attractive women sometimes face charges that they are succeeding because they are attractive rather than competent. And, in one of the few studies of physical attractiveness that has linked attractiveness ratings with social interaction, we find that women with more variable ratings were more satisfied with their social encounters.[76]

While it is not true of all studies on physical attractiveness, most use photographs which, prior to the study, are judged to fall into the beautiful or into the ugly category. Hence, in most cases, we are not reporting results from observations of live, moving, talking human beings in a particular environment and we are not generally dealing with subtle differences in physical attractiveness which lie between the extremes. Although there does seem to be a general consensus in this culture on who is and who isn't physically attractive, this methodological consideration should offer further consolation to those who fear their yearbook picture may have been placed in the wrong category. When we judge people's physical attractiveness, we usually consider a whole range of factors beyond what we might see in a single photograph—e.g., we observe the way they talk, the way they move, the way they treat us. Furthermore, our assessment of an individual's attractiveness may change over time. Research indicates that most people have had an experience when someone they thought was only moderately attractive actually became much more attractive to them.[77] In some cases, people noted that their perceptions changed because they modified the criteria they used to judge physical attractiveness; in others, they said they came to appreciate certain physical traits in the other person that they did not previously find attractive.

Situations also change judgments of physical attractiveness. For example, Mickey Gilley's song about how "all the girls get prettier at closing time" prompted some social psychologists to test the idea.[78] Information about the general attractiveness of patrons in several bars at different times leading up to closing time confirmed the idea that both men and women perceive a significant increase in attractiveness of others in the bar as closing time draws near. Although alcohol intake was not controlled in this study, there may still be some truth in the lyrics Gilley sings: "Ain't it funny, ain't it strange, the way a man's opinions change, when he starts to face that lonely night." Judgments of attractiveness in this context, then, change as the number of available women diminish. These judgments may also be affected by seeing someone considered to be extremely attractive just prior to meeting another person. College men, for instance, who viewed attractive women on television just prior to rating the attractiveness of some coeds rated the coeds lower on attractiveness than another group of men who did not see the women on television.[79]

In light of the general preference for a physically attractive partner, we might suspect dating patterns would reflect these preferences. Such a hypothesis would certainly be confirmed by a series of *computer dance studies* at the Universities of Texas, Illinois, and Minnesota. In these studies, physical attractiveness superseded a host of other variables in determining liking for one's partner and desire to date in the future. Although both men and women reported that the other's physical appearance was the most important contributor to their feelings of attraction, a number of studies show that men tend to place more value on youth and physical attractiveness when selecting a partner than do women. Women, in contrast, tend to value earning potential more than do men. In addition, one study demonstrated that the greater emphasis men place on physical attractiveness applies to both heterosexual and homosexual relationships.[80] In this study, homosexual and heterosexual men both rated partners' physical attractiveness as more important than than did homosexual and heterosexual women. The notion that men value physical attractiveness more than do women (and that heterosexual women place more value on the earning potential of their partners) may be surprising in today's social environment where gender equality is emphasized. These findings, however, have been replicated across a variety of age groups and cultures.[81] When it comes to initial mate preferences, men and women tend to act in more stereotypical ways than many would like to think.

If both women and men always pursued the most attractive partners they could find, people who were highly attractive would probably end up with more dating opportunities than they desired. There are times, however, when attractive persons are almost untouched in the mainstream of dating behavior. Why? Elaine Walster and her colleagues proposed what they called the matching hypothesis.[82] Since this hypothesis was presented, other studies confirm its validity. Essentially, the *matching hypothesis* argues that each person may be attracted to only the best-looking partners, but reality sets in when actual dates are made. You may face an unwanted rejection if you select only the best-looking person available, so the tendency is to select a person similar to yourself with respect to physical attractiveness. Hence, the procedure seems to be to try to maximize the attractiveness of our choice while simultaneously minimizing the possibilities of rejection. If you have high self-esteem, you might seek out highly attractive partners in spite of a considerable gap between your looks and your partner's. Self-esteem, in this case, will affect the perception of and possible reaction to rejection. Confirmation of the matching hypothesis has also been obtained by examining middle-aged, middle-class couples[83] as well as younger college-aged friends.[84] And in another research project it was found that couples who were similar in physical attractiveness during early stages of relationship development tended to make more courtship progress (achieve more breadth and depth of intimacy) over a nine-month period. Partners in the early phases of relationship development who were dissimilar in attractiveness were more likely to break up.[85]

Sometimes we find couples who appear to be mismatched with regard to their physical attractiveness. One study suggests that evaluations of males may change dramatically if they are viewed as married to someone very different in general physical attractiveness.[86] Unattractive men who were married to attractive women were judged, among other things, as making more money, as more successful in their occupation, and as more intelligent than an attractive man with an attractive wife. Judges must have reasoned that for an unattractive man to marry an attractive woman, he must have offset this imbalance by succeeding in other areas—e.g., making money.

In summary, strong attraction for a person is most likely if you view that person as physically attractive, and if he or she expresses positive evaluations toward you, tends to agree with your beliefs and attitudes, and is available for frequent contact. In addition to these factors, attraction for opposite-sexed pairs may be enhanced if the target person is seen as hard for others to get and easy for their partner in the relationship to get. Sometimes outside interference from parents may cause a couple to increase their attraction and resolve for each other, a phenomenon known as the *Romeo and Juliet effect*.[87]

SUMMARY

What forces bring people together to communicate and begin the process of building a relationship? How do we form impressions of others when we encounter them? What factors influence our judgments of other people as attractive? In short, what is the nature of the genesis of dialogue, what are those cognitive and behavioral processes enacted during the initial stages of encounters and relationships? These were the questions posed and addressed in this chapter.

People are drawn to each other for many reasons. We noted a few: (1) the impulse to receive stimulation; (2) the impulse to express experiences; (3) the impulse to assert and learn more about oneself; and (4) the impulse to enhance the enjoyment of certain activities.

Once in the immediate presence of others (and sometimes prior to co-presence), we begin to form impressions of the other person. What we see in others, and how we perceive them, may be influenced by a host of factors: (1) our own cultural, educational, and personal background; (2) our own needs, desires, and emotional states; (3) the method of self-presentation used by the other person; and (4) the way we choose to overtly describe covert feelings and impressions. Environmental stimuli (noted in Chapter 4) will also affect what we see in another person.

Once the factors that influence our perceptions have been identified, our analysis of the formation of impressions becomes more complex. A total picture evolves out of dynamic interaction between our own personality, the other's personality, the fragments of these personalities which each of us chooses to dribble out or magnify on a particular occasion, what others tell us, what modifications are imposed by the setting or time available, etc. While it is unrealistic to expect a precise mental roadmap of how person perception works, we have some general theories that are useful for description and explanation—attribution theory, implicit personality theory, Gestalt impression formation, the concept of central traits, inference processes, and stereotyping.

Sometimes certain forces are set in motion that cause us to feel particularly attracted to another person. On the basis of the research reviewed in this chapter, the following conditions seem to be most likely to provide a basis for attraction across most situations: (1) personal rewards derived from the other person; (2) proximity; (3) physical attractiveness; and (4) similarity of attitudes and beliefs. In some cases, however, the effects of any one of these factors may be neutralized or overridden by one or more of the other factors. Situational constraints and pressures will also affect the attraction process. It should also be clear that many of the processes discussed in this chapter are not limited to first encounters, strangers, or the commencement of an encounter. They were presented in this chapter because they may be more evident or dramatic during initiating and experimenting stages. Although this book has overtones of a distinct chronology, it is obvious that human communication cannot be rigidly fixed in an unchanging order. General patterns can be observed, but impression formation and attraction forces are obviously important at all stages of development and deterioration in relationships.

SELECTED READINGS

Personal Perception

Berger, C. R., and Kellermann, K. "Acquiring Social Information." In J. A. Daly and J. M. Wiemann, eds., *Communicating Strategically,* pp. 1–31. Hillsdale, NJ: Erlbaum, 1994.

Brown, R. *Social Psychology: The Second Edition.* New York: Free Press, 1986, pp. 131–199.

Cauthen, N. R., Robinson, I. E., and Krauss, H. H. "Stereotypes: A Review of the Literature, 1926–1968." *Journal of Social Psychology* 84 (1971): 103–125.

Fletcher, G. J. O., and Fitness, J. "Knowledge Structures and Explanations in Intimate Relationships." In S. Duck, ed., *Individuals in Relationships,* pp. 121–143. Newbury Park, CA: Sage, 1993.

Goffman, E. *The Presentation of Self in Everyday Life.* Garden City, NY: Doubleday Anchor, 1959.

Hastorf, A. H., Schneider, D. J., and Polefka, J. *Person Perception.* Reading, MA: Addison-Wesley, 1970.

Jones, E. E., and Davis, K. E. "From Acts to Dispositions: The Attribution Process in Person Perception." In L. Berkowitz, ed., *Advances in Experimental Social Psychology,* vol. 2. New York: Academic Press, 1965.

Jones, E. E., and Nisbett, R. E. "The Actor and the Observer: Divergent Perceptions of the Causes of Behavior." In E. E. Jones et al., eds., *Attribution: Perceiving the Causes of Behavior.* Morristown, NJ: General Learning Press, 1973.

Kelley, H. H. "The Processes of Causal Attribution." *American Psychologist* 28 (1973): 107–128.

Kleinke, C. L. *First Impressions: The Psychology of Encountering Others.* Englewood Cliffs, NJ: Prentice-Hall, 1975.

Laing, R. D., Phillipson, H., and Lee, A. R. *Interpersonal Perception: A Theory and a Method of Research.* New York: Springer, 1966.

Malloy, T. E., and Albright, L. "Interpersonal Perception in a Social Context." *Journal of Personality and Social Psychology* 58 (1990): 419–428.

Nisbett, R., and Ross, L. *Human Inference: Strategies and Shortcomings of Social Judgment.* Englewood Cliffs, NJ: Prentice-Hall, 1980.

Roloff, M. E., and Berger, C. R., eds. *Social Cognition and Communication.* Beverly Hills, CA: Sage, 1982.

Sarbin, T. R., Taft, R., and Bailey, D. E. *Clinical Inference and Cognitive Theory.* New York: Holt, Rinehart, & Winston, 1960.

Schleker, B. R., and Weigold, M. F. "Interpersonal Processes Involving Impression Regulation and Management." *Annual Review of Psychology* 43 (1992): 133–168.

Schneider, D. J. "Implicit Personality Theory: A Review." *Psychological Bulletin* 27 (1973): 294–309.

Scott, C. K., Fuhrman, R. W., and Wyer, R. S. "Information Processing in Close Relationships." In G. J. O. Fletcher and F. D. Fincham, eds., *Cognition in Close Relationships,* pp. 37–67. Hillsdale, NJ: Erlbaum, 1991.

Sedikides, C., Campbell, W. K., Reeder, G. D., and Elliot, A. J. "The Self-Serving Bias in Relational Context." *Journal of Personality and Social Psychology* 74 (1998): 378–386.

Swann, W. B., Jr., and Gill, M. J. "Confidence and Accuracy in Person Perception: Do We Know What We Think We Know About Our Relationship Partners?" *Journal of Personality and Social Psychology* 73 (1997): 747–757.

Tagiuri, R. "Person Perception." In G. Lindzey and E. Aronson, eds., *The Handbook of Social Psychology,* vol. 3. Reading, MA: Addison-Wesley, 1969.

Taylor, S. E., *Positive Illusions: Creative Self-Deception and the Healthy Mind.* New York: Basic Books, 1989.

Taylor, S. E. and Koivumaki, J. H. "The Perception of Self and Others: Acquaintanceship, Affect, and Actor-Observer Differences." *Journal of Personality and Social Psychology* 33 (1976): 403–408.

Zebrowitz, L. A. *Social Perception.* Buckingham, Great Britain: Open University Press, 1990.

Interpersonal Attraction

Athanaston, R., and Uoshioka, G. A. "The Spatial Character of Friendship Formation." *Environment and Behavior* 5 (1973): 43–65.

Berscheid, E., and Walster, E. H. *Interpersonal Attraction.* Reading, MA: Addison-Wesley, 1969.

———. "Physical Attractiveness." In L. Berkowitz, ed., *Advances in Experimental Social Psychology,* vol. 7, pp. 158–215. New York: Academic Press, 1974.

Burleson, B. R., and Denton, W. H. "A New Look at Similarity and Attraction in Marriage: Similarities in Social-Cognitive and Communication Skills as Predictors of Attraction and Satisfaction." *Communication Monographs* 59 (1992):268–287.

Buss, D. M. *The Evolution of Desire: Strategies of Human Mating.* New York: Basic Books, 1994.

Byrne, D. *The Attraction Paradigm.* New York: Academic Press, 1971.

"Chautauqua: The Role of Communication in the Similarity-Attraction Relationship." *Communication Monographs* 59 (1992): 164–212.

Hatfield, E., and Sprecher, S. *Mirror, Mirror: The Importance of Looks in Everyday Life.* Albany, NY: State University of New York Press, 1986.

Huston, T. L., ed. *Foundations of Interpersonal Attraction.* New York: Academic Press, 1974.

Lerner, M. J., and Agar, E. "The Consequences of Perceived Similarity: Attraction and Rejection, Approach and Avoidance." *Journal of Experimental Research in Personality* 6 (1972): 69–75.

Levinger, G. "A Three-Level Approach to Attraction: Toward an Understanding of Pair Relatedness." In T. L. Huston, ed., *Foundations of Interpersonal Attraction.* New York: Academic Press, 1974.

Lykken, D. T., and Tellegen, A. "Is Human Mating Adventitious or the Result of Lawful Choice? A Twin Study of Mate Selection." *Journal of Personality and Social Psychology* 65 (1993): 56–68.

McCroskey, J. C., and McCain, T. A. "The Measurement of Interpersonal Attraction." *Speech Monographs* 41 (1974): 261–266.

McCroskey, J. C., Richmond, V. P., and Daly, J. A. "The Development of a Measure of Perceived Homophily in Interpersonal Communication." *Human Communication Research* 1 (1975): 323–332.

Murstein, B. I. *Who Will Marry Whom? Theories and Research in Marital Choice.* New York: Springer, 1976.

Simpson, J. A., and Kenrick, D. T., eds. *Evolutionary Social Psychology.* Mahwah, NJ: Erlbaum, 1996.

Sprecher, S., and Duck, S. "Sweet Talk: The Importance of Perceived Communication for Romantic and Friendship Attraction Experienced During a Get-Acquainted Date."

Personality and Social Psychology Bulletin 20 (1994): 391–400.

Wheeler, L., and Kim, Y. "What Is Beautiful Is Culturally Good: The Physical Attractiveness Stereotype Has Different Content in Collec-

tivistic Cultures." *Personality and Social Psychology Bulletin* 23 (1997): 795–800.

Wilson, G., and Nias, D. "Beauty Can't Be Beat." *Psychology Today* 10 (1976): 96–98, 103.

NOTES

[1]L. Zunin, *Contact: The First Four Minutes* (Los Angeles: Nash, 1972).

[2]M. S. Davis, *Intimate Relations* (New York: Free Press, 1973), pp. 31–35.

[3]B. R. Schleker and M. F. Weigold, "Interpersonal Processes Involving Impression Regulation and Management," *Annual Review of Psychology* 43 (1992): 133–168.

[4]C. R. Berger, "Goals, Plans, and Mutual Understanding in Relationships." In S. Duck, ed., *Individuals in Relationships* (Newbury Park, CA: Sage, 1993), pp. 30–59; C. R. Berger, *Planning Strategic Interactions* (Mahwah, NJ: Erlbaum, 1997).

[5]C. H. Solano, "Loneliness and Perceptions of Control: General Traits Versus Specific Attributions." In M. Hojat and R. Crandall, eds., *Loneliness: Theory, Research and Theory* (Newbury Park, CA: Sage, 1989), pp. 201–214.

[6]S. Schachter, *The Psychology of Affiliation* (Stanford: Stanford University Press, 1959).

[7]D. T. Lykken and A. Tellegen, "Is Human Mating Adventitious or the Result of Lawful Choice? A Twin Study of Mate Selection," *Journal of Personality and Social Psychology* 65 (1993): 56–68.

[8]J. D. Vorauer and R. K. Ratner, "Who's Going to Make the First Move? Pluralistic Ignorance as an Impediment to Relationship Formation," *Journal of Social and Personal Relationships* 13 (1996): 483–506.

[9]Several of these and other barriers to relationship development are noted in S. B. Woll and P. C. Cozby, "Videodating and Other Alternatives to Traditional Methods of Relationship Initiation." In W. H. Jones and D. Perlman, eds., *Advances in Personal Relationships* (Greenwich, CT: JAI Press, 1987), vol. 1, pp. 69–108.

[10]M. J. Levesque and D. A. Kenny, "Accuracy of Behavioral Predictions at Zero Acquaintance: A Social Relations Analysis," *Journal of Personality and Social Psychology* 65 (1993): 1178–1187; W. B. Swann, Jr., and M. J. Gill, "Confidence and Accuracy in Person Perception: Do We Know What We Think We Know About Our Relationship Part-

ners?" *Journal of Personality and Social Psychology* 73 (1979): 747–757.

[11]The fact that we often make such rapid judgments needs little supporting evidence. Whether or not these judgments based on a glance are accurate is often questioned. Sudnow, on the other hand, argues that "for many activities, the single glance is a maximally appropriate unit of interpersonal observation." See D. Sudnow, "Temporal Parameters of Interpersonal Observation." In D. Sudnow, ed., *Studies in Social Interaction* (New York: Free Press, 1972), pp. 259–279.

[12]C. R. Berger, "Beyond Initial Interaction: Uncertainty, Understanding, and the Development of Interpersonal Relationships." In *Language and Social Psychology,* H. Giles and R. N. St. Clair, eds., (Baltimore, MD: University Park Press, 1979), pp. 122–144.

[13]D. Miell and S. Duck, "Strategies in Developing Friendships." In V. J. Derlega and B. A. Winstead, eds., *Friendship and Social Interaction* (New York: Springer-Verlag, 1986), pp. 129–143.

[14]C. R. Berger and K. Kellermann, "Acquiring Social Information." In J. A. Daly and J. M. Wiemann, eds., *Communicating Strategically* (Hillsdale, NJ: Erlbaum, 1994), pp. 1–31.

[15]B. R. Burleson, J. G. Delia, and J. L. Applegate, "The Socialization of Person-Centered Communication: Parental Contributions to the Social-Cognitive and Communication Skills of their Children." In M. A. Fitzpatrick and A. L. Vangelisti, eds., *Perspectives on Family Interaction* (Newbury Park, CA: Sage, 1995), pp. 34–76.

[16]M. Snyder and S. W. Uranowitz, "Reconstructing the Past: Some Cognitive Consequences of Person Perception," *Journal of Personality and Social Psychology* 36 (1978): 941–950.

[17]M. G. Frank and T. Gilovich, "Effect of Memory Perspective on Retrospective Causal Attributions," *Journal of Personality and Social Psychology* 57 (1989): 399–403; C. K. Scott, R. W. Fuhrman, and R. S. Wyer, "Information Processing in Close Relationships." In G. J. O. Fletcher and F. D. Fin-

cham, eds., *Cognition in Close Relationships* (Hillsdale, NJ: Erlbaum, 1991), pp. 37–67; E. R. Smith, "Mental Representation and Memory." In D. T. Gilbert, S. T. Fiske, and G. Lindzey, eds., *The Handbook of Social Psychology,* 4th ed. (Boston: McGraw-Hill, 1998), pp. 391–445.

[18]P. E. Vernon, "Some Characteristics of the Good Judge of Personality," *Journal of Social Psychology* 4 (1933): 42–58.

[19]S. Asch, "Forming Impressions of Personality," *Journal of Abnormal and Social Psychology* 41 (1946): 258–290.

[20]H. H. Kelley, "The Warm-Cold Variable in First Impressions of Persons," *Journal of Personality* 18 (1950): 431–439.

[21]J. Wishner, "Reanalysis of 'Impressions of Personality,' " *Psychological Review* 67 (1960): 96–112.

[22]C. Chiu, Y. Hong, and C. S. Dweck, "Lay Dispositionism and Implicit Theories of Personality," *Journal of Personality and Social Psychology* 73 (1997): 19–30.

[23]S. R. Levy, S. J. Stoessner, and C. S. Dweck, "Stereotype Formation and Endorsement: The Role of Implicit Theories," *Journal of Personality and Social Psychology* 74 (1998): 1421–1436.

[24]D. Dunning and D. A. Sherman, "Stereotypes and Tacit Inference," *Journal of Personality and Social Psychology* 73 (1997): 459–471.

[25]Y. Trope and E. P. Thompson, "Looking for Truth in All the Wrong Places? Asymmetric Search of Individuating Information About Stereotyped Group Members," *Journal of Personality and Social Psychology* 73 (1997): 229–241.

[26]T. R. Sarbin, P. Taft, and D. E. Bailey, *Clinical Inference and Cognitive Theory* (New York: Holt, Rinehart, & Winston, 1960).

[27]C. Sedikides, W. K. Campbell, G. D. Reeder, and A. J. Elliot, "The Self-Serving Bias in Relational Context," *Journal of Personality and Social Psychology* 74 (1998): 378–386.

[28]F. D. Fincham, S. R. Beach, and D. H. Baucom, "Attribution Processes in Distressed and Nondistressed Couples: 4. Self-Partner Attribution Differences," *Journal of Personality and Social Psychology* 52 (1987): 739–748; F. Grigg, G. J. O. Fletcher, and J. Fitness, "Spontaneous Attributions in Happy and Unhappy Dating Relationships," *Journal of Social and Personal Relationships* 6 (1989): 61–68; B. R. Karney, T. N. Bradbury, F. D. Fincham, and K. T. Sullivan, "The Role of Negative Affectivity in the Association Between Attributions and Marital Satisfaction," *Journal of Personality and Social Psychology* 66 (1994): 413–424; A. L. Vangelisti,

"Communication Problems in Committed Relationships: An Attributional Analysis." In J. H. Harvey, T. L. Orbuch, and A. L. Weber, eds., *Attributions, Accounts, and Close Relationships* (New York: Springer-Verlag, 1992): pp. 144–164.

[29]D. T. Miller and C. A. Porter, "Effects of Temporal Perspective on the Attribution Process," *Journal of Personality and Social Psychology* 39 (1980): 532–541.

[30]K. Fiedler, G. R. Semin, and C. Koppentsch, "Language Use and Attributional Biases in Close Relationships," *Personality and Social Psychology Bulletin* 17 (1991): 147–155.

[31]D. J. Hilton. "Conversational Processes and Causal Explanation," *Psychological Bulletin* 107 (1990): 65–81.

[32]J. P. Forgas, "On Being Happy and Mistaken: Mood Effects on the Fundamental Attribution Error," *Journal of Personality and Social Psychology* 75 (1998): 318–331.

[33]G. Fontaine, "Causal Attribution in Simulated Versus Real Situation: When Are People Logical, When Are They Not?" *Journal of Personality and Social Psychology* 32 (1975): 1021–1029.

[34]R. D. Laing, H. Phillipson, and A. R. Lee, *Interpersonal Perception: A Theory and A Method of Research* (New York: Springer Publishing Co., Inc., 1966, and Tavistock Pubs.).

[35]Copyright © 1970 by George R. Bach and Ronald M. Deutsch. From the book *Pairing,* published by Peter H. Wyden, Inc., a division of David McKay Co., Inc. Reprinted by permission of the publisher, pp. 83–85.

[36]R. K. Merton. "The Self-Fulfilling Prophecy," *Antioch Review* 8 (1948): 193–210.

[37]See, for example, G. Downey, A. L. Freitas, B. Michaelis, and H. Khouri, "The Self-Fulfilling Prophecy in Close Relationships: Rejection Sensitivity and Rejection by Romantic Partners," *Journal of Personality and Social Psychology* 75 (1998): 545–560.

[38]S. E. Taylor. *Positive Illusions: Creative Self-Deception and the Healthy Mind* (New York: Basic Books, 1989).

[39]M. W. Matlin and D. J. Stang, *The Pollyanna Principle: Selectivity In Language, Memory and Thought* (Cambridge, MA: Schenkman, 1979). Pollyanna was an irrepressibly cheerful child heroine who always seemed to find a bright side in even the most tragic circumstances. See E. H. Porter, *Pollyanna* (Boston: L. C. Page, 1913).

[40]For a review, see S. T. Fiske, "Attention and Weight in Person Perception: The Impact of

Negative and Extreme Behavior," *Journal of Personality and Social Psychology* 38 (1980): 889–908.

[41]Another explanation is that negative events have a greater impact on us than positive events do. If this is the case, the ability to focus on and recall negative events may help us to protect ourselves from potential harm.

[42]K. Kellermann, "The Negativity Effect in Interaction: It's All in Your Point of View," *Human Communication Research* 15 (1989): 147–183.

[43]Asch. "Forming Impressions," pp. 258–290.

[44]Copyright © 1970 by George R. Bach and Ronald M. Deutsch. From the book *Pairing,* published by Peter H. Wyden, Inc., a division of David McKay Co., Inc. Reprinted by permission of the publisher, pp. 174–175.

[45]C. De La Ronde and W. B. Swann, Jr., "Partner Verification: Restoring Shattered Images of Our Intimates," *Journal of Personality and Social Psychology* 75 (1998): 374–382.

[46]J. C. McCroskey and T. A. McCain, "The Measurement of Interpersonal Attraction," *Speech Monographs* 41 (1974): 261–266.

[47]R. L. Duran and L. Kelly, "The Influence of Communicative Competence on Perceived Task, Social, and Physical Attraction," *Communication Quarterly* 36 (1988): 41–49.

[48]W. B. Swann, Jr., J. G. Hixon, and C. De La Ronde, "Embracing the Bitter 'Truth': Negative Self-Concepts and Marital Commitment," *Psychological Science* 3 (1992): 118–121.

[49]W. G. Graziano, L. A. Jensen-Campbell, L. L. Shebilske, and S. R. Lundgren, "Social Influence, Sex Differences, and Judgments of Beauty: Putting the *Interpersonal* Back in Interpersonal Attraction," *Journal of Personality and Social Psychology* 65 (1993): 522–531.

[50]M. R. Parks, "Communication Networks and Relationships Life Cycles." In S. Duck, ed., *Handbook of Personal Relationships,* 2nd ed. (New York: John Wiley & Sons, 1997), pp. 351–372.; M. R. Parks and M. Adelman, "Communication Networks and the Development of Romantic Relationships: An Expansion of Uncertainty Reduction Theory," *Human Communication Research* 10 (1983): 55–79; M. R. Parks, C. M. Stan, and L. L. Eggert, "Romantic Involvement and Social Network Involvement," *Social Psychology Quarterly* 46 (1983): 116–131; S. Sprecher and D. Felmlee, "The Influence of Parents and Friends on the Quality and Stability of Romantic Relationships: A Three-Wave Longitudinal Investigation," *Journal of Marriage and the Family* 54 (1992): 888–900.

[51]D. Tannen, *You Just Don't Understand.* (New York: William Morrow, 1990).

[52]D. M. Buss, *The Evolution of Desire: Strategies of Human Mating.* (New York: Basic Books, 1994); J. A. Simpson and D. T. Kenrick, eds., *Evolutionary Social Psychology* (Mahwah, NJ: Erlbaum, 1996).

[53]C. Sedikides, M. B. Oliver, and W. K. Campbell, "Perceived Benefits and Costs of Romantic Relationships for Women and Men: Implications for Exchange Theory," *Personal Relationships* 1 (1994): 5–21.

[54]E. Walster et al., " 'Playing Hard To Get': Understanding an Elusive Phenomenon," *Journal of Personality and Social Psychology* 26 (1973): 113–121.

[55]R. A. Wright and R. J. Contrada, "Dating Selectivity and Interpersonal Attraction: Toward a Better Understanding of the 'Elusive Phenomenon'," *Journal of Social and Personal Relationships* 3 (1986): 131–148.

[56]R. E. Quinn. "Coping with Cupid: The Formation, Impact and Management of Romantic Relationships in Organizations," *Administrative Science Quarterly* 22 (1977): 30–45. Also see J. P. Dillard and K. Miller, "Intimate Relationships in Task Environments." In S. W. Duck, D. F. Hay, S. E. Hobfoll, W. Ickes, and B. M. Montgomery, eds., *Handbook of Personal Relationships* (Chichester: Wiley, 1988), pp. 449–465.

[57]See, for example, R. M. Houts, E. Robins, and T. L. Huston, "Compatibility and the Development of Premarital Relationships," *Journal of Marriage and the Family* 58 (1996): 7–20; E. C. Klohnen and G. A. Mendelsohn, "Partner Selection for Personality Characteristics: A Couple-Centered Approach," *Personality and Social Psychology Bulletin* 24 (1998): 268–278; J. C. McCroskey, V. P. Richmond, and J. A. Daly, "The Development of a Measure of Perceived Homophily in Interpersonal Communication," *Human Communication Research* 1 (1975): 323–332.

[58]D. Byrne, *The Attraction Paradigm* (New York: Academic Press, 1971); D. Byrne, "An Overview (and Underview) of Research and Theory within the Attraction Paradigm," *Journal of Social and Personal Relationships* 14 (1997): 417–431.

[59]For a review of some of these issues, see "Chautauqua: The Role of Communication in the Similarity-Attraction Relationship," *Communication Monographs* 59 (1992): 164–212.

[60]G. Marks, N. Miller, and G. Maruyama, "Effect of Targets' Physical Attractiveness on Assumptions of Similarity," *Journal of Personality and Social Psychology* 41 (1981): 198–206.

[61]D. W. Novak and M. J. Lerner, "Rejection as a Consequence of Perceived Similarity," *Journal of Personality and Social Psychology* 9 (1968): 147–152. For an extension of Novak and Lerner's findings, see also: M. J. Lerner and E. Agar, "The Consequences of Perceived Similarity: Attraction and Rejection, Approach and Avoidance," *Journal of Experimental Research in Personality* 6 (1972): 69–75.

[62]B. Park and C. Flink, "A Social Relations Analysis of Agreement in Liking Judgments," *Journal of Personality and Social Psychology* 56 (1989): 506–518.

[63]L. M. Uhr, "Personality Changes During Marriage" (Ph.D. diss. University of Michigan, 1957).

[64]F. M. Deutsch. L. Sullivan, C. Sage, and N. Basile, "The Relations Among Talking, Liking, and Similarity Between Friends," *Personality and Social Psychology Bulletin* 17 (1991): 406–411.

[65]M. J. Sunnafrank and G. R. Miller. "The Role of Initial Conversations in Determining Attraction to Similar and Dissimilar Strangers," *Human Communication Research* 8 (1981): 16–25.

[66]M. Sunnafrank, "Communicative Influences on Perceived Similarity and Attraction: An Expansion of the Interpersonal Goals Perspective," *Western Journal of Speech Communication* 50 (1986): 158–170.

[67]V. Blankenship, S. M. Hnat, T. G. Hess, and D. R. Brown, "Reciprocal Interaction and Similarity of Personality Attributes," *Journal of Social and Personal Relationships* 1 (1984): 415–432.

[68]S. Sprecher and S. Duck, "Sweet Talk: The Importance of Perceived Communication for Romantic and Friendship Attraction Experienced During a Get-Acquainted Date," *Personality and Social Psychology Bulletin* 20 (1994): 391–400.

[69]E. Aronson and D. Linder, "Gain and Loss of Esteem as Determinants of Interpersonal Attractiveness," *Journal of Experimental Social Psychology* 1 (1965): 156–171. See also: G. L. Clore, N. H. Wiggins, and S. Itkin, "Gain and Loss in Attraction: Attributions from Nonverbal Behavior," *Journal of Personality and Social Psychology* 31 (1975): 706–712; G. L. Clore, N. H. Wiggins, and S. Itkin, "Judging Attraction from Nonverbal Behavior The Gain Phenomenon," *Journal of Consulting and Clinical Psychology* 43 (1975): 491–497.

[70]C. R. Snyder and H. L. Fromkin, *Uniqueness: The Human Pursuit of Difference* (New York: Plenum, 1980).

[71]B. R. Burleson, W. Samter, and A. E. Lucchetti, "Similarity in Communication Values as a Predictor of Friendship Choices: Studies of Friends and Best Friends," *The Southern Communication Journal* 57 (1992): 260–276.

[72]B. R. Burleson and W. H. Denton, "A New Look at Similarity and Attraction in Marriage: Similarities in Social-Cognitive and Communication Skills as Predictors of Attraction and Satisfaction," *Communication Monographs* 59 (1992): 268–287.

[73]E. Berscheid and E. H. Walster, "Physical Attractiveness." In L. Berkowitz, ed., *Advances in Experimental Social Psychology*, vol. 7 (New York: Academic Press, 1974), 158–215.

[74]L. Wheeler and Y. Kim, "What Is Beautiful Is Culturally Good: The Physical Attractiveness Stereotype Has Different Content in Collectivistic Cultures," *Personality and Social Psychology Bulletin* 23 (1997): 795–800.

[75]Bersheid and Walster, *op. cit.*; Cf. pp. 200–201 for reference to an unpublished manuscript by the authors and R. Campbell, "Grow Old Along with Me," 1972.

[76]H. T. Reis, J. Nezlek, and L. Wheeler, "Physical Attractiveness in Social Interaction," *Journal of Personality and Social Psychology* 38 (1980): 604–617.

[77]K. J. Fudge and M. L. Knapp, "Interaction Appearance Theory: Changing Perceptions of Physical Attractiveness through Social Interaction" (unpublished manuscript, University of Texas, 1998).

[78]J. W. Pennebaker, M. A. Dyer, R. S. Caulkins, D. L. Litowitz, P. L. Ackreman, D. G. Anderrson, and K. M. McGraw, "Don't the Girls Get Prettier at Closing Time: A Country and Western Application to Psychology," *Personality and Social Psychology Bulletin* 5 (1979): 122–125. "Don't All the Girls Get Prettier At Closing Time" written by Baker Knight, Singleton Music Co: BMI and sung by Mickey Gilley, *The Best of Mickey Gilley*, vol. 2, 1975, Columbia.

[79]D. T. Kenrick and S. E. Gutierres, "Contrast Effects and Judgments of Physical Attractiveness: When Beauty Becomes a Social Problem," *Journal of Personality and Social Psychology* 38 (1980): 131–140.

[80]J. M. Bailey, S. Gaulin, Y. Agyei, and B. A. Gladue, "Effects of Gender and Sexual Orientation on Evolutionarily Relevant Aspects of Human Mating Psychology," *Journal of Personality and Social Psychology* 66 (1994): 1081–1093.

[81]D. M. Buss, "Sex Differences in Human Mate Preferences: Evolutionary Hypotheses Tested in 37 Cultures," *Behavioral and Brain Sciences* 12 (1989): 1–49; S. Sprecher, Q. Sullivan, and E. Hatfield,

"Mate Selection Preferences: Gender Differences Examined in a National Sample," *Journal of Personality and Social Psychology* 66 (1994): 1074–1080.

[82]E. Walster et al., "Importance of Physical Attractiveness in Dating Behavior," *Journal of Personality and Social Psychology* 4 (1966): 508–516.

[83]B. I. Murstein and P. Christy, "Physical Attractiveness and Marriage Adjustment In Middle-Aged Couples," *Journal of Personality and Social Psychology* 34 (1976): 537–542.

[84]L. L. Carli, R. Ganley, and A. Pierce-Otay, "Similarity and Satisfaction in Roommate Relationships," *Personality and Social Psychology Bulletin* 17 (1991): 419–426.

[85]G. L. White, "Physical Attractiveness and Courtship Progress," *Journal of Personality and Social Psychology* 39 (1980): 660–668.

[86]D. Bar-Tal and L. Saxe, "Perceptions of Similarly and Dissimilarly Physically Attractive Couples and Individuals," *Journal of Personality and Social Psychology* 33 (1976): 772–781.

[87]R. Driscoll, K. E. Davis, and M. E. Lipetz, "Parental Interference and Romantic Love: The Romeo and Juliet Effect," *Journal of Personality and Social Psychology* 24 (1972): 1–10.

6

Interaction Rituals

Dear Dr. Vangelisti,

I have a question. I'd like to ask about "breaking the ice" when meeting a woman for the first time. I don't want her to think I'm too straightforward but on the other hand shyness is just as bad if not worse. What I usually do is talk openly and tell her a lot about myself. I also try to get her to tell me about herself. My problem is that although everything seems normal at first, my relationships tend to drop off after only about a week. This drives me crazy and I spend most of my time wondering what I do to offend these women. Can you give me any ideas about what I might be doing wrong?

Eager to Please

The first few seconds of talk with another person can be extremely important in setting the tone for further conversation and contact. This chapter discusses some of the factors that may facilitate or inhibit communication during this time. The extent to which we violate or adhere to certain interaction rules and how we choose to formulate our greetings, address terms, relational openings, and small talk should provide a basis for explaining why some contacts appear to be "winners" and some seem to be "losers."

> *Relational life wavers between order and disorder, certainty and uncertainty, permanence and change. Rituals help to balance these competing forces by providing order and formality in regions of relational life that may be easily threatened by disorder and informality.*
>
> —Arthur P. Bochner

Sometimes we simply don't know what to say, when to say it, or how to say it. At other times the social situation seems almost to demand a certain kind of communication. It's as if both communicators are following a script written by someone else—a script each of them has performed before. And, although it often seems that we could make better use of our time than perform these rituals, we continue to "go through the motions." Interaction rituals may be short or long, performed by many or few, elaborate or plain, but they are an important part of the process of establishing, sustaining, and terminating relationships.[1]

Communication Rules

Interaction rituals are created and sustained by the existence of communication rules. A *communication rule* is a followable prescription that indicates what communication behavior (or range of communication behavior) is obligatory, preferred, or prohibited in certain social situations.[2] It is a probability statement about the expectations for the situation—what is the likelihood that X must be said or that Y must not be said? Some of these rules are limited to a single person—"When Harry starts to yell at me, I will stop talking to him." Other rules apply to the behavior of both partners in a relationship—"If we have a fight, we won't go to bed while we're still angry at each other." There are also rules that pertain to specific groups of people—when fathers want to show affection for their sons, they shouldn't kiss them on the lips. Then there are those rules that apply to most people in the society—when someone greets you, you should return the greeting. From these examples, we can see that the influence of communication rules is not limited to initial interactions. On the contrary, as we will see in Chapter 8, people involved in long-term relationships develop and negotiate rules that are unique to those relationships. Argyle and Henderson further argue that there are some rules that cut across different types of relationships. These researchers found that in Britain, Italy, Hong Kong, and Japan, people said that the following rules applied to most of their relationships: (1) partners should respect each other's privacy; (2) partners should look one another in the eye during conversation; (3) partners should not discuss with others what is said in confidence; (4) partners should not criticize one another in public; (5) partners should seek to repay debts, favors, and, compliments—no matter how small; and (6) partners should (or should not) engage in sexual activity with each other.[3] Regardless of how specific or general a rule is, when an individual, couple, group, or society follows a rule most of the time, it is considered a *communication norm*—the most typical behavior relative to the rule. People may acknowledge the existence of a rule but fail to follow it, so it doesn't become a norm. And sometimes people seem to be engaging in similar or normative behavior, but it is not rule-governed behavior—i.e., they may depart from the norm without any positive or negative sanctions. Rules may also develop about who can make the rules. A husband may agree that he spends too much money but disagree that his wife should tell him to stop spending so much.

We begin learning about communication rules as children. Some of these rules give direction concerning what we say—for example, we learn "Mama" is not a form of address appropriate for all human beings, or we learn what is acceptable to say and what is not ("Don't say that . . . it's not nice"). Other rules pertain to the structuring of conversations—we're taught not to talk when another person is talking[4] or not to start a conversation cold without some rapport building. We learn the implicit and explicit rules for getting the floor so we can talk, giving up the floor so the other will know it is his or her turn, maintaining our turn so another can't get in, and helping someone else to maintain his or her turn as we inject occasional comments without interrupting the conversational flow. We also learn rules that help us to manage certain conversational episodes. We know to be discrete when someone tells us a secret,[5] to act concerned when someone is hurting,[6] and to try stay relatively calm and rational when having an argument in public.[7] Researchers remind us that the application of any rule to a situation or a relationship varies[8]—most of us know romantic partners who have no qualms about fighting in public—and that these variations serve to define the nature of our relationships.

Rules develop in a variety of ways. Sometimes we talk openly about the rule-related issue and negotiate a rule acceptable to both parties. More often, though, rules are established in much more subtle ways. Metacommunication (see Chapter 1) may be the process that tells others how to behave relative to particular communicative responses. As a result of these "unspoken" processes used to establish agreed-upon rules of interaction, it is not uncommon for two people not to be able to state the specific rules that guide their behavior.

Common sense tells us that learning and obeying these rules is crucially linked to the way others evaluate us. Allgeier, for instance, found that an individual's ratings of interpersonal attraction and adjustment increased as that person more closely approached an equal share of the talk time in a conversation.[9] Berger and his colleagues documented the fact that when people violate the norms of small talk (not reciprocating appropriate information, not giving the right number of compliments, or not following an impersonal-to-personal sequence of information giving), communicators were judged to be less attractive and too unpredictable.[10]

Test yourself. Examine the following situations and jot down two answers for each one. One answer should be based on what communication behavior would be generally expected or appropriate; the other based on generally *un*expected or *in*appropriate communicative responses (rule violations).

1. You are in an intimate relationship with another person. He or she has just spent four hours preparing an elaborate gourmet meal for you. What do you say?

2. You are on the brink of becoming engaged to person A. However, circumstances forced you to take a long trip with person B. You were sexually intimate with person B, but both of you agree it was "a one-time thing." You still plan the engagement with person A. On your return, person A asks you what happened on your trip. What do you say?

3. You are introduced to a stranger. The stranger smiles and extends his or her hand to greet you. What do you do?

4. You enter an elevator. The only other person in the elevator is an attractive stranger of the opposite sex. What do you say or do?

Now ask some of your friends to respond to the foregoing episodes. Are there communication rules for these situations? Is there enough agreement on the appropriate behavior so we can assume there is a communication norm operating?

In an effort to predict the permissible communication in the episodes, you had to consider a number of factors: How well did the communicators know each other? What topic were they discussing? What messages preceded the one you were asked to predict? What was the setting in which the message was delivered and received? etc. Questions like these were the bases for a number of hypotheses developed by Roderick P. Hart and the senior author concerning the following interrelationships between speakers, listeners, situations, and expected messages.[11]

- When communicators are physically close, listeners expect more personal messages; less personal, or public, messages are expected when physical distance is greater.

- When the relationship between communicators is intimate, there is a greater demand for messages of affection; strangers are expected to supply messages that reflect less affection.

- When the speaker perceives the listener as higher in status, there is a greater demand for humility in message sending; when the listener is perceived as lower in status, dignity in message sending is expected—for example, his constituents did not expect Senator Muskie to cry when addressing them.

- When the speaker perceives the listener as highly ego-involved in the topic, there is a greater demand for respectful message sending—the speaker would not criticize his mother-in-law in front of his wife; if listener ego-involvement is perceived as low, nonpretentious messages are required—students in required courses would not appreciate messages implying they should be happy to be there.

- When the listener's self-image is highly involved in the message, there is a greater demand for complimentary messages—"I'd like to go out with you . . . I really would . . . but . . . "; when the listener's self-image is not at stake, undramatic messages are called for—the speaker would not expect the listener to get "heated" during idle chatter about the World Series.

- When the listener's basic attitudes are salient due to the situation or the topic of discussion, there is a greater demand for seriousness in message sending; if the listener's basic attitudes are irrelevant to the situation or discussion, more flippant messages may be required—a highly political listener would not expect to discuss the philosophy of Karl Marx at an orgy.

- When the speaker's role in a situation is clearly defined, there is a greater demand for his or her messages to be consistent with that role; a lack of clarity regarding the speaker's role will call for nonpresumptuous message sending. The self-appointed "coordinator" at an informal party is a good example of a violation of the latter.

- When there is a great deal of formality between the communicators, there is a greater demand for messages which could be described as "non-gauche"—"Hi. Queenie!" addressed to the Queen of England; informality requires informal messages.

Naturally, the preceding list represents only some of the many interpersonal conditions that help to structure the development of communication norms. You will no doubt think of others. At this point you may be troubled by what seems to be a communicator's book of etiquette. When you see that "you *can't* do this," "you *must* do this," or "you *aren't supposed* to do this," it is an understandable reaction to question these edicts—to think of the exceptions. After all, people do violate the rules we've discussed, sometimes with little or no punishment from those around them. Why?

Violating Communicative Rules

Norms are brought vividly to our attention when they are violated. Davis provides some excellent examples:

> In our society, a person can achieve the status of mental patient either by casually telling a mere acquaintance what would generally be considered his most intimate aspects or by arduously telling his closest friend what would

generally be considered his least intimate aspects. Thus, he could get himself committed to a mental hospital either by matter-of-factly describing to an acquaintance his disgusting anatomical details ("I have a terrible case of hemorrhoids. Let me show them to you") or by agonizingly confessing to his friend, after months of hinting that he would like to reveal to him his essential secret, something he has never told anyone before, that, more than anything else in the world, he hates the color blue ("it's everywhere! I can't stand it! I see it wherever I go!").[12]

A further illustration of what happens when conversational rules are violated is found in an assignment ethnomethodologist Harold Garfinkel gave his undergraduate students. Students were instructed to engage an acquaintance or a friend in ordinary conversation and, without indicating that anything was out of the ordinary, insist that the other person clarify the sense of his or her commonplace remarks. The following dialogues represent typical student experiences.[13]

Case One

"Hi, Ray. How is your girlfriend feeling?"

"What do you mean, how is she feeling? Do you mean physical or mental?"

"I mean how is she feeling? What's the matter with you?" (He looked peeved.)

"Nothing. Just explain a little clearer what do you mean?"

"Skip it. How are your Med School applications coming?"

"What do you mean, how are they?"

"You know what I mean."

"I really don't."

"What's the matter with you? Are you sick?"

Case Two

On Friday night my husband and I were watching television. My husband remarked that he was tired. I asked, "How are you tired? Physically, mentally, or just bored?"

"I don't know, I guess physically, mainly."

"You mean that your muscles ache, or your bones?"

"I guess so. Don't be too technical."

(After more watching)

"All these old movies have the same kind of old iron bedstead in them."

"What do you mean? Do you mean all old movies, or some of them, or just the ones you have seen?"

"What's the matter with you? You know what I mean."

"I wish you would be more specific."

"You know what I mean! Drop Dead!"

The foregoing conversations highlight how much we take for granted as we converse with others—how much we "let pass."[14] We assume that any important ambiguities in a person's discourse will be cleared up later. If we violate that rule too often (as illustrated in the cases presented), the other communicator will no doubt observe our violation and sanction us accordingly.

Like any rules, communicative rules require adherence. When the rule is broken, some type of sanctioning usually takes place—rejection, frustration, puzzled or disapproving looks, avoidance, reprimands, or simply a facial expression which visually says "You're weird!" While this is usual, it is not always the case. For instance, in many of our interactions there is a norm for politeness that discourages us from letting others know that their behavior is strange or inappropriate. Even if someone is talking too much or disclosing information that is too personal, we will sometimes listen attentively to avoid being rude.[15] In other cases, we may not sanction a rule violation because we see the violation as positive. Under the right circumstances, what seems to be excessive displays of affection or support from a loved one may be very much appreciated.[16] Also, there are times when we choose not to react negatively to rule violations because of a characteristic or behavior demonstrated by the rule violator.

One way to break communicative rules successfully, incurring little punishment, is to be perceived as a person who was not aware of the expectations for the situation,[17] or one who was aware but was incapable of doing anything about them. A person may be seen as irresponsible or naive ("He didn't know any better"). For example:

GRANDMA: How does my favorite boy like the nice warm sweater Grandma knitted for him?

CHILD: It's yucky.

Or he or she may be perceived as handicapped ("She couldn't help it") or as boxed in ("He had no alternative"). A person may also get away with rule violations if seen as "just having fun" ("She didn't mean it").

Sometimes one rule can be violated, but other contiguous rules are not violated, so that one's total behavior is considered balanced. A high school teacher may talk about sex in the classroom, but do so in an educational manner. Similarly, rules may be violated when people believe that accomplishing some other task (e.g., answering a phone call, comforting a crying baby) is more important than adhering to the rules.[18] As long as the violation does not violate the relationship, there should be less concern on the part of the message receiver(s).

Rule violations can also be offset by apologies,[19] but a more strategic method of defusing negative reactions is to acknowledge that the rule is about to be broken—a 25-year-old male says to a 45-year-old female stranger: "I know I probably shouldn't ask—and you don't have to answer if you don't want to—but how old are you?" Disclaimers of this type were the subject of study by Hewitt and Stokes.[20] They categorized the following types of disclaimers:

1. **Hedging.** This conveys: what follows is tentative and I'm willing to accept other views. "I'm no expert, of course, but . . ."; "I haven't thought this through very well, but . . ."; or "Let me play the devil's advocate here."

2. **Credentialing.** This conveys: I know you'll react unfavorably to what I'm about to say, but I'll try to establish special credentials that will soften that reaction. "Don't get me wrong, I like your work, but . . ." or, "I'm not prejudiced, some of my best friends are. . . ."

3. **Sin Licenses.** This conveys: I know you'll react negatively, but that's the way it has to be. "What I'm going to do is contrary to the letter of the law but not its spirit. . . ."

4. **Cognitive.** This conveys: I realize you may think I'm losing touch with facts or reality, so I'll acknowledge the fact, thereby showing I am in control. "I know this sounds crazy, but. . . ."

5. **Appeal for Suspended Judgment.** This conveys: I know you're going to be tempted to react unfavorably, but wait until you hear the whole story. "I don't want to make you angry by saying this, but . . ." or "Hear me out before you explode. . . ."

If the rule violation is perceived as an isolated instance, it has a greater chance of being accepted, particularly if the significant others (interaction partners and others involved in the situation) can find some unusual, but plausible explanation for the actions. For example, a person may break down and cry in front of a casual acquaintance who knows that that individual's brother just died of cancer.

A rule can be violated and unpleasant reactions circumvented by choosing the rule very carefully. If the violated rule is not deeply internalized or ego-related to the relevant, or significant, other(s) or it is not bound by severe sanctions (violations are expected), punishment will be minimal. Asking a total stranger on the street for a cigarette or forgetting the name of someone you were just introduced to would probably fall into this category. Notice how many times the slightest pause in regreeting a person you've been introduced to will cause them to help you by quickly restating their name. In some situations, people realize the rules are not widely known so that violators are given a greater range of behavior before the rule is considered violated.

For example, there seem to be few widely accepted rules for interactions involving one's former spouse. And people who are overtly solicitous with a handicapped person may, at first, be gently encouraged to interact in more conventional ways rather than reprimanded. Argyle found people reacting very negatively to violations that prohibited conversation from even taking place. These people considered the following to be totally disruptive: speaking an unknown language; being overly aggressive or disinterested; responding to an idea by changing the topic. The same people reacted less negatively to violations of rules that would be considered non-essential for conversation to take place.[21] The following were considered only mildly disruptive to conversations: lying on the floor; sitting too close; sitting too far away.

We also know that some people get away with rule violations because it is done with class or style—the violations are not perceived as too gross or too crude. Those who proffer sexual invitations in the initiating or early experimenting stages of a relationship are no doubt acutely aware of this need for sophistication. We would suspect that as the intensity of the conversation and the use of loaded language increases, there is a corresponding increase in the possibility that one or both participants will feel that a rule has been violated.

Shimanoff notes three other reasons why rule violations may not be negatively sanctioned: (1) the violator may be of a higher status and it may therefore be in the best interests of the other person to overlook the violation; (2) the violation may be viewed as a violation for the purpose of emphasis of humor; and (3) the act of giving a negative evaluation to someone may, itself, violate a rule of politeness so it is not proffered.[22]

In some situations, people do not care about negative reactions to rule violations. The violation may be used to disorient, frustrate, or elicit defensiveness in the other as a means to gain power over them. On other occasions, rule violations are used to get an early reading of the other person.[23] At such times the person may feel he or she has an adequate number of friends and thus choose to channel the energy into developing relationships with only those who react well in a difficult situation—for example, a rule violation. Also, the person may be extremely fearful of investing time and energy in a close relationship that may end up being hurtful. At such times, rigidity, rejection, and/or responses in line with the norm for the given situation by the recipient may not provide the necessary motivation to develop a closer relationship. Attempts by the recipient to counter the original rule violation with an even stronger violation may also work against attraction in situations of this type. These outcomes pertain to rules or conventions developed by a pair to fulfill their specific needs and desires. These rules can be easily changed (if both participants so desire) and sanctions are normally applied only by the other party, although in some cases "outside executioners" are shipped in.[24]

Most communicative rules are considered informal, nothing like *Robert's Rules of Order*. This informal nature may cause wide variations in adherence. Some people feel almost an obligation to break a rule once it is brought to their attention; others will adhere tenaciously for fear of not being correct. Most of us lie between such extremes. We recognize and can appreciate the fact that communicative rules add predictability, order, and structure to our world. We also recognize that they can be changed—that violations are not necessarily tantamount to social incompetence. We recognize that rules often make life easier—keeping us from having to make an interminable number of interpersonal decisions during each encounter; yet we know that rules are limited—that changes in factors such as the physical environment or in someone's mood[25] may leave us without any clear code of conduct. We understand how helpful a knowledge of communication rules can be when facing new social situations—giving us guidelines for achieving certain communication goals like acceptance, influence, understanding, and acknowledgment; and we realize the role communication rules play in the satisfaction of interpersonal needs—affection, ego support (or the lack of damage to it), inclusion, control, avoiding conflict, maintaining order, insuring interaction (or the absence of it), and so on.

With this understanding of the backbone of interaction rituals, communicative rules, the rest of the chapter will explore four common, but important rituals—greetings, forms of address, relationship openings, and small talk.

The Rhetoric of Hello

On the surface, interpersonal greetings seem to be a rather quick, simple, and routinized way of initiating communication. Generally we don't give much thought to what happens during those first few seconds of interaction unless something unusual happens[26]—receiving a warm smile and a "hi" from an unknown passerby or receiving a fully documented medical report when we query, "How are you?" For some time, scholars have regarded greetings and other similarly routinized social sequences (e.g., ordering food at a restaurant) as conversational *scripts* or sequences of actions that we carry out automatically, with very little thought.[27] More recently, however, an important qualification has been added to this description of scripts. Although they are routine and regular, conversational scripts are not static (unchanging). Instead they are flexible and adaptive.[28] In the case of greetings, this means that we adjust what we say to the person we are greeting—depending on our relationship with the person, the mood he or she is in, and how the person responds to us.

It is also important to remember that just because we normally don't pay much attention to greetings doesn't mean that they are simple or unimportant. In a very real sense, when we say hello (verbally and/or nonverbally), we have implicitly agreed to interfere with another's life. It could be argued, then, that this seemingly insignificant intrusion into another's life brings with it an added responsibility for the other's welfare. Perhaps this is one reason why city dwellers are sometimes described as cold when they do not respond to the well-meaning salutations of strangers; the city dwellers are expressing a need not to get involved. Consider how you feel when a person you know passes you and fails to acknowledge your existence. Conversely, consider how difficult it is for you to intentionally ignore a greeting from an acquaintance. The act of initiating communication is the first step in becoming a part of another person's life. Even passing greetings between strangers provide a form of social recognition, affirmation of a fellow human being's existence, and mutual access to one another.

For our purposes, the most important feature of the greeting ritual is what it tells us about the relationship between the interacting parties.

Greetings and Relationships

Since the manner in which a greeting is performed will help structure the dialogue to follow, it is not surprising that greetings convey information about the relationship. This information may appear in a variety of verbal and nonverbal behaviors. Strangers, for instance, might be more apt to engage in handshaking, formal forms of address (Mr.), and formal expressions like "Good morning"; "Nice to meet you"; or "Pardon me, but. . . ." Intimates may greet each other with an embrace or a kiss, avoid handshaking, use shortened verbalizations like "Hey!" or some specialized nonverbal gesture unique to themselves. One form of these specialized greetings has been labeled the "friendly insult greeting"—e.g., "Hi, dummy!" or "You rotten son-of-a-bitch, how ya doin?"[29] The "insult" is not intended to be taken literally at all, but the metamessage is that "we have such a close relationship, I am confident that you will understand that I mean the opposite of what I'm saying." Of course, there are times when it is not clear to the person being greeted that this is the case, so such greetings may be risky with all but the best of friends.

Status relationships may be noted in the ritual that requires a subordinate in the army to maintain a salute until it is returned by the greeted officer. Greetings by subordinates in executive suites may be proffered from a greater distance. Without belaboring the point, it should be clear that one of the things we say, when we say hello, is what the nature of our relationship is, so the forthcoming dialogue can follow suit. While our choice of words and behaviors in these situations depends, in part, on our efforts to be socially appropriate (polite) and conversationally efficient,[30] the nature of our relationship with the person we are greeting can override the usual norms for both politeness and efficiency. For instance, researchers have noted that intimates disregard some of the steps that people usually go through when they greet each other on the telephone.[31] While politeness norms suggest that people should identify themselves at the beginning of a phone conversation, frequently friends, family members, and lovers skip over this step. Because they tend to recognize each other's voices and speak to each other frequently, intimates don't always need to identify themselves or the purpose of their call.

When people have been parted for a period of time, it is often necessary to dramatize relationship features. An overly enthusiastic greeting may communicate that the absence has not changed what was previously a good relationship. Hence, the amount of time separating our greetings with a particular person may affect the expansiveness of the greeting. Goffman has proposed an *attenuation rule* which argues that the expansiveness of the greeting will gradually subside with each subsequent greeting, especially when an individual is forced to greet a person numerous times during the day—which is the case in many offices.[32] One of our colleagues, Robert E. Smith, felt it was also the case at the professional conventions of communication scholars which he attends—as his composition testifies:

Convention Book of Days

I

Heeeeyyyy! Jim!
Good to see you!
Looking fantastic
When did you get in?
Flight down went OK
How are things at the university?
Congratulations
That's great about Susan
Jimmy, first string, Wow
Barby, first clarinet, Great
Research going well?
Maybe dinner tomorrow
Heeeeyyyy! Bill . . .

II

Hi, Jim
Enjoying the convention?
Good paper last meeting
Cup of coffee, all right?

III

Hi, Jim

IV

(Buzz off, Jim)

This attenuation rule may also be applicable to the various stages of a relationship. For example, we would expect greetings in the early stages of a relationship to be more inflated or exaggerated than greetings between intimates. Relationships that are coming apart may also reflect a return to the more visibly formalized and stereotyped greetings. The very nature of the relationship between close friends, relatives, or married couples speaks so powerfully that the expansiveness of greeting behavior is allowed to subside and is instead expressed in many subtle and spontaneous ways. Kendon and Ferber have observed the following greeting sequence:[33]

1. **Sighting, Orientation, and Initiation of the Approach.**

2. **Distant Salutation.** This is the "official ratification" that a greeting sequence has been initiated and who the participants are. A wave, smile, or call may be used for recognition. Several types of head movements were noted. One, the "head dip," has also been observed in other situations as a marker to transitions between activities or shifts in psychological orientation. This movement was not observed if the greeter did not continue the approach.

3. **Approach.** As the greeters continued to move toward each other, gazing probably helped signal that channels were cleared for talking. An aversion of this gaze, however, was seen just prior to the close salutation stage. Grooming behavior and one or both arms positioned in front of the body were also observed at this point. When the participants were within ten feet of each other, mutual gazing, smiling, and a positioning of the head not seen in the sequence thus far were seen. The palms of the hands were sometimes turned toward the other person.

4. **Close Salutation.** As the participants negotiated a standing position, ritualistic comments like "Hi, Bob! How ya doin'?" were heard. And, if the situation called for body contact (handshakes, embraces), it would occur at this time.

While it would be literally impossible to catalogue each specific verbal and nonverbal greeting behavior for each type of person in every situation and every kind of relationship, a general taxonomy has been developed.[34]

Nonverbally, greetings are frequently initiated by a vertical or sideways motion of the head accompanied by eye contact. Kendon notes that a head toss probably invites further interaction—as does a tilting of the head back and/or raising of the eyebrows. But nods or a lowering of the head while making some other greeting gesture (e.g., wave) is likely to be just a greeting-in-passing. One of the functions of eye contact is signaling that the channels of communication are open. Should you not wish to pursue a conversation with a person, the avoidance of eye contact is imperative since a prolonged mutual glance almost obligates you to extend the encounter. Other eye-related greeting behaviors include winks or what is known as an *eyebrow flash,* a distinct up-and-down movement of the eyebrows which is barely detectable. Some observations from other cultures suggest that the eyebrow flash may be a universal behavior attendant to greetings.[35] The hands may also be very active in the greeting process. Salutes, waves, handshakes, handslaps, and various emblematic gestures such as the peace sign, raised fist, or thumbs up may be seen. The hands may also be engaged in grooming attendant to the greeting—running fingers through one's hair. Touching, in the form of embraces, kisses, or hitting on the arm is also common. The mouth may take the form of a smile or an oval shape which suggests a possible readiness for subsequent talk.

Sometimes we find ourselves in close contact with strangers and wish to signal that we do not want to greet them. Observations of people in such circumstances in a bar, shopping center, and on a college campus found the following nonverbal behaviors occurring in most of the situations: lip compression; lip bite; tongue-show; tongue-in-cheek; downward, lateral, and maximal lateral gaze avoidance; hand-to-face, hand-to-hand, hand-to-body, and hand-behind-head automanipulations; and postures involving flexion and adduction of upper limbs. These behaviors which signaled "stay away" or "greeting will not be well received" abruptly ceased after the strangers left the scene.[36]

Verbally, greetings may be classified along the following lines:

1. Verbal salutes—"Good morning."

2. Direct references to the other person by name, nickname, or personal pronoun—"Hi, babe!" or "Jeremiah!"

3. Questions of personal inquiry—"What's new with you?" or "How ya doin'?"

4. Verbalizations expressing a desire to continue a past relationship—"Long time no see" or "Nice seeing you *again.*"

5. Compliments—"You're sure looking good."

6. References to here-and-now surroundings—"May I get you another drink?" or "Can you tell me who did that painting?"

7. References to people or things, outside the immediate interaction setting— "How do you like this weather we're having?"

8. References to the other's behavior—"I noticed you were sitting all alone over here."

9. References to oneself—"Boy, have I had a rough day!" or "Hi, I'm Mark Knapp."

10. Apologies—"Excuse me, but. . . ."

11. Unexpected, humorous, or whimsical phrases designed to break the ice— "How's your sex life?" or "This is the best drink I've had since breakfast."

12. Immediate topic initiation which usually excludes any preliminary comments—"The reason I wanted to talk to you. . . ."

13. Single words or vocalizations that are essentially content-free—"Well!" or muted grunting sound.

The preceding list of behaviors is representative, but not necessarily exhaustive. Any given greeting may fall into several of the categories discussed. A legitimate question at this point might be: So what? So what if we go to all the trouble to dissect greeting behavior? In answer, the major advantage of this classification system is that it may eventually help us to understand more precisely what particular form greetings take at various stages of development and deterioration in human relationships. Once we are able to identify typical and regular patterns associated with specific stages and in specific situations, we have taken a giant step toward explaining the success or failure experienced later in the encounter. For instance, if you greet a close friend with behaviors typically found in interactions with strangers, a greater quantity of subsequent messages about the relationship itself may be required to make up for this unexpected behavior.

Forms of Address

Like greetings, the way we address another person may be brief, but it can say volumes about the relationship we have with that person. We are able to communicate our relative status to the other person, how well we are acquainted with him or her, whether we are angry or affectionate toward him or her, and whether the situation is a formal or informal one—all by the way we choose to address that person.[37] Fortunately, most of us have a variety of names and titles that provide several options as forms of address—Colonel Maxwell Q. Black, Colonel Black, Sir, Max, Maxie, "Ol' Stonedface." If a person offers a limited number of mutations of his or her name, others will often invent their own variations. This does not mean, of course, that we don't have trouble deciding how to address people. When we have difficulty determining our relative status or degree of intimacy to another, choices are frustrating—the familiar student dilemma: Dr., Professor, Mr., Mrs., Ms., Miss, Herbert or Mary Ellen? And what are the in-laws to be known as: Mr. and Mrs., Mom and Dad, Jim and Mavis, or should it wait until they can be Grandma and Grandpa?[38] As a rule, the more intimate we feel toward someone, the more we will be inclined to use less formal forms of address. The manifestations of this rule, and the exceptions to it, will be discussed in conjunction with the following continuum of formality for forms of address: (1) formal–impersonal; (2) ambiguous formality; (3) informal; and (4) intimate–affectionate.

Formal–Impersonal

The formal forms of address are generally used with strangers, new acquaintances, and those we perceive to have greater status than we do. In each case, the social distance between the communicators is high. Brown has identified what he feels is a universal norm underlying forms of address: Higher-status persons address subordinates with a form that people of equal status use when they are well acquainted or intimate (Bill or Willie); subordinates, on the other hand, must address the higher-status person with a form that people of equal status use when they are strangers or new acquaintances (Mr. Jennings).[39] This norm which incorporates indices of status and affection seems to have parallels in other behavior as well. For instance, Henley argues that people are most likely to initiate touching behavior with those of a status lower than their own—just as they do with people toward whom they feel affectionate.[40] Similarly, we've observed Ph.D.s calling the janitor they may see once or twice a week for thirty seconds by his nickname—"Hi, Mac." Researchers have argued that shorter names (like Mac) tend to be associated with approachability, whereas longer names (like Katherine or Alexander) tend to be linked to success and/or morality. Although this is clearly not always the case,[41] it may be part of the reason why people of a lower status are often addressed by their nicknames. Also, as we will note later, the use of nicknames generally is associated with people who feel more intimate with each other. Some observers of the current social scene have noted that women are more often called by their affectionate nickname (Billie, Georgie, Lilly) than men, who are more often known by an informal nickname (Bill or Bob, but not Billy or Bobby). In view of the parallels between affection and superiority presented thus far, such a finding (if it were true) would certainly have value for analyzing traditional perceptions of women in contemporary U.S. society.

Because formal names and titles often carry a sense of power or superiority, some researchers have investigated the extent to which we perceive certain names or titles as more masculine, or feminine, than others. For example, McConnell and Fazio found that people associated gender-marked, "man-suffixed" titles (e.g., chairman) with more masculine personality characteristics and "person-suffix" titles (e.g., chairperson) with relatively feminine characteristics.[42] They also found that individuals who had traditional beliefs about gender-roles were more influenced by gender-marked titles than were those with liberal beliefs. Given that formal titles provide information about our status, it is important to consider that the choices we make with regard to use of these titles also may send messages about our personality characteristics.

Formal forms of address are most often used when we perceive the other person's age, title, authority, eminence, or seniority as greatly above our own and when we feel this discrepancy needs to be manifested in the way we address the person. Formal forms of address will also manifest themselves when we fear the other person or when we want to build the addressee's ego through ingratiation strategies.

Ambiguous Formality

In the process of our life growth, our growth in school, or in our careers, we will periodically reach points where the perception of ourselves, relative to another in a particular situation, is vague. In short, we just don't know how to address someone. It might be a situation in which we feel a particular person doesn't warrant deference any longer because status differences have grown fuzzy—calling parents by their first names rather than "Mom" or "Dad," or calling a dissertation advisor by his or her first name. Imagine the dilemma for the Nixon cadre during and after the Watergate coverup—Mr. President? Mr. Nixon? Dick? Sir? Ahhh . . . ? It might also be a situation in which a person asks us to call him or her by his or her first name and we are reluctant to do so. There are any number of reasons why we will feel uncertainty or ambiguity about what to call someone. As a result, we may end up using any of the following strategies: (1) The most formal of the ambiguous forms of address includes Sir, Miss, Ma'am, Ms., etc. (2) The playful in-between is exemplified by "Doc" for a Ph.D. (3) The least formal response to the ambiguous situation is what Little and Gelles call the *Hey you form of address.*[43] A good example is the extended and amplified "Ahhhhh . . ." (with upraised finger) in place of a name or title.

Informal

The informal forms of address are usually derived from a person's first name—Jim is an informal form of James. In status-differentiated encounters the higher-status individual will usually ask the subordinate to call him or her by a less formal name. Many times, people try to speed up a relationship by deliberately using another person's first name when the situation calls for a more formal appellation. When you encounter a car salesperson and become offended by the salesperson's casual and frequent use of your first name, it may be because you perceive a needed formality for your relationship (strangers) and for the situation (business deals), not to mention the feeling that his or her usage immediately limits you to either subordinate or peer status at best.

Intimate–Affectionate

This represents the least formal of the forms used to address others. Ordinarily, this form is reserved for close friends or intimates. Even within this category, however, there seem to be subcategories of formality: (1) A further alteration of one's given name seems to be the most formal—Jimmy or Trish. Sometimes names do not have natural intimate forms so others will invent them—Marko for Mark. The usual manner of inventing these alterations is to add an *ie* or *y* to make an "ee" sound. Although most adult males regard this as too symbolic of childhood names, many exceptions do exist—Bobby Kennedy, Teddy Roosevelt, Jimmy Carter. A variation on given-name alteration is to use a person's middle name when it is not known to others and knowledge of it is symbolic of interpersonal closeness. (2) Nicknames that have been given because they are somehow associated with one's appearance, role, or activities represent the next lower level of formality—"Stretch," "Fireplug," "Chief," "Goose," or "Hands." Sometimes a name that starts out as a nickname becomes so commonly used in so many different relationships that it no longer has the uniqueness necessary to qualify as an intimate form of address—"Shaq" for basketball player Shaquille O'Neal. (3) Even more personal are those names that are considered traditional terms of endearment. These generally encompass terms designating the person as either sacred ("Angel"), an innocent small animal ("Chickadee") or child ("Babe," "Honey Child"), or a pleasant taste experience ("Sugar," "Honey"). (4) The most intimate forms of address seem to be those that have no apparent explanation, are often nonsensical, and are likely to be embarrassing if used in the presence of others—"Poopsie,""Booper," or "Snookums."

Although we would predict more personal forms of address between intimates, variations will appear, depending on how long intimacy has been established and what conditions exist in the environment for communicating. For instance, we are likely to find that longtime intimates may cease to use any mode of address. In addition, they may occasionally use the more formal forms, perhaps to emphasize closeness or just to be playful—"Thelma Z. Peters, I love you very much." Furthermore, the presence of others may cause an individual to address a close friend in a very formal manner—in a graduate student's oral examination, you might hear close friends addressing each other as Dr. and Professor. Obviously, the audience is not the friend and the friend understands. Formality may also change as the situation and roles change—Professor Ruggirello in the classroom becomes "Frank" in the touch football game.

As we mentioned earlier, the same form of address can be used to express anger or affection. Depending on the vocal inflection, the phrase "Look here, Baby Doll" could be demeaning and hateful or tender and loving. Naturally, the use of the intimate form greatly assists a demeaning vocal inflection in eliciting a defensive response. At other times anger or serious intent can be shown by simply increasing the degree of formality (and vocal volume). The following, familiar message construction seen in parent-child episodes illustrates this:

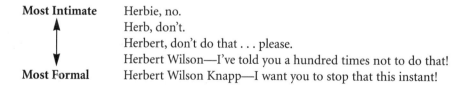

Most Intimate   Herbie, no.
⬆   Herb, don't.
⬇   Herbert, don't do that . . . please.
Most Formal   Herbert Wilson—I've told you a hundred times not to do that!
                 Herbert Wilson Knapp—I want you to stop that this instant!

Relationship "Openers"

How do you begin a relationship? Earlier in this chapter we noted that there are rules that help guide our communication choices. In most communication situations, we can recognize behaviors that are socially appropriate and others that are socially inappropriate. For instance, when greeting a superior, we tend to use more formal address terms than we would when greeting a peer. While rules such as these seem as if they should provide us with a prescription for how to begin relationships, they rarely do. In fact, often when we would like to initiate a relationship with someone, it is much easier for us to think of *in*appropriate behaviors than it is to think of appropriate ones. As a result, some people spend a great deal of time planning and rehearsing how to begin their first conversation with a man (woman). The classic example of this involves what many refer to as the "opening line."

Many prescriptions for good and bad opening lines are offered by the media and friends and acquaintances. However, many do not identify important contingencies such as the relationship between the communicators and the setting, the nonverbal cues used by communicators,[44] and the ability of each communicator to elicit disclosure from the other.[45] Those prescriptions that fail to recognize the importance of such factors tend to take on the characteristics of interpersonal burlesque. One book which says it will "lead you out of the singles jungle and into a happy marriage" is advertised by the following paragraph:

> From its initial, exclusive publication—at $95 a copy—to its rise to the top of the bestseller lists, this is the book that has helped women across the country escape the rut of a going-nowhere relationship—and start marrying the men of their choice. From the first date to getting to know a man, from dealing with your competition to steering romance into marriage, HOW TO MARRY THE MAN OF YOUR CHOICE will guide you directly to the altar—regardless of your looks, your past, your age![46]

Another book, which sports "50 Great Opening Lines," is advertised this way:

> The techniques in THE PICKING UP GIRLS KIT work for all men. You don't have to be brave, rich or good looking. Just walk up to the woman you have your eye on, use one of the simple techniques described in your kit, and you will pick her up. There is simply no way she can refuse you. WE GUARANTEE IT.[47]

From the never-fail fifty, we selected our favorite ten. You be the judge.

1. Do you have an aspirin?
2. Hi.
3. How long do you cook a leg of lamb?
4. Excuse me, I'm from out of town and I was wondering what people do around here at night.
5. What kind of dog is that? He's great-looking.
6. Wow! What a beautiful day.

7. Please pass the ketchup.

8. Didn't I meet you in Istanbul?

9. Who's your dentist?

10. Don't tell me a beautiful girl like you doesn't have a date tonight.

Another author who felt it necessary to justify his classification of "Hello" as a good opening line comments: "This is a fantastic opening line. I wish I could take credit for it. Probably millions of relationships between men and women have begun on this basis. If you feel more comfortable with 'Hi,' the results will be equally good."[48] This same author identifies the following as bad opening gambits between men and women:

1. Haven't I met you someplace before?

2. You are a beautiful person.

3. Let's go to bed.

4. I love you. Do you believe in love at first sight?

5. Do you think it will rain?

6. You look like a movie star.

7. Are you alone?

8. You look lonely.

9. Why are you here?

10. Where have I seen you before?

None but the most foolhardy would "guarantee success" with any message without some knowledge of who said it, to whom it was said, how it was said (vocal tone), whether, or how often, it had been said before, where it was said, what messages preceded it or would follow it. The assumptions underlying these pre-scriptions from the popular press are, however, important. Recipes for cookbook communication designed to initiate encounters are based on the belief that:

> *Only acceptable pickup line: "Hi, my name is [insert your name]. What's yours?"*
>
> Anonymous

(1) enough people have experienced difficulty in initiating communication to seek simple, guaranteed prescriptions, and (2) a number of people in this culture attach a great deal of importance to these initial behaviors, recognizing their role in facil-itating or inhibiting the communication that follows.

In an attempt to survey people who might actually use these opening lines and to categorize them according to different locations, psychologist Chris Kleinke asked several hundred college students in California and Massachusetts to write down all the opening lines they could think of that men might use with women at beaches, supermarkets, and bars.[49] After selecting the 100 most frequently cited openers, Kleinke asked 600 more students from the same two states to rate each line from "terrible" to "excellent." Both men and women respondents seemed to prefer the "direct" and "innocuous" lines over the "cute/flip" ones. But most men underestimated how much women were put off by the cute/flip approach. Some of the top-rated lines included:

In General Situations:
"I feel a little embarrassed, but I'd like to meet you." (direct)

At the Beach:
"The water is beautiful today, isn't it?" (innocuous)

At the Supermarket:
"Can you help me decide here? I'm a terrible shopper." (direct)

At the Bar:
"What do you think of the band?" (innocuous)

The bottom-rated lines included:

In General Situations:
"Is that really your hair?"
"Your place or mine?"
"You remind me of a woman I used to date."

At the Beach:
"Let me see your strap marks."

At the Supermarket:
"Do you really eat that junk?"

At the Bar:
"Bet I can outdrink you."

In another study, Murray found that the almost 3,000 opening lines he observed fell into three categories: questions (e.g., "How're you?"), advertisements/declarations (e.g., "My name is Heather"), and compliments (e.g., "I like your suit"). He also found that the use of sexual propositions and all three types of opening lines increased drastically from 10:00 P.M. to 11:00 P.M. and continued to increase at a slower rate until 1:00 A.M. Since his study was conducted in singles bars, this pattern is not surprising. As Murray himself notes, patterns of alcohol consumption, increased desperation (as closing time neared), and increases in perceived attraction (as desperation increased) probably account for this phenomenon.[50]

Although Murray's study focused on opening lines and sexual propositions in singles bars, the influence of alcohol on people's behavior during the early stages of relational development is apparent in other contexts as well. For instance, Mongeau and Johnson found that on first-dates, binge drinkers were more likely to become sexually involved than were nonbinge drinkers and that nonbinge drinkers, in turn, engaged in more sexual involvement that nondrinkers.[51] They also found that men reported more intimate sexual expectations and involvement than did women.

One final study of note asked adults as well as elementary, high school, and college students how they would initiate a friendly contact with a stranger of the same sex. The two most popular approaches reported were: (1) to ask the stranger to participate in an activity with you—e.g., children might ask the person to play with them during recess; and (2) to ask the person questions in order to find out more about him or her.[52]

One consistency that runs throughout all of these studies is that "good" opening lines rarely reveal the candid thoughts of the speaker. Granted, some people present themselves in a more direct, genuine way than do others.[53] But even the most direct lines (e.g., "I'd sure like to meet you") typically don't focus on relational or sexual issues. Douglas explains this by noting that although we might like to be more direct and efficient (e.g., "Do you find me physically attractive?"), we must balance our conversational efficiency with social appropriateness.[54] Certainly, it would be easier to reduce our uncertainty about potential relational partners by being more direct. However, since relational development is based on the wants and needs of *both* people, we must consider how the other person is going to respond to our direct inquiries.

In many cases, the response to an opening line is observable because the line is delivered and received in a face-to-face context. However, there are a number of different channels available to those seeking a romantic relationship, including personal ads, video dating services, match makers, and computer chat rooms. These alternative channels probably restrict some forms of communication (e.g., the ability to observe potential partners' nonverbal behavior) and allow for more freedom with regard to others (e.g., direct questions and impression management).[55] Although the communication that occurs between people who use these channels may differ from face-to-face interaction, it provides an idea of what some people think they want in a relational partner as well as what they believe others want. For instance, in studies of personal ads placed by heterosexual and homosexual men and women, several trends emerged: (1) heterosexual men wanted what heterosexual women offered—physical attractiveness; (2) heterosexual women sought what heterosexual men offered—financial security; (3) homosexual men emphasized physical attractiveness in their ads even more than did heterosexual men; and (4) homosexual women tended to deemphasize physical attractiveness as something to be sought or offered.[56]

While using a "bad" opening line may be a sure-fire way to discourage a relationship, using a "good" opening line doesn't ensure relationship development. Bell and Daly have found that people believe they use a number of other communication strategies to get people to like and appreciate them. These *affinity-seeking* strategies include behaviors that: (1) demonstrate one's *control and visibility* (e.g., being dynamic and interesting), (2) encourage *mutual trust* (e.g., consistently fulfilling commitments), (3) display *politeness* (e.g., adhering to conversational rules), (4) demonstrate *concern and caring* (e.g., listening to and supporting the other), (5) involve the other (e.g., including the other in activities), (6) show *self-involvement* (e.g., including oneself in the other's activities), and (7) focus on *commonalities* (e.g., pointing out similarities). People who were reported as using many of these affinity-seeking strategies were also rated as being more likable, socially successful, and satisfied with their lives. The use of other-oriented strategies (e.g., caring, listening, and including the other) seemed to best predict affinity. In addition, individuals' choice of affinity-seeking strategies depended on contextual and relational factors. People believed they used the different strategies in task-oriented situations than in social situations and they noted that status differences influenced their strategy choice.[57] These findings underline both the complexity and the mutuality of our initial interactions. When two people converse, both of them determine whether the conversation is successful and satisfying and both determine whether to continue the relationship. It is impossible to plan a conversation in its entirety (choosing the appropriate greeting, form of address, and affinity-seeking strategy) because we don't know how the other person will respond to us.[58] Communication rules provide us with a guideline, but it is a very general and necessarily flexible guideline.

After achieving contact and making our initial approach to conversation, the most common type of communication typically follows.

Small(?) Talk

What we commonly know as small talk has been discussed by other authors using terms like: *grooming talk, phatic communion, superficial talk, social cosmetics,* and *cliché conversation.* For some, this activity seems to be unimportant, even repugnant. Powell[59] correctly identified small talk as superficial, conventional, and perhaps the lowest level of communication about oneself. Indeed, small talk is characterized by breadth, not depth. We might expect to find a fair range of topics discussed, but very little motivation to reveal seldom-seen parts of one's inner self. Powell added, however, that small talk "represents the weakest response to the human dilemma." This opinion appears to be a gross miscalculation of the role of small talk in everyday life. The human condition is dependent on our ability to draw from a vast repertoire of topics, strategies, and feelings, in order to communicate at various levels of intimacy. Small talk represents a form of communication that is critical to developing relationships and thereby represents at times the strongest or most important response to "the human dilemma." In some contexts, such as the workplace, small talk is associated with trust.[60] In other situations small talk is almost the demanded form of communication—cocktail parties, family gatherings, first encounters. Without the ability to engage another in small talk in these situations, the human condition would surely suffer.

Personal careers may also suffer. Management Information Services (MIS) managers, according to one survey, had a high need to advance professionally and a low need to interact with others on a purely social level. As a result, one trade publication urged these managers to deliberately plan informal chitchat sessions with their non-data-processing colleagues or jeopardize their chances for promotion.[61] Although the specifics of exactly how to conduct these informal small-talk sessions were not presented, it is likely to be an important issue. Those people who castigate small talk are probably expressing a displeasure with the way in which it was conducted, not with the act of small talk per se. Like greetings, the act of engaging in small talk may be as important as the content of the exchange. Notice how engaging in small talk in the following example serves an important function in relationship building, even though the participants do not speak the same language:

> . . . a U.S. businessman who, while traveling to Europe for the first time, finds himself seated across from a Frenchman at lunch. Neither speaks the other's language, but each smiles a greeting. As the wine is served, the Frenchman raises his glass and gesturing to the American says, "Bon appetit!" The American does not understand and replies, "Ginzberg." No other words are exchanged at lunch. That evening at dinner, the two again sit at the same table and again the Frenchman greets the American with the wine, saying, "Bon appetit!" to which the American replies, "Ginzberg." The waiter notices this peculiar exchange and, after dinner, calls the American aside to explain that "the Frenchman is not giving his name—he is wishing you good appetite; he is saying that he hopes you enjoy your meal." The following day the American seeks out the Frenchman at lunch, wishing to correct his error. At the first opportunity the American raises his glass and says, "Bon appetit!" to which the Frenchman proudly replies, "Ginzberg."[62]

Even when communicators speak the same language, listening may not be the intent and the exchange of noises assumes precedence over substance.

The prevention of silence is, itself, an important conversational goal fulfilled by small talk. For some, it is difficult to accept the fact that there are communicative exchanges that shouldn't be taken too literally: Trivial conversation at parties doesn't mean everybody there (except us) was somehow devoid of intelligent things to say; and people who can't remember the topic of the sermon immediately upon leaving church may still have had a deeply religious experience. In many instances the literal translation of the words spoken is less important than the fact that words have been spoken. When a new student walks into a professor's office and sees him or her surrounded by papers, furiously pounding at the computer, and asks, "Are you busy?", the professor doesn't usually turn around and say, "No, I'm relaxing." The student's words were intended to be translated, "Hello! There's somebody here to see you. I want to talk to you. I realize I'm interrupting you. You may not want to talk to me or you may not have time so I'll ask a question that will give you the opportunity to ease out of this encounter by saying you're busy. I hope you appreciate the way I handled this interruption—so much so that you won't use the excuse I've given you." So, like this example of an opening line, small talk is often an end in itself. But small talk is also a means to an end—that is, it serves several important interpersonal functions.

Functions of Small Talk

Small talk is a way of maintaining a sense of community or fellowship with other human beings. It helps us cement our bond of humanness. Desmond Morris calls it a "friendly mutual aid system" akin to the grooming and licking rituals of non-human primates which provide feelings of comfort, security, and acceptance.[63] Hayakawa calls it "the language of social cohesion."[64] Keeping the lines of communication open with members of your own species and enjoying the togetherness of talking often take precedence over subject matter.

In the jargon of Schutz's interpersonal needs, we could say small talk is most effective in satisfying inclusion needs, since it is designed so that each party can (or must) contribute. Perhaps this is one reason that we find so little disagreement or conflict in small talk; supportiveness and affirmation are indispensable for maintaining effectively a sense of community with our fellow humans.

Small talk also serves as a proving ground for both new and established relationships. Small talk in this sense, then, becomes an "audition for friendship." We noted earlier how potential friends and acquaintances are visually filtered; during small talk we apply a verbal filter. Only after we are satisfied with the communication at the superficial level of small talk do we venture into "big talk"—communication characterized by greater focus and depth of personal disclosures. Sometimes we mistakenly associate seriousness exclusively with big talk. However, it is easy to think of many serious conversations (task-oriented business discussions or courtship games) that still offer only surface information about the participants. Other times, we make the mistake of assuming that big talk is more important than small talk for maintaining relationships. But Goldsmith and Baxter found that nearly half of all the conversations people reported having with acquaintances, friends, romantic partners, family members, and others, consisted of relatively informal, superficial talk.[65] Likewise, Duck and his colleagues found that intimates really spend a relatively small portion of their everyday conversation engaged in self-disclosive discussions.[66] While intimacy is usually a precursor to self-disclosure, self-disclosure doesn't always characterize intimate relationships. For instance, one of the necessary magic tricks for the person seeking instant intimacy is to give the illusion of serious self-revelation which can be shrugged off as superficial small talk, should the request for instant intimacy be denied; the other person has not truly become a confidant. In established relationships small talk may be dispensed with more quickly and easily, but it is a necessary prelude to more intimate dialogue. The frustration of this *Playboy* reader aptly illustrates the process:

> Because of a job transfer, my girlfriend and I live in different states; we see each other only on holidays and special trips. Every time we meet, we go through a ritual period of adjustment that wastes precious time and often causes discord. She insists that we fill each other in on the changes we have undergone. I would just as soon spend our time on the simple joys of being together and let the changes in our personalities surface gradually, but she sees this soul unveiling as vital to our relationship. We do love each other. How do we resolve our difficulties?—E. A., Omaha, Nebraska.[67]

It appears that the reader's girlfriend is hoping some initial small talk will assure her that surface changes have not occurred during their absence from each other and that this will allow them to escalate to their past-relationship-level talk once again.

Small talk provides a safe procedure for indicating who we are and how another can come to know us better. We're playing for time, trying to display our best features. If one of our many selves doesn't seem to work, we can always shift gears and bring out another self. For instance, one researcher found that women used the telephone strategically to influence the way their male dating partners perceived them.[68] These women made decisions about how often to call their dating partners, when to return calls, and what to talk about so that the men they were dating would not see them as overly aggressive. Small talk allows us to further reduce uncertainties about the other without revealing too much too soon. It can also allow others to focus more specifically on who we are. The fewer the uncertainties, the greater the chances of accurate predictions about the person—and the greater the chances of moving from small talk to big talk.

Another function of small talk is to serve as an interpersonal pacifier. It is a nonthreatening, time-killing activity devoid of the pressures involved in more analytical or introspective processes. In short, it can be a release, an escape valve, or a diversion from other kinds of talk which require more conscious thought.[69]

And finally, small talk provides a means for uncovering integrating topics, or, more simply, openings for more penetrating conversations and relationships. We now turn our attention to the nature of these topics, which is the information derived and exchanged during small talk.

Name, Rank, and Serial Number

When strangers meet for the first time, the first few minutes will usually be devoted to an exchange of demographic or biographical information—name, occupation, marital status, hometown.[70] They are attempting to obtain a sociological profile of the other person in the hope that certain similarities will be uncovered and form a common ground for conversational pursuit. The exchange of biographical information is more involved when the environmental cues do not provide much information about who a partner might be. In other situations, the environment allows participants to make more inferences with more certainty. For example, if you meet a person in a University building carrying books, you might not feel the need to ask if the person was a student, where the person goes to school, what general age range the person represents, and so forth. In some cases, the environmental forces will be so compelling that strangers will begin exchanging attitudes and opinions before seeking demographic data—two delegates who meet at a political gathering. During the early information exchange—a period Berger calls the *entry phase*—a norm often seems to be operating which says: If I provide you with some information about myself, you will reciprocate by giving me an equal amount of information about yourself. Or, in simpler terms, "I'll tell you my hometown if you tell me yours."

The reason biographical information is so predominant in a new relationship is that it is something each party is sure to know about himself or herself, and it is generally nonthreatening because it is nonarguable. Sure, we could start an argument over somebody's hometown, but we generally reserve that for later.

Other topics commonly encountered in initial small talk may be derived from the situation or surroundings. "I'm building a house and I was wondering what kind of insulation you selected for this room." The weather seems to be a topic everyone knows, is a part of every situation, and is generally nonthreatening. The topic of weather will probably occur more often in certain areas of the country and at certain times during the year. Some sections of the country seem to have local guidelines for small talk topics. In Lafayette, Indiana, for instance, it is not unusual to talk about the dearth of good restaurants in the area, the quality of the local newspaper, and the fact that it's a "good place to raise kids." Another currently popular ploy is to talk about how much you hate small talk and how people really aren't open with each other. Of course, talking *about* openness meets all the necessary criteria for small talk and is very different from actually *being* open by disclosing more intimate aspects of your personality. Finally, Beinstein's research shows how the topics for small talk will often reflect the environment, the time allowed for interaction, the distance between the participants, and the ostensible purpose for the meeting.[71] She obtained data on topics discussed in twenty-eight barber shops, thirty beauty shops, and thirty pharmacies in Philadelphia during the summer. It is no surprise that vacations were a frequent topic in all the shops, nor that beauticians talked with their customers mainly about fashions, nor that pharmacists talked with their customers mainly about health problems. The only surprise may have been that barbers talked about vacations more than sports.[72]

Once we have sufficiently stocked our biographical warehouse, we can begin to focus on those aspects that seem to be productive avenues for further conversation (increase the depth) or pursue additional areas that seem logically related (increase the breadth). Upon learning that a couple is not married and just living together, you may choose to slowly tap the conditions and value system that led to that decision or you may seek another different, but related area—"Yeah, a lot of things are changing nowadays. My sister got married with the understanding that she would not have any kids." More often than not, breadth is our choice with strangers and acquaintances; when depth is pursued, however, it is usually a brief foray unless the communicators already have a close relationship or unless special circumstances indicate that the other person needs and wants to uncover a particular inner area.

> *His own small talk, at any rate, was bigger than most people's large. "I believe it was Hegel who defined love as the ideality of the relatively of the reality of an infinitesimal portion of the absolute totality of the Infinite Being" he would chat at dinner.*
>
> Peter De Vries

Thus, through small talk we eventually obtain knowledge about the other person—hobbies, interests, likes, dislikes, tastes, future plans, other acquaintances and friends. Gradually, small talk will move past the highly superficial, biographical level, and information will be gained about attitudes, opinions, goals, and specific ways of behaving—how the person handles mistakes, conflict, play, and support for others. It is only when we begin to tap those things that a person does not reveal to just anybody—topics which are held in the middle layers of Altman and Taylor's Social Penetration Model (see Chapter 2)—that we have moved from small talk to big talk.

Berger points out the usefulness of this harvesting of biographical information in predicting possible attitudes a person might hold—similar backgrounds may suggest similar attitudes.[73] It seems we work backward too, predicting possible biographical information from perceived attitudes. If we disagree or agree with someone, we sometimes try to relate that back to some previously uncovered aspect of background similarity or dissimilarity. It is likely, however, that when we're surprised (background dissimilarities turn into attitude agreements or background similarities turn into attitude disagreements) we will be less inclined to recall our earlier store of information and attribute the situation, instead, to the current phase of the relationship.

Small talk also aids friends who have been separated to pick up their relationship again. When friends are separated, uncertainty increases and once again they have to start the feeling-out process. Since biographical data are the least apt to change, friends often start their small talk by asking what's been happening, what they've been doing since they last saw each other, etc. By telling friends what happened during a separation, we help them to "catch up" with our past and provide them with knowledge that may facilitate their interaction with us in the future.[74] Most of us engage in this type of small talk on a more limited basis with roommates, family, and lovers when we talk with them about what happened in our day. "Debriefing" a relational partner about the events of our day seems to have an important function in our relationships. Researchers have found that spouses who spent more time talking together about the events of their day tended to be more relationally satisfied.[75]

In an attempt to summarize some of the material discussed thus far, let's look at a study conducted by Berger and his colleagues.[76] Over 200 adult residents of a Chicago suburb were asked to imagine they were observing a two-hour conversation between people meeting for the first time. These "observers" sorted 150 preselected statements into eight fifteen-minute segments. They were also asked to place those statements that they felt would not occur in a two-hour conversation of this type into a separate category. Generally, the results confirm what we've been saying thus far: Demographic and superficial information about oneself tends to be disclosed to new acquaintances first; personal, sexual, and family problems are consistently placed in later time slots. Some noteworthy exceptions do exist—one's salary and age, although seemingly superficial information, are not disclosed early. In such cases, we might assume that speakers may not want listeners to infer deeper personality aspects from this biographical information. Table 6.1 presents a sampling of these results.

Whether you agree or disagree with the particular order of the preceding statements is irrelevant as long as you recognize that we all organize our revelations to others in some way. Some people may not mind mentioning their salary early in the conversation and even the people in this study—given additional information about the other person, e.g., an investment counselor for people in lower income brackets—may have revealed the salary information. The point is that *whatever* information you perceive to be more personal about yourself will most likely be

---

TABLE 6.1   Perceptions of When Information Might Be Revealed Between Strangers in a Two-Hour Conversation

---

Zero to Fifteen Minutes:

1. I'm a volunteer at a local hospital.
2. I'm from New York.
3. My son is a freshman at Penn State.
4. I have a dog, three cats, and a parakeet.

Fifteen to Thirty Minutes:

1. My wife is a good cook.
2. I've been skiing only once.
3. I like hunting for antiques.
4. I really enjoy playing tennis.
5. The Chicago Bears are a lousy football team.

Thirty to Forty-Five Minutes:

1. I've never really had a vacation.
2. I wish I knew more about politics.
3. Most of my clothes are blue or green.
4. One of my favorite authors is Norman Mailer.
5. I wear contact lenses.

Forty-Five to Sixty Minutes:

1. I am thirty-five years old.
2. It bothers me to see young women cursing and swearing.
3. My parents were much more politically conservative than I am.
4. I make it a point to see the doctor, dentist, and optometrist once a year.
5. I want to give my children all of the things I never had as a child.

Sixty to Seventy-Five Minutes:

1. I don't like people who smile all the time.
2. People who don't finish what they start always annoy me.
3. I don't believe in evolution.
4. I dislike my job so much I would like to quit tomorrow and move to a farm.
5. Any American who is a Communist should be deported from the country.

Seventy-Five to Ninety Minutes:

1. I don't believe that there is an afterlife, but I'm really not sure.
2. I hate lying in bed at night, listening to the clock tick.
3. I wish my church was more relevant to my life.
4. I believe in mercy-killing when there is absolutely no hope of survival.
5. My mother-in-law really dislikes me.

Ninety to One Hundred Five Minutes:

1. I have a violent temper.
2. I find it difficult to respond rationally when I am criticized.
3. I suspect people's motives when they compliment me.
4. I think we got married much too young.
5. There are times when I feel I have wasted my life.

One Hundred Five to One Hundred Twenty Minutes:

1. Sometimes I'm afraid I won't be able to control myself.
2. I wish my husband would feel free to cry as an emotional release.
3. I don't really like myself very much.
4. I often wonder why people don't like me.
5. My husband and I stay together for the sake of the children.

Statements Perceived as Not Occurring in a Two-Hour Conversation Between Previously Unacquainted Persons:

1. I had my first sexual experience when I was twenty-one.
2. I make $13,000 a year.
3. I'm suspicious of my husband's constant need to work late.
4. I have considered committing suicide on more than one occasion.
5. We got married earlier than we'd planned because I was pregnant.

revealed to another person only after the exchange of more superficial information. Naturally, there are exceptions. Bartenders, strangers on public transportation, and people who deliberately express a desire to listen to another person's troubles will experience a great deal more "unloading" of personal information during the early phases of the encounter. In many of these cases, there is no intent to build a relationship that would last beyond the needed catharsis. Relationships can and do develop under such circumstances, but they must, at some point, go back and exchange more superficial information.

Earlier, you will recall we suggested that while small talk disgruntles many people, it is not the small talk per se that bothers them, it is the way in which small talk is usually conducted. The following are a few of the many possible sources of this irritation: (1) You might engage in a great deal of demographic information exchange with no opportunity or motivation to pursue any of the possible commonalities. Sometimes fraternity or sorority rush parties impose these conditions. Just as you finish providing a biographical overview, it is time to switch partners and go through the same routine again. (2) You may encounter a person who is locked into one specific subject—and he or she doesn't even want to talk about that subject in much depth. Hence, breadth is cut off and the chances of finding integrating topics are decreased. If a person's lone topic happens to be themselves, small talk may seem especially boring. However, dissatisfaction may not accrue if that person's lone subject is also one you enjoy talking to death. (3) You may feel that there is an inequality of information exchange. You end up giving all the information and the other person does not reciprocate. Unless you are performing a counseling function, extremely high or low amounts of talking may not be perceived favorably during initial interaction. People who talked 80 percent of the time were judged to be domineering, outgoing, selfish, inconsiderate, inattentive, impolite, cold, and disliked by their interaction partner. People who talked 50 percent of the time were evaluated as likable, warm, attentive, and polite. Those who talked only 20 percent of the time were viewed as submissive, introverted, unselfish, and unintelligent.[77] Rightly or wrongly, our perception of how much help the other person is giving us in continuing the dialogue is closely related to our perception of whether the other wants to continue the conversation and the relationship. With new acquaintances and strangers, small talk allows us to avoid the anxiety caused by long silences. While this is confusing and/or irritating to the information giver, it may be that the receiver just doesn't understand the important role of questions in small talk. (4) You may also meet a person who violates the pleasantness norm in small talk, and brings the conversation dangerously close to conflict before the relationship can withstand the strain.

In summary, we have a form of public dialogue that serves a number of crucial personal and social functions, is omnipresent, is quantitatively superior to almost any other form of talk, and according to Malinowski, is pan-cultural[78]—and we choose to call it *small talk!* The covert question underlying all small talk is: Do you want our encounter and our relationship to continue? Should both parties agree to sustain their association, they will make some rather specific plans regarding when and where. Should either or both participants feel less enthusiastic about pursuing the relationship, the where and when of the next meeting will probably be left vague—"I'll probably run into you sometime." This vagueness serves the purpose of leaving the door open but does not commit either party to inviting the other in immediately. Obviously, additional encounters are used to help verify knowledge previously obtained or inferred and provide a mechanism to learn new things. Additional encounters are necessary in order to look for consistency or disparity across situations, between what was said and what was observed, between what the person says and what others say. One of the important mechanisms for initiating additional encounters is a previously identified topic of common ground—"Professor Knapp! How's the rhino expert? You know, I saw a TV program on the rhino the other night. Did you see it?"

SUMMARY

This chapter examined some of the ritualistic exchanges that affect our relationships with others. On the surface these behaviors don't seem too important to the development of our relationships, but they can be critical. Much of social interaction is influenced by rules—personal, relationship, group, and society rules for communicating. When communication is not satisfying, it may be that a rule has been violated. Ordinarily people receive negative reactions for not following the established rules of interaction, but we mentioned several ways in which rules could be (and are) violated without incurring unwanted sanctions. Sometimes these rules are so well learned that we don't pay much conscious attention to them yet we carry out entire sequences of behavior that are, to a great extent, rule-governed. We examined four of these patterned behaviors: greetings, forms of address, relational openings, and small talk.

Perhaps the most obvious and seemingly incidental act of initiating encounters is the greeting. Greetings, however, are anything but incidental, since they carry important relationship information concerning formality, status, and intimacy. Forms of address and opening lines, like greetings, also help to set the stage for the dialogue and relationship that will follow. While these three conversational rituals are relatively routine, it is important to remember that all three are also flexible. The beginning of any conversation is always mutually constructed by the participants.

In the same sense, we argued that the next phase of interaction which normally follows the opening line—small talk—is sometimes unfairly maligned. Several reasons were suggested why people might be nonplused by the way in which small talk is conducted, but it was also pointed out that effective small talk is critical to developing relationships and subsequent dialogue. Small talk helps us maintain a sense of community with our fellow human beings, provides a nonthreatening and revealing proving ground for new and/or established relationships, provides a safe procedure for indicating who we are and how others may come to know us, offers a diversion from uncomfortable "big" talk, and helps us to uncover integrating topics. The discovery of these integrating topics is a facilitative thread for bringing two strangers together, but it is also an important ingredient of small talk in existing relationships. The content of greetings and small talk will change as relationships ebb and flow, but the structure will be similar and the functional significance to the relationship will persist.

SELECTED READINGS

Communication Rules and Rituals

Bowers, J. W., Elliott, N. D., and Desmond, R. J. "Exploiting Pragmatic Rules: Devious Messages." *Human Communication Research* 3 (1977): 235–242.

Bruess, C. J. S., and Pearson, J. C. "Interpersonal Rituals in Marriage and Adult Friendship." *Communication Monographs* 64 (1997): 25–46.

Cushman, D., and Whiting, G. C. "An Approach to Communication Theory: Toward Consensus on Rules." *Journal of Communication* 22 (1972): 217–238.

Geller, D. M., Goodstein, L., Silver, M., and Sternberg, W. C. "On Being Ignored: The Effects of the Violation of Implicit Rules of Social Interaction." *Sociometry* 37 (1974): 541–556.

Goffman, E. *Interaction Ritual.* Garden City, NY: Doubleday, 1967.

———. *Relations in Public.* New York: Harper and Row, 1971.

Gouldner, A. W. "The Norm of Reciprocity: A Preliminary Statement." *American Sociological Review* 25 (1960): 161–178.

Hewitt, J., and Stokes, R. "Disclaimers." *American Sociological Review* 40 (1975): 1–11.

Honeycutt, J. M., Woods, B. L., and Fontenot, K. "The Endorsement of Communication Conflict Rules as a Function of Engagement, Marriage and Marital Ideology." *Journal of Social and Personal Relationships* 10 (1993): 285–304.

Hopper, R. "The Taken-for-Granted." *Human Communication Research* 7 (1981): 195–211.

Jones, E., and Gallois, C. "Spouses' Impressions of Rules for Communication in Public and Private Marital Conflicts." *Journal of Marriage and the Family* 51 (1989): 957–967.

Labov, W. "Rules for Ritual Insults." In D. Sudnow, ed., *Studies in Social Interaction,* pp. 120–169. New York: Free Press, 1972.

McLaughlin, M. L. *How Talk Is Organized.* Beverly Hills, CA: Sage, 1984, pp. 13–34.

Pearce, W. B. "Consensual Rules in Interpersonal Communication: A Reply to Cushman and Whiting." *Journal of Communication* 23 (1973):162–163.

———. "The Coordinated Management of Meaning: A Rules Based Theory of Interpersonal Communication." In G. R. Miller, ed., *Explorations in Interpersonal Communication.* Beverly Hills, CA: Sage, 1976.

Post, E. L. *Emily Post's Etiquette: The Blue Book of Social Usage.* 11th ed. New York: Funk & Wagnalls, 1965.

Rothenbuhler, E. W. *Ritual Communication: From Everyday Conversation to Mediated Ceremony.* Thousand Oaks, CA: Sage, 1998.

Scott, M., and Lyman, S. "Accounts." *American Sociological Review* 33 (1968): 46–62.

Shimanoff, S. B. *Communication Rules.* Beverly Hills, CA: Sage, 1980.

Stokes, R., and Hewitt, J. P. "Aligning Actions." *American Sociological Review* 41 (1976): 838–849.

Sudnow, D., ed. *Studies in Social Interaction.* New York: Free Press, 1972.

Wiemann, J. M., and Knapp, M. L. "Turn-Taking in Conversations." *Journal of Communication* 25 (1975): 75–92.

Greeting Behavior

Baxter, L. A. and Philpott, J. "Attribution-Based Strategies for Initiating and Terminating Friendships." *Communication Quarterly* 30 (1982): 217–224.

Coraro, W. A. " 'We're Friends, Right?': Children's Use of Access Rituals in a Nursery School." *Language in Society* 8 (1979): 315–336.

Firth, R. "Verbal and Bodily Rituals of Greeting and Parting." In J. S. LaFountaine, ed., *The Interpretation of Ritual.* London: Tavistock Publications, 1972.

Givens, D. "Greeting a Stranger: Some Commonly Used Nonverbal Signals of Aversiveness." *Semiotica* 22 (1978):351–367.

Goffman, E. *Relations in Public.* New York: Basic Books, 1971.

Hopper, R. *Telephone Conversation.* Bloomington, IN: Indiana University Press, 1992.

Kendon, A., and Ferber, A. "A Description of Some Human Greetings." In R. P. Michael and J. H. Crook, eds., *Comparative Behavior and Ecology of Primates.* London: Academic Press, 1973.

Knuf, J. "Greeting and Leave-Taking: A Bibliography of Resources for the Study of Ritualized Communication." *Research on Language and Social Interaction* 24 (1990/1991): 405–448.

Krivonos, P. D., and Knapp, M. L. "Initiating Communication: What Do You Say When You Say Hello?" *Central States Speech Journal* 26 (1975): 115–125.

Laver, J. "Communicative Functions of Phatic Communion." In A. Kendon, R. M. Harris, and M. R. Key, eds., *Organization of Behavior in Face-to-Face Interaction.* Chicago: Aldine, 1975.

Nofsinger, R. E. "The Demand Ticket: A Conversational Device for Getting the Floor." *Speech Monographs* 42 (1975): 1–9.

Powers, W. G., and Glenn, R. B. "Perceptions of Friendly Insult Greetings in Interpersonal Relationships." *Southern Speech Communication Journal* 44 (1979): 264–274.

Schegloff, E. A. "Sequencing in Conversational Openings." In J. J. Gumperz and D. Hymes, eds., *Directions in Sociolinguistics: The Ethnography of Communication,* pp. 346–380. New York: Holt, Rinehart & Winston, 1972.

Schiffrin, D. "Opening Encounters." *American Sociological Review* 42 (1977): 679–691.

Forms of Address

Brown, R., and Ford, M. "Address in American English." *Journal of Abnormal Social Psychology* 62 (1961): 375–385.

Brown, R., and Gilman, A. "The Pronouns of Solidarity and Power." *Style in Language,* edited by T. A. Sebeok. New York: John Wiley & Sons, 1960.

Fitch, K. L. "The Interplay of Linguistic Universals and Cultural Knowledge in Personal Address: Colombian *Madre* Terms." *Communication Monographs* 58 (1991): 254–272.

Harré, R., Morgan, J., and O'Neill, C. *Nicknames: Their Origins and Social Consequences.* London: Routledge and Kegan Paul, 1979.

Kramer, C. "Sex-Related Differences in Address Systems." *Anthropological Linguistics* 17 (1975): 198–210.

Kroger, R. O., Chang, K., and Leong, I. "Are the Rules of Address Universal?: A Test of Chinese Usage." *Journal of Cross Cultural Psychology* 10 (1979): 395–414.

Little, C. B., and Gelles, R. J. "The Social Psychological Implications of Forms of Address." *Sociometry* 38 (1975): 573–586.

Rausch, H. L., Marshall, K. A., and Featherman, J. M. "Relations at Three Early Stages of Marriage as Reflected by the Use of Personal Pronouns." *Family Process* 9 (1970): 69–82.

Slobin, D. I., Miller, S. H., and Porter, L. "Forms of Address and Social Relations in a Business Organization." *Journal of Personality and Social Psychology* 8 (1968): 289–293.

Small Talk

Beinstein, J. "Conversations in Public Places." *Journal of Communication* 25 (1975): 85–95.

___. "Small Talk as Social Gesture." *Journal of Communication* 25 (1975): 147–154.

Berger, C. R. "Proactive and Retroactive Attribution Processes in Interpersonal Communications." *Human Communication Research* 2 (1975): 33–50.

Berger, C. R., and Calabrese, R. J. "Some Exploration in Initial Interaction and Beyond:

Toward a Developmental Theory of Interpersonal Communication." *Human Communication Research* 1 (1975): 99–112.

Berger, C. R., Gardner, R. R., Clatterbuck, G. W., and Shulman, L. S. "Perceptions of Information Sequencing in Relationship Development." *Human Communication Research* 3 (1976): 29–46.

Duck, S., Rutt, D. J., Hurst, M. H., and Strejc, H. "Some Evident Truths about Conversations in Everyday Relationships: All Communications Are Not Created Equal." *Human Communication Research* 18 (1991): 228–267.

Goldsmith, D. J., and Baxter, L. A. "Constituting Relationships in Talk: A Taxonomy of Speech Events in Social and Personal Relationships." *Human Communication Research* 23 (1996): 87–114.

Gross, A. "Small Talk: The Second Language You Really Need." *Mademoiselle* (May 1974): 200–201, 262–263, 268.

Harrington, A. "Polluters of Time." *Harper's Magazine* 251 (1975): 28–29+.

Journal of Communication 27 (1977):158–196. This issue contains seven articles on a related subject—gossip.

Levin, J., and Arluke, A. *Gossip: The Inside Scoop.* New York: Plenum, 1987.

Tannen, D. *Talking Voices: Repetition, Dialogue, and Imagery in Conversational Discourse.* New York: Cambridge University Press, 1989.

Zunin, L. *Contact: The First Four Minutes.* Los Angeles: Nash Publishing, 1972.

NOTES

[1]For an extensive discussion of communication rituals, see E. W. Rothenbuhler, *Ritual Communication: From Everyday Conversation to Mediated Ceremony* (Thousand Oaks, CA: Sage, 1998).

[2]This definition is a modified version of one found in: S. B. Shimanoff, *Communication Rules* (Beverly Hills. CA: Sage, 1980), p. 57.

[3]M. Argyle and M. Henderson, *The Anatomy of Relationships* (London: Heinemann, 1985).

[4]It is worth noting that the rules governing the structure of a conversation may be as important to the overall relationship as the content. See J. M. Wiemann and M. L. Knapp, "Turn-Taking in Conversations," *Journal of Communication* 25 (1975): 75–92, which proposes: "Turn-taking in conversations not only helps us apportion the floor, but also serves a symbolic function of helping the interactants define their relationship."

[5]V. J. Derlega, S. Metts, S. Petronio, and S. T. Margulis, *Self Disclosure* (Newbury Park, CA: Sage, 1993).

[6]B. R. Burleson, "Comforting Messages: Feature, Functions, and Outcomes." In J. A. Daly and J. M. Wiemann, eds., *Strategic Interpersonal Communication* (Hillsdale, NJ: Erlbaum, 1994), pp. 135–161.

[7]E. Jones and C. Gallois, "Spouses' Impressions of Rules for Communication in Public and Private Marital Conflicts," *Journal of Marriage and the Family* 51 (1989): 957–967.

[8]See, for example, J. M. Honeycutt, B. L. Woods, and K. Fontenot, "The endorsement of Communication Conflict Rules as a Function of Engagement, Marriage and Marital Ideology," *Journal of Social and Personal Relationships* 10 (1993): 285–304.

[9]A. R. Allgeier, "The Effects of Differential Amounts of Talkativeness on Interpersonal Judgments" (Ph.D. diss., Purdue University, 1975).

[10]C. R. Berger, R. R. Gardner, M. R. Parks, L. Schulman, and G. R. Miller, "Interpersonal Epistemology and Interpersonal Communication." In G. R. Miller, ed., *Explorations in Interpersonal Communication* (Beverly Hills, CA: Sage, 1976), pp. 163–170.

[11]These hypotheses were developed during a pro-seminar at Purdue University that was taught by R. P. Hart and the senior author.

[12]Reprinted with permission of Macmillan Publishing Co., Inc. from *Intimate Relations* by Murray S. Davis. Copyright © 1973 by Murray S. Davis.

[13]H. Garfinkel, "Studies of the Routine Grounds of Everyday Activities," *Social Problems* 11 (1964): 225–250.

[14]R. Hopper, "The Taken-for-Granted," *Human Communication Research* 7 (1981): 195–211.

[15]J. A. Daly, D. J. Weber, A. L. Vangelisti, M. Maxwell, and H. L. Neel, "Concurrent Cognitions During Conversations: Protocol Analysis as a Means of Exploring Conversations," *Discourse Processes* 12 (1989): 227–244.

[16]W. A. Afifi and S. Metts, "Characteristics and Consequences of Expectation Violations in Close

Relationships," *Journal of Social and Personal Relationships* 15 (1998): 365–392.

[17]M. L. McLaughlin, *Conversation: How Talk Is Organized* (Beverly Hills, CA: Sage, 1984).

[18]C. A. Braithwaite, "Blood Money: The Routine Violation of Conversational Rules," *Communication Reports* 10 (1997): 63–73.

[19]N. Tavuchis, *Mea Culpa: A Sociology of Apology and Reconciliation* (Stanford, CA: Stanford University Press, 1991).

[20]J. Hewitt and R. Stokes, "Disclaimers," *American Sociological Review* 40 (1975): 1–11.

[21]M. Argyle, *Bodily Communication* (New York: International Universities Press, 1975), p. 65.

[22]Shimanoff, *Communication Rules*, pp. 98–99.

[23]See L. A. Baxter and W. Wilmot. "Secret Tests: Social Strategies for Acquiring Information About the State of the Relationship," *Human Communication Research* 11 (1984): 171–201, for a discussion of such "secret tests" in the context of romantic relationships.

[24]To show how communicative rules change, one writer observed: " . . . according to the rules of etiquette, as codified by Emily Post, divorced persons were supposed to meet socially as non-speaking strangers, the underlying theory being . . . that the divorce would not have been sought in the first place if the grievance of one of the parties had not been irreparable and unforgivable. But as divorces became more common, particularly with the advent and spread of 'friendly divorces,' this rule became difficult to enforce. In some social circles it would have meant that an awkwardly large number of people, including the friends of divorced persons, would find themselves in embarrassing situations. The old rule was therefore changed by consensus and later [re]formulated by Mrs. Post. Now it is quite proper for divorced persons to meet as friends." J. Bernard, *American Family Behavior* (New York: Harper & Row, 1942), pp. 210–211.

[25]J. P. Forgas, "Asking Nicely? The Effects of Mood on Responding to More or Less Polite Requests," *Personality and Social Psychology Bulletin* 24 (1998): 173–185.

[26]E. J. Langer. *Mindfulness* (Reading, MA: Addison-Wesley, 1989).

[27]R. C. Schank and R. P. Abelson, *Scripts, Plans, Goals and Understanding* (Hillsdale, NJ: Erlbaum, 1977).

[28]See R. C. Schank, *Dynamic Memory* (New York: Cambridge University Press, 1982) for the foundational ideas; K. Kellermann, "The Conversational MOP II. Progression through Scenes in Discourse," *Human Communication Research* 17 (1991): 385–414; K. Kellermann, "Communication: Inherently Strategic and Primarily Automatic," *Communication Monographs* 59 (1992): 244–300; and K. Kellermann, S. Broetzmann, T. Lim, and K. Kitao, "The Conversational MOP: Scenes in the Stream of Discourse," *Discourse Processes* 12 (1989): 27–62, for the application to initial interaction.

[29]W. G. Powers and R. B. Glenn, "Perceptions of Friendly Inside Greetings in Interpersonal Relationships," *Southern Speech Communication Journal* 44 (1979): 264–274.

[30]J. Laver, "Linguistic Routines and Politeness in Greeting and Parting." In F. Coulmas, ed., *Conversational Routine: Explorations in Standardized Communication Situations and Prepatterned Speech* (New York: Mouton, 1981), pp. 289–306; W. Douglas, "Affinity-Testing in Initial Interactions," *Journal of Social and Personal Relationships* 4 (1987): 3–15.

[31]R. Hopper, *Telephone Conversation* (Bloomington, IN: Indiana University Press, 1992); R. Hopper and K. Drummond, "Accomplishing Interpersonal Relationship: The Telephone Openings of Strangers and Intimates," *Western Journal of Communication* 56 (1992): 185–199.

[32]E. Goffman, *Relations in Public* (New York: Basic Books, 1971), pp. 84–85.

[33]A. Kendon and A. Ferber, "A Description of Some Human Greetings." In R. P. Michael and J. H. Cook, eds., *Comparative Behavior and Ecology of Primates* (London: Academic Press, 1973).

[34]P. D. Krivonos and M. L. Knapp, "Initiating Communication: What Do You Say When You Say Hello?" *Central States Speech Journal* 26 (1975): 115–125.

[35]I. Eibl-Eibesfeldt, "Similarities and Differences Between Cultures in Expressive Movement." In R. A. Hinde, ed., *Non-Verbal Communication*, (Cambridge: Royal Society and Cambridge University Press, 1972).

[36]D. Givens, "Greeting a Stranger: Some Commonly Used Nonverbal Signals of Aversiveness," *Semiotica* 22 (1978): 351–367.

[37]For a discussion of how universal knowledge (e.g., biological relationships) and cultural knowledge (e.g., the symbolic value attached to a person) about relationships affect the use of personal address terms, see K. L. Fitch, "The Interplay of Linguistic Universals and Cultural Knowledge in Personal Address: Colombian *Madre* Terms," *Communication Monographs* 58 (1991): 254–272.

[38]J. Jorgenson, "Situated Address and the Social Construction of 'In-Law' Relationships," *The Southern Communication Journal* 59 (1994): 196–204.

[39]R. Brown, *Social Psychology* (New York: Free Press, 1965), chapter 2. Also see: C. L. Kleinke, P. A. Staneski, and P. Weaver, "Evaluation of a Person Who Uses Another's Name in Ingratiating and Noningratiating Situations," *Journal of Experimental Social Psychology* 8 (1972): 457–466. Kleinke et al. propose that when we are dependent on a stranger (e.g., applicant to interviewer in job interview), and we use his or her first name, we run the risk of being perceived as insincere, phony, and less likable. Liking, however, may accrue when dependency is not an issue (e.g., noningratiation situation).

[40]N. M. Henley, "The Politics of Touch." In P. Brown, ed., *Radical Psychology,* (New York: Harper & Row, 1973), pp. 421–433. See also N. M. Henley, *Body Politics* (Englewood Cliffs, NJ: Prentice-Hall, 1977).

[41]Some researchers suggest that this generalization may be more accurate for men than for women because women's names often take a diminutive or feminine form (e.g., "ette" or "ie") at the end, even when they are relatively long. See Merhrabian and M. Piercy, "Affective and Personality Characteristics Inferred from Length of First Names," *Personality and Social Psychology Bulletin* 19 (1993): 755–758.

[42]A. R. McConnell and R. H. Fazio, "Women as Men and People: Effects of Gender-Marked Language," *Personality and Social Psychology Bulletin* 22 (1996): 1004–1013.

[43]C. B. Little and R. J. Gelles, "The Social Psychological Implications of Forms of Address," *Sociometry* 38 (1975): 573–586.

[44]M. M. Moore. "Nonverbal Courtship Patterns in Women: Context and Consequences," *Ethology and Sociobiology* 6 (1985): 237–247.

[45]D. R. Shaffer, C. Ruammake, and L. J. Pegalis, "The 'Opener': Highly Skilled as Interviewer or Interviewee," *Personality and Social Psychology Bulletin* 16 (1990): 511–520.

[46]M. Kent, *How to Marry the Man of Your Choice* (New York: Warner Books, 1984).

[47]E. Weber, *How to Pick Up Girls* (New York: Symphony Press, 1970), pp. 72–78.

[48]A. J. DuBrin, "The Meeting/Mating Game: How and Where To Play," *Single* 2 (1974): 48–51, 72–75.

[49]C. L. Kleinke, "How Not to Pick Up a Woman," *Psychology Today* 15 (1981): 18–19.

[50]T. E. Murray, "The Language of Singles Bars." *American Speech* 60 (1985): 17–30.

[51]P. A. Mongeau and K. L. Johnson, "Predicting Cross-Sex First-Date Sexual Expectations and Involvement: Contextual and Individual Difference Factors," *Personal Relationships* 2 (1995): 301–312.

[52]L. A. Baxter and J. Philpott, "Attribution-Based Strategies for Initiating and Terminating Friendships," *Communication Quarterly* 30 (1982): 217–224.

[53]W. C. Rowatt, M. R. Cunningham, and P. B. Druen, "Deception to Get a Date," *Personality and Social Psychology Bulletin* 24 (1998): 1228–1242.

[54]W. Douglas, "Affinity-Testing in Initial Interaction," *Journal of Social and Personal Relationships* 4 (1987): 3–16.

[55]M. B. Adelman and A. C. Ahuvia, "Mediated Channels for Mate Seeking: A Solution to Involuntary Singlehood?" *Critical Studies in Mass Communication* 8 (1991): 1–17.

[56]A. Feingold, "Gender Differences in Effects of Physical Attractiveness on Romantic Attraction: A Comparison Across Five Research Paradigms," *Journal of Personality and Social Psychology* 59 (1990): 981–993; R. Koester and L. Wheeler, "Self-Presentation in Personal Advertisements: The Influences of Implicit Notions of Attraction and Role Expectations," *Journal of Social and Personal Relationships* 5 (1988): 149–160; M. H. Gonzales and S. A. Meyers, " 'Your Mother Would Like Me': Self-Presentation in the Personals Ads of Heterosexual and Homosexual Men and Women," *Personality and Social Psychology Bulletin* 19(1993): 131–142.

[57]R. A. Bell and J. A. Daly, "The Affinity-Seeking Function of Communication," *Communication Monographs,* 51 (1984): 91–115; R. A. Bell, S. W. Trablay, and N. L. Buerkel-Rothfuss, "Interpersonal Attraction as a Communication Accomplishment: Development of a Measure of Affinity-Seeking Competence," *Western Journal of Speech Communication* 51 (1987): 1–18; J. A. Daly and P. O. Kreiser, "Affinity Seeking." In J. A. Daly and J. M. Wiemann, eds., *Strategic Interpersonal Communication* (Hillsdale, NJ: Erlbaum, 1994), pp. 109–134; J. M. Honeycutt and J. Patterson, "Affinity Strategies in Relationships: The Role of Gender and Imagined Interactions in Maintaining Liking Among College Roommates," *Personal Relationships* 4 (1997): 35–46.

[58]In fact, Berger, Karol, and Jordan found that plan complexity was inversely related to verbal fluency. (See C. R. Berger, S. H. Karol, and J. M. Jordan, "When a Lot of Knowledge Is a Dangerous Thing: The Debilitating Effects of Plan Complex-

ity on Verbal Fluency," *Human Communication Research* 16 (1989): 91–119.)

[59]J. S. Powell, *Why Am I Afraid To Tell You Who I Am?* (Chicago: Argus Communications, 1969).

[60]D. D. Levine. "Small Talk: A Big Communicative Function in the Organization?" Paper presented to the Eastern Communication Association Convention, 1987.

[61]J. Beeler. "Chitchat Seen Vital for MIS Heads," *Computerworld* 14 (April 7, 1980): 2.

[62]J. C. Condon, Jr., *Semantics and Communication* (New York: Macmillan, 1966), pp. 88–89.

[63]D. Morris, *The Naked Ape* (New York: Dell, 1969).

[64]S. I. Hayakawa, *Language in Thought and Action*, 4th ed. (New York: Harcourt Brace Jovanovich, 1978), ch. 6.

[65]D. J. Goldsmith and L. A. Baxter, "Constituting Relationships in Talk: A Taxonomy of Speech Events in Social and Personal Relationships," *Human Communication Research* 23 (1996): 87–114.

[66]S. Duck, D. J. Rutt, M. H. Hurst, and H. Strejc, "Some Evident Truths about Conversations in Everyday Relationships: All Communications Are Not Created Equal," *Human Communication Research* 18 (1991): 228–267.

[67]"The Playboy Advisor," *Playboy* (June 1973), p. 51.

[68]A. Sarch, "Making the Connection: Single Women's Use of the Telephone in Dating Relationships with Men," *Journal of Communication* 43 (1993): 128–144.

[69]J. Levin and A. Arluke, *Gossip: The Inside Scoop* (New York: Plenum, 1987), pp. 28–29.

[70]C. R. Berger and R. J. Calabrese, "Some Explorations in Initial Interaction and Beyond: Toward a Developmental Theory of Interpersonal Communication," *Human Communication Research* 1 (1975): 99–112.

[71]J. Beinstein, "Conversations in Public Places," *Journal of Communication* 25 (1975): 85–95.

[72]Other investigations on the types of topics people discuss have yielded similarly predictable results. Sherman and Haas, for example, have found that when women talk together, they tend to discuss relationship problems, family, health, reproductive concerns, weight, food, and clothing more frequently than men do. Men, on the other hand, focused more often on music, current events, and sports. (See M. A. Sherman and A. Haas, "Man to Man, Woman to Woman," *Psychology Today* (1984): 72–73.)

[73]C. R. Berger, "Proactive and Retroactive Attribution Processes in Interpersonal Communications," *Human Communication Research* 2 (1975): 33–50.

[74]S. J. Sigman, "Handling the Discontinuous Aspects of Continuous Social Relationships: Toward Research on the Persistence of Social Forms," *Communication Theory* 1 (1991): 106–127. Also see J. A. Gilbertson, K. Dindia, and M. Allen, "Relational Continuity Constructional Unites and the Maintenance of Relationships," *Journal of Social and Personal Relationships* 15 (1998): 774–790.

[75]A. L. Vangelisti and M. A. Banski, "Couples' Debriefing Conversations: The Impact of Gender, Occupation, and Demographic Characteristics," *Family Relations* 42 (1993): 149–157.

[76]C. R. Berger, R. R. Gardner, G. W. Clatterbuck and L. S. Schulman, "Perceptions of Information Sequencing in Relationship Development," *Human Communication Research* 3 (1976): 34–39.

[77]C. L. Kleinke, M. L. Kahn, and T. B. Tully, "First Impressions of Talking Rates in Opposite-Sex and Same-Sex Interactions," *Social Behavior and Personality* 7 (1979): 81–91. Also see C. L. Kleinke and T. B. Tully, "Influence of Talking Level on Perceptions of Counselors," *Journal of Counseling Psychology* 26 (1979): 23–29.

[78]B. Malinowski, "The Problem of Meaning in Primitive Languages." In C. K. Ogden and I. A. Richards, eds., *The Meaning of Meaning*, 10th ed., Supplement I, (London: Routledge & Kegan Paul, 1949), pp. 296–336.

The Foundations of Intimate Dialogue

Dear Dr. Knapp,

My best friend just broke up with his girlfriend. My problem is that ever since this happened, our friendship has gotten a little too close. Before, while he was still dating his girlfriend, we'd play basketball once a week and maybe go out partying on Friday or Saturday night. Now that she's gone, he wants to do everything together. Don't get me wrong—the guy is still my best friend—but I don't want to spend every minute of my life with him. He's even starting to annoy the women I date. It's embarrassing. I don't want to hurt his feelings, but this is really beginning to bug me. How do I tell him this without hurting his feelings and our friendship?

Bugged to Death

When relationships become more intimate, the expectations for the relationship change. Establishing a close proximity to the person you care about may be crucial in reaching greater intimacy, but maintaining opportunities for separate activities may be just as crucial for the continuance of those feelings of intimacy. In this chapter different types of intimacy are discussed, and several key factors associated with the development of intimacy are outlined. An understanding of these factors should provide additional insights into the way communication behavior changes as people develop closer relationships and why it changes.

> *The longing for interpersonal intimacy stays with every human being from infancy throughout life; and there is no human being who is not threatened by its loss.*
>
> —*Frieda Fromm-Reichmann*

The subject was pornography. There were many who claimed expertise, but they couldn't agree on a definition. Resolution of the problem was deemed critical enough to warrant consideration by the U.S. Supreme Court. Reporters grilled the lawyers and decision makers relentlessly: "What is the specific nature of pornography? How can we define it?" Finally, one Supreme Court Justice verbalized what so many others felt, but were afraid to say: "I can't tell you what it is, but I know it when I see it."

This chapter concerns advanced stages of human intimacy, stages which appear to have multitudinous definitions with little consensus. Many people feel they know or can identify it when they experience it; many others are much less certain. Like the pornography issue, there is certainly no shortage of public commentary on liking and loving. At one extreme are those who claim to know the answers, oftentimes giving conflicting advice. Our popular literature is saturated with case histories, testimonials, diagnostic tests, and advice on almost every conceivable aspect of intimate relationships. Readers learn from so-called experts how to "rekindle your dying marriage," how to "find out if your boss really likes you," or how "one out of every five women is looking for you as her no-strings-attached lover" as this outlandish book advertisement in a popular men's magazine claimed:

> . . . a distinguished American scientist shows you how three simple psychological insights can bring as many lovely young women to your bed as you could possibly wish for the rest of your life! . . . Not a single detail that you'll need (or want) to know is left out of this book. . . .
>
> Never again will you have to lose out because you might not be the type of guy certain women go for. . . . To put it all in a nut-shell: Once you learn to apply the principles of "SECRET FEMALE HYPNOTISM," you'll have the power to make women do *exactly as you wish.*

At the other extreme, are those who would rather remain uninformed. Former Senator William Proxmire, scorning what he called the "love racket," was quoted as saying that people don't want to know the answers to what comprises romantic love; they want it to remain a mystery. Not even Dear Abby is willing to wrestle with love's complexity: "When you're in love, you'll know it. You won't have to ask."

So much for the extremes. The following material will not reflect any simple insights, or answers that can explain the varieties of human intimacy; and we cannot provide any analysis that will completely strip the shroud of mystery from intimate relationships.

Loving and Liking

Many of the questions facing those who wish to study intimate relationships revolve around the oftentimes ambiguous terminology we use to label our experiences and feelings as they intensify toward another. Take the word *love,* for instance. We would probably be astonished if we told someone we loved them and they replied by asking: "What exactly do you mean by that?" When we are participants in the process of intimacy development, emotional distance is often difficult to achieve, and many of us seem to behave as if love had a single concrete referent which others will understand. On the other hand, we can look at the way others express love in a more detached manner and conclude that there are probably many ways of loving. Sociologist John Lee felt that the word *love* had many behavioral referents and that the assumption of a common referent was the biggest communication barrier between two people using the term. Both people say they are in love, but they may have very different ways of showing it because they are working with very different referents for the term. To test his idea, Lee sought answers from over one hundred people representing various walks of life. He asked them how they had met their beloved; what expectations they had for love; how they handled arguments, jealousy, breakups, reunions, sex, and absence; what their orientation toward life in general was; what their childhood was like; and many other questions. Listed below are six styles of loving which Lee identified. The first three he called *primary styles of love;* the last three are the result of mixing and combining elements of the primary styles.[1] Other combinations are obviously possible, but this list is sufficient to show that love may have many referents:

   1. Love of Beauty. These lovers are passionate and intense. They seem to have an immediate and powerful attraction to physical beauty. They have a clear concept of ideal beauty and get a noticeably heightened physiological reaction when they are confronted with persons approaching this ideal. They are eager for rapid self-disclosure and sexual intimacy. Sensations associated with touching the beloved are greatly enjoyed. The intensity this lover initially gives to a relationship must inevitably diminish, but successful long-term relationships can be achieved if satisfaction can be derived from relationship "highs" which occur less often and are, perhaps, less intense. Problems are normally associated with this lover's strong desire to find the ideal, which results in seeing things that aren't there. These lovers often experience strong emotional peaks and valleys.

   2. Playful Love. These lovers seem to derive the most pleasure from playing the game. They often consider love to be less important than, say, work, and believe in themselves so strongly that they feel they don't need much from others. As a result, they will not be very concerned about getting or giving involvement or dependency. Playing the game is often as rewarding as winning the prize. These lovers are interested in variety and good times and may have more than one lover at a time.

For people who are undemanding and self-sufficient, this style of love will be satisfying, but if one partner desires a deeper commitment, problems may arise. This advertisement for a book would be most likely to appeal to those who practice playful love: "Love is a game. Some play it poorly. And some play it well. If you want to play it brilliantly—so brilliantly you win almost every time—then its time you read *Connecting*."

3. Companionate Love. These lovers are patient; they let love grow naturally into a peaceful, enchanting affection. This love is based in friendship and companionship. They are generally not distressed by absences from their lover. The turbulence often generated by intense feelings or frivolity is not appealing to these lovers. In many ways they are less preoccupied with their partners than lovers with other styles. They can offer considerable stability and predictability, which may work well until such behavior is perceived as a dull routine by someone desirous of more variety and excitement.

4. Obsessive Love. This style combines the passion of the love of beauty with the desire to hold back feelings and manipulate the relationship found in playful love. These lovers are consumed by and possessive of their relationship. Their style is similar to what Peele and Brodsky call *addictive love*,[2] and is dangerously similar to drug addiction except that the lover is the object of dependency—a sort of interpersonal heroin. In this type of relationship, the slightest lack of enthusiasm by one partner will cause anxiety, pain, and/or jealousy in the other. These lovers need to be loved so much, they can't let the relationship take its course; they begrudge their partner's personal growth because they need the lover to fill their own self-emptiness. Their need for attention and affection is so strong and persistent it is virtually impossible to satisfy. They alternate between peaks of ecstasy and depths of despair. Breakups are akin to a withdrawal from drug dependency.

Limerance is a term used by Tennov to describe a state she says is commonly experienced by people who say they are in love.[3] But limerance, according to Tennov, is not love even though it has many characteristics of Lee's obsessive love.[4] People in the state of limerance are preoccupied with the object of their love during both sleeping and waking hours. Every look, gesture, and phrase may seem to be on a perpetual videotape projected on the mind. Complete dedication to the other person and a desire to absorb them physically, spiritually, and intellectually also characterizes limerance. People in this state continually hope for signs that the other person is feeling the same way and will ignore and overlook faults or whatever may cause problems while greatly magnifying the person's positive qualities. People in limerance will rearrange their lives in order to gain greater social and psychological proximity to the person they desire. Physiological symptoms may include stomach or chest pains, a general weakness, heart palpitations, etc. In short, you feel marvelously ill. Limerance thrives as long as there are obstacles to be overcome, and the "flatness" some couples feel after a relationship has been established for a time may mean limerance has run its course.

5. Realistic Love. These lovers combine the control and manipulation of playful love with companionate love. Compatibility is examined and sought on the basis of practicality. Lee uses the phrase *computer dating type* to describe this style. Logical thought and attempts to minimize the role of feelings in important decisions are valued. Careful planning based on the pros and cons not only characterizes courtship, but even separation may be carefully designed to occur at an "appropriate" time. Changes in life goals and the need for a less predictable relationship may pose challenges to the viability of this style.

6. Altruistic Love. These lovers view love as most major religions espouse—unselfish, patient, kind, generous, never jealous, never demanding reciprocity. Lee reports that while some of his interviewees had episodes in their lives that approached this style, he did not find any saints. Few interviewees seemed to exhibit this style consistently throughout their lives. And although it may seem appealing to have a lover who constantly places your needs (and the needs of all people) ahead of his or her own, this may also create a problem. For instance, someone who is always "above" the pull of self-satisfaction may appear to be more of a spectator in life's activities than a full-fledged participant.

The preceding styles of loving identified by Lee do a good job of making two important points—namely, (1) that love can manifest itself in many different ways; and (2) that different people may have different orientations or styles of loving.

We would expect love styles to manifest themselves differently depending on the degree of intimacy the couple feels and the length of time they have been together. The amount of experience you have with love in general or a particular style will also influence the likelihood a person will manifest it. Should each person in a love relationship have a similar style? There is evidence that couples with similar styles often do tend to find each other, but this does not seem to be the case with obsessive love and playful love. Do men and women gravitate toward a particular style? Among college students, men are overrepresented in playful love while women are found more often in companionate love. Certain love styles also seem more likely to be associated with perceived qualities of the relationship. For example, love of beauty and altrustic love, in one study, were more likely to be associated with greater relationship satisfaction, reward, investments, commitment, and less interest in alternative relationships. The opposite of these qualities were associated with playful love.[5]

Some research shows that women and men have different patterns of falling in love and tend to emphasize different styles. Women seem to fall in love earlier and more often than men as teenagers, but after about age twenty men fall in love easier. Men seem to be more interested in the passionate, game-playing styles of love, whereas women emphasize friendship and practicality with some degree of

Source: Esquire (December 1988)

possessiveness. Obviously, these general trends may not adequately represent the preferences of any given man, woman, or couple.

No matter what style of loving predominates for a person, there will be aspects of other styles which will be shown as well. To what extent do you think you show each of the styles identified by Lee? Select a person you love romantically and answer all the questions in Figure 7.1 with that person in mind.

Circle the number that best represents your attitude:
1 = Strongly Agree; 2 = Agree; 3 = Neutral; 4 = Disagree; 5 = Strongly Disagree.

1. My lover and I have the right physical "chemistry" between us.	1 2 3 4 5
2. I feel that my lover and I were meant for each other.	1 2 3 4 5
3. My lover and I really understand each other.	1 2 3 4 5
4. My lover fits my ideal standards of physical beauty/handsomeness.	1 2 3 4 5
5. I believe that what my lover doesn't know about me won't hurt him/her.	1 2 3 4 5
6. I have sometimes had to keep my lover from finding out about other lovers.	1 2 3 4 5
7. My lover would get upset if he/she knew of some of the things I've done with other people.	1 2 3 4 5
8. I enjoy playing the "game of love" with my lover and a number of other partners.	1 2 3 4 5
9. Our love is the best kind because it grew out of a long friendship.	1 2 3 4 5
10. Our friendship merged gradually into love over time.	1 2 3 4 5
11. Our love is really a deep friendship, not a mysterious, mystical emotion.	1 2 3 4 5
12. Our love relationship is the most satisfying because it developed from a good friendship.	1 2 3 4 5
13. A main consideration in choosing my lover was how he/she would reflect on my family.	1 2 3 4 5
14. An important factor in choosing my lover was whether or not he/she would be a good parent.	1 2 3 4 5
15. One consideration in choosing my lover was how he/she would reflect on my career.	1 2 3 4 5
16. Before getting very involved with my lover, I tried to figure out how compatible his/her hereditary background would be with mine in case we ever had children.	1 2 3 4 5
17. When my lover doesn't pay attention to me, I feel sick all over.	1 2 3 4 5
18. Since I've been in love with my lover, I've had trouble concentrating on anything else.	1 2 3 4 5
19. I cannot relax if I suspect that my lover is with someone else.	1 2 3 4 5
20. If my lover ignores me for a while, I sometimes do stupid things to try to get his/her attention back.	1 2 3 4 5
21. I would rather suffer myself than let my lover suffer.	1 2 3 4 5
22. I cannot be happy unless I place my lover's happiness before my own.	1 2 3 4 5
23. I am usually willing to sacrifice my own wishes to let my lover achieve his/hers.	1 2 3 4 5
24. I would endure all things for the sake of my lover.	1 2 3 4 5

SCORING: Add your ratings for statements 1–4. This is your score for love of beauty or passionate love. Your total for statements 5–8 is your score for playful or game-playing love. Your total score for statements 9–12 is your score for compassionate or friendship love. Your total for statements 13–16 is your score for realistic love. Your total for statements 17–20 is your score for obsessive love. Your total for statements 21–24 is your score for altruistic love. Lower scores indicate greater agreement with the scale (e.g., a score of 4 would reflect very strong and positive attitude toward this type of love; a score of 20 would reflect a strong negative attitude toward this type of love).

Source: C. Hendrick, S. S. Hendrick, and A. Dicke (1998). The Love Attitudes Scale: Short Form. *Journal of Social and Personal Relationships 15* (1988): 147–159. See also: C. Hendrick and S. S. Hendrick. A Theory and Method of Love. *Journal of Personality and Social Psychology 50* (1986): 392–402. Reprinted by permission of Sage Publications, Ltd.

Like Lee, Sternberg listened to people tell about their love relationships. His conclusion was that intimate relationships could be analyzed by examining three components: *intimacy,* which includes feelings of closeness, sharing, communication, and support; *passion,* which involves physiological arousal and an intense desire to be united with the loved one; and *commitment,* which involves both the short-term decision to love another and the longer term commitment to maintain it.[6] These three dimensions of love have been useful in other studies which have also tried to identify the central dimension of love.[7] This three-part, or triangular, theory provided Sternberg with a way of identifying the eight different types of love relationships which follow (see Figure 7.2).

The majority of our relationships are not likely to emphasize any of the three dimensions of Sternberg's theory—resulting in a state called *nonlove.* When intimacy is the only component, there is the kind of closeness associated with *liking.* When passion is the only component, there is a high degree of arousal but no intimacy or commitment. This type of relationship is *infatuated love.* When commitment is the sole dimension (no passion or intimacy), it is what Sternberg calls *empty love.* A couple may be committed to staying in a relationship but feel no passion or intimacy toward each other. This may occur at the end of a long-term relationship or at the beginning of one. Romantic love is a combination of intimacy and passion. It is liking plus physical attraction, but commitment is absent. Physical attraction is what some have called sexual desire and found it to be an important aspect of romantic love.[8] A short-term affair may have these features. Sternberg points out that the intimacy dimension of *romantic love* is itself a complex phenomenon. It is comprised of both general and specific feelings—for instance, feeling loved but also feeling loved by a person who is particularly good for you and a person who makes your relationship special. *Fatuous love* combines commitment and passion but excludes intimacy. This scenario might find a couple meeting and marrying within a week. But because they don't have the emotional support for long-term commitment provided by intimacy, the relationship may not last long. *Companionate love* has intimacy and commitment, but no passion. A long-term friendship or a marriage that has lost the physical attraction exemplifies this type of love. *Consummate love* contains all three dimensions. This kind of relationship, according to Sternberg, is difficult, but not impossible, to achieve. It is also difficult to maintain, but it is the kind of love that embodies the ideal for many seeking a love relationship.

To explain the foregoing eight types of relationships that result from combinations of Sternberg's three dimensions, it is necessary to talk as if a dimension did or did not exist. In reality, behaviors representing each dimension most likely occur in various degrees. Thus, passion may not be completely absent in companionate love, but may be of little influence in defining the nature of the relationship. In addition, these dimensions are changeable. Sometimes the magnitude of a given

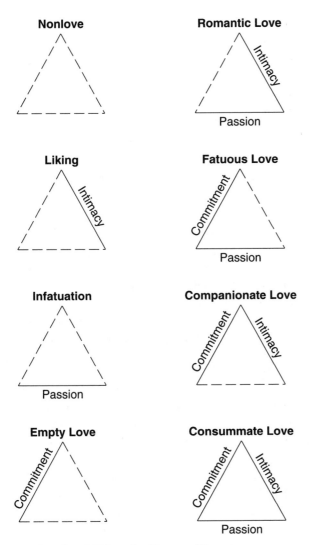

7.2 Sternberg's Triangular Theory of Love

relationship dimension may change quickly; sometimes it is a gradual process that occurs over many years. Passion and commitment, for example, may gradually reverse the amount of influence each plays in defining a marital relationship the longer it lasts. In one test of Sternberg's theory, passion did decline as the length of a relationship increased—but primarily for females. Although the researchers thought intimacy levels would also decrease over time, this was not the case. The amount of commitment was the best predictor of relationship satisfaction in long-term relationships.[9]

Efforts like the preceding to sort out the varieties of love inevitably bring us to the task of differentiating liking and loving. Some feel that love is just the end result of intensifying one's liking for another; others believe you can love someone and not like them. At this point, let's examine several attempts to unravel the liking/loving dichotomy.

He had forbidden me to call love the lotus that turns into lettuce . . .

Peter De Vries

Berscheid and Walster have contrasted liking with what they call passionate love (romantic and sexual attraction).[10] One distinguishing factor, they argue, may be the role of fantasy. Whereas liking may be based on a rather direct exchange of rewards between the participants, passionate love is often aroused by one's imagined fantasies—rewards are expected rather than actual. Should passionate love be heavily based on fantasy, a large letdown could be expected when reality-based information starts coming in during later stages of the relationship and the lesser rewards which can be obtained from this very real human being are realized. Other things being equal, liking will tend to increase as the time of interaction is extended. Passionate love, however, may erode over time, and as Berscheid and Walster put it, the best you can hope for after an extended period of time is an "afterglow." In this conceptual framework, *love may be necessary to propose marriage, but liking will be necessary to sustain it.* Finally, these authors note that *liking* is the attraction resulting from positive reinforcement received from another. *Loving,* however, is sometimes more complex. It is possible to fall in love with someone we know will cause us agony or suffering. According to Berscheid and Walster, it seems to be a process of experiencing some form of emotional arousal (either positive or negative) and having some rationale for labeling that arousal *love* which explains the many and seemingly conflicting emotions that may characterize love rather than liking. It may also help to clarify incidents where a person kills another he or she claims to love. A series of experiments in which subjects' physiological arousal was heightened by conditions representing fear, rejection, or frustration, and who were given some situational rationale to conclude that this arousal was related to a positive attraction to others, helped confirm the viability of this theory.

Women can tell if a man is the kind of man who likes women.

Anonymous

In a related set of studies, men experienced neutral (exercise), positive (comedy), or negative (anxiety) arousal. After arousal, these men viewed a videotape of either an attractive or unattractive woman whom they believed they would soon meet. Men with high arousal levels were more attracted to the attractive woman and more repulsed by the unattractive woman than similar men who did not experience high arousal. The aroused men had labeled their aroused state as sexual-romantic attraction or repulsion.[11] This type of research is based on the earlier work of Schachter, who proposed that any emotional experience depends on physiological arousal plus the individual's belief that he or she is experiencing a particular emotion—increased heart and respiration rate may be interpreted as either anger or joy, depending on what you see others in your immediate environment doing.[12] In summary, then, Berscheid and Walster's theory holds that individuals will experience passionate love if they are emotionally agitated and attribute their state to passionate love. When the arousal ceases or the individuals cease to attribute their internal emotional state to passionate love, love will fade. Taking this a step further, individuals can experience something that makes them feel elated (perhaps an A in Chemistry) and the unnamed emotional joy can later be labeled affection when they meet a friend. Thus, the emotional high from rewarding events can be transferred or generalized to other situations just as emotional lows can be projected onto people who were in no way responsible for them.

Whereas many argue that the differences between liking and loving are quantitative (loving is simply a more intense form of positive attraction), Rubin believes that there are qualitative differences.[13] *Liking*, according to Rubin, has two major components: affection and respect. *Affection* is liking based on mutual interacting characterized by warmth, closeness, and fondness. "You really make me feel good. You always seem to say the right thing and you're fun to be around. I really like you." *Respect* is liking based on another's admirable characteristics outside the interpersonal domain. It is a cooler, more distant sort of liking. "I've always liked my boss. Even though he is dour and hard sometimes, he is bright and responsible" or "I still like and respect you, but I don't love you anymore." Affection and respect are coexisting dimensions of liking; a liked person may not receive both attributions, although most of us would prefer some of both. The components of love, based on Rubin's conceptualization and research are: attachment, caring, and intimacy. *Attachment* consists of "powerful desires to be in the other's presence, to make physical contact, to be approved of, and to be cared for"—to be fulfilled by the other. *Caring* is the component in opposition to attachment, the view of love as giving rather than needing. When we care about another, their satisfaction and security becomes as important as our own. Intimacy is a postulate derived from the combination of attachment (self-fulfillment) and caring (self-surrender). Whereas these latter components are individual based, intimacy is the bond or link between the two people. It transcends the characteristics of each individual; it's the mixture.

Davis and Todd started their research with the assumption that love and friendship shared many characteristics but also differed on some crucial ones.[14] Their theory, shown in Figure 7.3, identifies eight characteristics of friendships. According to the theory, love relationships also contain these eight characteristics of friendship plus two other features: passion and caring. Their research based on this theory provides much support. Studies comparing best friendships and close friendships (same- and opposite-sexed) with lovers have largely resulted in what one would expect from the theory. Some exceptions have occurred, however. Being a "champion/advocate" does not seem to be a behavior particularly characteristic

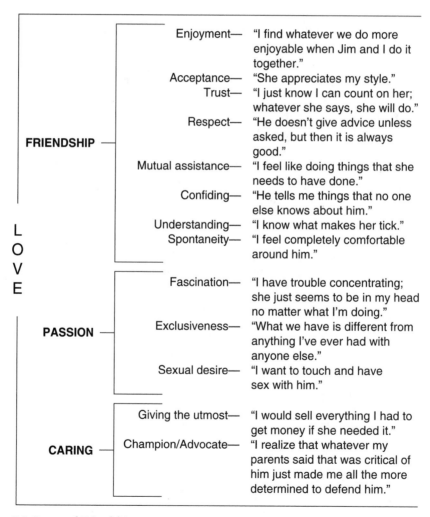

7.3 Love and Friendship

of lovers only; similarly, "enjoyment" appears to be more a factor in love relationships than friendships. This research indicates that "typical" love relationships differ from even very close friendships by having higher levels of fascination, exclusiveness, and sexual desire; a greater depth of caring (willing to give one's utmost when it is needed); and a greater potential for experiencing enjoyment. Love relationships also have greater potential for experiencing conflict, criticism, displeasure, anxiety, and ambivalence.

Fehr's research found that the best description of features characterizing a variety of close relationships (liking, romantic love, friendship, being-in-love, and love between family members) was a companionate cluster: *trust, caring, honesty, friendship,* and *respect*.[15] This underscores the idea that, in general, people believe there is a substantial amount of overlap in liking and loving, even though they are qualitatively different concepts. Passion, for example, is crucial to some love relationships but as a critical feature of love relationships in general, passion is less descriptive than the exchange of support and "warm fuzzies."

Amid all these distinctions between liking, loving, and types of love, it is worth noting that Maxwell found that relationship "closeness" seemed to involve similar behavior (self-reported) in close same-sex friendships, married couples (early stages and after twenty years), and between mothers and their young adult children.[16] Closeness was defined as: (1) separation distress; (2) disclosure; (3) naturalness; (4) similarity; (5) sharing attitudes, values, and interests; (6) following—i.e., seeking out and spending time with; (7) giving and receiving help; and (8) communicating about important issues. Other predicted but untested characteristics included discriminatory responses such as treating the other person as unique, developing synchrony and reciprocity of behavior, and the exchange of rewards.

The preceding theory and research has probably provided an overdose of terms and lists of characteristics. OK, omit the word probably. What does it all boil down to? The following conclusions seem warranted at this time:

1. There are many levels and types of liking and loving. Liking and loving are phenomena that seem to vary in both degree and kind—even though the components of "closeness" may be similar across some types of relationships.

2. Emotional intensity seems to be more characteristic of love relationships than friendships—particularly when first forming or when threats to the relationship are perceived.

3. The extent to which any characteristic or set of characteristics contributes to a relationship's definition is likely to change as the length of the relationship increases; some aspects will grow in importance, some will become less important.

4. Relationships described with the word *love* may be further understood by examining the degree of intimacy, commitment, and passion which characterizes the relationship.

5. Love relationships that last a long time are more likely to have a strong friendship component to them even though this may not have characterized the relationship when it began.

6. Liking and loving have many overlapping features.

7. It is also clear from the foregoing theory and research that we have a lot to learn about how various types and degrees of intimacy are communicated. Without focusing on specific behavior, Marston and his colleagues found that people experienced *intimacy* in the following ways: sex, openness, affection, supportiveness, togetherness, and quiet company; *passion* as romance and sexual intimacy; and *commitment* as supportiveness, expressions of love, fidelity, and expressions of commitment, consideration, and devotion.[17] Focusing specifically on nonverbal behavior, Guerrero identified differences between romantic relationships and friendships. Closer proximity, touch, gaze, and silence characterized the romantic relationships while more nodding and vocal signs of interest characterized communication in friendships.[18]

Given the overlapping features associated with various types of intimate relationships and the lack of clear referents associated with different intimacy terms, it is not surprising that we sometimes experience miscommunication and confusion during intimate exchanges. We know expressions of friendliness and caring can be misinterpreted as romantic behavior. Sometimes the reverse occurs. There are times when the ambiguity inherent in intimate dialogue serves a useful purpose, and we are not interested in being "clear." When clarity is important, communicators must be especially vigilant about signals which will be misread and provide the contextual information necessary to clarify intent.

> *The love we give away is the only love we keep.*
> Elbert Hubbard

There are still a lot of unanswered questions about the nature of liking and loving and how they are manifested. Even though we are not now in a position to solve these long-standing puzzles by putting all the right pieces in all the right places, we do have some pretty good guesses about the nature of the pieces. Let's call these the *foundations of intimacy:* (1) personality and early experiences; (2) situational and developmental factors; (3) cultural guidelines; (4) emotional arousal and labeling; (5) self-fulfillment; (6) self-surrender; and (7) commitment to a joint identity. Although we may not know precisely how it is accomplished, these foundations combine in complex ways to produce the variety of intimate relationships possible. Some combinations may even produce similar feelings in two individuals but very different behaviors. Part of the difficulty in understanding intimate relationships is that each foundation block is, at any time, subject to change by exerting influence on other foundation categories or by being influenced by forces from those other categories.

Foundations of Intimacy

Personality and Early Experiences

The participants in an intimate relationship bring to it their own unique experiences and behavioral orientations—commonly known as their personalities. While much of our temperament and behavior patterns are molded and influenced by our environment, there is some reason to believe that we enter the world with certain genetically based predispositions.[19] Whether innate or learned, these individual characteristics provide one source of explanation for how each of us approaches, avoids, sustains, and/or communicates intimacy.

If there are instincts or genetic predispositions, we need to examine the nature of early human experiences with attachment. Our early ancestors no doubt found value in close relationships because they provided protection and an opportunity for reproduction.[20] Using this knowledge as a backdrop for identifying acts of love among human beings today, Buss proposed the following: (1) Females are interested in males who can protect their young, so acts of love by men will be displays of resources which have the potential to be invested in the young; (2) males, on the other hand, are interested in women's reproductive capabilities, so acts of love by women will involve appearance-enhancing acts designed to show reproductive viability.[21] Obviously, males and females communicate a variety of acts which show love, but these two tendencies, according to Buss, are deeply rooted in our development as a species.

Another source of our adult behavior can be traced to our experiences as children. Commonly, researchers will examine the rewards and punishments parents administer and how these affect characteristics like social dependency or achievement needs. It is clear that early experiences with affection will certainly have an impact on later attempts to build intimate relationships; it is not clear, however, what that impact will be. For instance, let's assume a child has had some type of early emotional deprivation, perhaps a lack of parental closeness. From this background, that adult may consider the process of intensifying a relationship as negative. He or she may fear the dependency and vulnerability of a commitment to intimacy. "I've been burned before and I'm not going to let it happen again." That same background could, however, cause that adult to desperately seek out many friends and cling to intimates in an effort to offset early unpleasant experiences. It is not uncommon to find a person seeking a primary relationship with a person who symbolizes characteristics of one's mother or father. In some cases it may be because of pleasant experiences with the parent, but it may also be an effort to find someone to exercise one's neuroses on. One study found that the extent to which a person was optimistic about their own future marital relationship depended on whether they perceived their parents as having a good marriage. Optimism about future love relationships in general, though, was most accurately predicted by actual dating experiences.[22]

In an effort to identify specifically how our early childhood experiences with intimacy may influence our adult behavior, Hazan and Shaver studied patterns of attachment. Their research resulted in the identification of three adult attachment styles in romantic relationships: secure, avoidant, and anxious/ambivalent.[23] *Secure* lovers describe themselves as happy, friendly, trusting, and accepting of their partner despite known faults. They acknowledge that love rises and falls in many relationships, but also believe that in some relationships love never fades. *Avoidant* lovers say they fear intimacy and experience emotional extremes and jealousy. They believe romantic love is possibly an illusion, and if it does exist, it doesn't last long. They perceive that few potential partners exist for a satisfying love relationship and they worry that partners may ask them to be more intimate than they perceive they can be. *Anxious/Ambivalent* lovers seem to be a combination of what Lee called obsessive love and love of beauty. They report emotional extremes, obsession with the lover, jealousy, and extreme sexual attraction. They find it easy to fall in love, but they also believe it is rare to find a truly satisfying long-term love relationship. They worry that their partner doesn't want them or won't stay with them.

At first glance, one might think that everyone would prefer someone with a *secure* attachment style, but this does not seem to be the case. In fact, it is not unusual for dating partners to prefer those who have a similar style—e.g., a person with an anxious/ambivalent style preferring to date a person who is also anxious/ambivalent. Even though adults may manifest a dominant or preferred attachment style, the situation and the behavior of one's partner will surely influence and alter these tendencies emanating from early attachment experiences.[24]

Beginning early in childhood, some people believe men and women experience friendship differently. The widely held belief, and it is supported by some research, is that women friends talk more than men friends—especially about feelings and relationships. Male friends, on the other hand, are believed to base their friendships more on doing things together and when they do talk they mainly talk about sports and work. If disclosing feelings and talking about one's friendship are used as the standard for close, satisfying friendships, then one might conclude that male friendships are pretty empty. The puzzling part is that many men seem very satisfied with their male friendship and feel that they have a real sense of closeness in some of them. Supporting this view is some research which challenges the traditional portrayal of male friendships. This research argues that affect is not missing from or a minor part of men's friendships and that women not uncommonly rely on doing things together as an important part of some of their friendships as well. Perhaps more important than any differences in communication between men's and

Do the author's views fit your observations of male friendships? Can friendships be maintained by silence?

The Silent Friendships of Men*

What I enjoyed most about my conversations with John Campbell was that they hardly existed. We spoke—at the post office, at the village store, whenever he pulled over to the curb on his bike—two, three times a month. But we said very little. In the still, blank autumn afternoons like these, our silence abetted the season. One of us would open with some typically male, moderately hearty greeting; the other would follow with an observation about essentially nothing, like the lowering sky; the other would grunt or nod; John would pedal away, and that would be that.

When he died some weeks ago, of leukemia at age 77, I didn't say much either—just bowed my head. I went over to see his wife Jane, and again said little. I asked John's daughter Frances if I might have a picture of him, so that I could recall his tight, sweet-tempered face. She gave me the choice of the dashing John as a fighter pilot in World War II, the one with the goggles dangling from his neck, or the older John I knew, who sold real estate. I took the more recent shot.

"I saw *Private Ryan*," Francie told me. "Funny to think that when the Army Air Force came to the rescue of Tom Hanks and his infantrymen, that was Dad. He never spoke about the war."

That made sense to me. The silence of men in general is over-talked about and overcriticized. To be sure, men never open up as much as women want them to, but there is a wordless understanding in which we function fairly well—especially in friendships. There are a dozen guys whom I count as friends and who do the same with me, yet months pass without our speaking, and even when we do, we don't.

Old story: two women approach Calvin Coolidge. One says to the close-mouthed President, "Mr. Coolidge, I just bet my friend that I could get you to say three words." Says Coolidge: "You lose."

I believe, in fact, that most women would prefer a man to be glumly uncommunicative

than to spill his guts at the drop of a hat. That (one recalls with a shudder) was the goal of the so-called men's movement of Robert Bly et al. in the 1980s and early '90s, which exhorted men to express their feelings. If anyone doubts the perils of men expressing feelings, he should watch *The McLaughlin Group* or Cable Monica.

This drum-beating, male-retreating, back-to-the-woods nonsense is still going on, by the way. Last February a hundred men retreated to a pine forest in Louisiana owned by Benedictine monks to acuqire the ability to grieve. One reported that he had learned "to work my grief muscle." Thanks for sharing.

The push for men to express their feelings presumes that we have feelings, and we do have a few, but they remain submerged, and the airing of them often violates their authenticity. We are, as a gender, as dull as we seem. Contrary to the claptrap of the men's movement, men gain power through not talking. "The strength of the genie," said poet Richard Wilbur, "comes from being in a bottle." I'm no biologist, but my guess is that the male human animal was programmed for silence. One can make us talk counter to our genetic makeup, but it is like training kangaroos to box. It's mildly entertaining but pointless.

Older story: Wordsworth goes to visit Coleridge at his cottage, walks in, sits down and does not utter a word for three hours. Neither does Coleridge. Wordsworth then rises and, as he leaves, thanks his friend for a perfect evening.

There's a deep, basically serene well of silence in most men, which, for better and worse, is where we live. I do not mean to start claptrapping myself, but I often think that all our acts of aggression and wanna-fight posturing arise from that well as forms of overcompensation or panic. Unlike women, men are not social creatures, nor born administrators. It's nicely P.C. to think of God as female, but no woman would have

(continued)

Continued

thrown Lucifer out of heaven; would have offered him a desk job. Had Lucifer been a woman, she would have dropped all that "myself am hell" business and taken it.

I would go so far as to argue that men were programmed to be isolated from one another and that aloneness is our natural state. Silence in male friendships is our way of being alone with each other. Once men have established a friendship, that itself is the word. The affection is obvious, at least to us. A main component of our silence is an appreciation of the obvious.

Richard Rosenblatt, Time Magazine.

I may have spoken with my friend Campbell a total of a hundred times, yet I cannot recollect a single idea exchanged or the substance of a subject addressed. He knew that I wished him well, and I knew that he wished me the same. The day he died—before I learned that he had died—I called to him on his bike, mistaking a man of similar build and helmet for my friend. Later, when told of his death, I thought of that other man (I don't know why), and I pictured him pedaling away with a bright wave of the hand. See ya, John.

---

women's friendships is the lesson that there are many ways friends can communicate which provide energy necessary to develop and sustain close friendships.[25]

Another way of examining personality is to look at how it affects our perceptions of others. For instance, many believe that how well we are able to accept others is intimately linked to how well we accept ourselves. Hence, you may have more difficulty making close friends if you do not like yourself. Similarly, if you perceive yourself as unromantic or unlovable, you will probably find falling in love an infrequent experience. Low self-esteem seems to be a personality trait that will limit the frequency of intimate relationships. The chances of success are perceived as small by the individual with low self-esteem and, more often than not, these perceptions are confirmed. However, one research project concluded that those with low self-esteem were more likely to show "greater love, greater liking and more trust for their romantic partners and evaluate their love mates more favorably than those with high self-esteem."[26] This makes sense. If an individual has difficulty obtaining something, he or she would probably go to great lengths to hold onto it once it was obtained. The general lack of confidence stemming from low self-esteem will probably make it more difficult to build an intimate relationship with someone who closely approximates one's romantic ideal. It is not unusual, however, for many types of people, with many different personality configurations, to seek intimacy with those who have characteristics that are not only revered, but seemingly missing in their own lives—a mental midget marries a mental giant; the person with verbal diarrhea marries one with verbal constipation. There is a belief that somehow these characteristics will magically rub off on the person who lacks them. If the expectations for this personality osmosis are too great, it could lead (and has led) to bitter disappointment. On the other hand, idealizing one's partner, maintaining positive illusions about him or her, can be very beneficial to a relationship. It not only helps to maintain a relationship during times of stress, but one's partner may come to believe in and act out some of the aspects of your idealization. In this way, idealizing one's partner acts as a self-fulfilling prophecy—bringing about the relationship you desired.[27]

Finally, we can look at how our perception of another's personality may help to structure our own behavior. It is quite possible, for instance, that the personality you adopt in a relationship is heavily dependent on personality characteristics you perceive in the other person. What you see in the other person, however, is contingent on the type of relationship (as it realistically exists and as you would like it to be), the situation, and the other person's perceptions. For instance, some will see male aggressiveness as menacing; others will see it as masculine. In like manner, an aggressive woman may inspire dread or desire. Or you may delight in a self-confident, aggressive, verbose, independent, shrewd, and witty person as your closest friend and bridge partner; but you may be repelled at the thought of having such a personality with you on a daily basis as a roommate or spouse. Further, you may desire a given set of personality characteristics in a person with whom you want to form an intimate relationship, but such characteristics are only attractive isolated from your own personality. Oil and water are independently attractive and useful: merger, however, is costly for both.

Some people will enter relationships with high self-esteem, patience, tolerance, and adaptability; others may possess distinctly dissimilar personality profiles. Some will have a configuration of predispositions that will prepare them for a wide range of relationships with a wide range of people; others' predispositions will prepare them for a more limited range of people and types of relationships. Of course, this does not suggest that certain personality characteristics are better than others or that behavior patterns are unchangeable. It does suggest that when we examine the communicative patterns in advancing stages of a relationship (intimacy), we cannot ignore the contribution of the early experiences and personalities of the participants.

Situational and Developmental Factors

Circumstances can sometimes play a sizable role in the facilitation or inhibition of intimate relationships. Brenton relates the following example:

> An American woman who, with her husband, lived in an underdeveloped African country for several years told me how difficult it was to be accepted into its society; foreigners were forced to be only with each other. "I met people I wouldn't think of striking up friendships with here because of certain characteristics that turned me off," she said. "But the longer I stayed there the less important all that became. At first I deliberately overlooked things, then they didn't register so much because we became like one 'big family.'" Once back in the United States she met a few members of the "family" and found herself reacting to their negative qualities; she was no longer under the compulsion to make friends among a very limited group of individuals. She had compromised in Africa because of her need for people.[28]

In a similar way, people who work together sometimes develop relationships which are strongly influenced by factors associated with the work situation. When people spend much of their day in close proximity with others, work on tasks together, eat lunch or socialize during breaks together, it is not surprising that friendships develop. In time, co-workers may increase the intimacy of their talk (problems at work or in their life away from work) and expand the venues for talking (socializing after work).[29] Of course situational factors inherent in the work environment may act as inhibitors to relationship development as well. Working closely and talking with someone five days a week does provide a lot of information about that person in a relatively short period of time. It may or may not be information which prompts you to pursue a closer relationship.

Parents sometimes maneuver and pressure their children into circumstances that will restrict their intimacy choices. Sometimes such conditions will bring about premature or careless relationship choices; occasionally a child may marry a person who is not loved in order to spite the parents—to watch them squirm as the relationship begins its inevitable public demise. Regardless of how the situation materializes, some people simply find themselves thrown together; others find an almost conspiratorial set of external conditions that set up intimacy barriers. The term *spring fever* attributes one's feelings of intimacy to environmental changes associated with a new season of the year. While these situational forces no doubt contribute to one's feelings and perceptions, there are surely other contributing factors—the act of labeling one's emotional state with an intimacy term, biorhythmic cycles. Once an intimate relationship has been formed, its continuance may be heavily dependent on surrounding environmental circumstances. Many familiar statements of marital frustration reflect a maintenance of co-presence more than a sustenance of intimacy—"We had to stay together because of what separation might do to the kids," or "I know she treats me like scum, but I just couldn't handle things if she left."

Chronological age, by itself, is a relatively meaningless developmental barometer, but it is a fact that some situations, circumstances, or events are more likely to occur at certain times in one's life. For this reason we cannot ignore the interaction between one's stage in life and the extant circumstances. This interaction will often reveal differences in one's knowledge and understanding of, experience with, and predispositions for intimacy. Consider, for instance, the possible variants in meaning of the word *love* for a suburban child of six, a twenty-one-year-old bride for the first time, a middle-aged divorcee, and an older widow recently admitted to a nursing home. We all have some expectations for what a good friend or a lover should be like, and this is partly derived from how we perceive and react to events at various times in our life cycle. Children are generally told that they must love, who to love, and what expressions would constitute a satisfactory demonstration of love; adults are expected to *experience* love. Applying the standards we learn as children (loving Grandpa and Nana, or "I'll be your friend if you give me a cookie") to an adult experience may make the recognition of love difficult at first. At certain times in our lives a state of *intimacy readiness* may occur. Examples might be a lonely bachelor or an unhappily married woman, a college student with "Senior Clutch," or a person who might be described as in love with love. Obviously, there are other times when we are more lethargic or indifferent toward building intimate relationships—we already have a satisfactory number of concurrent relationships. Finally, it should be noted that as a relationship develops a history of its own, it may be possible to look back and see that at certain junctures behavioral manifestations of love were most important while at other times liking behavior was paramount for sustaining the intimate relationship.

An analysis of the environmental forces, the surrounding events, and each of our own developmental stages in life will certainly provide some of the necessary information for understanding and analyzing the nature of intimate relationships and intimate communication patterns.

Cultural Guidelines

Throughout our daily lives we are bombarded with messages about what constitutes the normative boundaries for assorted types of intimate relationships. Magazines, soap operas, advertisements, comic books, songs, novels, and movies serve to influence expectations, attitudes, and behaviors associated with human intimacy. These messages may reiterate the romantic ideal, espousing that love will conquer all adversity. As a result, some people seek utopian relationships which do not exist. Other messages may communicate this contemporary U.S. culture's encouragement of love and marriage—everyone is expected to fall in love; marriage is generally considered a good thing. They may propose the characteristics of people most suited for the development of intimate relationships—pairs who are physically attractive, single, opposite-sexed, similar in age and social background, who have known each other for an appropriate length of time, and who sexually desire each other. (This last characteristic in particular may be why people typically don't associate same-sexed relationships with intimate relationships.) Although our culture's standards are changing, there are still many people who feel that unmarried, middle-aged women must be unattractive, and generally failures; unmarried middle-aged men are still frequently categorized as either homosexuals or as individuals with mother complexes. Test yourself. Identify as many sources as you can that help to communicate the U.S. norm that in mixed-gender, romantic love the woman should be younger than the man. This norm, and the previously noted examples, have been widely communicated and have received cultural reinforcement in the past. This does not suggest that people in the United States don't receive counter-cultural messages nor that many people aren't adopting alternative (nontraditional) styles of intimacy. In time, some of these counter-normative messages may become the norm. One example of a transition from counter-normative behavior to more normative behavior concerns the familiar double standard regarding sexual behavior of men and women. Men, the previous norm told us, could experience sexual excitement and have intercourse without being in love; women, on the other hand, could not (without negative sanctioning) have sexual intercourse without being in love. Fortunately, behavioral standards that are similar for both sexes now receive greater acceptance, but this is a good example of how cultural guidelines encourage us to accept and label the same behavior in men and women differently. In fact, many cultural guidelines for the behavior of men and women in intimate relationships are in the process of changing. In the past, men were generally taught to shy away from overt emotional expressions; to express tenderness and affection in indirect, understated ways; to take responsibility for all important relationship decisions; to be the initiator of intimate behavior. All of these relationship teachings are being questioned in current mass media portrayals of male and female behavior.

There is an entire cultural litany for U.S. intimacy with numerous subcultural variations, but the foregoing examples should be enough to remind us of how our culture provides guidelines around which we are expected to structure our perceptions and behavior in intimate relationships.

Emotional Arousal and Labeling

Throughout most of this book we rely heavily on social and psychological factors to help us explain and understand interpersonal behavior. It would be a mistake, however, to ignore the role of body chemistry as a part of the process of experiencing intimate relationships.[30] For example, *oxytocin* is a hormone secreted by the pituitary gland which neuroscientists believe promotes close, intimate bonds. It has been shown to stimulate species contact; bonding and nurturing between parents and children; and affectionate and sexual behavior. PEA (*phenylethylamine*) is an amphetamine-related compound which triggers euphoria and energizes romantic lovers.

While there are many ways body chemistry works in tandem with social factors, none is more important than physiological arousal. Heightened emotions demand explanation—identifying labels. As soon as we've identified an emotional state as intense attraction for another person or as an extremely positive evaluation of another person, it will profoundly influence: (1) our expectations for the type of relationship we are entering—if we label what we're feeling as love, we will then expect a different set of behaviors (performed and received) than if we labeled the same feelings liking; (2) our perceptions of and consequent behavior toward the other person—what were faults before we labeled our feelings as love, now become mere idiosyncrasies; likewise, when we determine love is no longer an appropriate label for our feelings, idiosyncrasies may become faults again; (3) our motivation to expend energy for the relationship, the fervor and excitement with which we carry out the role prescribed by our label.

Patterson believes this process also operates in conjunction with various non-verbal behaviors shown in intimate and nonintimate situations.[31] Briefly, he suggests that sufficient amounts of eye contact, touching, and proximity will create an arousal state in the other person. If these behaviors are labeled positive (liking, love, relief) they will be returned or reciprocated; if they are labeled negative (dislike, embarrassment, anxiety) we will enact offsetting, opposite, or compensatory behavior. In this theory, the emotional arousal precedes the act of labeling it. The process may also be reversed. We may have a preexisting label (Elmo loves me) which may or may not fit Elmo's behavior toward us. According to this theory, a big discrepancy between what we expect and what we get is highly arousing and will bring forth compensatory behavior; if the discrepancy is only moderate, this is moderately arousing, pleasurable, and will elicit reciprocal behavior. Little or no discrepancy between the expected and observed behavior is not very arousing.[32] Both theories are useful. Each is probably suited to some situations and not others. Each points out the important connections between the physiological arousal associated with our emotions, the way we label it, and our consequent behavior.

> *When you're in love, you put up with things that, when you're out of love, you cite.*
>
> Miss Manners (Judith Martin)

Emotional responses are an important part of intimate relationships, but sometimes these relationships develop through an orderly, dispassionate, and sober process. Intimacy develops gradually as a result of the interpersonal reward schedules adopted by the participants. Various forms of liking and loving may develop in this fashion. Empathic ability may be very strong, and personal feelings for the other individual may be intensely felt. It is not, however, the same type of emotional drunkenness that so often characterizes romantic intimacy. The allusion to alcoholic intoxication was not a stylistic accident. The same brand of ecstasy and irrationality have often been noted both in love and inebriation. In this excerpt from one of Jimmy Buffett's songs we see the intermingling of the two conditions:

> . . . and commenced to get hot flashes
> Goosepimples was runnin' up and down my body
> Like . . . like I was in love
> In love for the first time—with anything that moved
> Animate, inanimate—it didn't matter
> It's like there's a great neon sign flashing on and off in my brain
> Sayin': Jimmy Buffett there's a great day a comin'
> Cause I was drunk. . . .[33]

Like alcoholic intoxication, romantic passion often has a sobering, reality-based morning after. The intensity level of the physiological arousal simply cannot be maintained indefinitely. Lederer and Jackson would probably add an emphatic "Thank God!" to that last statement since they feel that during these periods of unbridled passion, rationality is temporarily shelved and blinders are donned to ward off any unpleasant realities. They point out that the word *ecstasy,* a common label for one's emotions during a time of romantic love, is derived from a Greek word meaning *deranged* (in a state of being beyond all reason and self-control). Commenting further on potential distortions by a couple caught in this emotional tornado, Lederer and Jackson say: " . . . bad marriages, like death, are for others only . . . they are in such a passion (some call it romance), and are being driven so hard by the applause of society, that they cannot help themselves."[34] Permit us just one more analogy between those who treat themselves to alcohol and those who attribute their arousal to love. The drinker will often deny knowledge of any, and all, charges of abnormal behavior. We doubt the lover can be any better at transcending the situation when immersed in his or her emotions.

Exactly how we learn to label a particular, agitated emotional state as intimacy-related is not entirely clear. When, as children, we learn a word like *chair,* we can examine the referent by looking, touching, feeling, smelling, or even tasting. The referents for the term *intimate relationships* (lovers, close friends, intimates) and terms of intimacy (strong liking, loving, deep affection) are not available for sensory examination in the same way as a chair. We can observe others as lovers, close friends, or intimates and we can see how others exhibit strong liking, loving, and deep affection but we cannot experience the emotions behind our observations. Hence, we have to rely on what others tell us. Novelist Graham Greene echoed this idea when he said:

> Hatred seems to operate the same glands as love; it even produces the same actions. If we had not been taught how to interpret the story of the Passion, would we have been able to say from their actions alone whether it was the jealous Judas or the cowardly Peter who loved Christ?[35]

We also know that our parents give us some early guidance in labeling by providing the meaning for various physiological conditions—"You're just afraid of the dark," or "You're disappointed because your good friend can't go too." As noted previously, there is a wealth of parental guidance concerning love, but most often this guidance does not cover the emotions associated with passionate or romantic love. Parents probably assume their children can't experience such feelings until they grow up.

During late adolescence we have attained a fair grasp on the parameters of our own arousal tendencies and we begin to look for plausible labels to explain various states of arousal. The surrounding environmental and social conditions help a great deal. Sometimes parents may try to assist in this labeling process by identifying a relationship with an early romantic partner as "infatuation" or "just a crush" rather than "love." *Infatuation* generally refers to strong affective feelings which have been terminated—or soon will be terminated. As we mentioned before, if people accept the label, behaviors congruent with the label will most likely follow. The temporary nature of the term *infatuation* may, in turn, serve to shorten the duration of the relationship if one or both parties begin to act in concert with the label. Sometimes we opt for the socially approved label because the costs may be too high for selecting another label. For instance, a person who did not want to be burdened with the responsibilities associated with the label *love* might label arousal as sexual excitement at one point in life, and the same feelings as love at another point. No doubt there have been many instances in which the label *romantic love* has been astutely avoided as an explanation of one's arousal in the presence of a same-sexed friend.

It should be clear that the process of learning to identify the feelings of intimacy and to label them accurately is a process subject to considerable variation. This is because it is a process primarily learned by social comparisons. Besides variation, Brenton also observed the relativity in the labeling process in his extensive study of American friendship patterns:

> Describing their friendships to me, some people called them "close," though from my personal perspective I saw them as superficial. In time I realized how irrelevant my reaction was in relation to what was actually going on with *them*. To be sure, some wished for closer friendships and were distressed about this lack in their lives. But others were involved in as much closeness as they wanted to be involved in and could tolerate. Their version of closeness may not be my version or your version—but it is real and meaningful to them. So I came to believe that closeness is a relative value, not an absolute one, and that in the final analysis no one can define our friendships for us. We must, all of us, do that for ourselves—based on our awareness of ourselves, of our needs, and of the ways our friendships work in our lives.[36]

Brenton's observation reminds us of a communication truism—that meanings are not in the words we use, but in us.

One final note. Labeling our state of emotional arousal is an ongoing process. The discussion here has focused mainly on the period of entry into intimacy. As we linger longer in an intimate relationship, we continue to evaluate and label our emotions. As an intimate relationship progresses, there may be periodic peaks which resemble the early ecstasy. In fact, the concept of the anniversary is probably an attempt to remind us of such feelings. Mostly, however, enduring intimate relationships reveal more stable and less intense physiological arousal than that experienced during earlier phases of intimacy. As we give more (or less) to the relationship, as we have (or don't have) our needs satisfied, and as we commit more of ourselves to a joint (or individual) identity, we will reevaluate the relationship and relabel our feeling states. We may continue to use the word *love* to describe the relationship, but the type of love and the intensity may change dramatically over the years. Relationships that are coming apart, may do so—not because of arousal labeled hatred or dislike but—because there is a perceived absence of *any* arousal, or, at least, the absence of any arousal that might receive a positive label concerning our relationship to our partner.

> *. . . the Eskimos had fifty-two names for snow because it was important to them; there ought to be as many for love.*
>
> Margaret Atwood

Self-Fulfillment

Self-fulfillment, as a foundation for interpreting intimate relationships, is based on the assumption that the more our needs are fulfilled by the relationship, the greater will be our feelings of intimacy. We are, in essence, talking about the perceived rewards we receive—how effectively we perceive our partner as complementing our strengths and weaknesses; whether we find the needed similarity (or difference) in attitudes, values, physical attractiveness, sense of humor, and so forth. The following probably represent the most commonly discussed areas of need satisfaction in the pursuit of intimacy:

1. Affection Needs. The satisfaction of one's need for affection is a minimal and basic requirement for intimacy. This overlaps with what some call a sense of belonging. Various verbal and touching behavior might be an important manifestation in some relationships; in others, satisfaction of affection needs may also encompass sexual gratification. It should be obvious that the sex act, itself, does not necessarily mean the satisfaction of affection needs; and furthermore, sexual satisfaction doesn't always mean that affection needs are satisfied.

2. Self-Esteem Needs. The parties to an intimate relationship must recognize and deal with ways in which self-respect, recognition, appreciation, and status can be communicated, and how often messages of this type are required. It is hard to contribute effectively to the joint identity of the relationship if one or both partners are uncertain about or don't think much of their own identities.

3. Security Needs. In this context, security has a broad definition. It not only includes the rather primitive forms of security such as food, shelter, and friends; but it also includes a psychological security that is derived from the absence of threat, the presence of ego-supportive communications, and a healthy amount of predictiveness in the relationship and the environment.

4. Freedom Needs. As people grow more intimate with each other, it is almost inevitable that they will find it necessary to wrestle with questions concerning satisfaction of freedom needs. In some areas of activity, a person may want self-reliance and independence of action; in other areas, the same person may desire dependency and reliance on one's partner. Many times these issues are reflective of individual perceptions of how much exclusivity the developing relationship demands. Have you ever had what you considered to be a "dear friend" who was great except for one thing—the friend was like a parasite and you were the host? Your friend, by not satisfying your freedom needs, was engaging in behavior that might eventually cause you to weigh your need for the friendship against your need for freedom. Whatever one's needs in this area, self-fulfillment can only occur when each partner does not feel too limited or restrained by the relationship. Of course, if you feel no restraining forces from the relationship, you might well examine whether you have the kind of intimacy you thought you did. You can ensure your disappointment in a relationship by demanding total freedom and total intimacy at the same time.

5. Equality Needs. Although it is easy to write about the satisfaction of equality needs, it is considerably more difficult to specify what this means. Equality needs are linked to many of the other need areas previously mentioned. You may feel you need to be superior to your partner in some things; subordinate in others; and equal in others. Then, to make it even more confusing, on any given occasion you might want to be equal or subordinate in an area you had traditionally been superior in, etc. Equality in a relationship can also be affected by involvement with the relationship. An imbalance of involvement with the relationship may cause an imbalance of power in the relationship. And, interestingly, the person who is least interested in the relationship may, *for a time,* dictate the conditions of the relationship because the person who cares the most will defer most often to the wishes of the other. No matter what the intricate permutations of equality in a relationship might be, self-fulfillment will be enhanced if a person feels his or her needs for equality and/or inequality are generally met.

The rewards that lead to the satisfaction of the foregoing needs can be communicated in many ways. Such rewards may appear in very utilitarian forms—doing favors, doing chores, or giving gifts. There may be direct expressions of feelings—interest or encouragement; or there may be indirect expressions—moral support. Some rewards may come through physical expressions. Sometimes psychological stimulation is found in the other person—"I can learn from you"; or self-fulfillment may derive from being associated with someone talented in areas the partner in the relationship and others respect—intelligence or interpersonal skills. It is important to remember that needs do change, and the ways of satisfying these needs must also change at various times in the relationship.

Some people just don't seem to have much self-fulfillment on the dimensions previously listed. Why do they maintain their friendship or marriage? First, let's recall that we are dealing with individual perceptions and priorities. What we perceive as a reward, or a satisfier, for a particular need may not be what others perceive; furthermore, some individuals attach so much importance to certain needs that other needs do not require much fulfillment. In other words, freedom needs may be very important to one individual but not so important to another; what may seem to be a strong reward to one person in the freedom area may seem to be tokenism to another. So, in some situations outsiders may feel there is little self-fulfillment or need satisfaction while the participants feel that there is plenty.

In some situations people do stay together when they are obtaining little self-fulfillment. There may be strong external forces that cause the relationship to continue, and adaptations are made. Among these adaptations might be: (1) telling yourself that satisfactions will be forthcoming and this is just a phase of the relationship which can be explained; (2) seeking satisfactions from other relationships—complaining about your "terrible relationship" to others, seeking more satisfaction and rewards from children or other lovers; (3) waiting for the external forces to dissolve so exit from the relationship will be easier; or (4) taking your dissatisfaction out on your partner and feeding neurotically on the mutual misery.

In summary, participants in an intimate relationship have a desire for self-fulfillment by the other—a need to be cared for. The degree of intimacy one perceives will certainly be affected by the extent to which this self-fulfillment has been met. It would, however, be inappropriate to conclude from this discussion that if all needs aren't satisfied, a relationship is in trouble or the partners in a relationship are wrong for each other. Inevitably, we will always have some needs unfulfilled, maybe not always the same ones, but the point is not to expect all needs to be completely fulfilled at the same time. The nature of human relationships is that they are constantly in process. Sometimes an attempt to satisfy all one's needs may boomerang. For example, a couple has, by their own standards, a good relationship with many satisfactions. One of the partners feels a deficiency in self-esteem-building messages from the other partner. Rather than dealing with this problem within the relationship, the dissatisfied partner finds such messages flowing freely from others in exchange for a casual sexual encounter. When the spouse becomes aware of the sexual encounters, he or she perceives it as the breaking of a sacred covenant of the relationship and seeks to terminate the relationship.

Self-Surrender

The process of evaluation is perhaps our most common cognitive activity. Most of these evaluations are oriented toward a concern for our own feelings—"What does it mean to me?" *Self-surrender* is a process of evaluation in which the response is more likely to be: "What does this mean to the other person's feelings?" Self-fulfillment dealt with needing; self-surrender deals with giving. The assumption undergirding this foundation of intimacy is that the extent to which one is willing to give to another person is reflective of the degree of intimacy he or she feels. Psychiatrist Harry Stack Sullivan felt that a full extension of this concept brought one to a state of love:

> When the satisfaction or the security of another person becomes as significant to one as is one's own satisfaction or security, then the state of love exists.[37]

Realistically, few, if any, of us will reach a point where our communication shows a genuine concern for the other person that is *consistently* as great as our concern for our own satisfaction. It is clear, however, that some people are able to achieve a greater degree of this than others.

An analogy will illustrate the issue. Imagine you are in a deep hole without the means to get out. Some people who come by and see you will just look at you and ask how you got yourself into such a situation; others will point out that they would like to throw a rope, but there is no place to tie it; the people we feel closest to are those who immediately and unthinkingly throw the rope to us.

Commitment to a Joint Identity

Thus far, the foundations we've discussed have focused on the individual parties to the relationship—their personality, their emotional arousal, their need for caring and giving. The idea of a joint identity concerns something much more abstract—the bond or link between the two people. It is something different from a simple algebraic summation of both person's attributes, attitudes, and behavior. The blending of two individuals, like the blending of two chemicals, produces a new mixture. Indeed, there are still properties of the two original chemicals in the new mixture, but there is also a substance with characteristics unlike anything the original chemicals had. It is the amount of commitment to this new mixture, or new identity, that characterizes this foundation for assessing intimacy in a relationship.

For those engaged in cultivating this joint identity, it is possible to see a number of outward manifestations of their efforts. Sometimes these efforts will be very conscious and planned. For instance, the participants might discuss how the superstructure of the relationship far exceeds or transcends most of their individual needs and desires. This attempt to balance individuality and mutuality is a continuing concern for intimate partners. Often the very thing that enhances the joint identity will detract from the autonomy of one or both partners, and vice versa. Nevertheless, each partner must in some way demonstrate an ongoing commitment to the relationship as well as to himself or herself. Relationship commitment, like commitment to other things, requires an effort to become knowledgeable about it, devote time to it, make future plans based on it, speak favorably about it, and defend it against destructive forces. You can probably think of additional behaviors that show one's commitment to sustaining a relationship. Other manifestations of this joint identity may develop without a great deal of conscious programming. The partners find themselves using the same phrases and even similar vocal inflection patterns.

Mixed-sex pairs in our culture have used the marriage ritual to announce their movement toward a joint identity. A related issue concerns the accepted custom for the woman to adopt the man's last name and shed her own surname. If the name change was consistent with the joint identity concept, the two participants would adopt a totally new last name which might be preceded by their own family names—Mark L. Knapp-Landis and Lillian J. Davis-Landis.

> *I am good, you love me; therefore you are good.*
> *I am bad, you love me; therefore you are bad.*
>
> R. D. Laing

Same-sexed pairs often announce their movement toward a joint identity by consistently engaging in common activities. Two professors in the field of Speech Communication, Larry Barker and Robert Kibler, wrote so many articles and books together that their names were almost inextricably linked. When others in the field were referring to a work authored by either Kibler or Barker alone, there would often be some confusion as to whether it was jointly done. This points out the fact that when people engage in behavior that seems to affirm a joint identity, it is not always without complications. Roommates may live together but not want to be seen as a common package in some settings; spouses may want to be invited some places as a couple, but would prefer separate invitations to other functions. It is a common experience for the friends of a divorced couple to worry about whom to invite over first for fear the order of the invitations would communicate favoritism. Sometimes this dilemma is resolved by not inviting either person and results in both divorced individuals wondering whether the friends were really friends in the first place.

An example of the difficulties incurred by moving too quickly to establish a joint identity can be seen in the efforts made by businesses or organizations to fuse the corporate identity with the new employee's individual identity. New employees might feel a certain strain when it appears that they are being asked to commit themselves to this new identity before they even know the corporation. This situation usually occurs when the longtime employees try to pull the newly hireds into the "we" relationship too quickly—"We here at Purdue (IBM, or whatever) have always done it this way. . . ." It is not surprising to see many newly hireds respond with an "I-you" distancing move—"Well, I can understand why *you* have done it this way, but *I*. . . ."

Each of the seven foundations of intimacy, which have just been discussed, exerts its own influence on the *type* of intimacy you feel you have achieved and on the *intensity* with which you feel it. Whatever label you select to describe your intimate relationship with another person—deep affection, strong liking, romantic love, friendship—you should be able to account for your use of the label by examining your perception of the intimacy foundations in that particular relationship.[38] Obviously, there may be differences in your love for your grandfather, a lifelong friend, or your spouse; there may also be more similarities than you might imagine. Your own personal explanation for the qualitative and quantitative differences and similarities in your intimate relationships may be revealed as you ponder the influence of each intimacy foundation.

SUMMARY

This chapter focused on the intricacies of intimacy—the more advanced stages of a relationship which includes intensifying, integrating, and bonding. First, we examined the terminology typically used to describe these more advanced growth stages of relationships. While we didn't arrive at any neat, compact, and conclusive definitions, we uncovered some intriguing distinctions. One line of research, for instance, found at least six different *styles of loving;* another identified eight types of love relationships. These works suggest that the term *love* may have many referents and many overt manifestations. Although this last statement reverberates with triteness, we should recall how many times in this emotionally detached world of book reading, people act as if there were only one type of love and act accordingly. Furthermore, when people seeking a divorce say that they aren't in love, they may mean simply that they want a different type of love. A new intimate relationship may be the only way a person can shed old, displeasing habits and start over.

Next, distinctions between the terms *liking* and *loving* were sought. Love often involves a greater intensity of feelings and behaviors than liking, a quantitative difference; but there also seems to be a strong likelihood that qualitative differences between the two feeling states exist. Companionate features often accompany both liking and loving. We then outlined seven *foundations of intimacy* which we felt accounted for the variety of labels used to describe intimate relationships—labels such as deep affection, romantic love, friendship, strong liking. These foundations included: personality and early experiences; situational and developmental factors; cultural guidelines; emotional arousal and labeling; self-fulfillment; self-surrender; and commitment to a joint identity. These broad categories provide the parameters for explaining different relationships and different individual labels. Obviously, they fall far short of the specificity we might like to have—X type of love will most likely occur when the participants have A, B, and C personality characteristics, D and E early experiences, and have F and G needs fulfilled, etc.

SELECTED READINGS

Intimacy/Liking/Loving

Ackerman, D. *A Natural History of Love.* New York: Random House, 1994.

Adams, R. G., and Blieszner, R. "An Integrative Conceptual Framework for Friendship Research." *Journal of Social and Personal Relationships* 11 (1994): 163–184.

Aron, A. and Westbay, L. "Dimensions of the Prototype Love." *Journal of Personality and Social Psychology* 70 (1996): 535–551.

Beall, A. E. and Sternberg, R. J. "The Social Construction of Love." *Journal of Social and Personal Relationships* 12 (1995): 417–438.

Berscheid, E. and Reis, H. T. "Attraction and Close Relationships." In D. T. Gilbert, S. T. Fiske, and G. Lindzey, eds., *The Handbook of Social Psychology,* vol. 2, pp. 193–281, 4th ed. New York: McGraw-Hill, 1998.

Blieszner, R., and Adams, R. G. *Adult Friendship.* Newbury Park, CA: Sage, 1992.

Bochner, A. "Functions of Communication in Interpersonal Bonding." In C. Arnold and J. W. Bowers, eds., *Handbook of Rhetoric and Communication.* Boston: Allyn and Bacon, 1981.

Brehm, S. *Intimate Relationships.* 2nd ed. New York: McGraw-Hill, 1992.

Brenton, M. *Friendship.* New York: Stein & Day, 1974.

Buss, D. M. *The Evolution of Desire: Strategies of Human Mating.* New York: Basic Books, 1994.

Cunningham, J. D., and Antill, J. K. "Love in Developing Romantic Relationships." In S. Duck and R. Gilmour, eds., *Personal Relationships. 2: Developing Personal Relationships,* pp. 27–52. New York: Academic Press, 1981.

Daly, J. A., and Kreiser, P. O. "Affinity Seeking." In J. A. Daly and J. M. Wiemann, eds., *Strategic Interpersonal Communication,* pp. 109–134. Hillsdale, NJ: Erlbaum, 1994.

Davis, K. E., Kirkpatrick, L. A., Levy, M. B., and O'Hearn, R. E. "Stalking the Elusive Love Style: Attachment Styles, Love Styles, and Relationship Development." In R. Erber and R. Gilmour, eds., *Theoretical Frameworks for Personal Relationships,* pp. 179–210. Hillsdale, NJ: Erlbaum, 1994.

Davis, K. E., and Todd, M. J. "Friendship and Love Relationships." In K. E. Davis and T. O. Mitchell, eds., *Advances in Descriptive Psychology,* vol. 2. Greenwich, CT: J. A. I. Press, 1982.

Davis, M. S. *Intimate Relations.* New York: Free Press, 1973.

Fehr, B. *Friendship Processes.* Thousand Oaks, CA: Sage, 1996.

Fisher, H. *Anatomy of Love: The Natural History of Monogamy, Adultery and Divorce.* New York: Norton, 1992.

Fletcher, G. J. O., Simpson, J. A., Thomas, G., and Giles, L. "Ideals in Intimate Relationships." *Journal of Personality and Social Psychology* 76 (1999): 72–89.

Forgas, J. P., and Dobosz, B. "Dimensions of Romantic Involvement: Towards a Taxonomy of Heterosexual Relationships." *Social Psychology Quarterly* 43 (1980): 290–300.

Grote, N. K. and Frieze, I. H. " 'Remembrance of Things Past:' Perceptions of Marital Love from its Beginnings to the Present." *Journal of Social and Personal Relationships* 15 (1998): 91–109.

Guerrero, L. K. "Attachment-Style Differences in Intimacy and Involvement: A Test of the Four-Category Model." *Communication Monographs* 63 (1996): 269–292.

Guerrero, L. K. "Nonverbal Involvement Across Interactions with Same-Sex Friends, Opposite-Sex Friends and Romantic Partners: Consistency or Change?" *Journal of Social and Personal Relationships* 14 (1996): 31–58.

Hatfield, E., and Rapson, R. L. *Love, Sex, and Intimacy: Their Psychology, Biology, and History.* New York: Harper Collins, 1993.

Hatfield, E., and Walster, G. W. *A New Look at Love.* Lanham, MD: University Press of America, 1985.

Hazan, C., and Shaver, P. "Romantic Love Conceptualized as an Attachment Process." *Journal of Personality and Social Psychology* 42 (1987): 511–524.

Hecht, M. L., Marston, P. J., and Larkey, L. K. "Love Ways and Relationship Quality in Heterosexual Relationships." *Journal of Social and Personal Relationships* 11 (1994): 25–43.

Hendrick, C., and Hendrick, S. S. "A Theory and Method of Love." *Journal of Personality and Social Psychology* 50 (1986): 392–402.

Hendrick, C., Hendrick, S. S. and Dicke, A. "The Love Attitude Scale: Short Form." *Journal of Social and Personal Relationships* 15 (1998): 147–159.

Hendrick, S. S., and Hendrick, C. "Lovers as Friends." *Journal of Social and Personal Relationships* 10 (1993): 459–466.

Hendrick, S. S., and Hendrick, C. *Romantic Love.* Newbury Park, CA: Sage, 1992.

Hindy, C. G., and Schwarz, J. C. *If This Is Love, Why Do I Feel So Insecure?* New York: Atlantic Monthly Press, 1989.

Illouz, E. "Reason Within Passion: Love In Women's Magazines." *Critical Studies in Mass Communication* 8 (1991): 231–248.

Jeffries, V. "Virtue and Attraction: Validation of a Measure of Love." *Journal of Social and Personal Relationships* 10 (1993): 99–117.

Lederer, W. J., and Jackson, D. D. *The Mirages of Marriage.* New York: W. W. Norton, 1968.

Lee, J. A. *The Colors of Love.* Englewood Cliffs, NJ: Prentice-Hall, 1976.

Levy, M., and Davis, K. E. "Lovestyles and Attachment Styles Compared: Their Relations to Each Other and to Various Relationship Characteristics." *Journal of Social and Personal Relationships* 5 (1988): 439–471.

Lewis, M., and Rosenblum, L. A., eds. *Friendship and Peer Relations.* New York: Wiley, 1975.

Marston, P. J., Hecht, M. L., McDaniel, S., and Reeder, H. "The Subjective Experience of Intimacy, Passion, and Commitment in Heterosexual Loving Relationships." *Personal Relationships* 5 (1998): 15–30.

McCall, G. J., ed. *Social Relationships.* Chicago: Aldine Publishing, 1970.

Murray, S. L., Holmes, J. G., and Griffin, D. W. "The Self-Fulfilling Nature of Positive Illusions in Romantic Relationships: Love Is Not Blind, but Prescient." *Journal of Personality and Social Psychology* 71 (1996): 1155–1180.

Nardi, P. M., ed. *Men's Friendships.* Newbury Park, CA: Sage, 1992.

Nardi, P. M., and Sherrod, D. "Friendship in the Lives of Gay Men and Lesbians." *Journal of Social and Personal Relationships* 11 (1994): 185–199.

O'Connor, P. *Friendships Between Women: A Critical Review.* New York: Guilford, 1992.

Personal Relationships 3 (1996). Special Issue: On Understanding Love.

Prager, K. J. *The Psychology of Intimacy.* New York: Guilford, 1995.

Rawlins, W. K. *Friendship Matters: Communication, Dialectics, and the Life Course.* New York: Aldine, 1992.

Regan, P. "Of Lust and Love: Beliefs About the Role of Sexual Desire in Romantic Relationships." *Personal Relationships* 5 (1998): 139–157.

Register, L. M., and Henley, T. B. "The Phenomenology of Intimacy." *Journal of Social and Personal Relationships* 9 (1992): 467–481.

Rothman, E. K. *Hands and Hearts: A History of Courtship in America.* New York: Basic Books, 1984.

Scarf, M. *Intimate Partners: Patterns of Love and Marriage.* New York: Random House, 1987.

Seidman, S. *Romantic Longings: Love in America, 1830–1980.* Routledge, NY: SUNY Albany Press, 1991.

Seligman, C.; Fazio, R. H.; and Zanna, M. P. "Effects of Salience of Extrinsic Rewards on Liking and Loving." *Journal of Personality and Social Psychology* 38 (1980): 453–460.

Shaver, P. R., and Hazan, C. "A Biased Overview of the Study of Love." *Journal of Social and Personal Relationships* 5 (1988): 473–501.

Shaver, P., Hazan, C., and Bradshaw, D. "Love as Attachment: The Integration of Three Behavioral Systems." In R. J. Sternberg and M. Barnes, eds., *The Psychology of Love.* New Haven: Yale University Press, 1988.

Sias, P. M. and Cahill, D. J. "From Coworkers to Friends: The Development of Peer Friendships in the Workplace." *Western Journal of Communication* 62 (1998): 273–99.

Simpson, J. A. and Rholes, W. S., eds. *Attachment Theory and Close Relationships.* Mahwah, NJ: Earlbaum, 1998.

Sternberg, R. J. "Liking Versus Loving." *Psychological Bulletin* 102 (1987): 331–345.

———. "A Triangular Theory of Love." *Psychological Review* 93 (1986): 119–135.

———. *The Triangle of Love.* New York: Basic Books, 1988.

Sternberg, R. J., and Barnes, M. L. *The Psychology of Love.* New Haven: Yale University Press, 1988.

Sternberg, R. J., and Beall, A. E. "How Can We Know What Love Is? An Epistemological Analysis." In G. J. O. Fletcher and F. D. Fincham, eds., *Cognition in Close Relationships,* pp. 257–278. Hillsdale, NJ: Erlbaum, 1991.

Werking, K. *We're Just Good Friends: Women and Men in Nonromantic Relationships.* New York: Guilford, 1997.

NOTES

[1]J. A. Lee, "Love-styles." In R. Sternberg and M. Barnes, eds., *The Psychology of Love* (New Haven: Yale University Press, 1988), pp. 38–67; also J. A. Lee, *The Colors of Love* (Englewood Cliffs, NJ: Prentice-Hall, 1976).

[2]S. Peele and A. Brodsky, "Love Can Be an Addiction," *Psychology Today* 8 (1974): 23–26.

[3]D. Tennov, *Love and Limerance* (New York: Stein & Day, 1979).

[4]For example, see S. Spencer, *Endless Love* (New York: Knopf, 1979).

[5]G. D. Morrow, E. M. Clark, and K. F. Brock, "Individual and Partner Love Styles: Implications for the Quality of Romantic Involvements," *Journal of Social and Personal Relationships* 12 (1995): 363–387. S. S. Hendrick and C. Hendrick, "Gender Differences and Similarities in Sex and Love," *Personal Relationships* 2 (1995): 55–65.

[6]R. J. Sternberg, "The Triangle of Love." (New York: Basic Books, 1988).

[7]A. Aron and L. Westbay, "Dimensions of the Prototype of Love," *Journal of Personality and Social Psychology* 70 (1996): 535–555.

[8]P. C. Regan, "Of Lust and Love: Beliefs About the Role of Sexual Desire in Romantic Relationships," *Personal Relationships* 5 (1998): 139–157.

[9]M. Acker and M. H. Davis, "Intimacy, Passion and Commitment in Adult Romantic Relationships: A Test of the Triangular Theory of Love," *Journal of Social and Personal Relationships* 9 (1992): 21–50.

[10]E. Berscheid and E. Walster, "A Little Bit About Love." In T. L. Huston, ed., *Foundations of Interpersonal Attraction* (New York: Academic Press, 1974), pp. 355–381.

[11]G. L. White, S. Fishbein, and J. Rutstein, "Passionate Love and the Misattribution of Arousal," *Journal of Personality and Social Psychology* 41 (1981): 56–62.

[12]S. Schachter, "The Interaction of Cognitive and Physiological Determinants of Emotional State," *Advances in Experimental Social Psychology,* vol. 1, L. Berkowitz ed. (New York: Academic Press, 1964), pp. 49–80. Not all arousal-labeling experiments support Schachter's theory. Maslach found aroused people reporting negative emotions in both happy and angry situations. See C. Maslach, "Negative Emotional Biasing of Unexplained Arousal," *Journal of Personality and Social Psychology* 37 (1979): 953–969; C. D. Marshall and P. G. Zimbardo, "Affective Consequences of Inadequately Explained Physiological Arousal," *Journal of Personality and Social Psychology* 37 (1979): 970–988.

[13]Z. Rubin, *Liking and Loving* (New York: Holt, Rinehart, & Winston, 1973).

[14]K. E. Davis and M. J. Todd, "Friendship and Love Relationships." In K. E. Davis and T. O. Mitchell, eds., *Advances in Descriptive Psychology,* vol. 2 (Greenwich, CT: J. A. I. Press, 1982); K. E. Davis, "Near and Dear: Friendship and Love Compared," *Psychology Today* (February, 1985): 22–30. Also see: S. S. Hendrick and C. Hendrick, "Lovers as Friends," *Journal of Social and Personal Relationships* 10 (1993): 459–466.

[15]B. Fehr, "How Do I Love Thee? Let Me Consult My Prototype." In S. Duck, ed., *Individuals in Relationships* (Newbury Park, CA: Sage, 1993), pp. 87–120.

[16]G. M. Maxwell, "Behavior of Lovers: Measuring the Closeness of Relationships," *Journal of Social and Personal Relationships* 2 (1985): 215–238. Also see: M. R. Parks and K. Floyd, "Meanings for Closeness and Intimacy in Friendship," *Journal of Social and Personal Relationships* 13 (1996): 85–107.

[17]P. J. Marston, M. L. Hecht, M. L. Manke, S. McDaniel, and H. Reeder, "The Subjective Expe-

rience of Intimacy, Passion, and Commitment in Heterosexual Loving relationships," *Personal Relationships* 5 1998): 15–30.

[18]L. K. Guerrero, "Nonverbal Involvement Across Interactions with Same-Sex Friends, Opposite-Sex Friends and Romantic Partners: Consistency or Change?" *Journal of Social and Personal Relationships* 14 (1997): 31–58.

[19]A. Thomas, S. Chess, and H. G. Birch, "Origins of Personality," *Scientific American* (August 1970): 102–109.

[20]G. Wilson, *The Coolidge Effect: An Evolutionary Account of Human Sexuality* (New York: Morrow, 1981).

[21]D. M. Buss, *The Evolution of Desire: Strategies of Human Mating* (New York: Basic Books, 1994).

[22]K. B. Carnelley and R. Janoff-Bulman, "Optimism About Love Relationships: General vs. Specific Lessons from One's Personal Experiences," *Journal of Social and Personal Relationships* 9 (1992): 5–20.

[23]C. Hazan and P. Shaver, "Romantic Love Conceptualized as an Attachment Process," *Journal of Personality and Social Psychology,* 42 (1987): 511–524; P. Shaver, C. Hazan, and D. Bradshaw, "Love as Attachment: The Integration of Three Behavioral Systems." In R. J. Sternberg and M. Barnes, eds., *The Psychology of Love.* (New Haven: Yale University Press, 1988).

[24]M. W. Baldwin and B. Fehr, "On the Instability of Attachment Style Ratings," *Personal Relationships* 2 (1995): 247–261. Also: P. A. Frazier, A. L. Byer, A. R. Fischer, D. M. Wright, and K. A. DeBord, "Adult Attachment Style and Partner Choice: Correlational and Experimental Findings," *Personal Relationships* 3 (1996): 117–136.

[25]B. Fehr, *Friendship Processes* (Thousand Oaks, CA: Sage, 1996)

[26]"Seesaw Love," *Human Behavior* (August 1975): 35–36.

[27]S. L. Murray, J. G. Holmes, and D. W. Griffin, "The Self-Fulfilling Nature of Positive Illusions in Romantic Relationships: Love Is Not Blind, but Prescient," *Journal of Personality and Social Psychology* 71 (1996): 1155–1180.

[28]Copyright © 1974 by Myron Brenton. From the book *Friendship,* pp. 40–41. Reprinted with permission of Stein and Day Publishers and by permission of The Sterling Lord Agency, Inc.

[29]P. M. Sias and D. J. Cahill, "From Coworkers to Friends: The Development of Peer Friendships in the Workplace," *Western Journal of Communication* 62 (1998): 273–299.

[30]E. Hatfield and R. L. Rapson, *Love, Sex, and Intimacy: Their Psychology, Biology, and History* (New York: Harper Collins, 1993); H. Fisher, *Anatomy of Love: The Natural History of Monogamy, Adultery and Divorce* (New York: Norton, 1992); and D. Ackerman, *A Natural History of Love* (New York: Random House, 1994).

[31]M. L. Patterson, "An Arousal Model of Interpersonal Intimacy," *Psychological Review* 83 (1976): 235–245. This theory is similar to one discussed earlier in this chapter. See S. Schachter and J. Singer, "Cognitive, Social, and Physiological Determinants of Emotional State," *Psychological Review* 69 (1962): 379–399.

[32]D. N. Stern, "Mother and Infant at Play: The Dyadic Interaction Involving Facial, Vocal and Gaze Behavior." In M. Lewis and L. A. Rosenblum, eds., *The Effect of the Infant on Its Caregiver* (New York: John Wiley & Sons, 1974). Also see J. N. Cappella and J. O. Greene, "A Discrepancy-Arousal Explanation of Mutual Influence in Expressive Behavior for Adult and Infant-Adult Interaction," *Communication Monographs* 49 (1982): 89–114.

[33]Copyright © 1974 by ABC/Dunhill Records. Written by Lord Buckley and sung by Jimmy Buffett on the album: *Living and Dying In ¾ Time.*

[34]W. J. Lederer and D. D. Jackson. *The Mirages of Marriage* (New York: W. W. Norton, 1968), pp. 42–43.

[35]G. Greene, *The End of the Affair* (New York: Penguin Books, 1977). (Originally published, 1951, by Wm. Heinemann, London.)

[36]Copyright © 1974 by Myron Brenton. From the book *Friendship,* pp. 18–19. Reprinted with permission of Stein and Day Publishers and by permission of The Sterling Lord Agency, Inc.

[37]H. S. Sullivan, *Conceptions of Modern Psychiatry* (New York: W. W. Norton, 1953), pp. 42–43.

[38]A full understanding of love, like other types of intimate relationships, is highly contextual and requires an analysis of the specific feelings, thoughts, and actions of the people involved. See A. E. Beall and R. J. Sternberg, "The Social Construction of Love," *Journal of Social and Personal Relationships* 12 (1995): 417–438.

Interaction Patterns and the Maintenance of Relationships

CHAPTER **8**

Maintaining Relationships Through Dialogue:
Disclosures, Lies, and Fights

CHAPTER **9**

Maintaining Relationships Through Dialogue:
Commitment and Intimacy

8

Maintaining Relationships Through Dialogue: Disclosures, Lies, and Fights

Dear Dr. Vangelisti,

I have been going out with a certain guy for a little less than a month now. At the beginning of the relationship, we both were attracted to each other, felt we had a lot in common, and had a great time together. One night, though, we had a long talk and I told him a lot of very personal things about myself. He just listened. From that night on, the relationship has been declining for me. I can only see our differences now and when we go out I don't have such a great time anymore. We still spend a lot of time together, but this doesn't help the situation. I have shut myself off except for purely social conversation. Can anything be done to save this relationship?

Too Much Too Soon

There are many ways to be open with others. Perhaps this writer's problem stems from a tendency to be open with nonintimates in ways that are normally reserved for our more intimate relationships. Openness, or self-disclosure, is only one communication pattern that gradually changes as relationships become closer. This chapter discusses several of these communication patterns as they occur in close relationships including disclosing some personal information and withholding some; lying; and fighting fair.

> *Married life requires shared mystery even when all the facts are known.*
>
> —Richard Ford

This chapter and the next focus on the interaction patterns that are so critical to maintaining a close relationship. It is our belief that maintenance behavior is not something new to the ongoing dialogue that helped shape the relationship. Maintenance, from this perspective, is the way the partners deal with the critical and repeated acts of discourse that constitute their relationship. It is the way they deal with conflict; their ability to use small talk for relational purposes; the judicious use of disclosures as well as secrets; their ability to make their partner feel their commitment and affection; their ability to engineer the proper mixture of teamwork and team play; the ability to provide for one another's privacy as well as togetherness; and the ability to develop the proper balance of predictable and novel communication patterns.

Relationship maintenance, then, involves a blending of experiences and interactions, some of which are perceived as pleasant and some of which are not.

Not all relationships require the same kind of maintenance. Some friendships, for example, only require infrequent contact to sustain them, while others will be lost without regular care and feeding. In the same way, relationships that may need a great deal of maintenance at one point in time may need far less at another. *Maintenance* itself means different things to different people.[1] For example, it may require a far different set of skills to simply keep a relationship from disappearing than it does to keep a relationship at a point where it is satisfying to both parties. As noted above, maintenance behavior involves virtually any type of interaction characterizing the relationship. Maintenance can be performed, though, by using only a small subset of these behaviors at any given time. The ability to identify which subset of behaviors act in a relationship-maintaining way is, of course, part of the skill relationship caretakers must develop. Failure to maintain (appropriately care for) certain key communicative aspects of a relationship (e.g., conflict and affection) on a regular schedule may mean that eventually there will be need for repair or rejuvenation. When relationship-maintaining behavior is performed regularly for an extended period of time, it is difficult to appreciate its important effects. On the other hand, we are painfully aware of our relationship when it has not been properly maintained.

Self-Disclosure, Confidentiality, and Trust

The word *intimacy* is derived from Latin words meaning "to make known" and "innermost." For this reason, some people equate self-disclosure and intimacy. It is true that as people increase their affection for another, they seem to reveal more, previously hidden aspects about themselves; however, we also find people disclosing very private information to complete strangers. Self-disclosure seems to be a necessary condition for achieving intimacy, but it may also be possible to know a lot about someone and still not like them.

The Nature of Self-Disclosing Messages

Let's look at the composition of self-disclosing messages. By definition, self-disclosing messages reveal something about oneself. It might be relatively public information (twenty-nine-years old and born in Muskogee, Oklahoma), but intimate disclosures usually refer to more personal matters, things people probably wouldn't find out unless you told them, and things you don't tell many people.[2] Thus, your self-disclosures may reflect any breadth and depth combination, but intimate dialogue is primarily concerned with depth. Self-disclosures can focus on information, perceptions, or feelings; messages may be positive or negative, frequent or infrequent, long or short, accurate or inaccurate reflections of yourself, very intentional or under less conscious control. They may be well-timed or ill-timed. Disclosure may be extensive on a topic at one time and minimal on the same topic at another time.

Based on the studies of self-disclosure conducted over the last thirty years, we would suggest the dimensions in Table 8.1 be used in order to determine the nature and strength of the message for each partner to the relationship.

Self-disclosures of "greater magnitude" would be known by fewer people, be personally owned ("*I feel*" rather than the more general "*People feel*"), and be specific. Specificity may be related to the other person or to the other person's

---

TABLE 8.1   Dimensions of Self-Disclosure

Information

Many Know .... Few Know

Impersonal/Not Owned... Personal/Owned

Abstract .... Specific

Expectations for Self

Low Risk/Vulnerability .... High Risk/Vulnerability

Expectations for Other

Lack of Understanding/Acceptance .... High Understanding/Acceptance

Not Reciprocated .... Reciprocated

May Tell Others.. May Not Tell Others

behavior. It is more open and self-disclosive to say, "I feel _____ toward you, Merle" than it is to say, "I feel _____ toward people." Similarly, it is more revealing about yourself if you say, "You were late for our appointment" than to say, "You and I just operate by different rules." Self-disclosures of greater magnitude also involve more risk and make the discloser more vulnerable. Because of the discloser's perceived risk and vulnerability, he or she expects a comparable amount of understanding, acceptance, and assurance that the information will be kept confidential. If the recipient of the self-disclosure reciprocates with his or her own disclosure and it is of a similar magnitude, this in itself is likely to be a sign of mutual trust. Both interactants may go through the same motions, but not engage in reciprocated disclosures of the same magnitude. If this inequitable reciprocation is known, the trust and comfort level for the person engaging in the more vulnerable disclosure is likely to be less. Like any message, there are many ways to present a self-disclosing message. There are stylistic choices that may make your disclosure seem more open. For instance, disclosure *of* perceptions and/or feelings would probably be considered much more open and personal than disclosures *about* perceptions and/or feelings. Co-occurring nonverbal behavior will surely affect the perceived "depth" of the disclosure as well. It should also be noted that messages of self-disclosure are part of an ongoing process of interaction. From this perspective, the nature of self-disclosive messages at any given time will be affected by co-occurring behavior of each interactant.

Even though self-disclosure can be very important in forming and maintaining an intimate relationship,[3] it may not always be the best communication strategy. To determine whether a communication strategy is "best," we need to have some measure of correspondence between responses sought and responses obtained.

Self-Disclosure as Catharsis

One motivation for engaging in self-disclosing communication is to achieve some kind of catharsis, or communicative release. We may have some need to free ourselves of information which is eating away at us, a desire to get something "off our chest." While disclosing our deepest secrets and releasing our inhibitions does seem to have positive effects on our health, the primary motivation for such revelations is personal, not communicative.[4] The best one might argue is that the gains in one's personal health accruing from such disclosure may ultimately make them a better relationship partner.

Self-Disclosure as "The Need to Be Open"

Another motivation for disclosing personal information about yourself centers around the belief that it is best to "tell it like it is," "lay it on the line," and "reveal ourselves as we really are." Hiding and concealing information, according to this expressive orientation, is a reflection of being "hung up," "phony," or "a manipulator." To hold things in is dirty; letting them out is cleansing. From this perspective, "letting it all hang out" will lead to greater psychological adjustment as well as to closer relationships with fellow human beings. Here it is assumed that we can't communicate clearly if we have a lot to hide, that in true intimacy we need not weigh and measure our words because our partner will separate the wheat and chaff with the hands of a skilled craftsperson, keeping the grain and blowing the chaff away. Proponents of this orientation toward disclosure feel that when we keep things from others it is not for their sake but more for our own sake—fear of retaliation, guilt, and so on.

Admittedly, we have all seen and probably experienced instances in business, government, education, or family life where people have deliberately withheld information. The reasons could be for personal gain, to avoid a potentially negative reaction, or to "keep others from getting hurt." Often others are hurt more if they discover the information from another source. Rosenfeld believes males avoid self-disclosure in order to control their relationships while females refrain from it in order to avoid personal hurt and problems with interpersonal relationships.[5] Obviously, too little disclosure can be harmful, but too much disclosure can also be problematic.

> We have no secrets
> We tell each other everything
> About the lovers in our past
> And why they didn't last
> We share a cast of characters from A to Z
> We know each other's fantasies
> And though we know each other better when we explore
> Sometimes I wish
> Often I wish
> I never knew
> Some of those secrets of yours[6]

Indiscriminate or overzealous disclosure can cause difficulties for both the receiver and the communicator. The person who feels compelled to engage in a great deal of intimate self-disclosure in almost any setting is no more adjusted than the person who hides almost everything from everyone regardless of setting. These indiscriminately high disclosers are not adapting their messages to their audience. For these persons, intimate self-disclosures are so common, they are nearly reduced to the level of cocktail party chatter. Such indiscriminate self-disclosure drains the force out of and cheapens people's feelings.

"Today, kids tell it like it is."

Indeed, some roles even demand less disclosure from their interaction partners—doctor-patient and priest-confessor. Further, some friendships and marriages have low disclosure patterns and still manifest a high degree of satisfaction with the relationship. All of us should have someone with whom we can share our most personal feelings or our general life satisfaction may be low, but in the case of disclosure patterns, more is not necessarily (and probably isn't) best.

Self-Disclosure as a Communication Strategy

An important task facing couples who seek to establish a close relationship is the negotiation of privacy boundaries.[7] These negotiations involve what can/should be shared and what is/should be off-limits. The process of sharing more and more of yourself with another person inevitably highlights the offsetting need for a refuge from unwanted intrusions. It sounds simple enough, but these boundaries are not always clear—even to the person seeking privacy. Consider, for example, a man and a woman who have been sexually intimate for nearly two years even though they do not live together. One day, while the woman is in the shower shaving her legs, her boyfriend suddenly pulls aside the shower curtain and starts watching her. He says, "I just like to see you naked." Visibly upset, the woman tells her boyfriend to leave her alone. Later she tells him she felt "violated."

One of the most intense reveal-hide quandaries for romantic couples concerns what one does after having had an extramarital affair. There are two important decisions associated with this issue—whether to tell and, if the answer is yes, how to do it. If the motivation for telling this secret is to work at improving the marriage, there is a much better chance of a productive outcome than if the motivation is to punish or hurt the other person or simply to relieve guilt feelings. Many couples survive the disclosure of an affair and use it to form a better relationship. This doesn't mean that there won't be anger, pain, and conflict. But these are not uncommon elements in the quest for intimacy even if there is no extramarital affair. Some people (and therapists) maintain a more secretive position—e.g., "what you don't know won't hurt you." With certain circumstances and certain types of negotiated relationship rules, this may be an appropriate behavior. In other instances, the perpetrator's behavior change may negatively affect his or her spouse. And even though one person may not be hurt by what isn't known, the other person does know and that can affect the relationship too. Most people who report their experiences with an affair say the pain is not in the knowledge that one's partner had sex with another person, but in the private life that developed, the deceptions associated with that life, and the exchange of symbols associated with their intimacy—thereby reducing the intimacy value of such symbols for their relationship.

The second question has to do with how one talks about an affair if it is revealed. The repair process may take a long time—perhaps even years. But the central theme for the person having the affair should be that his or her primary interest is in putting the affair and all that it represented away and taking steps to improve the current relationship. The partner will want to hear negative things about the affair and at the same time positive signs of commitment (Chapter 9) about their relationship. A partner may indicate he or she wants to hear all the details, but the extent to which details are provided should be cast in the framework of whether such details are necessary to dispense with the affair and get on with building the current relationship, i.e., what purpose will knowledge of such details serve? Sometimes people say they want to hear things they don't. On the other hand, the person who had the affair usually overemphasizes the need to keep certain aspects secret. It is not so much that the person who finds out about an affair really wants to know all the gory details. They may only be trying to get confirmation that this is really an effort to expunge any ugly secrets from the marriage—e.g., is the revealer sincere in his or her intentions?

Self-disclosure, like any communication pattern, loses its capacity for accomplishing a variety of communicative goals if it is used indiscriminately. The critical question we should be asking ourselves is not, "What can I do to be totally open?" but "What do I want to accomplish and how can I do it best?" The latter question assumes that there is more than one alternative for what we want to say, further, sometimes we don't want to be as direct or personal as a total openness perspective might suggest. To be effective communicators, we will want to consider the timing of our disclosure, the other person's capacity to respond, the kind of relationship we have with the target person, long-term versus short-term effects, the motives for the disclosure, how much detail is called for, whether the disclosure is relevant to the current situation and feelings. We must remember that we can't say everything there is to say about anything anyway. Thus, we will be faced with selecting the information to be conveyed and the way to say it, whether we try to "tell it like it is" or not.

Because we have to be selective about what we say and how we say it, accuracy and reality become elusive goals in presenting ourselves to others and in perceiving what others are like.

> Owing to the very peculiar nature of knowledge about persons, relationships necessarily turn on somewhat misguided and misleading premises about other parties. Social order rests partly upon error, lies, deception and secrets, as well as upon accurate knowledge.[8]

Self-Disclosure as Manipulation

The irony of those who accuse secretive people of being manipulative is that self-disclosure can also be used as a manipulative device. We can deliberately disclose certain information to hurt, shock, or embarrass another person; we can take advantage of the reciprocity norm in order to try to elicit certain personal information or services from others. This latter strategy commonly occurs in attempts at *instant intimacy.* One version involves an effort to quickly move a new romantic relationship to what seems to be the intensifying stage. This can be done by one or both participants displaying the illusion that they have some special "vibes" that allow them to advance more quickly than most people. It is further illustrated by the way the two communicate with each other—using terms of endearment like "you sweet thing" and exchanging intimate disclosures, usually about sex or other past and ongoing relationships. This communicative behavior can then be the rationale for why they feel the way they do—they find it easy to talk to each other. This behavior is usually initiated by one person with what seems to be a personal disclosure (and maybe most people would think of it in that category) but the discloser does not consider it private, and he or she is not subject to much risk. Like so many instances of disclosure in relationships, *perceived* disclosure and *perceived* reciprocity of disclosure are often more critical than what actually takes place. In the case of instant intimacy, the entire procedure is, of course, designed to get the other person to reciprocate with disclosures dealing with sexual and relationship matters.[9] Once both parties have begun to verbally communicate as if they were at the intensifying stage, the intimate physical behavior that is also characteristic of the intensifying stage is legitimized. This strategy of talking to a person you don't know very well as if you did, in order to obtain the behavior characteristic of a friend or intimate, is not limited to romantic relationships. For instance, one woman we know uses this manipulative technique of rapid pseudo-disclosure when first going to a new hairdresser. In this case, the client is trying to establish a conversational climate characteristic of friends, assuming that a friend would give a better haircut than an acquaintance or stranger.

Self-Disclosure and Relationship Development

Certainly, self-disclosure contributes to the growth of a relationship that develops naturally and nonmanipulatively. As was noted in earlier chapters, less intimate information will be exchanged in the experimenting stage. As people begin forays into the intensifying stage, we will see a flurry of more personal self-disclosures. These disclosures, then, will increase as the relationship moves into the integrating stage. Since most of the research on self-disclosure has been conducted on stranger-stranger dyads, much of our knowledge about self-disclosure at more intimate stages must remain speculative. Figure 8.1 shows how the breadth and depth of self-disclosure changes as relationships vary in intimacy.

As noted earlier, one of the characteristics of self-disclosure is that it is often reciprocated—my self-disclosure has a good chance of eliciting a self-disclosure from you. In fact, our expectations are so firmly set for this reciprocity in the initial stages of a developing relationship that we often perceive reciprocal disclosures when they aren't there. It seems reasonable to argue that if we don't feel a mutuality

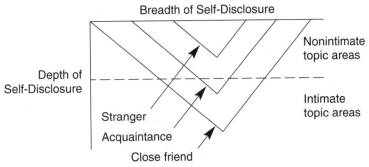

8.1 Breadth and Depth of Self-Disclosure for Three Types of Relationships[10]

of disclosure in the intensifying stage, we probably won't get to the integrating stage—unless, of course, some external force propels us there. As the relationship advances into intimacy, one disclosure may not be followed immediately by a reciprocal one, but if the mutual reciprocity doesn't balance out over a period of time, adaptations in disclosure patterns will be made.

As a relationship reaches for more intimacy, disclosures will probably be more frequent than in relationships that have established themselves and stabilized at an intimate stage. For instance, the feelings of intensifying intimacy may cause certain restraints to be released—frankness may often override tact; as intimacy is sustained, attempts to reinstate the constraints may be made in order to preserve the relationship and let it stabilize. Thus, as an intimate relationship grows from initiating to intimacy, disclosure frequency and depth will eventually reach a point of stabilization and probably taper off. Intimate relationships need to suppress some things or they may lose their intimacy. This does not mean, however, that the relationship has reached the circumscribing stage. It is an *act* of circumscribing, but this act does not typify or represent the common communication patterns of the intimate couple, nor does it signal a deterioration in the generally intimate character of the relationship.

Baxter and Wilmot found that there are "taboo" topics that may occur at virtually any relationship stage.[11] Some of these avoided topics include: extra-relationship activities, talking about rules and expected behavior, previous relationships, negative self-disclosures, and topics from the past that can be expected to cause problems. But the most frequently reported subject to avoid, according to the students interviewed, is the relationship itself. People in platonic relationships, relationships with romantic potential, and those in established romantic relationships all felt the relationship would suffer by being discussed. For people who want to maintain a relationship, this belief is quite natural. But it doesn't mean that the relationship is a topic that is ignored. It may be discussed in indirect ways or inferred from the nature of conversations on other topics. Baxter, herself, found quite a variety of techniques used by students to acquire information about their relationships.[12] Some of these methods included: (1) asking third parties; (2) trial intimacy moves—e.g., through self-disclosures, touch; (3) putting yourself down to see how the other will respond; (4) using hypothetical situations to see how the other will respond; (5) asking the partner to do something for you that shows sacrifice of time and energy; (6) separating for a while to see how the other responds; and (7) deliberately putting the partner in a situation where the nature of the relationship will be tested—e.g., encouraging partner to be with another person.

In long-established intimate relationships it is probably more difficult to identify what is personal and what is superficial, since the lines have been blurred (even to the participants) as the couple moves freely in and out of the two areas. Most of the research conducted on married couples shows more disclosure in couples who are more satisfied with their relationship.[13] However, it is significant that this disclosure doesn't seem to be just any kind of disclosure. The satisfied couples did not have as many *negative* disclosures of feelings." Often they resorted to more oblique ways of revealing negative perceptions—a husband who dislikes his wife interrupting him when he speaks may comment on the behavior of another couple observed at a party: "Wow, did you see how Caroline wouldn't let Larry get a word in edgewise?"

Trust and Self-Disclosure

Self-disclosure of intimate information is based on trust. According to Rempel et al., trust is the degree of confidence you feel when you think about the relationship.[14] Trust is composed of three primary perceptions: *predictability, dependability,* and *faith.* Predictability is the expectation that one's partner will act consistently in positive ways toward you; dependability means you can rely on your partner when it counts; and faith refers to the belief that your partner will continue to be responsive and caring in the future. High levels of trust are needed for intimate disclosures, but it is no guarantee of it. One of the reasons we see people disclosing highly personal information to strangers is that they realize there is minimal risk—the unknown and transient recipient usually cannot use the information against them. Ordinarily, disclosing highly personal information can make us vulnerable; it can give others power over us. This is why trust is so important. This is also why we try to get people to talk about themselves from the moment we meet them; we are trying to get to know where they stand, what they think and feel, so that we can have some control and find some predictability in the relationship. Recipients of self-disclosures should recognize the discloser's concerns—that the listener won't keep it confidential, that he or she won't reciprocate, that he or she won't understand or accept the disclosure. If we want a person to disclose more to us, we must make the person feel our appreciation for his or her trust in us and our acceptance and support for that person, not necessarily for the behavior or feeling which is the focus of the disclosure. This last issue is obviously easier said than done. It sometimes takes painstakingly long to get another person to understand that criticism of his or her behavior is not also a criticism of him or her as a person. It can be done, however.

Lying

At first glance, it may seem strange that we include lying as a behavior involved in maintaining a close relationship. After all, people report that they tell fewer lies to people with whom they have close relationships.[15] Nevertheless, decisions about truth-telling and lying are at the very heart of what constitutes a close relationship. For many, the familiar promise, "We won't lie to each other" is viewed as a covenant that will lead to and sustain greater intimacy. Without minimizing the importance of honesty in the maintenance of close relationships,[16] it is worth noting that each partner may have different referents for what "agreeing not to lie" means. For instance, does it mean I have to tell you things that I know would hurt you and you probably wouldn't find out anyway? Does it mean I have to tell you I hate your outfit (if that's the way I feel) when you ask for my opinion? If I tell you I went to bed with another person, is it lying not to tell you the details? If acts of omission, exaggeration, vagueness, evasiveness, and substitution are all a part of the act of lying, then everybody lies. If we can't avoid lying, then what is the kind of behavior we are trying to avoid with the "we won't lie to each other" promise?

For most couples, the real issue is whether a lie will have a damaging effect on the relationship and whether the motivation for lying was well-intended or not. Thus, when contemplating a lie, the following questions seem to be key: (1) Will this lie help both of us? If the lie is solely for the benefit of one partner, it is more likely to be viewed negatively and incur more relationship damage. Liar motivation is at issue here. The couple's short- and long-range mutual goals are the focus here. (2) Is the lie consistent with the rules of fairness in the relationship? That is, does one's partner operate by the same rules you do? Liar intentions are the concern now. If both partners agree that certain classes of lies are okay but others are not (e.g., lying about one's sexual prowess may be okay, but lying about having lunch with an ex-lover may not), then lies in the forbidden categories will incur more relationship damage. Sometimes, of course, a couple either assumes the other knows what categories are okay and what are not or they have not discussed the issue specifically. Thus, when an intentional lie in a category one partner believes is not acceptable occurs, the liar may argue that he or she was not aware of the rule and that it won't happen again. This is one way fairness rules about lying are negotiated. (3) Does your partner (the lied to) believe you have his or her best interests at heart—both generally and in this specific situation? If the answer is yes, the lie is likely to have less damage to the relationship. Even in situations where the liar clearly violates the couple's agreed-upon norms for lying (e.g., lying about an affair), the damage to the relationship will be offset if the offender can convince his or her partner that the lie was consistent with other instances that indicated a concern for the partner's welfare.

The best predictor of relationship termination as a result of a discovered lie is the perceived importance of the information lied about. This explains why those people who are more involved/committed to their relationship are going to have a greater emotional reaction to lies that impinge directly on the relationship.[17]

Over the last twenty years, there has been a tremendous quantity of research on lying and deception.[18] Only recently, though, has this research sought to identify the peculiar nature of lying in close relationships. There are at least three characteristics of close relationships that profoundly affect the nature of lying and distinguish it from lies to strangers or acquaintances.

The first characteristic has to do with the kind of *mutual influence* exerted by the partners to a close relationship. Even in lies to nonintimates, we may be more involved in the lie than we care to admit. It is easy to condemn lies that we feel we had no part in. But we can influence a person's decision to lie, and we can give tacit approval to it once it occurs. A familiar behavior of this type is the hostess who knows a guest is lying about "what a nice party this has been" but recognizes the intent is to avoid unpleasantness, so she cooperates in the deception. In other instances, a person may make it so clear that he or she is intolerant and inflexible regarding a certain behavior that this person's partner feels the necessity to lie when experiences with that behavior occur. Thus, we may be well advised to reflect on our own role in another's decision to lie before we determine how much punishment is deserved. Additionally, the role of the deceived in the deceiver's behavior is likely to affect the deceived person's motivation and accuracy in detecting the deception as well as the way the liar performs the lie. In close relationships, partners constantly negotiate interaction norms with the knowledge that each will play a role in the outcome. Lying is no different. When the outcome is an undesirable one, however, responsibility is frequently attributed to one's partner.

The second important characteristic of lies in close relationships concerns the increased possibility of *multiple exposure* to the lie. Lies to people we don't see that often do not require the same kind of development and/or repetition. This will surely affect the extent to which the liar will want to engage in a falsehood that requires long-term memory of details or whether it would be easier to engage in lies of omission.

The third characteristic of intimates is that they are quite *familiar* with one another's behavior. This raises the question of detection accuracy. Most of the research on detection of liars has been done with people who don't know each other very well. This research indicates that an untrained observer, looking at and listening to a stranger without the aid of any mechanical equipment, will be able to identify liars about half or slightly better than half the time. The percentage of accurate identification is, in reality, probably lower due to the fact that it is easier to deceive a person who has no reason to suspect that he or she is being lied to, and much of the research conducted asks subjects to "identify this person as a deceiver or nondeceiver"—an instruction which immediately forewarns subjects of possible deception.

Do you agree with the authors' views on lying?
Are there times in relationships when lying can be "good"?

The Lies That Bind*

The other day I lied to Amy. It wasn't a big lie, but it was big enough to assuage her doubts. Asked how I had spent the previous evening, I explained that work at the college had kept me late into the night. At another time, with perhaps a different person, another answer—a more truthful one—would have been offered. But not for Amy. Knowing that the evening was shared with a former girlfriend—albeit eating an innocent dinner at a very public restaurant—would have opened an old wound that has never fully healed. It all seems like a contradiction: our ties are forged by a strong symbiosis, and yet I realize I have continually lied to keep it so. The "truth," as I have discovered, often hurts and is less a prerequisite for a meaningful relationship than we may think.

This realization, a recent one, has come as quite a surprise for me. I once thought that love meant abandoning the lies of your life, those fences built to quarantine your real self from the everyday world. Falling in love meant the building of trust, honesty and openness, the coming together of two hearts, two minds. Love letters espoused such thoughts; marriage vows codified them. Certainly this was a delightful myth, sustained by advertisers, Dr. Ruth, pulp novels, Cosmopolitan magazine and B movies. Love, explained Erich Segal in his novel "Love Story," meant never having to say you're sorry. The translation was clear: love meant complete acceptance of wrongdoings, disappointments, hurts, character flaws and selfishness. And, for the most part, we have bought the script.

But the romantic language of love never included the vocabulary of the lie. Unspoken was the thought that love could also be tied to concealing the painful truths that trample sensitivities and whittle away at self-esteem.

In our attempt to idealize the notion of romance, we have lost a sense of our own vulnerability. And vulnerable we are, coping with a rapidly changing and confusing culture. In trying to understand our roles as men and women, a connection lost in the sweep of societal gender chaos, we are in danger of being overloaded. A lie can help keep the circuits intact.

Of course, lovers lie all the time, although they may fervently deny it. A close friend insists that honesty is paramount in his relationship with his wife—well, except for those small "white lies." Indeed, his are small lies about matters having to do with personal habits and predilections. The lies protect the vulnerable shell of his relationship and forestall confrontations. The lie has given him a retreat for doubts and indecisions.

Another friend wags a finger at me, complaining that I should have told Amy about my date with the former girlfriend. Even if it was hard to swallow, she said, Amy was entitled to a knowledge of "the real world."

Would my friend consider telling her husband about an old affair that had gone sour?

"Of course not," she replied. "It would destroy him and our marriage."

And that, of course, is the point. Some truths chip away at relationships, others chop them down whole. It is a matter of drawing lines, and we all draw different ones when it comes to the truth.

Most lies that I spin are inconsequential, simply intent on maintaining the day-to-day stability of my relationship. I have applauded Amy for her cooking, her new dress, her latest diet. Neither the cooking (overdone chicken with a peculiar white sauce), her dress (an obtuse floral pattern) or her weight loss (which effectively cut the appealing lines of her body) elicited much excitement. Or the truth. In each case, a lie served as a salve, not a sword.

There are also bigger lies about more important things. Amy has asked me on more than one occasion, "Do you love me?" If ranked, this inquiry would probably top the universal list. If I were always truthful, and sometimes I am not, I would confide to Amy the fluctuating tide of my emotions, a response that might stab into the heart of our relationship. But at those times I search for a more positive answer. And why not? When we talk about love, what do we say and what does it mean? Language is often too neutered to express complex feelings.

And yet, once such hard "truths" are out in the air, it's impossible to push them aside. Misspent words continue to haunt long after that particular emotion has changed into something else. So when Amy asks whether I love her, I always do, even if, at times, I don't. The lie is a support system that is part of the ritual of intimacy. It may not be truthful, but it is confirming. It is a paradox, indeed, that in writing this article, I have revealed my lies.

I should note that Amy herself is not a great believer of the lie. Amy is especially quick to point out when I try to lie to myself. She fails to understand that at times self-deception also plays a vital role in a healthy relationship.

I usually dabbled in self-deception each time the subject of marriage was broached. Ever since we met six years ago, Amy had wanted to marry; I opted for the status quo. As a single person, I had long valued the independence and freedom that a marriage might limit. But Amy astutely noted that if bachelorhood were a guiding principle, why then had I chosen a rather conventional monogamous relationship with her during these years? She was right, of course, and the contradiction between my words and life style was evident. But this longstanding lie gave me time to wear the skin of our relationship to see how it fit and felt. Had I been forced to confront my "true" feelings before, our relationship might not have survived, much less flourished. Finally I did reach a decision. Just recently, Amy and I were married, and our lives have never been more secure.

As intimacy deepens, the need for lying deepens also. The more that's exposed, the more there's a need to guard those unflattering secrets. A reflexive action to confide in people outside a relationship—a friend or professional counselor—comes from our emotional wellsprings, our need to protect and not harm the people we love. So we exchange confidences with friends that we could not share with a lover. We find the need to estrange ourselves from an intimate relationship in order to discover the problems that may exist within it. The reason is apparent; often a partner is least capable to help, caught herself (or himself) in the entanglements of intimacy and unable to provide perspective or detachment. In my case, I talk to my

(continued)

Continued

brother. I tell him of my fears, insecurities and doubts; the problems with commit-ment, monogamy and sex; the confusion that stems from loving too little or too much.

Within the confines of intimacy, however, such truths can hurt, and often needlessly. The problem of being truthful often centers on what in fact is truth. I have found that it is an entity in constant flux. Yesterday's truth may be less than truthful tomorrow. So perhaps a lie gives us the chance to be introspective about love in a way that truth can't. Perhaps, in a real way, it is a truer reflection of love. The lie allows us to question silently, letting us withhold judgment, at least for the time being. It may not necessarily make intimacy more valuable or answer deep-seeded problems. But perhaps it does.

*Paul Thaler, *New York Times Magazine.*

Lie Detection

Although research on detecting lying among friends and intimates is rare, Comadena found intimates generally more accurate than acquaintances. Friends, however, may exhibit more accuracy than spouses.[19] Spouses are committed to a relationship that may last a long time and involves daily contact. As a result, they may be more likely than good friends to develop a desensitization to behavior as-sociated with lying. Although people in close relationships may be able to detect lies their partner tells, there also may be a strong desire not to be an accurate de-tector, as this wife attests:

Little by little things were happening that didn't make sense, but I can remem-ber making excuses for them myself . . . I didn't want to believe there was any-thing to find out . . . so I was being deceived from two angles . . . I was deceiving myself . . . I didn't sit there when it was happening saying, "I am just fooling myself." You know, I, I, as I said, I made up a lot of excuses, and really believed them . . . I didn't confide in anyone, too, because I was afraid of what they would tell me. I wanted to believe everything was going to be fine and I wasn't being deceived. If I told someone else they might tell me I was being de-ceived and I didn't want to hear that. . . . But as much as I wanted to be a de-tective and find him out, I didn't want to either. Because the truth, I was afraid more of the truth than living in the lie kind of.[20]

If intimates do want to detect the lies of their partners, they have several ad-vantages. For example, in more intimate relationships the partners have a mental record or backlog for verbal checking and verification; further, they have a history of having observed the other in many different emotional situations. Hence, inti-

Reprinted with special permission of North America Syndicate.

mates should have a better idea of what behavior exceeds the boundaries of normality for their partner. Changes in behavior or activity patterns often trigger partner alertness if not suspicion. In addition, intimates have considerably more motivation to look closely for clues than acquaintances or mere observers. Although greater intimacy may give one an advantage in being able to perceive a partner's lies, greater intimacy may also make partners less attentive to the possibilities of lies.[21] Thus, unless intimates have a reason for expecting a lie, they may be less apt to notice it. The first lies to intimate partners are likely to be the easiest to get away with. After all, the relationship was built on trust, so there is no reason to be suspicious. Even if lie goes undetected, it may still have a significant impact on the relationship.[22] For example, a person who has engaged in an important deception in a close relationship may get mad at him or herself and take out their anger on their partner. Perceptions of their partner as being easily duped or as no more honest themselves may begin to take hold and alter feelings and discourse.

Although lie detection is no doubt an important skill on some occasions, there is always the danger of engaging in such acts too often. Those who go on a search-and-destroy mission for their partner's lies may find they have created more harm than good for the relationship. Suspicion can create suspicion to the point where neither person trusts the other and the lie detector has created the very thing he or she set out to destroy. In addition, it is likely that such a campaign against lies may only drive the worst offenders underground so they can refine their strategies. Besides, relationships often rely on certain kinds of deceptions for sustenance. To wipe out any ability to deceive another may wipe out some important structural foundations for the relationship. This doesn't mean we shouldn't probe, question, and investigate situations in which a lie seems to harm the relationship; it simply means we should try to preserve the assumption of truthfulness rather than replace it with an assumption of deceit. If you're like us, there are some things you'd rather not know the "truth" about.

> *Socrates: What Plato is about to say is false.*
> *Plato: Socrates has just spoken truly.*

Are there any behaviors that are always associated with lying behavior and nothing else? No. There are behaviors that liars in nonintimate relationships regularly exhibit, such as speech errors, higher pitch, more hesitations, fidgeting, etc., but intimates may attend to more idiosyncratic cues. The first author's wife, for example, listens for a barely audible gulp after a statement that is already suspected of being an untruth—e.g., "I dropped by the office to do some work," whereas "I stopped by the jeweler to check on your ring" would be the true statement. It is usually wise to look for clusters of behavior rather than a single cue. To say "I knew he was lying because he didn't look at me" is just as risky as saying "I knew he didn't have a large vocabulary because he used the word *liar* instead of *deceiver*." In order to increase the probability that we are accurate in detecting deception, we should look for clusters of cues—does his or her lack of eye contact fit with other things you've observed such as nervous movement and speech errors?

Some data are known on what seems to be stereotyped categories for lying behavior. Liars, for instance, will sometimes be observed exhibiting a cluster of *anxiety responses* due to guilt or psychological distress. These may include such behaviors as blushing, shaking, gulping, perspiring, voice tremors, speech errors, using fewer different words, and sending shorter messages. Sometimes observers key their observations on what they consider to be *excessive responses*. As noted earlier, excessive responses go beyond the boundaries of normal behavior for the individual being observed. It may be that the person is too inactive or too active; it might be that he or she talks excessively or engages in pronounced pauses and silences; it might be that he or she makes excessive eye contact (staring) or no eye contact at all; or it may be that he or she answers seemingly nonthreatening questions with extremely defensive remarks—"You're a little late this evening, dear. Where have you been?" "CAN'T I HAVE ONE PEACEFUL MOMENT BEFORE I GET THE THIRD DEGREE! IF YOU WANT TO KNOW MY WHEREABOUTS EVERY MOMENT OF THE DAY, HIRE A PRIVATE DETECTIVE!" Another category people sometimes observe in liars is *incongruous responses*. Liars sometimes have a hard time keeping their stories straight. Verbally, a person may contradict some known fact the receiver is aware of, or contradict his or her own earlier statement. Nonverbally, we might see some of the same inconsistency discussed earlier in this chapter—saying "I've always liked you" but exhibiting a host of nonverbal cues that attest otherwise. Finally, sometimes observers detect what might be called *indirect responses*. Verbal indirectness will take on the characteristics of some of the evasive tactics mentioned in Chapter 11—answering a question with a question, changing the subject. A person could also show verbal indirectness through vagueness—fewer verifiable factual assertions, fewer references to a verifiable past, fewer self-oriented statements for which a person could be held responsible, and more broad, sweeping generalizations. Nonverbally, indirectness may be seen, among other things, by not maintaining a direct body orientation when talking to another person or simply by increasing the distance between oneself and the listener. It should be clear from the preceding that many of the behaviors typically associated with liars are also manifested by people telling the truth. Thus, it is advisable to gather as much information about the situation as possible before charging the other with lying.

Constructive Conflict

In Chapter 1, we proposed that communication at increased stages of intimacy would be characterized by more overt, evaluative judgments of the other person. Further, intimate relationships are characterized by increased breadth and depth. The paradox, then, is that the possibilities for conflict may actually increase as the relationship grows more intimate.[23] Obviously, the frequency and intensity of conflict will vary from couple to couple. Marital couples described as "traditionals" have fairly clear rules and roles and seem to have less overt conflict.[24] Assuming a relationship remains intimate, the frequency of conflict in most relationships will probably level off as the participants deal with numerous issues or the same issues numerous times.

Conflict is neither good nor bad. The way people choose to engage each other in conflict, however, can be judged as positive or negative depending on how it affects the participants and the relationship. There is also some indication that the nature of premarital conflict will be a good predictor of marital happiness after the first two and one-half years of married life.[25]

During the early years of marriage the perceived negativity associated with conflict is strongly related to the likelihood of relationship dissolution—more so than the sheer number of fights. But an interesting reversal seems to occur after about eight years of marriage. At this point, the frequency of conflict becomes the best predictor of divorce. A high frequency of fighting between couples who have had eight years to negotiate a variety of issues associated with their relationship is a sign they may not have been very successful negotiators.[26]

For many couples, their "first big fight" can be a watershed event for the relationship. In a study which contrasted couples who broke up after their first big fight with those who stayed together, the first big fight provided a closer reading of the relationship:

> For survivors, the FBF [first big fight] typically renders explicit for the first time mutual feelings of commitment. Couples openly discuss previously unspoken concerns and gain a greater understanding of "where we stand" as a result. In contrast, those who broke up because of their FBF reported the onset of confusion about their relationship, the revelation of previously unknown aspects of their partner's personality, and the transformation of nonproblematic interaction into conversation that becomes at best, tense and sporadic. . . . The big difference between non-survivors and survivors was the way they perceived and handled conflict in their relationships. The survivors generally believed that a successful relationship required a joint effort in problem-solving, some sacrifice from both parties, and the ability and/or willingness to adjust one's own ways of doing things in order to mesh with the partner's way of doing things.[27]

The interpersonal costs of conflict can be high, but sometimes these apparent costs can be turned into profit. Profitable constructive conflict may: (1) provide a greater understanding of the other, oneself, and the relationship; (2) clarify similarities and dissimilarities; (3) assist people to learn methods for coping with future conflict; and (4) reveal areas where communicative effort and adaptation need to be strengthened. When conflict, or any force, threatens the continuance of a relationship, the participants learn a great deal about how solid the ties binding them are.

Although our major focus is on conflict between the parties to a relationship, conflict with an outside source can often serve to strengthen the relationship bond by necessitating the exchange of more rewards to protect against the outside threat. Consider the following: "Look what they did to us"; "Nobody treats my friend that way"; "I'm sorry you have to do this report, but the dodos upstairs sent down this edict. . . ."

Before the Fight

Before we get carried away with what may seem to be a "how to" manual for effective confrontation, let's face the fact that when our emotions are piqued, the probability that we will consciously try to plan our strategy for the ensuing conflict is severely lessened. For this reason, we could argue that those who are most effective in interpersonal conflict are those who foresee conflict and analytically weigh the nature of their partner and the nature of the conflict *prior to its appearance*. For instance, effective disputants surely consider the other's ability or inclination to deal with the problem (initiate, postpone, or delay indefinitely); the long- and short-range goals which they want to accomplish with the confrontation (catharsis or behavior change); the surrounding environment's contribution to the intensity of the confrontation (public locale or private); the mode of communication (written or oral).

Once we decide to enter the conflict situation, the *attitudes* we approach it with may be more important in determining the outcome or outcomes than any behavioral prescriptions. It seems that the most productive conflict will arise when both participants enter the encounter with the following orientations: (1) They recognize that not all conflicts can be resolved, that most will require more than a single encounter for a resolution satisfactory to both parties, and that they have the potential to solve this problem as a team. (2) They accept the fact that conflict is a natural part of all human relationships—that differences of opinion can, indeed, be helpful. (3) They have a desire to solve the problem arising out of a vested interest in the outcome (preserving the relationship) rather than just wanting to become a "winner." If one participant becomes the sole winner, the other becomes a loser, and when one party loses, the relationship loses. We knew a person, for instance, who had such a large vocabulary, breadth and depth of knowledge, and skill at formal debating techniques that he would always come away from a verbal duel seemingly unscathed—"victorious." However, nobody liked him. Who won? Conflict resides in the relationship, not in either individual. (4) They have an active concern for the feelings of the other person. (5) They maintain a flexibility that will allow them to see many possible outcomes other than personal victory—acquiescence, postponement, compromise.

Relationship partners who stay together long enough to expect periodic fights also tend to develop a sort of "code of conduct" for these fights. In one sense these rules are formulated to reduce potentially harmful fight behavior, but ironically, the rules themselves often become the source of disagreement which causes the participants to end up arguing about how they are arguing. Common examples of such rules include: "We will not fight in front of the kids (or friends)"; "We will not 'hit below the belt' "; "We will not leave the scene in the middle of an argument"; "We will not interrupt each other"; etc.

During the Fight

Now we arrive at the point where people are communicating during the conflict itself. What kind of strategies for conflict resolution are employed? Which of these strategies are best suited for constructive rather than destructive outcomes? To answer these questions, we are going to identify specific types of talk which typically characterize productive and unproductive fights. Before we do that, however, it is important to remember that in the absence of strategic thinking about conflict interaction, it is easy for us to be overtaken by excessive behavior associated with instinctive reactions to conflict. When we feel threatened, our "fight or flight" response is a natural first response. Unfortunately, many couples find themselves stuck in a distressingly extreme fight and/or flight pattern.[28] No doubt you will see the following patterns as too inaccurate and extreme to identify with. *Withdrawal* is a conflict pattern which arises when both parties want to flee the conflict. Both want relational peace and harmony so much that they almost never express negative feelings to each other. They see virtually all problems as "small" and are quick to find ways to keep from facing them. In such relationships, we would expect to find a relatively low level of intimacy coupled with an unspoken reservoir of tensions. It is not uncommon for those couples who withdraw from conflict to see themselves as martyrs who suffer in silence because they are "right" and their partner is "wrong." *Escalation* is the conflict pattern which develops when both parties want to fight rather than flee. In contrast to those who want to avoid conflict, these people want to pursue it. They have an urgency to express their anger and deal with problems immediately. When both parties respond to problems by exhibiting a desire to "get into the ring and settle it," we can expect the conflict to escalate. We can also expect both will be good at saying what's on their mind, but not so good at listening to their partner. It is not unusual that the fight-fight pattern produces repeated arguments about the same issues and leaves a residue of increased anger. Tragically, in some cases, couples sense the futility of their fight-fight pattern for solving problems and seek to remedy the situation by going to the other extreme and becoming withdrawers. The pattern in which one person pursues the fight while the other withdraws is no more productive than is the pattern where both persons manifest the same style of behavior. The pursuit-withdraw or withdraw-pursuit pattern feeds on itself, because in each case the responses are so predictable. The withdrawer can't understand why the pursuer is so upset by "little" things, and the pursuer can't understand why the withdrawer refuses to deal with problems.

Keep in mind that acts of withdrawal and pursuit are not, in and of themselves, "bad" for constructive conflict. The only thing wrong with any of the preceding patterns is that they represent adherence to predictable extremes of behavior and, as such, will not help couples effectively deal with disagreements. People who engage each other in productive conflict will manifest withdrawal as well as a desire to fervently pursue a problematic issue. With constructive problem-solvers, though, these behaviors are used strategically and as situationally adapted behavior—not as instinctively repeated and predictable behavior.

Exchanges during conflict between couples who are dissatisfied with their relationship are far more predictable than those of satisfied couples—e.g., criticism inevitably gets criticism in response; telling the other person what they are thinking inevitably gets disagreement in response; etc. Satisfied couples are more likely to provide novel responses. Gottman's work comparing the responses of satisfied and dissatisfied couples engaged in conflict provides us with concrete illustrations.[29] The dissatisfied couples tended to engage in more *cross-complaining*—i.e., one person's complaint would be countered with the partner's complaint:

H: I'm getting tired of eating hamburger every night.

W: Well, I'm getting tired of cooking every night . . . every morning and every afternoon!

Satisfied couples were more likely to acknowledge the validity of one another's complaint. Dissatisfied marital couples were also more likely to get bogged down in *arguments about how they were arguing*—for example:

H: You don't have to get so emotional about it.

W: I have to do something to make you pay attention when I'm talking. Otherwise, it's like talking to a brick wall.

H: I do pay attention, but I'm not going to pay attention when you get hysterical.

W: The only time you ever act like you're paying attention is when you are telling me not to do something.

Satisfied couples were able to break out of such sequences earlier (e.g., You're right, I was getting carried away) and get back to the original issue of disagreement. Dissatisfied couples generally communicated with more *negative affect*. The hostile vocal tone and facial expression accompanying a comment like, "You seem to be pretty calm considering what has happened," is likely to be taken as a criticism and responded to in a defensive manner. The same statement, without the accompanying negativity, is more likely to be perceived as a neutral or even concerned observation. Finally, dissatisfied couples tended to treat proposed solutions as they did the initial complaints—by *countering the partner's proposal with another proposal which was incompatible with it.* Satisfied couples were more likely to compromise, "give in," and look for mutually satisfying solutions.

> *Never ask a woman why's she's mad at you, as she*
> *will only get madder at your not knowing.*
>
> Anonymous

In addition to differences between satisfied and dissatisfied marital couples, there also seem to be differences in the conflict behavior of husbands and wives.

Unproductive conflict behavior is not the province of either the husband or wife. Husbands, as a group, reportedly have less ability to read nonverbal signals; less ability to deal with the communication of feelings; and less ability to remain involved in the conflict than their wives. Wives, on the other hand, show less skill as a group at knowing when to keep a problem off the interaction table and less ability in achieving emotional detachment during conflict.

One set of tactics for constructive conflict resolution hinges on identifying and specifically stating the source of the conflict rather than presenting it generally. Assuming that conflict is situation-bound and temporary, rather than personality-bound and lasting, improves greatly the chances for resolving the conflict. For instance, an individual's approach to a situation-bound problem will be influenced by the fact that the change desired is well within reach, not deeply hidden in the habits of the other. Sometimes, however, the real grievance is hidden because the trigger for the conflict is only a distant and minute manifestation of a deeper issue. An example of a hidden grievance was the dialogue about TV watching outlined in Chapter 1. When people fight about one person spending too much money, the "real" issue may be rooted in that person's need to buy love, to build self-esteem, to show who is in control, an expression of a value system that focuses on the here-and-now rather than the future—or a host of other feelings and attitudes. Novelist Diane Johnson gives perhaps the most detailed and vivid description of how much often lies beneath the surface in conflict situations[30]:

> The fights were all conducted in the same phrases but each phrase was just a formula, stood for pages and pages, a very long list, of hate and pain. I didn't understand this at the time, I admit. I didn't understand for example that every time Gavin said, "And then you bought that fucking chair," which he did say obsessively in the course of every fight, he really meant, "You defied me and went and did what you wanted just as you always do, causing me to feel unimportant and wretched and unattended, unlike my mother, who does what I want, which makes me feel manly, and, because it is an ugly chair which I hate, you are also assailing my comfort and my position in the household, making me feel unwanted and uncomfortable here: and by buying that hideous old secondhand chair when I had said not to, you were reproaching me financially, you were complaining that we couldn't afford a new one, another way of saying, as you constantly seem to, that now that we have all these loathsome brats I ought to disregard my personal development and think about earning money for them, something a man is not obliged to do, as I infer from my own family, where my father's career was sacrosanct and my mother's whole concern was my father, and instead you stick me with all these brats whom you don't even take care of properly, witness their dirty faces and wet pants, and have the nerve to complain to me about needing help and freedom when I did not ask you to bring these brats into the world and when I did, good naturedly, help you bring the chair home and help you upholster it, that's when I stuck the upholstery needle in my

eye you were not sorry although I could have been blinded which is another way of saying castration which is really your game isn't it, isn't it?

There were a number of other formulas: why don't you ever play with the children (me to G.); why don't you ever clean up around here (G. to me); you are rude to our friends (me to G.); you neglect our children and home (G. to me). We would trot these and others out at each quarrel like dominoes and line them up on the board. I was really dumb, I never did understand the game; I would dump over the board, screeching, "Why are you always bringing up that chair? Can't you forget it? Why do you want to ruin our family about some old chair, what a crazy obsession, sometimes I think you are crazy," and that's when he hit me. . . .

We are going to have peace even if we have to fight for it.

Dwight D. Eisenhower

Conflicts also arise when a person is feeling frustrated, irritable, or depressed because of some event totally unrelated to the person with whom he or she eventually argues. This emotional state simply spills over onto the person at hand and topics of friction are manufactured, even though these topics would be relatively unimportant on another occasion. Conflict may arise out of almost any topic area, but the three most common in marital disputes are *financial matters, communication,* and *sex.* Other frequent sources of dispute include: child raising; personal habits—sleeping and waking patterns, neatness, what and when to eat; responsibilities at home; how to spend leisure time; in-laws and friends; religion; alcohol and drugs; and jealousy. Any of these topics may be a source of superficial or serious disagreement, depending upon whether it is linked to basic values of the participants. Couples often fight about seemingly "little things" (see song insert on p. 278), but when such fights persist it is a sign that these "little things" are linked to important values. These sources of conflict are usually the result of behavior in the immediate present, but the past may enter in—"Remember when you did. . . . Well, I never forgave you for that and. . . ." Stockpiling sources of conflict from the past provides an almost limitless warehouse of problems which could be introduced; when this happens, the stockpiler's partner will worry more about defensive maneuvers than the problems themselves. Besides identifying the specific cause of the conflict, participants to a constructive outcome generally present the issues or problems one at a time. Admittedly, many issues may be intertwined, but if either participant in the argument feels an information overload, the problem becomes much more difficult to understand and resolve. An example of a subtle escalation to information overload is when one participant's complaint is met with a counter-complaint or a counter-demand over and over until the original complaint is forgotten.

It's the Little Things*

It's the way you stroke my hair
When I lie sleepin'
It's the way you tell me things
That I don't know
It's the way that you remember
I came home late for dinner
Eleven months and fourteen days ago
It's the little things
The itty bitty things
Like the way that you remind me
That I been growin' soft
It's the little things
The itty bitty things
It's the little things
That piss me off
It's the note you leave
On the breakfast table
With a list of things
To help me plan my day
It's the way you say we could have
If you'd done the things you should have
It's the little things darlin'
That make me feel this way
It's the little things
The little bitty things
Like the way that you remind me
That I been growin' soft
It's the little things
The itty bitty things
It's the little things
That piss me off

*Written by Robert Earl Keen © 1989 Keen Edge Music (BMI)/Administered by Bug. All rights reserved. Used by permission.

Another set of tactics associated with constructive conflict deals primarily with methods of information exchange and methods of encoding messages. Using this set of tactics, the participants will generally provide each other with enough feedback so that each one's viewpoint is understood by the other person. Obviously, disagreement may still exist when people understand each other, but many conflicts are grounded in misunderstanding. Sometimes when the emotional level of the argument is high, the participants will agree to guidelines for structuring the interaction; these are much like the formal rules used in bargaining. Although this is not a common practice in interpersonal encounters, where the rules are generally more implicit, sometimes the interactants must stop themselves from stepping on each other's words. In heated conflict situations any word has the potential to be explosive. The word *precious* does not seem particularly "loaded" out of context, but said in a sarcastic tone in the context of a controversial issue, it can be highly provocative—e.g., "Well, I hope you and your *precious* magazine are happy with each other!" In order to redirect or depress unproductive emotional intensity, some have suggested the use of a ground rule. Using this ground rule, you have to repeat what the other person said (to his or her satisfaction) before stating your own opinion. This drains a good deal of the emotion out of a heated debate and contributes to an understanding of the other's ideas. Generally, responses in constructive conflict are characterized by a spirit of inquiry rather than certainty—knowing what your partner thinks and feels, not knowing what your partner *should* think and feel. Chronic complaining and sarcasm are generally absent because the goal is solving a problem, not gaining superiority over the other person. Although there is less derogatory labeling of the other person ("slut," "chicken," "numbnut"), we find more statement labeling in constructive conflict. *Statement labeling* is simply the identification of a statement as a fact, feeling, or inference. Notice the differences in this example:

Inference Not Labeled	**Inference Labeled**
CLYDE: I saw your car parked in front of his house.	CLYDE: I saw a car that looked an awful lot like yours parked in front of his house and I just assumed it was yours.
EMMA: Oh you did, did you? Ol' Eagle-eye, huh? I suppose you got in the car to check the registration in the glove compartment? Or perhaps you checked the serial number?	EMMA: Well, you assumed wrong. It wasn't mine.

More pausing and reflection, rather than a constant rapid-fire exchange of opinions, are usually a part of constructive conflict. These time-outs serve both the speaker and the listener. The person who pauses may communicate that he or she is indeed giving serious thought to the ideas presented by the other. The pausing time can be useful for getting a grip on one's feelings or for deciding how to phrase an idea. It can also be useful for just cooling off or for considering the many ramifications of the other's messages. It can be valuable time to reflect on the pattern of resolution that previous arguments with this person have taken and how this conflict is likely to come out.

As a result of studying couples in conflict for the last fifteen years, Notarius and Markman have concluded that certain types of talk make constructive conflict more likely and certain types of talk make it less likely. For constructive conflict,[31] they suggest decreasing: (1) Negative problem talk—that is, the problem is presented in such a way that the speaker's position on the problem overshadows the problem itself. This can be done by a nasty tone of voice, sarcasm, pessimism, yelling, and so on. (2) Negative solution talk—i.e., presenting unreasonable, unrealistic, impractical solutions. Usually, it will be clear from the proposed solution that one's partner is somehow responsible for any perceived inadequacies in the proposed plans. (3) Mindreading—i.e., the assumption of complete knowledge of the other person's thoughts and motives. (4) Critical talk—i.e., evaluating oneself or one's partner by focusing on the flaws. Critical talk can be especially harmful because, as Notarius and Markman say: "One zinger will erase twenty acts of kindness." At the same time we are trying to decrease the frequency of the preceding, Notarius and Markman suggest we try to increase: (1) Listening talk—i.e., talk which shows you have at least heard and perhaps understood your partner's message. Making your partner feel understood does not mean you must agree with them. It may mean only that you communicate your involvement through nods, eye gaze, posture, and a verbalization which acknowledges what your partner has said (without a tone of voice or other comments which evaluate the worth of the message). (2) Positive problem talk—i.e., attempts to provide information about the problem in a focused, specific, and relatively neutral manner.

When trying to solve a problem, it is important to determine whether a problem is one that demands action or as one that demands listening, comforting, and stroking. There are some people who, upon hearing the basic outline of a problem, start trying to devise action plans for the two parties involved. No matter how many solutions people have in their bags of tricks, or how pragmatic those solutions, it is still a restricted communicative response pattern if action is the only type of response. Sometimes people just need to lay out a problem to another person who cares about them—the child who complains that another child has been mean to him or her may only want to be held and soothed. Compromise is the hallmark of constructive conflict and, more often than not, the ability to compromise arises out of the ability to understand that our partner's view of reality is just as real and just and as "right" as ours.

After the Fight

Participants to constructive conflict are aware that issues are in process—that the end of any given argument or confrontation does not neatly wrap up the issue forever. Following an argument on a certain issue are several common behaviors: (1) The confrontation is periodically reviewed after both participants have cooled off and gained distance—"Boy, you really had me worried the other night when you were yelling and your hand started curling around the butcher knife." (2) The participants apprise each other of progress reports on the agreed solutions—"Wait a minute, I thought we agreed to tell each other when we'd be late getting home?" (3) Reassurance rituals follow the argument—a bouquet of flowers with a card that reads "together again" or the familiar kiss (or shake) and make up. These reassurance rituals may also take the form of supportive statements for new behavior that reflects congruence with the agreed-on solution. They are an effort to reestablish the unity of the pair since the confrontation had numerous overtones of differentiating. The absence of such rituals may, of course, be the source of another conflict—"If you really cared about me, you would have. . . ." (4) Forecasts and tests are presented to one another that offer hypothetical situations to provide information on areas of potential conflict in a generally detached rather than involved climate—"What would you do if you were away from me and an attractive man wanted to sleep with you?" If a firm stand is taken in these hypothetical discussions, it may serve to strengthen the commitment of both parties to the behavior or attitude in question. It also follows, however, that if future behavior does not seem to be congruent with the earlier stated position, one party may be doubly angry.

One of the most important lessons to be learned about conflict resolution is the ability to let the other people *save face.*[32] People often say things they don't mean but this propensity is particularly evident during conflicts. If one participant holds the other to everything he or she says and obliges that person to defend it, he or she will. The defense may be judged logically feeble, but it won't lack for emotional vigor—a pattern not representative of constructive conflict. Even if it seems clear to one person that the other is totally wrong, it is very helpful in future dialogues if the fault is shared—"I guess I wasn't making myself very clear, and. . . ." Kicking a person when he or she is down is the antithesis of efforts at face-saving. A person interested in a constructive conclusion to an argument wouldn't conclude by periodically reviewing how right he or she was—"See! I told you. . . ."

The act of face saving often attempts to negate or minimize the importance, relevance, or even existence of the other person's potentially embarrassing or destructive behavior. *Forgiveness,* on the other hand, requires the acknowledgement of a behavior perceived by at least one person to be damaging to him or herself or to the relationship. By forgiving such behavior, the forgiver is not saying the behavior was acceptable. Instead, forgiveness is intended to communicate the desire to avoid retaliation, put the hurtful act away, and move on to more constructive acts for the relationship. Most of us want others to forgive us our mistakes, but many people find it difficult to forgive others. Forgiveness incorporates sympathy, compassion, and tenderness and this is not easy when another's behavior has hurt them. Saying you forgive someone and then acting in ways which show you have not is all too common and can make matters even worse. When the person supposed to be receiving forgiveness realizes he or she is still being punished for the transgression, they may think they have nothing to lose by committing another destructive act—usually initiated by an argument about whether they have truly been forgiven or not. Research shows that the people who are best able to forgive are those who are best able to empathize with the emotional and behavioral perspective of the transgressor.[33]

To avoid giving the wrong impression caused by our emphasis on conflict, we reiterate several important points: First, conflict is inevitably a part of intimate relationships. No matter how intimate our relationship is, it will have both constructive and destructive conflict. Since intimates are more committed to the relationship, they will try to minimize the destructive conflict, so we would predict less destructive conflict among intimates. Second, the behaviors that we detailed as representative of constructive conflict are simultaneously extraordinarily important, useful, and extremely hard to put into practice. Such behaviors are especially difficult to incorporate into your own style of conflict management, once conflict has begun. And since few of us have the motivation to practice conflict strategies in the absence of conflict, the best advice may be to practice observing, analyzing, and reflecting on the conflicts of others in an effort to gain a greater understanding of and control over your own behavior.[34]

SUMMARY

This chapter addressed three areas of communication that are crucial in the maintenance of relationships. In the area of self-disclosure, the primary question for relationship partners is what to reveal and what to keep secret. Relationships maintain themselves with the proper dosage of both. Disclosing personal information about oneself is typical of partners who desire increased intimacy. These acts of revelation about self are frequently reciprocated when each person wants to increase intimacy. And, although disclosures may be fewer in number as a relationship ages, self-disclosures still can be a potent force in gaining intimacy and trust. Each couple develops their own norms for the content, timing, style, and impact of self-revelations. Since disclosures from or about oneself can also be manipulative or hurtful, we proposed a model for assessing the nature of a disclosure for each partner. This model depicts self-disclosures varying on the following dimensions: how many people know the information and how many can be told; how personal or "owned" the information is; how specific it is; how much risk/vulnerability there is for the discloser; how much understanding/acceptance is expected from the target; and whether reciprocity is expected.

In the area of lying, the primary questions for relationship partners involve the establishment of rules concerning lies and identifying what behavior would constitute a violation of the rules. We don't like to talk about it in this manner, but lies can both help as well as destroy a relationship. In close relationships we identified three characteristics that affect the nature of lies and lie detection. *Mutual influence* was the phrase we used to indicate how each partner to a close relationship plays a part in the way lying develops and the impact it has on the relationship. Sometimes we do not want to face the possibility that our behavior precipitated lying on the part of our partner or that by "looking the other way" we give tacit approval to it. Close relationships also have the potential for multiple exposure to a lie. This is bound to affect both the liar's and the detector's strategies. Because trust is a characteristic of close relationships, a liar's first lies will not be suspected. But once suspicion is raised and there is a desire to uncover the lie, a person who knows the liar and his or her behavior best will probably be the best detector. Some stereotypical categories of lying behaviors were presented under the headings of anxiety responses, excessive responses, incongruous responses, and indirect responses.

In the area of fighting, the primary question for the relationship partners is how to engage in constructive conflict so the relationship will profit. Conflict in close relationships is a fact of life that, like lying, has the capacity to completely destroy a relationship or to strengthen it. Withdrawal from the interaction and a lack of sensitivity to feelings were two common problems associated with conflict resolution by couples in unsatisfactory marriages. Our discussion of constructive conflict identified many suggestions for positive behavior, but one of the most important is the overall attitude each partner brings to the conflict. If each partner believes he or she can solve the problem only as part of a team and that it is worth working on for the good of the relationship, many of the specific techniques we mentioned will come naturally.

SELECTED READINGS

Self-Disclosure, Confidentiality, and Trust

Baxter, L. A., and Wilmot, W. W. " 'Secret Tests': Social Strategies for Acquiring Information About the State of the Relationship." *Human Communication Research* 11 (1984): 171–201.

Bochner, A. P. "On the Efficacy of Openness in Close Relationships." In M. Burgoon, ed., *Communication Yearbook 5*, pp. 109–124. New Brunswick, NJ: Transaction, 1982.

Bok, S. *Secrets: On the Ethics of Concealment and Revelation.* New York: Vintage Books, 1983.

Bradac, J. J., Tardy, C. H., and Hosman, L. A. "Disclosure Styles and a Hint at Their Genesis." *Human Communication Research* 6 (1980): 228–238.

Brown, J. R., and Rogers, L. E. "Openness, Uncertainty, and Intimacy: An Epistemological Reformulation." In N. Coupland, H. Giles, and J. M. Wiemann, eds., *"Miscommunication" and Problematic Talk.* Newbury Park, CA: Sage, 1991.

Burgoon, J. "Privacy and Communication." In M. Burgoon, ed., *Communication Yearbook 6*, pp. 206–249. Beverly Hills, CA: Sage, 1982.

Chelune, G. J., ed. *Self-Disclosure.* San Francisco: Jossey-Bass, 1979.

Cozby, P. C. "Self-Disclosure: A Literature Review." *Psychological Bulletin* 79 (1973): 73–91.

Derlega, V. and Berg, J., eds. *Self-Disclosure: Theory Research and Therapy.* New York: Plenum, 1987.

Derlega, V. J., and Chaikin, A. L. *Sharing Intimacy: What We Reveal to Others and Why.* Englewood Cliffs, NJ: Prentice-Hall, 1975.

Derlega, V. J., Wilson, M., and Chaikin. A. L. "Friendship and Disclosure Reciprocity." *Journal of Personality and Social Psychology* 34 (1976): 578–582.

Dindia, K. "Self-Disclosure, Self-Identity, and Relationship Development: A Transactional/Dialectical Perspective." In S. Duck, ed., *Handbook of Personal Relationships,* 2nd ed. pp. 411–426. New York: Wiley, 1997.

Dindia, K., Fitzpatrick, M. A. and Kenny, D.A. "Self-Disclosure in Spouse and Stranger Interaction: A Social Relations Analysis." *Human Communication Research* 23 (1997): 388–412

Gilbert, S. J. "Empirical and Theoretical Extensions of Self-Disclosure." In G. R. Miller, ed., *Explorations in Interpersonal Communication,* pp. 197–215. Beverly Hills, CA: Sage, 1976.

Holmes, J. G. "Trust and the Appraisal Process in Close Relationships." In W. H. Jones and D. Perlman, eds., *Advances in Personal Relationships,* pp. 57–104. London: Jessica Kingsley, 1991.

Holmes, J. G., and Rempel, J. K. "Trust in Close Relationships." In C. Hendrick, ed., *Close Relationships,* pp. 187–220. Newbury Park, CA: Sage, 1989.

Holtgraves, T. "The Language of Self-Disclosure." In H. Giles and W. P. Robinson, eds., *Handbook of Language and Social Psychology,* pp. 191–207. New York: Wiley, 1990.

Jourard, S. *Self-Disclosure: The Experimental Investigation of the Transparent Self.* New York: John Wiley & Sons, 1971.

Luft, J. *Of Human Interaction.* Palo Alto, CA: National Press Books, 1969.

Parks, M. R. "Ideology in Interpersonal Communication: Off the Couch and Into the World." In M. Burgoon, ed., *Communication Yearbook 5,* pp. 79–107. New Brunswick, NJ: Transaction, 1982.

Pearce, W. B. "Trust in Interpersonal Communication." *Speech Monographs* 41 (1974): 236–244.

Pearce, W. B., and Sharp, S. M. "Self-Disclosing Communication." *Journal of Communication* 23 (1973): 409–425.

Petronio, S. "Communication Boundary Management: A Theoretical Model of Managing Disclosure of Private Information Between Marital Couples." *Communication Theory* 1 (1991): 311–335.

Priest, P. J. *Public Intimacies. Talk Show Participants and Tell-All TV.* Cresskill, NJ: Hampton Press, 1995.

Rawlins, W. K. "Openness as Problematic in Ongoing Friendships: Two Conversational Dilemmas." *Communication Monographs* 50 (1983): 1–13.

Rawlins, W. K., and Holl, M. "The Communicative Achievement of Friendship During Adolescence: Predicaments of Trust and Violation." *Western Journal of Speech Communication* 51 (1987): 345–363.

Rempel, J. K., Holmes, J. G., and Zanna, M. P. "Trust in Close Relationships." *Journal of Personality and Social Psychology* 49 (1985): 95–112.

Roloff, M. E. and Ifert, D. "Antecedents and Consequences of Explicit Agreements to Declare a Topic Taboo in Dating Relationships." *Personal Relationships* 6 (1998): 191–205.

Rosenfeld, L. B. "Self-Disclosure Avoidance: Why Am I Afraid To Tell You Who I Am." *Communication Monographs* 46 (1979): 63–74.

Schmidt, T. O., and Cornelius, R. R. "Self-Disclosure in Everyday Life." *Journal of Social and Personal Relationships* 4 (1987): 365–373.

Spencer, E. E. *Self-Disclosure in Family Conversational Interaction: Communication Between Parents and Older Adolescents.* Unpublished Ph.D. dissertation, University of Texas, 1992.

Vangelisti, A. "Family Secrets: Forms, Functions and Correlates." *Journal of Social and Personal Relationships* 11 (1994): 113–135.

Vangelisti. A. L. and Caughlin, J. P. "Revealing Family Secrets: The Influence of Topic, Function, and Relationships." *Journal of Social and Personal Relationships* 14 (1997): 679–705.

VanLear, C. A. "Testing a Cyclical Model of Communicative Openness in Relationship Development: Two Longitudinal Studies." *Communication Monographs* 58 (1991): 337–361.

Lying

Barnes, J. A. *A Pack of Lies: Towards a Sociology of Lying.* New York: Cambridge University Press, 1994.

Bok, S. *Lying: Moral Choice in Public and Private Life.* New York: Vintage Books, 1978.

Bolinger, D. "Truth Is a Linguistic Question." *Language* 49 (1973): 539–550.

Bowers, J. W., Elliott, N. D., and Desmond, R. J. "Exploiting Pragmatic Rules: Devious Messages." *Human Communication Research* 3 (1977): 235–242.

Buller, D. B., and Burgoon, J. K. "Deception: Strategic and Nonstrategic Communication." In J. A. Daly and J. M. Wiemann, eds., *Strategic Interpersonal Communication,* pp. 191–223. Hillsdale, NJ: Erlbaum, 1994.

Comadena, M. E. "Accuracy in Detecting Deception: Intimate and Friendship Relationships." In M. Burgoon, ed., *Communication Yearbook* 6, pp. 446–471. Beverly Hills, CA: Sage, 1982.

DePaulo, B. M. and Bell, K. L. "Truth and Investment: Lies Are Told to Those Who Care." *Journal of Personality and Social Psychology* 71 (1996): 703–716.

DePaulo, B. M. and Kashy D. A. "Everyday Lies in Close and Casual Relationships." *Journal of Personality and Social Psychology* 74 (1998): 63–79.

Ekman, P. *Telling Lies.* New York: Norton, 2nd ed., 1992.

Ekman, P. and O'Sullivan, M. "Who Can Catch a Liar?" *American Psychologist* 46 (1991): 913–920.

Hyman, R. "The Psychology of Deception." *Annual Review of Psychology* 40 (1989): 133–154.

Kalbfleisch, P. J. "Deceit, Distrust and the Social Milieu: Application of Deception Research in a Troubled World." *Journal of Applied Communication Research* 20 (1992): 308–334.

Knapp, M. L., and Comadena, M. E. "Telling It Like It Isn't: A Review of Theory and Research on Deceptive Communications." *Human Communication Research* 5 (1979): 270–285.

Knapp, M. L., Cody, M., and Reardon, K. "Nonverbal Signals." In C. Berger and S. Chaffee, eds., *Handbook of Communication Science.* Beverly Hills, CA: Sage, 1987, pp. 385–418.

Knapp, M. L., Hart, R. P., and Dennis, H. S. "An Exploration of Deception as a Communication Construct." *Human Communication Research* 1 (1974): 15–29.

Levine, T. R., and McCornack, S. A. "Linking Love and Lies: A Formal Test of the McCornack and Parks Model of Deception Detection." *Journal of Social and Personal Relationships* 9 (1992): 143–154.

McCornack, S. A., and Parks, M. R. "Deception, Detection and Relationship Development: The Other Side of Trust." In M. L. McLaughlin, ed., *Communication Yearbook* 9, pp. 377–389. Beverly Hills, CA: Sage, 1986.

Metts, S. "An Exploratory Investigation of Deception in Close Relationships." *Journal of Social and Personal Relationships* 6 (1989): 159–180.

Miller, G. R., Mongeau, P. A., and Sleight, C. "Fudging with Friends and Lying to Lovers: Deceptive Communication in Personal Relationships." *Journal of Social and Personal Relationships* 3 (1986): 495–512.

Miller, G. R., and Stiff, J. *Deceptive Communication.* Beverly Hills, CA: Sage, 1993.

Newman, J. B. "Doublespeak, Doubletalk and the Function of Language." *Quarterly Journal of Speech* 62 (1976): 78–81.

Nyberg, D. *The Unvarnished Truth-Telling and Deceiving in Ordinary Life.* Chicago: University of Chicago Press, 1993.

Robinson, W. P. *Deceit, Delusion, and Detection.* Thousand Oaks, CA: Sage, 1996.

Rodriguez, N., and Ryave, A. "Telling Lies in Everyday Life: Motivational and Organizational Consequences of Sequential Preferences." *Qualitative Sociology* 13 (1990): 195–210.

Rowatt, W. C., Cunningham, M. R., and Druen, P. B. "Deception to Get a Date." *Personality and Social Psychology Bulletin* 24 (1998): 1228–1242.

Sagarin, B. J., Rhoads, K. v.L., and Cialdini, R. B. "Deceiver's Distrust: Denigration as a Consequence of Undiscovered Deception." *Personality and Social Psychology Bulletin* 24 (1998): 1167–1176.

Stebbins, R. A. "Putting People On: Deception of Our Fellowman in Everyday Life." *Sociology and Social Research* 59 (1975): 189–200.

Werth, L. F. and Flaherty, J. "A Phenomenological Approach to Human Deception." In R. W. Mitchell and N. S. Thompson, eds., *Deception: Perspectives on Human and Nonhuman Deceit,* pp. 293–311. Albany, NY: SUNY Press, 1986

Zuckerman, M., DePaulo, B. M., and Rosenthal, P. "Verbal and Nonverbal Communication of Deception." In L. Berkowitz, ed., *Advances in Experimental Social Psychology,* vol. 14. New York: Academic Press, 1981.

Conflict

Alberts, J. K. "An Analysis of Couples' Conversational Complaints." *Communication Monographs* 55 (1988): 182–197.

Alberts, J. K., and Driscoll, G. "Containment Versus Escalation: The Trajectory of Couples' Conversational Complaints." *Western Journal of Communication* 56 (1992): 394–412.

Bach, G. R., and Wyden, P. *The Intimate Enemy.* New York: Avon Books, 1968.

Cahn, D. D., ed. *Intimates in Conflict. A Communication Perspective.* Hillsdale, NJ: Erlbaum, 1990.

Canary, D. J., Cupach, W. R., and Messman, S. J. *Relationship Conflict.* Thousand Oaks, CA: Sage, 1995.

Donohue, W. A. *Communication, Marital Dispute, and Divorce Mediation.* Hillsdale, NJ: Erlbaum, 1991.

Donohue, W. A., with Kolt, R. *Managing Interpersonal Conflict.* Newbury Park, CA: Sage, 1992.

Gottman, J. M. "Emotional Responsiveness in Marital Conversations." *Journal of Communication* 32 (1982): 108–120.

Gottman, J. M. *Marital Interaction.* New York: Academic Press, 1979.

Gottman, J. M. *What Predicts Divorce? The Relationship Between Marital Processes and Marital Outcomes.* Hillsdale, NJ: Erlbaum, 1994.

Grimshaw, A. D., ed. *Conflict Talk: Sociolinguistic Investigations of Arguments in Conversations.* New York: Cambridge University Press, 1990.

Krueger, D. L. and Smith, P. "Decision-Making Patterns of Couples: A Sequential Analysis." *Journal of Communication* 32 (1982): 121–134.

McGonagle, K. A., Kessler, R. C., and Gotlib, I. H. "The Effects of Marital Disagreement Style, Frequency, and Outcome on Marital Disruption." *Journal of Social and Personal Relationships* 10 (1993): 385–404.

McNeil, E. B. *The Nature of Human Conflict.* Englewood Cliffs, NJ: Prentice-Hall, 1965.

Messman, S. J. and Canary, D. J. "Patterns of Conflict in Personal Relationships." In B. H. Spitzberg and W. R. Cupach, eds., *The Dark Side of Close Relationships,* pp. 121-152. Mahwah, NJ: Erlbaum, 1998.

Metts, S. "Face and Facework: Implications for the Study of Personal Relationships." In S. Duck,
ed., *Handbook of Personal Relationships,* pp. 373–930. New York: Wiley, 1997.

Newell, S. E., and Stutman, R. K. "The Episodic Nature of Social Confrontation." In J. A. Anderson, ed., *Communication Yearbook 14,* pp. 359–392. Newbury Park, CA: Sage, 1991.

Noller, P., Feeney, J. A., Bonnell, D., and Callan, V. J. "A Study of Conflict in Early Marriage," *Journal of Social and Personal Relationships* 11 (1994): 233–252.

Notarius, C. I., Lashley, S. L., and Sullivan, D. J. "Angry at Your Partner?: Think Again." In R. J. Sternberg and M. Hojjat, eds., *Satisfaction in Close Relationships,* pp. 219–248. New York: Guilford, 1997.

Notarius, C., and Markman, H. *We Can Work It Out: Making Sense of Marital Conflict.* New York: Putnam's Sons, 1993.

Nye, R. D. *Conflict Among Humans.* New York: Springer Publishing Co., 1973.

Ohbuchi, K., Sachiko, C., and Fukishima, O. "Mitigation of Interpersonal Conflicts: Politeness and Time Pressure." *Personality and Social Psychology Bulletin* 10 (1996): 1035–1042.

Olson, D. H., and Ryder, R. G. "Inventory of Marital Conflicts (IMC): An Experimental Interaction Procedure." *Journal of Marriage and the Family* 32 (1970): 443–448.

Orvis, B. R., Kelley, H. H., and Butler, D. "Attributional Conflict in Young Couples." In J. H. Harvey, W. J. Ickes, and R. F. Kidd, eds., *New Directions in Attribution Research,* vol. 1, pp. 353–386. Hillside, NJ: Lawrence Erlbaum, 1976.

Peterson, D. R. "Conflict." In *Close Relationships,* ed. H. H. Kelley et al., pp. 360–396. New York: Freeman, 1983.

Rausch, H. L., Barry, W. A., Hertel, R. K., and Swaim, M. A. *Communication, Conflict, and Marriage.* San Francisco: Jossey-Bass, 1974.

Retzinger, S. M. *Violent Emotions: Shame and Rage in Marital Quarrels.* Newbury Park, CA: Sage, 1991.

Schaap, C., Buunk, B., and Kerkstra, A. "Marital Conflict Resolution." In P. Noller and M. A. Fitzpatrick, eds., *Perspectives on Marital Interaction,* pp. 203–270. Philadelphia: Multilingual Matters, Ltd., 1988.

Siegert, J. R., and Stamp, G. H. " 'Our First Big Fight' as a Milestone in the Development of Close Relationships." *Communication Monographs* 61 (1994): 345–360.

Sillars, A. L., and Wilmot, W. W. "Communication Strategies in Conflict and Mediation." In J. A. Daly and J. M. Wiemann, eds., *Strategic*

Interpersonal Communication, pp. 163–190. Newbury Park, CA: Sage, 1994.

Wile, D. B. *After the Fight: A Night in the Life of a Couple.* New York: Guilford, 1993.

NOTES

[1]D. J. Canary and L. Stafford, *Communication and Relational Maintenance* (New York: Academic Press, 1994).

[2]For each person these deeply personal topics or feelings vary. In fact, with any given person, the makeup of one's private secrets may change from $time_1$ to $time_2$. The following statements are what some people consider to be extremely personal and private—reserved for only the closest confidant. Consider to whom (if anyone) you'd reveal such information if were true of you. A stranger? An acquaintance? Your closest friend? (1) I can't urinate when others are close to me. (2) I feel so competitive I can't get close to anyone. (3) I feel inferior to you in this area. (4) I get violent sometimes. (5) I think women are ignorant. (6) I want to be a male ballet star. (7) I have a small penis. (8) I've had a mastectomy. (9) I ate my buggers as a child, but now I discreetly paste them under my desk.

[3]S. Sprecher, "The Effects of Self-Disclosure Given and Received on Affection for an Intimate Partner and Stability of the Relationship," *Journal of Social and Personal Relationships* 4 (1987): 115–127.

[4]J. W. Pennebaker, *Opening Up: The Healing Power of Expressing Emotions* (New York: Guilford, 1990).

[5]L. B. Rosenfeld, "Self-Disclosure Avoidance: Why I Am Afraid to Tell You Who I Am," *Communication Monographs* 46 (1979): 63–74. Also see: S. Petronio and J. N. Martin, "Ramifications of Revealing Private Information: A Gender Gap," *Journal of Clinical Psychology* 42 (1986): 499–506.

[6]"We Have No Secrets." Copyright 1972 by Quackenbush Music, Ltd. written by Carly Simon.

[7]See: S. Petronio, "Communication Boundary Management: A Theoretical Model of Managing Disclosure of Private Information Between Marital Couples," *Communication Theory* 1 (1991): 311–335; J. Burgoon, "Privacy and Communication." In M. Burgoon, ed., *Communication Yearbook 6* (Beverly Hills, CA: Sage, 1982) pp. 206–249; and T. J. Cottle, "Is Privacy Possible? Exposing Our-

selves in Public," *New Republic,* March 8, 1975, pp. 19, 21; and P. J. Priest, *Public Intimacies: Talk Show Participants and Tell-All TV* (Cresskill, NJ: Hampton Press, 1995).

[8]G. J. McCall and J. L. Simmons, *Identities and Interaction* (New York: Free Press, 1966), pp. 195–196.

[9]Similarity in the amount of disclosure and in the content of disclosure may have a positive effect on attraction. See: D. M. Daher and P. G. Banikotes, "Interpersonal Attraction and Rewarding Aspects of Disclosure Content and Level," *Journal of Personality and Social Psychology* 33 (1976): 492–296.

[10]Adapted from: Irwin Altman and W. W. Haythorn, "Interpersonal Exchange in Isolation," *Sociometry* 28 (1965): 422.

[11]L. A. Baxter and W. W. Wilmot, "Taboo Topics in Close Relationships," *Journal of Social and Personal Relationships* 2 (1985): 253–269. Also see: A. Vangelisti, "Family Secrets: Forms, Functions and Correlates," *Journal of Social and Personal Relationships* 11 (1994): 113–135 and M. E. Roloff and D. Ifert, "Antecedents and Consequences of Explicit Agreements to Declare a Topic Taboo in Dating Relationships." *Personal Relationships* 5 (1998): 191–205.

[12]L. A. Baxter, "Secret Tests: Social Strategies for Acquiring Information About the State of the Relationship," *Human Communication Research* 11 (1984): 171–201. For a discussion of reasons for revealing or hiding information about one's relationship from one's friends, see: L. A. Baxter and S. Widenmann, "Revealing and Not Revealing the Status of Romantic Relationships to Social Networks," *Journal of Social and Personal Relationships* 10 (1993): 321–337.

[13]A related study, not using married couples, found that positive disclosures resulted in more interpersonal attraction, regardless of the depth of disclosure. Cf. S. J. Gilbert and D. Horenstein, "The Communication of Self-Disclosure: Level versus Valence," *Human Communication Research* 1 (1975): 316–322.

[14]J. K. Rempel, J. G. Holmes, and M. P. Zanna, "Trust in Close Relationships," *Journal of Personality and Social Psychology* 49 (1985): 95–112; J. G. Holmes and J. K. Rempel, "Trust in Close Relationships." In C. Hendrick, ed., *Reviews of Personality and Social Psychology: Close Relationships*, vol. 10 (Newbury Park, CA: Sage, 1989), pp. 187–219.

[15]B. M. DePaulo and D. A. Kashy, "Everyday Lies in Close and Casual Relationships," *Journal of Personality and Social Psychology* 74 (1998): 63–79.

[16]H. LaFollette and G. Graham, "Honesty and Intimacy," *Journal of Social and Personal Relationships* 3 (1986): 3–18.

[17]S. A. McCornack and T. R. Levine, "When Lies Are Uncovered: Emotional and Relational Outcomes of Discovered Deception," *Communication Monographs* 57 (1990): 119–138.

[18]For summaries of research and writing on deception and lying, see: M. L. Knapp and M. E. Comadena, "Telling It Like It Isn't: A Review of Theory and Research on Deceptive Communications," *Human Communication Research* 5 (1979): 270–285; M. Zuckerman and R. Driver, "Telling Lies: Verbal and Nonverbal Correlates of Deception." In A. W. Siegman and S. Feldstein, eds., *Multichannel Integrations of Nonverbal Behavior* (Hillsdale, NJ: Erlbaum, 1985), pp. 129–147; P. Ekman, *Telling Lies* 2nd ed. (New York: Norton, 1992); M. L. Knapp, M. J. Cody, and K. K. Reardon "Nonverbal Signals." In C. R. Berger and S. H. Chaffee, eds., *Handbook of Communication Science* (Newbury Park, CA: Sage, 1987), pp. 385–418; G. R. Miller and J. Stiff, *Deceptive Communication* (Newbury Park, CA: Sage, 1993); W. P. Robinson, *Deceit, Delusion, and Detection* (Thousand Oaks, CA.: Sage, 1996); J. A. Barnes, *A Pack of Lies: Towards a Sociology of Lying.* (NY: Cambridge University Press, 1994); and D. Nyberg, *The Unvarnished Truth-Telling and Deceiving in Ordinary Life* (Chicago: University of Chicago Press, 1993).

[19]M. E. Comadena, "Accuracy in Detecting Deception: Intimate and Friendship Relationships." In M. Burgoon, ed. *Communication Yearbook 6* (Beverly Hills, CA: Sage, 1982), pp. 446–471. Also see: S. A. McCornack and M. R. Parks, "Deception Detection and Relationship Development: The Other Side of Trust." In M. L. McLaughlin, ed., *Communication Yearbook 9* (Beverly Hills, CA: Sage, 1986), pp. 377–389.

[20]L. F. Werth and J. Flaherty, "A Phenomenological Approach to Human Deception." In R. W. Mitchell and N. S. Thompson, eds., Deception:

Perspectives on Human and Nonhuman Deceit (Albany, NY: SUNY Press, 1986), p. 296.

[21]T. R. Levine and S. A. McCornack, "Linking Love and Lies: A Formal Test of the McCornack and Parks Model of Deception Detection," *Journal of Social and Personal Relationships* 9 (1992): 143–154.

[22]Sagarin, B. J., Rhoads, K. v.L., and Cialdini, R. B. "Deceiver's Distrust: Denigration as a Consequence of Undiscovered Deception," *Personality and Social Psychology Bulletin* 24 (1998): 1167–1176.

[23]This concept is known by many labels: confrontation; difference of opinion; friendly debate; knock-down, drag-out; discussion; little misunderstanding; spat; disagreement; argument. The choice of labels is often related to: (1) one's perception of the magnitude or intensity of the conflict or (2) one's need to reduce or increase the *actual* magnitude or intensity of the conflict—to make the conflict *seem* more trivial or more critical to the relationship than it actually is. Probably the most volatile conflicts take place: (1) when the issue is clearly linked to basic and deeply held values, and (2) when the relationship has few accumulated rewards.

[24]M. A. Fitzpatrick, "Negotiation, Problem Solving and Conflict in Various Types of Marriages." In P. Noller and M. A. Fitzpatrick, eds., *Perspectives on Marital Interaction* (Philadelphia: Multilingual Matters, 1988), pp. 245–270.

[25]C. Kelly, T. L. Huston, and R. M. Cate, "Premarital Relationship Correlates of the Erosion of Satisfaction in Marriage," *Journal of Social and Personal Relationships* 2 (1985): 167–178.

[26]K. A. McGonagle, R. C. Kessler, and I. H. Gotlib, "The Effects of Marital Disagreement Style, Frequency, and Outcome of Marital Disruption," *Journal of Social and Personal Relationships* 10 (1993): 385–404.

[27]J. R. Siegert and G. H. Stamp, " 'Our First Big Fight' As A Milestone in the Development of Close Relationships," *Communication Monographs* 61 (1994): 345–360.

[28]C. Notarius and H. Markman, *We Can Work It Out: Making Sense of Marital Conflict* (New York: Putnam, 1993); N. A. Klinetob and D. Smith, "Demand-Withdraw Communication in Marital Interaction: Tests of Interspousal Contingency and Gender Role Hypotheses," *Journal of Marriage and the Family* 58 (1996): 945-957; and G. Bodenmann, A. Kaiser, K. Hahlweg, and G. Fehm-Wolsdorf,

"Communication Patterns During Marital Conflict: A Cross-Cultural Replication," *Personal Relationships* 5 (1998): 343–356.

[29]J. M. Gottman, "Emotional Responsiveness in Marital Conversations." *Journal of Communication* 32 (1982): 108–120; and J. M. Gottman, *Marital Interaction* (New York: Academic Press, 1979).

[30]D. Johnson, *The Shadow Knows* (New York: Knopf, 1974), pp. 62–63. Copyright © 1974 by Diane Johnson. Reprinted by permission of Alfred A. Knopf, Inc.

[31]Notarius and Markman, *op. cit.*

[32]S. Metts, "Face and Facework: Implications for the Study of Personal Relationships." In S. Duck, ed., *Handbook of Personal Relationships,* 2nd ed. (New York: John Wiley & Sons, 1997), pp. 373–390.

[33]M. E. McCullough, E. L. Worthington, Jr., and K. C. Rachal, "Interpersonal Forgiving in Close Relationships," *Journal of Personality and Social Psychology* 73 (1997): 321–336.

[34]S. L. Braver and V. Rohrer, "Superiority of Vicarious over Direct Experience in Interpersonal Conflict Resolution," *Journal of Conflict Resolution* 22 (1978): 143–155.

CHAPTER 9

Maintaining Relationships Through Dialogue: Commitment and Intimacy

Dear Dr. Knapp,

My girlfriend is really nice except she keeps bugging me to say and do stuff to convince her I love her. I tell her I love her every time we are together. But that isn't enough for her. Then I get mad and that doesn't help. What's wrong with her? Is she insecure or something? What can I do? I do love her.

Stumped

There are many ways to communicate the degree of intimacy and commitment one feels for his or her partner. The phrase "I love you" is one way of communicating how you feel about your partner, and sometimes it will be enough. But intimates reveal the kind of relationship they have and want through the language and behavior evidenced in a variety of communicative situations. Some types of talk that are especially revealing about the nature of the relationship are explored in this chapter. The extent to which partners are able to construct dialogue that defines a mutually satisfactory relationship is the extent to which they are able to adequately maintain their relationship.

> . . . the communication dimension of an intimate relation has been considered and a third major force uncovered that transforms isolated individuals into interlinked intimates: the continual verbal and nonverbal statements they make to each other that they are intimates.
>
> —*Murray S. Davis*

The process of maintaining relationships, like the process of establishing relationships, is critically dependent on an understanding of the messages partners exchange. Messages which directly or indirectly communicate information about the closeness or intimacy of the relationship are especially important in determining why relationships are maintained and how satisfying they are to the participants. We begin our understanding of these messages with an examination of commitment and how it can be effectively communicated during the maintenance of close relationships.

Commitment and Commitment Talk

Commitment takes many forms. The form that comes most readily to mind is a kind of commitment based on each partner's degree of attraction for the relationship and each other—a *"want to"* type of commitment. But we know that people stay in relationships for other reasons as well. Sometimes commitment is based on what one or both partners feel they *"have to"* do—not what they want to do. This perspective may be associated with the perception that there aren't any good alternatives; that the relationship would be more difficult to end than to keep together; that too much has been invested in the relationship to terminate it; or that coping with the reactions of others would be too difficult. The decision to continue a relationship can also be based on feelings of obligation—an *"ought to"* orientation. This may be related to the kind of relationship ("Once you get married, you ought to stay married") or to the other person in the relationship ("I was the one who got him into this relationship, so I ought to stay with him").[1] While the obligatory nature of "ought to" commitment motives at first may seem less desirable than "want to" motives, it can be very important in sustaining relationships through difficult periods when "want to" motives are challenged. On the other hand, if a couple stays together solely because they think they ought to, they may not derive much satisfaction from it, as the following example illustrates:

> Yuri Uemura sat on the straw tatami mat of her living room and chatted cheerfully about her 40-year marriage to a man whom, she mused, she never particularly liked. "There was never any love between me and my husband," she said

blithely, recalling how he used to beat her. . . . In short, the Uemuras have a marriage that is as durable as it is unhappy, one couple's tribute to the Japanese sanctity of family.[2]

The important thing to remember about these three different types of commitments is that they will reflect and be reflected in different types of relationship talk. This can be seen in the following six dimensions associated with the strength of one's "want to" commitment.[3]

Perceiving a Rewarding Future

We use information gleaned from interaction with our partner to forecast the future. The extent to which we see a *rewarding future* with our partner increases the strength of our commitment to the relationship. Once the partners have sustained a relationship long enough for the nature of future talk to achieve some reality, the nature of subsequent future talk (and its effects) will change. Talk about the future takes many forms. It may be specifically directed at the future of the relationship, or it may be more general; it may focus on the immediate future or on long-range plans and goals; and it may emphasize the couple or only one partner. Each of these foci has the potential to signal a rewarding future. As with other patterns of communication, we would predict that attempts at constructing rewarding future talk would become more frequent when strain on the relationship is felt and there is a desire to "fix" it—e.g., "Let's move out of this place to somewhere we can start over. I'll get a job that allows me to be home more and we can have a baby."

Identifying with the Relationship

Our commitment is also gauged by the extent to which we *identify with the relationship*. Just as members of a corporation vary in the extent to which they believe in and accept the company's goals and values, members of a relationship vary in the degree to which they identify with it. In Chapter 2 we said that progress toward more intimacy brought the participants from an "I" orientation to a "We" orientation. Although we don't have terms to describe them, there are several gradations between I and We, and these are reflected here as the strength of one's identification with the relationship.

Perceiving Fewer Attractive Alternatives

The development of any relationship will require the elimination of some alternatives. And higher levels of commitment can be communicated by indicating that there are *fewer attractive alternatives*. In fact, one researcher found the best predictor of relationship failure was high attentiveness to alternatives. As the author put it, "Even if the grass is greener on the other side of the fence, happy gardeners will be less likely to notice."[4] Alternatives may be other potential relationships, but they can also be one's work, a hobby, etc. When these alternatives are attractive enough to replace some or all of the relationship, it can detract from the perceived commitment to that relationship.

A Willingness to Exert Effort for the Relationship

Most of us have many demands on our time. Those things we single out to devote time, energy, and resources to are perceived as the things we are most committed to. A *willingness to exert effort* on behalf of the relationship may be as varied as helping your partner study for a test or spending time listening to his or her problems.

Investing More in the Relationship

As a result of our efforts on behalf of the relationship, we accrue *greater investments* in the relationship. This, in itself, influences commitment. As investments increase, commitment to the relationship is also likely to increase.

Accepting Responsibility for Your Commitment

The last dimension deals with one's *responsibility for relationship commitment.* Commitment strength is related to perceptions that a person's behavior is freely chosen and that he or she is accountable for it. Even though it may be clear that external forces played an important role in the relationship, partners may still attribute their commitment to their free choice—which will have the effect of increasing perceived commitment.

When two people are widely discrepant about the preceding dimensions, there will probably be a lot of talk directed at the subject of commitment, and if the partners do not reduce the discrepancy, a change in the relationship is likely. But since these dimensions do not account for the possibility of strong "ought to" or "have to" motives, the relationship may continue with each partner having very different levels of commitment—e.g., one partner who is maintaining the relationship "for the sake of the kids." And if both partners are extremely committed to the relationship, they are not likely to find themselves closely bunched on the far right of Figure 9.1 for very long. The far right is a point that represents strong commitment, but it is not necessary to remain at this point once you have demonstrated your ability to get there. For example, once you have thoroughly identified with this relationship through a commitment to "We," you are then allowed to step back and enjoy a bit more of an "I" orientation. But if commitment is ever in question, this will again require movement toward the far right position on these dimensions. These dimensions are useful for assessing the development of a relationship, but it is not uncommon for people to report a less systematic development: "Commitment wasn't an issue. We just kept doing things and seeing each other and then one day . . . there we were." In situations like that, the dimensions in Figure 9.1 can be useful for retrospective analyses.

One final complicating factor about using these dimensions as a guide to commitment concerns the dynamics of interaction. Remember we are dealing with the behavior of two people. Imagine a situation in which both parties are strongly committed to the relationship. Each wants to expend a lot of effort on behalf of the relationship, but one person seems to be doing so much of this that the other person backs off. Since the partner engaging in frequent displays of effort for the relationship perceives little effort on the part of his or her partner, efforts may be intensified with no desired increase forthcoming from the other. Of course, talk about commitment will ensue, and since both partners feel a strong commitment, the type of behavior expected by each in the future can be negotiated. This example points out the importance of *initiation and reciprocity* to the communication of commitment. Initiating acts of commitment have an intensity to them that overshadows the reciprocity of the same act. If you are the first person to say, "I love you," and your partner says, "I love you too," you may perceive a less intense commitment from your partner if he or she doesn't initiate the sentiment on occasion.

Since the phrase "I love you" is such a crucial one in the talk of commitment, let's look at how it manifests itself in dialogue.[5] When dating couples tape-recorded private conversations about their relationship and about the first time "I love you" occurred in their relationship, three types of dialogue were revealed.

The first is called *declaration of love-reciprocation of love*. As the following conversations illustrate, both partners want to express their love, but the actual dialogue allows the pair to gradually work up to explicit declarations.

		Prediction of Future Rewards from This Relationship				
Low	1	2	3	4	5	High
		Identification With the Relationship/Sharing Values				
Low	1	2	3	4	5	High
		Unattractive Alternatives to the Relationship				
Low	1	2	3	4	5	High
		Willingness to Exert Effort on Behalf of the Relationship				
Low	1	2	3	4	5	High
		Amount Invested in the Relationship				
Low	1	2	3	4	5	High
		Personal Responsibility for Commitment to the Relationship				
Low	1	2	3	4	5	High

9.1 Cognitive/Affective Commitment to the Relationship

Example 1

MALE: We've been spending a lot of time together, and I've really begun to feel close.

FEMALE: Yeah, I've felt us growing together into something special. It feels good!

MALE: Maybe we're failing in love! (laughs)

FEMALE: I know, I love you.

MALE: I love you too. (pause) But, I don't know what we'll do now.

FEMALE: Let's just enjoy it. I don't know when I've been so happy!

MALE: Me, too!

In the following conversation, we have an example of *declaration of love-pseudo-reciprocation of love*. These are instances when the other partner's readiness to reciprocate "I love you" is incorrectly assessed.

Example 2

MALE: I've wondered how you feel about me.

FEMALE: Well, I know people see us together all the time.

MALE: I'm beginning to—well—want you around all the time.

FEMALE: You're very special to me.

MALE: I love you.

FEMALE: I do, too. (pause) Now I'm really confused though. I mean, I feel close to you, but I've always considered you a friend. I guess more than a friend now. I don't know.

MALE: Yeah, well, I thought there was something wrong.

The third type is a *declaration of love-refutation of love*. Here the declarer again misconstrues the partner's readiness to reciprocate, but instead of simply being "confused" as in Example 2, the partner is clearly unready to reciprocate.

Example 3

FEMALE: You know, I've really enjoyed our summer. You know, dating and stuff.

MALE: Yeah, well, me too.

FEMALE: I love you, Jack.

MALE: Well, (pause) there's no way you could "love" me after only knowing me only a couple of months.

FEMALE: I love you, anyway.

MALE: I'm sorry, I'm not sure, and I feel pressured.

FEMALE: Well, you're playing with my emotions! I'm gonna treat you so you'll eventually fall in love with me!

MALE: But I'm not ready for that! I think we should just cool off for awhile and not see each other.

FEMALE: (sobbing) Oh, I give up!

Once a relationship has achieved intimacy and become stabilized, how is the phrase "I love you" manifested? The following discussions by married couples reveal situations where "I love you" is suspect as a forecast for a request or to take the edge off bad news; to recapture feelings of commitment; and to gain assurance that commitment is still there.

Example 4

FEMALE: Let's see, oh, I know how we say it. It was like this: You called me from work and said: "Joan? I love you" and I said: "I know, me too, what's wrong!?"

MALE: What!? Why'd you say that!?

FEMALE: Well, when you start off by telling me you love me you usually did something wrong. Oh, I know, it was 'cause we couldn't go out to eat dinner to celebrate our anniversary.

MALE: Well, I love you, too.

FEMALE: I know, (laughs)

Example 5

MALE: You know, I think we got in the habit of saying "I love you" as—as, well, as a way to assure each other we still care, and in the madness of the midst of both of our careers, the relationship is still the most important thing. Sure, on the phone, we'd both say: "I love you, see you later," and as a way to call each other like: "Hi, love."

FEMALE: Yeah.

MALE: But remember when you got that great job and I saw you walking toward me on campus?

FEMALE: Yeah, I was excited.

MALE: We hugged and both said: "I love you." That was different.

FEMALE: I guess we both knew we had jobs we always wanted, but yeah, that meant a lot. It meant *we* were still the most important thing.

Example 6

FEMALE: I don't know. This is interesting. Do you still love me?

MALE: Why do you ask?

FEMALE: Well, I guess I haven't heard you say it in a while.

MALE: Of course I love you.

FEMALE: I love you, too. I guess it just feels good to hear it once in a while.

MALE: Yeah. Now that you mention it, it *does* feel good!

In troubled relationships, the "I love you" phrase may not be enough to convince one's partner he or she is loved. It has become an empty phrase because there have not been enough follow-up behaviors that specifically testify to the declaration of love. Specific behaviors that complement more abstract statements of commitment are always important, but especially so in relationships that are questioning the extent of one's commitment. These "follow-through" acts and all of the dialogue in the preceding examples of "I love you talk" point to the importance of *how* commitment talk is performed. *In fact, the way we enact our commitment talk is at least as important, if not more so, than the content itself.* As we noted with the initiation process, *intensity* has a lot to do with the perceived strength of the commitment talk. This may involve rapt attention and focus achieved through long mutual gazes and close proximity; voice volume ("He just kept yelling 'I love Linda' as we walked down the street. It was embarrassing, but it meant a lot to me"); or absolute statements ("I'll *always* love you," or "I'll *never* leave you"). It is important to note that the intensity of commitment talk may be different for establishing a relationship and maintaining it. The absolute statements may taper off as the length of a relationship increases and there is a more rational endorsement of the tentative nature of life and love in general. The use of absolute statements often appears in the early phases of intensifying as an abundance of superlatives— "You have the *greatest* mind of any woman I've ever met." Although this behavior seems to taper off as the relationship stabilizes at a high level of intimacy, it can recur quickly if it appears there is trouble in the relationship and at least one person wants to save it. This pattern is consistent with the idea put forth earlier that as we move toward intimacy we move on a continuum from rigid to flexible in our communication. This idea, however, also suggests that there are certain critical points within advanced stages of intimacy where rigidity rears its ugly head. Interestingly, the absolutism of the courtship pattern can be very beneficial in cementing the commitment of the two parties. It only becomes a problem if the superlatives and "all-ness" terms are interpreted rigidly and used against the other later—"You said you'd do *anything* I wanted . . . well, I want. . . ."

Repetition is another way of performing commitment talk that has the potential for increasing its impact on the relationship. During the early attempts to reach for more intimacy, couples often repeat their commitment over and over—using virtually the same words each time. The first time a person tells you that he or she loves you, it has strong dramatic import. Commitment continues to take the form of "I love you" until, like any word or phrase, it begins to lose its effectiveness. When

From *The Road to Hell* © 1991 by Matt Groening. All rights reserved. Reprinted by permission of Acme Features Syndicate.

a person begins to say the words *I love you* like a programmed robot, there will probably be a move to show love in new ways by actions or dialogue which say *I love you* in different ways. In short, the constant repetition of this one phrase has diminished reward value, and new forms of proof are often called for. This is why we may be deceived by analyzing conventional statements about closeness in a relationship when we examine people who have been stabilized at a high level of intimacy for a long time. These couples will have many different ways of stating their commitment, and the frequency will no doubt taper off with intimacy sustained by "reminders" of commitment. When the relationship is threatened or when a partner's commitment is questioned and there is a desire to rejuvenate the relationship, frequent repetition of commitment (often in stereotypical forms used earlier to build the relationship) will recur.

Messages of commitment also vary in the extent to which they reflect *effort* by the communicator. Willingness to expend effort for the relationship was discussed earlier in the context of what is said; here we are dealing with *how* it is said (or done). When others feel we are "working" hard at showing our commitment, the strength of the message more likely will be seen as greater. This doesn't mean you will necessarily respond positively to it. It may be an ardent lover you don't love.

Commitment talk may also gain strength from *explicitness*. It is harder to back down from messages for which there can be little misinterpretation. Vagueness and equivocation signal less commitment. Obviously, in long-term relationships, commitment talk may seem less explicit to an outsider, but the participants can read into such statements an explicitness of an earlier time. Sometimes this process even allows some rewriting of history—allowing two people who have decided to live out their remaining years together to mentally recall a past that wasn't there—e.g., "Bill and I have always given each other 110 percent." Explicitness of commitment talk in the presence of others may sometimes be embarrassing, but it also serves as testimony that a person is willing to stand behind you socially as well as personally.

When commitment is *codified*, it has the effect of making it more permanent—it is a lasting relationship symbol. Writing down one's commitment is commonly done in letters and poems. But since the 1970s, many couples have also attempted to formalize the conventional marriage contract. These efforts have taken the form of agreements specifying the division of household responsibilities; rules for sharing income and expenses; expectations for relationships with others outside the marriage; clauses for changing, renewing, and terminating the contract; as well as others. These efforts are attempts to minimize potentially vast differences in expectations between marriage partners and/or to protect one's resources if the relationship should fail. In addition, such specificities make interpretation of the marriage contract easier than was the traditional contract which was couched in such lofty, ambiguous terminology that it was subject to almost any interpretation. Some feel that almost any kind of formalized contract is an admission of one's inability to deal with issues as they arise. For these people, contracts suggest a lack of faith and trust in the relationship itself and the parties to the relationship. They may simply want to live together without any type of contract or legally binding document. Over time, however, an informal, unwritten contract or set of rules may develop even for these people. There are obviously many reasons for these formal prenuptial agreements, but our concern is with the possible rhetorical implications of these contracts.

Any time we make a rule we begin to limit our alternatives for dealing with unexpected or unforeseen circumstances. When we write that rule down, we make it more permanent. When we ask that our rule be made a legally binding document, we have made it even more difficult to adapt to new and changing circumstances. On one hand, this rigidity serves as testimony to the strength of commitment. Simultaneously, however, it adds a permanence—a hardening that may increase the probabilities of maladaptive communication strategies emerging. For instance, sometimes couples feel that the contract signifies ownership. Either explicitly or implicitly, messages may be based upon the fact that the other person "belongs to me"—"You're my wife and you'll do as I tell you." Some feel the contract tends to increase one's laxity in communicating. That is, the energy expended during courtship can now be forgotten, the hunt is over, the quarry has been captured, relaxation is the order of the day. Still others believe that the contract legitimizes intrusion into the other's behavior, thoughts, and feelings to the extent that the other person feels no personal identity or freedom—"Now that we've married I can open all your mail, demand to know where you are every minute," etc. In short, some believe that the existence of a formal relationship contract brings about communication patterns that would never be used in a similar but contract-free relationship. The fact is, however, that nobody knows if this belief is true. There is no research that specifically indicates the prevalence of certain communication patterns in contract relationships that do not exist in contract-free relationships. Indeed, the existence of the contract probably does influence the way the participants talk to each other, but exactly how much influence and what form that influence takes are yet to be determined. There is certainly a reasonable possibility that there are maladaptive patterns which stem from formal contracts; obviously, other equally maladaptive patterns may arise out of relationships without contracts. The value of some formal contracts for explicitly revealing intentions and expectations, for announcing the mutual commitment to one another, and for fusing the relationship forms a positive base for communicating.

If a person wanted to know how to more effectively communicate his or her commitment, we would suggest the following. The absence of or opposite of these may also mean commitment is not being effectively communicated:

1. Repeat your commitment over and over in different ways. (Follow "I love you" talk with specific acts that prove it.)
2. Use unqualified, absolute statements.
3. Talk about future relationship rewards.
4. Make public statements of your commitment to the relationship.
5. Make your statements of commitment to the relationship more permanent— e.g., in writing.

6. Do things that show effort—that you've gone to a lot of trouble.

7. Initiate at least as much as you respond—showing you don't always wait for the other person to express his or her commitment first.

Personal Idioms

Intimates have some unique speech patterns that distinguish them from nonintimates. Intimates normally have a greater sociological, psychological, and communicative history to their talk. Sometimes, then, they can present a great deal of information in a very few words. The following quote expresses the issue of simplification quite well:

> . . . the speech of intimates is played out against the backdrop of assumptions common to the speakers, against a set of closely shared interests and identifications, against a system of shared expectations; in short, it presupposes a "local cultural identity" which reduces the need for the speakers to elaborate their intent verbally and to make it explicit.[6]

As a result of their relationship history, intimates often develop an interpersonal jargon with private symbols and private meanings, known only to the intimate pair. In addition, they develop words and phrases commonly used by others that have special meanings for them. In such cases, intimates can refer to things in a public gathering that most people interpret one way but that the intimates interpret another—perhaps exchanging a knowing glance or wink to confirm the "special" interpretation. Galvin and Brommel provide this exemplary testimony from one of their informants.

> My sister and I have a long history of intimacy. Since early childhood, we have shared unique communication behavior. Our intimate namecalling is truly unique. Gail refers to me as "Sis," "K. C.," or "Coops." I, in return, call her "Kitten," "G. K.," or "Li'l Coops." As a result of doing many activities together, we acquired the duplex nickname of "The Coop Sisters." Occasionally, my mother refers to me by the name Loree. This is my middle name and the name of her grandmother whom she loved deeply. She is the only one who calls me this. "G. K." and I have always shared some type of personal jargon. This ritual began with our secret language of "witchtalk." "Witchtalk" meant saying the exact opposite of what one really meant. Now, in our current jargon, a romantic relationship is "official" only if one has been kissed by the male and "the bone" refers to a male who is sexually exciting. We also share a peculiar handshake which can be interpreted as meaning "I agree with you 100 percent" or "I can identify with you."[7]

These "personal idioms" serve at least two useful functions for the intimates. First, they serve to make the pair a more cohesive unit—to reinforce the identity of the couple as something special or unique. This special language sets them off from those who "don't know the language." The private jargon developed by less intimate groups like fraternal organizations, prisoners, and soldiers also supports group cohesiveness. Second, personal idioms help a couple define relationship norms. There are many issues that intimates need to address—e.g., how shall we refer to sex, sexual organs, things we don't like about each other, affectionate feelings, etc.? Sometimes personal idioms are an effective substitute for more direct, explicit terminology.

Our interest in these personal idioms prompted us to conduct two studies.[8] In the conduct of these studies, we collected 545 idioms from couples ranging in age from 20 to 76. The personal idioms reported to us were classified into the following categories:

1. **Expressions of Affection.** These phrases expressed love, reassured, or complimented one's partner. "So Much" and "Hunch Nickle" as well as pulling on the right ear lobe were all idioms reported to mean, "I love you."

2. **Teasing Insults.** This category combines playfulness and derogation—usually through the tactic of "kidding." "Futtbutt" which referred to a woman's buttocks and "Animal" which was used to refer to unduly aggressive behavior are examples. Perhaps the act of making a partner's idiosyncrasy the subject of everyday teasing comments or gestures is a way to tell the partner the behavior is bothersome without threatening the equilibrium of the relationship.

3. **Partner Nicknames.** These terms of address included such names as "Boo," "Honski," "Bake," "Tooty," and "Mopsy."

4. **Names for Others.** These were names used for people outside the relationship. For example, "Pizza King" was the label given to a next-door neighbor's lover; "Mr. Finch" designated a person trying to compensate for small size; and "Motz" was a slow, disorganized person.

5. **Requests and Routines.** Sometimes it was necessary for the couple to communicate something in front of others without actually saying it. Thus, "What's new?" was interpreted by one couple as "I'm bored and ready to leave"; for another couple, "Let's go for a bike ride" meant "Let's go outside and smoke some dope." Sometimes these routines were within the confines of the relationship. "Week Thursday," for instance, meant "I'll attend to it at my convenience."

6. **Confrontations.** These idioms, like the Teasing Insults, showed displeasure or criticism of the partner's behavior but the teasing or playful element of the former category was absent. "Jelly Beans" was a brief way to say, "You're talking over my head and I don't understand you"; "Pulling a Mrs. Oswald" indicated "You've

made lukewarm soup again." Twisting one's wedding ring was a nonverbal command to the partner: "Don't you dare do (or say) that."

7. Sexual Invitations. Ways of proposing sexual intercourse included such phrases as "Let's go home and watch some TV" and "Aren't you getting awfully hot?"

8. Sexual References and Euphemisms. These idioms referred to male genitals ("Bozo," "Bodacious"), female genitals ("Wuzzer"), or sexual intercourse ("Boogie-Woogie").

Does the use of personal idioms contribute to a couple's satisfaction or closeness? Two studies indicate this may occur, but certain types of idioms are probably less related to satisfying relationships than others.[9] Requests, teasing insults, and confrontations, for example, seem to be less related to intimacy.

Sometimes friends and romantic partners will use the speech register we more frequently associate with parents talking to their infants—that is, parentese or babytalk. Personal idioms commonly occur as a part of this speech pattern as in these examples. You'll have to supply the vocal intonation:

> "Hewo, I wuv you, Jellybean."
> "Oh, Punkin, are you okay?"
> "I'm sorryyy. Please forgive meee. I looove you."
> "Awww, is my lil' Jer-Bear not feeling well?"

Babytalk among friends and romantic partners is more likely used to express affection or to signal playfulness. Even though babytalk can be used sarcastically or to create distance, it's primary function seems to be the establishment and maintenance of emotional closeness.[10]

The use of personal idioms is likely to decline as the length of the relationship increases. Their frequency and impact on the relationship seem most powerful at the early stages of a developing relationship. They can, of course, have a powerfully negative impact when used with a partner who is trying to reduce or eliminate any signals which would suggest closeness and intimacy. Idioms tend to develop and receive use during the period when people want to emphasize commitment to the relationship the most—from serious dating through about the first three years of cohabitation or marriage. When personal idioms are no longer used, it may be due to one or more of these reasons: (1) situational changes—e.g., an idiom that mimicked one partner's mother was dropped when the mother died; (2) stated displeasure with the idiom by a partner; (3) relationship changes—e.g., feeling the relationship is "cemented" or feeling that matters previously represented by an idiom can be addressed more directly; (4) need changes—e.g., the couple no longer feels the need to communicate the information represented by the idiom; or (5) the need for variety—e.g., the idiom simply became tiresome or was replaced by another one.

The idioms develop in a variety of ways. Sometimes they are derived from slurred words, baby talk, etc. One respondent said, "In college we used to say 'peat-heart' which later became 'peep' and is now 'peepee.' " Personal characteristics can be a source for idioms such as the woman who complained too often about how fat her butt was and gained the name "Futtbutt." Idioms also come from pleasantly memorable events, songs, or books. For instance, one person said, "I saw one character in a Peanuts comic strip call another his 'sweet little Baboo' and I liked it." Another source includes people previously known by one or both partner prior to the couple's relationship. As one person reported, "Motz is an old neighborhood character out of my childhood who hung out at the local candy store. He was a funny guy who was very slow and kind of dumb." Many personal idioms arise out of the need to remedy a situation or solve a problem—whether it is deciding what to call sexual organs or how to ask the other person if they're ready to leave a party without being rude to the host.

The expression of ideas in a "different way"—whether it is through the use of personal idioms or some other way—is perhaps the most evident difference in speech patterns between intimates and nonintimates. In fact, close friends or intimates sometimes look upon these highly personalized verbal exchange patterns as private possessions. Hence, it can be disturbing to hear (or hear about) a close friend or intimate talking in a similar manner with another of his or her friends. Goffman says this is particularly true if the intimate does not know the other friend.[11]

Giving Compliments and Gifts

One person told us that her husband gives her at least one compliment a day. They have been married over thirty-five years. Even if we assume this couple's experience is unusual, it raises the question of whether complimenting is a speech act that has the ability to serve important maintenance functions in close relationships. After all, compliments tell others what we value, and that, in turn, provides a guide for what might make us happy. But compliments, like criticism, can be threatening. They are an evaluation of another person. You may say you like how I do the dishes. This may not be something I want to be complimented on or wish to become the family expert on, lest I be the person stuck with the job forever. And we know people sometimes use compliments manipulatively so we sometimes maintain a healthy distrust of compliments—especially with those whom we suspect have something to gain from us.

We conducted several studies of the compliments people give and found that more than half of the nearly 1000 compliments we examined were directed at friends, relatives, and lovers.[12] We not only give more to those we feel close to, but over 75 percent of the givers and receivers reported positive feelings from the act. Although complimenters acknowledged that compliments can be used manipulatively and as part of "meaningless" politeness routines, over two-thirds of the compliments we collected were said to be deserved or earned. What things seem to get complimented most? Appearance, attire, and performance (which may include work, play, verbal, or activities related to domestic skills). The most meaningful compliments, however, focused on the whole person or the person's personality—e.g., "Your courage was what first attracted me to you."

As long as the compliment is perceived as sincere and addresses something valued by the receiver, it may go a long way toward maintaining intimacy. In fact, some couples spend a lot of time complimenting themselves on maintaining a good relationship—e.g., "We sure are a good team." In this way both partners are rewarded for their efforts directed toward maintaining the relationship.

Like compliments, the giving of gifts is a way of periodically making a statement about the relationship. The gift statement, like other statements designed to maintain the relationship at a desired level of intimacy, may be effectively or ineffectively performed.

When gifts are given can be a crucial determinant of their impact on the relationship. There are times when gifts are normally expected, such as Christmas and birthdays. *Not* giving a gift on these occasions is potentially a strong negative statement about the relationship. Still, some couples may establish their own norms which do not sanction the absence of gift-giving on traditional gift-giving occasions. Giving a gift to a person you feel close to when it is not expected is like getting an unexpected compliment. It has the potential to communicate a special concern for the relationship, because there was no obligatory day of perceived celebration which precipitated it. Yet sometimes the obligatory occasion is generated by the relationship and gifts are used to "make up" after an unpleasant fight or to lift the spirits of a partner who feels "down." In such cases, the gift carries the message that the giver wants to restore the feelings of closeness between them. Earlier in this chapter we noted that the overuse of the phrase "I love you" could drain it of its value as a statement of intimacy. The person who gives gifts so often that they no longer seem "special" runs a similar risk. Needless to say, showering too many gifts on a loved one is not in the top 1000 concerns for most couples.

The gift-giver is faced with a number of decisions about the nature of the gift and the process of giving it which affect the way it is received. What makes a good gift? The general answer is that it should be tailored to the needs and desires of the recipient while, at the same time, serving as a relationship statement. This could mean that a husband could give his wife, the ardent gardener, a shovel for her birthday and have it well received. For this to happen, however, the wife must be desirous of the shovel and perceive such a gift as thoughtful and caring commentary on their relationship. The danger, of course, is that the gift is received as "impersonal" and symbolic of the husband's desire to encourage more work on the part of his wife. Besides, buying things in another person's area of expertise runs the risk of presuming you know what they, the experts, need. When partners are choosy about gifts in the area they feel particularly skilled, it is wise to set clear expectations for the giver's behavior or to graciously accept what is given.

Gift-givers sometimes act as if they are tailoring the gift to the interests of the other person, but on closer examination, the gift is also given to the giver as well—e.g., a husband who gives his wife a sexy "teddy" for her birthday. As long as the wife sees this as a statement of relational closeness, the shared nature of the gift will not be a concern. Anniversaries are occasions when gifts are often expected to have a shared nature to them—e.g., a trip to a place where something important to the relationship happened or an audio tape of songs which recall special times in the history of the relationship. Like any statement about the relationship, the best gifts reflect effort and involvement on the part of the giver and are devoid of any perceived obligations attached to them.

During the process of giving and receiving gifts, couples will negotiate their own norms. When one person responds unenthusiatically to a gift and thus hurts the feelings of the giver enough to withdraw from future gift-giving, the demand for discussing personal norms is strong. Subsequent to forgetting a gift-giving occasion, a couple may agree that it is appropriate for forecasts to be given (e.g., "My birthday is next Friday"), while another couple may find this detracts from the positive impact of gift-giving (e.g., "You only give me gifts because I tell you to"). One couple may treat Valentine's Day as an occasion for intense celebration; another may agree to "skip" Valentine's Day because it is not unique to their relationship. When gifts are exchanged, there will inevitably be differences in cost, effort, number, etc. Over time, couples may agree on the acceptable ratio—for example, "We always spend about the same on each other" or "You'll always spend three times more on me than I will on you." The process of negotiating these norms, and the relative pleasure or displeasure associated with the giving and receiving of the gifts, is a good example of the concept of relationship maintenance.

Giving Comfort

Life does not always go smoothly. Each partner to a close relationship experiences his or her share of emotional distress. Sources of hurt may be external to the relationship or centered within it. Generally, this not-uncommon pain is caused by failing at something integral to one's self-concept or being rejected by someone who is valued. Those who share a close relationship expect their partner to help them through these periods of stress through the adroit use of comforting messages.[13] In fact, we can reasonably expect that a couple's skill with comforting messages is a crucial barometer of intimacy, and each partner's ability to manage this style of communication will have a lot to do with how the relationship is maintained.

When the need for comfort has been determined and the helper is committed to providing comfort, it is important to find an environment conducive to comforting, to initiate the comforting when the recipient is ready, and to adapt the messages to the history and capabilities of the person as well as the nature of the hurt. At a minimum, the comforter's behavior should be focused on lessening or alleviating the other's unpleasant feelings. If, in the process, the comforter is also able to get the person to better understand what happened to them and pursue ways of feeling better, optimum results will be achieved.

Because people in close relationships have developed expectations for the way their partner communicates and because these people may be willing to accept communication behavior from their partner that they wouldn't accept from most people, it is hard to pinpoint the "ideal" comforting strategy for intimates. We can, however, identify those patterns which have been useful for a wide range of people with varying levels of intimacy. These involve: (1) talk about feelings; (2) talk about the value of the person being helped; and (3) signals which underscore the authenticity of the helper's responses.

The success or failure of comforting behavior often hinges on whether and how the helper talks about feelings. To ignore, dismiss as somehow uncalled for, or even to condemn the feelings of the injured person is, as a rule, problematic. Nevertheless, these responses are not uncommon. Consider the effect of the following efforts at comforting:

> "You shouldn't be so upset about what he said to you."
>
>   or
>
> "Hey, don't take it so hard. These things happen. It's no big deal."

At a minimum, people like to have their feelings recognized and accepted. Sometimes that is sufficient in itself. For example:

> "I'm sorry you don't feel good. I'd feel the same way. It's ok. (Hug) Go ahead and cry."

Sometimes the recognition and acceptance of the other's feelings serve as a prelude to a more extended interaction which is designed to accomplish other goals—namely, reinforcing the value of the other and the sincere involvement of the helper. For example:

> "I know it must hurt . . . and you have a right to be angry. He had no business talking to you that way. You've always been a class act—never saying anything bad about him and this is the gratitude he shows! I love you very much and I'm

Reprinted with special permission of North America Syndicate.

in this thing with you. If you want to look for another job, I'll help you. You need to work in a place that appreciates you."

In the preceding example, the comforter indicates acknowledgment and acceptance of the person's feelings, but goes on to explore the reasons for the hurt and the inherent goodness of the person. Exploring the reasons for the hurt may lead to an interaction which will help the distressed person gain insight and understanding about what happened. Effective comforting is often characterized by the comforter's ability to establish conditions favorable to effective coping and problem-solving by the person who feels the hurt. The need to emphasize the value of the distressed person stems from the fact that they may be questioning their own worth, and that is why they feel distressed. Another important feature of the last example is its attempt to show that the helper is thoroughly involved and that his or her responses are genuine—not just "going through the motions" of helping. The helper expresses commitment to the relationship by proposing a shared course of action and by condemning the person who made the injurious remarks. The condemnation of the person making the injurious remarks serves a useful purpose, but it may be perceived as somewhat presumptuous by the injured person. After all, the comforter was not the person who was mistreated. As a result, it is not uncommon for the distressed person to argue with the comforter about how evil the source of pain is and even go so far as to defend it. What is important for the comforter in a close relationship, though, is to make sure he or she is clearly aligned with their partner—communicating the message that anyone who hurts the partner is, in essence, hurting both. Once that is established, there is no need to further berate the person who caused the hurt unless the partner encourages it.

Persuasion

We don't always like to think of ourselves as a person who tries to "change" our partner, but, like it or not, people in close relationships are constantly trying to influence the thoughts, feelings, and actions of their partners. It is the stuff and substance of negotiating a relationship. Whenever we ask for something, give advice, criticize, or complain, we have entered a persuasive environment. What are the typical areas of intended influence in close relationships? In one study, people in close relationships identified six primary persuasive goals:

1. giving advice about your partner's lifestyle ("Tell your father we don't want his money");
2. giving advice about your partner's health ("You've got to stop smoking");
3. recommending a change in the relationship ("Let's spend some time apart");
4. requesting a change in your partner's political stance ("If you vote for him, you're voting to give away more of the money we make");
5. asking your partner to share an activity ("I wish you'd jog with me"); and
6. asking your partner for help ("I wish you'd help me clean this place on Saturdays").[14]

With these goals in mind, how do people in close relationships actually go about trying to influence their partners? What strategies do they use? There is no shortage of information about persuasive strategies and processes.[15] Table 9.1, for example, highlights a variety of approaches available to men and women trying to maintain relationships through persuasion.[16]

In close relationships, both men and women use a variety of persuasive strategies but there can be dramatic differences in the behavior of men and women in abusive relationships. Battered and abused women, for example, try to cope with a relationship in which they have little power and control by using persuasive techniques designed to seek more power and control. Although women in non-abusive relationships try, at times, to seek power too, it is done within a relationship in which power and control do not seem permanently imbalanced—and that makes a difference. Battered women will sometimes use more indirect tactics like ingratiation, promises, alluring and deceptive behavior, and sometimes they seek power by using aggressive strategies such as threats and warnings. Women whose husbands do not batter them are more likely to hint, disagree, and discuss issues—strategies which rely on assumptions of shared power and shared perspectives in the relationship.[17]

Even though we have much to learn about persuasion in close relationships, it is reasonable to expect that the degree of intimacy or closeness itself will play a role in the enactment of persuasive strategies. For example, persuasion theory tells us it is crucial to establish trust in order to increase the possibilities of accomplishing persuasive goals. Trust, as it happens, also accompanies increased feelings of intimacy. With this in mind, the strategy designated as "Ask" in Table 9.1 would seem

TABLE 9.1 **Persuasive Strategies Used to Get Cooperation**	
Strategy	*Description*
Ask	Without giving any particular reasons, simply ask your partner for cooperation
Present Information	Present facts or evidence in support of your appeal
Mention Personal Benefits	Show how one or both of you would benefit
Mention Benefits to Others	Show your partner how his or her cooperation will benefit others
Butter Up	Make your partner feel important/wonderful
Mention Relationship	Use the relationship as a reason for cooperating—e.g., "As my best friend, I hope you'll do this for me"
Bargain with Favor	Offer to do a favor in exchange for cooperation
Bargain with Object	Offer your partner a highly desired physical object or money
Mention Similar Behavior	Tell you partner about others who have done or would do the same thing
Make Moral Appeal	Appeal to a moral value—e.g., "It's the right thing to do"
Emotional Appeal	Cry, beg, throw a tantrum, sulk, or use some other emotional display
Criticize	Attack your partner on a personal level, trying to make them feel personally inadequate
Deceive	Mislead your partner
Threaten	Inform your partner of the negative things that will result from not cooperating
Force	Physically assault your partner or use some other means of force

well suited to those who feel greater closeness in their relationship. Elaborate and lengthy justifications, explanations, and inducements do not seem to capture the essence of persuasion between intimates. We might also expect that greater intimacy would carry with it the expectation that partners would perceive more obligations to *grant* resources and wishes to their partner. Similarly, there may be a greater felt obligation among intimates to *offer* resources to their partner without any request being made.[18] If this is true, increasing intimacy means an increasing expectation that your partner will attend to at least some of your needs without enactment of overt persuasion. All these assumptions about what intimates expect and will do also suggest that if expected behavior is not forthcoming, it will trigger an influence attempt in the form of a complaint or criticism.[19] Different degrees of intimacy or closeness also accentuate the role of mutual goals as a part of the persuasive goals of a single partner. The greater the intimacy and interdependency, the greater the difficulty in distinguishing between the persuasive efforts and outcomes of an individual and a couple. For intimates, the specter of the relationship is never far from any effort on the part of one partner to influence the other.

The process of building a close relationship also means a growing familiarity with the expected responses of one's partner. This knowledge provides a foundation for the design of persuasive messages. Sometimes the unique characteristics and responses of one's partner in an intimate relationship may prompt the use of strategies which are not well understood by outsiders. Familiarity with one's partner will also give valuable information about what language to use and avoid, what is the best and worst timing for persuasive attempts, what topics are more subject to change and what topics aren't, what responses signal that it is best to "back off" and what responses signal receptivity, and so on. This is not to suggest that familiarity provides a foolproof basis for predicting which strategies are going to work. It does suggest that the familiarity gained in long-term, intimate relationships is an important factor in determining the selection of persuasive strategies.

Because relationship partners typically spend more time with each other in closer proximity as intimacy increases, this will also affect the manner in which persuasion unfolds in those relationships. As proximity increases, relationship partners will have opportunities to use multiple strategies, change strategies that don't work, return to an issue at another time, bring up the subject in a different context (e.g., when friends or relatives are present), revisit an issue which was not initially resisted but upon reflection needs to be, repeat a persuasive message over and over to a captive audience, and so on. In short, proximity will exert its own influence on how people in developing relationships influence each other.

> *More than anything else, women want you to make them laugh.*
>
> Anonymous

The effectiveness of persuasive strategies used during the maintenance of close relationships will depend on a variety of factors. As we have noted, persuaders in this context have several potential advantages: (1) audience familiarity; (2) repeated opportunities to accomplish their goals; (3) the trust implicit in close relationships; and (4) the obligations to cooperate associated with building intimacy. Of course, all these factors can backfire as well. This can occur when the persuader uses strategies which are perceived by his or her partner as a lack of audience familiarity—e.g., "You know I can't stand it when you use that word!"; when the repeated opportunities for persuasion are abused—e.g., "You keep hammering on the same thing and I'm sick of it!"; when the persuader is perceived as taking advantage of the trust and/or obligations inherent in the relationship. No matter what you are trying to accomplish through persuasion, it is important for your partner to feel that you have an overriding concern for the relationship; that your individual goals are, in some way, linked to your mutual relationship goals; that you are not too frequently putting the importance of your personal goals above the importance of your partner; that you have specific ideas about how your goals can be accomplished and what each of you can contribute in order for them to come about; and that you are not interested in short-term goals at the expense of long-term relationship damage (e.g., using threats, emotional blackmail, or excessive negativity). The beauty and wonder of close relationships, though, is that "ineffective" strategies often become an integral and understood part of the dialogue—e.g., "Oh yeah, Mildred screamed and yelled and told me she was moving out tomorrow if I didn't change. And I will make some changes. But she does that almost every time she wants me to do something. We're very much in love. She's been doing this for fifteen years."

Sex Talk

We talk *about* sex with acquaintances, friends, and romantic partners. In addition, romantic partners negotiate ways of *initiating*, *accepting*, and *refusing* sexual intercourse. They must also negotiate the appropriate type of talk (if any) *during* sexual intercourse. All these types of sex talk can have profound effects on the relationship. Similarly, ineffective relationship talk can profoundly affect a couple's sexual behavior.[20]

Like other areas requiring relationship maintenance, problems can arise from too much or too little talk. When a person is described as "preoccupied with sex" because his or her conversations are so often filled with sex-related information or when a person won't talk about sexual matters when the topic is appropriate, these communicative orientations are likely to require modification for effective relationship maintenance. Sexual topics include such things as: discussing one's body parts; sexual preferences; sexual experiences; sexual fantasies; safe sex; sexual responsiveness; and sexual receptiveness. During sex, talk may focus on what feels good and not so good; what you want your partner to do or not do; and what verbal and/or nonverbal behavior will increase or decrease arousal.

Most research seems to suggest that during the early stages of relationships, men initiate sexual intercourse and women play the role of accepting or refusing.[21] As the length of a romantic heterosexual relationship increases, the couples will develop a more complex initiation pattern suited to the particularized culture they develop. This may or may not involve more initiation efforts on the part of the woman. We also know that the frequency of sexual intercourse as a marker of intimacy decreases as the relationship establishes itself as an intimate one. Like other types of communication we have discussed, quantity gradually gives way to quality in long-term relationships. In troubled relationships, however, one or both part-ners may want to increase the frequency of sexual behavior in order to reestablish closeness.

The question of how people go about initiating and responding to sex has re-ceived some attention.[22] We know it is a mistake to assume it will "happen natu-rally" all the time, because so many people report problems in accomplishing this act. Some of these problems are related to making difficult distinctions between affectionate behavior and sexual behavior. They may be separate activities or one and the same. Sometimes the intensity associated with touching, kissing, hug-ging, and so on, will effectively distinguish the two; sometimes it is the time avail-able; and sometimes it is necessary to clarify potentially ambiguous nonverbal cues with verbal behavior—e.g., "I just want to hug." Sometimes the misinterpretation of signals is not related to misperceiving affection and sex but to the misperception of sexual signals. There are many reasons why we communicate ambiguously and indirectly when we initiate and respond to requests for sex. While serving some im-portant purposes, this also increases the possibilities for misinterpretation. For ex-ample, sexual invitations may begin with various kinds of nonverbal posturing or sexual innuendo. This approach makes one's interest in sex a possible topic for dis-cussion but does not formally make a proposal for sex.[23] If the target of these "in-terest" signals responds with similar signals of interest, this provides a context for increasing the clarity of the sexual invitation, if, indeed, that is the intended goal. If interest signals are not reciprocated, this keeps both parties from having to face the possible difficulties involved in a direct and unambiguous rejection. Temporary or "incomplete" rejections are also subject to misinterpretation—e.g., "I don't want to ruin our relationship right now by having sex. I want it to be the right person and the right time and I've got to figure all this out." This response can also be an effective "test" in that a person who wants a long-term relationship and might qual-ify as the "right" person would not persist in requesting sex at this time. Dating and married couples also gravitate toward ambiguous messages because they don't want to "ruin the mood" or "hurt feelings." "Having a headache" became so famil-iar as a way of politely saying "no" to sex that it is now a cultural stereotype.

Sometimes a person is not sure whether he or she wants to engage in sex and these mixed messages confuse the partner.[24] In a study that asked women if they had ever said no to a request for sex but meant yes, 39 percent of 610 college women said they had.[25] Most said they had only a few times responded in this way. These women reported offering token resistance because they didn't want to be labeled loose or promiscuous; because they were afraid of a sexually transmitted disease; because it was against their beliefs; and because they were angry with their part-ner—e.g., "I wanted him to beg because I was angry with him." Women also re-ported agreeing to have sex when they didn't really want to. Contrary to those who believe men want to have sex at any time under any circumstances, psychologists at Penn State University found that men, too, give token resistance (saying "no" and meaning "yes") and token compliance (saying "yes" and meaning "no") at about the same frequency as reported by the college women. Lest these findings be misunderstood, it should be noted that predominantly, a "no" means "no" and should be taken as such. On the other hand, we have to acknowledge that some "mixed signals" can occur; these may create problems in understanding one another's intentions. Additional talk or less ambiguous talk should be helpful in clarifying these responses. In heterosexual negotiations about sexual activity, it is not uncommon for both males and females to contribute to the resulting misinterpretations. In trying to resist an invitation for sex, women may not always be direct. For example:

Direct:	"Please don't do that."
	"I don't want to do this."
Less Direct:	"I don't think I know you well enough for this."
	"I can't do this unless you are committed to me."
Indirect:	"It's getting late."
	"I'm seeing someone else."

The less direct the woman's message, the greater the likelihood the man will not understand it as communicating resistance. For example, 38 percent of the men who judged the resistance statement, "I don't think I know you well enough for this" said it meant "She wants to go further, but wants me to know that she usually only does this with people she has known longer." Thirty-five per cent of the men responding to the statement, "I'm seeing someone else" thought it meant, "She might want to go further, but wants me to be discreet, so that the other guy doesn't find out." Women say they use less direct and indirect strategies for communicating resistance because they are worried about offending, hurting, or angering the man. While such concerns are worth considering, they should not override making one's intentions clear.[26]

Most of the research targeted at identifying specific signals or strategies associated with the initiation of sex and the response to these initiations has not examined the sequential development of the process.[27] Instead, various verbal and nonverbal signals are listed. For example, various kinds of intimate touching, pressing bodies together so they touch at as many places as possible, kissing "deeply" or on many body parts, and looking at the other person in a sexy manner, are all mentioned as common nonverbal signals. Verbal signals may vary in directness and include such comments as: "I'd like to be alone with you," "You sure look sexy in that outfit," "Let's make love." As noted in the section on personal idioms, intimate couples often have unique phrases for verbally signaling a desire for sex. There are so many factors that help define the situation as sexual for long-term intimates that the repertoire of initiating behaviors may not be as large as they exhibited at earlier relationship stages. Mutuality of action in close relationships may even make the idea of initiation and response inappropriate. For example, who is the initiator when one person in a close relationship indicates a "readiness" for sex which, in turn, prompts the other partner to initiate it? Also, consider the couple who gets in the habit of having sex Saturday and Sunday mornings after they wake up. In this context, initiation and acceptance/rejection behaviors look very different. In addition, couples who share a bedroom and bathroom area also have a situation that offers opportunities for seeing the other person in a very private way, which may also increase the chances of sexual behavior at times when both partners are in this area. Sexual communication involves signals emanating from the partners (e.g., grooming/dress, touching, talking, etc.); signals emanating from the environment (e.g., privacy, bad weather outside, quiet, dark, etc.); timing (e.g., choosing the right moment; time since last sexual intercourse); and individual factors (e.g., how relaxed and spontaneous each feels and the role of one's olfactory, visual, and tactile senses, etc.). When one's partner is also ready for sexual behavior, a good indicator is the extent to which the initiation behavior is reciprocated or at least countered with an act of equal intimacy. The lack of reciprocation, acting interested in something else, being "too tired" and verbally indicating "no" are common ways to decline sex.

Like other messages that can be associated with intimacy, sex has many meanings. It may be a way to communicate love, pleasure, dominance, relief of frustration or loneliness, or revenge. It may also have different meanings at different stages of a relationship. Saying you "enjoy sex" during the early years of a long-term relationship may indeed mean you enjoy the sex itself; after thirty years of sex with the same partner, saying you "enjoy sex" may simply mean you enjoy being close to your partner. If sex is going to be an act that effectively maintains an intimate relationship, each partner needs to be committed to negotiating an effective way of initiation, acceptance, and rejection of signals related to sex. Each must also make an effort to infuse these overtures, the sexual act itself, and the afterplay with the meaning that most closely fits the desired relationship definition. Couples would also be well advised to spend more time talking with each other about each other's particular sexual thoughts, emotions, and behavior rather than relying on the many stereotypes of men and women in general, which may or may not be accurate for any individual.

Intimate Play

Play is a form of behavior that can be extremely important to the maintenance of the relationship as a whole. In one study, playfulness was found to be a strong correlate of relationship closeness in same-sex friendships and in opposite-sex romantic relationships.[28] Some of the personal idioms discussed earlier were specifically designed for play. Play is a type of behavior that can provide a source of mutual pleasure and can help maintain the equilibrium of a relationship. Tensions inevitably build up, and play behavior can redirect these energies toward activity that is for the mutual enjoyment of the partners without conscious planning by the partners. It is not uncommon for couples to report play behavior with their partner prior to sex. Even the tensions created during safe-sex and condom-use talk are sometimes alleviated through various forms of play, such as children's games, parody, and sexual teasing.[29] "Trying to have fun" together does not qualify as intimate play because the ambiguity of whether this is play or something more serious has been removed—and the benefits of play with it. Play is also a way to express thoughts that would normally be suppressed.[30] As such, it becomes an effective problem-solving activity. It can also serve as a source of arousal when the relationship is in need of such stimulation. Play is not likely to occur if more basic relationship needs are not met.

As important as play can be, it is infrequently flagged as "play" behavior. Instead, invitations to play involve abrupt topic changes, exaggerating or expanding normal behavior, outrageous or put-on behavior, invitations to engage in some playful activity, and nonverbal cues that indirectly suggest that the current activity is being dropped in favor of something less serious. Sometimes one partner will play *for* his or her partner (the other is a willing audience member); sometimes one partner will play *with* the partner (both are willing participants in play); and sometimes only one partner is willing to play—a situation that involves playing *at* one's partner.[31] The latter case is not likely to reap the same benefits of play derived from the first two for the relationship.

Intimacy Without Words

The language of intimacy does not hinge entirely on the spoken word, as the following example vividly points out:

> On the screen, a man and woman who are about to become lovers often follow this scenario: (1) they are talking to each other about matters external to their relationship; (2) they suddenly catch and hold each other's glance; (3) their involvement drains from their talk; (4) one says something like, "I think I'm in love with you," though this step may be omitted; (5) they lapse into silence; (6) while their eye-to-eye contact continues, they gradually move closer together (7) they touch, embrace, and kiss (while turning off eye contact by closing their eyes in order to sharpen their reception of close—more intimate—communication by tuning out distant distractions). The scene dissolves, though in recent films it continues somewhat longer while the couple rotate to

a horizontal position in which they carry on their kinesic conversation somewhat further. In either case, the audience is expected to assume that, in the in-
finitesimal interval before the next scene, their relationship has spurted to a
higher level, for we next see them engaging in such hard-core intimate communication as holding hands during a romp through the woods.[32]

The potential impact of nonverbal messages in relationships with a long history is probably stronger than in short-term relationships because the participants
know the language better. Couples who are low in marital satisfaction typically
misunderstand each other's nonverbal signals more (although the husband is by far
the least accurate); look at each other more than do satisfied couples—particularly
when negative messages are involved; look more while speaking than do partners
in satisfied marriages; and see negative nonverbal signals as more intentional, controllable, and stable than do satisfied couples. In any close relationship, the negative nonverbal signals are more likely to draw attention and demand explanation.[33]

Sometimes our reliance on multiple sensory input for our interpersonal messages can be a barrier when we are forced to reduce the input channels—the long-
distance telephone call (where vocal cues are the sole nonverbal input) may prompt
one intimate to query, "Are you OK? Is anything wrong?" As we suggested earlier in
this book, strangers and acquaintances will rely much more on widely understood,
stereotyped, and precisely coded messages—words, emblematic and illustrative
gestures,[34] and the most conventional facial expressions. Intimacy is brought about
by, and brings about, the use of a broader spectrum of nonverbal messages.

Since the nonverbal messages in intimate relationships become less stereotyped, it becomes more difficult to generalize about what nonverbal behavior in
such relationships might be like. We can, however, assume that two people who feel
they have an intimate relationship will exhibit indices of affection more often.
Thus, we can outline some common nonverbal behaviors associated with greater
liking, warmth, or affection, and predict that they will occur more frequently in intimate relationships. With each of the nonverbal behaviors discussed in the following paragraphs, it is evident that the behaviors themselves fit the terminology
commonly used to describe intimate situations—private, personal, proximate, permeable. This is logical, for if intimacy is the "closest" type of relationship, its nonverbal manifestations should psychologically or physically reflect closeness and
efforts to reduce separating distances. One qualification is in order. In Chapter 7
Rubin's conceptualization of the term *liking* was reported. You will recall that he
designated two dimensions: affection and respect. Certainly if one likes another
only on the respect dimension, some of the behaviors we are about to mention
would be modified, absent, or totally reversed—we expect less touching directed at
a person we respect but do not feel any affection for.

Touching is an act that reduces physical distance of the parts touched to zero;
naturally, we would expect more touching, longer touches, and touching in a

greater number of places among intimates. The type of touch employed in intimate relationships is also different from that used in more superficial relationships; it generally includes more stroking and caressing than patting. Obviously, touching one another plays an integral role in the behaviors characteristic of intimate relationships—giving encouragement, expressing tenderness, showing emotional support, aiding in grooming (combing hair; adjusting clothes), replacing a long verbalization. Intimates show more permeability on the verbal level which is manifested by self disclosures; they also manifest permeability on the nonverbal level by allowing their partners access to body parts unavailable to nonintimates. One common exception to this norm involves the kiss on the lips. Ordinarily, such a kiss would be limited to intimates or those with whom we would like greater intimacy, but social-polite kisses can also be observed between new acquaintances—a TV talk show host giving a "peck" to contestants. Some feel that sexual touching is the highest form of human intimacy; interestingly, however, others find it easier to give access to their body than to give access to their feelings—"Sure I went to bed with her, but I didn't tell her I loved her. We hardly said anything."

Morris believes that heterosexual couples in Western cultures normally go through a sequence of steps—like courtship patterns of other animals—on the road to sexual intimacy.[35] Notice that each step, aside from the first three, involves some kind of touching: (1) eye to body; (2) eye to eye; (3) voice to voice; (4) hand to hand; (5) arm to shoulder; (6) arm to waist; (7) mouth to mouth; (8) hand to head; (9) hand to body; (10) mouth to breast; (11) hand to genitals; (12) genitals to genitals and/or mouth to genitals. Morris feels that these steps generally follow the same order, although he admits there are variations. One form of skipping steps, or moving to a level of intimacy beyond what would be expected, is found in socially formalized types of bodily contact—the goodnight kiss or the hand-to-hand introduction.

> *. . . Mrs. Arpeggio darted her husband a look not to be missed, by which we must have sensed without seeing her, as if by marital radar.*
>
> Peter De Vries

But Watzlawick suggests that there may be perceived differences in the appropriate sequence of courtship steps even though people with different cultural experiences agree on the behaviors making up the steps[36]:

> During the last years of World War II and the early postwar years, hundreds of thousands of U.S. soldiers were stationed in or passed through Great Britain. . . . Both American soldiers and British girls accused one another of being sexually brash. Investigation of this curious double charge brought light

on an interesting punctuation problem. In both cultures, courtship behavior from the first eye contact to the ultimate consummation went through approximately thirty steps, but the sequence of these steps was different. Kissing, for instance comes relatively early in the North American pattern (occupying, let us say, step 5) and relatively late in the English pattern (at step 25 let us assume), where it is considered highly erotic behavior. So when the U.S. soldier somehow felt that the time was right for a harmless kiss, not only did the girl feel cheated out of twenty steps of what for her would have been proper behavior on his part, she also felt she had to make a quick decision: break off the relationship and run; or get ready for intercourse. If she chose the latter, the soldier was confronted with behavior that according to his cultural rules could only be called shameless at this early stage of the relationship.

Since pupil dilation seems to occur under conditions of emotional arousal, sexual arousal, interest, and attentiveness, we would certainly look for a greater frequency of this behavior among intimates. Further, mutual eye glances, eye contact, or the colloquial "making eyes" should occur more often and for longer periods of time. If we look at the functions served by mutual eye contact, it is easy to see why such a predication makes sense: Mutual eye gazing can signal that communication channels are open rather than closed. It can psychologically reduce the physical distance between the communicators—pulling them closer to each other. It is a useful method for getting visual feedback. Research suggests that we look at those things that are rewarding to us or toward which (whom) we have a positive attitude. Keep in mind, however, that there may be exceptions here, too. Long-term intimates may have many other ways to communicate messages formerly communicated through eye gaze. They may also show less eye gaze due to the fact that they have agreed (perhaps implicitly) to communicate deference through reduced eye gaze. Like the verbal patterns mentioned earlier, we would expect eye gaze to peak during early formation of an intimate relationship, stabilize at a lower level, and peak again during relationship crises.

Mehrabian's research on nonverbal immediacy (see Chapter 3) isolated a number of other behaviors one might expect to see among some intimates.[37] Again, such behaviors are most likely to be seen during times when relationship commitment is perceived to be in greatest demand. These behaviors include: nodding, leaning forward, maintaining open arms and body positions, direct body orientation to the other person, and postural congruence. Positive facial expressions (happiness, interest, joy, amusement) might also reflect greater intimacy than do negative expressions. It should be noted, however, that frequency of behavior may not always be a very telling indicator. You may smile only on rare occasions, but those occasions may contribute heavily toward the perceptions of intimacy in your relationship. In addition, intimates who face a daily parade of positive and negative experiences may show fewer positive facial expressions when in each other's presence than people who have a friendly relationship. In a friendly relationship you can be "on your best behavior" during the occasions when you are with the other person. The same pattern may characterize the behavior of a person during courtship so the person's neutral and negative behavior is a virtual surprise once co-habitation begins.

The stereotyped intimate vocalizations may include a lower pitch, softer voice, slower rate, and a somewhat slurred enunciation.[38] Long-term intimates may communicate equally intimate messages on the vocal level with fewer stereotypical behaviors. The absence of vocal sounds (silence) is also a potentially important part of intimate communications. Words, in fact, sometimes act to create a greater distance than silence in some intimate contacts—sexual intercourse. As relationships grow, participants continue to exchange information until they become more and more comfortable being silent in one another's presence. Silences are often very uncomfortable at early stages of a relationship. They cause people to desperately scan their minds for some appropriate small talk to fill them. These silences may be perceived by participants as suggesting too strongly a communication pattern characteristic of intimacy. Hence, the extent to which we feel comfortable with another in silence can be vivid testimony to how well we know him or her. Of course, it can also be vivid testimony to how much we dislike a person or how little interest we have in getting to know a person. Thus, silence may reflect distance as well as closeness.[39] Silences are usually charged with the words and deeds preceding them so a silence can generate a tremendous range of meanings, some of which are listed in Table 9.2.

Just as there are norms governing public silences (in churches, courtrooms, libraries, hospitals, at funerals), intimates may also have their own norms for when and where silences should occur. It may be during the playing of "Silverbird" rather than the "Star Spangled Banner," the place may be the bedroom instead of the courtroom, but interpersonal norms for silences seem to be a common corollary of intimacy.

TABLE 9.2 Some Meanings of Silence	
Agreement	Disagreement ("Silent Treatment")
Thoughtfulness	Ignorance
Revelation (We often say much about the people we are describing by what we choose to omit.)	Secrecy ("If he didn't have something to hide, he'd speak up.")
Warmth (Binding the participants)	Coldness (Separating the participants)
Submission	Attack (Not answering a letter—or worse, not answering a comment directed at you.)
Gaining attention	Boredom
Consideration	Inconsideration

Up to this point we've focused entirely on nonverbal behavior that is directly tied to the human body itself. Clothing and other apparel may also show the merging of intimates' identities.

Although we would predict that communication between intimates would be more accurate, the sending of nonverbal, emotional messages (like verbal ones) is not a perfected art. We sometimes send confusing messages. Some people, in fact, have particularly severe problems which either keep them from communicating intimate messages or propel them toward intimate messages when they don't want to send them.

Beier reports these observations of newlyweds who were asked to portray different moods to see how well others could identify them:

> I shall never forget two examples of this discordance. One girl, who tried like everyone else to appear angry, fearful, seductive, indifferent, happy and sad—and who subsequently edited her own performances for authenticity—appeared to her judges as angry in every case. Imagine what a difficult world she must have lived in. No matter where she set the thermostat of her emotional climate, everyone else always felt it was sweltering hot. Another girl in our experiment demonstrated a similar one-dimensionality; only in her case, whatever else she thought she was doing, she invariably impressed her judges as seductive. Even when she wanted to be angry, men whistled at her.[40]

SUMMARY

This chapter has focused on those communicative behaviors involved in the maintenance of relationship commitment and intimacy. In addition to commitment, we discussed personal idioms, compliments, gifts, comforting, persuasion, sex talk, intimate play, and intimacy without words.

Each of the verbal and nonverbal behaviors noted may be more prominent during periods when commitment to intimacy is in greater demand—e.g., during early attempts to establish intimacy and during relationship crises when intimacy needs to be reasserted. In addition, we noted that intimates can (and do) negotiate very different behavioral patterns from those shown by most people. With these qualifications in mind, this chapter suggested the following:

1. Commitment is communicated by addressing the future rewards in the relationship; by identifying with the relationship; by rejecting competing alternatives to the relationship; by showing a willingness to exert effort on behalf of the relationship; by investing a lot in the relationship; and by accepting personal responsibility for commitment to the relationship.

2. The communication of commitment involves repeating your commitment; using unqualified ways of expressing your commitment; talking about future rewards; making public statement of your commitment; taking action to make your declarations of commitment more permanent, as in writing them down; showing effort in your commitment talk; and initiating commitment talk as much as providing responses to your partner's initiations.

3. The communication of intimacy can be done through the use of personal idioms and private meanings unique to the intimate couple.

4. Compliments and gifts tell the other person what you value. A good gift, like a good compliment, is tailored to the needs and desires of the recipient. When you believe gifts and compliments are deserved and given without some ulterior motive, they more effectively serve relationship maintenance.

5. Comforting messages help relationship partners when they are feeling "down" or hurt. The most important goal in comforting is to sincerely involve yourself in the recognition and acceptance of your partner's feelings in an effort to lessen the hurt. Subsequently, comforting messages should also help your partner understand and cope with what happened and to feel better about themselves.

6. Persuasive messages focus on efforts to change your partner's thoughts, feelings, behavior, or the relationship itself. This involves giving advice, asking for help, challenging attitudes and beliefs, complaining, criticizing, and so on. Relationship maintenance through persuasion depends on each partner's ability to tap into a reservoir of knowledge about the other; their ability to use the close proximity of the target to their advantage; and their ability to integrate the trust and felt obligations inherent in the relationship into their strategies.

7. Sex talk is often a major problem in close romantic relationships because the methods used to initiate and respond are so often subject to misinterpretation. Effective maintenance requires being sensitive to distinctions between communicating affection and communicating sex. When the ambiguity of nonverbal messages creates problems, verbal clarity is in order.

8. Play is a valuable behavior for building and maintaining close relationships. It enables couples to enact "time-outs" when necessary. Play is also instrumental in couples dealing with tensions, expressing difficult messages, providing mutual pleasure, and solving problems.

9. Nonverbal messages are important at all stages of intimacy, but being able to read these signals effectively is critical to long-term satisfaction.

Throughout this chapter, we have not tried to separate or distinguish same-sexed pairs from different-sexed pairs in terms of the behavior discussed. This may be unsettling to some; confusing to others. The goal of signaling intimacy is one shared by same-sexed and different-sexed pairs. Differences in the way some of these signals are manifested may occur, but in some cases the messages will be similar. Traditionally, our society has not referred to same-sexed pairs as intimates because it might connote a sexual relationship. As a result, some of the differences in expressing intimacy to members of the same sex may be a result of social sanctions more than anything else. Instead of saying, "I love you" repeatedly, then, same-sexed relationships may substitute another phrase which is designed to express intimacy and repeat it.

Obviously, some communication patterns common to intimate relationships have not been discussed. We noted earlier in the book, for instance, that we would expect to see an increasing number of pair-references over self-references. And, although the topic of feedback was implicit in much of the material covered, it should be clear that feedback is important as a way of giving help to another. After all, if we want to learn how our behavior matches up with our intentions, who is more suited to provide believable testimony than the one we feel closest to?

As a relationship begins to escalate toward intimacy, an increasing number of behaviors (outlined in this chapter) are manifested as intimate dialogue. At first there will probably be a cautious testing to see if the other person wants to move the relationship to a more intimate level. If one person injudiciously and wrongly assumes that the relationship is more intimate than it really is and begins behaving as if it were, we may see the other person helping the imprudent partner save face. Rather than bluntly telling the person that he or she has inaccurately perceived the situation, the partner may communicate this idea by saying: "It's not you. . . . I just don't want to get involved with anyone right now," or "Yeah, we really do have fun . . . but I've got so much work to do right now, I don't know how long it's going to be before I can get out again." It should also be evident that intimates occasionally exhibit behaviors that are more characteristic of acquaintances or even strangers. Less intimate, nonverbal behavior and extreme forms of politeness may appear as a function of playfulness, but it will also vividly remind the participants from whence and how far they've come.

SELECTED READINGS

Commitment

Adams, J. M., and Jones, W. H. "The Conceptualization of Marital Commitment." *Journal of Personality and Social Psychology* 72 (1997): 1177–1196.

Braithwaite, D. O., and Baxter, L. A. " 'I Do' Again: The Relational Dialectics of Renewing Marriage Vows." *Journal of Social and Personal Relationships* 12 (1995): 177–198.

Brickman, P. *Commitment, Conflict, and Caring.* Englewood Cliffs, NJ: Prentice-Hall.

Bui, K-V. T., Peplau, L. A., and Hill, C. T. "Testing the Rusbult Model of Relationship Commitment and Stability in a 15-Year Study of Hetero-sexual Couples." *Personality and Social Psychology Bulletin* 22 (1996): 1244–1257.

Fehr, B. "Laypeople's Conceptions of Commitment." *Journal of Personality and Social Psychology* 76 (1999): 90–103.

Johnson, M. P. "Commitment: A Conceptual Structure and Empirical Application." *The Sociological Quarterly* 14 (1973): 395–406.

Johnson, M. P. "Commitment to Personal Relationships." In W. H. Jones and D. Perlman, eds., *Advances in Personal Relationships*, pp. 117–143. London: Jessica Kingsley, 1991.

Knapp, M. L., and Taylor, E. H. "Commitment and Its Communication in Romantic Relationships." In A. L. Weber and J. H. Harvey, eds., *Perspectives on Close Relationships,* pp. 153–175. Needham Heights, MA: Allyn and Bacon, 1994.

Lund, M. "The Development of Investment and Commitment Scales for Predicting Continuity of Personal Relationships." *Journal of Social and Personal Relationships* 2 (1985): 3–24.

Lydon, J., Pierce, T., and O'Regan, S. "Coping with Moral Commitment to Long-Distance Dating Relationships." *Journal of Personality and Social Psychology* 73 (1997): 104–113.

Michaels, J. W., Acock, A. C., and Edwards, J. N. "Social Exchange and Equity Determinants of Relationship Commitment." *Journal of Social and Personal Relationships* 3 (1986): 161–176.

Miller, R. S. "Inattentive and Contented: Relationship Commitment and Attention to Alternatives." *Journal of Personality and Social Psychology* 73 (1997): 758–766.

Nock, S. L. "Commitment and Dependency in Marriage." *Journal of Marriage and the Family* 57 (1995): 503–514.

Rusbult, C. E. "A Longitudinal Test of the Investment Model: The Development (and Deterioration) of Satisfaction and Commitment in Heterosexual Involvements." *Journal of Personality and Social Psychology* 45 (1983): 101–117.

Rusbult, C. E., and Buunk, B. P. "Commitment Processes in Close Relationships: An Interdependence Analysis." *Journal of Social and Personal Relationships* 10 (1993): 175–204.

Stein, C. H. "Felt Obligation in Adult Family Relationships." In S. Duck, ed., *Social Context and Relationships,* pp. 78–99. Newbury Park, CA: Sage, 1993.

Surra, C. A., Arizzi, P., and Asmussen, L. A. "The Association Between Reasons for Commitment and the Development and Outcome of Marital Relationships." *Journal of Social and Personal Relationships* 5 (1988): 47–63.

Swenson, C. H., and Trahaug, G. "Commitment and the Long-Term Marriage Relationship." *Journal of Marriage and the Family* 47 (1985): 939–945.

VanLange, P. A. M., Agnew, C. R., Harinck, F., and Steemers, G. E. M. "From Game Theory to Real Life: How Social Value Orientation Affects Willingness to Sacrifice in Ongoing Close Relationships." *Journal of Personality and Social Psychology* 73 (1997): 1330–1344.

Personal Idioms

Bell, R. A., and Healey, J. G. "Idiomatic Communication and Interpersonal Solidarity in Friends' Relational Cultures." *Human Communication Research* 18 (1992): 307–335.

Bell, R. A., Buerkel-Rothfuss, N. L., and Gore, K. E. " 'Did You Bring the Yarmulke for the Cabbage Patch Kid?' The Idiomatic Communication of Young Lovers." *Human Communication Research* 14 (1987): 47–67.

Bombar, M. L., and Littig, L. W. "Babytalk as a Communication of Intimate Attachment: An Initial Study in Adult Romances and Friendships." *Personal Relationships* 3 (1996): 137–158.

Bruess, C. J. S., and Pearson, J. C. " 'Sweet Pea' and 'Pussy Cat': An Examination of Idiom Use and Marital Satisfaction Over the Life Cycle." *Journal of Social and Personal Relationships* 10 (1993): 609–615.

Hopper, R., Knapp, M. L., and Scott, L. "Couples' Personal Idioms: Exploring Intimate Talk." *Journal of Communication* 31 (1981): 23–33.

Compliments and Gifts

Cheal, D. J. "The Social Dimensions of Gift Behavior." *Journal of Social and Personal Relationships* 3 (1986): 423–439.

Deutsch, M. "The Interpretation of Praise and Criticism as a Function of Their Social Context." In D. Barnlund, ed., *Interpersonal Communication.* New York: Houghton Mifflin, 1968.

Knapp, M. L., Hopper, R., and Bell, R. A. "Compliments: A Descriptive Taxonomy." *Journal of Communication* 34 (1984): 12–31.

Mauss, M. *The Gift.* Glencoe, IL: Free Press, 1954.

Comforting

Applegate, J. L. "Adaptive Communication in Educational Contexts." *Communication Education* 29 (1980): 158–170.

Burleson, B. R. "Comforting Communication." In H. E. Sypher and J. L. Applegate, eds., *Communication by Children and Adults: Social Cognitive and Strategic Processes,* pp. 63–104. Beverly Hills, CA: Sage, 1984.

Burleson, B. R. "Comforting Messages: Features, Functions, and Outcomes." In J. A. Daly and

J. M. Wiemann, eds., *Strategic Interpersonal Communication*, pp. 135–161. Hillsdale, NJ: Erlbaum, 1994.

Burleson, B. R. "The Production of Comforting Messages: Social-Cognitive Foundations." *Journal of Language and Social Psychology* 4 (1985): 253–273.

Clark, C. *Misery and Company: Sympathy in Everyday Life.* Chicago, IL: University of Chicago Press, 1997.

Perrine, R. M. "On Being Supportive: The Emotional Consequences of Listening to Another's Distress." *Journal of Social and Personal Relationships* 10 (1993): 371–384.

Rogers, C. R. "The Necessary and Sufficient Conditions of Therapeutic Personality Change." *Journal of Consulting Psychology* 21 (1957): 95–103.

Persuasion

Alberts, J. K. "An Analysis of Couples' Conversational Complaints." *Communication Monographs* 55 (1988): 184–197.

Cody, M. J., Canary, D. J., and Smith, S. W. "Compliance-Gaining Goals: An Inductive Analysis of Actors' Goal Types, Strategies, and Successes." In J. A. Daly and J. M. Wiemann, eds., *Strategic Interpersonal Communication*, pp. 135–161. Hillsdale, NJ: Erlbaum, 1994.

Dillard, J. P. "Types of Influence Goals in Personal Relationships." *Journal of Social and Personal Relationships* 6 (1989): 293–308.

Dillard, J. P., Kinney, T. A., and Cruz, M. G. "Influence, Appraisals, and Emotions in Close Relationships." *Communication Monographs* 63 (1996): 105–130.

Falbo, T., and Peplau, L. A. "Power Strategies in Intimate Relationships." *Journal of Personality and Social Psychology* 38 (1980): 618–628.

Roloff, M. E., Janiszewski, C. A., McGrath, M. A., Burns, C. S., and Manrai, L. A. "Acquiring Resources from Intimates: When Obligation Substitutes for Persuasion." *Human Communication Research* 14 (1988): 364–396.

Rudd, J. E., and Burant, P. A. "A Study of Women's Compliance-Gaining Behaviors in Violent and Non-Violent Relationships." *Communication Research Reports* 12 (1995): 134–144.

Rule, B. G., and Bisanz, G. L. "Goals and Strategies of Persuasion: A Cognitive Schema for Understanding Social Events." In M. P. Zanna, J. M. Olson, and C. P. Herman, eds., *Social Influence: The Ontario Symposium Vol. 5,* pp. 185–206. Hillsdale, NJ: Erlbaum, 1994.

Sagrestano, L. M., Christensen, A., and Heavey, C. L. "Social Influence Techniques During Marital Conflict." *Personal Relationships* 5 (1998): 75–89.

Seibold, D. R., Cantrill, J. G., and Meyers, R. A. "Communication and Interpersonal Influence." In M. L. Knapp and G. R. Miller, eds., *Handbook of Interpersonal Communication,* 2nd ed., pp. 542–588. Newbury Park, CA: Sage, 1994.

Steil, J. M., and Weltman, K. "Influence Strategies at Home and at Work: A Study of Sixty Dual-Career Couples." *Journal of Social and Personal Relationships* 9 (1992): 65–88.

Tracy, K., Van Dusen, D., and Robinson, S. " 'Good' and 'Bad' Criticism: A Descriptive Analysis." *Journal of Communication* 37 (1987): 46–59.

Sexual Communication

Brown, M., and Auerback, A. "Communication Patterns in Initiation of Marital Sex." *Medical Aspects of Human Sexuality* 15 (1981): 105–117.

Buss, D. "Casual Sex." In D. Buss, *The Evolution of Desire,* pp. 73–96. NY: Basic Books, 1994.

Christopher, F. S., and Frandsen, M. M. "Strategies of Influence in Sex and Dating." *Journal of Social and Personal Relationships* 7 (1990): 89–105.

Cupach, W. R., and Comstock, J. "Satisfaction with Sexual Communication in Marriage: Links to Sexual Satisfaction and Dyadic Adjustment." *Journal of Social and Personal Relationships* 7 (1990): 179–186.

Cupach, W. R., and Metts, S. "Sexuality and Communication in Close Relationships." In K. McKinney and S. Sprecher, eds., *Sexuality in Close Relationships,* pp. 93–110. Hillsdale, NJ: Erlbaum, 1991.

Edgar, T., and Fitzpatrick, M. A. "Communicating Sexual Desire: Message Tactics for Having and Avoiding Intercourse." In J. P. Dillard, ed., *Seeking Compliance,* pp. 107–112. Scottsdale, Ariz.: Gorsuch Scarisbrick, 1990.

Grauerholz, E., and Serpe, R. T. "Initiation and Response: The Dynamics of Sexual Interaction." *Sex Roles* 12 (1985): 1041–1059.

Koeppel, L. B., Montagne-Miller, Y., O'Hair, D., and Cody, M. J. "Friendly? Flirting? Wrong?" In P. J. Kalbfleisch, ed., *Interpersonal Commu-*

nication: Evolving Interpersonal Relationships, pp. 13–32. Hillsdale, NJ: Erlbaum, 1993.

Lim, G. Y., and Roloff, M. E. "Attributing Sexual Consent." *Journal of Applied Communication Research* 27 (1999): 1–23.

McCormick. N. B. "Come-ons and Put-Offs: Unmarried Students' Strategies for Having and Avoiding Sexual Intercourse." *Psychology of Women Quarterly* 4 (1979): 194–211.

McKinney, K., and Sprecher, S., eds. *Sexuality in Close Relationships*. Hillsdale, NJ: Erlbaum, 1991.

Motley, M. T., and Reeder, H. M. "Unwanted Escalation of Sexual Intimacy: Male and Female Perceptions of Connotations and Relational Consequences of Resistance Messages." *Communication Monographs* 62 (1995): 355–382.

O'Sullivan, L. F., and Gaines, M. E. "Decision-Making in College Students' Heterosexual Dating Relationships: Ambivalence About Engaging in Sexual Activity." *Journal of Social and Personal Relationships* 15 (1998): 347–363.

Perper, T. *Sex Signals: The Biology of Love.* Philadelphia, PA: ISI Press, 1985.

Perper, T., and Weis, D. L. "Proceptive and Rejective Strategies of U.S. and Canadian Women." *Journal of Sex Research* 23 (1987): 455–480.

Sprecher, S., and McKinney, K. "Sexuality in Close Relationships." In A. L. Weber and J. H. Harvey, eds., *Perspectives on Close Relationships*, pp. 193–216. Needham Heights, MA: Allyn and Bacon, 1994.

Play

Adelman, M. B. "Play and Incongruity: Framing Safe-Sex Talk." *Health Communication* 3 (1991): 139–155.

Baxter, L. A. "Forms and Functions of Intimate Play in Personal Relationships." *Human Communication Research* 18 (1992): 336–363.

Betcher, R. W. "Intimate Play and Marital Adaptation." *Psychiatry* 44 (1981): 13–33.

Glenn, P. J., and Knapp, M. L. "The Interactive Framing of Play in Adult Conversations." *Communication Quarterly* 35 (1987): 48–66.

Nonverbal Behavior

Knapp, M. L. "Dyadic Relationship Development." In J. M. Wiemann and R. P. Harrison, eds., *Nonverbal Interaction*, Beverly Hills, CA: Sage, 1983.

Knapp M. L., and Hall J. A. *Nonverbal Communication in Human Interaction.* Fort Worth: Holt, Rinehart, & Winston, 1997.

McCormick, N. B., and Jones A. I. "Gender Differences in Nonverbal Flirtation." *Journal of Sex Education and Therapy* 15 (1989): 271–282.

Moore, M. M. "Nonverbal Courtship Patterns in Women: Context and Consequences." *Ethology and Sociobiology* 6 (1985): 237–247.

Noller, P. *Nonverbal Communication and Marital Interaction.* New York: Pergamon Press, 1984.

Patterson, M. L. "Functions of Nonverbal Behavior in Close Relationships." In S. Duck, ed., *Handbook of Personal Relationships*, pp. 41–56. New York: Wiley, 1988.

NOTES

[1]M. P. Johnson, "Commitment: A Conceptual Structure and Empirical Application," *The Sociological Quarterly* 14 (1973): 395–406. Also see: M. P. Johnson, "Commitment to Personal Relationships." In W. H. Jones and D. Perlman, eds., *Advances in Personal Relationships* (London: Jessica Kingsley, 1991), pp. 117–143. Also see: J. M. Adams and W. H. Jones, "The Conceptualization of Marital Commitment: An Integrative Analysis," *Journal of Personality and Social Psychology* 72 (1997): 1177–1196.

[2]N. D. Kristof, "Who Needs Love? In Japan, Many Couples Don't." *New York Times,* February 11, 1996, A1, A6.

[3]M. L. Knapp and E. H. Taylor, "Commitment and Its Communication in Romantic Relationships." In A. L. Weber and J. H. Harvey, eds., *Perspectives on Close Relationships* (Needham Heights, MA: Allyn & Bacon, 1994), pp. 153–175.

[4]R. S. Miller, "Inattentive and Contented: Relationship Commitment and Attention to Alternatives," *Journal of Personality and Social Psychology* 73 (1997): 758–766.

[5]W. F. Owen, "Mutual Interaction of Discourse Structures and Relational Pragmatics in Conversational Influence Attempts," *Southern Speech Communication Journal* 52 (1987): 103–127.

[6]B. Bernstein, "Elaborated and Restricted Codes: Their Social Origins and Some Consequences," *American Anthropologist* 66 (1964): 60–61.

[7]K. M. Galvin and B. J. Brommel, *Family Communication: Cohesion and Change* (Glenview, IL: Scott, Foresman, 1982), p. 5.

[8]R. Hopper, M. L. Knapp, and L. Scott, "Couples' Personal Idioms: Exploring Intimate Talk," *Journal of Communication* 31 (1981): 23–33.

[9]R. A. Bell, N. L. Buerkel-Rothfuss, and K. E. Gore, " 'Did You Bring the Yarmulke for the Cabbage Patch Kid?' The Idiomatic Communication of Young Lovers," *Human Communication Research* 14 (1987): 47–67. C. J. S. Bruess and J. C. Pearson, " 'Sweet Pea' and 'Pussy Cat': An Examination of Idiom Use and Marital Satisfaction Over the Life Cycle," *Journal of Social and Personal Relationships* 10 (1993): 609–615.

[10]M. L. Bombar and L. W. Littig, Jr., "Babytalk as a Communication of Intimate Attachment: An Initial Study in Adult Romances and Friendships." *Personal Relationships* 3 (1996): 137–158.

[11]E. Goffman, *Presentation of Self in Everyday Life* (Garden City, NY: Doubleday Anchor, 1959), p. 50.

[12]M. L. Knapp, R. Hopper, and P. A. Bell, "Compliments: A Descriptive Taxonomy," *Journal of Communication* 34 (1984): 12–31; M. L. Knapp, R. Hopper, and R. A. Bell, "I Really Loved Your Article, But You Missed Your Deadline," *Psychology Today* 19 (1985): 24–28.

[13]B. R. Burleson, "Comforting Messages: Features, Functions, and Outcomes." In J. A. Daly and J. M. Wiemann, eds., *Strategic Interpersonal Communication* (Hillsdale, NJ: Erlbaum, 1994), pp. 135–161.

[14]J. P. Dillard, "Types of Influence Goals in Personal Relationships," *Journal of Social and Personal Relationships* 6 (1989): 293–308.

[15]D. R. Siebold, J. G. Cantrill, and R. A. Meyers, "Communication and Interpersonal Influence." In M. L. Knapp and G. R. Miller, eds., *Handbook of Interpersonal Communication,* 2nd ed. (Newbury Park, CA: Sage, 1994), pp. 542–588.

[16]This table is a modified version of the strategies presented in: B. G. Rule and G. L. Bisanz, "Goals and Strategies of Persuasion: A Cognitive Schema for Understanding Social Events." In M. P. Zanna, J. M. Olson, and C. P. Herman, eds., *Social Influence: The Ontario Symposium,* vol. 5. (Hillsdale, NJ: Erlbaum, 1987), pp. 185–206. Also see: B. G. Rule, G. L. Bisanz, and M. Kohn, "Anatomy of a Persuasion Schema: Targets, Goals, and Strategies," *Journal of Personality and Social Psychology* 48 (1985): 1127–1140.

[17]J. E. Rudd and P. A. Burant, "A Study of Women's Compliance-Gaining Behaviors in Violent and Non-Violent Relationships," *Communication Research Reports* 12 (1995): 134–144.

[18]M. E. Roloff, C. A. Janiszewski, M. A. McGrath, C. S. Burns, and L. A. Manrai, "Acquiring Resources from Intimates: When Obligation Substitutes for Persuasion," *Human Communication Research* 14 (1988): 364–396.

[19]See: J. K. Alberts, "An Analysis of Couples' Conversational Complaints," *Communication Monographs* 55 (1988): 182–197. J. K. Alberts, "A Descriptive Taxonomy of Couples' Complaint Interactions," *Southern Communication Journal* 54 (1989): 125–143; and K. Tracy, D. Van Dusen, and S. Robinson, " 'Good' and 'Bad' Criticism: A Descriptive Analysis," *Journal of Communication* 37 (1987): 46–59.

[20]W. R. Cupach and J. Comstock, "Satisfaction with Sexual Communication in Marriage: Links to Sexual Satisfaction and Dyadic Adjustment," *Journal of Social and Personal Relationships* 7 (1990): 179–186.

[21]N. B. McCormick, "Come-ons and Put-offs: Unmarried Students' Strategies for Having and Avoiding Sexual Intercourse," *Psychology of Women Quarterly* 4 (1979): 194–211; E. Grauerholz and R. T. Serpe, "Initiation and Response: The Dynamics of Sexual Interaction," *Sex Roles* 12 (1985): 1041–1059; M. Brown and A. Auerback, "Communication Patterns in Initiation of Marital Sex," *Medical Aspects of Human Sexuality* 15 (1981): 105–117.

[22]McCormick, "Come-ons . . . " 1979; C. J. Jesser, "Male Responses to Direct Verbal Initiatives of Females," *Journal of Sex Research* 14 (1978): 118–128; T. Edgar and M. A. Fitzpatrick, "Communicating Sexual Desire: Message Tactics for Having and Avoiding Intercourse." In J. P. Dillard, ed., *Seeking Compliance: The Production of Interpersonal Influence Messages,* (Scottsdale, Ariz.: Gorsuch Scarisbrick, 1990), pp. 107–112; S. Metts and W. R. Cupach, "The Role of Communication in Human Sexuality." In K. McKinney and S. Sprecher, eds., *Human Sexuality: The Societal and Interpersonal Context* (Norwood, NJ: Ablex, 1989).

[23]It should be noted that the ambiguity of some sexual messages is at the core of many disputes about sexual harassment and rape. This underscores the importance of understanding the multiinterpretation potential of messages about or related to sex.

[24]L. F. O'Sullivan and M. E. Gaines, "Decision-Making in College Students' Heterosexual Dating Relationships: Ambivalence About Engaging in Sexual Activity," *Journal of Social and Personal Relationships* 15 (1998): 347–363.

[25]C. L. Muehlenhard and L. C. Hollabaugh, "Do Women Sometimes Say No When They Mean Yes? The Prevalence and Correlates of Women's Token Resistance to Sex," *Journal of Personality and Social Psychology* 54 (1988): 872–879. R. L. Shotland and B. A. Hunter, "Women's 'Token Resistance' and Compliant Sexual Behaviors Are Related to Uncertain Sexual Intentions and Rape." *Personality and Social Psychology Bulletin* 21 (1995): 226–236; B. A. Hunter and R. L. Shotland, " 'Token Resistance' and Compliance to Sexual Intercourse: Similarities and Differences in Men's and Women's Behavior," *Personality and Social Psychology Bulletin* (under review).

[26]M. T. Motley and H. M. Reeder, "Unwanted Escalation of Sexual Intimacy: Male and Female Perceptions of Connotations and Relational Consequences of Resistance Messages," *Communication Monographs* 62 (1995): 355–382. Also see: G. Y. Lim and M. E. Roloff, "Attributing Sexual Consent," *Journal of Applied Communication Research* 27 (1999): 1–23.

[27]A few studies have viewed sexual interaction as a process. See: Grauerholz and Serpe, 1985; and T. Perper, and D. L. Weis, "Proceptive and Rejective Strategies of U.S. and Canadian Women," *The Journal of Sex Research* 23 (1987): 455–480.

[28]L. A. Baxter, "Forms and Functions of Intimate Play in Personal Relationships," *Human Communication Research* 18 (1992): 336–363.

[29]M. B. Adelman, "Play and Incongruity: Framing Safe-Sex Talk," *Health Communications* 3 (1991): 139–155.

[30]R. W. Betcher, "Intimate Play and Marital Adaptation," *Psychiatry* 44 (1981): 13–33.

[31]For an analysis of the structure of play, see: P. J. Glenn and M. L. Knapp, "The Interactive Framing of Play in Adult Conversations," *Communication Quarterly* 35 (1987): 48–66.

[32]Reprinted with permission of Macmillan Publishing Co., Inc., from *Intimate Relations* by Murray S. Davis. Copyright © 1973 by Murray S. Davis.

[33]P. Noller, *Nonverbal Communication and Marital Interaction* (New York: Pergamon Press, 1984); V. Manusov, "An Application of Attribution Principles to Nonverbal Behavior In Romantic Dyads," *Communication Monographs* 57 (1990): 104–118.

[34]*Emblems* and *illustrators* are technical terms. Briefly, *emblems* are gestures that have an almost direct verbal translation such as the hand formation used to indicate "A-OK." *Illustrators* are nonverbal acts that are directly tied to, or accompany speech and illustrate what is being said verbally. For further elaboration of these and other nonverbal behaviors, see P. Ekman and W. V. Friesen, "The Repertoire of Nonverbal Behavior: Categories, Origins, Usage, and Coding," *Semiotica* 1 (1969): 49–98.

[35]D. Morris, *Intimate Behavior* (New York: Random House, 1971), pp. 71–101.

[36]P. Watzlawick, *How Real Is Real?* (New York: Random House, 1976), pp. 63–64.

[37]A. Mehrabian, *Nonverbal Communication* (Chicago: Aldine Publishing Co., 1972).

[38]J. R. Davitz, *The Communication of Emotional Meaning* (New York: McGraw Hill. 1964), p. 63.

[39]There have been many words written about silence. If you wish to pursue the topic, the following should provide a diverse introduction: J. V. Jensen, "Communicative Functions of Silence," *ETC: A Review of General Semantics* 30 (1973): 249–257; T. J. Bruneau, "Communicative Silences: Forms and Functions," *Journal of Communication* 23 (1973): 17–46; R. L. Johannesen, "The Functions of Silence: A Plea for Communication Research," *Western Speech* 38 (1974): 25–35; A. Jaworski, *The Power of Silence: Social and Pragmatic Perspectives* (Newbury Park, CA: Sage, 1993).

[40]E. G. Beier, "Nonverbal Communication: How We Send Emotional Messages," *Psychology Today* 8 (1974): 53–56.

V

Interaction Patterns for Coming Apart

CHAPTER 10

Communication and the Process of Relationship Disengagement

Dear Dr. Vangelisti,

How do you know when a relationship is over? This seems like a very simple question, but I think I may be staying in a relationship that has already ended. I've been involved in this relationship for almost six years. It was great for the first five years. Sure, we had a few rough times, but we always seemed to work things out. The last six months have been terrible. I went to Europe to study for a semester and now that I've returned everything has changed. We seem unaware of each others' needs and feelings. It is like we are bored with each other. We have not had any big fights or anything. We just seem to be drifting apart. What happened?

Confused

There are many reasons why relationships come apart. In this case it may have been a combination of the two people spending so much time away from each other, each pursuing different interests, and growing in different directions during that time. In previous chapters we've discussed how people get together. This chapter and the next focus on how relationships come apart and how people communicate the feelings and ideas associated with relationship disengagement.

> *So sorry and sad,*
> *But that's part of the deal*
> *When the tingle becomes a chill**

The bonds that hold people in relationships can dissolve with abrupt suddenness; they can be eaten away over a period of years as if small but regular doses of poison were at work; or they can loosen as the people in the relationship drift apart. The end of a relationship may be intensely volatile and threatening; it may resemble long-simmering coals which never seem to get around to bursting into flames. Or as life-giving energies are increasingly withheld from the relationship, the participants may just grow weary of a dull and unrewarding co-presence.

Terminating Relationships

Obviously, messages that communicate distancing, disengagement, and de-escalation are not limited to the termination stage of a relationship. They can and do occur in all the other interaction stages as well.

There are instances when a relationship begins to deteriorate before it starts; that is, one person does not return the normal approaching features of the greeting ritual. A common example is found in the numerous distancing moves performed by urban shoppers when approached by a street person or beggar; the shoppers avoid eye contact and verbalizations, stiffen up, and try to physically move away from the greeter. The avoidance of a greeting from an acquaintance or friend is an especially severe step toward relationship de-escalation, providing the snub cannot be effectively explained as accidental—"Oh, Jeez, I didn't see you," or "Wow, I didn't even realize you were talking to me, my mind was a million miles away." The reason that the absence of a greeting to an acquaintance or friend can be so devastating is that, among other things, the greeting ritual acknowledges the other's humanity and existence, a courtesy expected by all but one's most detestable enemies.

People may move directly to the avoiding or terminating stages following a greeting ritual. Since neither party has much time and energy invested in the relationship at this point, one person will not notice if the other unilaterally arranges things so that future contact is avoided. In large gatherings when an individual is meeting many new people, it is not uncommon for both parties to agree effervescently to "try to get together sometime" without the least commitment to such a course of action. Often both parties will accurately send and receive the metamessage: "Nice to meet and be with you at this time, but we probably won't be together again. If we are, that's fine." Sometimes, of course, one party either misses the metamessage or sincerely wishes to extend the duration of the association.

Obviously, many things may occur during the initiating stage that make the development of the relationship slower or decay-prone—greeting a person with the wrong name, exhibiting inappropriate greeting behavior for the type of relationship established, or observing some stigmatizing feature which runs against expectations for a desirable person with whom to build a relationship (height, weight, disfigurement, race).

There may be similar complications for two individuals who find themselves at the experimenting stage. When small talk is in order and one or both persons either clam up, argue, jabber meaninglessly, or in some other way avoid fulfilling the interpersonal contract, relationship development is naturally put in greater jeopardy. Sometimes the two participants simply cannot find an integrating topic; or when integrating topics have been established, a simple phrase may serve to shatter and disintegrate—"Yes, my husband always says. . . ." uttered in a context where at least one party expected the other to be unmarried. At other times, de-escalation from experimenting may not be intentional, but because of other commitments, other friends, living arrangements, or differing lifestyles, it may be difficult to arrange meetings and the couple may drift into the avoiding stage.

For most of us, the most vivid referent for a terminated relationship centers on a relationship that grew beyond the experimenting stage into intensifying, integrating, or bonding. Our involvement in these relationships is stronger and the withdrawal process is likely to be more dramatic. But even relationships that have been intimate manifest termination signals before the termination stage. Just as we are made aware of our eventual biological death prior to old age and as some conversational partners nervously look at their watch soon after a conversation begins, established intimate relationships may also provide some early signs of possible termination.

Reasons for Breaking Up

Virtually anything that creates relationship stress could be considered a source of relationship dissolution. Marriage therapists and clinical psychologists seem to agree, however, that a breakdown in communication is one of the major forces that pulls relationships apart. A 1979 survey of marriage counselors identified the following ten as the most common trouble areas for couples.[1] In order of frequency, these included: (1) a breakdown in communication; (2) the loss of shared goals or interests; (3) sexual incompatibility; (4) infidelity; (5) the excitement or fun has gone out of the marriage; (6) money; (7) conflicts about children; (8) alcohol or drug abuse; (9) women's equality issues; and (10) in-laws. More recent studies have confirmed the perceived centrality of communication to healthy marital functioning.[2] For example, a national survey of adults in the Unites States indicated that people felt the most common cause of marital dissolution was a lack of effective communication.[3] In fact, individuals noted that ineffective communication was more likely to lead to relational demise than money problems, interference from relatives/in-laws, sexual problems, previous relationships, or children. Another investigation that followed couples over the first three years of marriage revealed that satisfaction with communication was more often associated with overall marital satisfaction than were several other indices (e.g., satisfaction with finances, with ability to visit with friends and family, sexual satisfaction, etc.).[4] In most of these studies, communication "problems" or "breakdowns" generally referred to the fact that couples didn't seem to talk to each other about matters that were central to the continuance of a close relationship—e.g., indicating what you feel, what you want from the relationship, etc. The work of Gottman,[5] Markman,[6] Belsky,[7] and other researchers[8] suggests another communication pattern that is symptomatic of eventual relationship termination. Distressed couples tend to exchange and perceive a lot of negativity in their interaction. When compared with nondistressed couples, their communication includes more sarcasm, more negative feelings reciprocated, and more interpretations of the other's behavior as showing negativity. Distressed couples also engage in more "problem escalation" in which partners alternate between one presenting a problem and the other responding negatively to it.[9] Longitudinal studies show that couples become less happy and more likely to divorce when partners are more hostile toward each other,[10] when they invalidate each other's communication,[11] when husbands reject their wives' influence, and when wives initiate problem solving with negative behavior.[12]

Of course, it would be a mistake to assume that communication is the only "cause" of relationship decay. Relationships usually come apart for a variety of reasons involving: (1) Dissatisfaction with one's *partner*—e.g., not receiving the expected rewards from the partner. (2) Disillusionment with the *relationship*—e.g., the purposes for forming the relationship have been accomplished. (3) Difficulties with *individual characteristics*—e.g., psychological or behavioral tendencies that interfere with the maintenance of rewarding relationships.[13] (4) Problems with *others* who form the relationship network—e.g., in-laws, friends, former or current lovers. (5) Inability to deal with the strain imposed by *circumstances*—e.g., relocation.

A study involving students at four colleges provides some information about why dating couples break up.[14] The reasons aren't always that different from those expressed by married couples. Table 10.1 presents these reasons and the percentage of men and women who agreed that the breakup could be attributed to one or more of these reasons.

TABLE 10.1 Reasons for the Termination of Dating Relationships[17]		
Reason	*Women's Reports*	*Men's Reports*
Becoming bored with the relationship	76.7%	76.7%
Differences in interests	72.8	61.1
Woman's desire to be independent	73.7	50.0
Man's desire to be independent	46.8	61.1
Differences in backgrounds	44.2	46.8
Conflicting sexual attitudes	48.1	42.9
Conflicting marriage ideas	43.4	28.9
Woman's interest in someone else	40.3	31.2
Living too far apart	28.2	41.0
Man's interest in someone else	18.2	28.6
Pressure from woman's parents	18.2	13.0
Differences in intelligence	19.5	10.4
Pressure from man's parents	10.4	9.1

The percentage differences in Table 10.1 between men and women remind us that there are two, sometimes very different, sides to every breakup. In this study of dating couples, women were somewhat more likely to initiate the end of the relationship, but there was also a strong tendency for both men and women to view themselves as the initiator rather than their partner. Perhaps this desire to take the responsibility for the breakup ("it was my desire to be independent") is an effort to offset the stigma associated with a person who was so unsuitable as to be rejected. Just because women were credited with initiating more breakups than men may not mean they are less tolerant of relationship problems. Instead, it may mean that they are more observant of those problems. Another investigation published ten years after this one concluded that "men appear to be less aware of and/or less willing to accept responsibility in the dissolution process."[15] It is also possible, however, that women are simply more direct in their expression of a need to end a relationship. Some men who say their partner initiated the breakup may be dissatisfied with the relationship, but instead of overtly initiating a breakup they engage in behavior that eventually drives the woman to do the job. Thus, it isn't always the least involved partner who officially seeks the termination. The more involved partner can be influenced by the less involved partner's frustrating and unrewarding behavior.[16] In such cases, the broken-up-with can take the position, "I wanted to stay together, but she (he) wanted to end it." The "blame," then, falls on the partner—not the self.

Breakups also affect people's post-relationship feelings in different ways. Sometimes the behavior of one person will reflect the opposite of the other—the extent that one person feels relief in the breakup, the other feels regret. Some individuals cope with the loss by relating to others more, whereas others become more reserved.[18] In the dating couples previously discussed, men seemed to have a more difficult time reconciling themselves to the fact that the relationship was over and that they were no longer loved by their partner than did women. When men initiated the breakup, though, the couple was more likely to maintain a relationship at a lower level of intimacy—friends. Many of the differences we see in post-relationship feelings are attributable to people's perceptions of their relationship and their ability to deal with loss. Researchers have found that people who were more committed to their relationship (e.g., those who perceived their relationships to be closer, who had more lengthy relationships, and who perceived they had fewer relationship alternatives,) tended to be more distressed following a breakup.[19] In contrast, individuals who had more resources to cope with their breakup (e.g., those who felt they had more social support, who perceived the breakup was controllable, and who had higher self-esteem) were likely to be less distressed and to feel that they recovered from the breakup.[20] Regardless of how each person initially responds to the dissolution of a relationship, it is important to remember that these initial responses, feelings, needs, and attributions tend to change over time.[21]

A study of gay and lesbian couples further reveals that the reasons partners give for disengagement do not seem to be affected by couples' sexual orientation.[22] In this study, gays and lesbians who had recently experienced a separation from their partners were asked to provide the major reason why their relationship ended and to rate the distress they felt about the separation. The data provided by these couples then were compared to similar data collected from heterosexual couples. The study's findings show that those in gay or lesbian relationships did not differ from heterosexual couples in reasons for their separation or in the level of distress they experienced. Although gay and lesbian couples face some different social and relational challenges than heterosexual couples do, the reasons people in these relationships give for breaking up and the distress they feel about losing their relationship appear to be quite similar.

Although there seems to be a fairly consistent set of reasons for breakups, there are many differences in the way relationships come apart.[23] Some relationships take years to end. For a number of reasons, the partners may be ambivalent about whether they want to leave one another and may attempt several reconciliations. Other relationships die quickly. Dissolution is wrought in a deliberate, unambiguous manner. Davis distinguishes between those relationships that simply "pass away" and those that seem to manifest a "sudden death."[24]

Passing Away

Relationships, says Davis, may slowly lose their vitality for innumerable reasons, but the following three reasons seem to be especially crucial—and typical. For people bent on maintaining a relationship, these three reasons represent especially difficult forces for the relationship to withstand. The presence of any of the following situations, however, should not connote a feeling of inevitable termination. It may be that a knowledge of these potential problems and motivation to develop skills for dealing with them is the best insurance against these factors leading to a breakup.

1. A new intimate may enter the relationship scene. If the standing relationship was made up of a same-sexed pair, and the new friend is of that same sex, one person may face the problem of integrating a threesome in which two are compatible with him or her but neither of these two is compatible with each other. If a new intimate of the opposite sex enters an established heterosexual relationship, he or she may pose such dilemmas for the original pair as: deciding with whom to spend how much time and energy; trying to communicate with the old intimate in the same way, yet still develop a set of activities with the new intimate that cannot be freely communicated to the old intimate; making decisions regarding the type and frequency of favors for each intimate; and realizing that the process of integrating with the new intimate will eventually cause oneself to become a new person. Social psychologist Caryl Rusbult and her colleagues note that individuals' responses to dilemmas such as these will depend on (a) how satisfied they were with the relationship before the other person emerged, (b) the amount of resources they have invested in the relationship, and (c) the quality of the best available alternative to the relationship.[25] Keep in mind we are talking about a situation in which people feel the same sense of commitment to the new relationship as they did to the old.

The entrance of a new intimate or "rival" into the life of an established relationship may cause jealousy. Jealousy is a reaction to a perceived loss or threat to a relationship. The cause of this threat may be actual or imagined. Furthermore, the amount of jealousy people feel depends, in part, on the extent to which they perceive the new intimate has characteristics that are important to the way they define themselves. For example, one study[26] showed that women, on average, noted that it was important to their self-definitions that they satisfied their partners' desires. As a consequence, women felt more jealous when a rival had characteristics they thought were desirable to their partner. Men, in contrast, noted that they were more jealous when a rival performed better than they did on a dimension they felt was important—when the rival possessed some ability that was relevant to the way the men defined themselves.

The jealousy brought about by the perception of a new intimate may encompass several types:

- **Time Jealousy**—The feeling that one does not have enough time with the partner.

- **Person Jealousy**—One partner may be threatened (or irritated) by a specific person the other has chosen to relate to but not be threatened by others.

- **Opportunity/Situation Jealousy**—One person may have unique opportunities/experiences that exclude the partner, who then feels cheated, or one person may be invited to participate in experiences with people at times or in places that exclude the partner.[27]

Some degree of jealousy may benefit a relationship by showing care and concern, but it may also lead to unhealthy responses—e.g., wallowing in self-pity, planning revenge, or even threatening violence.[28] Jealousy, like love, is a physiological reaction which, when labeled, calls forth a learned script for appropriate behavior. It is important to note, however, the way people define "appropriate behavior" depends on a number of factors including their immediate goals and how secure they feel about their relationship. The degree to which individuals *experience* jealousy is not always clearly reflected by the way they *express* jealousy.[29] For instance, people who feel jealous during the initial stages of relationship development may pretend not to be jealous because they are worried about how their partner will react to their feelings. In contrast, those who have progressed beyond the initial stages may feel more confident about openly expressing jealousy to their partner.

Ordinarily those who are most dependent, insecure, and subscribe strongly to a value system supporting possessiveness of private property and total togetherness in relationships are most likely to experience jealousy.[30] But researchers have also found that the sort of relationships people are in affect the degree to which they feel jealous. For example, one survey of nearly 25,000 people revealed that those who had been divorced or separated felt more jealous in their relationships than those who were married or widowed. In addition, individuals who were cohabitating with their partners tended to be more jealous than those who were married. One explanation for these findings is that the people who felt more jealousy also felt less commitment in their relationships than they would like.[31] Another explanation is that those who were more jealous believed they had less control and predictability in their relationships.[32] As a result of feeling more uncertain, these individuals may have begun to perceive their relationships in different (i.e., more threatening, more negative, even more fearful) ways.

How do people cope with jealous feelings? Men are more likely to work on repairing their damaged self-esteem, whereas women seem to concentrate on repairing the damaged relationship. Jealousy, though, is rarely an individual's problem—it typically involves a *relationship*—and the most effective method of coping is an exchange of expectations, assumptions, and feelings relating to the behavior in question. This allows both partners to work on adjustments if both are committed to preserving the relationship.

2. Interaction distance (availability for interaction) may expand and, over time, will cause a relationship to fade. For many relationships, where at least one party would like to maintain the intimacy level, the following pattern is understandable and predictable: (a) An intense siege of messages about the relationship precedes the act of increasing distance between the participants (anticipating, no doubt, the possible effects of the separation on the relationship). (b) An initial spurt of communication activity (daily letter writing and telephoning), which is designed to maintain the previous intimacy level, follows the separation. (c) Gradually, over time, the intimacy level previously known attenuates. Some of the strong debilitating forces brought about by expanded interaction distance include: decreased physical and psychological stimulation; awkward and infrequent receiving and giving of favors; curtailed or indirect information exchange on all topics (especially the relationship); and experiences and activities performed without the intimate, which can eventually cause misalignment of previously synchronized attitudes and behaviors. Research suggests that the restricted communication experienced by long-distance dating partners is often accompanied by a tendency to idealize the relationship.[33] It is very possible that this idealization is part of what helps some people to maintain long-distance relationships for a time. But viewing the relationship in an idealized, unrealistic way may also make for a difficult transition period if and when the partners decrease the distance between them. Obviously, all this does not suggest that the relationship cannot be maintained at a different stage; it simply points to the difficulty of maintaining (for a length of time) a fairly intimate relationship without proximity.

3. The normal processes of individual psychological and physical development over the course of the relationship may sap strength from the relationship. The more narrowly focused and rigidly defined our relationship is, the more vulnerable change makes it. People may grow at different rates and in different directions. What may have attracted them to each other at one point in their lives may become a point of difference should, say, one person's values change in a certain area. Over time, a quality that initially seemed "exciting and different" may become "unpredictable and weird."[34] Things happen. Physical beauty changes. One person learns and constantly observes the most irritating and unpleasant aspects of the other person along with the desirable behaviors. Events such as the entrance of a child into the relationship, a sickness or an accident, a promotion or a demotion, a new job, or a new location occur and may profoundly alter the congruence of attitudes, interests, and habits. It seems that as a relationship deteriorates, the balance of attractions and level of involvement for the two parties becomes unequal, whereas during the process of becoming more intimate the attractions and involvement seem to be more balanced.

It has been observed that intimate communications will sometimes decrease (and acquaintance messages increase) in an aging intimate relationship because one or both partners do not expend the energy necessary to maintain the intimacy level. "He doesn't show affection for me like he used to." If the absence of messages consonant with an intimate relationship violates expectations for the relationship, difficulties are surely on the horizon. For various reasons, however, some people who have previously held an intimate relationship are satisfied with a relationship maintained at the acquaintance level. Love, as the preceding chapters said, takes many forms, and companionship is, for some, a viable form.

More often than not, the changes just discussed are slow and subtle, with many ups and downs. Each person will be gathering data—"If you really loved me, you'd . . ."; but the magnitude of the changes may not be recognized or admitted for some time. Once the differences are highlighted, it may be even longer before one or both persons arrive at a satisfactory answer to the question of whether the changes can be "lived with" or whether there are grounds for moving the relationship to another stage or to termination. After people answer this question, their dependence on their partner, desire to avoid conflict, concern for their partner, or fear of being alone may extend the process of coming apart even further.[35]

Sudden Death

If the preceding factors are analogous to a relationship slowly bleeding to death, the following is like an unexpected decapitation. Certainly the *actual* death of one partner would be an example of a relationship suddenly dissolving, but Davis provides several other instances in which relationships experience sudden death.

1. In some instances, the partners to a relationship have lost feelings of intimacy, but continue to act out their roles because certain ties make it difficult to sever the relationship. Once these ties are loosened through the efforts of both persons, the relationship is quickly over, sometimes to the shock of people who knew them. Perhaps the constraining bond may be the fact that both persons work in the same office and must cooperate in order to accomplish business goals; perhaps it is the feeling that "we need to stay together for the sake of the children." Interpersonal unpleasantries are repressed and sometimes cause such inner turmoil that the hostility leaks out for others to see anyway. In any case, once the work environment can be changed or the children have become self-sufficient, the relationship may terminate suddenly.

When the researchers who conducted the previously discussed study of dating couples asked their 103 students to identify the time at which the breakup occurred, the data revealed that the school calendar may act as a relationship tie which delays or facilitates breakups. Most of the 400 breakups reported occurred at the end of the school year (May/June), the beginning of the school year (September), and during the Christmas vacation in December/January. When breakups were initiated by the less involved partner they usually occurred at the end of the school year, over the summer, or at the beginning of the school year; when the more involved partner initiated the breakup, it usually occurred during the school year. The authors comment on their findings by saying:

> This pattern of breakups suggests that factors external to a relationship (leaving for vacations, arriving at school, graduation, etc.) may interact with internal factors (such as conflicting values or goals) to cause relationships to end at particular times. For example, changes in living arrangements and schedules at the beginning or end of a semester may make it easier to meet new dating partners (e.g., in a new class) or make it more difficult to maintain previous ties (e.g., when schedules conflict or one moves away). Such changes may raise issues concerning the future of a relationship: Should we get an apartment together? Should we spend our vacation apart? Should I accept a job out of state? Should we get together after vacation? If one has already been considering terminating a relationship, such changes may make it easier to call the relationship off. For example, it is probably easier to say, "While we're apart we ought to date others" than to say, "I've grown tired of you and would rather not date you any more." If one is to attribute the impending breakup to external circumstances, one may be able to avoid some of the ambivalence, embarrassment, and guilt that may be associated with calling a relationship off.[36]

2. Sometimes one person wants to terminate the relationship and the other does not. If the unwilling partner is skillful enough, he or she can keep the relationship in a state of limbo almost indefinitely—by promising "I'll change" at critical junctures or instituting various rejuvenation techniques such as a weekend at a resort. As a result of the unevenness inherent to such a relationship and the knowledge that it is not working for oneself, the dissatisfied partner often decides to act unilaterally and swiftly, trying to avoid any prolongation attempts by the other. Such action is not taken without the possibility of real stress for the terminator. For instance, the terminator must often try to accomplish this maneuver while at the same time avoiding extreme hostility from the other and pangs of guilt for oneself. Hence, rather than take the initiative, the terminator will sometimes try to increase the costs for the unwilling partner sufficiently so that termination will soon become a bilateral decision.

Almost anything is easier to get into then out of.
Mrs. Frederick Lewis Allen

---

3. A variation on the preceding situation concerns relationships in which expectations for the rate of relationship development differ, which again prompts one person to lay the relationship to rest. If one person feels the development is too fast, he or she may request a slowdown, trying to keep the relationship at its current level while waiting to "see how things develop." If the other person does not provide the necessary slowdown mechanisms, a rapid, injudicious decision, often rejection, may be forced. Equally injudicious, of course, is a reluctant acceptance to advance the relationship when one's motivation is feeling guilty rather than feeling intimacy. Relationship escalation based primarily on the need gratification of one person (as in this case) may not have much staying power. The whole episode described here is dangerously similar to the coping strategy of some children— "If you don't play my way, I'll take my bat and go home." When the pace of a relationship's development is too slow, the antithesis of sudden death may appear—the agonizingly slow process in which one or both parties moves toward termination out of boredom or disgust.

Since it isn't always crystal clear for people in a relationship when one of them is ready to advance the relationship, and since pushing advancement at the wrong time can be destructive, escalation efforts often have escape valves. That is, after having suggested an escalation, one can, if necessary, indicate "I didn't think you really meant it *that* way" or "You didn't think I was serious, did you?" or upon rejection, "Who cares? I wasn't really into him/her anyway."

4. Another instance of sudden death may occur when neither party wants to end the relationship, but due to some unforeseen event, a quick termination is precipitated. It may be an argument that gets out of hand when things are said which cut deeply and cannot be forgotten easily. Or it may be that a smooth-running relationship acquires a deadly amount of friction when two people begin competing in the same job environment or for the same award.

5. As was mentioned in previous chapters, intimates develop formal and informal covenants or rules of conduct between themselves; some of these are trivial and easily changeable, some are considered more sacred and inviolable.[37] The latter are usually closely linked to one's core beliefs or expectations and form the foundation and linkages for other dimensions of the relationship. If one of these sacred covenants is broken, it dramatically increases the chances of a sudden termination of the relationship.[38] One reason for this is that there are generally few, if any, adequate excuses ("I was drunk") or methods of correction ("I'll never do it again") which can satisfactorily offset the damage brought about by the violation.

Duck has suggested four phases leading to the dissolution of relationships (see Figure 10.1).[39] While these phases may be more appropriate for some relationships than others, they do point out important issues which relationship partners often have to deal with. In the *Intra-Psychic Phase,* the major activity is the assessment of the other person's behavior and evaluating the extent to which that behavior provides a justification for terminating the relationship. In the *Dyadic Phase,* the partners discuss the perceived problems associated with the relationship. The major

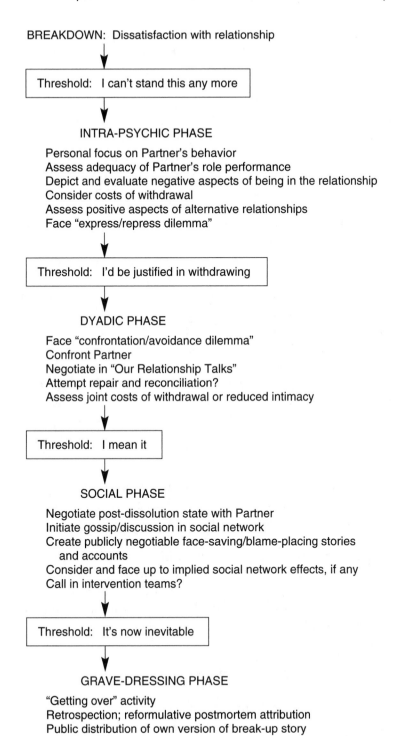

BREAKDOWN: Dissatisfaction with relationship

Threshold: I can't stand this any more

INTRA-PSYCHIC PHASE

Personal focus on Partner's behavior
Assess adequacy of Partner's role performance
Depict and evaluate negative aspects of being in the relationship
Consider costs of withdrawal
Assess positive aspects of alternative relationships
Face "express/repress dilemma"

Threshold: I'd be justified in withdrawing

DYADIC PHASE

Face "confrontation/avoidance dilemma"
Confront Partner
Negotiate in "Our Relationship Talks"
Attempt repair and reconciliation?
Assess joint costs of withdrawal or reduced intimacy

Threshold: I mean it

SOCIAL PHASE

Negotiate post-dissolution state with Partner
Initiate gossip/discussion in social network
Create publicly negotiable face-saving/blame-placing stories
    and accounts
Consider and face up to implied social network effects, if any
Call in intervention teams?

Threshold: It's now inevitable

GRAVE-DRESSING PHASE

"Getting over" activity
Retrospection; reformulative postmortem attribution
Public distribution of own version of break-up story

10.1 Phases of Dissolving Personal Relationships[40]

question underlying this interaction is, "Should the relationship be repaired, redefined or dissolved?" In the *Social Phase,* the participants concern themselves with the public acknowledgement to the social networks associated with the relationship that the relationship is being dissolved. In the *Grave-Dressing Phase,* the major activities are focused on physically, psychologically, and socially ending the relationship. One common concern during this phase is to reconceptualize the relationship so that what happened "makes sense" to each participant.

Making sense of the prior relationship and its dissolution is important for both partners. Much of this sense-making occurs when participants develop an account or story about what caused the breakup.[41] Explaining why the breakup happened helps partners "work through" the changes brought on by relational dissolution. Indeed, Harvey, Orbuch, and Weber argued that those who fail to create an account of their breakup tend to have more difficulty coping with the losses they experience.[42] During the Social and Grave-Dressing Phases, when participants disclose their breakup account to others, they begin to bridge the gap that often exists between their private thoughts about the relationship and their social world. By explaining "what went wrong," they are able to hear themselves think aloud, confide their feelings in others, deal with new information, and maintain relationships with their social network.[43]

The fact that a relationship has passed away slowly or has experienced a sudden demise does not necessarily finalize one's association with it. Sometimes postparting problems can linger long after the relationship has formally disengaged. Partners may get mental or emotional flashes of the past relationship when they encounter shared places or activities. A word or phrase spoken by another person may resemble something the departed one used to say. Perhaps old memories return when one partner is confronted with a task he or she had previously cooperated on, or the other person used to perform alone. In addition to this *pentimento,*[44] partners may find post-relationship blues in the process of trying to disengage the social circles and relatives without experiencing more interpersonal trauma. Then, there are the dilemmas of building new relationships by trying to unlearn the subtleties of the private language (and modes of thinking) developed and used with one's previous partner. These relationship remnants are bound to characterize relationship termination. It is important to review and reflect on one's own needs and communication patterns for application to future relationships. There is a point, however, where work on new relationships will heavily blot out the old; if not, the reruns may become pathological.

Communication During Relationship Decay: Return of the Stranger

In an effort to find out what specific types of strategies people use when they want to break off a relationship, Cody asked students to recall a heterosexual relationship in which they had taken the initiative in breaking off.[45] Students were asked to write down what they said and/or did to accomplish that task. The students used relationships that had been going on for as long as two years, but the average length was about six months. Although this study was conducted with students, the range of strategies reported would appear to apply to other populations. Abbreviated statements listed in Table 10.2 encapsulate the variety of responses provided. The

---

TABLE 10.2   Disengagement Strategies[46]

Positive tone:

1. I told him/her that I was very, very sorry about breaking off the relationship.
2. I told him/her that I regretted very much having to break off the relationship.
3. I told him/her that I cared very, very much for him/her.
4. I told him/her that I was very scared too and didn't want to hurt his/her feelings.
5. I tried very hard to prevent us from leaving on a "sour note."
6. I tried very hard to prevent us from having "hard feelings" about the breakup.

Negative identity management:

7. I told him/her that I was going to date other people and that I thought she/he should date others also.
8. I told him/her life was too short and that we should date other people in order to enjoy life.
9. I told him/her that I thought we should date around and left it at that.
10. I told him/her that it was the best thing for both of us, that we need more time to date others and that I wanted to be sure to find the right person.
11. I told him/her that I wanted to be happy and that we should date other people.
12. I said that I thought we might ruin our relationship altogether if we didn't start dating around a little because I was not happy.

Justification:

13. I fully explained why I felt dissatisfied with the relationship, that it hasn't been growing and that I believe we will both be happier if we didn't date anymore.
14. I said that a good relationship meets the needs of both people and that ours isn't meeting my needs. I said that I didn't want to change him/her and I would have to if he/she were going to meet my needs. So I don't think we should see each other anymore.
15. I fully explained how I felt and that I wanted to break things off. I explained that a relationship was no good unless it makes both people happy and that I wasn't happy and that I didn't want to date anymore.
16. I said that I was really changing inside and I didn't quite feel good about our relationship anymore. I said that we'd better stop seeing each other.
17. I honestly conveyed my wishes not to date anymore.
18. I fully explained my reasons for why we shouldn't see each other anymore.

(continued)

TABLE 10.2 **Continued**

Behavioral de-escalation:

19. I didn't say anything to the partner, I avoided contact with him/her as much as possible.

20. Without explaining my intentions to break off the relationship, I avoided scheduling future meetings with him/her.

21. I never brought up the topic of breaking off the relationship, I just never called the person again and never retuned any of his/her calls.

22. I never verbally said anything to the partner, but I discouraged our seeing each other again.

De-escalation:

23. I told him/her that there should be mutual love and understanding in a relationship and that at the moment I didn't feel as close as I should. I then said that I think we should lay off awhile and see if we wanted to get back together. If we wanted to get back together, we will.

24. I said that we are very close and that we shouldn't be anything but honest and open. If one is not happy, then the other wouldn't be happy either. I think the best thing for us is to let things cool off for awhile and see if we want to continue.

25. I told him/her that I needed to be honest with him/her and suggested that we break it off for awhile and see what happens.

26. I said that the relationship was becoming a strain on me and that we're just going to call it off for now. Maybe some day we can get back together and things will work out.

27. I told him/her that while I was happy most of the time I sometimes felt that I can't do all the things I wanted to. I then said that we should call it quits for now and if we still wanted to get back together we will.

28. I said that we have become too dependent upon each other and have nothing to offer to this relationship and that if we take a period of time to do other things we would be capable of continuing the relationship in the future.

statements formed five groupings: (1) Positive Tone; (2) Negative Identity Management; (3) Justification; (4) Behavioral De-escalation; and (5) De-escalation.

The strategies for terminating a relationship listed in Table 10.2 were then used by Cody to further investigate relationship decay. He found, for instance, that people in intimate relationships were more likely to justify their intentions and employ de-escalation and positive-tone strategies than those disengaging from less intimate relationships. In these less intimate relationships behavioral de-escalation was more likely to be employed. Cody also felt that the causes for the breakups would affect the strategies used, so he asked students to identify the causes of their breakup (Table 10.3) and correlated the causes selected with the strategies selected. Some of these findings include: (1) Students who perceived the relationship problems as the fault of their partner chose justification strategies and avoided positive tone and de-escalation. In such instances the disengager would be expected not to employ strategies that would increase the likelihood of future contacts. (2) When the relationship problem was perceived as a partner's inability or lack of interest in compromising (taking the other for granted; didn't contribute enough to the relationship), the disengager was more likely to use justification and de-escalation strategies and less likely to use positive-tone strategies. (3) It was only when the breakup was initiated by feelings of constraint or lack of freedom that the negative-identity strategy was used along with de-escalation, positive tone, and justification. A later study conducted by Banks, Altendorf, Greene, and Cody not only replicated

TABLE 10.3 Causes Precipitating Relational Disengagements[49]

1. I realized that he/she had too many faults (personality and otherwise).
2. I felt his/her personality was incompatible with mine.
3. I felt that she/he was too demanding.
4. The partner behaved in ways that embarrassed me.
5. Generally, the partner's behaviors and/or personality was more to blame for the breakup than anything else.
6. I realized she/he was unwilling to make enough contributions to the relationship.
7. I felt that he/she no longer behaved towards me as romantically as she/he once did.
8. I felt that he/she took me for granted.
9. I felt that he/she wasn't willing to compromise for the good of the relationship.
10. I simply felt that the relationship was beginning to constrain me, and I felt a lack of freedom.
11. Although I still cared for the partner, I wanted to start dating other people.
12. While this relationship was a good one, I started to get bored with it.
13. The partner made too many contributions and I started to feel suffocated.
14. I felt that she/he was becoming too possessive of me.
15. Although I still liked the partner, I felt that the romance had gone out of the relationship.
16. I was primarily interested in having a good time and not with initiating a relationship.
17. I felt that he/she was too dependent upon me.
18. The two of us simply developed different interests and had less in common.
19. I realized that I couldn't trust him/her.
20. One of us moved away and we couldn't see each other very much.
21. Most of my friends (or all of them) didn't like him/her (most of his/her friends didn't like me), causing problems that detracted from the relationship.
22. Generally, the relationship itself didn't seem right, and the faults of the relationship could not be blamed on any one person in the relationship.
23. My parents didn't approve of him/her (or her/his parents didn't approve of me).
24. The partner showed too much physical affection (or was too aggressive).

these findings, but also found that the quality of relational partners' networks influenced strategy choice. Partners who reported high levels of overlap in their social networks were more likely to employ positive tone, de-escalation, and justification strategies.[47] Like intimacy, being involved in one another's social network seems to encourage consideration for the other's feelings and accountability for one's own behavior during a breakup.

While the preceding two studies validate the notion that these strategies are recalled by individuals who experience a breakup, the actual process of disengagement is probably much less conscious and much more complex. Recalled strategies may not accurately reflect all of the subtleties of the breakup process.[48]

In Chapter 1 eight general characteristics of communication were outlined, which would most likely be found in the very early stages of communicating with an unknown quantity—a stranger. As relationships decay, partners to the relationship seem to design messages in such a way that interaction patterns gradually take on the same "stranger" characteristics—messages that are narrow, stylized, difficult, rigid, awkward, public, hesitant, and that suspend judgments. Some of these message qualities may evidence signs of distance before others. For example, some couples may quit talking about their goals for the future or their sexual desires before they begin to suspend judgments. Others may continue to discuss their sexual desires, but may withhold their judgments and opinions on a variety of issues to gain a sense of power or superiority over their partners.[50] Boiling this down, it seems that people communicate de-escalation of a relationship by producing messages that communicate: (1) an increasing physical and psychological distance; and (2) an increasing disassociation with the other person. These messages can be direct and unambiguous, or they can be indirect and subtle. When emotional confrontations about relationship termination are not desired, the initiator may try to avoid the partner (e.g., stop frequenting familiar places, stop asking about the partner)[51] or may use strategies that take some of the blame for the dissolution (e.g., apologizing, expressing regret).[52] Confrontations can also be avoided by using distance and disassociation signals to "hint" at the need for relationship disengagement. These more indirect approaches may represent a perceived need to protect oneself, a desire to protect one's partner, or a feeling of doubt that the termination is really desired. And, although indirect approaches typically extend the time it takes to accomplish a breakup, indirectness was a very common strategy reported by students in terminating friendships—although the students felt it would be less likely with very close friendships.[53] In most cases, the process probably shows fluctuations between indirect and direct strategies.

Distance

Distance may be communicated by various withdrawal strategies or by the erection of barriers to symbolize withdrawal. We would expect, for instance, to see actual physical distance between the interacting communicators increase. We would also predict an increase in the time between interactions as well as a shorter duration for each encounter (less total communication). Perhaps early stages of decay may manifest lengthy interactions, but if they remain unrewarding, less time will be awarded such discussions. In this same regard, the participants may make it harder to contact one another by sending nonspecific messages about where and when contact can be made—"Where can I reach you?" "Don't bother, I'll call you." or "When will you be coming over to pick up your stuff?" "Whenever I feel like it."

Distance may also be communicated by the communication content, or, in Mehrabian's terms, *nonimmediacy* (not liking). We would expect less variety in the topics discussed and probably less information volunteered about one's personal activities and self. For the participants in a disintegrating relationship, a rationale will be increasingly perceived for *not* exchanging the same amount of information as when the relationship's future looked bright and secure. After all, how much are you willing to invest in a stock that seems on the verge of bankruptcy? As a reflection of this communicative closure, a lot more statements like "Don't worry about that. It doesn't concern you" or "I can't talk to you about anything anymore without you getting surly" will be transmitted. If the relationship was well advanced, amount of talk about the relationship might be fairly high initially, but again, if such talk continues to produce sour results, its frequency will taper off quickly. Our guess is that the same general usage level of superlatives and absolute statements that the pair exhibited in the growth process will be found at this stage—but now the statements are heavily laden with negativity. For instance, instead of, "You're the *only* one for me—the *greatest*" we might hear, "You *never* think of my needs—*never* have—you're the *most* self-centered person I've *ever* known." Speaking of needs, it should be a natural part of this process to see fewer favors exchanged. Not only is the motivation for favor-giving decreasing, but many times unsolicited favors by the other are discouraged. They may simply activate the psychological forces behind the norm of reciprocity which can produce a feeling of indebtedness at a time when one is trying to clear the books.

Finally, distance can be communicated through nonverbal behaviors. Some of the more obvious nonverbal manifestations might include: (1) less direct body orientation; (2) less total eye contact; (3) eye contact for shorter durations, except in those instances where it is used to intimidate or threaten during verbal communication or preceding physical combat; (4) less touching; (5) a colder vocal tone; and (6) silences filled with discomfort, embarrassment, and disaffection rather than warmth.

The following reports illustrate the wife's need to achieve nonverbal distance during a time when she was contemplating divorce. They also show how the husband's account of the same behavior was very different. He either failed to recognize the wife's marital dissatisfaction, recognized it and didn't want to face it, or didn't see the connection between cuddling and the decreasing intimacy in the marriage. The wife said,

> Steve always put his arm around me to cuddle before we went to sleep. I wasn't in the mood for it and for the first time I told him so. I can't stand being on the verge of divorce and still cuddling every night. He just turned over and went to sleep.

Her husband described the same event as follows:

> Joanne and I have always held each other before going to sleep, so I put my arm around her as usual. She said, "I'm not in the mood," so I thought, "OK" and went to sleep.[54]

Disassociation

Disassociation is usually reflected in an increasing concern for oneself, and a resulting decrease in concern for the relationship. This focus on self results in communicative behaviors that flow naturally from such an orientation. For instance, if your main concern was preserving the self (to the exclusion or minimization of the process of preserving the relationship), you would be inclined toward less compromise in disagreements, adopting the illusory, "I win, you lose" stance, with its corollary that there is only one view of reality which is "right." The reason we use the word *illusory* is that so many times the strategies used to "win" only produce tremendous costs to the self-proclaimed "victor." As these costs for communicating orally mount, movement toward the stagnating stage can be expected.

Disassociation is also reflected in an increase in individual experiences and fewer activities jointly performed by the partners to the relationship. In the same manner, language which ties the pair into a single unit will be increasingly abandoned—more "I," "me," "my," and "mine" expressions replace the "we," "our," and "us." When the pair terms are used, it is likely to be in the context of pointing out how "we are different in the following ways" leading to the oft-spoken and ironic conclusion that "I guess I never really knew you." Since the prognosis for the relationship's future is tenuous at best, the past tense is used most often in communicating in an attempt to rewrite the relationship's history so that current actions make sense. The only necessary future-tense discussions concern what kind, if any, of a relationship the future holds.

The attempt to emphasize differences and accentuate individuality may take many forms—buying clothes that illustrate differences; showing preferences for food or art work that obviously deviate from known preferences of the other; pursuing contrary interests; widespread verbalization of certain inharmonious attitudinal positions. Individuality can also be reflected in speech patterns. Word choice,

10.2 Magritte's "The Lovers" aptly illustrates the feeling of distance and disassociation

accent, rate of speaking, or even the amount of talk may show increasing divergence when at least one partner attempts to disassociate himself or herself from the other person.[55] As noted earlier in this chapter, communication during relationship decay tends to move increasingly toward the type of communication used with strangers. As one person disassociates himself or herself from a particular other—communication takes on more interpersonal etiquette; more formal names and titles; the avoidance of endearment terms.

A note on the complexity of the foregoing behaviors seems to be in order. Identifying a relationship on the decline through observation of its communication patterns is difficult. This is because the observers need, but often don't have, a baseline measure of typical communication against which current patterns can be compared. Suppose observers see, for instance, that a couple exhibits several distancing and disassociation features in their communication behavior. Perhaps this simply reflects a form of adaptation made by this particular couple and not a signal of relationship decay. Or, observers might see a certain amount of distancing and disassociation maneuvers when the observed people are trying to move a relationship back (perhaps from intensifying to experimenting) but are not trying to terminate it. In order to communicate this desired change in the relationship ("Can't we just be friends instead of lovers?") the couple finds it necessary to turn down their proximity and integration sensors—just as it is necessary in the termination process. It's a matter of degree. In another instance, observers may see distancing or disassociation behavior, but the relational partners themselves may not even be aware that they are sending distancing or disassociation messages. Ironically, one partner may accuse the other of such behavior only to increase the chances of such behavior appearing, whether it was extant in the first place or not.

Every exit is an entry somewhere else.
Tom Stoppard

Similarly, it is sometimes nearly impossible to sort out cause-effect relationships—when the wife began going skiing alone, was this in itself an act of disassociation, or was an enjoyable activity for the wife the start of many new associations, friends, etc., which eventually turned a simple hobby into a divisive force in the relationship?

A final qualification concerns the fact that in every relationship, even the most intimate one, there will be some messages that communicate distance and disassociation. The critical question is: When are these de-escalation messages of sufficient strength or quantity to indicate that a relationship has taken a downward spiral? Until research supplies more specific answers, the answer will probably continue to emanate from the feelings of each individual. Our guess is that if we listen to our feelings (rather than what we or others *think* we should feel) those feelings will signal warnings, maybe not to the degree of danger or to the cause of the danger but to the need for some scrutiny of the relationship.

The Farewell Address

Unlike other speeches called farewell addresses, the relationship farewell address is not restricted to a certain time frame. It may extend over a period of hours, days, or months. It does, however, have some features that are common to other farewell speeches and to the goodbye ritual we perform so many times everyday. Probably the most important commonality is the belief by the participants and others that the act of leave-taking is not a separate, isolated unit of discourse. The farewell address will reflect facets of the total relationship history, although those facets are often magnified to the point where the participants may very well see their exhibited behavior as a distortion or misrepresentation of their "normal" style. For example, a leave-taking may be characterized by a lot of yelling and nastiness which the pair feels is atypical of their relationship, but which is more typical than they wish to admit.

In a study of everyday leave-taking in human transactions, three functions of leave-taking behaviors were identified: (1) summarizing the substance of the discourse; (2) signaling the impending decreased access between the communicators; and (3) signaling supportiveness.[56] Although this study focused on specific conversations, the three functions form a useful paradigm for analysis even when the situation observed changes from a conversation to an ongoing relationship. For instance, the termination of some conversations calls for the recapitulation or summarizing of salient points—as in the case of a professor counseling a student on how to study more effectively for his or her exams. Similarly, some relationship farewells require an historical summary, usually emphasizing the unpleasant aspects of the relationship to provide a rationale for the imminent action.

The final moments of a conversation also show the second function of conversational leave-taking—verbal and nonverbal efforts to communicate the impending decrease in communicative access. Put another way, we let people know we are going to be absent from them for awhile. The latter phases of a relationship also communicate this decreased access. As we've noted, there are many ways of showing decreased access by increasing psychological and physical distance. A farewell address may, however, be more explicit—"After July 1, we will only have to see each other once a month. Oh, maybe we'll run into each other accidentally someplace, but I'm not going out with you again." Perhaps the strongest act that communicates the certainty of decreased access for disengaging married couples is that of deciding how to divide household objects and/or time spent with children.

The third function of conversational leave-taking is to signal a form of supportiveness for what has transpired ("Thanks for your time. I think you really helped me"). It also offsets inaccessibility signals by suggesting future contact ("OK, let's do this again sometime"), and communicates the idea that the conversation is terminated, but not the relationship. Have you ever noticed how many future plans people make that never come about—but it doesn't matter? All that really matters between friends is that they continue to talk about a future. When the farewell address is designed to communicate the fact that there will be no future relationship, this function obviously cannot be achieved. However, many farewell addresses leave open the possibility for some kind of future relationship—even if it is something slightly more than stranger status.[57] As a result, signs of supportiveness may be evident in the farewell rhetoric of decaying relationships. The parties may agree to be friendly and helpful to each other when occasional future contact is made; they may reflect on the decaying process supportively—"It could have been a lot worse if you hadn't . . . and I want you to know I appreciate it. . . ." The parties may express welfare concern—"Yeah, well . . . take care of yourself. . . ." Once separation has formally occurred, it is not at all unusual to hear reminiscences such as: "Sure we had some bad scenes, but. . . ." In fact, supportiveness may be just as critical for relationship termination as it is for conversation termination—which may help to explain why nonsupportive terminations so often take a high psychological toll.

A comparison between conversational and relational leave-taking is worthy of note. In conversations there are two very common methods of verbally explaining why one is leaving. One of these is called an *internal legitimizer* because the leaver takes sole responsibility for the act of leaving—"Well, I think that is all I have to say." The other pattern is called an *external legitimizer* because the justification for leaving is derived from forces external to the leaver—"I can see other people are waiting to see you, so I'll be going." Leaving a relationship can also be expressed or justified from internal or external perspectives. Some people will reflect on personal behaviors and attitudes that may have contributed to the deterioration of the relationship; others are more inclined to focus their reflection on people and events external to themselves. Although research suggests that dissatisfied couples tend to give internal, stable explanations for the negative events in their relationship (e.g., ". . . because she is insensitive to my needs"),[58] it is very possible that once partners terminate the relationship, their explanations will change (e.g., ". . . because we were both hurting"). The notion that people often focus on internal or external causes for relational dissolution does not suggest that combination of the two perspectives is unheard of; in reality, most relationships are abandoned because of a combination of internal and external forces. The perspective emphasized will probably depend on relational factors such as the duration of the association, the relationship stage, and the degree to which the partner feels invested in the relationship. Individual factors such as the partner's personality, mood (e.g., sad or guilty)[59] and mental state (e.g., depressed or lonely)[60] should also affect the explanation he or she formulates.

Finally, let's examine the familiar farewell, or goodbye, itself. Although the term *goodbye* is possibly our most common referent for leave-taking expressions, it is not really common in daily exchanges. It probably has a greater frequency in children's leave-taking than in adults; and some form of it is probably used more to terminate telephone conversations than face-to-face encounters. The feature most relevant to our current analysis, however, is the hypothesized finality communicated by the term *goodbye* in face-to-face transactions. Goffman believes we now use *goodbye* primarily in situations where the interactants will be apart for an extended period of time.[61] Further, we would expect *goodbye* to be found in more formal situations than informal situations. Thus, it seems reasonable to hypothesize that the farewell address is more likely to contain *goodbyes* that simultaneously communicate formality, finality, and extended absence.

The following is a composite developed by Davis which illustrates a number of the issues that may characterize the termination of an intimate relationship.

> We just can't go on like this! I don't want to see you again. I don't want to speak to you again. Don't ask me what I'm going to do. Don't ask me for any more favors. Here's your ring back. You can have the house and the furniture. I'll take the baby. You'll have to call Tim and Ann and tell them we won't be able to come to dinner. I'll stay at a hotel tonight and send over tomorrow for my personal belongings. And you'll be hearing from my lawyer within a week. We're through![62]

SUMMARY

Our goal in this chapter has been to elaborate on those processes enacted when relationships come apart. We briefly outlined how relationship termination may occur in less intimate associations, but the major emphases in the chapter dealt with terminations of more intimate relationships. These relationships may pass away or, because of special circumstances, experience a sudden death. After the relationships have been officially terminated, the participants may continue to experience relationship flashbacks, which should gradually attenuate over time.

The second part of this chapter identified the general nature of communication during relationship decay as an increasing psychological and physical distance and continued disassociation from the other person. In short, communication behavior in decaying relationships will increasingly reflect patterns associated with strangers rather than those associated with intimates. Specifically, as a relationship moves toward termination, we would expect to find:

- Increasing physical distance between the interactants
- Increasing time between interactions
- Shorter encounters
- Less personal information exchanged
- Less relationship talk
- Fewer favors given and/or asked for
- Less verbal immediacy
- Superlatives and absolutistic statements couched in negative rather than positive evaluations
- Less nonverbal immediacy—less touching, colder vocal tone, less eye contact
- An increasing concern for self rather than for the relationship or the other person
- Less compromising due to an increasing win-lose orientation
- More individual rather than mutual activities
- Decreasing use of endearment terms and private language—a return to a less particularized set of etiquette norms
- Differences accentuated in clothes, food, and other preferences; and many, many more

While we might agree that the preceding list of behaviors seems to occur in disintegrating relationships, this does not suggest we won't find some evidence of the same behaviors in relationships that are growing or moving back to earlier stages.

These behaviors, however, will not be common in intimate relationships. The question of whether these behaviors are associated with a dying relationship or with one that has a temporary virus can be answered by looking at the frequency with which a given behavior occurs and seeing whether other behaviors seem to be communicating the same distancing and disassociation messages. We might find, for instance, relational partners who have infrequent verbal interactions, but send many nonverbal messages of affection. Hence, for this couple, one behavior that might communicate distance is offset by others that communicate closeness.

To further illustrate the similarities between communication in encounters and relationships, we looked at relationship farewells through the lens of research data on saying goodbye in conversations. Parallels were suggested along functional lines—in both conversations and relationships evidence of the need to summarize, to clarify the impending decreased access, and to show supportiveness during the goodbye ritual was found.

SELECTED READINGS

Relationship Termination

Baxter, L. A. "Strategies for Ending Relationships: Two Studies." *Western Journal of Speech Communication* 46 (1982): 223–241.

Baxter, L. A., and Philpott, J. "Attribution-Based Strategies for Initiating and Terminating Friendships." *Communication Quarterly* 30 (1982): 217–224.

Burnett, R., McGhee, P., and Clarke, D. D. *Accounting for Relationships: Explanation, Representation, and Knowledge.* London: Methuen, 1987.

Cody, M. J. "A Typology of Disengagement Strategies and an Examination of the Role Intimacy Reactions to Inequity and Relational Problems Play in Strategy Selection." *Communication Monographs* 49 (1982): 148–170.

Cupach, W. R., and Metts, S. "Accounts of Relational Dissolution: A Comparison of Marital and Nonmarital Relationships." *Communication Monographs* 53 (1986): 311–334.

Davis, M. S. *Intimate Relations.* New York: Free Press, 1973, pp. 245–283.

Duck, S. "A Topography of Relationship Disengagement and Dissolution." In S. Duck, ed., *Personal Relationships 4: Dissolving Personal Relationships,* pp. 1–30. New York: Academic Press, 1982.

Duck, S. "Toward a Research Map for the Study of Relationship Breakdown." In S. Duck and R.

Gilmour, eds., *Personal Relationships 3: Personal Relationships in Disorder,* pp. 1–29. New York: Academic Press, 1981.

Duck, S., ed. *Personal Relationships 4: Dissolving Personal Relationships.* New York: Academic Press, 1982.

Emmers, T. M., and Hart, R. D. "Romantic Relationship Disengagement and Coping Rituals." *Communication Research* 13 (1996): 8–18.

Hill, C. T., Rubin, Z., and Peplau, L. A. "Breakups Before Marriage: The End of 103 Affairs." *Journal of Social Issues* 32 (1976): 147–168.

Lee, L. "Sequences in Separation: A Framework for Investigating Endings of the Personal (Romantic) Relationship." *Journal of Social and Personal Relationships* 1 (1984): 49–73.

Levinger, G. "A Social Exchange View on the Dissolution of Pair Relationships." In R. L. Burgess and T. L. Huston, eds., *Social Exchange in Developing Relationships,* pp. 169–193. New York: Academic Press, 1979.

Miller, G. R., and Parks, M. R. "Communication in Dissolving Relationships." In S. Duck, ed., *Personal Relationships 4: Dissolving Personal Relationships,* pp. 127–154. New York: Academic Press, 1982.

Orbuch, T. L., ed. *Close Relationship Loss: Theoretical Approaches.* New York: Springer-Verlag, 1993.

Owen, W. F. "Metaphors in Accounts of Romantic Relationship Termination." In P. J. Kalbfleisch, ed., *Interpersonal Communication: Evolving Interpersonal Relationships,* pp. 261–278. Hillsdale, NJ: Erlbaum, 1993.

Vaughn, D. *Uncoupling: How Relationships Come Apart.* New York: Vintage Books, 1987.

Weber, A. L., Harvey, J. H., and Orbuch, T. L. "What Went Wrong: Communicating Accounts of Relationships Conflict." In M. L. McLaughlin, M. J. Cody, and S. J. Read, eds., *Explaining One's Self to Others: Reason-Giving in a Social Context,* pp. 261–280. Hillsdale, NJ: Erlbaum, 1992.

Leave-Taking

Adato, A. "Leave-Taking: A Study of Commonsense Knowledge of Social Structure." *Anthropological Quarterly* 48 (1975): 255–271.

Albert, S., and Kessler, S. "Ending Social Encounters." *Journal of Experimental Social Psychology* 14 (1978): 541–553.

———. "Processes for Ending Social Encounters: The Conceptual Archaeology of a Temporal Place." *Journal for the Theory of Social Behavior* 6 (1976): 147–170.

Firth, R. "Verbal and Bodily Rituals of Greeting and Parting." In J. S. LaFountaine, ed., *The Interpretation of Ritual.* London: Tavistock Publications, 1972.

Goffman, E. *Relations in Public.* New York: Basic Books, 1971, pp. 79–91.

Knapp, M. L., Hart, R. P., Friedrich, G. W., and Shulman, G. M. "The Rhetoric of Goodbye: Verbal and Nonverbal Correlates of Human Leave-Taking." *Speech Monographs* 40 (1973): 182–198.

Knuf, J. "Greeting and Leave-Taking: A Bibliography of Resources for the Study of Ritualized Communication." *Research on Language and Social Interaction* 24 (1990/1991): 405–448.

Laver, J. "Communicative Functions of Phatic Communion." In A. Kendon, R. M. Harris, and M. R. Key, eds., *Organization of Behavior in Face-to-Face Interaction.* Chicago: Aldine Publishing Co., 1975.

Schegloff, E. A., and Sacks, H. "Opening Up Closings." *Semiotica* 4 (1973): 289–327.

Sigman, S. J. "Handling the Discontinuous Aspects of Continuous Social Relationships: Toward Research on the Persistence of Social Forms." *Communication Theory* 1 (1991): 106–127.

Tarrant, J. J., Feinberg, G., and Feinberg, M. *Leave-taking.* New York: Simon and Schuster, 1978.

Divorce

Amato, P. R. "Explaining the Intergenerational Transmission of Divorce." *Journal of Marriage and the Family* 58 (1996): 628–640.

Gottman, J. M. *What Predicts Divorce?: The Relationship between Marital Processes and Marital Outcomes.* Hillsdale, NJ: Erlbaum, 1994.

Hagestad, G. O., and Smyer, M. A. "Dissolving Long-Term Relationships: Patterns of Divorcing in Middle Age." In S. Duck, ed., *Personal Relationships 4: Dissolving Personal Relationships,* pp. 155–188. New York: Academic Press, 1982.

Kaslow, F. W., and Schwartz, L. L. *The Dynamics of Divorce.* New York: Brunner/Mazel, 1987, pp. 38–41.

Kurdek, L. A. "Predicting Marital Dissolution: A 5-Year Prospective Longitudinal Study of Newlywed Couples." *Journal of Personality and Social Psychology* 64 (1993): 221–242.

Levinger, G. "A Social Psychological Perspective on Marital Dissolution." *Journal of Social Issues* 32 (1976): 21–47.

———. "Marital Cohesiveness and Dissolution: An Integrative Review." *Journal of Marriage and the Family* 27 (1965): 21–47.

———. "Sources of Dissatisfaction Among Applicants for Divorce." *American Journal of Orthopsychiatry* 36 (1966): 803–807.

Levinger, G., and Moles, O. C., eds. *Divorce and Separation.* New York: Basic Books, 1979.

Lykken, D. T. "How Relationships Begin and End." In A. L. Vangelisti, H. T. Reis, and M. A. Fitzpatrick, eds., *Stability and Change in Relationships.* New York: Cambridge University Press, in press.

Matthews, L., Wickrama, K., and Conger, R. "Predicting Marital Instability from Spouse and Observer Reports of Marital Interaction." *Journal of Marriage and the Family* 58 (1996): 641–655.

Ponzetti, J. J., and Cate, R. M. "The Divorce Process: Toward a Typology of Marital Dissolution." *Journal of Divorce* 11 (1988): 1–20.

Riessman, C. K. *Divorce Talk: Women and Men Make Sense of Personal Relationships.* New Brunswick, NJ: Rutgers University Press, 1990.

Textor, M., ed. *The Divorce and Divorce Therapy Handbook.* Northvale. NJ: Jason Aronson. 1989.

Weiss, P. *Marital Separation.* New York: Basic Books, 1975.

Jealousy

Adams, V. "Getting at the Heart of Jealous Love." *Psychology Today* 13 (1980): 38, 41–44, 47, 102, 105–106.

Bernard, J. "Jealousy in Marriage." *Medical Aspects of Human Sexuality* 5 (1971): 200–215.

Clanton, G., and Smith, L. G., eds. *Jealousy.* Englewood Cliffs, NJ: Prentice-Hall, 1977.

DeSteno, D. A., and Salovey, P. "Jealousy and the Characteristics of One's Rival: A Self-Evaluation Maintenance Perspective." *Personality and Social Psychology Bulletin* 22 (1996): 920–932.

Dijkstra, P., and Buunk, B. P. "Jealousy as a Function of Rival Characteristics: An Evolutionary Perspective." *Personality and Social Psychology Bulletin* 24 (1998):1158–1166.

Guerrero, L. K., and Andersen, P. A. "Jealousy Experience and Expression in Romantic Relationships." In P. A. Andersen and L. K. Guerrero, eds., *Handbook of Communication and Emotion: Research, Theory, Applications, and Contexts,* pp. 155–188. San Diego, Ca: Academic Press, 1998.

Pittman, F. *Private Lies: Infidelity and the Betrayal of Intimacy.* New York: W. W. Norton, 1989.

Salovey, P. *The Psychology of Jealousy and Envy.* New York: Guilford, 1991.

White, G. L., and Mullen, P. E. *Jealousy: Theory, Research and Clinical Strategies.* New York: The Guilford Press, 1989.

NOTES

[1]C. Safran, "Troubles That Pull Couples Apart: A Redbook Report," *Redbook* (January 1979): 83, 138–141.

[2]B. L. Fisher, P. R. Giblin, and M. H. Hoopes, "Healthy Family Functioning: What Therapists Say and What Families Want," *Journal of Marital and Family* 8 (1982): 273–284; F. W. Kaslow and L. L. Schwartz, *The Dynamics of Divorce* (New York: Bruner/Mazel, 1987), pp. 38–41; H. J. Markman, M. J. Renick, F. J. Floyd, S. M. Stanley, and M. Clements, "Preventing Marital Distress through Communication and Conflict Management Training: A 4- and 5-Year Follow-Up," *Journal of Consulting and Clinical Psychology* 61 (1993): 70–77; F. Walsh, "Conceptualization of Normal Family Processes." In F. Walsh, ed., *Normal Family Processes* 2nd ed. (New York: Guilford, 1993), pp. 3–69. For reviews, see: P. Noller and M. A. Fitzpatrick, "Marital Communication in the Eighties," *Journal of Marriage and the Family* 52 (1990): 832–843; P. Noller and H. H. Guthrie, "Studying Communication in Marriage." In W. Jones and D. Perlman, eds., *Advances in Personal Relationships,* vol. 3 (London: Jessica Kingsley, 1991), pp. 37–73.

[3]"How Americans Communicate: A National Survey." Prepared by Roper Starch for the National Communication Association, 1998.

[4]A. L. Vangelisti and T. L. Huston, "Maintaining Marital Satisfaction and Love." In D. J. Canary and L. Stafford, eds., *Communication and Relational Maintenance* (San Diego, CA: Academic, 1994), pp. 165–186.

[5]J. M. Gottman, *Marital Interaction: Experimental Investigations* (New York: Academic Press, 1979); J. M. Gottman, *What Predicts Divorce? The Relationship Between Marital Processes and Marital Outcomes* (Hillsdale, NJ: Erlbaum, 1994).

[6]H. Markman, "The Longitudinal Study of Couples' Interactions: Implications for Understanding and Predicting the Development of Marital Distress." In K. Halweg and N. Jacobson, eds., *Marital Interaction: Analysis and Modification* (New York: Guilford, 1984), pp. 253–281.

[7]J. Belsky and K. H. Hsieh, "Patterns of Marital Change During the Early Childhood Years: Parent Personality, Coparenting, and Division-of-Labor Correlates," *Journal of Family Psychology* 12 (1998):511–528.

[8]B. R. Karney and T. N. Bradbury, "Neuroticism, Marital Interaction, and the Trajectory of Marital Satisfaction," *Journal of Personality and Social Psychology* 72 (1997):1075–1092; K. A. McGonagle, R. C. Kessler, and I. H. Gotlib, "The Effects of Marital Disagreement Style, Frequency, and Outcome on Marital Disruption," *Journal of Social and Personal Relationships* 10 (1993): 385–404; P. Noller, "Negative Communications in Marriage," *Journal of Social and Personal Relationships* 2 (1985): 289–301.

[9]D. Revenstorf, K. Hahlweg, L. Schindler, and B. Vogel, "Interaction Analysis of Marital Conflict." In

K. Hahlweg and N. S. Jacobson, eds., *Marital Interaction: Analysis and Modification* (New York: Guilford, 1984), pp. 159–181.

[10]L. Matthews, K. Wickrama, and R. Conger, "Predicting Marital Instability from Spouse and Observer Reports of Marital Interaction," *Journal of Marriage and the Family* 58 (1996): 641–655.

[11]H. Markman and K. Hahlweg, "The Prediction and Prevention of Marital Distress," *Clinical Psychology Review* 13 (1993): 29–43.

[12]J. Gottman, J. Coan, S. Carrere, and C. Swanson, "Predicting Marital Happiness and Stability from Newlywed Interactions," *Journal of Marriage and the Family* 60 (1998): 5–22.

[13]V. Jockin, M. McGue, and D. T. Lykken, "Personality and Divorce: A Genetic Analysis," *Journal of Personality and Social Psychology* 71 (1996): 288–299; D. T. Lykken, "How Relationships Begin and End." In A. L. Vangelisti, H. T. Reis, and M. A. Fitzpatrick, eds., *Stability and Change in Relationships* (New York: Cambridge University Press, in press).

[14]C. T. Hill, Z. Rubin, and L. A. Peplau, "Breakups Before Marriage: The End of 103 Affairs," *Journal of Social Issues* 32 (1976): 147–168.

[15]W. R. Cupach and S. Metts, "Accounts of Relational Dissolution: A Comparison of Marital and Nonmarital Relationships," *Communication Monographs* 53 (1986): 328.

[16]D. Vaughn, *Uncoupling: How Relationships Come Apart* (New York: Vintage Books, 1987), pp. 169–175, 194–196, 241–244.

[17]Source: Adapted from "Breakups Before Marriage: The End of 103 Affairs," by Charles T. Hill, Zick Rubin and Letitia Ann Peplau, in *Divorce and Separation,* edited by George Levinger and Oliver C. Moles. © 1979 by The Society for the Psychological Study of Social Issues. By permission of Basic Books, Publishers, Inc.

[18]J. D. Freezel and P. E. Shepherd, "Cross-Generational Coping with Interpersonal Relationship Loss," *Western Journal of Speech Communication* 51 (1987): 317–327.

[19]J. Simpson, "The Dissolution of Romantic Relationships: Factors Involved in Relationship Stability and Emotional Distress," *Journal of Personality and Social Psychology* 53 (1987): 683–692.

[20]P. A. Frazier and S. W. Cook, "Correlates of Distress Following Heterosexual Relationship Dissolution," *Journal of Social and Personal Relationships* 10 (1993): 55–67.

[21]R. Burnett, P. McGhee, and D. D. Clarke, *Accounting for Relationships: Explanation, Representation, and Knowledge* (London: Methuen, 1987); L. R. Propst and L. Fries, "Problems and Needs of Adults." In M. Textor, ed., *The Divorce and Divorce Therapy Handbook* (Northvale, NJ: Jason Aronson, 1989), pp. 45–60; T. Stephen, "Attribution and Adjustment to Relationship Termination," *Journal of Social and Personal Relationships* 4 (1987): 47–61.

[22]L. A. Kurdek, "Adjusting to Relationship Dissolution in Gay, Lesbian, and Heterosexual Partners," *Personal Relationships* 4 (1997): 145–161.

[23]J. J. Ponzetti and R. M. Cate, "The Divorce Process: Toward a Typology of Marital Dissolution," *Journal of Divorce* 11 (1988): 1–20.

[24]M. S. Davis, *Intimate Relations* (New York: Free Press, 1973), chapter 8.

[25]C. E. Rusbult, S. M. Drigotas, and J. Verette, "The Investment Model: An Interdependence Analysis of Commitment Processes and Relationship Maintenance Phenomena." In D. J. Canary and L. Stafford, eds., *Communication and Relational Maintenance* (San Diego, CA: Academic, 1994), pp. 115–139; C. E. Rusbult, I. M. Zembrodt, and L. K. Gunn, "Exit, Voice, Loyalty, and Neglect: Responses to Dissatisfaction in Romantic Involvements," *Journal of Personality and Social Psychology* 43 (1982): 1230–1242.

[26]D. A. DeSteno and P. Salovey, "Jealousy and the Characteristics of One's Rival: A Self-Evaluation Maintenance Perspective," *Personality and Social Psychology Bulletin* 22 (1996): 920–932.

[27]G. Clanton and L. G. Smith, eds., *Jealousy* (Englewood Cliffs, NJ: Prentice-Hall, 1977), p. 188.

[28]F. Pittman, *Private Lies: Infidelity and the Betrayal of Intimacy* (New York: Norton, 1989); for a list of tactics partners may use to "retain" their partners in the face of relational threats, see D. M. Buss and T. K. Shackelford, "From Vigilance to Violence: Mate Retention Tactics in Married Couples," *Journal of Personality and Social Psychology* 72 (1997): 346–361.

[29]L. K. Guerrero, and P. A. Andersen, "Jealousy Experience and Expression in Romantic Relationships." In P. A. Andersen and L. K. Guerrero, eds., *Handbook of Communication and Emotion: Research, Theory, Applications, and Contexts* (San Diego, Ca: Academic Press, 1998) pp. 155–188.

[30]See, for example, L. K. Guerrero "Attachment-Style Differences in the Experience and Expression of Romantic Jealousy," *Personal Relationships* 5 (1998): 273–291; D. J. Sharpsteen, "The Effects of Relationship and Self-Esteem Threats on the Likelihood of Romantic Jealousy," *Journal of Social and Personal Relationships* 12 (1995): 89–101.

[31]P. Salovey and J. Rodin, "The Heart of Jealousy," *Psychology Today* (September, 1985), pp. 22–29.

[32]C. Ellis and E. Weinstein, "Jealousy and the Social Psychology of Emotional Experience," *Journal of Social and Personal Relationships* 3 (1986): 337–357.

[33]L. Stafford and J. R. Reske, "Idealization and Communication in Long-Distance Premarital Relationships," *Family Relations* 39 (1990): 274–279.

[34]D. H. Felmlee, "Fatal Attractions: Affection and Disaffection in Intimate Relationships," *Journal of Social and Personal Relationships* 12 (1995): 295–311; D. H. Felmlee, " 'Be Careful What You Wish For . . .': A Quantitative and Qualitative Investigation of 'Fatal Attractions'," *Personal Relationships* 5 (1998): 235–253.

[35]S. M. Drigotas and C. E. Rusbult, "Should I Stay or Should I Go? A Dependence Model of Breakups," *Journal of Personality and Social Psychology* 62 (1992): 62–87; L. Lee, "Sequences in Separation: A Framework for Investigating Endings of the Personal (Romantic) Relationship," *Journal of Social and Personal Relationships* 1 (1984): 49–73; D. Vaughn, "The Long Goodbye." *Psychology Today* (July, 1987), pp. 37–42.

[36]Hill, Rubin, and Peplau, "Breakups Before Marriage: The End of 103 Affairs," *op cit*, pp. 156–157.

[37]W. H. Jones and M. P. Burdette, "Betrayal in Relationships." In A. L. Weber and J. H. Harvey, eds., *Perspectives on Close Relationships* (Boston: Allyn and Bacon, 1994), pp. 243–262.

[38]D. Vaughn, *Uncoupling: How Relationships Come Apart*. pp. 132–134.

[39]S. Duck, "A Topography of Relationship Disengagement and Dissolution." In S. Duck, ed., *Personal Relationships 4: Dissolving Personal Relationships* (New York: Academic Press, 1982), pp. 1–30.

[40]Reprinted with permission from Steve Duck, "A Topography of Relationship Disengagement and Dissolution." In S. Duck, ed., *Personal Relationships 4: Dissolving Personal Relationships*, (New York: Academic Press, 1982), p. 16. Copyright: Academic Press Inc. [London] Ltd.

[41]J. H. Harvey, A. L. Weber, and T. L. Orbuch, *Interpersonal Accounts: A Social Psychological Perspective* (Oxford: Basil Blackwell, 1990).

[42]J. H. Harvey, T. L. Orbuch, and A. L. Weber, "A Social Psychological Model of Account-Making in Response to Severe Stress," *Journal of Language and Social Psychology* 9 (1990): 191–207.

[43]A. L. Weber, J. H., Harvey, and T. L. Orbuch, "What Went Wrong: Communicating Accounts of Relationship Conflict." In M. L. McLaughlin, M. J. Cody, and S. J. Read, eds., *Explaining One's Self to Others: Reason-Giving in a Social Context* (Hillsdale, NJ: Erlbaum, 1992), pp. 261–280.

[44]Author Lillian Hellman prefaces her book, *Pentimento,* with the following definition: "Old paint on canvas, as it ages, sometimes becomes transparent. When that happens it is possible, in some pictures, to see the original lines: a tree will show through a woman's dress, a child makes way for a dog, a large boat is no longer on an open sea. That is called pentimento, because the painter 're-pented,' changed his mind. Perhaps it would be as well to say that the old conception, replaced by a later choice, is a way of seeing and then seeing again."

[45]M. Cody, "A Typology of Disengagement Strategies and an Examination of the Role of Intimacy, Reactions to Inequity and Relational Problems Play in Strategy Selection," *Communication Monographs* 49 (1982): 148–170.

[46]Source: From M. J. Cody, "A Typology of Disengagement Strategies and an Examination of the Role Intimacy Reactions to Inequity and Relational Problems Play in Strategy Selection," *Communication Monographs* 49 (1982): 163.

[47]S. P. Banks, D. M. Altendorf, J. O. Greene, and M. J. Cody, "An Examination of Relationship Disengagement: Perceptions, Breakup Strategies and Outcomes," *Western Journal of Speech Communication* 51 (1987): 19–41.

[48]See, for example: R. Hopper and K. Drummond, "Emergent Goals at a Relational Turning Point: The Case of Gordon and Denise," *Journal of Language and Social Psychology* 9 (1991): 39–65.

[49]Source: From M. J. Cody, "A Typology of Disengagement Strategies and an Examination of the Role Intimacy Reactions to Inequity and Relational Problems Play in Strategy Selection," *Communication Monographs* 49 (1982): 162.

[50]J. Ayres, "Perceived Use of Evaluative Statements in Developing, Stable, and Deteriorating Relationships with a Person of the Same or Opposite Sex," *Western Journal of Speech Communication* 46 (1982): 20–31; L. A. Baxter, "Relationship Disengagement: An Examination of the Reversal Hypothesis," *Western Journal of Speech Communication* 7 (1983): 85–98.

[51]T. M. Emmers and R. D. Hart, "Romantic Relationship Disengagement and Coping Rituals," *Communication Research* 13 (1996): 8–18.

[52]Indeed, Metts argued that initiators may increase their use of such "polite" strategies as the

loss incurred from ending the relationship increases (see S. Metts, "The Language of Disengagement: A Face-Management Perspective." In T. L. Orbuch, ed., *Close Relationship Loss.* New York: Springer-Verlag, 1992).

[53]L. A. Baxter, "Strategies for Ending Relationships: Two Studies," *Western Journal of Speech Communication* 46 (1982): 223–241.

[54]D. R. Peterson, "Assessing Interpersonal Relationships by Means of Interaction Records," *Behavioral Assessment* 1 (1979): 225.

[55]R. L. Street and H. Giles, "Speech Accommodation Theory." In M. E. Roloff and C. R Berger, eds., *Social Cognition and Communication* (Beverly Hills, CA: Sage, 1982), pp. 193–226.

[56]M. L. Knapp, R. P. Hart, G. W. Friedrich, and G. M. Shulman, "The Rhetoric of Goodbye: Verbal and Nonverbal Correlates of Human Leave-Taking," *Speech Monographs* 40 (1973): 182–198. For additional information on human leave-taking, see A. Adato, "Leave Taking: A Study of Commonsense Knowledge Social Structure," *Anthropological Quarterly* 48 (1975): 255–271; S. J. Sigman, "Handling the Discontinuous Aspects of Continuous Social Relationships: Toward Research on the Persistence of Social Forms," *Communication Theory* 1 (1991): 106–127.

[57]Davis (*Intimate Relations,* p. 271), rightly notes that the term *friends* is often used euphemistically between ex-intimates to connote a relationship which manifests characteristics of acquaintances.

[58]See, for example, F. D. Fincham and T. N. Bradbury, "Marital Satisfaction, Depression, and Attributions: A Longitudinal Analysis," *Journal of Personality and Social Psychology* 64 (1993): 442–452.

[59]J. P. Forgas, "Sad and Guilty? Affective Influences on the Explanation of Conflict in Close Relationships," *Journal of Personality and Social Psychology* 66 (1994): 56–68.

[60]C. A. Anderson, R. S. Miller, A. L. Riger, J. C. Dill, and C. Sedikides, "Behavioral and Characterological Attributional Styles as Predictors of Depression and Loneliness: Review, Refinement, and Test," *Journal of Personality and Social Psychology* 66 (1994): 549–558.

[61]E. Goffman, *Relations in Public* (New York: Basic Books, 1971), p. 83.

[62]Reprinted with permission of Macmillan Publishing Co., Inc., from *Intimate Relations* by Murray S. Davis. Copyright © 1973 by Murray S. Davis, page 270.

11

The Dialogue of Distance and De-escalation

Dear Dr. Vangelisti,

This guy and I have been going together for a long time. We both love each other. However he is a very moody person. He is quick to jump down my throat for stupid things. When I try to defend myself and explain, a bigger disagreement breaks out. When I say I'm sorry (to avoid a fight), he tells me he doesn't like "pansies" and he knows why I'm saying that I'm sorry. He says I should tell him how I feel, but I know he'll ignore me or we'll have a fight. I don't know what to do. He's so good in so many ways, but I feel helpless in situations like this.

Perplexed Pansy

Some patterns of communication are more likely to be associated with the deterioration of relationships than others. The pattern described above may create a momentary distance between the man and woman, but if practiced often enough it may lead to a more permanent separation. The woman is asked to state how she feels, but when she does, she feels she is punished. This and other potentially troublesome patterns of communication are discussed in this chapter.

> *The conversation was like some crazy folding chair I couldn't get straight.*
>
> —Peter De Vries
>
> *Bad is never good until worse happens.*
>
> —Danish Proverb

There are many ways to express caring for another person—e.g., a gift, a telephone call, a back rub. But sometimes one person's perception of what constitutes a display of affection and caring does not match his or her partner's perception. Consider the husband who resents his wife being late for appointments—"If she cared about me, she wouldn't be late like this." In the husband's family, being on time was a sign of caring, and tardiness required an extended apology. Although the wife is aware of her husband's concern for her being on time, she doesn't associate it with her caring or not caring for him. Her family was chronically late to everything and so is she. In this case, then, the husband's and the wife's rules for sending and receiving messages of affection do not correspond. Similarly, a husband who works long hours may think, "If my wife cares about me, she'll appreciate my working so hard for her." The wife, however, says to herself, "If my husband really loved me, he would want to spend more time with me and not so much time at work."

On other occasions, these messages of caring and affection are communicated in ways agreed to by both relationship partners—but the painful channels involved may ultimately hurt the relationship. For instance, a wife criticizes her husband's behavior to such an extent that it is hard for him to do anything to please her. As a result, he sometimes breaks things or threatens suicide or takes an overdose of drugs. This behavior elicits a great deal of caring and kindly behavior from the wife. Both agree that the wife's behavior during these times is a sign she really loves her husband. When the husband is no longer "out of control," the wife returns to her critical behavior—expressing her resentment for his previous irresponsibility. A related example concerns a husband who can't lose weight because both husband and wife agree that: (1) the wife's love for her husband is shown when she cooks rich and big meals; and (2) the husband's love for his wife is shown by the gusto he displays in eating large quantities of her cooking. In each example, the couple was relying on painful channels of communication for sending and receiving messages of caring and affection.[1]

All the preceding examples illustrate patterns of communication that may lead to divisiveness in a relationship. Sometimes our relationship messages are rooted in different rules, and at other times the partners agree on the rules, but these rules reinforce pain in the relationship. These are only two of many communication patterns that tend to precipitate relationship de-escalation. The remainder of this chapter will be devoted to the explication of a variety of these patterns.

Some Potentially Destructive Patterns of Communication: An Interpersonal Chamber of Horrors

Even though some people's communication patterns seem to "drive us crazy," we should remind ourselves that *any* communication pattern has the potential for being perceived as destructive. An extremely paranoid person might perceive a hurried "hello" as a negative evaluation of his or her personality. Although we can agree that perceived destructiveness is in the mind of the observer, we also know that some communication patterns elicit reactions such as fear, distrust, hurt, confusion, vengeance, and decreased self-worth which numerous experts and laypersons feel are unproductive for relationship growth. These patterns will be the focus for the remainder of this chapter. They are problematic because they represent extremes—either they are extreme behavioral styles or they are practiced extremely often. The extremes we'll be dealing with are: *helpful-critical, active-passive, aggressive-evasive, dominating-submissive,* and *certain-provisional.* As we discuss these various patterns, keep in mind that these specific categories are not mutually exclusive; that is, a pattern may be aggressive and also critical or an attempt at domination may be made by being evasive.

Even though a pattern may be destructive for many people, there is always the possibility that a particular configuration of events, time, and personalities will not activate a pattern's destructive potential. For some of the patterns discussed, the question of whether it is toxic rests on the frequency with which it appears. A pattern may be very effective in accomplishing one's goals one day but very ineffective if used repeatedly. Obviously, there are many other contingencies that affect our reactions to various styles of communicating. When we are physically tired or hungry, we may become antagonistic toward statements that ordinarily would not upset us. People who have had a lot of exposure to a given style of communicating will react differently than someone meeting up with it for the first time. The question of whether any given style of communicating will be considered "abnormal," "frustrating," "insane," or whatever is also a function of the climate of the times, a function of what society or a given subculture defines as normal communication. Was the U.S. military spokesman's infamous comment during the Vietnam War— "We had to destroy the village in order to save it"—symptomatic of the climate of the times, or an isolated instance of craziness in message sending? Communication patterns can be offensive, confusing, or damaging simply because of individual differences, perhaps the inability of a person to carry off certain styles. For instance, one person we know tries to be sarcastic but can't emphasize the contrast between voice and words sufficiently, so most people simply glare at him, stupefied, not knowing if he is serious, or kidding, or what. The issue of communicative effectiveness, or competence, will be discussed more extensively in Chapter 12, but a knowledge of these contingencies (and we've mentioned only a few) should make us less prone to condemn a word, phrase, tactic, game, or pattern as "bad" without placing it in a specific context with specific people.

In spite of the preceding qualifications, some will still have a tendency to see the following patterns of communication as vile and ruinous and therefore in need of eradication. A number of people would argue that eradication is impossible, that antidotes (especially when applied with missionary zeal) will only give rise to a new disease. Penicillin can eradicate some bacteria, but for those who are allergic to it, the cure only brings greater costs. The words of Koestler's fictional revolutionary make the same point:

> All our principles were right, but our results were wrong. This is a diseased century. We diagnosed the disease and its causes with microscopic exactness, but wherever we applied the healing knife a new sore appeared. Our will was hard and pure, we should have been loved by the people. But they hate us.[2]

And some people would argue that eradication of these so-called destructive patterns of communication would be dysfunctional, that the process of learning to cope with life's tragedies is healthy. Our own personal view is that we should approach these potentially destructive patterns of communication as follows:

1. We should recognize and accept the fact that we will probably never communicate perfectly, but that we should continue trying to do so.

2. We should recognize and accept the fact that others (like us) will probably never communicate perfectly, but we should continue to help them in their efforts to do so—for example, by not being a receptive victim to a destructively manipulative strategy or by resisting the temptation to match (or supercede) the destructiveness of messages directed to us.[3]

3. We should, therefore, recognize and accept the idea that the responsibility for interpersonal destruction cannot ever rest entirely with one person—"I criticize you because you won't leave me alone." "I won't leave you alone because you criticize me."

4. We should try to minimize the usage of any communicative strategy that consistently fails to achieve the results we would like.[4]

5. When we are trapped (or go voluntarily) into a destructive spiral, we should try to learn enough about what happened to us so that we can better cope with it next time.

Helpful–Critical Patterns

Helpful

Initially, it may be hard to conceive of a helpful pattern of communication that is potentially divisive. There are at least two instances, however, that might qualify.

Both are attempts to "save" or "protect" others by being helpful. One instance is when a person does not need or request help, but the other person insists on giving it. The second instance is when a person requests help, and the other person agrees to provide the help, but does not deliver.

With all the best intentions, our partners in a close relationship sometimes insist on helping us when we don't ask for their help, nor need it. Consider a situation in which one partner always "helps" the other person tell a funny story at parties. The helper definitely helps to make the story funny, but the other person wants to, and is perfectly capable of, effectively telling the story by him or herself. "Helpful" intrusions like this tend to rob the other person of the personal satisfactions associated with performing a task and diminish any self-esteem which might be associated with successfully accomplishing a goal.[5]

A popular and often infuriating mechanism necessary to foretell another's need for help is mindreading. *Mindreading* is an attempt by one person to predict and state to another what the other person is feeling or thinking, how he or she will react, what he or she will accept or reject, what his or her motivations are, and so forth. It can be particularly irritating when the mindreader "helps" an individual by publicly stating the person's thoughts or feelings to a third person in a public setting. If the person denies the accuracy of the mindreader or expresses displeasure with the act of mindreading itself, the mindreader can show a bewildered distress at the ungrateful reaction to "a sincere effort to help you." The following comments might come from helpful mindreaders in different situations:

- You can't fool me. I can read you like a book.
- You're not hurt, you're just embarrassed.
- I can tell you're upset and have had a bad day. No? (Patronizing chuckle which dismisses the denial) Oh, now, don't try to hide it . . . sit down and tell me about it. . . .
- Judging from the way you're acting, your period must be due soon.
- What you need is a drink.
- I know you're trying not to bring it up, but I know you're thinking about it. You're still mad at me for what I said yesterday.

It doesn't really matter whether the mindreader is accurate or not; the act itself can be aggravating and even more aggravating when accurate. It is true that, as intimacy grows, our knowledge of the other also grows, and the other will welcome educated guesses sometimes. With less intimacy we will probably embrace the strategy less. Most of us want to feel that there is some unpredictability and mystery about us. Even if there isn't much, it can be maddening to be told there isn't any. Furthermore, mindreading is often acted out in a patronizing manner, a manner which, when practiced often enough, tends to drain responsibility for self and knowledge of self from the person being "helped."

The other instance of destructively helpful behavior is when help is requested and promised, but is either withheld or perceived as unusable. The sequence might go like this: (1) A student feels that the class material is understandable, studies diligently, yet scores low on examinations. (2) The student requests help with the problem from the instructor. (3) The instructor indicates a "willingness to help any student having problems." (4) The instructor is unable to make any of the appointments to discuss the matter, or after a lengthy elaboration of the problem by the student, the instructor quickly terminates the conference by telling the student to "study harder." (5) Now the student gets sullen or angry. (6) This prompts the instructor to show indignation and disappointment in the student—"Boy, that's the thanks I get. I was only trying to help."[6]

Critical

The hypercritical pattern is rarely masked by an exterior of helpfulness or protectiveness. It is more often raw negativity—the greatest contribution to negativism since the minus sign. If there is a chance (and there always is) of finding a flaw, it will be found and brought up.

> Wanna go out Friday night?
> Sure.
> What do you want to do?
> How about going to a movie?
> There's nothin' on except those dumb musicals and horror shows.
> There's a basketball game at the stadium.
> You want to fight those crowds? Besides, there's no way we'll win.
> Why don't we go out to eat?
> That'd be great if we had the kind of money they hit you for . . . and Burger
>   Queen isn't my idea of eating out.
> Well, we could stay home and watch TV. I could make some popcorn.
> Yeah . . . but we always do that.
> OK. *You* do what you want and *I'll* go out with somebody else.

A variation on the above sequence may occur when the first person's complaint is countered with a complaint by the second person—"Why do we always have to have hamburger? I'm getting tired of it." "Well, if you'd get a better job and make more money we could afford steak." A second variation occurs when the criticism is frozen in time—"You got a D in college math and now you want to be responsible for paying the bills and keeping the checkbook balanced? Ha!" This pattern uses the past as a weapon to prove "you'll always be a criminal." Since positive things are hard for hypercritical people to see and still maintain their critical stance, forgiveness on the part of the hypercritical partner is often painfully slow. If all we learn from the past is what to hold against another, the study of interpersonal histories isn't worth much.

The critical disaster seeker who looks at the world through black colored glasses is certainly not without impact on those who are on the receiving end. Constant negativity, even if it isn't directed at the other person, can have a dampening, depressing effect. Humor (other than sarcasm) is a rare commodity. Constant negative statements can make the receiver feel so bad, he or she provides even more stimuli for the complainer to latch onto; it can make the receiver begin to feel negative, and feel that the other isn't much fun to be around.

Sometimes people will focus their negativity and criticism on the other person's personality or behavior. This may be motivated by a desire to hurt the other person.[7] This goal is most effectively achieved by publicly calling attention to some aspect of the other's behavior of which he or she is only vaguely aware and which is at variance with his or her self-concept. Take, for example, a son talking about his father at a party: "Have you ever noticed how my dad talks endlessly and in great detail about himself and his activities, as if everyone should hang on every word? When his tiresome monologue terminates, and somebody else starts talking, he either leaves the room, acts restless and inattentive, or tries to change the subject back to himself." The focus of hypercritical behavior on another's personality may also be motivated by an attempt to see how far one can push another. One person may be trying to see how much criticism, no matter how unreasonable, the other will take in order to avoid giving up the relationship. This is indeed an insidious way of testing another's commitment to the relationship. Ironically, sometimes those who are most critical and negative are those who are most in need of close, positive, and uncritical relationships.

Active–Passive Patterns

Active

The level of intensity with which two people approach their encounters may also be carried to divisive extremes. At one extreme is what may sometimes amount to the equivalent of a Siamese twin, someone who is always with you. Interpersonal hyperactivity can be characterized by a person who is constantly seeking any interaction with anyone. Being together is an important end in itself. Sometimes it is not enough simply to be together; it is necessary to be friends.[8] In such cases, we would expect a barrage of "getting close" activity very soon after contact—confiding secrets, using nicknames. It is hard to ignore such intensity, and hard for many to adjust to and like for sustained periods of time. Interactions with such people are often characterized by a high degree of talkativeness; extraversion; a never-ending list of questions; intense involvement in almost every topic, even the most mundane; and an exhibitionistic participation which at times includes frequent fever-pitched emotional highs and lows. The frequency of questions that probe every minute detail of the other's experience may also be perceived as an interrogation representing a lack of trust rather than as a sincere interest in what, for many people, is unnecessary filler. If this perceived lack of trust develops, the hyperactive strategy elicits just the opposite reaction from what was desired. Even without the element of trust entering the picture, this extremely active style may cause others to recoil and withdraw. Such reactions may be a result of others feeling that the extroverted, hypertalkative person is trying too hard, forcing them to pay attention or listen, and evidencing a certain desperation in seeking attention or affection.[9] Others may fear getting involved with a person whose desperation could reflect instability.

Passive

At the other end of the scale is the passive person—withdrawn, uninvolved, introverted—a regular passenger on the line of least resistance. This behavior may appear only at certain times—at the inception of a disagreement, when a sensitive topic is brought up; sometimes it is more characteristic of a person's general communicative (life) style. In either case, it is common for the person exhibiting a passive style to leave the field of interaction. The person may do this by remaining in the same area, but adopting strategies that negate his or her presence while simultaneously denying the validity of the other's argument. Examples are: responding continually with silence, pseudo-agreement to reduce the length of the other's argument ("Right." "Um-hmm." "Sure."), or indifference and lack of commitment ("Do what you want." "I don't care."). The passive person may dramatize the need to withdraw or avoid others by announcing departure at an inappropriate juncture—saying "I'm going to bed" in the middle of another's statement. Equally upsetting, but more devious, is the technique of using sullenness and withdrawal as a means of testing the other person's relationship commitment—seeing how long it will take before the other will try to draw him or her back into participation and coldly observing what methods are used.

Keep in mind that we are not condemning the need to withdraw, to be alone, or people with a generally quiet, retiring demeanor. We are saying that a chronic pattern of passivity or withdrawal is *one* style that can be very troublesome for relationship maintenance.

A related pattern of interaction often reported to counselors and therapists involves this approach-withdrawal sequence. In the following example, there is no attempt by the passive partner to redirect the approaching person to another form of satisfaction. In the words of therapist Pierre Mornell:

> Although she has her own needs for privacy and quiet at night, I've found most wives—at least a majority of those who seek my help for their troubled marriages—do want "something more" from their husbands in those hours when they come together.

This need for *something* more is directly or indirectly conveyed to the man. Basically she is saying, overtly and covertly, "Give me something I'm not getting."

He, in turn, experiences her demands (for longer talks, or an honest expression of feelings, or spending more time with the kids or her, or his being more active in sharing the domestic load, or her desire for better sex) as MORE PRESSURE. (Pressure he needs like a hole in the head.) And in the face of that pressure, direct or indirect on his wife's part, he withdraws. He retreats. He lapses into sullen silence.

What is her reaction?

As I said, it was her husband's withdrawal that made her furious in the first place. So, more agitated, she comes back at him with greater demands for "something he's not giving her." This causes him to retreat further. She becomes more pressured, even abusive. He retreats further. She becomes hysterical, bitchy. He lapses into complete silence, total passivity. She goes wild. The battle escalates. The self-defeating pattern continues and gets worse, if that's possible. And it is possible. The pattern can last years. Lifetimes![10]

Keep in mind that this same sequence can occur with a female withdrawing and a male who wants "something he's not getting." Similarly, the pattern may occur in same-sex dyads. The important point is to understand the potentially destructive power of the *pattern* if it is practiced too often or at the wrong time.

Aggressive–Evasive Patterns

The primary distinction between the aggressive and the evasive styles of behavior is the degree of directness. The aggressive style is characterized by a straightforward, head-on orientation in which the aggressor takes full responsibility for his or her messages. Hostility and control are the bywords for this pattern.[11] Evasive strategies, on the other hand, are typified by tangents, misdirection, vagueness, and confusion. Message responsibility is often shirked by the sender. You may not like the aggressive pattern, but at least you know where you stand.

Aggressive

Rosenfield, Hayes, and Frentz have discussed a process they call hassling.[12] *Hassling* is identified as a five-step progressive and destructive sequence. The steps in this sequence are: (1) repartée; (2) cliché; (3) name-calling; (4) provocation; and (5) physiological degeneration. This sequence will be used as a basis for elaborating on the nature of an aggressive communication pattern.

Repartée. The earliest signs of antagonism between combatants appear in the form of witty remarks. These remarks are clever attempts to put the other person down and, like a game of tag, to be the last one to touch or hit the other so as not to be "it." Consider, for example, this father–son exchange as the son is leaving the house one evening:

FATHER: Too bad you can't stay longer. I've got some interesting people for you to meet—your family.

SON: Oh really? Do you know them?

FATHER: Yeah, all except one gypsy who doesn't spend much time in any one place.

SON: Well, sometimes you gotta be quick if you want to catch the best.

Cliché.   This stage seems to grow out of the first, but differs in the originality of the retorts. The participants are no longer listening very carefully and have to resort to canned or programmed comments.

FATHER: Is that right?

SON: You got it, man.

FATHER: Oh yeah?

SON: Yeah.

FATHER: *Very* funny.

SON: Ha! I'll bet.

Namecalling.   At this point the assailants begin to use more potent verbiage, trying to humiliate and ridicule with stigmatizing labels. In some cases this means the use of ethnic slurs. In the conversational sequence we've been following between the father and son we might hear labels like: hypocrite, child, bum, leech, pig, freak. Namecalling is only one example of destructive labeling. In the process of the deterioration of a relationship, the participants are often prone to look for data to justify their bad feelings and explain their crumbling relationship. It is not uncommon to look for this data in the behavior of the other person. Hence, behavior that may have seemed odd, strange, or atypical during the growth stages may now be labeled as crazy, neurotic, or insane. What was once merely suspicion may now be labeled paranoia. Emotional acts may now be designated as hysteria. If the other person's behavior was "down" or "blue" before, it might now be labeled a state of depression. The same thing happens in the course of one's life span. When you're young you repeat yourself and forget things, but when you get old the same behavior may qualify you for the label *senile.* Unfortunately, these labels are often hard to shed, especially when more than one person begins to use the label and when *you* wonder if there might be some validity to it.

Provocation.   While all the stages mentioned thus far operate on the assumption that "if you can't compete, get out of the interaction," the provocation stage is the strongest test. Both participants know that this is the last chance to designate a "winner" using only words as weapons. This stage is characterized by insults, threats, and accusations. Insults and threats may also follow a progressively assertive sequence. What started out as a nonverbal signal (mock smile, eyes rolled upward and accompanied by an upward spiral gesture made with the index finger) may eventually manifest itself as "That's the dumbest thing I've ever heard, as if it made any difference anyway." Threats may also reflect a developmental pattern. "I'm liable to get mad . . . really mad . . . so don't push me . . . you just try to get away with it—see what it gets you . . . OK, but I'll remember this" may turn into more dramatic appeals peppered with what has traditionally been called obscene terminology—"One more crack like that and I'm going to beat the shit out of you." The degree of emphasis applied at this stage is contingent on how effective one's remarks have been at previous stages and to what extent a person has suppressed his or her anger up to this point.

Physiological Degeneration.   At this stage, the participants' faces tighten while their bodies ready for what seems to be the only alternative—a physical fight. Sometimes when the dialogue reaches the fight stage and there is a clear physical inequity, a temper tantrum might result instead of a fight—a husband or lover putting his fist through a door or a child throwing a fit in front of his or her parents. Others who arrive at this stage and feel they can't win a physical encounter may break down, showing they have already been sufficiently abused.

While the preceding five stages do seem to represent the basic elements of the aggressive pattern, the following should be noted: (1) While we often see the aggressive pattern in the sequence presented, the pattern can be entered at any stage in the sequence—an aggression may start with insults and move quickly into physical contact. (2) While there is a certain compelling force driving the participants toward greater intensity, they can step out of the sequence at any point. Obviously, the ability to step out is sometimes easier in the early stages, but it is not hard to understand why an opponent might be more than willing (even helpful) to allow the other to withdraw at the provocation stage. (3) Stages may also be skipped. But as soon as one person verbalizes thoughts and feelings, the other will usually know where the process was picked up and what is expected in return. (4) *Most important, while aggressive tendencies are usually directed at other people, the stimulus for anger is, more often than we may realize or want to admit, something about our own behavior we're displeased with.*

Experts believe that one in three women in the United States will be seriously assaulted (hit, kicked, bitten, and so on) by a male partner sometime during their lifetime. This includes women from all walks of life and at all stages of relationships (e.g., dating, cohabiting, married). In the face of such information, we feel it is important to discuss this form of aggression further. In some cases of physical abuse, there does not seem to be an identifiable pattern. Abuse is reported to occur unpredictably. In other cases, however, there seems to be a recurring cycle or pattern.[13] Battered wives, for example, have reported that the cycle of abuse begins with minor battering for which the wife often blames herself. Then more severe battering occurs—causing serious injury. Next, the husband promises to change, gives gifts, acts charming, and in general, plays on her feelings of guilt and sympathy. The wife hopes this temporary behavior will become permanent and remains in the relationship—only to become the victim of another incident of the husband's out-of-control rage. Perhaps one question most frequently asked by people who have not faced this kind of aggression is why the victims stay in the relationship so long after the first beating. Some of the most commonly mentioned reasons include: (1) the fear that leaving may only bring on additional violence; (2) the real or perceived lack of support, protection, and safety from friends and community agencies; (3) the feeling of isolation that sometimes keeps the battered woman from gaining knowledge and support; (4) a rock-bottom self-esteem which argues that she deserves what she gets; and (5) a paradoxical bonding or dependency with the batterer—a person who, when he is good, provides just what she needs—and he is often good following the physical violence. It should also be noted that physical abuse is only one kind of abuse in relationships of this type. For example, restricting freedom to go places and do things; threats to hurt the person financially, making decisions for the other person; requiring sexual behavior against the partner's protestations; intimidation through looks, yelling, smashing things, and physically abusing pets. Contrary to what some of these wives believe, this kind of behavior should not be considered typical or tolerable—even though many of these husbands and wives have observed frequent incidents of such violence in other families. There are no doubt many explanations for physically abusing a person you purportedly care about, but the most frequently cited reasons attributed to male abusers are fear of abandonment and fear of rejection.

Up to this point we have focused on physical aggression and abuse by men directed toward women. It should be noted that threats of violence and acts of abuse are reported by male relationship partners at about the same percentage as female victims. Physical aggression by women is also a tragic response pattern, but our discussion focused on male abusers because this type of abuse usually holds the potential for greater physical harm.

Evasive

Evasiveness, even though it is less direct than the aggressive pattern, can be equally damaging to a relationship if used often enough. Remember that some evasive strategies can be, on any given occasion, the best alternative for communicating—particularly when you perceive all your options for response will elicit negative reactions.[14] This discussion will focus on four general methods of evasion:

(1) changing the focus of responsibility, (2) changing the direction of the conversation; (3) changing the level of the conversation; and (4) sending incongruous messages.

Changing the Focus of Responsibility. This method uses another person or object to distract or divert attention away from oneself. The purpose of this technique is not simply to change the focus of conversation. Generally, evasive maneuvers have three purposes in common: (1) avoiding responsibility and control over one's own behavior; (2) giving an excuse to provide a rational explanation for one's behavior; and (3) making someone or something else look like the sole destructive element. Responsibility and control for one's behavior can be dumped on any number of sources—"The boss makes me bring all this work home. I don't want to," or "I know I don't go out much anymore, but Charles is an alcoholic, you know," or "My parents (wife, boyfriend) won't let me." The model seems to be something like this:

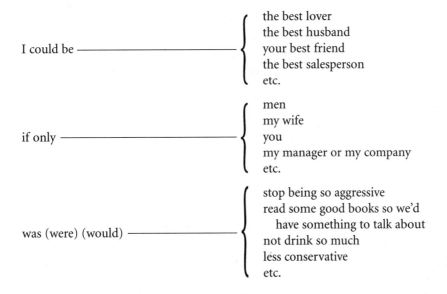

Berne illustrates the evasive pattern in games he calls "See What You Made Me Do," and "If It Weren't for You." "See What You Made Me Do" has its roots in the familiar situation where one person is engrossed in some activity and is interrupted. The innocent question of a child to her father, "What are you doing, Daddy?" may precede the father hitting his hand with a hammer. This, then, provides the rationale for "See what you made me do." When such behavior becomes a way of life, it can easily degenerate into other forms of blame ("You got me into this," or "I didn't bring it up, you did.") or vengeance ("I told you so," or "See what you've done now."). "If It Weren't for You" is a similar tactic. Let's assume a professional woman architect resigns her job because she wants to have children and stay home and raise them. When the home and child-rearing activities fail to provide the needed professional stimulation, the woman moans, "If it weren't for my kids, I'd go back to work."

Changing the Direction of the Conversation.   There are numerous strategies that can be used to avoid threatening conversations by shifting topics or focus. Washburne, in a delightful piece, outlines several methods for not answering questions.[15] While there are overtones of humor in the following strategies, there are serious consequences for relationships characterized by frequent incomplete and tangential transactions. Washburne says there are three basic methods for giving answers that are not answers: (1) "not answering at all"; (2) "managing the question"; and (3) "managing the questioner." Such answers give the appearance of cooperating, but never seem to address the question directly. These tactics, Washburne says, leave the questioner either satisfied, restrained by politeness from pursuing the matter, or thoroughly confused.

The first method is called "not answering at all." The simplest form is to ignore, or apparently not hear, the question. Watzlawick provides an example of how silence can be used to communicate disagreement without having to be held responsible for it.[16]

> THERAPIST: Well, now what kind of weekend did you have after our session Friday evening?
>
> HUSBAND: Oh, I would say, a very good one, wouldn't you, Jean?
>
> WIFE: (remains silent)

What makes this tactic so difficult for the husband to cope with is that the wife has made her point, but if she is questioned about her silence indicating disagreement, she has numerous escape routes—"Oh, was I supposed to say something?" "Did I say that?" or "Oh . . . I was just trying to remember." She can deny her communicative intent and in turn accuse the questioner of making unwarranted inferences or of mindreading. As Watzlawick says, this is a situation in which "agreement cannot be reached, disagreement cannot be tolerated, so a stand is taken without really taking a stand." Engineering a distraction is another way of not responding. Following the question, the receiver may spill a drink, knock over a vase, drop a lighted cigarette into the depths of a sofa, or point out some external event such as "how rough" the kids are playing outside. Pipe smokers have an arsenal of equipment for creating possible distractions and a lengthy lighting ritual for delaying responses—time which can be used to plan one's defense if all else fails.

The second method Washburne calls "managing the question." There are numerous ways to manage a question. Intentionally *misunderstanding* the question is an obvious means to avoid answering—"Is your car paid for?" "You know, I really got a bargain with this car. They were asking . . . but. . . ." *Limitation* is the process of taking a broad question and answering only that aspect of it with which you feel comfortable—"How did you like my meatloaf?" "I particularly liked the sauce. It must have taken you a long time to make it. . . ." The *non sequitur,* as the label implies, is a response that is not logically related to the question. Some people seem to have a mouthful of topics that they can launch into no matter what the question. Usually these monologues are lengthy enough so that the questioner either gives up or forgets the original question. Such monologues might begin with: "This reminds me of . . . " or "I can best respond to that by recalling a similar situation . . . " A political candidate may be addressing an audience when a heckler yells out, "What are you proposing to do with all the waste from the nuclear plants you propose building?" Using the non sequitur strategy, the candidate may pause, smile, and say, "Today's my birthday and I've vowed not to get mad at anybody." *Restatement* is the act of seeming to restate the question (for the sake of clarity), but converting it to one you find easier to deal with—"Are we going into a depression?" "As I understand your question, you are really asking about the present state of the business cycle. Business income is the highest in history. . . ." A similar evasive maneuver is *the more fundamental question*—"Are you a liberal?" "Well, before we can deal with my own personal stance, we need to consider the more fundamental question, what does *liberal* mean?" Professors are often cited for a technique Washburne calls the *hypothetical answer.* When asked a question, a direct answer is avoided by explaining all the various alternative perspectives without identifying with any one of them. *Is this really a question?* is an approach that attempts to annihilate the question itself by pointing out that it is actually several questions, that there are false premises, and so forth. Once the question has been sufficiently dissected, the respondent can discuss any sub-question desired. The *moot question approach* asserts that the question is almost impossible to answer and that there is no sense pondering the imponderable. For example, a mother says, "Why do you suppose our son gets so upset and runs to his room every time you start to talk to him?" The father replies, "Look, you're asking a question the best minds of the world can't answer—what makes kids tick. There's no sense spending a lot of time trying to figure out what causes people to act the way they do—it's so complex and there are so many factors involved we'd only get into more trouble by considering it." The last method of managing the question is called *the assertion of nothing.* A friend is asked to comment on a new outfit that the wearer obviously likes and the friend doesn't: "Boy, that is *some* outfit!" The voice emphasis makes otherwise empty words seem full of meaning. It should be remembered that some of these methods we use to deliberately avoid answering questions are the same methods we use when we are trying to answer questions.[17] For example, when someone asks, "Are you going to Bob's party?" you may reply, "Does a submarine have screen doors?" Although most of us would assume the person isn't going to Bob's party, the reply certainly qualifies as a non sequitur and does not directly answer the question. Other indirect responses are more closely related to the question, but still avoid clearly and unambiguously affirming or negating the question—e.g., "Are you going to Bob's party?" "Bob and I are best friends." or "Are you going to Bob's party?" "I have a really important test to take in the morning." The receiver is expected to infer the answer through an understanding of how the reply connects back to the question.

Bavelas and her colleagues have found that people's evasive, indirect, or ambiguous messages are the result of a person facing an avoidance-avoidance conflict.[18] In short, the communicator is faced with a situation in which any direct message, whether it is a lie or the truth, will get negative consequences. As a result, the communicator engages in what Bavelas calls, "equivocal communication." Let's say a husband has found some old letters that reveal his wife had an affair several years ago and, on the basis of the evidence, says: "You must have really loved him." The wife knows the content of the letters so she wants to avoid saying no because she knows the husband will then point to various sentences. On the other hand she wants to avoid saying yes because she knows how much that would hurt her husband and she wants their relationship to remain intact. She chooses instead to equivocate by saying, "I hardly knew him." The implication is that no matter what the letters say, the only kind of love that would be threatening would be one which involved knowing the other person well and this was not the case. The husband may still feel rotten, but he may also be secretly happy he didn't get a direct, straightforward, unequivocal response. As this example illustrates, evasive or equivocal responses can be appropriate and useful in avoidance-avoidance conflict situations. When they are overused or used repeatedly in situations when one's partner wants a direct response, they are likely to precipitate further problems with the relationship.

Washburne's third method to change the direction of the conversation is to "manage the questioner." One effective way to do this is to put the questioner on the defensive. This can be done by a rather direct insult such as "The very fact that you'd ask that question shows how uninformed you are on this topic," or in a friendly tone, you might say, "You probably didn't mean to ask that . . . what you really want to know is . . ." Another maneuver that Chapman calls "Whine and Decline" is an effort to bring up a topic you know will irritate your partner in order to stimulate a climate of conflict.[19] This, then, provides the rationale for avoiding any subjects or behavior the partner may have wished to initiate. Specifically, one spouse who wants to avoid sexual intercourse begins the pre-bedtime preparations with something like "I know you don't like to discuss it, but I think we really must decide something about. . . ." After the ensuing battle, the initiator can then not only justifiably decline the sexual advances, but feign previous interest—"Every time I feel affectionate, you seem to figure out some way to blow up and ruin it. . . ." Another way to manage the questioner is to relieve the questioner of his or her role so that you can become the questioner. Such a sequence might go something like this: "What happened at the convention?" "Oh, it was very dull. I wish I'd stayed home. What did you and the kids do?" The last, but far from the least effective way to manage your fellow interactant, is to use compliments or praise. Sometimes it can be very disarming. Your partner may forget the original topic or question, and the whole tone of the conversation can dramatically change with comments like "Where did you learn to argue so effectively?" or "You always seem to hit the nail right on the head. How did you develop this ability?"

Changing the Level of the Conversation. Conversational smoke-screens can also develop when people shift the level of discussion on a concrete–abstract continuum. One variation is to bring a very high level, philosophical discussion down to the "but what would happen if we actually put this into practice" level. The more frequent occurrence is shifting from a specific analysis to a more general, abstract one. A student wants to know why a professor can't spend more time helping him or her, and the professor launches into a discussion of criteria for promotion, various perspectives on student–teacher relations, and how this all relates to the philosophy of education.

Conversational level can also be varied on a serious–joking continuum. A person can camouflage an inability to deal with humor or light conversational banter by shifting from a nonserious to a serious dimension—an example is a person who gives an oral sociological or historical treatise on the use of obscene language during a "bull session." On an occasional basis such behavior may gain one the label of "conversational boor"; frequent practice will likely breed impatience, frustration, and eventual avoidance on the part of receivers who dislike being sobered up during a humor binge. Sometimes we find people replying to a serious comment or question in a way that indicates their refusal to respond seriously—"Son, do you use marijuana?" "Gee, Dad, how did you know? I've been hooked since I was thirteen. My habit is up to $100 a day. I wanna quit, but I just can't. I'll probably be on the hard stuff in no time."[20] If the father takes the son's comment seriously, he risks the charge of naiveté; if he retorts with anger at the mockery, the son can protest unfair punishment—"Hey, whatdya want? I admitted it, didn't I?"

Sending Incongruous Messages. When a speaker sends two simultaneous messages that communicate vastly different things, he or she is sending incongruous or discrepant messages. *Sarcasm,* for instance, relies on one's ability to contrast a message sent in nonverbal channels (voice, face, hands) with the words used—saying "This is a great book, Professors Knapp and Vangelisti" accompanied by nonverbal signals that leave considerable doubt about the veracity of the words alone. Contradictory messages are also sent when the speaker has no intention of being cutting or sarcastic. Consider the parent who, with clenched fists, a reddened and strained face, and a harsh vocal tone, towers over his or her child and screams threateningly, "Damn it, Lester, don't you know that I love you!" The parent's verbalization may have been very sincere, and the contradictory nonverbal signals may have been unconsciously added; nonetheless, the child gets two very different messages. The game Berne calls "Rapo" is built on contradictory messages of approach-avoidance or acceptance-rejection or both. In the case of Rapo, however, the contradictory messages are not communicated simultaneously, even though they may coexist in the mind of the perpetrator. An example is one person who flirts with another until the target begins to respond fully and positively to what is perceived as an amorous set of messages. Then the game player abruptly changes the message and rejects the responder with an "How dare you!" or "I just don't understand men (women)." Gratification for the game player may come not only from the discomfort caused the victim, but from perpetrating an act that further confirms his or her low estimation of the opposite sex. Laing has identified several other instances of these double-edged messages which he says, given the right conditions, can produce enough confusion in another person to "drive them crazy."[21] The right conditions include a high frequency of occurrence, an intimate relationship between the communicators, and the presence of no other people to whom the receiver can turn for discussion and possible clarification of the confusion. Some methods Laing described for sending inconsistent messages include: (1) communicating on two unrelated levels at the same time—intellectually and sexually; (2) constantly switching from one emotional wavelength to another while on the same topic; and (3) switching from one topic to another while remaining on the same emotional wavelength—discussing the death of a loved one in an automobile accident in the same emotional tone you would discuss what you had for breakfast.

Thus far we've been talking primarily about the construction of the incongruous messages. We haven't said much about the receiver's options following the confusing presentation. Some messages might be incongruous, but at least there is a choice of possible responses; other messages, however, are constructed so that the receiver is left without a legitimate choice. The receiver is faced with a double bind—damned if you do, damned if you don't.[22] The double bind occurs when person A puts person B in such a position that regardless of what person B says or does, sanctioning will be the result.[23] The enormity of the dilemma is seen when we consider that no matter what we do, we cannot keep from communicating—and to communicate is to be punished. Consider these examples:

Injunctions	*Response Choices*	*Punitive Reactions to Choices*
You should be less obedient.	OK, I Will.	See? You obey my every whim.
	No, I won't.	You do what I tell you to do! *or* You must not care much for me if you won't do as I ask.
You ought to love more.	OK, I will.	You can't just turn love off and me on like that. You're just saying that because I asked you to.
	I'm sorry, I can't.	Then you'd better learn! *or* If that's all you think of me, then let's forget it.

You can think of other choices "open" to the respondent, but since the injunction is paradoxical, there will be something wrong with these choices too. "Be spontaneous" and "I want you to dominate me" are familiar injunctions that are well within the genre of the examples above. Notice how the plea for domination defines the relationship as complementary and symmetrical at the same time. (*See* pages 80–81 for a discussion of complementary and symmetrical relationships.) This is the nature of a paradox. A final illustration of how double binds manifest themselves in everyday conversation is presented by the following hypothetical situation. "Red" Doyle is the coach of a football team, the Boone Bombers. He is discussing a just-completed play with one of his players, Bill "Concrete" Connolly. Connolly, according to his instructions for the play, blocked an opponent named Greene. An opposing linebacker, named Jenkins, rushed past Connolly and tackled Connolly's quarterback for a fifteen-yard loss. Notice how Coach Doyle is able to create double binds that cover Connolly's thinking, feeling, and acting.[24]

"Jenkins really murdered us on that last play. We've got to stop him. Were you trying to block him?"

Connolly might legitimately assume, at this point, that blocking Jenkins would have been rewarded and not blocking him would have been punished. Since he hadn't blocked Jenkins, Connolly tries to alibi.

"Yeah, Coach," said Connolly meekly. "I was going to, but . . . " he began in a slow, uncertain voice.

Only to find out his assumption was totally wrong, Connolly is punished for his actions.

Coach Doyle forcefully threw his cap on the ground, and while looking Connolly straight in the eyes, said in a firm, punitive tone: "Going to? You can't block every man on the field, superman. This is a game of discipline and of following orders. Since when do you decide who to block? Are you the new coach?"

"No, Coach, I only thought . . . "

This is the opening Coach Doyle uses to punish his player for thinking. He frightens Connolly into not thinking for himself, but intimates that the player should think about how to protect his quarterback.

"You only thought! How nice! I'll thank you not to think. I can do all the thinking around here."

After having communicated the seriousness of this matter—a matter where fear of authority, guilt, and remorse are appropriate emotions—Coach Doyle shifts gears again and punishes his player for being frightened and discouraged.

As Connolly lowered his head, turned, and looked hurt, Coach Doyle began to laugh. "Look at you. Just look at you. Has my concrete turned to marshmallow?"

Given the nature of the double bind in the context of a relationship that is important to the person put in the double bind, it is not hard to see how many believe it can lead to schizophrenia and other pathologies. Some try to reduce the inconsistency of double binds and paradoxical messages by increasing their own consistency of response. A person, for instance, might interpret all messages received as suspicious, untrustworthy, and filled with hidden meanings. If this behavior is continued, it will eventually gain that person the label of paranoid. Another person might react to all messages as unimportant, irrelevant, and laughable. This may cause others to diagnose that person's behavior as a disorder called hebephrenia. Still another person may simply withdraw into himself or herself, a process which in its extreme form is known as catatonia.

Some believe that constant exposure to a learning context where the goal is to escape punishment rather than to seek rewards is more damaging than the confusion caused by the double bind itself. Suffice to say, the combination of negativity, confusion, and punishment can be lethal. Fortunately, most of us will arrest the process before it becomes pathological. This can be done by invalidating some of the conditions prerequisite to driving one crazy—for example, by reducing the amount of exposure by leaving the environment which produces the double binds, and talking to others about one's confusion in an effort to see the process more objectively.

Therapists have reported an interesting twist in coping with double binds, something like a reverse double bind. Watzlawick, Beavin, and Jackson report a couple who came to therapy because they argued too much.[25] The couple were told by the therapist that they argued so much because they loved each other so much. To disprove this "absurd" and "ridiculous" theory, the couple stopped arguing— only to find they got along much better. Watzlawick gives this example of how a double-bind situation was reversed by "schizophrenic communication."

. . . take the example of an alcoholic father who demands that he be seen as a loving, respectable parent and not as the violent drunkard which he is—and, of course, knows himself to be. When this man threatens his children with punishment if they show fear when he comes home drunk, the children are placed in a particular dilemma which requires a denial of their perceptions in order to support Father's deception. Suppose further that this father, after having terrorized his children into going along with his make-believe, suddenly does an about-face and accuses them of trying to deceive him about their fear. Now they are faced with two alternatives, both of which entail punishment. If they betray their fear, they will be punished for implying that he is a dangerous drunk. If they conceal their fear, they will be punished for their "insincerity." And, of course, if they were capable of protesting and saying, "Look what you are doing to us," they would again be punished. . . . What possible adaptive reaction, short of a catatonic stupor, is there to the paradox posed by a double bind? . . . One of the children could conceivably run away from home, claiming that he had actually seen a "huge black gorilla breathing fire" in the house. . . . The child's message, i.e., his symptom, denies that it is a communication about Father and it further denies that it is a denial. In other words, the child's fear now has a reason, but of a kind which implies that it is not a real reason. After all, there are no black gorillas at large. . . . Now paradox is countered with paradox and Father is himself in a double bind, as he can no longer coerce his child into concealing his fear. After all, the child is not afraid of him and who can argue with a child's fantasy? Nor can the father label the metaphor, as this would be tantamount to admitting that he looks like a dangerous beast—which is the very thing that Father demands be overlooked.[26]

Dominating–Submissive Patterns

In most relationships behaviors that show dominance or submission fluctuate with the topic being discussed, who has the expertise or experience, the roles required for a given task, interpersonal needs of the participants, amount of energy, and many other factors. However, when either dominance or submission becomes a habitual response—an inflexible communicative pattern—it can easily tear a relationship apart.

Dominating

The dominant extreme is comprised of a person who plays a constant game of winning and losing. Life is a continual parade of competitive events in which one person wins power and another loses it. In order to hold power over others (or a particular other), a person will try to become the primary source of important rewards and punishments; try to assert his or her "expertise" on a wide variety of topics; and generally try to maintain control over resources that directly affect the relationship—e.g., money, information, ability to perform certain asks, etc. For the person seeking dominance, differences between people are often evaluated not simply as differences, but as marks of superiority or inferiority, strengths and weaknesses.

Encounters are often more like contests or jousting matches. Many times the dominance-prone individual is unaware of the behavior he or she manifests. There may be such a predominant concern for oneself that others are seen only as props. A person exhibiting this pattern may even believe he or she is doing things for others when he or she is not—buying expensive tickets to a concert featuring a performer the dominator really likes, but the partner could easily live without seeing. Many times the driving force behind this need for dominance and power is insecurity—"Since nobody thinks I'm a good decision maker, I'll show them."

There are a number of communication patterns characteristic of the dominant style, but the implicit assumption behind all of them is that the other person is somehow not quite adequate. The other person is either dumb, childish, inexperienced, unsophisticated, tasteless, uninformed, or possessed of some other inferior quality. With such an assumption, it is easy to predict communicative manifestations. All the important decisions need the "superior" person's input; sometimes the benevolent dictator will allow the partner to make some "unimportant" decisions in order to "keep them happy" and let them feel that they have a role in determining things. Commands and ultimatums are often the order of the day, usually framed around two polarized alternatives—"Do this and not that," or "I don't care what you want, we're going to . . ." or "It's either my way or not at all." Since life is seen as a competitive arena, we might also expect to hear an abundance of trade-offs if the authoritarian edicts don't work—"OK, you can do that, but if you do, you're going to have to . . ." or "I'll let you get away with it, but in turn I'm going to . . ." Naturally any analysis of specific communication behaviors associated with dominance should recognize that dominance can be exhibited in many ways. Dominance displays that involve talking loud, fast, and often may subside as the partner shows acceptance of the other's dominant role. Dominance may appear differently as different issues are discussed, and some dominance patterns may be highly idiosyncratic and known only to the interacting pair—e.g., "When he sits up in his chair and speaks very slowly, I know I'd better give him what he wants."

Sometimes dominance displayed in rather straightforward, stereotypical ways is rebuffed and more indirect methods are tried. It is the interpersonal equivalent of guerrilla warfare. Strategies Chapman calls "You Can Never Repay Me" and "Torture Rack" are two of these indirect methods at domination.[27] The key to domination in "You Can Never Repay Me" is some basis for the dominator to claim he or she has made great sacrifices for the other and the only way to be repaid is by an endless deference to demands. These demands are often accompanied by whimpering resignation which attempts to produce feelings of guilt and eventual submission in the other—"Go ahead and enjoy yourself; after all, your happiness is what I've worked and slaved for all these years." "Torture Rack" uses some form of physical ailment (headaches, backaches) to induce submission by the other person. Submission is forced because the ailment always seems to intensify when the dominant person's wishes are thwarted in the least—"Don't let my suffering change your plans. . . ."

It should be clear by now that the ideal situation for the autocrat is one where he or she speaks and the other listens and obeys. However, there are instances in which the dominator must cope with a partner who does not conform through subservience. These situations are not unlike those confronting authorities in organizations who wish to discourage individuals from seeking reform. O'Day outlined what he called a series of intimidation rituals in organizational settings.[28] O'Day's paradigm seems to be just as useful for analyzing any interpersonal situation in which an uncooperative person must be dealt with by someone who wants to maintain his or her dominance. Generally, the communicative goals of the authoritarian are: (1) to keep the other person from getting any additional support; (2) to make it look as if the authoritarian is blameless; and (3) to neutralize the other person without letting him or her become a martyr. O'Day says such efforts usually follow four escalating phases: (1) nullification; (2) isolation; (3) defamation; and (4) expulsion.

Nullification.   Here the reformer, or person to be dominated, is expected to give up simply on the word of the authority—"Take my word for it, you're wrong" or "Do as you're told and you'll be OK." If necessary, the dominant person might resort to something like, "Ok, I'll look into it" in order to defuse the other person's request and, if necessary, cover up anything that might support the other's contention.

Isolation.   If the dominator's authority continues to be questioned, attempts are made to isolate the questioner. This might be difficult if the stage of the relationship does not permit opportunities for such isolation. A husband might try to keep his wife from talking to the neighbors, her mother, friends. A mother might try to keep her daughter from talking to her peers about an issue that might challenge the mother's knowledge and authority. Even children who dominate their parents learn how to "divide and rule"—"Dad is always picking on me, Mom" may start a process that ends up with Mom and Dad fighting and Junior triumphantly looking on from the sidelines.

Defamation.   Continued persistence by the person challenging the authoritarian in the face of these indirect attempts at suppression may bring about more direct efforts. This phase, for instance, calls for the dominator to question the motives of the challenger, to point out various problems which have caused the person to "act this way" recently, to find every instance of an error on the part of the other person and blow it up to show a lack of competence.

Expulsion. Although this might be a ready alternative for less intimate relationships which manifest this situation, expulsion comes only as a last resort in more intimate relationships. The problem with expulsion is that other people are often brought in for observations of the situation. If the authoritarian can terminate a relationship without the possibility of anything approaching a formal review, then expulsion would be a more desirable alternative.

Submissive

In direct opposition, but with no less potential for relationship destruction, is the perpetually-submissive-response type. Exaggeration of dependency, abdication of responsibility, and self-deprecating remarks characterize this communicative style. Wanting to be led by others is a common manifestation where submissive types seek subordinate positions rather than positions where some responsibility might be involved. When it isn't possible to seek such positions, the submissive person might complain: "I didn't ask to be promoted to this higher level position . . . I knew I couldn't do it. . . ." Comments that reflect one's inadequacies abound in the talk of the submissive person: "How stupid I am" or "What an idiot I was for. . . ." Since a person using this pattern has a low self-concept and has little confidence in his or her abilities, it is common to give in to the slightest request from another. In short, the behavior seems to be the archetype of "I'm Not OK, You're OK."[29]

Speakers who are reticent to talk, whose speech rate literally invites interruptions, who express themselves tentatively by using qualifiers and hedges, who are unassertive and uncertain, are manifesting the characteristics of what some have called "powerless speech." Generally women's speech is not, as some used to believe, characterized by these features. And men do not generally exemplify "powerful speech" either.[30] Language choices and speech styles which characterize power or the lack of power are usually a function of the situation, your role in that situation, your interaction history, your interpersonal needs, and the nature of your partners speech. On the other hand, when one relationship partner *consistently* exhibits submissiveness through powerless speech, relationship stress is an expected result.

Initially it might seem strangely attractive to some to be in a relationship with a submissive other. After all, wouldn't it be nice to be paired up with a slave? Most people we've known, however, who have found themselves in this position don't agree. Consider that if you want to build an intimate relationship, you must fuse with and become part of the other—absorbing some of your slave. But the slave provides little in the way of challenges or stimulation and relinquishes responsibilities. It is ironic that the dominating pattern previously discussed may be so effectively instituted by a dominator that a helpless follower develops. Then, if the dominant person wants the pattern to change ("Why don't you get out on your own and take some responsibility for yourself . . . ?"), he or she may find the slave unwilling or unable to change. This sets up a pattern where the parasitic monster created by domination now begins to burden rather than please the creator.

Certain–Provisional Patterns

The last extreme and potentially destructive communication patterns we will discuss revolve around the issue of predictability. At one extreme, the communicator consistently expresses a certainty about the way things are; at the other extreme the communicator sees the world and the people in it as an ever-changing, unfathomable web of interconnections.

Certain

The certainty pattern is so much a part of our everyday experience that we have a familiar label for a person exhibiting this behavior—a know-it-all. Some people believe that the less we know about something, the more certain we seem to feel and act. Know-it-alls believe, or at least act as if they believe, that it is possible to know and say everything about something. It probably is impossible to know everything about something. Try this simple experiment with a friend or acquaintance. To make it easier, don't pick something complex like a human being; pick something very concrete and structurally simple like a pencil or a door. Now try to say or write everything that could be said about the object you chose. Were you able to say everything about it—atomic structure, evolutionary origins, uses, etc.? As noted in Chapter 5, we perceive only a portion of what is out there. Further, we communicate about an even smaller portion than what we have perceived. For this reason, it can be especially annoying when someone selects an occasional behavior we perform and turns it into an unqualified, stable personality trait. Let's assume person A and person B are friends and have exchanged constructive criticism on numerous occasions previously. Now we find person A, on this occasion, to be hot, tired, and particularly sensitive to criticism about body odor. Person B makes a derogatory remark about person A's body odor. Person A explodes. Now, person B says, "You know, one of your big problems is you can't take criticism." The unqualified, nonspecific nature of this comment and A's current disposition will probably turn this molehill into Mount Everest in a very short while.

Other variations on the know-it-all style include: the person who behaves, not as if he or she were saying everything on the subject, but at least everything important on the subject. This, of course, denies the importance of other people's perceptions. Then there is the "nothing new under the sun" approach—everything has been thought of and/or done before in some form. Usually, the person exhibiting this style will find so much predictability in life (often on a post hoc basis) that he or she may manifest a slow, methodical unexciting, and possibly uninteresting demeanor. There are other variations of the know-it-all style, but the preceding should provide a broad sampling.

We tend to be on guard when we encounter this pattern of extreme certainty because outward appearances suggest that the other person has THE answer. If that is the case, if no further data are needed, of what value is our input? However, the outward manifestations of certainty and assuredness may only mask an insecurity and a deeply felt need to be right.

An interesting twist on this certainty mechanism is the ability of our certain attitudes to bring about confirming evidence. This, of course, only provides further testimony to our skills at accurately perceiving and predicting life around us. This situation, in which the process of predicting an outcome brings about that outcome, is called the *self-fulfilling prophecy.*[31] This process begins with a false definition of a situation: A father believes that parents and teenagers cannot get along, that war is inevitable. The next step is for the father to begin behaving as if this assumption were a fact—looking for things that show hostility on the part of his son and preparing his defenses. The third step is the impact the father's behavior has on the son—the son notices what he thinks is an increased hostility on the part of his father and responds with what he considers defensive maneuvers. The final step is the proof for the father. Now that the father can interpret his son's behavior as hostile, he can pat himself on the back for the accuracy of his initial prediction, little realizing that his own behavior is closely linked to his son's. In short, a faulty assumption triggered a new behavior which made the original faulty assumption appear to come true. Thus, many of the "facts" we are so certain about (and which support our prejudices) may be largely a consequence of our behavior reflecting our own attitudes. Although the following dialogue was designed originally to be humorous, it aptly illustrates how, sadly, we can initiate our own destruction:

YOU: Well, our first big fight.

MATE: Yes.

YOU: (Pause) Do you think we have anything left?

MATE: What do you mean?

YOU: I mean do you think we still have a relationship?

MATE: Of course. (Pause) Why—don't you think so?

YOU: Well, I thought so before, at any rate.

MATE: What's that supposed to mean?

YOU: That I thought so before.

MATE: And you don't think so now?

YOU: (Pause) I don't know. What do you think?

MATE: (Pause) I don't know. I thought so before.

YOU: But now you're maybe not so sure, is that it?

MATE: (Pause) I don't know. Maybe not.

YOU: Well, since you're obviously planning to break up with me sooner or later, you might as well do it sooner and not prolong the agony.[32]

Provisional

The antithesis of the overly certain pattern is found in the person who expresses constant uncertainty, provisionalism, and qualification. Life, and the everyday decisions which need to be made, are so complex and unpredictable, the provisional person won't do or say anything "for sure." We've all had fascinating (and frustrating) discussions about what we know "for certain" or what is the "truth" of any particular observation; furthermore, if most of us err on this certainty-provisional continuum it is probably on the side of too much certainty. However, there are those who become almost inactive because they feel there are so many contingencies that need consideration before any given decision can be made. Closure is a rare commodity. Tasks and decisions are more often left up in the air. Everything is questioned extensively and intensively. Taking a stand is nearly impossible because the other alternatives or other points of view seem equally viable. Even one's observations of direct sensory experiences are sometimes qualified—in the midst of a heavy downpour saying, "*It seems to me* that it's raining" rather than "It *is* raining." It should be clearly understood that we are not suggesting the consideration of contingencies or the qualifying of one's remarks are signs of ineffective communication or strategies that will destroy a relationship. We are saying that the inability to make a decision based on all the alternatives considered can lead to an inaction which others will find hard to cope with over a long period of time. We are also saying that people will be frustrated with this style of communication if they rarely hear the provisional person say something definite or unqualified.

SUMMARY

This chapter detailed some specific extreme communication patterns that past experience and professional testimony suggest are common sources of relationship destruction. Obviously, any pattern has the potential to build or destroy, but the following, because they represent extremes or because they are applied extremely often, are specially suited to elicit unproductive responses—fear, distrust, defensiveness, confusion, vengeance, decreased self-worth, hurt. We should, however, be careful not to condemn these patterns as inherently and consistently "bad." *On any given occasion, using one of these patterns may be the best rhetorical choice an individual could make.*

First we discussed the *helpful–critical patterns*. The "helpful" pattern was analyzed from two perspectives: (1) that of a person not requesting help but having another try to give it by "reading the other's mind"; and (2) that of a person requesting help, which another person consents to give but then does not provide. The critical pattern concerned the fault-finder or complainer.

Other extremes were represented by the *active–passive patterns*. A person who is oversocial—who forces himself or herself on you—can be just as destructive to a relationship as the person who represents the antithesis—someone who is frequently withdrawn, indifferent, and silent.

The *aggressive–evasive patterns* were discussed. Aggressiveness can be divisive and provoke an individual to physical violence. The aggressive counterpart may be less direct, but evasiveness can be equally damaging. There are many manifestations of evasion in interactions. We discussed four major methods: (1) the process of changing the focus of responsibility away from oneself and onto another or others; (2) the process of changing the direction of the conversation by either not answering, managing the question, or managing the questioner; (3) the process of changing the level of conversation by treating a serious response lightheartedly or vice versa, or by trying to bring a very abstract discussion down to a concrete level or vice versa; and (4) the process of sending incongruous messages and putting people in double binds.

In discussing the *dominant–submissive patterns*, we noted that the dominant style assumes that the other is somehow not quite adequate in some area or areas and therefore needs to be shown THE way. Domination can be sought directly through commands and ultimatums or indirectly by such games as "Torture Rack" or "You Can Never Repay Me." We suggested a process through which a dominant individual may seek to squelch "insubordination"—nullification, isolation, defamation, and expulsion. The submissive style can elicit undesirable responses in a relationship due to its exaggeration of dependency, avoidance of responsibility, and self-deprecating remarks.

The last pair of extremes presented varied on the amount of predictability felt—*certain and provisional patterns*. The certain approach may overgeneralize, exhibit absolutism in verbal behavior, avoid qualifications or be characterized by feeling that one is saying all that is important to say. In some cases, this know-it-all approach manifests itself in a self-fulfilling prophecy. For the provisional pattern, life is far too unpredictable to ever know or say anything "for sure." Hence, a decisionless state of limbo is maintained.

Throughout this chapter we've tried to emphasize the fact that relationships crumble through the efforts of two people—not one. There will always be those issues that give rise to relationship crises (tardiness, sloppiness, impoliteness, or some personal hygiene issue). We need to realize and accept our own communicative imperfections and those of others; minimize the use of strategies that consistently get poor results for us; and try to learn from our mistakes.

SELECTED READINGS

Problematic Patterns and Schemes

Berne, E. *Games People Play.* New York: Grove Press, 1964.

———. *What Do You Say After You Say Hello?* New York: Grove Press, 1972.

Chapman A. H. *Put-Offs and Come-Ons.* New York: G. P. Putnam's Sons, 1968.

Gilbert, D. T. "Overhelping." *Journal of Personality and Social Psychology* 70 (1966): 678–690.

Harris, T. *I'm O.K., You're O.K.* New York: Harper & Row, 1967.

James, M., and Jongeward, D. *Born to Win.* Reading, MA: Addison-Wesley. 1971.

Leary, M. R., Springer, C., Negel, L., Ansell, E., and Evans, K. "The Causes, Phenomenology, and Consequences of Hurt Feelings." *Journal of Personality and Social Psychology* 74 (1998): 1225–1237.

Lederer, W. J., and Jackson, D. D. *The Mirages of Marriage.* New York: W. W. Norton, 1968.

Mortenson, C. D. *Problematic Communication: The Construction of Invisible Walls.* Westport, CT: Praeger, 1994.

O'Connor, K. M., and Garnevale, P. J. "A Nasty but Effective Negotiation Strategy: Misrepresentation of a Common-Value Issue." *Personality and Social Psychology Bulletin* 23 (1997): 504–515.

Potter, S. *The Complete Upmanship.* New York: Holt, Rinehart, & Winston, 1970.

Ruesch, J. "The Tangential Response." In P. H. Hoch and J. Zubin, eds., *Psychotherapy of Communication,* New York: Grune & Stratton, 1958.

Shostrom, E. L. *Man, The Manipulator.* New York: Abingdon Press, 1967.

Sieburg, E. "Confirming and Disconfirming Organizational Communication." In J. L. Owen, P. A. Page, and G. I. Zimmerman, eds. *Communication in Organizations.* New York: West Publishing, 1976.

Spitzberg, B. H., and Cupach, W. R., eds., *The Dark Side of Close Relationships.* Mahwah, NJ: Erlbaum, 1998.

Stamp, G. H., Vangelisti, A. L., and Daly, J. A. "The Creation of Defensiveness in Social Interaction." *Communication Quarterly* 40 (1992): 177–190.

Vangelisti, A. L., and Crumley, L. P. "Reactions to Messages That Hurt: The Influence of Relational Contexts." *Communication Monographs* 65 (1998): 173–196.

Self-Fulfilling Prophesies

Blanck, P. D., ed. *Interpersonal Expectations: Theory, Research, and Applications,* New York: Cambridge University Press, 1993.

Merton, R. "The Self-Fulfilling Prophecy." *Antioch Review* 8 (1948): 193–210.

Rosenthal, R. *Experimenter Effects in Behavioral Research.* New York: Appleton-Century-Crofts, 1966.

——— and Jacobson, L. *Pygmalion in the Classroom.* New York: Holt, Rinehart, & Winston, 1968.

Double Binds and Incongruous Messages

Bugental, D. E. "Interpretations of Naturally Occurring Discrepancies Between Words and Intonation: Modes of Inconsistency Resolution." *Journal of Personality and Social Psychology* 30 (1974): 125–133.

DePaulo, B. M., Rosenthal, R., Eisenstat, R., Rogers, P. L., and Finkelstein, S. "Decoding Discrepant Nonverbal Cues." *Journal of Personality and Social Psychology* 36 (1978): 313–323.

Fleming, J., and Darley, J. "Mixed Messages: The Multiple Avoidance Problem and Strategic Communication." *Social Cognition* 9 (1991): 25–46.

Heller, J. *Catch 22.* New York: Simon & Schuster, 1961.

Leathers, D. G. "The Impact of Multichannel Message Inconsistency on Verbal and Nonverbal Decoding Behaviors." *Communication Monographs* 46 (1979): 88–100.

Mehrabian, A. *Nonverbal Communication.* Chicago: Aldine, 1972.

Noller, P. "Negative Communication in Marriage." *Journal of Social and Personal Relationships* 2 (1985): 289–301.

Schuham, A. "The Double Bind Hypothesis a Decade Later." *Psychological Bulletin* 68 (1967): 409–416.

Sluzki, C. E., and Ransom, D. C., eds. *Double Bind: The Foundation of the Communicational Approach to the Family.* New York: Grune & Stratton, 1976.

Volkmar, F. R., and Siegel, A. E. "Responses to Consistent and Discrepant Social Communications." In R. S. Feldman, ed., *Development of Nonverbal Behavior in Children,* pp. 231–255. New York: Springer-Verlag, 1982.

Wagner, H., and Pease, K. "The Verbal Communication of Inconsistency Between Attitudes Held and Attitudes Expressed." *Journal of Personality* 44 (1976): 1–15.

Watzlawick, P. *How Real Is Real?* New York: Random House, 1976.

Watzlawick, P., Beavin, J. H., and Jackson, D. D. *Pragmatics of Human Communication.* New York: W. W. Norton, 1967.

Weigert, A. *Mixed Emotions: Certain Steps Toward Understanding Ambivalence.* Albany, NY: SUNY Press, 1991.

Physical Abuse and Aggression

Arriaga, X. B., and Rusbult, C. E. "Standing in My Partner's Shoes: Partner Perspective Taking and Reactions to Accomodative Dilemmas." *Personality and Social Psychology Bulletin* 24 (1998): 927–948.

deTurck, M. A. "When Communication Fails: Physical Aggression in Marriage as a Compliance Gaining Strategy." *Communication Monographs* 53 (1987): 106–112.

Harris, L. M., Gergen, K. J., and Lannamann, J. W. "Aggression Rituals." *Communication Monographs* 53 (1986): 252–265.

Johnson, M. P. "Patriarchal Terrorism and Common Couple Violence Against Women." *Journal of Marriage and the Family* 57 (1995): 283–294.

Lloyd, S. A. "Conflict Types and Strategies in Violent Marriages." *Journal of Family Violence* 5 (1990): 269–284.

Marshall, L. L. "Physical and Psychological Abuse." In W. R. Cupach and B. H. Spitzberg, eds., *The Dark Side of Interpersonal Communication,* pp. 281–311. Hillsdale, NJ: Erlbaum, 1994.

Marshall, L. L., and Vitanza, S. A. "Physical Abuse in Close Relationship: Myths and Realities." In A. L. Weber and J. H. Harvey, eds., *Perspectives on Close Relationships,* pp. 263–284. Boston: Allyn and Bacon, 1994.

O'Leary, K. D., and Vivian, D. "Physical Aggression in Marriage." In F. D. Fincham and T. N. Bradbury, eds., *The Psychology of Marriage,* pp. 323-348. New York: Guilford, 1990.

Stamp, G. H., and Sabourin, T. C. "Accounting for Violence: An Analysis of Male Spousal Abuse Narratives." *Journal of Applied Communication Research* 23 (1995): 284–307.

Straus, M. A., Gelles, R. J., and Steinmetz, S. K. *Behind Closed Doors: Violence in the American Family.* Garden City, NY: Doubleday, 1980.

Sugarman, D. B., and Hotaling, G. T. "Dating Violence: Prevalence, Context and Risk Markers." In M. A. Pirog-Good and J. E. Stets, eds., *Violence in Dating Relationships: Emerging Social Issues.* New York: Praeger, 1989.

Tolman, R. M., and Bennett, L. W. "A Review of Quantitative Research on Men Who Batter." *Journal of Interpersonal Violence,* 5 (1990): 87–118.

Umberson, D., Anderson, K., Glick, J., and Shapiro, A. "Domestic Violence, Personal Control, and Gender." *Journal of Marriage and the Family* 60 (1998): 442–452.

Dominance and Power

Adorno, T. W., Frenkel-Brunswick, E., Levinson, D. J., and Sanford, R. N. *The Authoritarian Personality.* New York: Harper & Row, 1950.

Berger, C. R. "Power, Dominance, and Social Interaction." In M. L. Knapp and G. R. Miller, eds., *Handbook of Interpersonal Communication* (2nd. ed.), pp. 450–507. Thousand Oaks, CA: Sage, 1994.

Blau, P. M. *Exchange and Power in Social Life.* New York: Wiley, 1964.

Bradac, J. J., Wiemann, J. M., and Schaefer, K. "The Language of Control in Interpersonal Communication." In J. A. Daly and J. M. Wiemann, eds., *Strategic Interpersonal Communication,* pp. 91–108. Hillsdale, NJ: Earlbaum, 1994.

Burgoon, J. K., Johnson, M. L., and Koch, P. T. "The Nature and Measurement of Interpersonal Dominance." *Communication Monographs* 65 (1998): 308–335.

Christie, R., and Geis, F. L. *Studies in Machiavellianism.* New York: Academic Press, 1970.

Ellyson, S. L., and Dovidio, J. F., eds. *Power Dominance and Nonverbal Behavior.* New York: Springer-Verlag, 1985.

Emerson, R. M. "Power-dependance Relations." *American Sociological Review* 27 (1962): 31–41.

Falbo, T., and Peplau, L. A. "Power Strategies in Intimate Relationships." *Journal of Personality and Social Psychology* 38 (1980): 618–628.

Huston, T. L. "Power." In H. H. Kelley et al., eds., *Close Relationships,* pp. 173–219. New York: Freeman, 1983.

Infante, D. A. "Aggressiveness." In J. C. McCroskey and J. A. Daly, eds., *Personality and Interpersonal Communication,* pp. 157–192. Newbury Park, CA: Sage, 1987.

Jones, E. E. *Ingratiation: A Social Analysis.* New York: Appelton-Century-Crofts, 1964.

Liska, J. "Dominance-seeking Language Strategies: Please Eat the Floor, Dogbreath, or I'll Rip Your Lungs Out, OK?" In S. A. Deetz, ed., *Communication Yearbook 15*, pp. 427–456. Newbury Park, CA: Sage, 1992.

Mason, A., and Blankenship, V. "Power and Affiliation Motivation, Stress, and Abuse in Intimate Relationships." *Journal of Personality and Social Psychology* 52 (1987): 203-210.

Murphy, C., and Cascardi, M. "Psychological Aggression and Abuse in Marriage." In R. L. Hampton, ed., *Issues in Children's and Families' Lives: Family Violence, vol. II*, pp. 1–25. Newbury Park, CA: Sage, 1993.

Ng, S. H., and Bradac, J. J. *Language and Power.* Thousand Oaks, CA: Sage, 1993.

Rogers-Millar, L. E., and Millar, F. E. "Domineeringness and Dominance: A Transactional View." *Human Communication Research* 5 (1979): 238–246.

Winter, D. G. *The Power Motive.* New York: Free Press, 1973.

NOTES

[1] J. Strayhorn, "Social-Exchange Theory: Cognitive Restructuring in Marital Therapy," *Family Process* 17 (1978): 437–448.

[2] A. Koestler, *Darkness at Noon* (New York: Modern Library, 1941), p. 58.

[3] X. B. Arriaga and C. E. Rusbult, "Standing in My Partner's Shoes: Partner Perspective Taking and Reactions to Accomodative Dilemmas," *Personality and Social Psychology Bulletin* 24 (1998): 927–948.

[4] The "results we would like" are often hard to determine, since in the rapid give and take of daily interpersonal communication, we desire multiple goals, any one of which may drift in and out of our conscious awareness at any given time. For instance, I want to "win" this argument and I want to maintain your friendship. I may only realize how important my friendship goal was after I have verbally decimated my former friend and the current loser. In Chapter 8 a similar problem was discussed—a person wanting to be open and to disclose something critical about another's behavior, but not wanting to hurt them . . . or be hurt by them.

[5] D. Gilbert and D. H. Silvera, "Overhelping," *Journal of Personality and Social Psychology* 70 (1966): 678–690.

[6] For an elaboration of this interpersonal sequence and other "games people play," see: E. Berne, *Games People Play* (New York: Grove Press, 1964).

[7] M. R. Leary, C. Springer, L. Negel, E. Ansell, and K. Evans, "The Causes, Phenomenology, and Consequences of Hurt Feelings," *Journal of Personality and Social Psychology* 74 (1998): 1225–1237; A. L. Vangelisti and L. P. Crumley, "Reactions to Messages That Hurt: The Influence of Relational Contexts," *Communication Monographs* 65 (1998): 173–196.

[8] What we are describing here is closely aligned with what Schutz calls the *oversocial* and *overpersonal* types; this assessment is based on these people's interpersonal needs. *Undersocial* and *underpersonal* types merge with what we've called *passive*. Schutz's description of the Abdicrat and Autocrat will be integrated in the Domination-Submission category. See: W. C. Schutz, *The Interpersonal Underworld* (Palo Alto, CA: Science & Behavior Books, 1966).

[9] C. Derber, *The Pursuit of Attention: Power and Individualism in Everyday Life* (Boston: G. K. Hall, 1979). Also see: A. L. Vangelisti, M. L. Knapp, and J. A. Daly, "Conversational Narcissism," *Communication Monographs* 57 (1990): 251–274.

[10] P. Mornell, *Passive Men, Wild Women.* (New York: Ballantine, 1979). See also A. Christensen and C. L. Heavey, "Gender and Social Structure in the Demand/Withdrawal Pattern of Marital Conflict," *Journal of Personality and Social Psychology* 59 (1990): 73–81.

[11] J. E. Stets and M. A. Pirog-Good, "Interpersonal Control and Courtship Aggression," *Journal of Social and Personal Relationships* 7 (1990): 371–394.

[12] L. W. Rosenfield, L. S. Hayes, and T. S. Frentz, *The Communicative Experience* (Boston: Allyn and Bacon, 1976), pp. 167–170.

[13] L. E. A. Walker, *The Battered Woman* (New York: Harper & Row, 1979); G. H. Stamp and T. C. Sabourin, "Accounting for Violence: An Analysis of Male Spousal Abuse Narratives," *Journal of Applied Communication Research* 23 (1995): 284–307; M. P. Johnson, "Patriarchal Terrorism and Common Couple Violence Against Women," *Journal of Marriage and the Family* 57 (1995): 283–294; D. Umbcrson, K. Anderson, J. Glick, and A. Shapiro, "Domestic

Violence, Personal Control, and Gender," *Journal of Marriage and the Family* 60 (1998): 442–452.

[14]When politicians are evasive with listeners who are very "issue involved," the ambiguity allows these listeners to read their own beliefs into the statement. If the ambiguous statement is presented with great intensity, firmness, and certainty to uninvolved listeners, the listeners may feel the speaker "really knows her (or his) subject." See: C. J. Orr and K. E. Burkins, "The Endorsement of Evasive Leaders: An Exploratory Study," *Central States Speech Journal* 27 (1976): 230–239. Nofsinger points out that in everyday conversation we expect others to cooperate in helping make sense out of our utterances. Hence, what might seem like an indirect or evasive response is sometimes generously interpreted by the receiver as an answer that follows logically—Q: "Are notebooks allowed during the final exam?" A: "Are porcupines allowed in balloon factories?" See: R. E. Nofsinger, Jr., "On Answering Questions Indirectly: Some Rules in the Grammar of Doing Conversation," *Human Communication Research* 2 (1976): 172–181. Also see: T. Holtgraves, "Interpersonal Foundations of Conversational Indirectness." In S. R. Fussell and R. J. Kreuz, eds., *Social and Cognitive Approaches to Interpersonal Communication.* (Mahwah, NJ: Erlbaum, 1998), pp. 71–89. Bavelas has shown that indirect and evasive messages are most likely to be produced when the communicator perceives the situation as one in which other message choices have negative aspects to them. See: J. B. Bavelas, "Situations that Lead to Disqualification," *Human Communication Research* 9 (1983): 130–145.

[15]C. Washburne, "Retortmanship: How to Avoid Answering Questions," *ETC: A Review of General Semantics* 26 (1969): 69–75.

[16]P. Watzlawick, *An Anthology of Human Communication: Text and Two-Hour Tape* (Palo Alto, CA: Science & Behavior Books, 1964), p. 18.

[17]J. W. Bowers, N. D. Elliott, and R. J. Desmond, "Exploiting Pragmatic Rules: Devious Messages," *Human Communication Research* 3 (1977): 235–242.

[18]J. B. Bavelas, A. Black, N. Chovil, and J. Mullett, *Equivocal Communication* (Newbury Park, CA: Sage, 1990).

[19]A. H. Chapman, *Put-Offs and Come-Ons* (New York: G. P. Putnam's Sons, 1968), pp. 14–16. This book outlines many games that reflect put-off forces—fear, anger, and competitive hostility. The come-on forces (forces which draw people together) are also discussed extensively.

[20]For an elaboration of various kinds of put-ons like this one, see: R. A. Stebbins, "Putting People On: Deception of Our Fellowman in Everyday Life," *Sociology and Social Research* 59 (1975): 189–200.

[21]R. D. Laing, *The Self and Others* (Chicago: Quadrangle Press, 1962), p. 131.

[22]P. Watzlawick, J. H. Beavin, and D. D. Jackson, *Pragmatics of Human Communication* (New York: W. W. Norton, 1967), pp. 194–229. The double bind is today sometimes referred to as *catch-22* after the novel by the same name. The novel deals with a person who tries to avoid flying missions by showing how he is afraid—even "crazy." He is told that people who fly these missions are indeed crazy and it would be abnormal not to be afraid. Hence, he must be sane and must fly the missions.

[23]For further perspectives on the double bind, see also: C. E. Sluzki and D. C. Ransom, eds., *Double Bind: The Foundation of the Communicational Approach to the Family* (New York: Grune & Stratton, 1976); A. Mehrabian, "Inconsistent Messages and Sarcasm," in *Nonverbal Communication* (Chicago: Aldine Publishing, 1972), pp. 104–132; and A. Schuham, "The Double-Bind Hypothesis a Decade Later," *Psychological Bulletin* 68 (1967): 409–416.

[24]P. Watzlawick presents a similar analysis in *An Anthology of Human Communication: Text and Two-Hour Tape* (Palo Alto, CA: Science & Behavior Books, 1964), pp. 41–42.

[25]Watzlawick, *Pragmatics of Human Communication*, pp. 251–252.

[26]Watzlawick, P. *An Anthology of Human Communication*, pp. 39–40.

[27]Chapman, *Put-Offs and Come-Ons*, pp. 17–18; 28–32.

[28]R. O'Day, "Intimidation Rituals: Reactions to Reform," *Journal of Applied Behavioral Science* 10 (1974): 373–386.

[29]T. Harris, *I'm O.K., You're O.K.* (New York: Harper & Row, 1967).

[30]S. H. Ng and J. J. Bradac, *Language and Power* (Beverly Hills, CA: Sage, 1993).

[31]R. Merton, "The Self-Fulfilling Prophecy," *Antioch Review* 8 (1948): 193–210. For an analysis of how this process works in the classroom, see also: R. Rosenthal and L. Jacobson, *Pygmalion in the Classroom* (New York: Holt, Rinehart, & Winston, 1968); also see: P. D. Blanck, ed., *Interpersonal Expectations: Theory, Research, and Applications* (New York: Cambridge University Press, 1993).

[32]D. Greenberg, *How to Make Yourself Miserable* (New York: Random House, 1968).

Toward More Effective Communication in Relationships

CHAPTER **12**

Evaluating and Developing Effective Communication in Relationships

Evaluating and Developing Effective Communication in Relationships

Dear Dr. Knapp,

I have difficulty talking to people I really care about. I get along fine with most people and have lots of "friends" at work. But when it comes to someone I love, I just can't say what I really feel. It doesn't matter whether the person is female or male. If I'm upset with someone I care about, I never confront the person. When I want to say "I love you," I freeze up. Sometimes I deal with this by writing people notes. Most of the time though, I'll sit there quietly when I would really like to express my feelings. How can I be the life of the party with people I barely know but a social reject with people I care about the most?

Caring but Clumsy

The standards for a communicator's success or failure may not be the same from situation to situation. The people who make the evaluations, the reasons for making the evaluations, and the things that are evaluated all may vary greatly from the school environment to the home environment. These and other factors that form the basis of our judgments about effective communication in relationships are covered in the first part of this chapter. Then the link between our perceptions of communication and our perceptions of relationships is discussed. A number of suggestions for improving our communication abilities in the context of our relationships are noted. In addition, because becoming an effective communicator is a very complex, never-ending process, the ingredients necessary for developing effective communication skills are covered. The chapter concludes with several ways we can strive for more communicative successes in our relationships.

> *Making a judicious evaluation requires that the critic be aware of the intricacies of human communication and cognizant that he can never know everything about the communication situation.*
>
> —Robert Cathcart

Let's begin with some statements about the behavior of effective communicators, statements with which many of you will no doubt agree:

1. An effective communicator avoids ambiguity and abstract words; he or she addresses issues clearly.
2. An effective communicator would not throw a childish temper tantrum and deliberately yell abuses at another person.
3. An effective communicator knows that the best way to get people to do something is to praise them, make them feel important, and tell them what they want to hear.

On the surface, the foregoing statements seem sound and reasonable. After all, most introductory communication textbooks tell you to speak clearly, sometimes supporting their contention with footnotes from ancient, revered rhetoricians like Aristotle or Quintilian. (Effective sales texts frequently make the same point without the footnotes.) The second statement might seem to some to be so obviously and intuitively true that evidence to support it would be superfluous. The last statement reflects a key thread in the communicative philosophy of Dale Carnegie, whose influence on American communicators was—and is—immense.

Let's look at the statements again. Since none of them is qualified by phrases such as *most of the time* or *usually* or *often* or *probably,* we need find only one exception to the statement's contention to disagree with it. You can probably find other exceptions, but let's look at these: (1) It's generally good advice to make messages clear, but there are times when people might need to be deliberately vague in order to accomplish their objectives.[1] A politician who speaks to several different constituencies may find too much specificity antithetical to getting elected; a fiancée may wish to spare her future husband the unambiguous and "gory" details of her previous love affairs; an adult son may not want to disclose the specifics of his financial affairs to his parents. Too much clarity in initiating labor–management negotiations may create a polarization that is difficult to undo. Sometimes people are more likely to agree with a proposition stated in a fairly abstract way and disagree when the specifics of that proposition are made known. And, strange as it seems, sometimes people even attribute greater credibility to those who communicate messages they don't understand—thinking the communicator is so much more intelligent and that is the reason they are unable to grasp what he or she is saying. Some people get a lot of mileage out of this phenomenon until it becomes clear that other so-called intelligent people can't even sort through the vagueness and jargon used by this person. (2) Of course, we wouldn't suggest the rigidity and imprudent behavior associated with a temper tantrum for everyday communicative fare. It can, however, be an effective strategy for accomplishing one's goal—for the person who continually seeks compromise and conciliation through sensitivity and understanding from another person who stiffly rejects any of the responses. The first person may "give up" and "blow up," a stimulus which can then elicit the same spirit of conciliation earlier sought. It is a dangerous, risky, and seldom recommended ploy, however, because it can just as easily (if not more easily) result in further antagonism and polarization. But it has worked. In abbreviated form it might look like this:

HE: Please . . . (reaches to touch)

SHE: No. (pulls away)

HE: I'm sorry . . .

SHE: Ha! Forget it.

HE: I want to help . . .

SHE: You can't . . .

(. . . etc. and eventually)

HE: ALL RIGHT! . . . GOD DAMN IT! . . . I'VE HAD IT! . . . YOU CAN COUNT ME OUT! . . . (throws magazine across room) . . . I'M TIRED OF TRYING! (kicks coffee table and heads for the door)

SHE: C'mon, now . . . I didn't mean for you to get so upset . . . I'm sorry I was so nasty . . . (reaches to touch) . . . sit down and let's talk. . . .

(3) For the third statement we might look at a long-term marital relationship. Suppose the wife was seeking a promotion at work and asked her husband for feedback on her resume. A number of things could go wrong—the wife may see the praise as excessive and may, as a result, mistrust her husband's feedback; if she receives only praise from her husband and receives a more critical response from her boss, she may lose respect for her husband's opinions in this area.

The point of this find-the-exception-to-the-rule exercise is that almost any advice that purports to be a key to success in relational communication will—with some person, in some situation, at some time—be impotent or ineffective. We've already noted that even patterns normally considered pathological may sometimes be effective strategies when all other avenues are blocked (see Chapter 11). The only reason the so-called temper tantrum succeeded in the dialogue just discussed was because of the particular relationship between the parties and the messages that preceded it. Any pattern of relational communication can be successful or unsuccessful, effective or ineffective. Yes, sometimes effective communication will be threatening, withdrawing, and inflexible. To be sure, some patterns are better suited for more frequent successes in a wider variety of situations than others; they'll be discussed later. For now, let's take a closer look at the concept of communicative success, or effectiveness in our relationships.

The Relativity of Effective Communication

Success is not an absolute concept. That is, we don't all use the same standards to evaluate our successes in any endeavor.[2] Some feel that they are successful in their careers if they are able to attain the job or position they want. Some feel they are successful if they earn a lot of money. Still others feel successful if they work for a prestigious organization—regardless of position or salary. Evaluating the success or effectiveness of the communication that occurs in our relationships is also relative; a judgment that any individual is communicating effectively (or is an effective communicator) is dependent on who is doing the evaluating, when it is done, what is evaluated, and how and why it is done.

Who Is Evaluating Communicative Success?

Montgomery notes that different criteria for effective communication are established and maintained by different societies, relationships, and individuals.[3] For example, a society's beliefs and values affect the standards its people use to judge communication. Research comparing evaluations made by those who live in the United States and those who live in other countries (e.g., Columbia, Korea) suggest that there are differences in the ways members of these societies judge interaction.[4] Furthermore, within the United States, various ethnic groups evaluate certain aspects of verbal and nonverbal communication in different ways.[5] Montgomery argues that many of today's western societies tend to value positive communication over negative communication, that they see intimacy and openness as central components of close relationships, and that they believe that individuals should have control over what happens in their relationships. These assumptions may not always be accurate. There are times when negative communication is very important to relationships, when openness can create relational discord, and when individuals are simply unable to "work" hard enough to control their relational outcomes.

Even so, criteria such as these sometimes affect the ways members of a particular society evaluate relational communication.

The criteria used to assess effective communication also may differ from one relationship to the next. Relational partners often negotiate standards for communication that are both unique to their relationship and different from those held by their society. Some couples value conflict; others view conflict as a very destructive form of communication.[6] Some families believe that members should all have similar values; others place a high premium on individuality.[7] Because they are unique, these shared relational standards can serve to reinforce intimacy between relational partners. (Recall, in Chapter 9, our discussion of personal idioms.) It is also possible, however, for partners to develop destructive relational standards. Research has demonstrated, for example, that negative communication within the marital dyad often predicts later dissatisfaction in the relationship.[8] Similarly, couples who have unrealistic expectations for their relationship (e.g., "We should never argue with each other") tend to be less satisfied.[9] Although it is difficult to determine whether standards such as these actually *cause* dissatisfaction in the relationship, we can conclude that they are not usually associated with "healthy" or "satisfying" relationships.

Finally, individuals often develop and maintain their own idiosyncratic criteria for quality communication. Different standards for effective communication may be used by people with different interests, priorities, values, and experiences. Furthermore, perceptual differences can arise even when people have agreed to use the same criteria—co-workers may view behavior differently than best friends or lovers. When individuals themselves are the evaluators, they may be able to consider their own abilities and past accomplishments and arrive at an evaluation emphasizing effectiveness because "it was the best I could have done." Often, this is a perceptual luxury which may not be afforded an outside observer—or even a very intimate relational partner. Our acceptance and receptivity to judgments of our effectiveness are also colored by the person(s) doing the evaluating. We sometimes look at evaluative feedback differently when it is sought from a specific person than when it is not sought but volunteered by the evaluator. Whether we consider the people evaluating our effectiveness as better or worse at communicating than ourselves may also make a difference in how we receive or accept the evaluation.

When Is Communicative Success Evaluated?

Several time-related considerations can also affect our judgment of effective communication. These include: (1) the specific situation(s) or circumstances involved, (2) the stage of the relationship under consideration, (3) the life stage of the communicator, and (4) the time in history.

In examining any communication situation, a number of questions must be addressed. Am I to evaluate your ability as a communicator during our interaction, immediately after the interaction, or six months from now? And if I do all three, will the judgments be similar? Should they be? Some research methodology is based on the assumption that these measures at different times should be similar in order to be considered accurate. Anyone who subscribes to the view that people and things are in a process of continual change would probably find such a belief problematic. The question, however, remains: Will I evaluate your effectiveness at one point in time or at many points? If I select only one point, I might evaluate you following a personal tragedy or while enacting a new role which you may feel is not representative of your usual behavior. Sometimes people do use a single instance to generalize a person's overall effectiveness—"Did you hear what she said to her boyfriend? I can't imagine even associating with someone who is so insensitive!" Sometimes the reverse is true, people use the frequency with which a pattern or outcome occurs as a standard of success or failure. This latter point of view leads to another question: Can we communicate effectively in every situation and every relationship? If not, how often do we have to demonstrate effectiveness to be considered generally successful?

Implicit in the preceding chapters is the assumption that any consideration of effective relational communication must take into account the stage of one's relationship with the other person. To be judged effective with a stranger, I might have to conform more closely to accepted cultural norms; with my friends, however, there may be tacit agreement to break certain of these norms to indicate our closeness. Thus, if we communicate differently at different stages of our relationship with another, judgments of communicative competence must consider the expectations for communicative behavior at that stage in the relationship. Suppose, for instance, both participants to a relationship want to terminate it. Both parties are reflecting on their differences. Can we say this is "ineffective communication" or a "communication breakdown"—or just a natural and expected pattern for ending a relationship? If one or both parties do not want the relationship to deteriorate, we will have to determine whether our judgment of effectiveness will be based on the behavior of both parties or on the behavior of either one individually.

Another consideration for the timing of evaluations focuses on our life stages. Most people don't hold children to the same standards for effectiveness as they hold adults. Although, admittedly, some do. Traditionally, most of the standards for communicative competence in children have focused on mastery of the rules of language—grammar, syntax, sentence construction. Rarely are such concerns the focus for measuring communicative competence in adults. Suffice to say, people's stage of life will influence the criteria used by those evaluating their effectiveness in communication.

Delia and Clark have identified five periods of development that boys experience as they develop proficiency in listener-adapted communication skills.[10] At first the child is unable to perceive that listeners have certain characteristics that play an important role in their efforts to accomplish certain communicative tasks. Gradually, the child perceives the communication-relevant characteristics in listeners, but still does not connect these characteristics with specific communication tasks. Then the child learns to associate listener characteristics with his or her communicative efforts, but the knowledge of how to control and alter messages to offset or support certain listener characteristics is not yet available. In time the child tries to adapt to different kinds of listeners and situations through the use of very general adaptation strategies—e.g., altering tone of voice or including a phrase to show deference. The final stage is one of refinement in which more control over the communication situation is manifested in the use of specific listener-adapted strategies based on inferences about the attitudes, qualities, and possible reactions of the listener. Given these very different developmental skills, it would seem most appropriate to apply different standards for communicative success at different periods in the life of the child. Although we don't have comparable information for middle-aged and older adults, it seems reasonable to assume that listener-adapted communication skills may show changes at other life periods as well.

There also seem to be different priorities given to various communication styles at different times in history[11]—the formal, grandiose eloquence of yesteryear would seem strangely out of place today; the dictum that "good marital communication is devoid of conflict" seems to be a standard of bygone days; and although Harry Truman's proclivity to be open and "tell it like it is" can now be admired, it was often considered a tragic mistake during his presidency. Some periods in history have emphasized (some would say overemphasized) either the rational-calculating-task oriented style or the affective-feeling oriented style.[12] Suffice to say, the climate of the times also influences our judgments of what is "good" and "bad" communication.

Success can eliminate as many options as failure.
Tom Robbins

What Is Evaluated for Communicative Success?

By far, the most common approach currently used for assessing communicative effectiveness in relationships is the correspondence between what relational partners set out to accomplish and the extent to which they accomplish it—did they get the response they desired? For example, if you wanted to have somebody understand something, how well did he or she seem to understand it? If you wanted to influence somebody or make that person do something, did he or she do it? If you wanted someone to evaluate you in a certain way, was it done? If you wanted to entertain somebody, was he or she entertained?

Aside from the obvious difficulty in verifying each desired response through ordinary feedback, there are other sources of potential variation in this "response sought–response obtained" paradigm: (1) Communicators may have multiple goals.[13] Is the accomplishment of any one or all of them considered successful? Can communicators partially accomplish each goal and still be successful? Must successful communicators be able to select strategies that can accomodate incompatible goals?[14] If communicators obtain a response from themselves (relief) by "getting something off my chest," is that effective communication? Can communicators fail to achieve their objective, but achieve an unexpected goal and still be successful? This last question raises the issue of whether we are always aware of what we want to accomplish with our communications. How can we know what another knew or didn't know as he or she entered an encounter? Does anyone's overt behavior accurately reflect what he or she knew or didn't know? (2) Some feel there is an ethical or moral dimension to effective communication, a communicator may accomplish a goal, but if that goal is not one that is considered ethical or moral success is obviated. For example, if someone wanted to hurt you, lie to you, decrease your self-worth, or confuse you, that person might do so and still be considered an ineffective communicator by some. (3) Some feel that one's own effectiveness is inextricably linked to the goal attainment of the other person—*you* can't be considered effective unless the *other person* has attained his or her interaction goals. You may think you did "a great job." The other person felt rotten. Hence, under these conditions, you would not be considered successful. Of course, not all communicative goals are self-serving; you may have as one of your goals "not to make the other person feel rotten." Listeners may sometimes seem to be dissatisfied and still be accomplishing their goals—you may not like to "give in" to your relational partner during a disagreement, but in a public setting it may be the most appropriate (and least hurtful) thing to do. Sometimes listeners feel completely satisfied, but no other observer of the interaction would agree. Listeners also change or modify their goals during the interaction. Someone might be so uncompromisingly dogmatic that you, as listener, will adjust your original goals and feel "lucky" to have accomplished what little you did—given the other person's behavior. (4) In well-established relationships another situation adds a different hue to the response sought–response obtained paradigm. Perhaps the speaker wants to communicate the message: "Allow me an opportunity to be an ineffective communicator." For example, without verbalizing it, a person might get across this message: "I've had a rotten day; a rotten week; I'm tired and frustrated; I'm going to be ranting and raving, using obscene language, making outlandish claims, saying things I don't mean . . . and all I want from you is agreement and support!" If this communication sequence is understood by the listener and acted out by the communicator—if one person wants to vent his or her emotions under a rhetorical guise and another is party to it—is this communicator effective or ineffective?

Sometimes criteria for effectiveness are based on quantity of response—frequent eye contact or frequent verbalizations indicating supportiveness. The quantitative criteria for effectiveness seem to ignore the possibility that more may not always be better; too much eye contact may be negatively perceived as staring or too much indiscriminate supportiveness may eventually be perceived as insincerity. Most of us have encountered the person we felt was just "too smooth." Thus, we're faced with the fact that on some occasions we can't give enough of a particular behavior; on other occasions a small amount may be too much.

The size and diversity of a communicator's repertoire may distinguish more effective from less effective communicators. Indeed, the greater the number of alternative strategies at your disposal, the greater your chances of accomplishing your goal. But some people on some occasions will get the communicative job done because they keep hammering away with a limited range of strategies. These people will predictably have less overall success in a variety of situations and relationships, though.

Another judgment within the province of what is to be evaluated for communicative success comes from the twofold process of diagnosing, or analyzing, a situation versus executing, or carrying out, the behaviors deemed appropriate from the analysis. Some people are most perceptive analysts or critics, but find it difficult to enact the behaviors that are called for:

> We brought you truth, and in our mouth it sounded like a lie. We brought you freedom, and it looks in our hands like a whip. We brought you the living life, and where our voice is heard the trees wither and there is a rustling of dry leaves. We brought you the promise of the future, but our tongue stammered and barked. . . .[15]

Others manifest behaviors that are judged effective, but relate a diagnosis of the situation in seemingly superficial terms. Part of the process of diagnosis is the ability to predict responses. Miller points out that when we make predictions about the consequences of our messages, we deal with information on three levels:

1. **a cultural level**—judging our predictions against culture-specific norms (e.g., anticipating little political success in the United States by running on a Marxist ticket);
2. **a sociological level**—basing our predictions on what we know about a person's reference groups (e.g., most Catholics oppose abortion);
3. **a psychological level**—making predictions based on a specific individual and how that individual differs from the cultural norms and the general characteristics of his or her reference groups.[16]

These levels lead to still other questions: Must we be proficient at all levels of prediction before we are considered effective? Indeed, since knowledge at each level of prediction has some presuppositions for the next level, is it even possible to be a better predictor at level one (the cultural level) than at level three (the psychological level)?

Research on the decoding abilities of married couples underlines the notion that being able to accurately diagnose or analyze a situation is only part of what it takes to be a successful communicator. Although accurately detecting a partner's feelings and intentions certainly can be helpful to relationships, studies show that accuracy is not always associated with relational satisfactions.[17] Indeed, Sillars notes that there are several conditions when accuracy might even be harmful to relationships.[18] These include:

1. **irreconcilable differences**—when clarifying partners' views on an issue will not help to resolve the differences between them.
2. **benevolent misconceptions**—when maintaining certain misconceptions helps to facilitate relational satisfaction and stability.[19]
3. **blunt, unpleasant truths**—when being completely "truthful" or "honest" creates pain or distress for one or both partners.

Under each of these three conditions, increased accuracy may lead partners to feel more dissatisfied and less secure about their relationship. Knowing how to communicate about issues that are particularly distressing or that make one or both partners feel insecure may be a more important criterion for effective communication than accuracy when couples find themselves in situations such as these.

There seems to be an almost interminable list of dimensions upon which to seek a judgment of effectiveness. For instance, we might look at pronunciation, vocabulary, nonverbal behavior, effective verbal content, message organization, use of logic, written messages, public speeches. Clearly, a communicator can be judged effective in one mode, level, or type of communication and less effective in another. President Lyndon Johnson was said to be very persuasive in private settings and with one or two other people but much less effective when he addressed large groups. Some of our most effective novelists and poets manifest considerably less eloquence when speaking orally. Some communication skills appear to transcend modes and levels, whereas others are mode- or level-specific.

Finally, as we consider what to evaluate, we should account for individual differences. Certainly, known differences in an individual's physical or mental capabilities should contribute to an alteration of our criteria for communicative success. Further, as adults, all of us have developed a style of communicating based on past interaction rewards and models. This does not mean a style is an inflexible response pattern; instead it designates the boundaries around which we typically operate. As we consider what communicative adaptations we need to make to another person, we also need to realize that not all the behaviors we feel will be effective will fit our style. We recall a rather dull, puritanical professor who tried to "identify" and become more "relevant" with his students. He chose to increase the use of *damn* and *hell* in his lectures—a feature alien to his normal style. Instead of enhancing his credibility, he only succeeded in arousing sympathy from some students and outright laughter from others at the disharmony produced by the two contrasting styles. Similarly, in the context of a close relationship, if one partner tries to modify his or her communicative style in a way that is unnatural (perhaps as a last-ditch effort to "save" a relationship), the efforts may be perceived by his or her partner as awkward or even irritating.

How Is the Evaluation of Communicative Success Performed?

There are just about as many ways to gather data on communicative success as there are ways to evaluate those data. Criteria and standards for effectiveness will be influenced by and influence how we gather data on communicative success. If, for instance, you are a participant observer, part of your evaluation of another is colored by your own behavior. Would you be inclined to say your behavior contributed to another's *ineffectiveness?* Will you obtain only audio, only video, only written, or some combination of these types of messages to analyze effectiveness? Will you obtain evaluations from other people, paper and pencil tests, or physiological measures? Will your standards of effectiveness change if the only location for gathering the data you need is also heavily saturated with communication "noise"? Such questions are nearly endless. We've raised them only to show that the methods for gathering the corpus for communicative evaluations also impinge on our ultimate judgments of effectiveness.

Why Is the Evaluation of Communicative Success Performed?

People perform evaluations of others' communication for a variety of reasons. The motivation for performing the evaluation and the uses to which that evaluation will be put certainly affect what will be evaluated. The behavior of the person being observed may be altered if he or she is aware of the evaluation and its consequences. If an individual is only aware of the evaluation after it is finished, his or her acceptance of that evaluation may be influenced by a knowledge of why it took place. Sometimes evaluations are conducted for a reason not apparent to the person evaluated—researchers who fail to report the results of their evaluations back to those who provided the information to the researcher. Sometimes assessments of communicative success are closely linked to the success in work or the mental well-being of the person being evaluated—performance reviews for promotion, firing, grading, or self-help evaluations in therapy or evaluations for a politician who wants to improve his or her ability to communicate with various constituencies. Other times, relational partners may do their own, personal evaluation to decide whether they want to increase relational intimacy ("Would she really be supportive of me if I were to have a crisis?") or to end a relationship ("If he would just pay more attention to me when I need to talk, I'd be happier"). In most cases, these sorts of evaluations are done without consulting the partner for his or her input. As a result, very important relational decisions can be made based on incomplete information and without the other partner even knowing about them.

Is Evaluation of Communicative Success Possible?

The preceding contingencies for judging communicative effectiveness in relationships were not designed to show that legitimate judgments of effectiveness can't be made but only to reiterate the difficulty, relativity, and complexity resident in such judgments. Once we agree to (or are subjected to) a set of standards—with all their strengths, shortcomings, and arbitrary rules—we then know better (still not for sure) what to expect and how to achieve effectiveness. This should not suggest that these standards or evaluative criteria are the "best." Surely we will operate with many sets of standards as we go about our lives; we will have to adapt to each of these standards and none of them will be exactly the same. It should be clear that absolutes are hard to come by in this business of communicating. We've discussed success in terms of listener satisfaction, speaker goals, and a priori standards among other things. We've suggested that your success as a communicator in your relationships will depend on how you adapt to each moment-to-moment change in people, places, topics, and events. You'll read newspaper columns and paperback books which purport to give easy answers to extremely complex problems with, we hope, a new appreciation for what was left unanalyzed, what was analyzed superficially, and what might have been analyzed using standards for communicative success different from those discussed here.

Although the following summary definition of effective communication may not satisfy everyone in every situation, it seems to be the composite that encompasses the major perspectives we've discussed:

> Communication behavior is evaluated as effective when a person (or persons) is perceived as having appropriately adapted to the self-other-topic-situation interface in order to achieve a desired response or responses.

Scholars note that communication competence involves control (an ability to put forth and achieve goals), adaptation (an ability to respond to the social environment), and collaboration (an ability to sustain interaction with others).[20] If a person is perceived to exhibit effective communication behavior in a variety of situations involving different people, topics, and goals, he or she is likely to be called an "effective communicator"—without reference to a specific situation.

Since the act of perceiving is so critical to understanding what constitutes effective communication, the next section will address the following question: How do we perceive effective communication?

Perceptions of Effective Communication

Our judgments of communicative effectiveness are intertwined with our judgments of interpersonal relationships in general. For example, it is hard to make a judgment about the communication between a guard and a prisoner apart from our perceptions of the relationship between guards and prisoners in general. Wish, Deutsch, and Kaplan conducted a study that provides some information on the dimensions underlying perceptions of interpersonal relationships.[21] They asked people to make some judgments: (1) about their own relationships—between themselves and their close friends; (2) about what typical role relations might be like—between husband and wife, parent and young child, teammates (during a game), nurse and invalid; and (3) about their own relationships as a child—between themselves and their mothers. When all the responses were analyzed, it seemed that these subjects tended to view interpersonal relationships along four major dimensions: (1) cooperative–friendly versus competitive–hostile; (2) equal versus unequal; (3) intense versus superficial; and (4) socioemotional–informal versus task oriented–formal.

To show how these dimensions combine, here are some sample relationship ratings:

Competitive–hostile and Unequal	guard and prisoner
Competitive–hostile and Equal	political opponents
Cooperative–friendly and Equal	close friends; husband and wife
Cooperative–friendly and Unequal	teacher and pupil; nurse and invalid
Superficial and Task–formal	salesperson and regular customer
Superficial and Socioemotional–informal	second cousins; spouse's parents
Intense and Socioemotional–informal	husband and wife; close friends
Intense and Task–formal	teacher and pupil; business partners

As might be expected, not all the participants in the study seemed to interpret each dimension in the same way, nor did they attach the same importance to each dimension. Some felt that people in a hostile relationship avoided each other and that occasional interactions were marked by formality and superficiality. Others felt that a hostile relationship meant clashing head-on with intense and emotional interactions. Returning to the paradigm outlining various stages of interaction in a relationship (see Chapter 2), we can see that these different perceptions were simply recalling different stages in a deteriorating relationship. Younger and single respondents tended to attach more importance to the socioemotional–informal versus task oriented–formal dimension whereas older and married subjects attached more importance to the cooperative–friendly versus competitive–hostile dimension. Further, respondents felt the intense versus superficial dimension was more important in evaluating their own relationships, but the cooperative–friendly versus competitive–hostile dimension was more important in viewing others. Finally, as we intimated earlier, our perceptions of what dimensions are important will change as we move through different stages of life. We may, at some points in life, emphasize the quality of relationships; but as certain events affect our lives, we may perceive the friendly or hostile dimensions as most critical in evaluating our own relationships or the relationships of others.

At any life stage, our perceptions of communication effectiveness are going to be influenced by our expectations for and assumptions about our relationships. A number of researchers have noted, for example, that unrealistic relationship expectations are often associated with relational dissatisfaction.[22] When a partner strongly holds beliefs such as, "Spouses should be able to sense each other's needs and thoughts as if they could read each other's mind" or "Spouses should be completely supportive of all of each other's ideas and actions," it is inevitable that he or she will be disappointed. Any communication behavior that does not comply with these very strict standards will fall short of what a partner "should" be communicating. Perceptions of the communication will, therefore, be negative and perhaps even detrimental to the relationship—regardless of the intentions of the speaker.

Although relational contingencies have a strong influence on what we perceive to be effective and appropriate communication, it is also possible to discuss our perceptions of communication on a more general level. Feingold, for instance, tried to identify the general characteristics of an effective communicator.[23] After an extensive review of typical prescriptions for effective communication behavior, he developed a questionnaire which was administered to over 600 people from various walks of life. Some were asked to fill out the questionnaire about a person they felt was generally an effective communicator; others were asked to complete the form with a specific *in*effective communicator in mind. The dimensions along which these respondents tended to judge communicative ability included: (1) other-versus self-orientation;[24] (2) similarity versus dissimilarity to receiver; (3) clarity versus vagueness; and (4) message vigilance–attention versus message neglect–inattention.

The following six statements, taken from Feingold's questionnaire, tended to discriminate most clearly between the effective and ineffective communicators being judged. According to this study, then, we would be most likely to report that people we know who demonstrate effective communication in their relationships do the following things frequently and that those we classify as ineffective relational communicators seldom do them:

1. This person says the right thing at the right time.
2. This person adapts his or her communication to others.
3. This person avoids using language that might be offensive.
4. This person reveals something about his or her feelings when he or she is talking.
5. This person is aware of the effect of his or her communication on his or her partner.
6. This person is not difficult to understand.

Rx for Effective Communication

What is the best advice we can give to people who want to improve their ability to communicate in their relationships? Scholars and lay people alike have addressed this question in various ways for the last 2000 years. There seems to be an almost inexhaustible supply of lists that give advice on how to improve communicative behavior. Some of this advice has been excellent; some of it has been just shy of inane. Sometimes these prescriptive statements contain a kernel of sound advice, but suffer from inflexibility ("A good communicator *never* criticizes"), vagueness ("A good communicator uses self-disclosure"), or incomplete explanations ("Use facts instead of inferences").

One way to reduce our tendency to make these overly simple prescriptions is to appreciate what a complex task we accomplish when we communicate with another person. It is very easy for two people to misunderstand each other. And unfortunately, many relational problems begin with misunderstanding.[25] A wife who comes home from work every day in a bad mood may not clearly explain to her husband that the source of her moodiness is work-related stress. Even though she would like to talk about her problems, her husband may avoid interacting with her. He may reason that her moodiness is a signal that she "needs space" at the end of the work day. She, in turn, may see his avoidance not as consideration, but as a sign that he doesn't care. This interpretation is likely to increase her stress level and her moodiness. Over time, when the husband sees that his efforts to reduce his wife's stress are not effective, he may begin to assume that her moodiness is directed at him—and by this time, some of it is.

Obviously, in trying to remedy this case, a simple prescription (e.g., "A good communicator is expressive") is not very useful. It may be more helpful to describe the misunderstanding and then to discuss some of the ways misunderstandings such as this one can be prevented—or at least minimized. Fincham, Fernades, and Humphreys define four pathways to miscommunication:[26]

1. The speaker's intent and the message do not correspond. Imagine if in our previous example, the husband had asked his wife what was bothering her. Although sincere, his message would likely be misunderstood if he used a sarcastic or disinterested tone in his voice. This sort of miscommunication can create problems for couples even though the speaker has very positive intentions.

2. The listener infers the wrong intent from the message even though the speaker encodes it properly. Now visualize the husband asking his wife what was bothering her, but using all of the appropriate nonverbal signals. A misunderstanding would still occur if the wife inferred that her husband was only acting concerned because he wanted something—money, sex, an uninterrupted evening of quiet television watching.

3. Both the speaker and the listener make errors. This is probably a good description of the miscommunication that happened between the couple in our initial example. The wife did not send a clear message to her husband about the source of her stress, or about her desire to discuss her problems. The husband did not check his assumptions about what was bothering his wife or about her desire to be left alone at the end of the work day. As a consequence, both partners ended up feeling unheard or uncared for.

4. Both the speaker and the listener perform their task adequately and neither makes an error. Although counterintuitive, it is possible for misunderstanding to occur when both partners clearly communicate what they intend. This is often due to the fact that partners have different rules or beliefs about communication. For instance, it is possible that the husband in our example had one belief about how to interpret moodiness ("When people act moody, they are sending the message that they want to be left alone"), and the wife had another ("When people act moody, they are sending the message that they want attention"). If partners are unaware of such differences, it may be difficult for them to unravel their miscommunications.

While you can probably think of some additional pathways to miscommunication, the four presented here help to illustrate why it is problematic to make overly simple prescriptions for improving the way we interact. Many misunderstandings are too complex to be addressed by such prescriptions. Does this mean that all advice about effective communication is useless? Certainly not. A number of scholars have made concerted attempts to study effective (and ineffective) communication. Although their findings may not apply to all situations, they provide us with tools we can use to diagnose our communication problems and improve our communication skills. For instance, Wiemann's research on initial interactions found that effective communicators were perceived as (1) other-oriented—empathic, affiliative, supportive, and relaxed; (2) flexible—capable of adapting during an encounter or across different types of encounters; and (3) interaction-oriented—capable of managing "procedural" aspects of the encounter so that it flows smoothly.[27] Effective interaction management refers to the ease with which speaking turns are exchanged and the appropriate degree of control or responsibility over topics initiated and discussed. The fascinating contribution of Wiemann's research to our understanding of communicative competence is his finding that management of the interaction can be extremely important. Relatively minute changes in management behaviors (interruptions, pauses longer than three seconds, unilateral topic changes) resulted in large variations in evaluations of competence by subjects tested. As listeners and relational partners, then, we are apparently attending to and evaluating a host of fleeting, subtle, habitual, and non-content features of another's communicative behavior. Unless, for some reason, these behaviors are magnified (making it a content issue: "Why don't you ever let me finish without interrupting me?"), neither listener nor speaker are very much aware of these actions.[28]

Hart's approach to effective communication also emphasizes the complex interplay between listener judgements and speaker behaviors.[29] As listeners, we come away from our encounters with evaluations—many of them unspoken—"She's really weird. . . . I can't understand a word she says"; "I got the impression all he wanted to do was get the conversation over with as soon as possible"; "He's a pretty slick salesman, but I have this nagging feeling that he really doesn't give a damn about *my* needs"; or "She didn't sound like she believed what she was saying, so why should I?" As a result of weighing and analyzing reactions just like these, Hart developed five principles which he feels need to be enacted for effective communication to occur. These principles, of course, are not instilled in listeners simply because a speaker states them—just because you tell me you're interested in my welfare doesn't necessarily make me feel it. So, Hart also proposed *some* of the possible ways to demonstrate these principles. Obviously, as we've said so many times before, different relationships, different people, different topics, and different situations will dictate what ways are best for making a relational partner feel that a principle has been enacted. The methods that work for one situation may fail miserably in the next. Of the five principles, Hart says, each principle should be given approximately equal attention in any given encounter. However, there will be exceptions—the unfaithful wife who must stress the relationship principle above all others; or the job interviewee who must stress expertise before showing how it will help the company. See Table 12.1.

Looking at Hart's effective communication principles another way, they seem to address themselves to the matters of *profit* (for the speaker and the listener);

TABLE 12.1 Hart's Principles for Achieving Effective Communication[30]			
Principle	**Some Ways to Show It**	**Samples**	**If Principle Is Violated, Speaker Is Seen as:**
I am committed to you and will try to deal with your immediate existence, (i.e., "I'm going to talk *with* you, not at you.")	• use audience involvement • adjust to feedback • use analogies to connect your "worlds" • attach youself to their values • use familiar, practical examples • show immediate benefits to be derived from the interaction • adapt to situational changes, etc.	• "Well, son, majority rule is like if you and I want to go for ice cream and Mommy doesn't. We'd go because we outnumber her." • "I think my stand on consumer protection proves I'm the person for the job." • "I get the feeling you're still not convinced. What do you think we ought to do about the problem?"	• *Paternalistic* (e.g., true believer or authoritarian parent) • *Ego-tripper* (e.g., a braggart or know-it-all) • *Irrelevant* (e.g., a required course in Latin)
I am committed to my message, (i.e., "I mean what I say and I know what I'm talking about.")	• cite personal experiences • take a firm stand on the issue • appear factually knowledgeable • show your stake in the interaction • show you've made an investment in the subject, etc.	• "Now listen, I've been to Ethiopia and I've seen those people starving." • "The average giraffe is usually mute and has 12,000 bones in its neck." • "You may not vote for me, but I'm in this race 'til the bitter end."	• *Phony* (e.g., all talk, no action) • *Wishy-washy* (e.g., a sycophant) • *Dumb* (e.g., doesn't know what he or she is talking about)
I hope that both of us will profit from this interaction, (i.e., "I'm talking to you for our mutual benefit.")	• teach them something they hadn't known • detail the *concrete* benefits to be derived from listening to you • establish common ground • depict interaction as profitable or entertaining for you, etc.	• "Hey, it's been great talking to you." • "Just think, honey, a whole week by ourselves at the beach with nobody else around." • "If you don't heed my warnings about pollution, your very lives will be in danger."	• *Boring* (e.g., a lecture on East Indian toothpicks) • *Suspicious* (e.g., a "free" giveaway from a used-car dealer)

			If Principle Is Violated, Speaker
Principle	***Some Ways to Show It***	**Samples**	***Is Seen as:***
I want to interact with you and hope that our relationship will continue, (i.e., "We will make communication and, perhaps, a relationship.")	• dialogue with audience • show that they can affect you • link your proposal to their future well-being • don't rush through the interaction • specify your future intentions, etc.	• "As you go to college, John, remember that we'll miss you and that you can count on us." • "Hey, let's get together again soon. Next week?" • "If you have trouble with the radio, Mr. Smith, bring it back. We've been in business for fifty years and will be here for another fifty."	• *Parasitic* (e.g., a fly-by-night salesperson) • *Dogmatic* (e.g., Chair of the Board with 51% of the stock)
I want you to understand fully the practical implications of my message, (i.e., "I'm talking about things that can be understood and utilized.")	• don't overload the listener with more information than he or she can handle • avoid difficult abstractions • summarize; reorient the listener when necessary • move from easily understood information to complex information • use details to vivify your thoughts, etc.	• "If you remember nothing else, just remember that I love you." • "As Linus says, 'Happiness is a warm puppy.'" • "And so, folks, remember our motto: 'If you're looking for safety, dependability, and beauty, buy a Volkswagon.'"	• *Incomprehensible* (e.g., explaining "responsibility" to a two-year-old) • *Confused* (e.g., a bumbling professor lecturing on perfect communication)

commitment (to the message and the listener); *quality* (of the interaction and the relationship); and *tangibility* (of the message). We might perceive each dimension as present or absent; high or low. For instance, the ultimate speaker profit may be seen as exploitative whereas the absence of any perceived speaker profit might be viewed as altruistic. A speaker "loss" might elicit perceptions of sympathy, pity, or stupidity. Listener profits may be seen as very beneficial, useful, absent, or even injurious. Listeners' commitment may be identified by examining attentiveness, interest, and sensitivity. Extreme message commitment may be seen in a person who is perceived as very certain and obstinate or very uncertain and changeable. When we perceive the quality of our interaction, we are usually looking at questions of whether it was effortless and refreshing or laborious and weary. Relationship quality, in this context, seems to deal with not only an accepting-rejecting dimension, but also a time dimension—lasting versus transient. Indeed, researchers have found that relational commitment—the dedication to continue the relationship even in the face of difficulties—is a very important factor in determining long-term relational quality.[31] Further, many efforts to rejuvenate and repair distressed relationships focus on enhancing each partner's commitment to the other's communication messages.[32] One survey of marital and relational counselors found that one of the most common problems of distressed couples involves a lack of commitment to one another's message—partners are unwilling and/or unable to take the other's perspective when listening.[33] For this reason, most forms of couples' therapy involve, at least to some extent, training in skills such as diagnosing the partner's feelings, summarizing and restating those feelings, and demonstrating acceptance through vocal tone, facial expression, and posture.[34] These types of communication skills not only enable partners to express their commitment to one another's messages, but also help them to make their own messages more clear and tangible.

By now it should be apparent that we can (carefully) make some prescriptive statements about how to improve the way we communicate with our relational partners. Granted, some partners may establish rules or norms that render these statements inappropriate for their relationships. For many of us, though, the statements will provide a guideline as to how to enhance the quality of our interactions and decrease misunderstanding.

One of the most common recommendations made by researchers and clinicians involves validating our relational partners. Validation, according to Gottman, is letting your partner know that you understand him or her.[35] In Hart's words (see Table 12.1), validation touches on your commitment to your partner ("I am committed to you and will try to deal with your immediate existence") as well as your commitment to the interaction ("I want to interact with you and hope that our relationship will continue"). By validating the other, you demonstrate that you care about his or her message—that you are willing to attend to the message and put time and effort into understanding it. Validation may be comprised of small, seemingly unimportant behaviors such as nodding or making eye contact with your partner when he or she speaks (rather than reading or watching television). However, it may also involve more global behaviors such as expressing appreciation to your partner when he or she does something you enjoy (e.g., makes a nice meal, gives you a massage). In the latter case, your partner's message is often an unspoken one (e.g., "I did something for you to make you happy"), reflected in behavior rather than words. Validating something your partner does, though, can be just as important as validating something your partner says. When we fail to validate the other, we create a context where he or she may very well feel unheard and unloved.

Of course, showing the other person that you understand him or her is only one part of the equation. You also want to speak so that your partner understands what you say. As noted at the beginning of this chapter, though, sending a clear, unambiguous message is not always the most effective way to get someone to understand you. Many times, in the midst of conflict, partners send very clear messages (e.g., "You are such a selfish pig!") that they later regret. Furthermore, some messages that sound clear to listeners actually don't say what the speaker intended them to say (e.g., "We never go out anymore" might actually mean "I'd like to spend some quiet time alone with you"). If your goal is to speak so that your partner understands you, you need to formulate your messages with an awareness of how they may be interpreted. For instance, when couples discuss "touchy topics" (e.g., a desire for change in their sexual interaction, dissatisfaction with the way household tasks are divided), both partners are typically ready to defend themselves. As a consequence, messages are often interpreted in a more negative way than they were intended. It is also very easy during these types of conversations to send messages that place blame or responsibility on the other. Researchers and clinicians make several recommendations to minimize partners' feelings of defensiveness and increase the likelihood that they will understand each other. One of the most common recommendations is that partners "take responsibility" for their feelings when they communicate. Rather than blame the other person for how you feel (e.g., "You make me feel so stupid!"), this means that you express your feelings using "I statements" (e.g., "I feel really stupid when . . . "). Another common recommendation is that partners make an attempt to place statements that may be interpreted as negative (e.g., "I wish you'd spend more time with my family") in a positive relational context (e.g., "I really liked it when you went out to dinner with my family the other night and I wish you'd do that more often"). Fincham and his colleagues explain that "balancing" negative messages with positive messages often helps your partner to be more receptive to what you say.[36]

Some people may object to the idea of modifying their messages so that their partner will understand them. They may feel if their partner really cared about them, they wouldn't have to watch what they say—that if they really had an "intimate" relationship they would be able to express themselves without worrying about the way their partner would react. The problem with this perspective is that: (1) it assumes that our partners will always understand our intentions and (2) it fails to recognize the fact that our communication influences others—that what we say has an effect on our listeners.

Notarius and Markman argue that it is critical for each partner to recognize the impact his or her messages have on the other.[37] From the speaker's perspective, this means that messages sometimes need to be "edited" in order to be understood.

From the listener's perspective, it means that assumptions about the meaning of a message sometimes need to be checked (e.g., "Did you have a bad day at school or did I do something to upset you?"). In short, both partners need to adjust their communication behaviors to the other in order to communicate effectively. In Hart's terms, these adjustments not only make the speaker's messages tangible (understandable) to the listener, but they bring the speaker's desire for a quality relationship (one that is rewarding to both participants) to the forefront.

Becoming an Effective Communicator

Communicators are born. We humans seem to be brought into this world with the capacity to learn and use language. People who are effective communicators in their relationships, however, are made, not born. How? The following four ingredients—knowledge, experiences, motivation, and attitudes—seem to adequately cover the necessities for developing social competence and/or effective communication in relationships.

Knowledge

To become an effective communicator, it seems reasonable to expect that a person should develop a sizable, well-rounded knowledge base. Part of this knowledge is *content knowledge* ("knowing what" or "knowing that") and can be obtained from books, lectures, and experiences of others. Another part of any well-rounded knowledge base is *procedural knowledge* ("knowing how") which involves an understanding of what effective communicators do.[38] For many of our interactions with others, a broad liberal arts education seems to be extremely helpful. An extensive and intensive educational base helps build a knowledge of people's behavior, our environmental surroundings, group behavior, cultural norms, history, and the arts. This knowledge, in turn, certainly assists in developing much needed predictive ability concerning cultural and sociological expectations; it also helps to build expertise and confidence in message sending. In our close relationships, however, we also need an extensive knowledge of our relational partners—their usual responses to certain situations, their assumptions about relationships, their family histories, etc. Without this intimate, individualized knowledge we really don't have an intimate relationship. With this knowledge (and, perhaps more important, a conscious awareness of this knowledge) we are better able to respond and adapt to the daily events that make up a close relationship. Since much of our message sending in our relationships is preceded and/or followed by reflection on why we did or did not behave in a certain way, it is important to build a mental reference library of information which may help clarify why we interact as we do. This book was designed for that purpose. Vicarious learning through books, lectures, and the experiences of others is indeed an important source of knowledge, but for optimum development, it should be supplemented with knowledge obtained from actual experiences in life's laboratory.

Experiences

Communicative experiences may be obtained by observing others (building diagnosis skills) and by participating with others (building performance skills). From early childhood throughout life, we imitate communicative responses and model our behavior after others. Some of this behavior is so subtle we learn it with little conscious effort—using eye behavior to signal one's desire for a speaking turn. Mostly, however, learning effective relational communication, like developing proficiency at any skill, is hard work. The most effective communicators probably expose themselves to many different communicative situations and are not afraid to try novel experiences and challenges.

> *It is not doing things, but understanding what you*
> *do that brings real excitement and lasting pleasure.*
>
> Robertson Davies

There are many reasons why a wide variety of communicative experiences can be helpful in building one's effectiveness. For instance, without the knowledge of different people and different situations, flexibility and adaptation are impaired. You may learn how to interact with one type of person, perhaps the type who agrees with you, but may be extremely ineffectual when cast in a role outside this limited group. Children, because of limited experiences, do not have the same predictive abilities as some adults—but adults who constrict their experiences may find similar limitations. More experience may mean the possibility of some initial communicative and relational failures, but ultimately these failures can be turned into a far greater success than that enjoyed by the person who safely sticks with only easy communicative experiences and easy relationships. The person with a greater experiential base will increase his or her chances of learning realistic expectations for communicative success. Accuracy in person perception should increase. There should also be an increase in understanding one's own interaction needs and goals in various relationships and ways that can and cannot achieve these goals.

Bochner identified five ways in which communication functions in relationships: (1) to foster favorable impressions; (2) to organize relationships—negotiating and living by certain rules; (3) to validate and support a view of reality common to you and your partner; (4) to express your feelings and thoughts; and (5) to protect yourself—those areas where you are most subject to being hurt.[39] Since the specific ways whereby we use communication to accomplish these goals change with different types of relationships and different people, a broad base of experiences with many types of relationships and different types of people may be helpful in preparing for effective communication in any one relationship.

The widely experienced person should have an appreciation for the complexity of the process of communication and the complexity of people in general. If it is true that we tend to fear the things we know the least about, perhaps we should get to know other people better—and get to know ourselves better at the same time through those people. It may mean that our appreciation for our fellow human beings' shortcomings and strengths (and our own) will help us reduce maladaptive behaviors.

It should be clear that a broad-based set of experiences needs a great deal of self-motivated practice and helpful feedback to be useful. Becoming an effective communicator in any relationship is a never-ending process—a constant process of analysis that continues as long as (and sometimes longer than) the relationship does. Seeking and analyzing feedback on our communicative behavior from our relational partners, from experts, and from diagnostic tests (including videotaped episodes) will surely help us develop more realistic expectations of our own skills. Learning how to communicate more effectively should become somewhat like driving a car—behavior that is largely habitual and that contributes to a smooth operation, but with constant vigilance for that ever-present possibility that will require adaptation to changing relational circumstances.

Motivation

The desire to communicate effectively is probably as important, if not more important, than all the behavioral prescriptions we might employ. If we strongly desire to have a person or a group of persons understand something, believe something, or do something, it is not at all unlikely that the necessary behavioral techniques will follow. Also, on a more general level, our desire to approach and engage ourselves in social situations (rather than to avoid or extricate ourselves) will influence the type and quality of communication behaviors we employ.[40] For example, when relational partners withdraw from a situation involving conflict, certain sorts of messages may be sent—"I don't care enough about this relationship to continue the discussion," "I don't see the issue as an important one," or "I want you to work harder on this relationship than I do so that I know you really love me." In many cases, the lack of willingness to engage in dialogue with one's partner results in misunderstanding about what each partner wants and needs from the relationship. Over time, these sorts of misunderstandings can redefine the relationship in ways that neither partner originally intended.

If a lack of motivation to communicate with one's relational partner potentially creates feelings of distance, the motivation to succeed in our relational communication should, in most cases, enhance relational closeness. Recall Hart's approach to effective communication: Demonstrating to our partner that we are motivated and we *want* to interact with him or her is one factor in determining how effective we are. Suffice to say, when we are sufficiently motivated to succeed, when we are able to visualize ourselves succeeding, when we get an inner feeling of pleasure out of communicating effectively with our relational partners, we have taken a giant step toward becoming an effective communicator.

Attitudes

Attitudes, too, can be critical to effectiveness in communicating with others. Certainly we could predict potential differences in effectiveness between communicators who enter a relational situation with these different attitudes:

A My communicative behavior is going to be important in this situation.

A_1 I have so much to be concerned with I can't worry about something as abstract as "communication."

B This is going to be a tough situation, so I'd better be on guard and watch carefully what they say and what I say.

B_1 This is going to be a tough situation. I know I'll goof it up.

C I'm not anxious to go, but I may learn something.

C_1 There's nothing I can get out of this situation.

Furthermore, if we believe that being able to communicate effectively with others is closely linked to becoming a "better person," we might expect to see an increasing security in our own identities as communicative efforts are rewarded. Security in our own identities will, in turn, contribute positively to our communicative efforts.

Becoming an effective communicator in our relationships involves continual efforts to improve our understanding, analytical skills, and performance skills. Some are easier to learn than others. Irving Lee, a noted teacher and scholar of human communication, said that the development of communication skills involved the following five activities.[41] They are listed according to how difficult they are to master—*with the easiest activities listed first and the most difficult last.*

1. We have to acquaint ourselves with what is known about the subject of our communication—theories, facts, etc.

2. We have to learn to recognize proficiencies as well as shortcomings and defects in the communication behavior of others.

3. We have to learn to recognize proficiencies as well as shortcomings and defects in the communication behavior of ourself.

4. We have to learn to develop skills in prescribing methods for improving our own communication.

5. We have to learn to develop skills in prescribing methods for improving the communication behavior of others.

Writing Your Own Story

You, the reader, are about to finish a book on how people communicate during the various twists and turns that their relationships take. Some of you will remember a lot from this book; some won't remember much. Some of you will sell your book, whereas others will use it as a future resource. Two things, however, will be the same for everyone who has read this book: (1) everyone will continue to have communication experiences in their relationships that they want to understand and analyze; and (2) everyone's ability to analyze those experiences and to recall information will be greatly assisted with a simple memory jogging device. Newspaper reporters, novelists, and anyone who has had a high school English course is familiar with a set of questions—"who," "what," "where," "when," "how," and "why"—that is designed to uncover key information for telling and understanding a story.

We think these same questions will be useful in understanding the communication in your own relationship story. It will help you explain why you feel especially good or bad at a particular time and clarify puzzling communicative transactions. Notice how many familiar comments people make about the communication in their relationships can be categorized in this simple system. While this system will not provide ready solutions to problems, it should be very helpful in the first stage of problem-solving—identifying the nature of the problem. A final note concerns the absence of "why" questions. We feel that a focus on the other aspects of the communicative experience will naturally stimulate why questions.

> ### *Who initiated the communication?*
>
> "I am always the one who says 'I love you' first. How come you never think to say it first?"
>
> "You brought it up; not me."
>
> "It's not my fault we don't talk about it. You never bring it up."
>
> "I like it when you start talking about what happened to you during the day because then I feel more like talking about my day."

What was or was not said/done?

"You never respond when I talk to you."

"You always have something positive to say and I like that."

"You never tell me I look nice.

Where was something said/done?

"Why did you have to say it in front of my mother?"

"You can't expect me to talk about that here."

"Let's talk about this when we're alone."

When was or was not something said/done?

"Getting flowers from you when there was no special occasion was the last thing I expected."

"You seem to know when I need comforting."

"You didn't have to bring that up now; you know I've got this other thing on my mind."

"You knew I was expecting you to ask me about that when I said . . . "

"It's too late for apologies now; you should have contacted me earlier."

How was it said/done?

"The way you said it—so abruptly—I just didn't believe you."

"The intensity in the way you expressed yourself overwhelmed me."

"I feel accepted and understood when you focus on me like that."

How often was something said/done?

"Saying you love me every day really makes me feel good."

"You used to want a lot of sex; now you don't seem interested as much."

Communicating Effectively Together

What is the "bottom line" for effective communication in relationships? It should be clear to you, by this point, that we are not going to provide you with a specific formula for relational success (and that you should be wary of anyone who does offer such a formula). There are, however, several principles of effective communication in relationships that can be gleaned from the material presented in this chapter as well as other literature on couples' therapy and counseling. We offer these principles not as an "answer" to relational problems, but as a guideline or tool that you can use to help you through the difficulties (and the rewards) that relationships bring.

1. Be both flexible and stubborn. Combine a willingness to adapt with a basic, gut-level refusal to give up on the relationship. As we've repeatedly noted in this book, people change, situations change, and values change. These changes and others will often require modifications in how and what individuals communicate to their relational partners. Without an ability (and a willingness) to adapt to the changing communicative needs of their relationships, people may be unable to maintain close and satisfying romantic partnerships. The flexibility we are talking about here is not weak or submissive (e.g., "Of course I'll change dear—whatever you want."). Instead, it is coupled with a stubborn determination to make the relationship work (e.g., "I'm willing to do what it takes to keep us together.").

2. Talk openly about your feelings, attitudes, and opinions. In any relationship, there will be some things that both partners decide to keep to themselves. When we advise you to "talk openly" with your relational partner, we are not saying that you need to express every feeling, all the time, in every situation (e.g., it's probably not a good idea to initiate a discussion about the state of your relationship right after your partner has flunked an exam). Nor are we suggesting that you should express yourself without considering the effect of what you say on your partner (e.g., "You really look fat in that outfit!"). Expressing your feelings, alone, will not solve all of your relationship problems. When we advise you to talk openly with your partner, we hope to remind you that communication is the "life-blood" of romantic relationships. If you want another person to love you, you must allow that person to know you and to respond to your wants and needs.

3. Respond to your partner in ways that show respect, value, and caring. One of the quickest ways to silence relational talk is to be unresponsive. Even when discussing "routine" issues, such as how the day went or what needs to get done tomorrow, people usually feel bad if their relational partner does not act interested in what they are saying. When the topics of discussion are more intimate (e.g., feelings about the relationship, sexual desires), we are even more sensitive to our partner's responses. It is important to note here that romantic partners may "listen" to each other without acting responsive. Responsiveness involves more than just hearing a relational partner's words. It also involves showing that you value your partner and what he or she is saying. Responsive behaviors may include eye contact, paraphrasing, head nodding, or touch. Regardless of the specific behaviors you demonstrate, the important thing is that your partner feels like you care enough to listen.

4. Attend to the important. Even the most responsive people will encounter difficulties if they fail to respond to the things their partner feels are important. In most cases, it is easy to respond to the things that we, ourselves, feel are important to the relationship. Since we usually know what these things are, we can attend to and prioritize them as central aspects of the relationship. It is more difficult, however, to identify the things our partner feels are important. At the beginning of relationships, partners may be so eager to please one another that they fail to express their wants and needs. Later, when their needs have not been met, they may become resentful—assuming that "If she really loved me, she would know that this is important to me!" "Attending to the important" involves taking the time and effort necessary to discover what both you and your partner feel are central aspects of your relationship. It also involves letting go of things that are unimportant. Sometimes partners spend a great deal of energy on parts of their relationship that don't mean very much to either one of them. Other times, they fix their attention on "little things" about their relationship that they find annoying. When partners focus on aspects of their relationship that they feel are unimportant or trivial, they have less time and fewer resources to devote to the things they really care about. Also, in many cases, seemingly trivial issues mask more important concerns. A heated argument about who drank the last soda or who left the toilet seat up actually may represent partners' worries about whether they are receiving the respect or consideration that they need. Focusing on seemingly trivial issues may prevent partners from uncovering and attending to their more significant concerns. Those more important concerns may involve affection, an ability to self-disclose, sexuality, or even career aspirations. What do you and your partner believe are the important components of a "good" relationship? What do the two of you define as "good" relational communication? What do you want out of your relationship? These are questions that you and your partner need to answer (and continue answering) together.

5. Work at the relationship, but remember to have fun. Generous amounts of both serious effort and silliness are often needed to create a close, satisfying romantic relationship. After reading this book, it should be clear to you that intimate relationships usually require a great deal of time and effort. But "all work and no play" can make almost any relationship tiring. Create space in your life to enjoy your relationship. Find activities that you both like and take the time to do them. Laugh together. Remind yourselves of what initially made you fall in love. Talk about your dreams. One of the main reasons people come together in romantic relationships is because they enjoy each other. Allow that sense of fun and enjoyment to be one of the reasons you stay together.

SUMMARY

This chapter was deliberately designed to follow the chapters outlining communicative behavior at various stages of a relationship. Our hope was that an understanding of messages produced at different points in a relationship would provide a framework within which effective relational communication could be viewed. As we so frequently stated, no pattern, no style, no word is always going to guarantee that a communicator will effectively communicate. The only "sure-fire," "never-fail," "key" to success is to analyze sufficiently each situation so that messages can be adapted accordingly. Success in relational communication ventures depends on a number of factors. Some of these include: (1) who makes the judgment of effectiveness; (2) at what point or points in time (relationship, life, history, conversation) the judgment is made; (3) what the judge(s) chooses to evaluate—obtaining a desired response, being ethically sound, helping the other to achieve his or her goals, certain verbal and/or nonverbal behavior, quantity of cues produced, number and diversity of strategies employed, ability across different modes, etc.; (4) how the judgment is made—the conditions for testing or observation; and (5) why the judgment was made and whether the subject is aware of the evaluation.

In the belief that people cannot completely separate their judgments of relationships from their judgments of people's communication within relationships, we reviewed the Wish et al. study, which provided a look at broad categories often used to examine relationships. We also discussed the notion that people's assumptions and expectations of their relationships affect the way they perceive their partners' communication. In addition, a study by Feingold examined perceptions of communicative behavior. Almost every one of six statements found by his study to discriminate reliably between the behavior of effective communicators and the behavior of ineffective communicators focused in one form or another on proper adaptation.

Another part of this chapter presented statements of advice for those interested in improving their communicative abilities. This was an effort to identify those suggestions that, although subject to variation in any given situation and/or relationship, seem to be generalizable across situations more than other suggestions. We made a concerted attempt to get a variety of approaches without sacrificing intellectual quality and usefulness. To provide a context for the discussion, we presented Fincham et al.'s pathways to miscommunication. Then we looked at Wiemann's research, which reiterated the fact that effective communicators seem to be other-oriented and flexible but added a dimension, interaction-oriented—one's ability to manage the "administrative" aspects of the conversation (turn-taking, topic initiation) as well as the substantive aspects. In addition, we examined Hart's work, which suggested five principles to guide the effective communicator. These principles were grounded in the communicators' ability to make partners feel that they: (1) are committed to them and are trying to deal with their immediate existence; (2) are committed to their own message; (3) hope both participants will profit from the interaction; (4) want to interact with the other and hope that the relationship will continue; and (5) want the listeners to understand fully the practical implications of the message. Finally, the section concluded with an application of some of these ideas about effective communication to the context of personal relationships. Some of the common communication difficulties faced by couples were discussed and suggestions as to how partners might effectively deal with those difficulties were provided.

After developing a better understanding of what an effective relational communicator is (from research and credible prescriptions), we sought some explanation of how a person might achieve this status. We suggested that one needed a firm knowledge base, a continuous variety of experiences, strong intrinsic motivation, and a set of positive attitudes regarding oneself and one's communicative acts.

We also provide a set of questions that we hope will serve as a memory jogging device for people who are interested in analyzing and understanding their own communication. Journalists and novelists often use the questions, "who," "what," "where," "when," "how," and "why" to help them understand a story. We believe that these same questions will help you analyze and explain the communication in your own relationship story.

We concluded the chapter with a discussion of what might be termed the "bottom line" for effective communication in relationships. Although we recognize that it is impossible to provide "ten easy steps" to competent relational communication, we hope that some of these comments will provide a more clear understanding of how your communication influences the quality of your close relationships.

SELECTED READINGS

Evaluating Communication

Asher, S. R. "Children's Ability to Appraise Their Own and Another Person's Communication Performance." *Developmental Psychology* 12 (1976): 24–32.

Asher, S. R., and Parke, R. D. "Influence of Sampling and Comparison Processes on the Development of Communication Effectiveness." *Journal of Educational Psychology* 67 (1975): 64–75.

Burleson, B. R., and Denton, W. H. "The Relationship Between Communication Skill and Marital Satisfaction: Some Moderating Effects." *Journal of Marriage and the Family* 59 (1997): 884–902.

Burleson, B. R., and Samter, W. "A Social Skills Approach to Relationship Maintenance: How Individual Differences in Communication Skills Affect the Achievement of Relationship Functions." In D. J. Canary and L. Stafford, eds., *Communication and Relational Maintenance*, pp. 61–90. San Diego, CA: Academic, 1994.

Christie, R., and Geis, F. L. *Studies in Machiavellianism*. New York: Academic Press, 1970.

Delia, J. G., and Clark, R. A. "Cognitive Complexity, Social Perception and the Development of Listener-Adapted Communication in Six-, Eight-, and Twelve-Year Old Boys." *Communication Monographs* 44 (1977): 326–345.

Delia, J. G., and Swanson, D. L. "The Nature of Human Communication." In R. L. Applebaum, and R. P. Hart, eds., *Modcom: Modules in Speech Communication*. Chicago: Science Research Associates, 1976.

Feingold, P. C. "Toward a Paradigm of Effective Communication: An Empirical Study of Perceived Communicative Effectiveness." Ph.D. dissertation, Purdue University, 1976.

Flavell, J. H. *The Development of Role-Taking and Communication Skills in Children*. New York: John Wiley & Sons, 1968.

Foote, N. N., and Cottrell. L. S. *Identity and Interpersonal Competency.* Chicago: University of Chicago Press, 1955.

Habermas, J. "Toward a Theory of Communicative Competence." In H. P. Dreitzel, ed., *Recent Sociology.* No. 2. New York: Macmillan, 1970.

Hale, C. L. "Cognitive Complexity-Simplicity as a Determinant of Communication Effectiveness." *Communication Monographs* 47 (1980): 304–311.

Hymes, D. *On Communicative Competence.* Philadelphia: University of Pennsylvania Press, 1970.

Ickes, W., ed. *Empathic Accuracy.* New York: Guilford, 1997.

Johnson, F. L. "Communicative Competence and the Berstein Perspective." *Communication Quarterly* 27 (1979): 12–19.

Krauss, R. M., and Glucksberg, S. "The Development of Communication: Competence as a Function of Age." *Child Development* 40 (1969): 255–266.

Larson, C. E., Backlund, M., Redmond, M., and Barbour, A. *Assessing Functional Communication.* Urbana, IL: ERIC Clearinghouse on Reading and Communication Skills, 1978.

Longabaugh, R. "The Structure of Interpersonal Behavior." *Sociometry* 29 (1966): 441–460.

Mehrabian, A., and Ksionzky, S. "Categories of Social Behavior." *Comparative Group Studies* 3 (1972): 425–436.

Montgomery, B. M. "Quality Communication in Personal Relationships." In S. W. Duck, ed., *Handbook of Personal Relationships,* pp. 343–359. New York: John Wiley & Sons, 1988.

Montgomery, B. M. "Communication in Close Relationships." In A. L. Weber and J. H. Harvey, eds., *Perspectives on Close Relationships,* pp. 67–87. Boston: Allyn and Bacon, 1994.

Mortensen, C. D. *Miscommunication.* Thousand Oaks, CA: Sage, 1997.

Norton, R. W. "Foundations of a Communicator Style Construct." *Human Communication Research* 4 (1978): 99–112.

Pearson, J. C., and Daniels, T. D. " 'Oh, What Tangled Webs We Weave': Concerns About Current Conceptions of Communication Competence." *Communication Reports* 1 (1988): 95–100.

Perotti, V. S., and DeWine, S. "Competence in Communication: An Examination of Three Instruments." *Management Communication Quarterly* 1 (1987): 272–287.

Spitzberg, B. H. "The Dialectics of (In)competence." *Journal of Social and Personal Relationships* 10 (1993): 137–158.

Thomas, G., Fletcher, G. J. O., and Lange, C. "On-Line Empathic Accuracy in Marital Interaction." *Journal of Personality and Social Psychology* 72 (1997): 839–850.

Weinstein, E. A. "The Development of Interpersonal Competence." In D. A. Goslin, ed., *Handbook of Socialization Theory and Research.* Chicago: Rand McNally, 1969.

_____."Toward a Theory of Interpersonal Tactics." In C. W. Blackman and P. F. Secord, eds., *Problems in Social Psychology.* New York: McGraw-Hill, 1966.

Wish, M., Deutsch, M., and Kaplan, S. J. "Perceived Dimensions of Interpersonal Relations." *Journal of Personality and Social Psychology* 33 (1976): 409–420.

Developing Communication Skills

Allen, R. R., and Brown, K. L., eds. *Developing Communication Competence in Children.* Skokie, IL: National Textbook, 1976.

Argyris, C. "Explorations in Interpersonal Competence—I." *Journal of Applied Behavioral Science* 1 (1965): 58–83.

———. *Interpersonal Competence and Organizational Effectiveness.* Homewood, IL: Irwin-Dorsey, 1962.

Bledsoe, J. L. "Your Four Communicating Styles." *Training* (March 1976): 18–21.

Bochner, A. P., and Kelly, C. W. "Interpersonal Competence: Rationale, Philosophy, and Implementation of a Conceptual Framework." *Speech Teacher* 23 (1974): 279–301.

Fincham, F. D., Fernades, L. O. L., and Humphreys, K. *Communicating in Relationships: A Guide for Couples and Professionals.* Champaign, IL: Research Press, 1993.

Fry, C. L. "Training Children to Communicate with Listeners Who Have Varying Listener Requirements." *Journal of Genetic Psychology* 114 (1969): 153–166.

Gottman, J. M. *Why Marriages Succeed or Fail.* New York: Simon & Schuster, 1994.

Greene, J. O., and Burleson, B. R., eds., *Handbook of Communication and Social Interaction Skills.* Mahwah, NJ: Erlbaum, in press.

Hart, R. P., and Burks, D. M. "Rhetorical Sensitivity and Social Interaction." *Speech Monographs* 39 (1972): 75–91.

Hart, R. P., Carlson, R. E., and Eadie, W. F. "Attitudes Toward Communication and the Assessment of Rhetorical Sensitivity." *Communication Monographs* 47 (1980): 1–22.

Holland, J. L., and Baird, L. L. "An Interpersonal Competency Scale." *Educational and Psychological Measurement* 28 (1968): 503–510.

Notarius, C., and Markman, H. J. *We Can Work It Out: Making Sense of Marital Conflict.* New York: Putnam, 1993.

Parks, M. R. "Communicative Competence and Interpersonal Control." In M. L. Knapp and G. R. Miller, eds., *Handbook of Interpersonal Communication,* pp. 589–617. Thousand Oaks, CA: Sage, 1994.

Ring, K., and Wallston, K. "A Test to Measure Performance Styles in Interpersonal Relations." *Psychology Reports* 22 (1968): 147–154.

Rosenthal, R., ed. *Skill in Nonverbal Communication: Individual Differences.* Cambridge, MA: Oelgeschalger, Gunn & Hain, 1979.

Shannon, J., and Guerney, B., Jr. "Interpersonal Effects of Interpersonal Behavior." *Journal of Personality and Social Psychology* 26 (1973): 142–150.

Shantz, C. U., and Wilson, K. E. "Training Communication Skills in Young Children." *Child Development* 43 (1972): 693–698.

Snavely, W. B. "The Impact of Social Style upon Person Perception in Primary Relationships." *Communication Quarterly* 29 (1981): 132–143.

Snyder, M. "The Self-monitoring of Expressive Behavior." *Journal of Personality and Social Psychology* 30 (1974): 526–537.

Spitzberg, B. H., and Cupach, W. R. *Interpersonal Communication Competence.* Beverly Hills, CA: Sage, 1984.

Spitzberg, B. H., and Cupach, W. R., *Handbook in Interpersonal Communication Competence.* New York: Springer-Verlag, 1989.

Walters, B. *How to Talk to Practically Anybody About Practically Anything.* New York: Dell Publishing Co., 1970.

Wiemann, J. M. "Explication and Test of a Model of Communicative Competence." *Human Communication Research* 3 (1977): 195–213.

Zemke, R., "From Factor Analysis and Clinical Psychology: Better Ways to Help Train People to Win in Interpersonal Relations." *Training* (August 1976): 12–16.

NOTES

[1]M. L. Williams and B. Goss, "Equivocation: Character Insurance," *Human Communication Research* 1 (1975): 265–270; See also: C. J. Orr and K. E. Burkins, "The Endorsement of Evasive Leaders: An Exploratory Study," *Central States Speech Journal* 27 (1976): 230–239; M. L. Williams, "The Effect of Deliberate Vagueness on Receiver Recall and Agreement," *Central States Speech Journal* 31 (1980): 30–41; J. B. Bavelas, A. Black, N. Chovil, J. Mullett, *Equivocal Communication* (Newbury Park, CA: Sage, 1990).

[2]J. C. Pearson, *Lasting Love: What Keeps Couples Together* (Dubuque, IA: W. C. Brown, 1992).

[3]B. M. Montgomery, "Quality Communication in Personal Relationships." In S. W. Duck, ed., *Handbook of Personal Relationships.* (New York: John Wiley & Sons, 1988), pp. 343–359; B. M. Montgomery, "Communication in Close Relationships." In A. L. Weber and J. H. Harvey, eds., *Perspectives on Close Relationships* (Boston: Allyn and Bacon, 1994), pp. 67–87.

[4]See, for example, N. Ambady, J. Koo, F. Lee, and R. Rosenthal, "More Thank Words: Linguistic and Nonlinguistic Politeness in Two Cultures," 70 (1996): 996–1011; K. L. Fitch, "A Cross-Cultural Study of Directive Sequences and Some Implications of Compliance-Gaining Research," *Communication Monographs* 61 (1994): 185–209; M. S. Kim and S. R. Wilson, "A Cross-Cultural Comparison of Implicit Theories of Requesting," *Communication Monographs* 61 (1994): 210–235.

[5]J. N. Martin, M. R. Hammer, and L. Bradford, "The Influence of Cultural and Situational Contexts on Hispanic and Non-Hispanic Communication Competence Behaviors," *Communication Quarterly* 42 (1994): 160–179; S. G. Timmer, J. Veroff, and S. Hatchett, "Family Ties and Marital Happiness: The Different Marital Experiences of Black and White Newlywed Couples," *Journal of Social and Personal Relationships* 13 (1996); 335–359.

[6]M. A. Fitzpatrick "A Typological Approach to Communication In Relationships," Ph.D. diss.

(Philadelphia: Temple University, 1977); J. M. Gottman, "The Roles of Conflict Engagement, Escalation, and Avoidance in Marital Interaction: A Longitudinal View of Five Types of Couples," *Journal of Consulting and Clinical Psychology* 61 (1993): 6–15.

[7]M. A. Fitzpatrick and L. D. Ritchie, "Communication Schemata within the Family: Multiple Perspectives on Family Interaction," *Human Communication Research* 20 (1994): 275–301; L. D. Ritchie and M. A. Fitzpatrick, "Family Communication Patterns: Measuring Intrapersonal Perceptions of Interpersonal Relationships," *Communication Research* 17 (1990); 523–544.

[8]J. M. Gottman, J. Coan, S. Carrere, and C. Swanson, "Predicting Marital Happiness and Stability from Newlywed Interactions," *Journal of Marriage and the Family* 60 (1998): 5–22; J. M. Gottman and L. J. Krokoff, "Marital Interaction and Satisfaction: A Longitudinal View," *Journal of Consulting and Clinical Psychology* 57 (1989): 47–52; T. L. Huston and A. L. Vangelisti, "Socioemotional Behavior and Satisfaction in Marital Relationships: A Longitudinal Study," *Journal of Personality and Social Psychology* 41 (1991): 721–733.

[9]J. Epstein and R. J. Eidelson, "Unrealistic Beliefs of Clinical Couples: Their Relationship to Expectations, Goals, and Satisfaction," *American Journal of Family Therapy* 9 (1981): 13–22.

[10]J. G. Delia and R. A. Clark, "Cognitive Complexity, Social Perception and the Development of Listener-Adapted Communication in Six-, Eight-, Ten-, and Twelve-Year Old Boys," *Communication Monographs* 44 (1977): 326–345.

[11]T. Stephen, "Communication in the Shifting Context of Intimacy: Marriage, Meaning, and Modernity," *Communication Theory* 4 (1994): 191–218.

[12]B. H. Spitzberg and R. L Duran, "Toward an Ideological Deconstruction of Competence," paper presented at the annual meeting of the International Communication Association, Australia, July, 1994.

[13]K. Tracy and J. P. Moran III, "Conversational Relevance in Multiple Goal Settings." In R. T. Craig and K. Tracy, eds., *Conversational Coherence: Form, Structure, and Strategy* (Beverly Hills, CA: Sage, 1983), pp. 116–135.

[14]For a commentary on this and other similar issues, see. B. H. Spitzberg, "The Dialectics of (In)Competence," *Journal of Social and Personal Relationships* 10 (1993): 137–158.

[15]A. Koestler, *Darkness at Noon* (New York: Modern Library, 1941), p. 58.

[16]G. R. Miller. "Interpersonal Communication: A Conceptual Perspective," *Communication* 2 (1975): 93–105. For further elaboration of this material, see: G. R. Miller and M. Steinberg, *Between People* (Stanford, CA: Science Research Associates, 1975).

[17]B. R. Burleson and W. H. Denton, "The Relationship Between Communication Skill and Marital Satisfaction: Some Moderating Effects," *Journal of Marriage and the Family* 59 (1997): 884–902; W. Ickes, *Empathic Accuracy* (New York: Guilford, 1997); G. Thomas, G. J. O. Fletcher, and C. Lange, "On-Line Empathic Accuracy in Marital Interaction," *Journal of Personality and Social Psychology* 72 (1997): 839–850.

[18]A. L. Sillars, "Interpersonal Perception in Relationships." In W. Ickes, ed., *Compatible and Incompatible Relationships* (New York: Springer-Verlag, 1985), pp. 277–305.

[19]See also S. L. Murray and J. G. Holmes, "A Leap of Faith? Positive Illusions in Romantic Relationships," *Personality and Social Psychology Bulletin* 23 (1997): 586–604; S. L. Murray, J. G. Holmes, and D. W. Griffin, "The Benefits of Positive Illusions: Idealization and the Construction of Satisfaction in Close Relationships," *Journal of Personality and Social Psychology* 70 (1996): 79–98.

[20]B. H. Spitzberg and W. R. Cupach, Handbook of *Interpersonal Competence Research* (New York: Springer-Verlag, 1989); also see M. R. Parks, "Communicative Competence and Interpersonal Control." In M. L. Knapp and G. R. Miller, eds., *Handbook of Interpersonal Communication* (Thousand Oaks, CA: Sage, 1994), pp. 589–617.

[21]M. Wish, M. Deutsch, and S. J. Kaplan, "Perceived Dimensions of Interpersonal Relations," *Journal of Personality and Social Psychology* 33 (1976): 409–420. For similar research, see also: R. Longabaugh, "The Structure of Interpersonal Behavior," *Sociometry* 29 (1966): 441–460; and C. E. Osgood, "Speculations on the Structure of Interpersonal Intentions," *Behavioral Science* 15 (1970): 237–254.

[22]D. H. Baucom and N. Epstein, *Cognitive-Behavioral Marital Therapy.* (New York: Brunner/Mazel, 1990); N. Epstein and R. J. Eidelson, "Unrealistic Beliefs of Clinical Couples: Their Relationship to Expectation, Goals, and Satisfaction," *American Journal of Family Therapy* 9 (1981): 13–22; G. J. O. Fletcher, J. A. Simpson, G. Thomas and L. Giles, "Ideals in Intimate Relationships," *Journal of Personality and Social Psychology* 76 (1999): 72–69; S. Metts and W. R. Cupach, "The Influence of Relationship Beliefs and Problem-

Solving Responses on Satisfaction in Romantic Relationships," *Human Communication Research* 17 (1990): 170–185; A. L. Vangelisti and J. A. Daly, "Gender Differences in Standards for Romantic Relationships," *Personal Relationships* 4 (1997) 203–219.

[23]P. C. Feingold, "Toward a Paradigm of Effective Communication: An Empirical Study of Perceived Communicative Effectiveness" (Ph.D. diss., Purdue University 1976).

[24]This does not mean, of course, that effective communicators are always found in one category. For instance, effective communicators seem to be generally perceived as other-oriented. Like any orientation, however, it can be overdone. If communicators consistently send you-oriented messages or verbal stares, it may create some of the discomfort engendered by nonverbal staring. See: R. J. Cline and B. M. Johnson, "The Verbal Stare: Focus of Attention in Conversation," *Communication Monographs* 43 (1976): 1–10.

[25]A. T. Beck, *Love is Never Enough* (New York: Harper & Row, 1988); L. H. Gordon, "Intimacy: The Art of Working Out Your Relationships," *Psychology Today* 26 (Sept/Oct, 1993): 40–43.

[26]F. D. Fincham, L. O. L. Fernades, and K. Humphreys, *Communicating in Relationships: A Guide for Couples and Professionals* (Champaign, IL: Research Press, 1993).

[27]J. M. Wiemann, "Explication and Test of a Model of Communicative Competence," *Human Communication Research* 3 (1977): 195–213.

[28]Research by Street and Murphy has detailed a related, but distinct ability called Interpersonal Orientation (see: R. L. Street, Jr., and T. L. Murphy, "Interpersonal Orientation and Speech Behavior," *Communication Monographs* 54 (1987): 42–62).

[29]Some of these ideas can be found in R. P. Hart, G. W. Friedrich, and B. Brummett, *Public Communication,* 2nd ed. (New York: Harper & Row, 1983).

[30]Source: Reproduced and adapted from R. P. Hart (lecture notes, University of Texas, Department of Speech Communication) 1991.]

[31]J. M. Adams and W. H. Jones, "The Conceptualization of Marital Commitment: An Integrative Analysis," *Journal of Personality and Social Psychology* 72 (1997): 1177–1196; M. Lund, "The Development of Investment and Commitment Scales for Predicting Continuity of Personal Relationships," *Journal of Social and Personal Relationships* 2 (1985): 3–23; C. E. Rusbult and B. P. Buunk, "Commitment Processes in Close Relationships: An Interdependence Analysis," *Journal of Social and Personal Relationships* 10 (1993): 175–204.

[32]M. L. Knapp and E. H. Taylor, "Commitment and Its Communication in Romantic Relationships." In A. L. Weber and J. H. Harvey, eds., *Perspectives on Close Relationships* (Boston: Allyn and Bacon, 1994), pp. 153–175; W. W. Wilmot, "Relationship Rejuvenation." In D. J. Canary and L. Stafford, eds., *Communication and Relational Maintenance* (San Diego, CA: Academic, 1994), pp. 255–273.

[33]A. L. Vangelisti, "Couples' Communication Problems: The Counselor's Perspective," *Journal of Applied Communication Research* 22 (1994): 106–126.

[34]See, for example, D. H. Baucom and N. Epstein, *Cognitive-Behavioral Marital Therapy* (New York: Brunner/Mazel, 1990); L. S. Greenburg, C. L. Ford, L. S. Alden, and S. M. Johnson, "In-Session Change in Emotionally Focused Therapy," *Journal of Clinical and Consulting Psychology* 61 (1993): 78–84; M. J. Renick, S. L. Blumberg, and H. J. Markman, "The Prevention and Relationship Enhancement Program (PREP): An Empirically Based Preventitive Intervention Program for Couples," *Family Relations* 41 (1992): 141–147.

[35]J. M. Gottman, *Why Marriages Succeed or Fail* (New York: Simon & Schuster, 1994).

[36]F. D. Fincham et al., op. cit., 1993.

[37]C. Notarius and H. J. Markman, *We Can Work It Out: Making Sense of Marital Conflict* (New York: Putnam, 1993).

[38]B. H. Spitzberg and W. R. Cupach, *Handbook of Interpersonal Competence Research* (New York: Springer-Verlag, 1989).

[39]A. Bochner, "Functions of Communication in Interpersonal Bonding." In C. Arnold and J. W. Bowers, eds., *Handbook of Rhetoric and Communication* (Boston: Allyn and Bacon, 1984).

[40]B. H. Spitzberg and W. R. Cupach, *Interpersonal Communication Competence* (Beverly Hills, CA: Sage, 1984).

[41]Reported in: W. V. Haney, *Communication: Patterns and Incidents* (Homewood, IL: Richard D. Irwin, 1960), p. viii.

Author Index

Subject Index